# International Handbooks on Information Systems

*Series Editors*

Peter Bernus, Jacek Błażewicz, Günter J. Schmidt, Michael J. Shaw



For further volumes:
http://www.springer.com/series/3795

# Titles in the Series

M. Shaw, R. Blanning, T. Strader and A. Whinston (Eds.)
**Handbook on Electronic Commerce**
ISBN 978-3-540-65882-1

J. Błażewicz, K. Ecker, B. Plateau and D. Trystram (Eds.)
**Handbook on Parallel and Distributed Processing**
ISBN 978-3-540-66441-3

H.H. Adelsberger, Kinshuk, J.M. Pawlowski and D. Sampson (Eds.)
**Handbook on Information Technologies for Education and Training**
ISBN 978-3-540-74154-1, 2nd Edition

C.W. Holsapple (Ed.)
**Handbook on Knowledge Management 1 Knowledge Matters**
ISBN 978-3-540-43527-3

C.W. Holsapple (Ed.)
**Handbook on Knowledge Management 2 Knowledge Directions**
ISBN 978-3-540-43848-9

J. Błażewicz, W. Kubiak, I. Morzy and M. Rusinkiewicz (Eds.)
**Handbook on Data Management in Information Systems**
ISBN 978-3-540-43893-9

P. Bernus, P. Nemes and G. Schmidt (Eds.)
**Handbook on Enterprise Architecture**
ISBN 978-3-540-00343-4

S. Staab and R. Studer (Eds.)
**Handbook on Ontologies**
ISBN 978-3-540-70999-2, 2nd Edition

S.O. Kimbrough and D.J. Wu (Eds.)
**Formal Modelling in Electronic Commerce**
ISBN 978-3-540-21431-1

P. Bernus, K. Merlins and G. Schmidt (Eds.)
**Handbook on Architectures of Information Systems**
ISBN 978-3-540-25472-0, 2nd Edition

S. Kirn, O. Herzog, P. Lockemann and O. Spaniol (Eds.)
**Multiagent Engineering**
ISBN 978-3-540-31406-6

J. Błażewicz, K. Ecker, E. Pesch, G. Schmidt and J. Weglarz (Eds.)
**Handbook on Scheduling**
ISBN 978-3-540-28046-0

F. Burstein and C.W. Holsapple (Eds.)
**Handbook on Decision Support Systems 1**
ISBN 978-3-540-48712-8

F. Burstein and C.W. Holsapple (Eds.)
**Handbook on Decision Support Systems 2**
ISBN 978-3-540-48715-9

D. Seese, Ch. Weinhardt and F. Schlottmann (Eds.)
**Handbook on Information Technology in Finance**
ISBN 978-3-540-49486-7

T.C. Edwin Cheng and Tsan-Ming Choi (Eds.)
**Innovative Quick Response Programs in Logistics and Supply Chain Management**
ISBN 978-3-642-04312-3

J. vom Brocke and M. Rosemann (Eds.)
**Handbook on Business Process Management 1**
ISBN 978-3-642-00415-5

J. vom Brocke and M. Rosemann (Eds.)
**Handbook on Business Process Management 2**
ISBN 978-3-642-01981-4

Jan vom Brocke • Michael Rosemann
Editors

# Handbook on Business Process Management 2

## Strategic Alignment, Governance, People and Culture

Springer

*Editors*
Prof. Dr. Jan vom Brocke
University of Liechtenstein
Institute of Information Systems
Fürst-Franz-Josef-Strasse 21
9420 Vaduz
Principality of Liechtenstein
jan.vom.brocke@uni.li

Prof. Dr. Michael Rosemann
Queensland University of Technology
Faculty of Science and Technology
126 Margaret Street
Brisbane Qld 4000
Australia
m.rosemann@qut.edu.au

ISBN: 978-3-642-26456-6 ISBN: 978-3-642-01982-1(eBook)
DOI 10.1007/978-3-642-01982-1
Springer Heidelberg Dordrecht London New York



*Cover design:* SPi Publisher Services

Printed on acid-free paper

Springer is part of Springer Science+Business Media (www.springer.com)

*to my wonderful wife Christina*

from Jan

*to Louise, Noah and Sophie – with love*

from Michael

# Foreword

Business Process Management (BPM) has emerged as a comprehensive consolidation of disciplines sharing the belief that a process-centered approach leads to substantial improvements in both performance and compliance of a system. Apart from productivity-gains, BPM has the power to innovate and continuously transform businesses and entire cross-organizational value chains. The paradigm of "process thinking" is by no means an invention of the last two decades but has already been postulated by early economists like Adam Smith or engineers like Frederick Taylor.

A wide uptake of the process paradigm began at an early stage in the manufacturing sector, either as a central principle in planning approaches such as MRP II or as a factory layout principle. Yet, it took an amazingly long period of time before the service industries actually recognized the significance of processes as an important organizational variable. The ever-increasing pressure in the ultimate journey for corporate excellence and innovation went along with the conception of a "process" as a unit of analysis and increasingly appeared in various disciplines.

As part of quality management, the critical role of process quality led to a plethora of process analysis techniques that culminated in the rigorous set of Six Sigma methods. In the information technology discipline, the process became an integral part of Enterprise Architectures and conceptual modeling frameworks. Processes became a "first class citizen" in process-aware software solutions, and in particular, in dedicated BPM-systems formerly known as workflow management systems. Reference models, such as ITIL or SCOR, postulated the idea of best (process) practices, and the accounting discipline started to consider processes as a controlling object (Activity-based Costing). Universities are now slowly starting to build Business Process Management courses into their curricula while positions such as business process analysts or chief process officers are increasingly appearing in organizational charts.

However, while the role of processes has been widely recognized, an all encompassing discipline promoting the importance of process and providing integrated BPM methodologies has been lacking for a long time. This may be a major reason why process thinking is still not as common as cost awareness, employee focus, or ethical considerations.

BPM is now proposed as the spanning discipline that largely integrates and completes what previous disciplines have achieved. As such, it consolidates how to best manage the (re-)design of individual business processes and how to develop a foundational Business Process Management capability in organizations catering for a variety of purposes and contexts.

The high demand for BPM has encouraged a number of authors to contribute and capture different facets in the form of textbooks. Despite a substantial list of references, the BPM community is still short of a publication that provides a consolidated understanding of the true scope and contents of a comprehensively defined Business Process Management.

It has been our motivation to fill the gap for a point of reference that reflects the holistic nature of BPM without compromising the detail. In order to structure this Handbook, we define BPM as consisting of six core factors, i.e., Strategic Alignment, Governance, Methods, Information System, People and Culture. These six factors had been derived as part of a multi-year global research study on the essential factors of BPM maturity.

We now present a Handbook that covers these six factors in two volumes comprising more than 1,500 pages from over 100 authors, including the world-leading experts of the field. Different approaches of BPM are presented reflecting the diversity of the field. At the same time, we tried to provide some guidance, i.e., by means of the six core elements, to make it easy to open up the various facets of BPM according to individual preferences. We provide further comments details in the "how to read this book" section.

Both volumes together reflect the scope of BPM. Each volume has been organized to have its own focus. The first volume includes the introduction to BPM and concentrates on its Methods and Process-aware Information Systems. The second volume captures in three sections Strategic Alignment, Governance, and People, and Culture. Both volumes include contributions, combine the latest outcomes of high-standing BPM research with the practical experiences gained in global BPM projects.

This second volume is clustered in three sections.

1. The first section is dedicated to the important field of Strategic Alignment in BPM. In a set of nine chapters, both perspectives of (a) linking BPM initiatives to the organizational strategy and (b) utilizing BPM as an opportunity for competitive differentiation are covered.
2. The second section covers the various issues of Governance relevant to successfully implementing and executing BPM. In a total of nine chapters, guiding principles that clearly define roles and responsibilities and decision-making processes for BPM, are discussed on both a program and project management level. Specific organizational concepts are presented, such as the BPM Center of Excellence. Related practical cases are given, including Texas Instruments, Procter and Gamble, and ThyssenKrupp Presta.

3. The third section is assigned to the still widely unrecognized but yet vital field of People and Culture. In eight chapters, the fundamental contributions to the role of the human factor within BPM are considered. First, educational issues are covered like expertise management and BPM training. Then, specific issues, such as knowledge and creativity in BPM, are added to the agenda. Again, practical cases round up this section, such as the Hilti case on the cultural leverage in BPM.

We are very grateful to the outstanding, carefully crafted and responsibly revised contributions of the authors of this Handbook. All contributions have undergone a rigorous review process involving two independent experts in two to three rounds of the review. The unconditional commitment to a high quality Handbook required, unfortunately, in some cases rejections or substantial revisions. In any case, all authors have been very responsive in the way they addressed the requested changes. We are very much aware of the sum of the work that went into this book and cannot appropriately express our gratitude in the brevity of such a foreword.

While producing this Handbook, the authors' enthusiasm was truly interrupted as the BPM community was confronted with and saddened by the tragic loss of two of the most inspirational BPM thought leaders the world has seen. Michael Hammer, founder of the Business Process Reengineering discipline and maybe the most successful promoter of the process paradigm passed away in September 2008. Shortly after, Geary A. Rummler, a pioneer in terms of the role of business process as part of the corporate search for organizational performance died in October 2008. We are honored that this Handbook features some of the last inspirations of these two admirable individuals; we also recognize that the BPM community will be a poorer place without them.

A special expression of our gratefulness goes to Karin-Theresia Federl and Christian Sonnenberg, Institute of Information Systems, University Liechtenstein, who brought order and discipline to the myriad of activities that were required as part of the compilation of this Handbook. We hope that this Handbook on Business Process Management will provide a much appreciated, sustainable summary of the state-of-the-art of this truly exciting discipline and that it will have the much desired positive impact for its future development and uptake.

*Jan vom Brocke & Michael Rosemann, June 2010*
Vaduz, Liechtenstein, and Brisbane, Australia

# How to Read this Handbook

This book brings together input from BPM experts worldwide. It incorporates a rich set of viewpoints all leading towards an holistic picture of BPM. Compiling this Handbook, we did not intend to force all authors to go under one unique doctrine. On the contrary, we felt that it is rather the richness of approaches and viewpoints covered that makes this book a unique contribution. While keeping the original nature of each piece, we provide support in navigating through the various chapters.

- *BPM Core Elements:* We identified six core elements of BPM that all authors are using as a framework to position their contribution. You will find an introductory chapter in volume 1 of this Handbook explaining these elements in detail.
- *BPM Cross-References:* We asked each author to thoroughly read corresponding chapters and to include cross-references to related sections of the BPM Handbook. In addition, further cross-references have been included by the editors.
- *BPM Index:* Both volumes have a detailed index. In order to support a maximum of integration in each volume the keywords of the other volume are also incorporated.
- *BPM Who-is-Who:* We added an extended author index to each volume serving as a who-is-who. This section illustrates the individual background of each author that might be helpful in contextualizing the various contributions to the BPM Handbook.

We truly hope that these mechanisms help you in choosing the very the chapters of this BPM Handbook most suitable for your individual interest.

# Contents

## Part II Governance



## Part III People and Culture

# Contributors


**Chris Aitken** Brisbane, Australia, c.aitken@qic.com

**Wasana Bandara** Brisbane, Australia, w.bandara@qut.edu.au

**Ulrike Baumöl** Hagen, Germany, ulrike.baumoel@fernuni-hagen.de

**Jyoti M. Bhat** Bangalore, India, JYOTIMB@infosys.com

**Eric Brabänder** Saarbrücken, Germany, eric.brabaender@ids-scheer.com

**Markus Brenner** Stuttgart, Germany, mbrenner@horvath-partners.com

**Ryan Brinkworth** Dubai, United Arab Emirates, ryan.brinkworth@emirates.com

**Tobias Bucher** St. Gallen, Switzerland, tobias.bucher@unisg.ch

**Roger Burlton** Ontario, Canada, rburlton@uniserve.com

**Heitor Caulliraux** Rio de Janeiro, Brazil, heitor.caulliraux@gpi.ufrj.br

**Jim Champy** Boston, MA, USA, Jim.Champy@ps.net

**André Coners** Hagen, Germany, Coners@fh-swf.de

**Paul Coogans** Brisbane, Australia, p.coogans@qic.com

**David Court** Sydney, Australia, david.court@aftrs.edu.au

**Tonia de Bruin** Brisbane, Australia, tonia.debruin@ssa.qld.gov.au

**Gaby Doebeli** Brisbane, Australia, gaby.doebeli@onthenet.com.au

**Didier Elzinga** Adelaide, Australia, didier.elzinga@rsp.com.au

**Jude Fernandez** Bangalore, India, judef@infosys.com

**Peter Fettke** Saarbrücken, Germany, peter.fettke@iwi.dfki.de

**Sukriti Goel** Bangalore, India, sukriti_goel@infosys.com

**Guido Governatori** Brisbane, Australia, guido.governatori@nicta.com.au

**Alain Guillemain** Brisbane, Australia, a.guillemain@qic.com

**Keith Harrison-Broninski** Bath, United Kingdom, khb@rolemodellers.com

**Diana Heckl** Frankfurt/a.M., German, d.heckl@frankfurt-school.de

**Alexandra Kokkonen** Brisbane, Australia, akokkone@yahoo.com.au

**Dax D. Jacobson** Waltham, MA, USA, djacobson@bentley.edu

**Leandro Jesus** Rio de Janeiro, Brazil, leandro.jesus@elogroup.com.br

**Dimitris Karagiannis** Vienna, Austria, dk@dke.univie.ac.at

**Daniel Karrer** Rio de Janeiro, Brazil, daniel.karrer@elogroup.com.br

**Mathias Kirchmer** Philadelphia, PA, USA, mathias.kirchmer@accenture.com

**Bo Østerberg Kristensen** Schaan, Liechtenstein, bo.kristensen@hilti.com

**Manish Kumar** Bangalore, India, manish_kumar28@infosys.com

**Yvonne Lederer Antonucci** Chester, PA, USA, yantonucci@widener.edu

**Peter Loos** Saarbrücken, Germany, peter.loos@iwi.dfki.de

**André Macieira** Rio de Janeiro, Brazil, andre.macieira@elogroup.com.br

**M. Lynne Markus** Waltham, MA, USA, mlmarkus@bentley.edu

**Jürgen Moormann** Frankfurt/a. M., Germany, j.moormann@frankfurt-school.de

**Stefan Novotny** Eschen, Principality of Liechtenstein, Stefan.novotny@thyssenkrupp.com

**Martin Petry** Schaan, Liechtenstein, martin.petry@hilti.com

**Nicholas Rohmann** Munich, Germany, nrohmann@4cgroup.com

**Michael Rosemann** Brisbane, Australia, m.rosemann@qut.edu.au

**Shazia Sadiq** Brisbane, Australia, shazia@itee.uq.edu.au

**August-Wilhelm Scheer** Saarbrücken, Germany, scheer@iwi.uni-sb.de

**Stefan Seidel** Vaduz, Principality of Liechtenstein, stefan.seidel@uni.li

**Robert Shapiro** Wellfleet, MA, USA, rshapiro@processanalytica.com

**Katherine Shortland** Sydney, Australia, Katherine.Shortland@aftrs.edu.au

**Theresa Sinnl** Vaduz, Principality of Liechtenstein, theresa.sinnl@uni.li

**Christian Sonnenberg** Vaduz, Principality of Liechtenstein, christian.sonnenberg@uni.li

**Andrew Spanyi** Oakville, Ontario, Canada, andrew@spanyi.com

**Christine Stephenson** Dubai, United Arab Emirates, christine.stephenson@emirates.com

**Roger Tregear** Canberra, Australia, r.tregear@leonardo.com.au

**Jan vom Brocke** Vaduz, Principality of Liechtenstein, jan.vom.brocke@uni.li

**Robert Winter** St. Gallen, Switzerland, robert.winter@unisg.ch

**Robert Woitsch** Vienna, Austria, robert.woitsch@dke.univie.ac.at

**Michael zur Mühlen** Hoboken, NJ, USA, mzurmühlen@stevens.edu

**Jörg Zwicker** Saarbrücken, Germany, joerg.zwicker@iwi.dfki.de

# Part I
# Strategic Alignment

## Strategic Alignment

Business Process Management requires an alignment with the organizational strategy. Only such a tight alignment ensures relevance of BPM and a valuable contribution to the corporate long-term priorities. Strategic alignment does not have to be a unidirectional undertaking in the typical sense that a BPM strategy is oriented toward the corporate strategy. Successful Business Process Management can also shape corporate strategy when improved process performance provides an opportunity to become a competitive differentiator.

While the significance of strategic alignment is widely acknowledged, its operationalization remains a largely open question in the BPM community. Very often a gap between the overall strategy and the more operational issues of process operations can be observed. So how can we demonstrate the strategic relevance of process-related initiatives, or, the other way around, how can we ensure strategy conform process design?

In the first chapter in this section, Roger Burlton refers to this dilemma appropriately as "Lost in Translation." In his contribution, he starts off unfolding the nature of this problem and continues providing specific methodological support for strategically aligning BPM. His approach also provides a framework for the subsequent chapters. With this in mind, we have a closer look at the different strategic options BPM might offer. The study from Mathias Kirchmer, in the second chapter, focuses on innovation and agility as cornerstones of many corporate strategies. It particularly discusses the role of process automation as a means to leverage these objectives. A complementary view is presented by Markus Brenner and André Coners in the third chapter. Considering processes as a key resource for strategic management, they introduce the idea of process capital management. The approach is illustrated by means of a real life example from Lufthansa.

In order to implement the strategic objectives, the "right" processes have to be identified to be dealt with in the "right" way. For this purpose, frameworks are needed facilitating the selection of process and action. The fourth chapter by Chris

Aitken, Christine Stephenson, and Ryan Brinkworth gives an overview of various criteria to be applied for classifying processes. The results are summarized in a comprehensive framework that may serve as a starting point for developing an individual corporate process schema. However, such frameworks have to be individualized for the specific context (e.g., products, customers, competition, etc.) of an organization. This aspect is analyzed in the fifth chapter by Tobias Bucher and Robert Winter. Drawing from empirical studies, a taxonomy of Business Process Management approaches is presented, which intends to support choosing the right BPM approach for the specific contextual situation of an organization.

In terms of choosing the right process, the assessment of processes plays an important role. Drawing from Management Accounting and Performance Measurement in particular, Process Performance Management is essential for quantifying the capabilities of BPM and processes in the light of strategic requirements. An overview of contemporary approaches in this area is given by Diana Heckl and Jürgen Moormann in the sixth chapter. As one major source for such measurement systems, data generated by process-aware information systems can be used for the cost-effective, real-time assessment of processes. The class of methods that takes full benefit of such process data is called Process Analytics. An overview about Business Process Analytics is given by Michael zur Mühlen and Robert Shapiro in the seventh chapter.

The strategic focus on corporate performance is increasingly constrained by conformance requirements that make process design a balancing act between performance and conformance. The eighth chapter is dedicated to this topic and covers the field of managing the regulatory compliance in business processes. This contribution by Shazia Sadiq and Guido Governatori describes a methodology for aligning business and control objectives and zooms into the role of BPM as a driver in achieving regulatory compliance.

Considering the various strategic implications, management has to take decisions on alternative BPM initiatives to be implemented in an organization. For this purpose a value assessment of these alternatives is required in order to rank initiatives according to their strategic contribution. The ninth chapter by Wasana Bandara, Alain Guillemain, and Paul Coogans gives an example on how to prioritize initiatives on process improvements. This chapter gives an overview of related methods and reports on the related practical experiences within the financial services sector. By doing so, it rounds up the section on strategic alignment in BPM.

1. Delivering Business Strategy through Process Management
   by Roger Burlton

2. Management of Process Excellence
   by Mathias Kirchmer

3. Process Capital as Strategic Success Factor: The Lufthansa Example
   by Markus Brenner and André Coners

4. Process Classification Frameworks
   by Chris Aitken, Christine Stephenson, and Ryan Brinkworth

5. Taxonomy of Business Process Management Approaches
   by Tobias Bucher and Robert Winter
6. Process Performance Management
   by Diana Heckl and Jürgen Moormann
7. Business Process Analytics
   by Michael zur Mühlen and Robert Shapiro
8. Managing Regulatory Compliance in Business Processes
   by Shazia Sadiq and Guido Governatori
9. Prioritizing Process Improvement: An Example from the Australian Financial Services Sector
   by Wasana Bandara, Alain Guillemain, and Paul Coogans

# Delivering Business Strategy Through Process Management

**Roger Burlton**

**Abstract** There is no shortage of planning activities in organizations today. However, the concept of a process to develop the connections between an organization's intent and its capabilities to enable that intent is woefully weak and inconsistent in most cases. This chapter strives to outline how an organization can develop a more rigorous statement of strategic intent as the starting point for all investments in change. It delves into what is needed to ensure that the hope expressed in such strategic plans and annual reports is actionable and becomes a reality. It provides a structured and repeatable method to articulate environmental pressures, intent, stakeholder interests, strategy, business processes, and various other capabilities and the relationship among them with integrity. It provides a process for establishing the business process architecture of the organization and uses it as the alignment linchpin to provide traceability from choices made in prioritized programs of change in technology, human capability, policy, and other supporting mechanisms back to their raison d'être: the enterprise strategy.

## 1 Introduction

This chapter will describe what organizations must do if they wish to see their bold statements of intent and strategic direction realized through the mechanism of business processes. In enterprise after enterprise in all sectors and countries, there is no shortage of strategic plans and documented statements of positioning. In addition, there is no shortage of human effort and financial resources expended on programs, initiatives, and projects for change within many different professional domains. There is a large gap, however, between the performance and behavioral outcomes anticipated and the reality of what sees the light of day.

R. Burlton
BPTrends Associates, Process Renewal Group, Vancouver, BC, Canada
e-mail: rburlton@uniserve.com

J. vom Brocke and M. Rosemann (eds.), *Handbook on Business Process Management 2*, International Handbooks on Information Systems,
DOI 10.1007/978-3-642-01982-1_1, © Springer-Verlag Berlin Heidelberg 2010

In my view, the prime role of Business Process Management (BPM) at this enterprise level is to ensure that the various developed capabilities are aligned with one another and together they deliver traceable process performance back to the stated strategic goals and objectives of the "Organization-in-Focus" (OIF). The prime role of enterprise level process management, then, is to ensure that capability investment decisions for change and ongoing management of process operations are always in sync with a set of agreed strategic criteria. Our processes should act as the coordinator to ensure that we optimally allocate scarce resources consistent with delivering enhanced value to the customers of the OIF within the constraints of other stakeholders' requirements.

The chapter is an update to my book: BPM: Profiting from Process (Burlton 2001) that shows a framework for establishing or validating strategic intent in a form that can be leveraged. It will identify means for identifying and resolving potential conflicts among various stakeholders' expectations, products, services, and business drivers. It will show how customer relationship lifecycles can be used to ensure that we focus on the core value proposition, value chains, and value streams against which all other internal efforts and capabilities should be assessed. It will define the processes to manage the relationships with all stakeholders and to support the core value chain to customers. It will establish a set of reconciled stakeholder-based criteria to help prioritize and manage changes downstream.

The chapter will consider the role of industry reference frameworks, which along with stakeholder and asset lifecycles will produce a stable process architecture defining what the OIF does today and will do in the future. This architecture, along with the strategic and stakeholder criteria developed earlier, will ensure that improvements in how the processes perform are prioritized and resourced according to traceable strategic drivers resulting in an aligned program of change.

It will briefly discuss the performance management aspects of BPM made possible by the process architecture and the stakeholder analysis and how these, plus the strategic objectives of the OIF, provide the basis for a better balanced scorecard and human motivation system.

Also, the chapter will briefly introduce the connection to the capability aspects of the enterprise including technology, human competencies, organizational design, facilities, equipment and locations, policies and business rules, and knowledge sharing.

## 2 Lost in Translation

### 2.1 *Today's Reality*

By now, we all know that many grand ideas are never realized. Classically, somewhere in the range of half of all ideas described in strategic plans never see the light of day and a high proportion of those that do are late or misaligned, thereby robbing the enterprise of the opportunity promised in some form of compelling business case. These are sad numbers and they have led many organizations to be very wary of strategic planning, sometimes seen as not worth the effort. Consequently, many of these organizations have reverted to disconnected functional and tactical planning instead. These functionally-oriented approaches, however, have actually led to value streams and workflows full of disconnects and waste.

Today, moreover, everything an enterprise does is interconnected and the rippling effect of a change in one domain or department can spill over to many others with severe unintended consequences. We still see plans developed by functional managers that largely disregard their peers' needs and are blind to the ultimate value proposition to customers. The assumptions made by these domain managers are often self-serving due to incentives, to be that way. They may optimize their parts while sub optimizing the whole. This should be no surprise since their motivation, as driven by formal accountability mechanisms, encourages localized behavior.

Functional managers request services and capabilities from enabling parts of the organization such as Information Services and Human Resource departments based on their functional needs, and in many cases, the functional groups own the budget for change making it difficult to paint a bigger picture from an enterprise capability perspective. The resource allocation processes often drive support groups to become tactical order takers at the expense of their own future credibility. This is how many organizations ended up with 20 or 30 applications and databases, all supposedly containing the same but redundant customer information that cannot be consolidated.

In this vein, a number of management styles have proven to be sub-optimal

- Management by order-taking
- Management by decibel level
- Management by bullying and ridicule
- Management by hope and slogans

There is a better way than taking an all too prevalent inside-out approach that ignores enterprise strategic intent and customer value creation.

## 2.2 *The Outside-in Perspective: The One that Counts*

Customers and consumers do not care at all about our insides. As a matter of fact, no external stakeholders do. They only value what they get and how they are treated. There are many approaches to becoming capable that have been in existence for some time that recognize this. Fortunately these are becoming better and better recognized, especially in difficult economic or competitive circumstances.

- Lean Management and its predecessors, Kaizen and value analysis, are completely built around the concept of starting by understanding what the customer values and assessing all activity in order to eliminate "waste" or unnecessary nonvalue-added work.
- Michael Porter brought us the concept of Value Chains whereby we evaluated how well all the key aspects of work could be planned to optimize the whole company not just the parts of an enterprise.

- Kaplan and Norton brought us the powerful models of Value Proposition (Kaplan and Norton 2001) to help organizations sort out the predominant style and thinking they needed to differentiate themselves in the marketplace.

If we take a customer-centric approach, then all of these methods just reflect the common sense that places the consideration of "ends" before "means." Fortunately, we are starting to see organizations take aligned strategy and capability management more seriously.

- A BPTrends survey in 2006 and again in 2007 asked the question "What does BPM mean to your organization?" Approximately 40% responded that it is "A top-down methodology designed to organize, manage and measure the organization based on the organization's core processes" (BPTrends 2009).
- Under the industry leadership of John Zachman, mature levels of Enterprise Architecture have become more than just technology planning for IT organizations (Zachman 2009).
- Kaplan and Norton's Balanced Scorecard is becoming adopted as a way of seeing more than just a financial perspective on corporate performance (Kaplan and Norton 2006).
- Compliance programs such as Sarbanes Oxley and Basel II, as well as many others, can be implemented to help cross functional management of value chains as well as meeting compliance regulations.
- The concept of Customer Relationship Management has the potential to be more than a technology, if it starts with customer relationship values and not software as its perspective. Other forms of Enterprise Resource Planning (ERP) have the same potential.
- Service Oriented Architecture (SOA) starts with the goal of reusable software assets across a set of enterprise processes.

Our risk is perhaps now having too many choices of potentially competing and confusing cross functional programs that will vie for management attention and lead to a hope that one of these is sufficient and can solve all problems and deliver on the enterprise strategy with traceability of performance and alignment of capabilities. To stay connected to intent they will all require a common process perspective.

## 2.3 Methodology Implications

With so many pressures and options facing managers, an integrative approach seems necessary. Modern methods not only recognize the need to work at many levels in many domains but also to remain connected among themselves.

The BPTrends Associates Pyramid conceived by Paul Harmon in Fig. 1 shows an Enterprise level that deals with an overall strategic alignment and management of the process asset with governance, prioritization, and resource allocation for process transformation. The Process level takes individual processes or activities and scopes, analyzes, and designs new ways of working with a healthy dose of

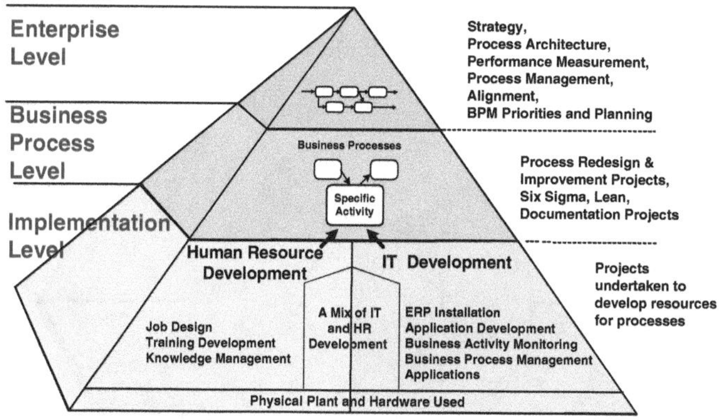


**Fig. 1** The BPTrends associates pyramid

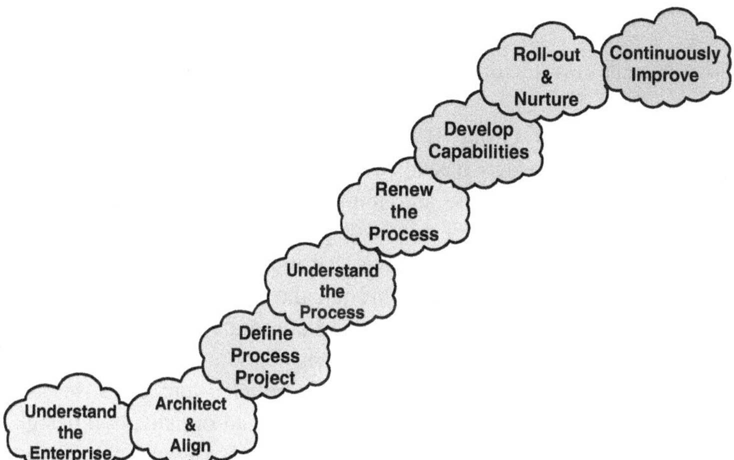


**Fig. 2** Process Renewal Group Business Process Management Framework

project management thrown in. The Implementation level builds the technological, human, and infrastructural resources required for the processes to work and intent to be achieved. These can be done independently, but strategic alignment is best served starting at the top and working down selectively within the scope of the architecture.[1]

[1]Harmon (2010) provides an in-depth discussion of these levels with regard to the scope and evolution of Business Process Management.

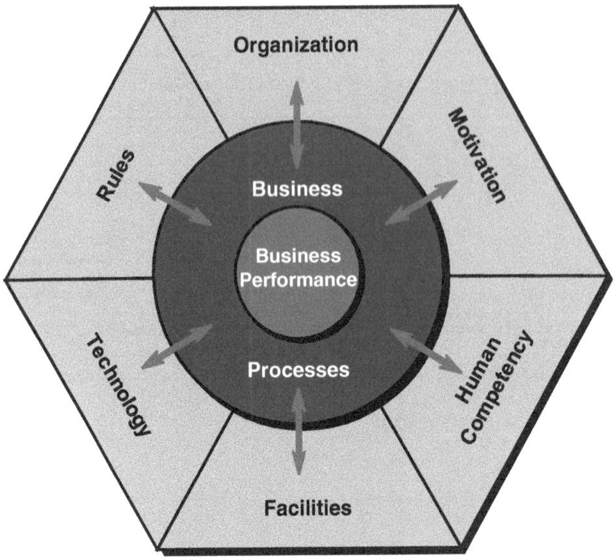


**Fig. 3** The Burlton Process Hexagon: Using business processes as aligner of capabilities

The Process Renewal Group (PRG) Methodology, shown in Fig. 2, that I developed over a decade ago has always provided a multi-level approach that connects the enterprise, process, and implementation aspects of the BPTrends Pyramid and adds the postproject aspect of governance and continuous improvement. The Burlton Hexagon, Fig. 3 shows that processes are mechanisms that are measurable and deliver performance through the definition of the process KPIs in support of the stakeholder relationship and corporate objectives. It also shows that work flows by themselves are not sufficient. The processes must also consider the constraints or empowerment delivered by policies and rules, technologies, facilities, human competencies, human motivation, and organization design.

At all levels of the pyramid, alignment among the hexagonal components must be established and maintained. In addition, with processes being managed as corporate assets at the enterprise level, traceability of the hexagonal components to strategic intent is mandatory.

## 3 An Integrative Model from Drivers Through Aligned Capability

Processes and other future capability needs are compared to current capabilities of various sorts; gaps are identified, aligned, and prioritized and programs of change established. Capability enhancement programs and projects are resourced and conducted. Traceability of changes is carefully monitored against strategic intent.

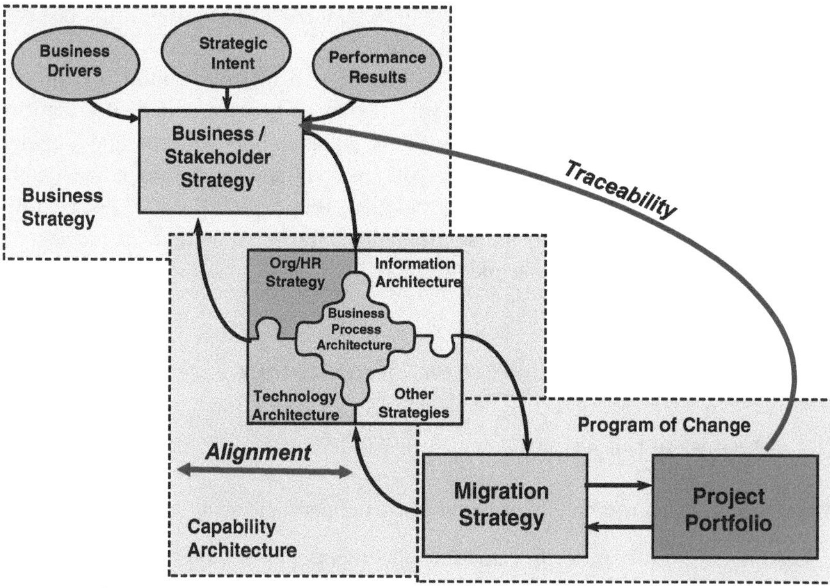


**Fig. 4** PRG's strategic integrity model

Figure 4's approach is supported by the first two clouds (the enterprise phases) in the PRG methodology as well by the BPTrends Enterprise level work (Fig. 2).

The chapter will describe, in turn, the activities and deliverables that the first enterprise cloud (Understand the Enterprise) will cover:

- (1.1) Validate Strategic Direction: OIF Scope, External Influences/Drivers, Strategic Intent, Strategic Key Performance Indicators (KPIs)
- (1.2) Determine Stakeholder Relationships: Stakeholders, Stakeholder Products and Services, Stakeholder Relationship Attributes, Stakeholder Relationship KPIs
- (1.3) Consolidate Strategic Criteria: Criteria for Process Design and Decision Making

The activities of the second enterprise cloud (Architect and Align) are:

- (2.1) Architect Business Processes: Value Chain/Value Stream/Process Architecture Map
- (2.2) Identify Measures of Performance: Value Chain/Value Stream/Process KPIs
- (2.3) Align Process Governance: Value Chain/Value Stream/Process Governance Roles and Responsibilities
- (2.4) Prioritize Processes: Process Priorities for Change
- (2.5) Align Process Capabilities: Process/Human/Technology/Facility Dependencies
- (2.6) Establish Enterprise Transformation Portfolio: Transformation Program

I will deal with each of this in order with only a brief discussion of the last two (2.5 and 2.6), which will be covered elsewhere.

It should be recognized that the two phases will naturally build off, of one another in a never ending cycle from year to year. The next round of enterprise strategy formulation may be constrained or enhanced by current and planned capabilities from the previous round. If you are fortunate, then your new capabilities will be leverageable into new strategic plans that exploit them. Consequently, the activities in the two clouds are significantly iterative although, for the sake of explanation, I will show these sequentially.

## *3.1 Validate Strategic Direction (Methodology 1.1)*

### 3.1.1 Purpose of the Activity

The purpose of this methodology activity is to understand and validate:

- The planning horizon for the strategic statements
- The scope of the enterprise "Organization in Focus" (OIF)
- External and internal business drivers
- The strategic intent of the OIF
- Organizational principles
- Known OIF strategies
- OIF scorecards
- The strategic criteria for future decision-making in all the following process work

It is important to note that when it comes to the perspective of managing processes as enterprise assets, the work of the architects has a context that is traceable to the intended direction of the OIF. Consequently, the effort conducted at this point is not to be confused with actually developing corporate strategy, but instead it is to understand what has been done and be sure that the interpretation of it is a commonly understood and accepted one. Lack of agreement is a warning flag that cannot be ignored since processes have purposes and the analysis of performance and capability gaps must be assessed against a common set of accepted criteria. If some members of the senior management team see the OIF as being all about customer relationships and others believe that cost reduction and operations should be the emphasis, then the remainder of the enterprise level BPM work will thrash and stall.

### 3.1.2 Strategic Concepts

A good starting point and repeatable metamodel for this work has been evolving over the past several years, thanks to the work of the Business Rules Group. This work is now published as the Business Motivation Model (BMM) standard (OMG

2009) by the Object Management Group. One only has to look at any number of strategic documents across organizations to find that words such as "Mission" and "Vision" become confused. "Goals" and "Objectives" are freely used interchangeably despite their differences. Even the term "Strategy" itself is inconsistently applied. This problem of lack of precise wording has made it difficult to document statements of direction in any repeatable fashion. It also means that it is difficult to communicate higher statements of intent and approach to lower levels of the enterprise and to ensure traceability of performance tracking from bottom to top.

The BMM, shown as Fig. 5, defines both the structure of the strategic concepts as well as the semantics of the terms used. It not only covers the traditional components of strategic planning, but also includes the concepts of Influencers (stakeholders in the remainder of the chapter) and Assessments. These will be covered in later sections. An important feature of this model is the perspective offered on its components by Reference Elements. The ones of most interest from the point of view of BPM are Organizational and Process. The message is that every level of the organization and also the processes of the organization should have a model with a consistent structure as depicted by the BMM framework.

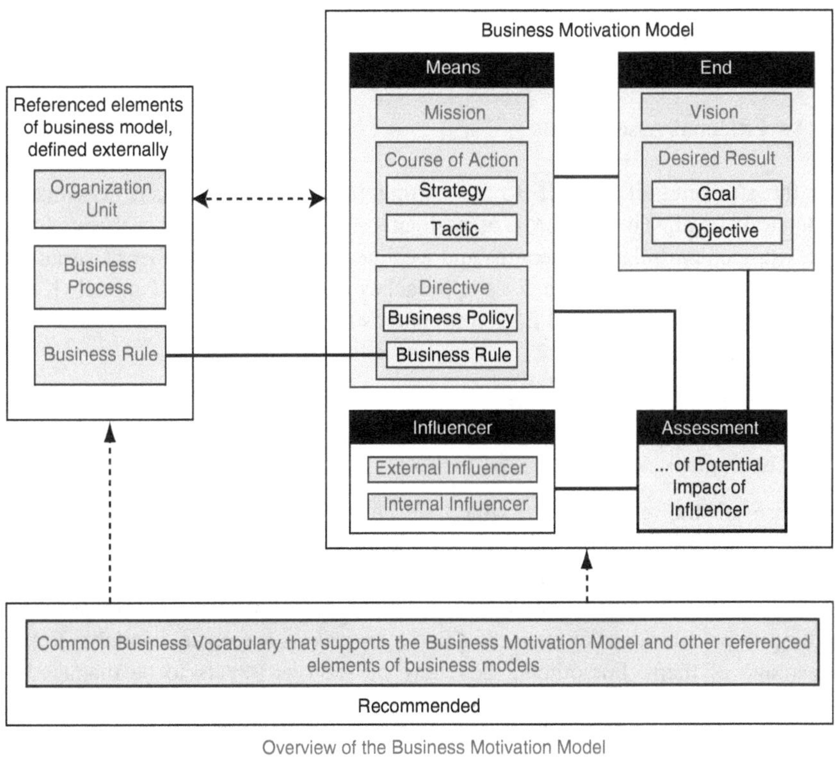


**Fig. 5** Object Management Group's Business Motivation Model

### 3.1.3 Scope of the Strategic Models

The BMM implies, as does common sense, that every part of the enterprise from the whole to specific units should be able to articulate its Mission, Vision, Goals and Objectives as well as other driving motivations. The same is true for each and every process. Of course, the set of organizational and process attributes should also be connected, aligned, and traceable among one another.

At the enterprise level, a good starting point is to determine the scope of what is being addressed. Once again, I will refer to this as the OIF. The OIF can be wide or narrow, but must be clear. Some choices are:

- Group of corporations
- Corporation
- Division
- Department
- Internal group

The advantages of a wider scope are better integrity of overall value creation and customer value chain benefits; however, going too big can become time-consuming due to complexity and is almost always political. The advantages of a more narrow scope are easier effort and less political struggles internally; however, sub-optimization is a common risk.

### 3.1.4 External Assessments

For the strategies of the OIF to have grounding, external assessments must be understood by all. These external assessments can be opportunities or threats for us depending on our relative strengths and weaknesses. One of a number of variations of business environmental analysis approaches is labeled the PEST model (Kotter and Schlesinger 1991). The PEST components are:

- Political
- Economic
- Social
- Technological

These are the realities from which we cannot escape. Separately or taken in combination, the enterprise strategy must honestly assess its ability to deal with them or better yet, be able to anticipate a range of external possibilities for them and be ready should they occur. For some, the drivers may represent great opportunities waiting to be exploited for business gain so long as resources are available to take advantage of them. For others, they may be seen as threats to be managed to mitigate risk. The response, strategically, will depend on whether the enterprise has internal strengths that can help leverage new business opportunity or mitigate the threat. Alternately, if there are internal weaknesses, it must determine how to overcome them to prevent business erosion or lost opportunities.

### 3.1.5 Strategic Analysis of External Assessments

There are a number of ways, described below, to discover strategies to deal with the opportunities and threats posed by the external drivers. A few of these are Business Scenario Analysis, Value Proposition, and the Balanced Scorecard. All have their strengths and are more powerful when used in conjunction based on a common process architecture framework.

Business Scenario Analysis

Responding to threats and opportunities as they happen is required but risky. Many organizations are trying to mitigate this as well as build more agile capabilities by using Business Scenario Analysis (Schwartz 1991) techniques originally developed by Shell Oil in the sixties. This approach assumes that no set of drivers is totally predictable so a range of possibilities should be considered from pessimistic through optimistic and assembled into possible scenarios. These are then used to test proposals for solutions and design for differing possibilities under "what-if" situations. It emphasizes the planning elements (drivers) that have highest impacts and greatest uncertainty. Although there will be a range for each element, some will be more likely than others. Some will be inevitable, some strong possibilities, and others just possibilities.

Value Proposition

A key component that subtly but strongly will drive the strategy and also the management of processes is the determination of the value proposition. Kaplan and Norton have stated that "The Core of any business strategy is the customer value proposition, which describes the unique mix of product and service attributes that a company offers. It defines how the organization will differentiate itself from competitors to attract, retain and deepen relationships with targeted customers. The Value proposition is crucial because it helps an organization connect its internal processes to improved outcomes with its customers." (Kaplan and Norton 2001)

The value proposition observes that no organization can be best at everything and that although it must be competent in all things it has to lead with one of:

- Operational Excellence
  Customers value the efficiency and reliability of what the organization provides. Utility companies would fall into this category for the most part.
- Customer Intimacy
  Customers value the relationship with the organization above anything else. The products and services are secondary and can change based on the trust relationship with the organization. Knowledge-intensive industries such as personal financial advisors would fall into this category for the most part.

- Product Leadership
  Customers value the uniqueness and novelty of the company's offerings. The company will primarily focus on fast time to market and innovation. Certain innovators such as some fashion or electronics companies would qualify.

Different companies can operate with differing propositions in the same industry. Each of them, however, reaches out in different ways of interacting with customers and consumers in the market. Finding the appropriate proposition can be hard and political, but the process architecture depends on it and the allocation of resources for capability change demands it.

#### Balanced Scorecard

Kaplan and Norton also developed the concept of Balanced Scorecard as a response to the shortcomings of traditional financially oriented and backward-looking measurement systems observed in most companies. They arrived at the concept that organizations should also be looking at a quadrant of measures that adds customer measures, process measures, and learning and innovation measures to the traditional lagging ones. Over the years, I have been using a slightly wider view of the measurement system to ensure alignment among all stakeholders, all processes, and all capabilities, and building a traceability line of sight up and down the set of organizational units (Atkinson et al. 1997). Sometimes referred to as an "Accountability Scorecard," others and I have found it more suitable than a classic Balanced Scorecard when it comes to ensuring process performance traceability. The traceability line states that poor capability means ineffective or inefficient processes that affect customers and other stakeholder relationships negatively and ultimately poor bottom-line performance at the enterprise level. Likewise, strength at all levels drives hard to match business performance.

### 3.1.6 Documenting the Strategic Intent

Experience has proven that following the structure of the BMM from the OMG shown earlier is useful in documenting the OIF's strategic statements in a form that will help the enterprise level BPM work to be conducted with integrity. Separating ends (vision, goals, and objectives) revise to means (mission, strategies, and tactics) crystallizes the articulation of the guides for the establishment of process prioritization and design later.

There are other strategic factors of interest such as principles and values but this set is a great starting point as an irrefutable context for relationship management and process management that follows. The strategy becomes more tangible when we add an analysis of the products and services we currently exchange, and we want to exchange in the future with each of our external stakeholders in the next activity.

## *3.2 Determine Stakeholder Relationships (Methodology 1.2)*

### 3.2.1 Purpose of the Activity

The purpose of the stakeholder analysis activity is to understand or determine:

- Customer segmentation
- Other stakeholder types and sub-types
- Today's and tomorrow's products, services and information given to and received from each stakeholder type (interactions)
- The starting point for process architecture development and process analysis
- The health of the current interactions between stakeholder and OIF
- Consensus on the types of external relationships
- The expected goals of the relationships
- The performance indicators and objectives of the relationship
- The capabilities required to be successful

Especially useful will be the ends, means, and assessment attributes described in the last section for the OIF, but applied in a more focused way for each stakeholder relationship.

The first questions to be answered regarding external connections are "Who cares about us?" and "Who do we care about?" Some stakeholders interact with us on a regular basis and exchange things with us. Some stakeholders may not interact with us much, but certainly affect what we do or are affected by what we do. Others may be interested but are not as close as the first two groups. We need to care about all of them and get them to care about us. Once we understand them we can decide what we need to do to optimize our part in the ecosystem within which we all participate. It all starts with gaining agreement on the classification of the various types of stakeholders that we wish to see. It is important to note that this classification most likely will not be identical to the classic marketing segmentation used for advertising or sales campaigns. The segmentation thought process is more based on how we interact with or deal with the types. For example, we may organize and structure sales messaging for selling to the banking marketing segment and the telecommunications market with different teams. However, the way we do the work and the sales approach itself may not need to differ even if the sales proposal terms themselves do. In this case, we would say for the purposes of process management that the stakeholder is the same at the higher level of composition, even if the ads themselves differ. Be careful regarding the stakeholder segmentation names used and the definitions of them, since this can be the source of major semantic, cultural and political disconnection.

The classic starting top levels of stakeholder types prior to decomposition are:

- Customers and Consumers: those we are in business to serve.
  This category is often not as simple as it may seem since there may be many intermediaries or channels to market, many types of products and services for different markets and differences among buyers, influencers, and users.

- Owners: those who invest in or direct our activity.
  This category includes all the investors, boards of directors, and senior executives. Again there will likely be sub levels depending on degree of control.
- Staff: those who work on serving and supporting the enterprise and its stakeholders.
  Staff is considered to be an external stakeholder type since members are part of the enterprise due to their own free will and will have to be attracted and satisfied personally as well as assume internal roles once hired. There may be several types based on the permanency of their tenure or association with collective bargaining units.
- Suppliers: those who provide products, services, and resources to us.
  Suppliers may be segmented according to their nature of supply.
- Community: those who govern, guide, or influence what and how we do what we do.
  This can be a very broad category with many segments since those who provide regulatory and compliance requirements and certification will be different to those who may be simply influencers on us or for us.
- Competitors: those who fight in our markets for our customers.
  Competitors may be targets for capacity enhancement through the acquisition of them or of us by them.
- Enterprise: the enterprise itself.
  This category is somewhat esoteric in that it considers the enterprise to be a different stakeholder than its staff or owners or customers, in that its perspective is sustainability and freedom to act in the best interest of its longer-term well-being.
- Overlaps and Oddballs: those who play conflicting roles.
  There will always be other types that do not fit the normal sectors. There will also be those that play multiple roles, such as customers or suppliers who compete with you or competitors who own part of your company.

These are all decomposable into sub-types, but there will be a practical limit to breaking down too far to the point where the further levels are not useful for enterprise level work. Each can also be weighted so that some will be considered more heavily when it comes to influencing choices and design decisions. The weighting is a strategic choice. You will have to ask yourself the question if the five customers that make up 75% of your business volume should be considered the same as those who make up the remainder. Your value proposition should help you, since weights will differ among each possible choice. Remember if you do not weight them, you are saying they are all equally strategic and important.

### 3.2.2 The Stakeholder Business Context

The Stakeholder Business Context is a model of stakeholder interactions and exchange well-being. It is represented by drawing a simple diagram of the actual and planned exchanges delivered to and received from each stakeholder type and the "OIF". We can show all current and future exchanges including:

- Products delivered or received
- Services provided or received
- Information exchanged
- Knowledge shared
- Commitments (formal and informal) made
- State changes of various assets or relationships

When building a context model, we expect to find that an incoming item will often be paired with one or more outgoing exchange items. For example, a request for credit may come in and a rejection or acceptance may go out in response.

A triage-like assessment of each exchange can be made to get a good start on understanding relationship issues and opportunities. Taken together, it becomes obvious which relationships are in good health overall, and which need serious attention in terms of the processes that support them or are supported by them. A form of strategic Ishikawa or Fishbone diagram is produced but the real value of the exercise lies in the common insights gained across a typically diverse and silo'd group of internal decision makers.

### 3.2.3 Stakeholder Relationship Analysis

We will need a gage of current versus future performance gap to discover the capabilities needed and the extent of change. Start with gaining an agreement on the future we want to see with each stakeholder type, determine how to measure the success and progress toward it, and then derive the capabilities or critical factors required to close the gaps.

### 3.2.4 Stakeholder Expectations and Goals

A useful technique for sorting out the stakeholder vision is called Time Machine Visioning. In this "back to the future" scenario, the architect and strategist imagine themselves going to the future they would like to see at the planning horizon time when all results are in and the process is performing as desired. Statements are postulated as to what each stakeholder type would say, or better yet what you want them to say. It then becomes the OIF's role to do everything necessary to make the statements come true. The statements become the voice of the customer and the other stakeholders as well. These are referred to as the stakeholder expectations, which are indeed our goals for the relationship. The technique defines value criteria and keeps everyone aimed squarely at the purpose of the initiative but the criteria must be used as the guide to all design decisions. This is not to say that all stakeholders will love what we want for them, but since it is our business we must choose. It is also good practice to write the statements as if the stakeholder were actually saying it in real sentences that may start with words such as "As a result of the success of the enterprise transformation program, we can now say . . ." James G. Barnes' book, "Secrets of Customer Relationship Management" (Barnes 2001), offers a set of categories for these statements that can be reused and interpreted in this exercise. This approach applies equally well when examining a single process for its stakeholder goals.

### 3.2.5 Measurement of Relationship Performance

The stakeholder goal statements are the basis for the determination of the performance indicators required to be able to monitor success of the relationship and progress toward success. These will now become contributing KPIs toward the strategic intent ones. They measure value creation from the perspective of the stakeholder as well as the OIF. Both sides must realize value from the relationship to attain its expectations. These will be a combination of effectiveness, efficiency, and adaptability. To avoid sub-optimization, one KPI will not do.

The goal statements are also the basis for establishing the relationship objectives. That is the target values of the KPIs that the organization will aim for. These will be set for the same timing as the time machine destinations. They may also be established for interim points in time as milestones to be achieved along the way. These KPIs now become part of the Balanced Scorecard which in turn will be supported by process measures that will be derived from the process architecture.

### 3.2.6 Critical Success Factors (CSFs) and Required Capability for Relationship Success

The gap in current versus target goals and objectives will indicate the state of the relationship change required and the extent of capability changes needed. The changes in each Burlton hexagon segment will be greater and more of segments will be affected when the performance relationship gap is larger. Small performance gaps will not require launching major new systems but a big gap may. Small gaps will not require significant organizational changes but large ones may depend on them.

In order to discover the CSFs, make sure you answer the following question: "In order to achieve our vision and improvement targets from where we are today it is absolutely vital that . . . . . . . . . . . . . ...." Obtain three to five responses from the perspective of each stakeholder type. Consider all aspects of the hexagon as well as dependencies on other processes. The responses should be linked to strategic intent and the stakeholder goals and objectives discovered earlier.

Taken together, the results of the stakeholder analysis will provide additional strategies and criteria for later decision making as well as the beginning of the design of the process architecture. There will be conflicts among stakeholder perspectives that will have to be sorted out. This is the time to do it; not later when inconsistencies are typically discovered.

## *3.3 Consolidate Strategic Criteria (Methodology 1.3)*

### 3.3.1 Purpose of the Activity

The purpose of this methodology activity is to:

- Discover and reconcile inconsistencies and conflicts among stakeholder views
- Gain agreement on the decision making criteria to be used to:
  - Assess alternatives and prioritize resource allocation
  - Remove personal biases toward solution design in the latter
- Balance the enterprise intent with the stakeholder criteria

This activity provides assurance that the process architects will subsequently design an architecture that truly helps the enterprise manage the capabilities required to attain its corporate objectives with the appropriate value proposition. It will validate the fit among strategic components and among potentially conflicting stakeholder perspectives as well as be sure that both levels are connected.

Ideally, this will be a simple negotiation that will also summarize the results into a brief OIF and Stakeholder Charter upon which programs of change will be chosen. It will also be the starting point for defining the process architecture that will define the structure and organization of OIF processes.

## *3.4 Architect Business Processes (Methodology 2.1)*

### 3.4.1 Purpose of the Activity

The purpose of this methodology activity is to determine:

- All value chains, value streams, processes, and sub processes of value to the enterprise stakeholders
- The relevance of any published industry frameworks to the OIF
- The Core Processes of value to the customers of the organization
- The Guiding and Enabling Processes supporting the Core Processes
- High Level Process Map and Attributes
- The KPIs of the architected processes

The BPTrends pyramid articulates the levels of process work we can conduct. Our challenge is to optimize process performance at all of these levels. However, the Process Architecture that describes what we do, in terms of what is important to those for whom we do it, starts at the top. Its existence provides significant benefits to those levels below, since it automatically provides context and scope for each. Since the performance scorecard must provide traceability from what everyone does every day to full process results to the stakeholder value to strategic objectives, there is no other way to connect these dots with integrity without a sound and elegant architecture.

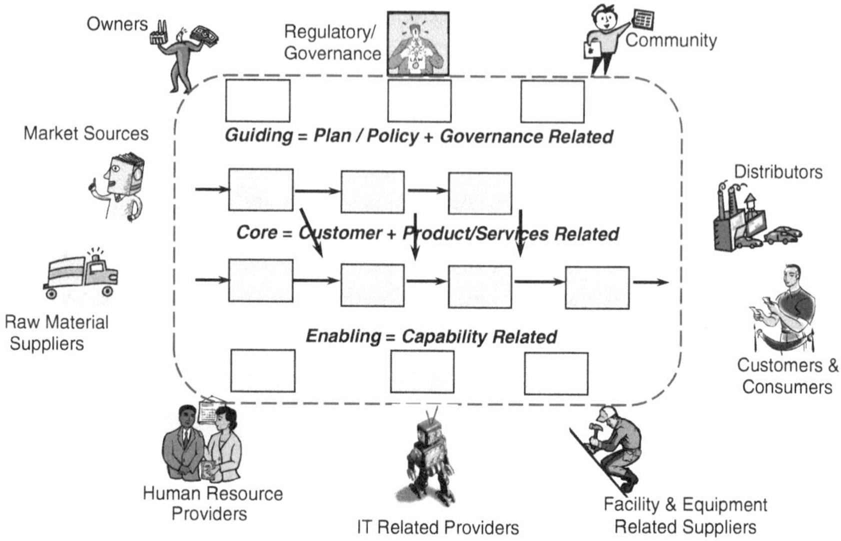


**Fig. 6** Stakeholder-driven processes

The architecture is built from the perspective of a clear "OIF" with defined boundaries and responsibilities. An architectural level process is a repeatable series of activities performed to produce a result of value for one or more of the stakeholders of the OIF sitting outside its walls. It starts with an understanding of the exchanges developed earlier as part of stakeholder analysis conducted earlier. Common sense will tell us that everything coming into the OIF must come from an external stakeholder and be received by at least one process, and likewise everything leaving the OIF must go to an external stakeholder and be produced by at least one process. This is the essence of integrity.

The interactions that come from and go to the customers, consumers, and main value chain partners will mostly define our Core Processes. The ones that involve owners, regulatory, or influencing stakeholders will define our Guiding Processes. Those who send and receive reusable resources such as technologies, people, and facilities, will establish our Enabling Processes. The typical depiction of these with Guiding at the top, Core in the middle, and Enabling at the bottom is shown in Fig. 6.

A well-formed architecture will exhibit a set of processes consistent with well-formed naming conventions. The first of these is simply that each process, activities and tasks, should be named by an active *verb–noun* combination. Just as a sentence needs verbs to indicate action or transformation, so does a process. In addition, the name should be strong and not be some non-descript or lazy verb. The process name should unambiguously communicate the intent of the process not its start or some vague action. That means that non verb structures cannot be tolerated. Gerunds and other noun forms with endings such as …ing, …ent, …tion and …al must not be used.

"Marketing" is not a name for a process. "Procurement" is not a name for a process. "Evaluation" is not a name for a process. "Approval" is not a name for a process. All of these are unclear and in many cases extremely confusing with imprecise starts and stops and a strong association with an organizational function. Process names must be crisp, unambiguous, and convey commonly understood meanings. This means that despite what some process modeling academics have shown in their works, the following lazy or vague verbs such as manage, handle, process, and do, should be avoided if possible, and replaced by something definitive that is outcome oriented. Rather than saying "handle order," say "fulfill order," which shows the result of the process. Rather than saying "manage IT," say provide IT capability. Show the process value proposition in its name and do not clump several processes together under a functional heading. This is not a trivial suggestion. Do it, and you will thank me later.[2]

### 3.4.2 Lifecycle Approach to Building the Architecture

Processes move stakeholder relationships through a lifecycle of state changes – from unawareness through termination of the relationship. They also move enterprise assets and other items of interest through a lifecycle of their own – from idea through retirement or termination. There is a time when our customers do not know we exist. There is also a time when they will no longer be customers or potential customers for whatever reason. There is a time when a product has not yet been thought of. There is also a time when it has been retired from service. In between these extremes are a series of state changes that require someone to do something to move them to the next progressive state. These are processes in value streams that that have to be made to work, otherwise potential customers will not be identified, qualified, or sold to. These are also processes that take product ideas and test them, launch them, and sell them. Among the relationship cycles and the asset cycles, there may be redundancies. The customer cycle will sell products, as will the product cycle. The lifecycle approach is typically easy for staff to articulate one at a time and it avoids the normal problems of seeing processes within organizational boundaries since it looks at the life of a relationship from the stakeholder perspective and not the internal organizational one. The lifecycle approach does not miss much, and is easier for subject matter staff to work through methodically and for architects to facilitate.

[2]Methodological aspects of how to architect high quality business processes are covered elsewhere in this handbook. Reijers et al. (2010) present a framework for realizing high quality process models and discusses additional parameters for deriving a well-formed architecture. Koschmider and Oberweis (2010) suggest an approach to design business processes with a recommendation-based editor. This approach can help overcoming productivity barriers and low process model quality by reducing the need for the user to study the modeling notation. Becker et al. (2010) point out that it is not only important to create models which can be readily understood by humans, but also by computers in order to improve decision making on process architectures.

### 3.4.3 Reference Frameworks Approach to Building the Architecture

In the past decade, we have witnessed the growth of a number of industry and specific value chain frameworks or reference models that articulate a set of best practices for viewing and managing the work of organizations. These frameworks serve the purpose of providing a starter kit or a point of comparison for organizations that want a consistent way of evaluating themselves against a benchmark. Typically organized as a hierarchy of functions, processes, and activities with or without dependencies among them, provide names, descriptions, performance indicators and other attributes that may be reused. These frameworks are not always relevant due to the peculiar nature of the business. They may also use names that clash culturally. Few organizations can expect to simply take the reference models and apply them without thought or some amount of assessment and modification. For process areas that simply require a best practice, these often work well. After all, if you are building capability that will not differentiate you no matter how good you are in it, why would you want to stray from what is proven? Why would you not examine the documented results of work performed by many intelligent professionals who typically would have collaborated over a long period of time to reach consensus and subsequently had the ideas tested in the real world. However, in the areas that you have chosen to be the basis for competition or differentiation, taking on the industry's best practice alone will make you the same as the industry at best. Is that "best" good enough for you? If not, you have to develop your own models or variations and then keep quiet about them.

Generic Enterprise Models

There are a number of models intended to describe organizations of all types in all sectors. The best example of these is the Process Classification Framework from The American Productivity and Quality Center (APQC) (APQC 2009). The PCF is very general in nature since it does not try to be industry specific. It is, however, a useful reference in that it is comprehensive, covering not only core processes but also, enabling, guiding, and managing the ones that some other frameworks overlook. It tends, however, to be more functionally oriented in places where it takes an area such as the finance function and drills into its activities rather than seeing these as components of other wider processes viewed from an outside-in stakeholder perspective. Nonetheless, it is a useful reference, but cannot be relied upon alone to replace good enterprise analysis of processes.[3]

[3]Aitken et al. (2010) propose a generic approach to develop organizational models based on process classification frameworks such as the APQC framework.

### Industry-Specific Models

There are a number of industry models in place and emerging that aim to describe an industry in its whole. The implicit assumption is that every player in the industry is essentially the same as all the others at the basic level. One of these is e-TOM from the Telemanagement Forum (tmforum 2009) which describes a generic telecommunications organization. In places it is remarkably useful as a process reference, especially in the area of provisioning and similar engineering-like processes. In others, however, like the APQC framework, it is very functional in its orientation. Nonetheless, it does contain just about everything a Telco might wish to do if you look hard enough.

### Domain-Specific Models

There are a number of models developed surrounding particular functions within the organization and the processes within them. Some of the best examples of these can be seen in the IT function. Most prevalent is ITIL (IT Infrastructure Library) (IT Governance Institute 2009) which is a framework of best practices supporting IT services management. It is particularly strong in the areas of service support and weaker in the general IT management aspects for which one might supplement with other models. Its use is very widespread in the IT community and recognized as best practice. Another model that works well in the IT Domain is COBIT 4.1 (Control OBjectives for Information and related Technology), which was originally developed as an IT audit framework by the non-profit ISACA organization but is now being recognized more for IT management in general (IT Governance Institute 2009). It is a good partner model for ITIL, especially as the two frameworks start to converge in their latest releases (ISACA 2009).

### Process, Lifecycle, and Value Chain Models

The longest running framework that takes the perspective of end-to-end processes as the point of view would be SCOR (Supply-Chain Operations Reference) (Supply Chain Council 2009). Its purpose is to examine all work in a connected process chain from the supplier's supplier through to the customer's customer across and within enterprises. In existence for about a decade and supported by over 800 member organizations, it is well respected and highly adopted in companies and industries with significant logistics challenges, especially across multiple partners. A growing perspective, however, is that supply chains exist in various guises beyond the movement of physical goods and advocates of SCOR will use it for nontraditional process customer – supplier challenges.

The VRM (Value Reference Model) has a wider perspective than SCOR although it also tackles supply chains (Value Chain Group 2009). It has added product development and customer relations perspectives as well and, when taken together, these provide a wide value creation framework more universal than SCOR. These describe the normal process sequences and dependencies in order to take and deliver an order, get a product to the market and optimize a customer relationship. They do not cover the general management of the business or the provisioning of resources. While weak on these guiding and enabling processes, these two are quite robust in their areas of focus.

A government-oriented services framework has been developed by the Government of Canada. GSRM (Governments Strategic Reference Model) takes the lifecycle perspective of a generic government service from concept through decommissioning (Treasury Board of Canada Secretariat 2009). Its patterns are intended for use by governments to manage the life of services at each of the stages of maturity.

### 3.4.4 Architecture Consolidation

Both the process lifecycle and the process frameworks approaches have merit. Their combination is unbeatable in completeness, richness, and relevance. Both approaches tend to delve to a level of detail that is deeper than the single page snapshot that is often seen in the first view of process architecture diagrams. Careful layering is needed to ensure that a manageable architecture is derived. A rough guideline of ten to 15 core processes and an equivalent number of guiding and enabling processes for a total of about 30 should exist at the top layer, showing that the value chains and value streams have been found to be useful. This mile-wide and inch-deep perspective ensures that we see the full picture at all levels. Each of these top level processes can be broken into a similar number of subprocesses depicted in its own diagram.

Keep in mind that the structure and semantics of the architecture will be political, there will be a functional bias and it will be confusing for those not exposed to process thinking. Be prepared to make those managers aware before trying to sell the models to them. You are changing the semantics and, to some degree, the culture of the enterprise as you do this, so be patient and give it enough time to steep.

## 3.5 *Identify Measures of Performance (Methodology 2.2)*

### 3.5.1 Purpose of the Activity

The purpose of this methodology activity is to:

- Identify the performance indicators to be used for each process
- Associate the process architecture KPIs with the strategic objectives and stakeholder measures

- Determine traceability of measures across and from the start to the end of the value streams and chains
- Identify which measures appear in processes later in the chain that are caused by those ones earlier

Measurement attributes at this level must be consistent with or contribute toward the enterprise balanced scorecard. They will have a vertical perspective connecting to the more strategic measures and a horizontal one connecting to the prior and following processes as well. Both are important.

## Top Down and Horizontal Perspectives

By now, we should have a good start toward the strategic measures of the OIF and the ways to measure stakeholder relationship success. If not, we must go back and get this clear or the process architecture level will have no measurement context or criteria. For each process at the top level of the architecture, we determine which processes are relevant in support of the strategic direction of the OIF, which are of value to the stakeholders, and the KPIs for each process in terms of the support for the higher level strategic and stakeholder KPIs. We must also establish the KPIs for each process that can only be captured in a later process if there are any. For example, the measures of customer satisfaction or dissatisfaction with the taking of an order may only be measured in a downstream process that receives and settles returned goods from the customer. Effectiveness measures typically fall into this category only becoming apparent later in the value stream. We can also set the targeted performance objectives for the process at this time. Remember that an objective is a KPI with a target level by a defined time.

It is critical to have well-formed KPIs since in many cases the ones proposed are not truly measurable. A well-formed KPI has the following characteristics:

- Relevant: supports the assessment of a purpose, vision, or goal
- Comparable: has a Unit of Measure
- Time-bound: is associated with a period of time or a point in time
- Measurable: reliable data can be attained without bias or excessive time and cost
- Trustworthy: people feel confident that it is accurate

Finding a combination of KPI types is the best practice since focusing on one type alone often leads to sub-optimization in the others for the same process. For example, becoming too efficient can affect resource availability and hence service to customers. In addition, the performance of an early process may affect those that follow in a way that diminishes the downstream process' performance due to questions not asked or inattention to data quality. Once again, three types of measures are efficiency, effectiveness, and adaptability. Look for one of each for each process.

Efficiency measures are traditional based in more traditional industrial engineering disciplines and are typically the easiest to measure since they can be easily counted up, divided, and compared at all levels of a process decomposition.

Effectiveness measures are those that are associated with the value received by the process customer or output recipient. Effectiveness measures are typically harder to measure since they require the receiver's perception of value to be known. They have their basis in total quality management disciplines such as Lean, and consequently, measuring effectiveness at lower levels of process decomposition may not be useful if it truly is the whole stream that is important to the receiver. In these cases, proxies that stand in for the overall KPI may have to be found.

Efficiency and Effectiveness measures do not question the product or service or capability that is being produced. They assume that these are stable. Adaptability measures are those that are associated with timing of the product and service availability or the ease of capability change.

Measurement sounds much easier than it is and a means of gathering reliable measurement data is sometimes the biggest issue. Some information may not be affordable or even possible to capture in a timely fashion. Some may be highly suspect in terms of bias and reliability. Sampling theory requires statistical significance. It also questions relevance as to the time the sample is taken. All too often, projecting the sample results to the full population from which the sample is taken will be biased by the time of the day or year when the sample is taken. The anthropic principle (Bostrom 2002) tells us that the act of measuring often changes the measurement results due to motivational or physical factors involved in the measuring. For example, watching staff conduct the work will surely result in different behavior than when no one is around. In considering the KPIs, we must consider the feasibility of the means of gathering reliable data in addition to the unit of measure itself. To find out more about designing individual measurement systems, the reader is advised to consult Heckl and Moormann (2010), which explores different approaches for measuring process performance and demonstrates how measurement systems can be derived, which account for specific organizational contexts.

## *3.6 Align Process Governance (Methodology 2.3)*

### 3.6.1 Purpose of the Activity

The purpose of this methodology activity is to:

- Ensure clear responsibility for all processes
- Establish sustainable process governance and start-to-end management
- Start to define an organizational migration path

Process Governance can be confused with process management supporting services normally found in a process support group or center of expertise that provides capability and consulting to process projects. That is not what this section will deal with. Other chapters in the book will look at those issues of support and enablement [e.g., Markus and Jacobson (2010), Rosemann (2010), and Scheer and Brabänder (2010)]. Here we will discuss the activities required to take responsibility for continually optimizing and managing the process assets of the OIF; its performance and timely improvement. We must answer "Who will manage process execution and govern performance and improvement on a sustainable basis and how will this be done?"

There are a number of key roles that must be played in order to assure that processes continue to be effective assets at their best. At this point, the reader may have expected a discussion on process ownership. Instead we will discuss a wider set of concepts since "ownership" as a uni-dimensional concept is proving to be too simplistic given that the management and governance aspects of processes are far more complex than that. The term "owner" will not be used here since the emotion and resistance from non-"owners" of processes, who are day-to-day managers of staff that work in the process, can be too great and often lead to a conflict of motivational alignment at the personal manager level. I will articulate a set of roles that are required in order to maintain optimal process performance at multiple levels of the value chain, value stream, process, and activity responsibility. As in data management, which abandoned the term "owner" years ago since the data asset is a corporate one and therefore not owned but shared, I will use the term "steward" for the change executive role.

In mature organizations, specific process instances will be executed and managed operationally in multiple locations. They will be monitored for performance and consistently improved across all locations, and along with the total set of all processes, governed for optimization and alignment. This will require a number of roles to be clearly differentiated:

- A *process lead* is responsible for ensuring the completion of a specific process instance for a specific customer or requestor all the way from the initiation through to the closing event and result delivery.
- A *process manager* plans, directs, and monitors defined sets of processes, instances, and resources and adjusts them to produce expected outputs and business results day to day. Sets of instances may pertain to specific locations, transactions, projects, clients, accounts, etc. The process lead, will typically line-report to this manager operationally.
- A *process steward* is responsible for the designs of a related enterprise process and its guides and enablers. He or she plans and sponsors their development and deployment universally. The steward also monitors their performance and assesses their continued fitness in the light of market conditions and recommends funding of changes.

- A *process executive* governs a logical group of enterprise processes at the value stream or value chain levels of complex and large enterprises. The *executive* will ultimately be responsible for both performance and change oversight.

Other optional roles are:

- A *stewardship coordinator* supports, enables, and coaches the stewards and provides executives and stewards with required services.
- A *process management council or forum* brings together stewards and executives for standards setting, coordination, change prioritization, and change issue resolution.

These can be seen graphically in Fig. 7.

Note that these are roles and not positions and the titles may vary from enterprise to enterprise. In large complex organizations, they may be assumed by different people. However, in simpler enterprises, multiple roles may be assumed by one person. For example, the process steward and process manager will most likely be the same person when the process only runs and is managed in one place as opposed to multiple locations.

To assure overall knowledge sharing, motivation, and consistency as well as architecture control and overall synchronization, a process management council can be formed for governance purposes. It processes stewards and executives and is supported by the stewardship coordinator who may be from the center of expertise.

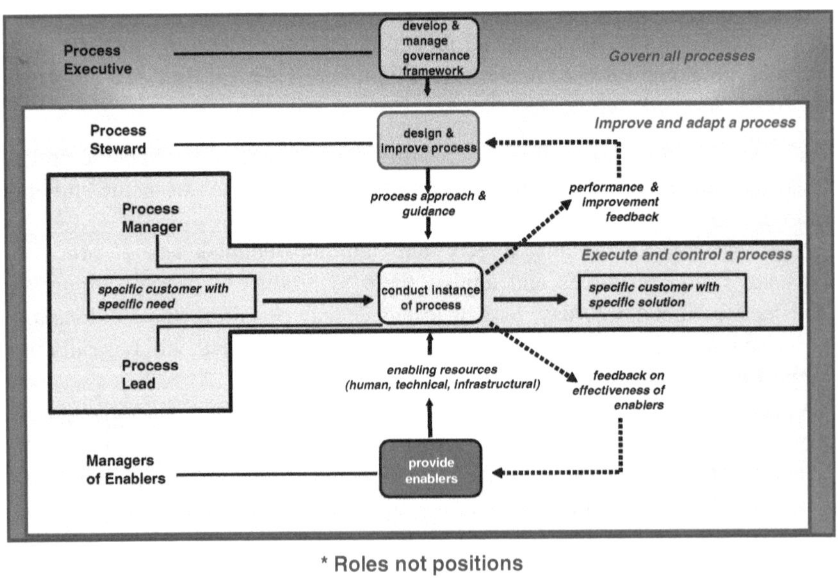


Fig. 7 Process governance roles. Roles not positions

### 3.6.2 Motivation Alignment and Stewardship Support

The deliverables from the last three sections must come together and be in complete alignment. Governance without an agreed process architecture means we have no consistency in what we are managing. A process architecture with no measures for performance paints a nice picture with no ways of assessing results. Governance with measurement and reporting is required in order to have process accountability for managers, stewards, and executives. Conflict between the goals of the processes and the personal performance plans of the stewards is a certain recipe for dysfunction. Governance will not last long because no one will care about it.

Another challenge is that the process executives and stewards typically need help in becoming effective even at the best of times when their motivation is in synch with the stakeholders receiving value from the process. These are new and unfamiliar roles that are often overlaid on existing responsibilities and often seen as more work. The BPM Center of Expertise, if experienced enough, can be important contributors in enabling sound process governance.

With the governance model in place, it is now possible to prioritize opportunities for process and capability renewal, according to process performance and outcomes, and manage cross functional change.

## *3.7 Prioritize Processes (Methodology 2.4)*

### 3.7.1 Purpose of the Activity

The purpose of this methodology activity is to:

- Determine which processes are critical to the achievement of Strategic Business Objectives and Stakeholder Value Creation
- Identify the gaps in process performance
- Find the processes most in need of improvement relative to future needs
- Begin the ranking of processes and related capabilities for renewal

Now that we know the criteria for what is important to the enterprise and its stakeholders and what our processes are, we can circle back and connect up the stakeholder values and performance requirements to give us a ranking of where our biggest return on investment for change will come from. An example of how to prioritize business processes for improvement projects is provided by Bandara et al. (2010).

This will comprise an assessment of process value ranking and process performance gap analysis. The best opportunities for raising enterprise performance will be in processes that have both the highest potential value to stakeholders in support of our strategic intent and those that also have the largest performance gap today, from where we need them to be at the end of our planning horizon. In order to do this, we can produce a series of matrices and grids of process-value contribution versus potential process-performance gap that are carefully aligned. We may do this in a very formal manner or in a more subjective way if time pressures demand.

### 3.7.2 Matrix Alignment Approach

The Process/Stakeholder Value Matrix

By cross referencing the stakeholders value proposition to the processes in the architecture in a matrix, we can assess the value that each process should or could provide to each stakeholder relationship. When summed up and weighted by stakeholder relationship importance, defined earlier, we can identify the level of *GAIN*. Figure 8 illustrates how this may be structured. This evaluation uses the OIF strategic intent and stakeholder analysis results, especially the stakeholder goals and objectives, to assess which processes are most important, important or not critical in attaining the target for the future state of the relationships. A scale of 1–3 can be applied for each process and the sum of all scores for each process, factored by the stakeholder weighting, will allow a ranking scale of most value-added process to the strategic intent to the least value added.

The Process/Stakeholder Performance Gap Matrix

The Process/Stakeholder Performance Gap Matrix is similar to the Process/Stakeholder Value Matrix in structure. It contains the same rows and columns and is weighted the same as well. The intersecting cells, however, hold a different assessment. This time they reflect the potential performance gap of the process

| Stakeholder Criteria * | Weight | Proc 1 | Proc 2 | Proc 3 | Proc 4 | Proc 5 | Proc 6 | Proc 7 | Proc 8 | ... |
|---|---|---|---|---|---|---|---|---|---|---|
| | | | | | | | | | | |
| Stakeholder 1 | 1 | 2 | | 2 | 3 | 1 | | 1 | 3 | |
| Stakeholder 2 | 1 | | 1 | 2 | 2 | 3 | 1 | 3 | | |
| Stakeholder 3 | 1 | 3 | 3 | | 1 | | 3 | 1 | 3 | |
| Stakeholder 4 | 1 | 3 | | 2 | | 2 | | | 1 | |
| Stakeholder 5 | 1 | 2 | 1 | 1 | 2 | 3 | 3 | 2 | | |
| All others | | +11 | +8 | +10 | +11 | +7 | +6 | +9 | +10 | |
| Summary | | 21 | 13 | 17 | 19 | 16 | 13 | 16 | 17 | ... |
| Ranking | | 1 | 9 | 3 | 2 | 6 | 9 | 6 | 3 | |

**gain**

Inherent Value

**Version 1: Degree of Potential Process Value Contribution**

Low (1) Medium (2) High (3) Blank=Marginal or No Relationship (0)

**Fig. 8** Process/Stakeholder value matrix

while holding constant the value or importance of the process in the first matrix. The question is one of how well will today's process design, and its current supporting capabilities, be able to meet the future stakeholder performance need? Note that today's performance may not have a large gap but future requirements may mean that current capabilities will not meet changing requirements and hence a gap is recognized. This is referred to as the level of *PAIN* as shown in Fig. 9.

## Pain and Gain

By assembling the results of the two matrices' rankings, we can map Pain rank versus Gain rank and produce a quadrant of High and Low Gain versus High and Low Pain as depicted in Fig. 10.

The High Pain/High Gain quadrant is clearly where the greatest advantage can be realized and most of the resources should be allocated. Processes here solve the largest performance problems that are most important to the value proposition and intent of the OIF strategic intent. Low Gain/High Pain processes are not as rewarding, enterprise wide and a second choice. High Gain/Low Pain is where we would like all of the most important processes to end up but we must be careful not to fall behind on these and remain aware of potential threats and opportunities. Low Gain/Low Pain means that that our less important processes that work well should be simply in continuous improvement mode. The findings from the grid must still be vetted and adjusted from cost/benefit, dependency, political, and other types of feasibility perspectives to build the transformation plan.

A fast-track version of this grid can be performed using a nine-block triage approach that uses enterprise value proposition and company vision, goals, and objectives as the Gain perspective; whereby the three Gain categories are whether

| Process * Performance | Weight | Proc 1 | Proc 2 | Proc 3 | Proc 4 | Proc 5 | Proc 6 | Proc 7 | Proc 8 | ... |
|---|---|---|---|---|---|---|---|---|---|---|
| | | | | | | | | | | |
| Stakeholder 1 | 1 | 3 | 1 | 2 | 3 | 1 | | 1 | 3 | |
| Stakeholder 2 | 1 | 3 | 1 | 3 | | | 2 | 2 | 1 | |
| Stakeholder 3 | 1 | 3 | 1 | 2 | 2 | 2 | 3 | | 3 | |
| Stakeholder 4 | 1 | 3 | | 2 | 2 | 2 | 1 | 2 | | |
| Stakeholder 5 | 1 | | 1 | 1 | 2 | 3 | | 1 | 2 | |
| All others | | +47 | +17 | +46 | +43 | +38 | +34 | +24 | +40 | |
| Summary | | 59 | 21 | 56 | 52 | 46 | 40 | 30 | 49 | ... |
| Ranking | | 1 | 13 | 2 | 3 | 5 | 9 | 11 | 4 | |

**Version 2: Health of Existing Process / Opportunity**
Small Gap (1) Moderate Gap (2) Significant Gap (3)

**pain**
**Performance Gap**

**Fig. 9** Process/Stakeholder performance-gap matrix

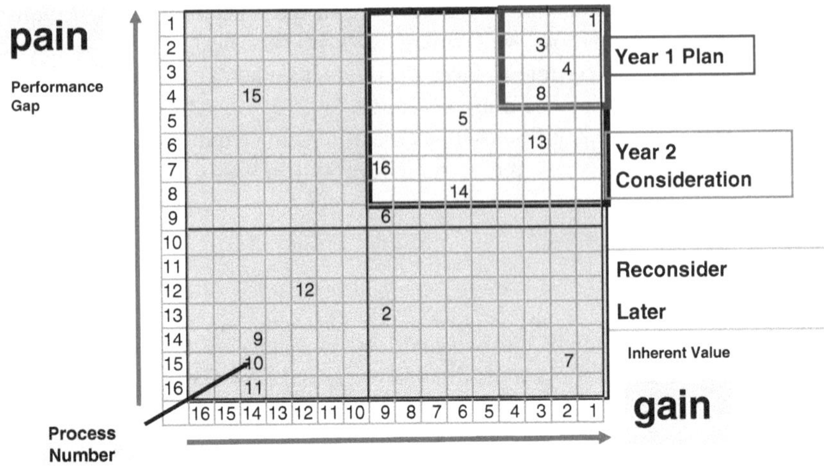


Fig. 10 Process/capability migration strategy grid

or not each process is a differentiator toward world class performance, is a best practice requirement, or simply a commodity process that will never make a big difference, no matter how well we make it perform. The Pain perspective is also triaged into potential performance gap from biggest at the top to smallest at the bottom. Together they provide another way to pick priorities.

## 3.8 *Align Process Capabilities (Methodology 2.5)*

### 3.8.1 Purpose of the Activity

This method activity determines the information needed in order to be able to conduct the envisioned processes and identifies the gaps in information quality; assesses the contribution of knowledge to the processes; identifies barriers to process performance due to overly constraining, inappropriate or inadequate guides; determines which policies and core rules can and cannot be changed, initiates the knowledge and policy changes; and determines the supporting capabilities and assets (strategic technologies, human competencies and physical facilities) needed to conduct the envisioned processes in the optimal manner for their stakeholders. The tasks performed during this activity are:

- Determine Enterprise Information Fit/Gap
- Determine Knowledge Fit/Gap
- Identify Policy Fit/Gap
- Identify Technology Fit/Gap
- Determine Human Competency Fit/Gap
- Establish Physical Facility Fit/Gap

Detailed methods for this part of the method will be covered elsewhere in this book but without our prior foundational strategic and process methodological work all of these will be misaligned and change will not be delivered holistically.

## *3.9 Establish Enterprise Transformation Portfolio (Methodology 2.6)*

### 3.9.1 Purpose of the Activity

This method activity identifies all existing projects of any type currently underway, all planned and funded projects of any type, all planned and unfunded projects of any type, and current budgets and commitments-to-complete; it maps and assesses the fitness of existing and planned projects against priority processes and the required enabling capabilities. In addition, this activity determines any constraints that will hinder changes in the priority processes, produces funding criteria for continuation or freezing of existing projects and initiation of new ones, recommends approval or freezing projects; and produces the Enterprise Transformation Portfolio.

The tasks performed during this activity are:

- Validate Priorities
- Identify Existing Programs/Projects
- Rationalize Current with Required Future Initiatives
- Create/Update Enterprise Transformation Program

Detailed methods for this part of the method will be covered elsewhere in this book, but if this work is not managed continuously starting with the strategy, process, capability, and architectural activities described in this chapter, then it will quickly revert to a process of fielding and reacting to internal special interests and politically biased misaligned resource allocation.

# 4 Conclusion

The work described in this chapter is the foundation for managing a modern enterprise; one that is customer-focused, strategically-aligned, and process-centric. Customers do not care about our departments, functions, or organization chart and should not be exposed to the navigational problems across them. Business strategies are not paper documents to be ignored. They must be used and connected to everything that everyone does everyday. Business processes are the only things that connect the dots to create stakeholder value consistent with enterprise strategic intent. This fundamental shift in work toward linked performance management and change management must become a relentless pursuit for change agents. It will happen sooner or later to all organizations that survive. What I have attempted to describe here is a simple and common sense approach to remain true to the ideals of managing by process for stakeholder outcomes, not by function for internal reward.

## References

Aitken C, Stephenson C, Brinkworth R (2010) Process classification frameworks. In: vom Brocke J, Rosemann M (eds) Handbook on business process management, vol 2. Springer, Heidelberg

APQC (2009) www.apqc.org

Atkinson AA, Waterhouse JH, Wells RB (1997) A stakeholder approach to strategic performance measurement. Sloan Manage Rev 38(3):25–37

Bandara W et al. (2010) Prioritizing process improvement: An example from the Australian financial services sector. In: vom Brocke J, Rosemann M (eds) Handbook on business process management, vol 2. Springer, Heidelberg

Barnes JG (2001) Secrets of customer relationship management: it's all about how you make them feel. McGraw-Hill, New York

Becker J, Pfeiffer D, Falk T, Räckers M (2010) Semantic business process management. In: vom Brocke J, Rosemann M (eds) Handbook on business process management, vol 1. Springer, Heidelberg

Bostrom N (2002) Anthropic bias: observation selection effects in science and philosophy. Routledge, New York

BPTrends (2009) www.bptrends.com

Burlton RT (2001) Business process management: profiting from process. Sams Publishing, Indianapolis, IN

Harmon P (2010) The scope and evolution of business process managment. In: vom Brocke J, Rosemann M (eds) Handbook on business process management, vol 1. Springer, Heidelberg

Heckl D, Moormann J (2010) Process performance management. In: vom Brocke J, Rosemann M (eds) Handbook on business process management, vol 2. Springer, Heidelberg

IT Governance Institute (2009) www.itgi.org

ISACA (2009) www.isaca.org/cobitmappings

Kaplan RS, Norton DP (2001) The Strategy-Focused Organization: How Balanced Scorecard Companies Thrive in the New Business Environment. Boston, MA: Harvard Business School Press

Kaplan RS, Norton DP (2006) A review of Alignment: Using the Balanced Scorecard to Create Corporate Synergies. Boston, MA: Harvard Business School Press

Koschmider A, Oberweis A (2010) Designing business processes with a recommendation-based editor. In: vom Brocke J, Rosemann M (eds) Handbook on business process management, vol 1. Springer, Heidelberg

Kotter J, Schlesinger L (1991) Choosing strategies for change. Harv Bus Rev 1991, 24–29

Markus ML, Jacobson DD (2010) Business process goverance. In: vom Brocke J, Rosemann M (eds) Handbook on process management, vol 2. Springer, Heidelberg

OMG (2009) www.omg.org

Reijers HA, Mendling J, Recker J (2010) Business process quality management. In: vom Brocke J, Rosemann M (eds) Handbook on business process management, vol 1. Springer, Heidelberg

Robert S, Kaplan, David P Norton (2006) Alignment - Mit der Balanced Scorecard Synergien schaffen

Rosemann M (2010) The service portfolio of a BPM center of excellence. In: vom Brocke J, Rosemann M (eds) Handbook on business process management, vol 2. Springer, Heidelberg

Scheer A-W, Brabänder M (2010) The process of business process management. In: vom Brocke J, Rosemann M (eds) Handbook on business process management, vol 2. Springer, Heidelberg
Schwartz P (1991) The art of the long view: planning for the future in an uncertain world. Doubleday, New York
Supply Chain Council (2009) www.supply-chain.org/
tmforum (2009) www.tmforum.org
Treasury Board of Canada Secretariat (2009) www.tbs-sct.gc.ca/btep-pto/documents/2004/patterns-patrons/patterns-patrons00-eng.asp
Value Chain Group (2009) www.value-chain.org/
Zachman J (2009) www.zachmaninternational.com

# Management of Process Excellence

**Mathias Kirchmer**

**Abstract** In order to be successful, enterprises have to adapt quickly to new opportunities and threats. They have to take smart decisions and execute fast. Innovation and agility become main success factors. The Management of Process Excellence (MPE) is a key enabler. It leads to a functioning "real-time enterprise". MPE links enterprise strategy with people and technology for the highest operational performance. Technologies such as Service Oriented Architectures (SOA) or the Web 2.0 support this approach. Knowledge assets such as reference models increase productivity again. The resulting next generation enterprise is ready for long-term success. This chapter discusses MPE, an approach to achieve agility and innovation through Business Process Management. It describes the relation between process management and innovation and how next generation process automation can support that effort. Finally, an appropriate process governance approach for MPE is presented.

## 1 Management of Process Excellence (MPE) Requirements and Approach

The *requirements* for the Management of Process Excellence (MPE) (Kirchmer 2008) result from its specific goals. MPE takes a holistic Business Process Management (BPM) approach and focuses it on achieving two key goals:

- Innovation
- Agility

M. Kirchmer
Executive Partner, Accenture, Philadelphia, PA, USA
e-mail: mathias.kirchmer@accenture.com

J. vom Brocke and M. Rosemann (eds.), *Handbook on Business Process Management 2*, International Handbooks on Information Systems,
DOI 10.1007/978-3-642-01982-1_2, 

Consequently, MPE is closely linked to an organization's strategy. It transfers strategic requirements into operational working processes, fast and effectively. A company following a traditional BPM approach may launch a process automation initiative to achieve a cost reduction. However, when later on new products have to be launched, the automated processes may not be flexible enough to handle that situation. An organization following an MPE approach would, from the beginning on, drive an automation initiative in a way that leads to a flexible process execution, using technologies that allow an easy adaptation to changing requirements,while still achieving the desired cost effects. This flexibility can, for example, be achieved by using a process repository with all process-related documentation as basis for the automation. The resulting transparency enables the required flexibility.

MPE must achieve two important key outcomes:

- Enable smart decisions regarding strategy and operations – in other words, high-quality decisions made in a timely manner
- Ensure the fast execution of the actions resulting from those decisions

MPE Not only does clarify strategic direction, align resources, and increase discipline, as "traditional" BPM approaches do but it also provides quality information in the required time frame to support the right decisions on all levels of an organization and delivers the infrastructure necessary to ensure the fast execution of resulting tasks, making change easier.

MPE must ensure the desired results at the lowest cost level, reflecting management's desire to get "more for less" (Spanyi 2006). Only the economically feasible approach is relevant in practice. Therefore, MPE requires the use of available standards and best practices wherever possible, based on an approach known as "open BPM" (Kirchmer 2007). This "open" approach leads to high flexibility around the process lifecycle because of the integration of the various process-management phases. This is achieved in a cost-efficient way by establishing an appropriate process management organization and governance to identify and roll out the necessary standards applied through Open BPM. Examples are architecture standards or standards for modeling methods and tools, process automation engines, or business activity monitoring (BAM) systems.

The MPE *approach* is illustrated in Fig. 1. It has been developed based on Scheer's ARIS Three Level Framework for Process Excellence (Jost and Scheer 2002; Kirchmer and Scheer 2004; Scheer 1998a, 1998b), a widely used general approach for business process lifecycle management. In addition to this and other general approaches (e.g., Kirchmer and Scheer 2004), MPE places explicit focus on innovation and agility. Every phase of the process lifecycle has to be aligned with those objectives; other process goals are reflected as "sub-objectives". The entire "process of process management" is organized appropriately. This creates the basis for a high-performance business. MPE underlines BPM's role of enabler for innovation and agility.

MPE begins with the business process strategy of an organization. The process strategy transfers the overall business strategy into appropriate process structures.

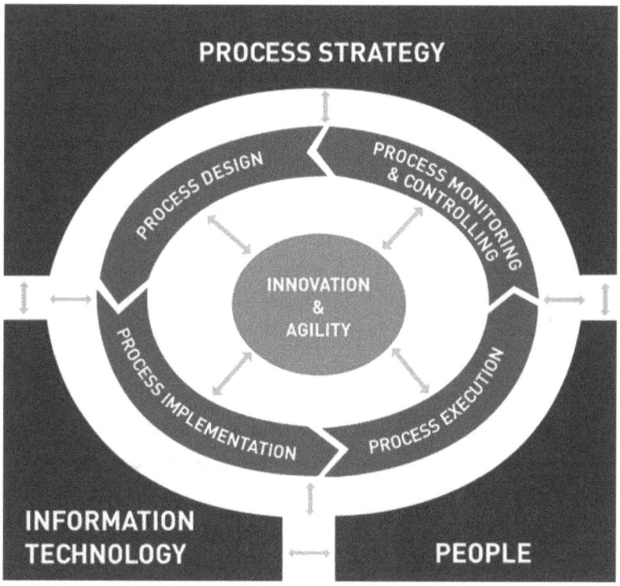


**Fig. 1** MPE approach

First, the main business processes of a company are identified. Next, innovations and their general process impacts are defined, delivering the basis for the definition of the business process structure and the related process goals. Result is a process map identifying a company's end-to-end processes. Innovation areas as well as processes and sub-processes that are especially important to achieve competitive advantage are identified using this process map. The overall goals can be described using concepts such as the "balanced scorecard" (Kaplan and Norton 1996). The underlying application system architecture is planned accordingly, supporting the required agility. This means flexible application architecture with componentized systems are preferred to huge monolithic applications that are difficult to adjust. All aspects combined set the guideline and strategic direction for a process-centric organization focused on innovation and agility. The guideline and direction deliver the overall structure for all process-related activities in the following phases of MPE. The process strategy provides basis for the overall governance for the organization of process management.

The strategic guideline is passed to the process design phase, where the business processes are specified in detail. Here, the approach of the "process factory" is used to develop process models as efficiently and effectively as possible to ensure the highest agility in the day-to-day process management activities. A process factory is an "industrialized" environment to support the development and the systematic reuse of process models (Kirchmer 2008). Core is an integrated process model repository that stores the process-related "knowledge assets" in an easy-to-use format. Thus, a process design can be quickly modified and used as input in the other phases of the process life cycle. Every process initiative delivers its design results in the repository format so that it can be reused in other initiatives. An important aspect is the use of process reference models as starting points for process design (Fettke and Loos 2007). This reduces modeling time and increases model quality. A process factory is necessary to ensure a quick move from strategy to the implementation and execution phase while still having sufficient time to focus on desired process innovations. In the design phase, business processes must be specified in detailed and consistent descriptions, which can be used to drive the process implementation and execution. In other words, the created knowledge assets must include all relevant information about the processes to be executed to support the close link between strategy and execution. The result is a process blueprint consisting of business process models that form the enterprise's process knowledge assets and drive the following phases of the business process life cycle.

Based on these process models, all physical and information-processing activities of a process are implemented within an enterprise and across organizational boundaries. The results are intra- and inter-enterprise processes, ready for execution. The implementation can be carried out based on IT to support the following automated execution or manual execution through people. Generally, it is a mixture of both: automation may deliver the necessary speed and efficiency to be agile; manual steps provide the required flexibility and adaptability. Some parts of a process may even need to be executed in teams [e.g., brainstorming activities in a research department (Harmon 2007)] to ensure the appropriate creativity to support innovation activities. This implementation phase includes the software configuration or development, as well as the people change management, consisting of information, communication, and training (Kirchmer and Scheer 2003). For the implementation phase, it is important to have the process design in a format that enables a very time-efficient implementation, so that the execution can start quickly. This can be ensured through the aforementioned process factory approach. During the implementation phase, the organization goes through a transformation process to achieve the defined innovation and agility.

During the process execution phase, processes are executed based on the implemented IT or people resources. The software systems can be standard application packages, such as enterprise resource planning (ERP), supply chain management (SCM), or customer relationship management (CRM) systems, that primarily support best practice processes. Alternatively, processes can be executed based on more flexible application solutions, such as next-generation business process automation systems, based on a service-oriented architecture (SOA). An MPE approache has to ensure that all processes identified in the process strategy as "innovation candidates" are executed using application systems with the highest flexibility so that they can be easily adjusted to the necessary change. The people-based execution may be supported by continuous learning and talent management initiatives, for example, through computer-based training approaches or regular face-to-face training initiatives. The execution has to deliver the targeted innovation and agility.

The actual executed processes are measured and controlled in the process monitoring and controlling phase of MPE. In order to do that efficiently, systems for BAM should be used. If there are negative differences observed between the actual values and the planned KPIs that were defined based on the goals identified in the process strategy, action must be taken. Either a "continuous process improvement" (CPI) is initiated through the process design phase (the design is improved to meet the defined goals and passed on to implementation and then to execution) or the situation is resolved on a strategic level if the business environment has changed significantly. This phase of MPE overlaps with the execution phase. In this monitoring and controlling phase, process performance improvement methodologies, such as Six Sigma (Snee and Hoerl 2003; Harmon 2003), Lean, or combinations of such approaches (George 2003), can be implemented. This phase delivers necessary information about the execution to ensure smart decisions based on process KPIs. It enables a continuous focus on the goals defined in the process strategy and helps measure the success of the implemented innovation and agility.

An organization can begin a BPM initiative at any of the phases of MPE. Of course, the typical entry point is process strategy, followed by the analysis and design of processes. However, there are more and more organizations starting with the monitoring and controlling of existing processes, which lead to strategy and process design. The implementation of a process-based software solution can also serve as a starting point. The decision about the MPE starting point should be based on the company-specific situation: the current needs and budgeted initiatives, the political situation, the staffing situation, and similar aspects.

In many cases, companies select a two-step approach and begin with a pilot project focused on one or two processes. The first nucleus of a process organization, for example, in the form of a Center of Excellence is established. Based on the result, the entire MPE approach can be rolled out. Whatever starting point is chosen, it is important to envision the entire MPE concept, so every initiative becomes a building block of a successful overall MPE approach.

The design phase, including the process strategy, and the implementation phase comprise the process build-time activities. In this instance, companies created the ability to act fast in order to achieve MPE's goal of "fast execution." The process execution, as well as the monitoring and controlling phase, consist of the run-time activities of the process life cycle. They deliver the necessary information to ensure timely and high-quality decisions.

All phases of MPE should be supported by available BPM software, especially modeling software and repositories (as required by the process factory). The data volume to be handled by BPM activities and MPE's specific demand for speed and high-quality information make this request even more important. The necessary integration and consistency of process-related knowledge, especially the business process models, cannot be achieved manually.

## 2 Innovation: Key Target of MPE

To master the continuous changes and new developments of today's business environment, innovation – especially business process innovation – has become a core focus area for successful organizations. To ensure long-term survival, an enterprise must make innovation part of day-to-day business. Only then, can enterprises attain desired revenue and profit stability and growth and high performance. Consequently, business processes have to be managed in a way to support and drive innovation. MPE makes innovation a key target. But what exactly do processes and innovation have to do with each other? That question has to be clarified to be able to organize MPE appropriately.

More and more companies are built on the principles of process innovation. Dell, for example, did not invent the PC. But it did invent new business processes to bring PCs to market, eliminating unnecessary steps in the supply chain, while offering more flexibility and control to the customer. These processes have become Dell's main differentiator in the competitive marketplace. Process innovation was the basis for starting and growing this company. Amazon.com did not invent the book, but it introduced a now-popular process of buying books online from the comfort of your living room. This is a process innovation based on the Internet with its new technical capabilities. eBay did not invent the auction, but its online, easy-to-use processes increased the popularity of the auction. This is again a process innovation as the basis for a new business.

Traditional companies are also focusing on process innovation. For example, enterprises in the machinery industries offer more convenient and reliable service processes based on Internet connections to their clients or directly to the delivered equipment. Airlines have simplified the ticketing process to reduce cost and increase, or at least stabilize, service levels through online ticketing. This is a process innovation that eventually became the standard, an industry best practice. Banks reduce cost and improve their service levels through online banking.

Business process innovation is clearly of the highest importance for every company. But what is it all about? How do "innovation" and "business processes" really fit together? Innovation is defined as the act of "introducing something new." A useful structure of innovation is proposed by Davila et al. (2006). According to them, innovation has two major directions:

- Business model innovation
- Technology innovation

Business model innovation includes a new or modified value proposition, new business processes (especially in the supply chain), or new target customers and markets. Let us look at a few examples. Levis Strauss & Co. introduced denim jeans. Because of the company's new process of putting rivets in pants for strength, jeans were introduced as working clothes for farmers and factory workers. Since the first introduction of the denim jeans, the company's value proposition has changed and evolved as denim jeans have become an expensive fashion product. In its PC offerings, Dell's value proposition was the convenient custom configuration and ordering of products – the supply chain processes eliminated dealer networks and enabled individual configuration by the client, while the target customers remained, more or less, the same as those of competitors. The opening of new markets for existing offerings is another kind of business model innovation. If a company has always sold to the US market, but now decides to also deliver products to Europe, this is a form of business model innovation (new market). Sometimes, the profit formula is considered as an additional component of the business model; however, it may also be seen as part of other elements (e.g., aspect of the general value proposition).

Technology innovation has the following levers: offerings, including products and services; process technologies; and enabling technologies. New product technologies (e.g., the introduction of digital cameras) are some of the most obvious forms of innovation. Process technologies support efficient and effective business processes. ERP systems, for example, were able to make specific processes more efficient and effective. Supporting technologies improve either product or process technologies. For example, the development of efficient relational databases supported the development of integrated application software, especially the aforementioned ERP systems.

Innovation in the fields of processes and process technologies show the direct link between "process" and "innovation." But the other forms of innovation also lead to new processes. New value propositions and expansion into new markets require appropriate business processes. A product innovation generally leads to new production or distribution processes. The result is an indirect link between "business processes" and "innovation." Basically, any form of innovation requires new or modified business processes and needs business process innovation: processes with new structures, more accurate, granular or timely data, new organizational responsibilities, new functions or superior process deliverables. MPE supports innovation by encouraging an innovation focus in each phase of the process life cycle: the process management is organized in a way that it makes the changes required by innovation easy, for example, by identifying the innovation areas already in the process strategy, applying the concept of the process factory in the design, using flexible automation architectures like SOA, or measuring processes effectively through BAM.

The levers of innovation are shown in Fig. 2.

But how does an enterprise organize innovation? Once again, the answer is BPM: the management of innovation within an enterprise is a business process in and of itself. This process must be defined, implemented, executed and controlled just like any other business process. It goes through the same process life cycle. The "innovation process" has to be a key process to be managed by MPE.

An example of one such innovation process is shown in Fig. 3. The process develops from the preparation of an innovation initiative, to the "idea finding" activities, and finally to the execution of the innovation idea. The innovation manager identifies relevant mega trends and, based on those, the relevant innovation fields. These innovation fields guide the definition of the company-specific innovation

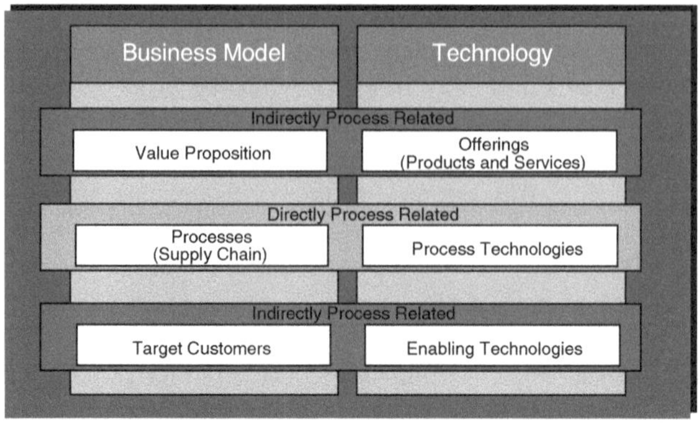


**Fig. 2** Levers of innovation and the relation to processes

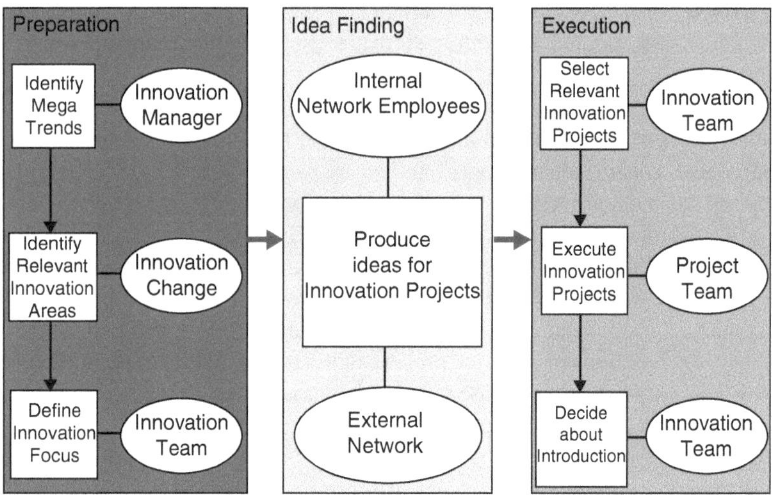


**Fig. 3** Example of an innovation process

focus. This focus directs the "idea finding", using internal and external resources. The innovation ideas are evaluated, and the most interesting ones become innovation projects. These projects develop prototypes and business cases based on the innovation idea. Then, the innovation team can decide which innovation ideas will be brought to market, or the ideas that will actually become innovations.

Owing to the importance of process innovation, the innovation process must support this form of innovation effectively. For many traditional companies, this will require a big shift because they formerly thought of innovation in terms of technology innovation, especially product innovation. This shift can be supported by selecting the appropriate external partners, like universities or research institutions, to participate in the innovation process.

When implementing and improving an innovation process, it is of highest importance to accelerate the time until the innovation can be introduced into the market. This reduces innovation cost and increases the probability of high-revenue effects (George et al. 2005; Johnson and Suskewicz 2008). An MPE approach has to optimize the innovation process regarding cycle times.

Hammer, the renowned BPM thought leader, recognized that operational innovation, or business process innovation, is not easy to achieve. For a successful innovation process, he recommends six key factors (Hammer 2005):

- Business process focus, from the beginning of an innovation initiative
- Definition of process owners, including a senior executive who can make change happen
- Full-time design team
- Managerial engagement, ensuring the implementation of the innovation
- Building buy-in
- Bias for action

Once a process innovation has been implemented, one must recognize that the interrelation with other processes may require additional change. Therefore, one process innovation initiative may immediately trigger the next process change project.

The innovation process can be centralized in an organization or carried out in decentralized units. The more effective approach has to be defined based on a company's specific strategy. This is especially true for organizations working in a global business environment an important topic (Bartlett and Ghoshal 2002).

MPE provides a business infrastructure with the flexibility necessary to facilitate innovation, especially business process innovation. It sets the parameters so that an organization is able to react to change efficiently and effectively. Process innovation is simply a special driver of such change.

## 3 Information Technology Enabling the Execution of MPE

Most business processes within an organization are at least partially supported by IT. The IT support influences the management of those processes and can encourage or hinder innovation and agility. ERP, CRM, SCM, or similar systems are present in one or the other way in almost every enterprise. Many executives are already considering new IT architectures based on SOA or are in the midst of such an implementation. Some companies even take these ideas to the next level, such as those working toward the use of Web 2.0 applications. But what does it all mean? How do these IT components fit into MPE – or better, why does MPE require their use?

During the last 10–15 years, an increasing number of business processes have been supported by standard software packages, such as ERP, SCM or CRM systems (Kirchmer 1999). The most popular are ERP systems, covering the majority of a company's operational activities, such as sales, material management, production planning and control, maintenance, asset management, finance, financial controlling, human resources, etc. The use of standard software has numerous advantages when compared to individually developed software systems.

A key advantage of these "traditional" standard software solutions is that they not only deliver technology to execute a specific process but also provide best business practices. The software reflects its vendor's business knowledge regarding a certain topic or industry, as well as the experience of the vendor with other customers in the same area.

The successful use of standard software, such as ERP systems, implies the design and execution of business processes according to the delivered best practices of the software solution. If you buy an ERP system, you don't just purchase a piece of technology; you also buy a set of predefined business processes. In turn, you have to adapt at least part of your organization to the requirements of the software-based business processes. For example, you may be forced to create some material master data before you send out a procurement order. ERP systems include a process definition that is more or less coded in the software. The software only allows very limited changes or adjustments of its process definition. These adjustments can be done during the software configuration through the setting of specific parameters. This is a key task of ERP implementation activities.

Modifications to the delivered process logic often result in modification to software that lead in most cases, to tremendous cost. Many of the advantages of standard software are lost if you decide to modify that software. However, most of the standard systems allow the integration of "add-on software" through predefined interfaces. But this is, in many cases, insufficient, especially for the support of a process that is critical to achieving competitive advantage that is important for process innovation. As a result, new business processes are not adequately supported by traditional software solutions, which leads to negative impacts on the process performance. This is obviously not consistent with an MPE approach.

Key processes tend to be strongly influenced by a company's specific offerings (products or services) and the related market demands, so standard software applications such as ERP cannot deliver the required best-possible IT support because they reflect the needs of wider user communities. SOA offer a solution for those needs. They enable separation of the business process design and support through appropriate software applications or application components delivered as so-called services (we will use "service" as synonym for an application software component, delivering specific results needed to support one or several functions of a business process). This means that application software can be used exactly as required by business processes. SOA provides the environment to link the required application components and exchange data as necessary to support the overlying business processes design (Kirchmer and Scheer 2004; Woods 2003; Kalakota and Robinson 2003; Woods and Mattern 2006). This enables the execution of next-practice business processes, that of business process innovation. In other words, it is IT for business process innovation, as Woods and Mattern, some of the first authors of a book about SOA, describe SOA (2006) – a perfect fit to support the goals of innovation and agility of MPE.

The use of SOA can lead to significant reductions in IT maintenance costs because expensive program-to-program interfaces of traditional software environments are avoided. All software components are simply linked into the integration environment of the SOA (Woods and Mattern 2006). This resolves many of the issues of extending ERP systems through add-on applications supporting enterprise-specific processes or sub-processes.

These integration capabilities are also the basis for the reuse of software components in the case of custom developments, thus resulting in cost savings. Once a software component or service is developed, it can be used to support several processes. It can be part of another integrated process-oriented software system.

The true value of SOA, however, is only delivered when the environment is used to support business change, to enable agility and process innovation. MPE enables this business-driven use of SOA by integrating it in the "process factory" and use the process models stored in the repository to drive the SOA configuration. The process design can be improved and cost and time efficiently implemented, through the selection and adjustment of the application components needed to support the specific processes. New "services" can be added, and others deleted or modified, according to the requirements of the business processes. The same procedure can be used to realize completely new or strongly modified processes, thus enabling business process innovation. SOA can be used to support the fast execution of process designs, reflecting strategic directions. Thus, SOA plays a critical role of transferring strategy into operational performance through MPE.

New IT architectures are clearly driven by the World Wide Web (WWW). The common opinion that the Internet hype would end after the burst of the dot-com bubble in 2001 has been proven wrong. On the contrary, Web capabilities have continuously improved, and the ability to bring people and organizations together in communities has become more important than ever (Fingar 2006). The new generation of WWW capabilities is often called "Web 2.0." Web 2.0 can be perceived as the second generation of Web-based communities and hosted services, which aim to facilitate creativity, collaboration, and the sharing of ideas and data between users. The term was created and promoted in a conference organized by O'Reilly Media in 2004 (O'Reilly 2005).

There are already many current initiatives to transfer the capabilities of Web 2.0 into the business world, targeting enterprise clients. The result is the "Enterprise 2.0" (McAffee 2006). Enterprise 2.0 is a company using the capabilities of Web 2.0 for its business purposes (Kemsley 2010).

The Enterprise 2.0+ is highly integrated with the business environment, as shown in Fig. 4. A company may be member of many online communities. Imagine using an environment like Youtube to exchange business process models. Instead of posting videos, companies could post process models representing their organization's best business practices or other interesting process ideas. This could facilitate the exchange of business experiences within and across specific industries – which would become an important factor to support MPE's design of innovative processes.

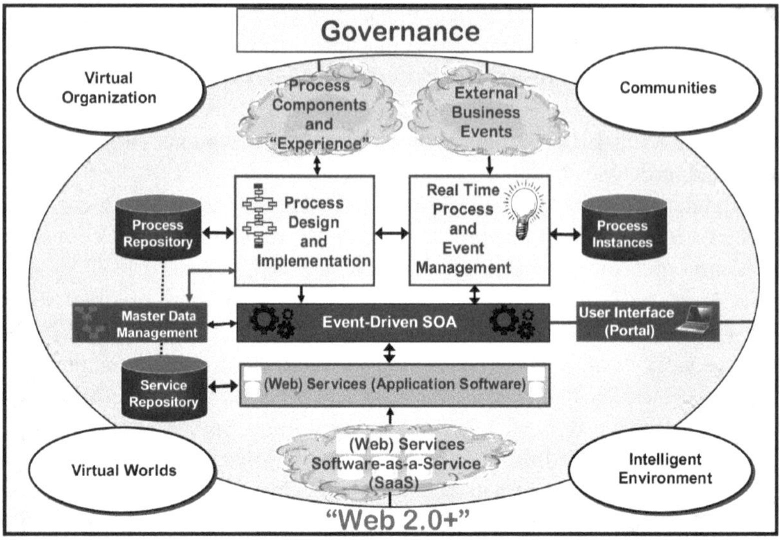


**Fig. 4** Enterprise 2.0+ – Integrated with business environment

The Web 2.0 environment could be utilized to make the Enterprise 2.0+ part of a powerful virtual organization. For example, one could create an innovation network around the company, including customers, partners, research institutes, universities, etc. The exchange of ideas could be organized through blogs.

Until now, most information systems received necessary data through human interaction. For example, a person enters the shipping data of orders. This is often very costly and leads to delays. New technologies, such as radio frequency identification (RFID), enable the automated creation of that data. For example, once containers are loaded into a ship, this information is automatically transferred through RFID into a software system and from there becomes available through the Web. The result is an "intelligent environment" or the "internet of things" (Fleisch et al. 2005; Mattern 2005), which ultimately leads to business processes that enable innovation and high performance.

This intelligent environment closes the gap between the real and the virtual world step by step. Once you have more and more information about the real world digitized, you can start using this information as building blocks for a virtual world, allowing the realistic test of new business process as described above. And, the boundaries between the real and virtual worlds then begin the blur.

The Enterprise 2.0+ is clearly a perfect environment for MPE. It permanently delivers the information necessary for timely decisions and supports the almost real-time execution of the resulting actions. Strategy and operational performance are closely integrated. Agility and innovation are strongly encouraged. Therefore, MPE requires an early adaptation of the Enterprise 2.0 approach.

A key challenge of Enterprise 2.0+ is finding the appropriate governance model. Web 2.0 empowers people and encourages creativity. But how do you ensure that they still work toward the company's goals? A traditional governance model, consisting of many inflexible rules and policies, does not work in such an environment. The Enterprise 2.0+ could utilize a governance model similar to that of the online encyclopedia Wikipedia. Users are guided through common goals and control themselves. However, it is clear that an enterprise is more complex, so the governance has to be more refined. But the direction is demonstrated by Web 2.0 communities like Wikipedia.

## 4 Business Process Governance for MPE

Business process governance (BPG) is a set of guidelines focused on organizing all BPM activities and initiatives of an organization in order to manage all of its business processes (Kirchmer 2005; Kirchmer and Spanyi 2007; Markus and Jacobson 2010). The resulting governance framework provides the frame of reference to guide organizational units of an enterprise and ensure responsibility and accountability for adhering to the BPM approach, thus to follow the MPE philosophy. Therefore, the definition of appropriate governance and governance organizations is a key element of MPE and a differentiator to other approaches. Scheer and Brabänder (2010) suggest an alternative view on business process governance by proposing an "accountability framework".

BPG involves the following components:

- A high-level model of an organization's key processes
- Clarification of high-level goals to frame the definition of KPIs that will be used to monitor the performance of these business processes; this includes innovation-related goals
- Accountability for the innovation, improvement, and management of business processes
- A clear formal structure for the description of business processes and the related aspects (enterprise or business process architecture)
- An outline of the infrastructure necessary for MPE
- Aligned recognition and reward systems
- The set of priorities in innovating and improving key business processes

The primary objective of BPG is to set the stage for the effective deployment of BPM to create value for customers, shareholders, and other stakeholders. BPG ensures that BPM delivers consistent business results to satisfy and exceed the expectations of an organization. BPG is responsible for the management of the BPM process. This means you implement MPE through BPG (Kirchmer 2008). MPE again drives the success of all other business processes, specifically core processes relevant for a company's competitive positioning. The relation between BPG and BPM is explained in Fig. 5.

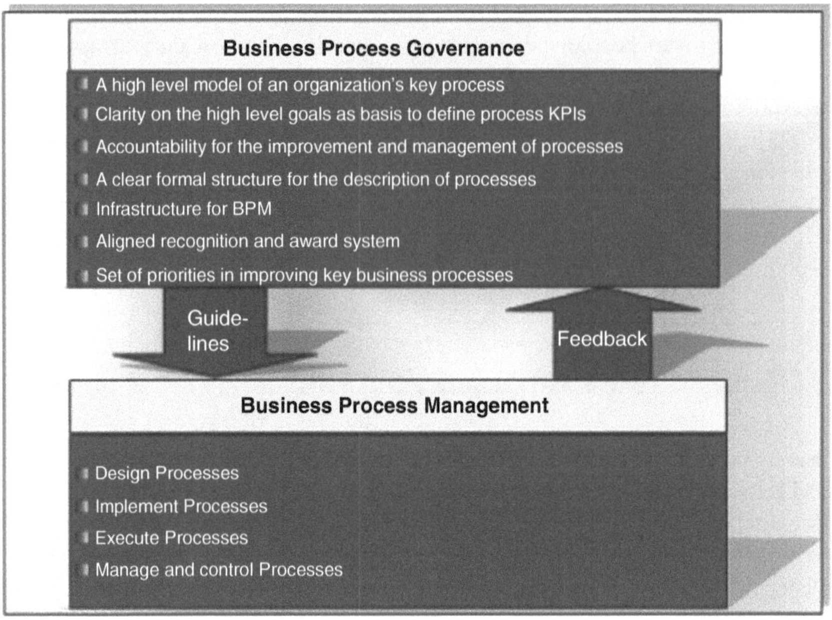


**Fig. 5** Relation of BPG and Business Process Management

BPG is relevant for all phases of MPE: design, implementation, execution, as well as monitoring and controlling of processes. Each phase of MPE is guided by BPG, leading to its overall orchestration. These guidelines may target the content of process models (e.g., identifying and mitigating risks) or purely formal aspects of BPM (e.g., each function of a process model must be assigned to the responsible and accountable organizational unit).

An example of a BPG guideline for process design is "graphically identify operational risk in process models." A process implementation example is "deploying the related business application software (ERP, SCM, CRM, etc.) to support the business processes" (Kirchmer and Scheer 2004) (resulting in a "process-oriented implementation"). "Any change of the process workflow must be approved by the managers of the involved departments" is an example of a guideline for process execution. "Benchmarks for process KPIs have to be checked and, if necessary, updated every 6 months" guides the CPI in the controlling phase of MPE.

What is the broader background of BPG? BPG is the required foundation to assure the sustainability of process innovation and improvements and the continuous focus on creating value for all stakeholders, such as customers, business partners, employees, and shareholders. The importance of governance has already been recognized in one-time improvements to individual business processes, such as order to cash, source to pay or new product development. Its importance increases significantly when an organization decides to deploy MPE on an enterprise level for competitive advantage.

BPG ensures and guides the enterprise-specific execution of MPE. It is an essential component of leadership; therefore, general principles for execution of strategies and management tasks must be considered when defining BPG for an organization (Bossidy and Charan 2002):

- Know your people and your business
- Insist on realism
- Set clear goals and priorities
- Follow through
- Reward the doers
- Expand the capabilities of your employees

To develop BPG for an organization, it is crucial that the leadership team knows the people and the business of an enterprise within the context of key business processes. A focus on realism and achieving a shared understanding of the organization's business processes are required when developing BPG guidelines; otherwise, the guidelines are worthless. At a minimum, the leadership team must have a common understanding of the high-level business processes, including clarity on organizational responsibilities, deliverables, inputs, outputs, key functional steps, dependencies, and KPIs. Within BPG, clear goals and priorities must be set so that people's efforts in executing MPE activities are as effective as possible and that appropriate attention is set on innovation and agility. BPG ensures that business performance management activities create value, and the "doers" or people, who get them done, are rewarded. This really makes BPM a part of the how the organization completes work. BPG should include guidelines for training and education to expand the capabilities of employees, and call attention to the importance of cross-functional collaboration to properly equip people involved in BPM.

The leaders of organizations that chose to deploy MPE as a management discipline appreciate that value is created and work is accomplished via the organization's business processes. They recognize the importance of MPE to topics, such as strategy, growth, and the integration of mergers and acquisitions. These topics typically preoccupy the thoughts of leadership teams – the people of an organization responsible for making MPE happen – in high-performance businesses.

Thoughtful leaders recognize that MPE enables the clearer formulation and execution of strategy. As far back as 1985, Michael Porter emphasized the concept of the value chain and noted, "Activities, then, are the basics of competitive advantage. Overall advantage or disadvantage results from all of a company's activities, not only a few" and then went on to say, "The essence of strategy is choosing to perform activities differently than rivals do" (Porter 1996). Organizational strategy drives the design of BPG and MPE enables the execution of strategy. This aspect supports MPE's key role as the link between strategy and operations, which will drive high performance for the organization.

When it comes to sustainable organic growth and innovation, leaders also recognize that MPE is equally important. Rapid, sustainable growth requires a systemic view of the business and broad collaboration, which requires immense effort from many firms. The design of BPG must recognize that focusing on goals, such as flawless delivery responsiveness, is essential in providing existing products or services to existing or new markets.

When growth is planned through mergers or acquisitions, the integration phase is essential to success. Perceptive leaders appreciate that an important reason for the success of mergers or acquisitions is the ability of the merged firm to perform for and meet the needs of their customers. It is in the "integration phase" that MPE can play an enabling role. This is related to the fact that merged firms often have an opportunity to gather specific information on comparative core business processes and their relative health, and address customer facing issues in the premerger due diligence period. MPE makes M&A initiatives innovation projects, creating a new organization that uses systematically synergies between the merging companies by providing the transparency, for example, though the process repositories used in the process factory.

BPG plays a key role in MPE and enabling high performance for an enterprise. Organizations elect to invest energy in establishing BPG because it is the management infrastructure that enables them to address critical topics, such as strategy, growth, and the integration of mergers and acquisitions through the improvement and management of the corporation's core business processes. BPG sets the stage to achieve competitive advantage through MPE. It moves MPE to a consequent support of innovation and agility.

In the previously described concept of the Enterprise 2.0+, BPG must be adapted by focusing on goals and general directions regarding the MPE activities, while still addressing the aforementioned topics. BPG has to offer sufficient freedom – and also sufficient direction – to people to truly use the benefits of Web 2.0 capabilities. Creativity and collaboration need to be applied to achieve the organization's goals and provide value to the relevant stakeholders.

BPG is, in organizations, often addressed through a specialized Center of Excellence (CoE). The CoE delivers process management services to the organizations, provides the necessary standards, and enforces BPG rules and guidelines. The CoE organizes the "Process of Process Management" and its roll out in the form of a project portfolio. The main aspects to be considered while setting up a CoE are shown in Fig. 6. Rosemann provides a detailed discussion on the service portfolio of BPM centers of excellence (Rosemann 2010), and Jesus et al. show how a center of excellence has been implemented at a Brazilian company (Jesus et al. 2010).

CoE in an MPE environment enforces the consequent realization of agility and innovation. For example, it selects and enforces standards around the process life cycle, supporting the "process factory", such as an enterprise wide repository, or provides flexible process execution and controlling solutions to the entire organization.

BPG provides to an MPE environment enough freedom to achieve innovation and agility and combines it with sufficient structure to ensure the alignment with the overall strategy. It makes MPE the key link between strategy and operations enabling sustainable high performance.

MPE expands a BPM approach through a consistent focus on innovation and agility. It enables smart decisions and a fast execution of the resulting actions. MPE is based on an industrialized management of all phases of a process life cycle in an integrated way that links business strategy with operations through a systematic use

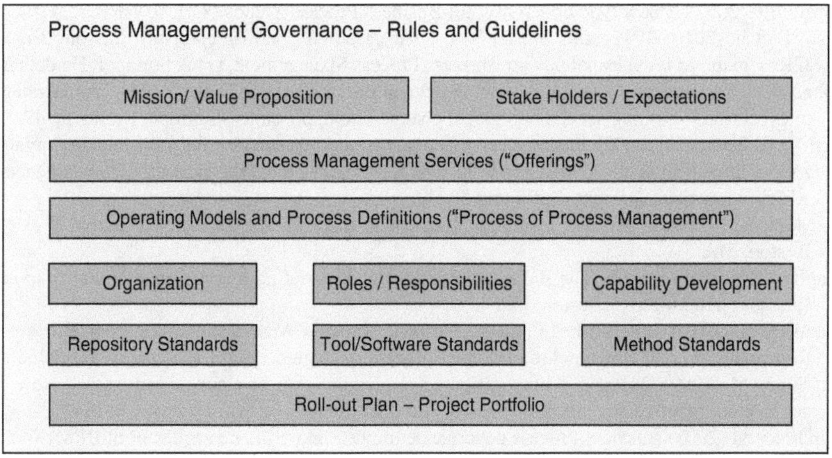


**Fig. 6** Main aspects of a governance and process management center of excellence

of process assets. The focus of MPE on innovation is paramount since process innovation is of the highest importance for most organizations. Key enablers are flexible IT systems architectures like SOA. The appropriate governance for MPE delivers enough structure to focus the approach and leaves the necessary freedom for creative solutions.

## References

Bartlett CA, Ghoshal S (2002) Managing across boarders – The transnational solution. Harvard Business School Press, Boston, MA

Bossidy L, Charan R (2002) Execution: the discipline of getting things done. Crown Business, New York

Davila T, Epstein MJ, Shelton R (2006) Making innovation work. Wharton School Publishing, Upper Saddle River, NJ

Fettke P, Loos P (eds) (2007) Reference modeling for business systems analysis. IDEA Group, Hershey, PA

Fingar P (2006) Extreme competition – Innovation and the great 21st Century business reformation. Meghan-Kiffer, Tampa, FL

Fleisch E, Christ O, Dierkes M (2005) Die betriebswirtschaftliche Vision des Internets der Dinge. In: Fleisch E, Mattern F (eds) Das Internet der Dinge – Ubiquitous Computing und RFID in der Praxis. Springer, Berlin, pp 3–37

George ML (2003) Lean six sigma for service – Conquer complexity and achieve major cost reductions in less than a year. McGraw-Hill, New York

George M, Works J, Watson-Hemphill K (2005) Fast innovation – Achieving superior differentiation, speed to market, and increased profitability. McGraw-Hill, New York

Hammer M (2005) Six steps to operational innovation. In: Harvard Business School Working Knowledge for Business, hbswk.hbs.edu, 8/30/2005

Harmon P (2003) Business process change management – a manager's guide to improving, redesigning, and automating processes. Morgan Kaufmann, San Francisco, CA

Harmon P (2007) A new type of activity. In: Business Process Trends (ed.) Newsletter, 5(19)
Jesus L et al. (2010) BPM center of excellence. The case of a Brazilian company. In: vom Brocke J, Rosemann M (eds) Handbook on Business Process Management, vol 2. Springer, Heidelberg
Johnson M, Suskewicz J (2008) Accelerating innovation. In: Pantaleo D, Pal N (eds) From strategy to execution – Turning accelerated global change into opportunity. Springer, Berlin, pp 49–64
Jost W, Scheer A-W (2002) Business process management: a core task for any company organization. In: Scheer A-W, Abolhassan F, Jost W, Kirchmer M (eds) Business process excellence – ARIS in practice. Springer, Berlin, pp 33–43
Kalakota R, Robinson M (2003) Service blueprint: a roadmap for execution. Addison-Wesley, Boston, MA
Kaplan R, Norton D (1996) The Balanced Scorecard – Translating Strategy into Action. Harvard Business School Press, Boston, MA
Kemsley S (2010) Enterprise 2.0 meets Business Process Management. In: vom Brocke J, Rosemann M (eds) Handbook on business process management, vol 1. Springer, Heidelberg
Kirchmer M (1999) Business process oriented implementation of standard software – How to achieve competitive advantage efficiently and effectively, 2nd edn. Springer, Berlin
Kirchmer M (2005) Business Process governance: orchestrating the management of BPM. White paper, Berwyn, PA
Kirchmer M (2007) Knowledge communication empowers SOA for business agility. In: The 11th World Multi-Conference on systemics, cybernetics and informatics, July 8–11, 2007, Orlando, FL, Proceedings, Volume III, pp 301–307, 2007
Kirchmer M (2008) High performance through process excellence – from strategy to operations. Springer, Berlin
Kirchmer M, Scheer A-W (2003) Change management – Key for business process excellence. In: Scheer A-W, Abolhassan F, Jost W, Kirchmer M (eds) Business process change management – ARIS in practice. Springer, Berlin, pp 1–14
Kirchmer M, Scheer A-W (2004) Business process automation – Combining best and next practices. In: Scheer A-W, Abolhassan F, Jost W, Kirchmer M (eds) Business process automation – ARIS in practice. Springer, Berlin, pp 1–15
Kirchmer M, Spanyi A (2007) Business process governance, 2nd edn. White paper, Berwyn, PA
Markus ML, Jacobson DD (2010) Business process goverance. In: vom Brocke J, Rosemann M (eds) Handbook on business process management, vol 2. Springer, Heidelberg
Mattern F (2005) Die technische Basis fuer das Internet der Dinge. In: Fleisch E, Mattern F (eds) Das Internet der Dinge – Ubiquitous Computing und RFID in der Praxis. Springer, Berlin, pp 39–66
McAffee A (2006) Enterprise 2.0: the dawn of emergent collaboration. MIT Sloan Manage Rev 47(3) pp 21–28
O'Reilly T (2005) What is Web 2.0 – Design patterns and business models for the next generation of software. In: www.oreilly.com, 9/30/2005.
Porter M (1996) "What is strategy?" Harv Bus Rev, November–December 1996
Rosemann M (2010) The service portfolio of a BPM center of excellence. In: vom Brocke J, Rosemann M (eds) Handbook on business process management, vol 2. Springer, Heidelberg
Scheer A-W (1998a) ARIS – Business process frameworks, 2nd edn. Springer, Berlin
Scheer A-W (1998b) ARIS – Business process modeling, 2nd edn. Springer, Berlin
Scheer A-W, Brabänder E (2010) The process of business process management. In: vom Brocke J, Rosemann M (eds) Handbook on business process management, vol 2. Springer, Heidelberg
Snee R, Hoerl R (2003) Leading six sigma – A step-by-step guide based on experience with ge and other six sigma companies. Prentice-Hall, Upper Saddle River, NJ
Spanyi A (2006) More for less – The power of process management. Meghan-Kiffer, Tampa, FL
Woods D (2003) Enterprise service architectures. SOA, Beijing
Woods D, Mattern T (2006) Enterprise SOA – Designing IT for business innovation. O'Reilly, Bejing

# Process Capital as Strategic Success Factor: The Lufthansa Example

**Markus Brenner and André Coners**

**Abstract** The high importance of processes regarding a company's success has been known for a long time. However, the level of importance of processes, especially in comparison with other success factors, has not been in focus in a consequent matter yet. The research regarding "intangible assets" now provides a new perspective. According to recent research findings, "process capital" is one of the most important assets of a company. In consequence, process capital has to be built up and managed and has to be a major focus of corporate strategy. On the one hand, the process capital can be the basis for strategy development. On the other hand, process capital is essential for strategy implementation. Process capital management (PCM) is the concept that, in addition to a "classical" process management, also focuses on developing and preserving intangible assets. This chapter gives an introduction to process capital. Then, the correlation between process capital and strategy is analyzed. Furthermore, a suggestion is made regarding the further development of process management toward PCM. Finally, the importance of process capital is illustrated by means of a real-life example from Lufthansa.

## 1 Processes as Intangible Assets ("Process Capital")

It is almost general knowledge that processes are important to a company's success. However, it is rare to focus attention on the level of mimportance of processes. Therefore, a systematic approach to processes, in part regarding their impact upon corporate success, is necessary in order to manage process potential to its full extent. Generally speaking, corporate success can be attributed to the existence – and efficient and effective utilization – of a company's resources. Analyzing the determinants of corporate success – known as success factors – is part of success research

M. Brenner (✉)
Horváth and Partners Management Consultants, Stuttgart, Germany
e-mail: mbrenner@horvath-partners.com

J. vom Brocke and M. Rosemann (eds.), *Handbook on Business Process Management 2*, International Handbooks on Information Systems,
DOI 10.1007/978-3-642-01982-1_3, 

(e.g., Rockart 1979). We distinguish between two types of success factors: internal factors such as resources and external factors such as market share. When looking at company resources, we distinguish between three categories: financial resources, material resources, and immaterial resources (known as intangible assets). Empirical testing has shown that intangible assets induce significant reactions on the capital market (cf. Lev and Sougiannis 1999). Intangible assets can be defined as "the non-material and non-financial resources a company can exploit for longer than the current reporting year" (Günther et al. 2004, p. 162). In the following definition from the Schmalenbach Gesellschaft, which is derived on the basis of Edvinsson's and Malone's system (cf. Edvinsson and Malone 1997, p. 65), intangibles are broken down into seven categories (cf. WGARIA 2005, p. 68). Within this definition, process capital is exemplified as a category of intangible assets (see Fig. 1). Accordingly, process capital is understood as "Intangible values that relate to an entity's organization, primarily in terms of structure and process" (WGARIA 2005, p. 69). "Examples include a well-functioning distribution and/or communication network as well as effective quality management processes" (WGARIA 2005, p. 69).

In another definition, processes are seen as a main component of "organizational infrastructure." This organizational infrastructure embodies "business processes and systems that transform "lifeless things," tangible and intangible, to bundles of assets generating cash flows and conferring competitive positions" (Lev and Daum 2003, p. 7). These authors attach great importance to organizational infrastructure: "[. . .] organizational infrastructure, when operating effectively, is the major intangible of the firm" (Lev and Daum 2003, p. 7).

In consequence, process capital is created by the existence or development of processes which represent economic advantages. As a result, the company's intangible assets are increased.

A detailed definition of process capital distinguishes between the two components of *process structure* (cf. Becker and Kahn 2003) in the sense of an operational structure and *process performance* (Heckl and Moormann 2010). From the perspective of a company, the existence of defined processes that

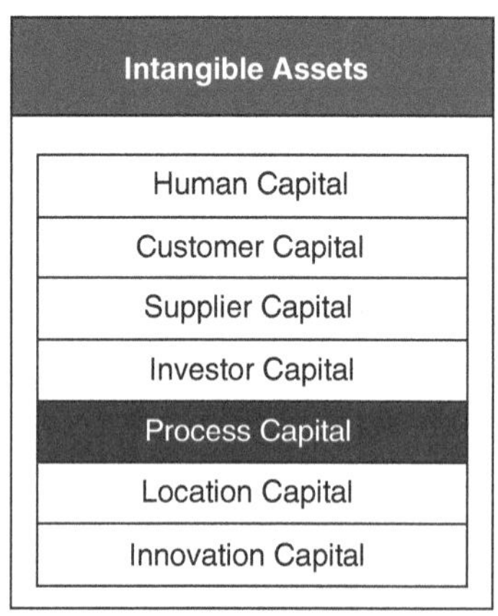


**Fig. 1** Process capital as a category of intangible assets based on: WGARIA 2005, p. 68

conform to corporate business targets represents a "value". On the basis of the business model a company chooses, the aim is to have and to develop the "right" processes in terms of strategic and operative efficiency and effectiveness targets. Thus, for example, HAMMER stresses the effectiveness target: "Processes are what create the results that a company delivers to its customers" (Hammer 2007, p. 53). The existence of the "right" processes enables the company (cf. Mayer 2005, p. 2) in the following:

- To recognize the relevant market trends and to translate these into products faster than the competition
- To recognize its target markets and target customer groups and to address and coordinate them appropriately
- To establish support processes which provide effective support for the business model and demonstrate benchmarkable efficiency
- To manage the value-adding processes in such a way as to ensure an optimal division between which activities are carried out internally and which are outsourced
- To organize the collaboration with value-adding partners along commercial aspects

The existence of a defined and (ideally) well-documented process structure alone does not suffice to ensure corporate success and "sustainability" or whether process capital retains its value over time. Rather, the important aim here lies in shaping the processes to conform to the targets they must achieve in terms of costs, time, and quality. This is known as process performance management (Heckl and Moormann 2010). Process performance has a direct impact upon the central key performance indicators of turnover and costs (cf. Mayer 2005, p. 5). Defined processes which satisfy their performance targets are the embodiment of sustainable process capital. If we understand process capital in these terms, it becomes "[...] a sustainable strategic competitive advantage, a dynamic core competency of a company" (Osterloh and Frost 2006, p. 7).

As such, process capital is seen as an extremely important success factor – based on its contribution to company success – compared with the other categories of intangible assets, as shown in empirical studies (cf. Günther et al. 2005, p. 101ff.). Against this background, value-based corporate management should go beyond material assets (e.g., management and controlling of fixed asset investments) and focus on managing and controlling intangible assets, especially process capital. One key aspect should not be ignored: according to OSTERLOH/FROST, process capital only exists when process structure and performance can be deployed to create value, or at least to preserve it. This is the case when processes are aligned with corporate strategy in terms of structure and performance. This then gives rise to the question of how to design and shape processes so that they help the company to reach its strategic financial and customer targets. Consequently, these targets should form the starting point for designing all processes – from the innovation process, through the processes for supply chain, operations, market, and customer relationship, to the processes for internal services. With Business Process Management

(BPM), a management concept already exists to this end. However, BPM lacks the goal of preserving and further developing process capital as an intangible asset.

The main focus of this chapter is to describe the correlation between process capital and strategy. This correlation will be illustrated by means of a real-life example from Deutsche Lufthansa AG (hereafter Lufthansa). Furthermore, a suggestion regarding the further development of BPM toward process capital management (PCM) is made.

# 2 The Correlation Between Strategy and Process Capital

## *2.1 Overview*

The choice and form of a corporate strategy, which set appropriate targets are seen as a significant success factor in both academia and industry. In the 80s and 90s of the last century, two main perspectives arose from the mass of systematization approaches and became established in the business world: Porter's market-based approach (cf. Porter 1998) and the resource-based approach of Prahalad and Hamel (1990). Great importance is attached to the resource-based approach as a method of creating competitive advantage: "Establishing competitive advantage involves formulating and implementing a strategy that exploits the uniqueness of a firm's portfolio of resources and capabilities" (Grant 2005, p. 136f). In contrast, Porter places the approach of delimiting the relevant market and market-based design of products and services at the heart of the strategy discussion. This discussion focuses on a promising two-pronged strategic orientation on the goals of cost and quality leadership (cf. Porter 1998, p. 45). In the meantime, there is a broadly accepted view that both approaches can interact with each other: "Strategy is concerned with matching a firm's resources and capabilities to the opportunities that arise in the external environment" (Grant 2005, p. 132). In the following, we share this integrating view of the strategic approaches. Nevertheless, as process capital deals with the company's resources, there is a strong emphasis on the resource-based view throughout this article.

If we look at the plethora of publications on strategic management (cf. Mintzberg et al. 1998 for an overview of the different schools of thought), we can identify two main questions: How do we substantiate strategy content and how do we implement the defined strategy in the company's daily business? A company's existing process capital, or that which needs to be built up, plays an important role in answering these questions. As Chandler said, "Structure follows strategy" (Chandler 1962, p. 14), and this is often used to exemplify how interdependent strategy and organization, and hence processes, are. If we see strategy as the means of implementing corporate goals, then it becomes clear that we need processes with which we can plan, execute, and monitor measures toward strategy implementation (Burlton 2010). Consequently, processes and process targets must be derived from strategy.

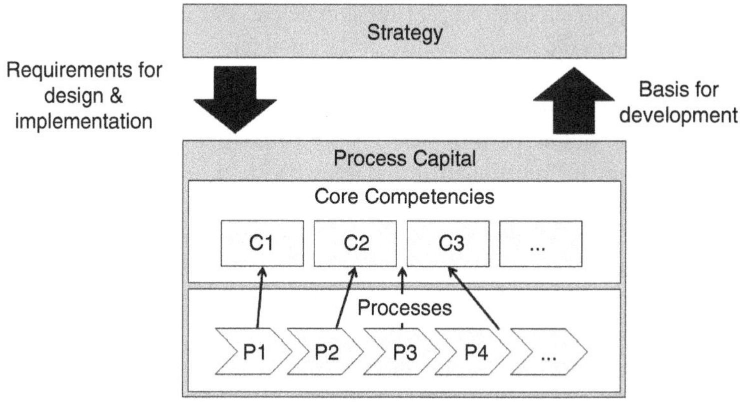


**Fig. 2** The interrelationship between strategy and process capital

An empirical study gave a fitting summary: "Get your strategic objectives aligned with business processes" (Hung 2006, p. 37).

However, processes should also be seen as strategic success factors when substantiating the content of strategies. Indeed, it is often the case that the key success factor for business models is the company's ability to master core competencies. Among other things, running a successful "no-frills" airline depends on efficiently mastering aircraft turnaround and thus reducing ground time. Numerous other examples in industry could be given here to prove the hypothesis of a positive correlation between corporate success and process capital, where processes are seen as core competencies (one prime example would be Google's internet-based search process). Thus, existing and future process capital must be taken into consideration when formulating strategy. Figure 2 summarizes the interrelationship between strategy and process capital.

On the one hand, the process capital, which consists of processes that are part of a company's core competencies, can be the basis for strategy development. On the other hand, the defined strategy gives rise to parameters for process structure and performance. We can talk about interdependence.

On the basis of the literature cited here, we can assume that both the ability to regard processes as an organization's core competency when formulating strategy, especially the processes that are "visible" for the recipient, and the ability to accurately design and shape process structures and process performance on the basis of the strategy a company chooses represent success factors. We explain these success factors in more detail in the following sections.

## 2.2 *Core Competencies in Process Capital*

The underlying idea of aligning strategy with the strengths of a company in the sense of *core competencies*, for example, certain processes, results from the resource-based approach to strategy. Core competencies can be processes that will play a central role in the future because of the company's strategic orientation and are already well-established in the company – or can be developed to be so. As a rule, it is difficult for other companies to create or acquire these processes in terms of their structure and/or performance. These limited resources are difficult to imitate and cannot be substituted (cf. Barney 1991, p. 105 f.) and as such are particularly valuable. Consequently, they are also called strategic resources or strategic success factors. Generally, not all of a company's processes fall into this category. Hence, support processes are regularly well-documented and described by standard IT applications. These outsourceable processes have little impact upon strategy development and implementation.

What do impact upon the development of core competencies, however, are the so-called *core processes*. "Core processes are processes that cross functional boundaries, produce an output that is strategically important to the organization's success, and have a high impact on customer satisfaction" (Hung 2000, p. 4). Insofar as the process capital which exists in an organization is unique, cannot be imitated, and comprises processes which generate value (core processes), we can consider the idea of aligning strategy with this process capital.

In the following section, we take a look at how process capital can be used to implement strategies.

## 2.3 Strategy Implementation Using Process Capital

The strategic level represents the "initiating and shaping factor in corporate management" (Ahlrichs and Knuppertz 2006, p. 23). Successful strategy implementation requires its prior operationalization. This, in turn, raises the question of which processes contribute to reaching targets and realizing the strategic plan, and to what extent. This can be seen in the fact that processes are one of the four perspectives of the Balanced Scorecard, which is used as an instrument of strategy implementation (cf. Kaplan and Norton 1996).

However, there is a major deficit in traditional corporate management: Strategic and operative planning is usually separated and lacks rigorous and consistent linkage. As such, the strategic plan is developed as a requirement for annual operative planning (budgeting) and for mid-term planning in the form of planning premises and target values. While the operative planning budgets and financial performance indicators focus on *individual organizational units,* in terms of strategic targeting, we often focus on quantitative and qualitative indicator variables at *overall company level.* This schism in organizational bearing within the planning system can lead to operative plans being developed whose contribution to strategy implementation cannot be measured. In contrast, however, we can use a process orientation to combine the strategic and operative planning levels by focusing on *processes which cross functional and organizational boundaries* from strategic targeting all the way through to operative realization (cf. Ahlrichs and Knuppertz 2006, p. 21). The processes are aligned with both strategic and operative targets.

When it comes to implementing strategies, the strategies themselves should be used to derive process-related target values. Hence, if a company decides to pursue the strategy of quality leadership, all its processes must focus on securing the desired level of quality. The operational processes work toward creating a top-quality product. For marketing and customer relationship processes, this desire for quality must be reflected in customer dealings. Within the innovation process, all efforts should be focused on developing top-class products which are difficult for competitors to imitate in terms of the degree of novelty. Since the mid-nineties, the *Balanced Scorecard* has become an established instrument for deriving requirements from strategy. By using the Balanced Scorecard in combination with a further tool known as the *Strategy Map*, it becomes possible to substantiate strategies and to document the specific target values which act as yardsticks for the implementation phase. From the aspect of processes, the process perspective defined in the Balanced Scorecard, together with the targets it stipulates, is of particular importance for the strategic fields of action. Companies that use the Balanced Scorecard already have a first focus on processes for the Key Performance Indicator-based implementation of their strategies – because of the integrated business process perspective.

This, however, does not appear to suffice as only the main targets with strategic relevance are considered in a Balanced Scorecard. It is precisely that focus on few targets that KAPLAN/NORTON see as a success factor of the Balanced Scorecard. Yet, when we derive the strategic demands upon processes, we actually want to define comprehensive targets for all strategically relevant processes and be able to measure the extent to which those targets are reached. To do this, we need to use KPIs to determine the contribution of process capital to strategy implementation, or the extent to which strategic goals are reached, and to compare this with target values.

It is for this reason that we wish to introduce an instrument known as the *Strategic Process Alignment matrix* (SPA matrix) as a method of aligning processes with corporate strategy. The SPA matrix establishes formal, KPI-based relations between strategy and those processes with strategic relevance. Thus, strategic requirements upon process performance should be portrayed and made measurable. To do this, we use a matrix to systematically compare the strategic goals, which for example, can be taken from a Strategy Map with the core processes. In this way, we can assess the contribution of process capital to strategy based on the criteria of "process relevance" and "degree of target achievement." Process relevance represents a weighting in percent of how relevant a process is for reaching the strategic goal. As several processes are relevant for achieving a specific strategic goal, we have to weigh the impact of the different processes upon the goal as a whole when estimating the percentage values. Hence, we analyze and estimate the extent to which a process should contribute to reaching a specific strategic target.

Subsequently, the concrete demand upon the process is specified in the form of a performance indicator, which measures target achievement, and a target value. This is done for each strategic target and "relevant" process. By comparing actual and target values and carrying out deviation analyzes, we can monitor and manage the conformity of process performance with strategic targets. Thus, the SPA matrix provides management with a strategy-based process cockpit. In the example of SPA

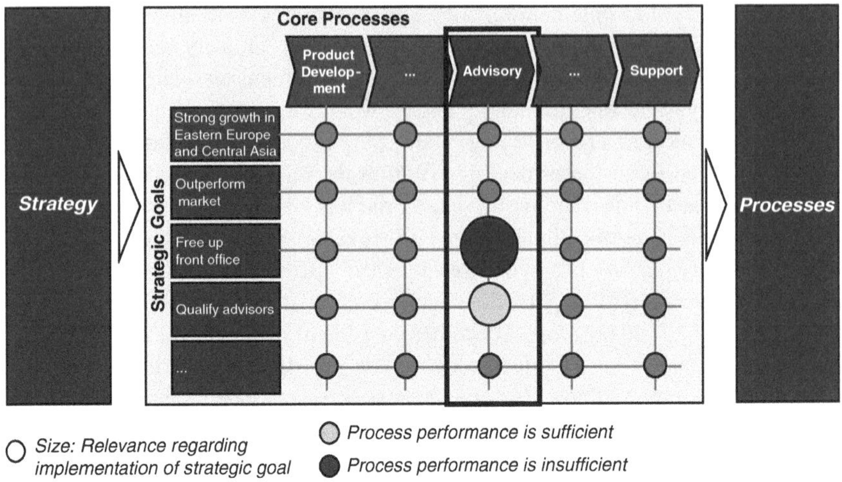


**Fig. 3** Example depiction of the SPA matrix

matrix portrayed in Fig. 3, the strategic goals were developed in Balanced Scorecard workshops. After the finalization of the company's Strategy Map, another accompanying workshop was initiated: Within "SPA" workshops, executed with the management team, the implications for each process regarding each strategic goal were discussed. As an example, the advisory process of a bank which has a relatively high relevance for the strategic goal "Free up front office" fails to meet strategic requirements. This might be due to the fact that this process still has too many high-maintenance communication interfaces to the back office, which in turn might be measured using the performance indicator "Number of interfaces in process."

By using the SPA matrix, companies are able to track process performance from a strategic point of view. Nevertheless, the following question still remains: how can companies design their management system so that it systematically creates process-based values?

# 3 Process Capital Management

## *3.1 Overview*

After the previous chapters focused on the importance of process capital, we shall now show how process capital can be built up and managed systematically. Before presenting and detailing the necessary tasks and activities, we first need to analyze the term PCM in terms of what is commonly called BPM. "Traditional" process management (BPM) represents a management approach which describes how to manage processes using strategic and operative targets. The same applies to PCM. In addition to the classical "management" of processes, however, PCM goes one

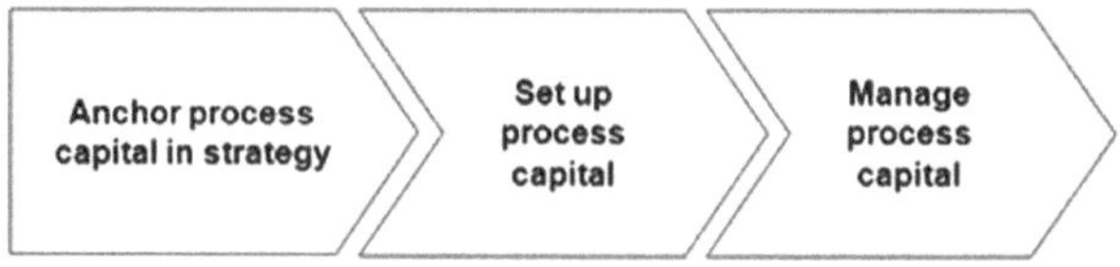


**Fig. 4** Tasks of PCM

step further by also focusing on developing and preserving intangible assets. This means that also and especially the relationships of process capital to the other intangible asset categories, for example, human capital, are considered and controlled using an integrative management approach (Fig. 4).

Once the concept of process capital has been firmly anchored in strategy, one of the major tasks consists of actually building up that process capital. Subsequently, we need to implement an appropriate management control system to secure the long-term existence of the process capital stock. These tasks have to be substantiated and shaped in the form of a PCM control loop. This control loop should ensure process capital is involved in planning, developing, and managing the process capital stock and ensure that those developments are fed back retrospectively into the planning process. On a sideline note, the tasks of PCM should be institutionalized in the company's organization (e.g., by a process management unit in collaboration with the controlling department) in order to secure the sustainability of PCM.

In the following subsections, we describe the tasks mentioned here in more detail.

## 3.2 Anchoring Process Capitals in the Strategy

One of the first tasks we need to carry out is to integrate a "perspective" focusing on process capital into the strategy development and planning process. To do this, we must first know and formally describe the company's processes. Explicit steps aimed at checking the process-based core competencies and their impact upon related financial and market performance indicators must be included in the strategic planning process. On the one hand, the *strategy development* phase involves testing the extent to which core competencies arising from the process model might support the strategic options being evaluated. The objectives underlying this step are first to prioritize potential strategic actions based on an analysis of the existing process capital in connection with the strategic options on hand. Second, we need to find out which elements of process capital can be developed using specific measures so as to provide process-based support for the prioritized strategic options.

One further aspect of integrating process capital into the company's strategy can be found in the phase aimed at *operationalizing strategy*. By using the SPA matrix described above, we can substantiate the strategy by capturing the requirements for each strategically important process. This then results in performance indicators and target values which are used in the next phase of strategy implementation to track progress at process level. Should deviations from target values occur, these can be recognized at an early stage, and we can take the appropriate decisions to modify *strategy implementation*. Special attention needs to be paid to the company's core processes. If there is not enough de facto mastery of these processes in terms of target values, we need to build up the appropriate process capital needed for strategy implementation.

## 3.3 Building up Process Capital

We can build up the process capital needed to secure strategy implementation by carrying out process design and optimization measures (*business process optimization*). In this way, the process structure and performance required (usually at short notice) for strategy implementation can be created. However, this is not enough to secure sustainable process capital, as carrying out process transformations is not only extremely resource-intensive, but also representing a considerable burden upon the company's employees. For this reason, it is advisable to create an environment which is conducive to systematically developing process capital as a permanent core competency for the company. Several factors play an important role here: process culture, change management, and human capital. *Process culture* should be seen as taking overriding priority and should be closely connected with the company's organizational structures, in the sense of being the "complete and self-evident classification and execution of all business activities in the form of processes" (Ahlrichs and Knuppertz 2006, p. 43). In this way, employees are not connected with one another primarily through the company's hierarchy, but rather through the processes. The resultant reduction in the number of organizational interfaces can lead to more efficient communication and a more flexible corporate structure.

Alongside process culture, *change management* represents a significant contribution to establishing process capital. On the one hand, building up process capital involves changing "hard facts," such as the structure of processes and the organizational structure. On the other hand, "soft factors" also change, for example the behavior of employees as process owners. Special importance to processes of learning and change, which focus on ensuring that an organization is capable of adapting (for example, by employee multi-skilling) to dynamic changes in the conditions affecting process execution (for example, change in strategy, collapse in demand, etc.) is attached here. This also makes another category of intangible assets particularly important for sustainable process capital: *human capital*, insofar as this shapes, executes, and controls the processes. A reduction in the number of hierarchy levels, accompanied by a focus on end-to-end processes, can, for example, strengthen the employees' personal sense of responsibility, which ought to result in the creation of creativity potentials because of the existence of a common mindset. Against this background, raising innovation capital can in turn lead to

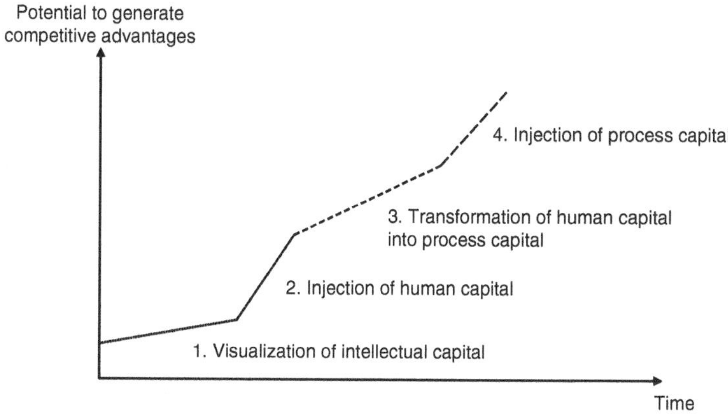


**Fig. 5** Generating process capital based on: Edvinsson (2000), p.15

the development of new, innovative processes (cf. Becker and Kahn 2003, p. 8). Human capital is a major platform for building up process capital, as can be seen in Fig. 5.

Initially, we need to establish an awareness of the existence of intellectual capital in the organization ("Visualization of intellectual capital"). We must create an in-depth understanding among staff about actual and target processes using employee programs and change management methods. This will enable process capital to develop into practical and applicable knowledge which can be used to create value in the company. By combining this with human capital ("Injection of human capital"), the organization's processes can be enhanced and improved. These newly (documented and) acquired skills and knowledge result in actual process capital as a core competency firmly anchored in the organization ("Transformation of human capital into process capital"). As these competencies can be traced back to methods and techniques, they are no longer tied to individual employees and are hence firmly and permanently anchored in the company (portrayed as the "Injection of process capital" in Fig. 5).

## *3.4 Managing Process Capital*

Companies wishing to build up process capital must permanently analyze their processes in terms of performance: process flows need to be questioned and, if necessary, modified to fit new situations. We can use PCM here to comprise planning, and organizational and control measures for managing the value chain in terms of costs, time, quality, and – as a consequence – customer satisfaction.

Here, process controlling plays a central role, which can be seen as aligning planning, control, and management to those processes being examined (cf. Heckl and Moormann 2010). The main task of process controlling is to make processes measurable and hence to provide the institutionalized information necessary for process control. To do this, process controlling instruments can be used. Depending on their specific data and analysis focus, these can be classified on the basis of whether they serve to measure strategic or operative performance. Examples of strategically oriented instruments include the SPA matrix mentioned earlier and activity-based costing (ABC), a tool for strategic cost management (cf. Kaplan and Anderson 2004). To measure and analyze operative process performance, we could, for example, carry out business activity monitoring (cf. Wang 1999) and data mining using process-related databases (cf. van der Aalst et al. 2003). The aim here is to facilitate early recognition of problems in process flows in order to be able to initiate suitable and timely countermeasures.

The information provided should contain statements about the efficiency and effectiveness of the processes. To this end, it is necessary to define and measure performance indicators which influence the success of the processes (cf. Heckl and Moormann 2010). Alongside financial indicators such as process cost rates, these are mainly nonfinancial variables which focus on time (e.g., run time) and quality (e.g., error rate for process output). Process controlling does not only comprise measuring and reporting performance indicators, however. In fact, it actually reflects the "classical" understanding of controlling in that it deals with planning and monitoring targets, as well as initiating countermeasures. In terms of process controlling, this means we need to define process targets, to regularly measure the extent to which those targets are reached, and, if necessary, to set appropriate reactions to deviations from plan in motion. In this way, we can firmly anchor the development of processes into the company (cf. Neumann et al. 2003, p. 234).

Last but not least: for a concise overview about the development stage of process capital, a process maturity model – such as Hammer's Process and Enterprise Maturity Model (PEMM) (cf. Hammer 2007) – can be applied. Subsequently, a target/actual comparison of the process maturity level or a benchmarking project results in measures for maintaining process capital.

## 4 Case Study: Lufthansa AG

### *4.1 Example of Lufthansa's Process Capital*

Case study research can be regarded as a common approach to verifying or negating scientific statements (cf. Yin 2008). In the following, we try to illustrate the PCM concept by means of Lufthansa. All information regarding the Lufthansa case study is on the basis of publicly available documents. The authors have interpreted core competencies and processes as process capital. Many of its core competencies, which are mandatory for Lufthansa's strategy, can be contributed to process capital. As the airline industry in Europe has been characterized by a movement toward concentration in recent years, one of Lufthansa's important strategic goals is to grow, either organically, or through co-operations and takeovers. Consequently, through its complete acquisition of the Swiss airline Swiss, together with shareholdings in other aviation businesses, such as Jet Blue and its involvement in Austrian Airlines, Lufthansa has been able to gain considerable ground in important markets. However, integrating another airline into its own network is not an easy task. Lufthansa has proven to have the right processes for such integration work. In particular, the takeover of Swiss and its subsequent integration into Lufthansa's route network can be seen as a prime example of the importance of process capital. Integrating other airlines into one's own route network is a substantial undertaking as each and every airline has its own very individual characteristics. Alongside such factors as having different aircraft types, integrating the systems (route network, IT systems, etc.) represents an especially challenging hurdle. The availability of a process which can incorporate other airlines into Lufthansa's network represents a key core process for Lufthansa. Lufthansa is able to tap into prior experience. Back in 1997, the company was the initiator and founding member of the airline network Star Alliance. The skills and abilities Lufthansa developed here in a multitude of operation processes and in particular the process of integration manifest themselves as process capital. The company can now rely upon this resource for takeovers and other integration activities, using it to create value.

Besides this process capital necessary for integration work, there is another prime example for process capital in the company's daily business. Lufthansa's aircraft maintenance processes, which are core processes, are best practice in the aviation world. As one result, Lufthansa has one of the highest reputations regarding safety in the market and is considered to be quality leader. As another result, Lufthansa's strategy is influenced by these maintenance processes. These processes are not used only to maintain its own fleet. Instead, Lufthansa formed a separate unit, Lufthansa Technik, which offers maintenance services to the market.

## 4.2 *Strategy Implementation at Lufthansa Based on Process Capital*

Let us now use the example of Lufthansa to demonstrate how process capital can be used to implement strategy. One of the most important strategic goals for Lufthansa is quality and innovation leadership. Considering the SPA matrix from Sect. 2.3, these goals would be in the vertical dimension of the matrix. First, we must check to see which processes are relevant to achieve these goals and to determine the requirements toward these processes. As an example, the processes "Passenger handling," "In-flight service," and "Operations" are used. These processes all contribute significantly to the strategic goals of quality and innovation leadership. In a second step, the goals have to be specified for each process and changes or improvements defined. Regarding the processes used as example, the following process changes were defined by Lufthansa:

### 4.2.1 Passenger Handling

Handling passengers consists of all land and airside processes until the passenger has boarded the aircraft. Lufthansa has derived measures from strategy to significantly improve this process. Regarding quality, the company has designed a top-class product. Specific services for top customers, such as special lounges and limousine transfer to the aircraft (for first class passengers and members of the HON level in the frequent flier program), mean Lufthansa now leads the industry in this field. Regarding innovation, home-printed boarding passes and check-in by mobile phone offer convenient ways to check in. It is obvious that in order to be able to offer the same high-end travel experience for all customers worldwide, or at least for customers to feel this is what they are receiving (service quality), the appropriate processes must be defined at every individual stage (process structure) and carried out in the same way (process performance). This means the current strategy is implemented by setting up a suitable process structure and by monitoring process performance. After successful implementation, these processes form key factors which distinguish Lufthansa from its competitors and the process capital represents a corresponding value for the company.

### 4.2.2 In-Flight Service

Another example is the in-flight service process. Lufthansa invested huge amounts of time and money on improving seating. The airline was among the first to offer flat seats throughout the international business class. These seats allow travelers to sleep more comfortably and better. Another innovation regarding customer experience was the introduction of in-flight internet access.

### 4.2.3 Operations

Not only in passenger-related processes is innovation a goal which Lufthansa implements in its processes. Several process innovations have been introduced: By the use of the "Aircraft Addressing Communication and Reporting System", data of aircraft operating worldwide are sent to the Traffic Control Center in Frankfurt and analyzed. Potential faults can immediately be detected. Lufthansa also introduced what is known as the "electronic flight bag." This system, developed by the subsidiary Lufthansa Systems, replaces lots of paper-based documentation which has to be available in the cockpit (e.g., maps). Each year, up to 16 million pieces of paper can be replaced with up-to-date information.

All these examples improve Lufthansa's processes significantly with goals out of strategy. Lufthansa can increase quality and customer satisfaction. Innovative processes also result in higher efficiency. Finally, in order to secure the process performance and the sustainability of process capital, a PCM has to be established. As a consequence, process capital is generated and represents an asset for the airline.

# 5 Summary and Outlook

Countless publications from both academia and industry deal with the importance of *processes* for corporate success. In most cases, selected examples of process optimizations and process management success stories are described without really proving what share of corporate success can actually be attributed to processes. This essay looks at this topic from a different perspective: using intangible assets – which have come to the fore in recent years – as a starting point, the intangible category of process capital is subjected to close scrutiny.

On the basis of a definition of the term process capital and a description of the correlation between process capital and strategy, this essay shows how process capital can be built up as a strategic success factor and managed permanently and consistently. Here, it is important to remember that while extensive literature can be found on other areas of research into intangibles, such as human capital, to date, there have been very few investigations into process capital. As such, this article should demonstrate the need for further research and provide impulses for a more detailed analysis of the topic. There is particular need for research into the positive correlation between process capital and PCM and corporate success postulated in this article. The use of empirical research methods (e.g., interviews with experts) would lend itself to this end.

# References


Ahlrichs F, Knuppertz T (2006) Controlling von Geschäftsprozessen: Prozessorientierte Unternehmenssteuerung umsetzen. Schäffer Poeschel, Stuttgart

Barney J (1991) Firm resources and contained competitive advantage. J Manage 19(1):99–120

Becker J, Kahn D (2003) The process in focus. In: Becker J, Kugeler M, Rosemann M (eds) Process management: a guide for the design of business processes. Springer, Berlin, pp 1–12

Burlton RT (2010) Delivering business strategy through process management. In: vom Brocke J, Rosemann M (eds) Handbook on business process management, vol 2. Springer, Heidelberg

Chandler A (1962) Strategy and structure. MIT, Cambridge

Edvinsson L (2000) Some perspectives on intangibles and intellectual capital 2000. J Intellect Capital 1(1):12–16

Edvinsson L, Malone MS (1997) Intellectual capital: realizing your company's true value by finding its hidden roots. HarperBusiness, New York

Grant RM (2005) Contemporary strategy analysis. Blackwell, Malden, MA

Günther T, Kirchner-Khairy S, Zurwehme A (2004) Measuring intangible resources for managerial accounting purposes. In: Horvath P, Möller K (eds) Intangibles in der Unternehmenssteuerung. Vahlen, München, pp 159–185

Günther T, Beyer D, Menninger J (2005) Does relevance influence reporting about environmental and intangible success factors ? – Empirical results from a survey of "new economy" executives. Schmalenbach Bus Rev Special Issue 2/05, 101–138

Hammer M (2007) The agenda. Random House, New York

Heckl D, Moormann J (2010) Process performance managment. In: vom Brocke J, Rosemann M (eds) Handbook on business process management, vol 2. Springer, Heidelberg

Hung R (2000) An empirical examination of the relationship between business process management and business performance: a study of Australia's top 100 companies. Dissertation, University of Sydney, Sydney

Hung RY-Y (2006) Business process management as competitive advantage: a review and empirical study. Total Qual Manage 17(1):21–40

Kaplan RS, Anderson SR (2004) Time-driven activity-based costing. Harv Bus Rev 11:131–138

Kaplan RS, Norton DP (1996) Balanced scorecard: translating strategy into action. Harvard Business School Press, Boston, MA

Lev B, Daum JH (2003) Intangible Assets and the need for holistic and more future-oriented approach to enterprise management and corporate reporting. URL=http://www.juergendaum.de/articles/PAPER%2010-PMA_IC_symp_lev_daum.pdf

Lev B, Sougiannis T (1999) Penetrating the book-to-market black box: the R&D-effect. J Bus Financ Account 26:419–449

Mayer R (2005) Prozessmanagement: Erfolg durch Steigerung der Prozessperformance. In: Horváth & Partners (ed), Prozessmanagement umsetzen. Schäffer Poeschel, Stuttgart, pp 1–6

Mintzberg H, Ahlstrand B, Lampel J (1998) Strategy safari: a guided tour through the wilds of strategic management. Free Press, New York

Neumann S, Probst C, Wernsmann C (2003) Continuous process management. In: Becker J, Kugeler M, Rosemann M (eds) Process management: a guide for the design of business processes. Springer, Berlin, pp 233–250

Osterloh M, Frost J (2006) Prozessmanagement als Kernkompetenz: Wie Sie Business Reengineering strategisch nutzen können. Gabler Verlag, Wiesbaden

Porter ME (1998) Competitive strategy: techniques for analyzing industries and competitors. Free Press, New York

Prahalad CG, Hamel G (1990) The core competence of the corporation. Harv Bus Rev 3:79–91

Rockart JF (1979) Chief executives define their own data needs. Harv Bus Rev 57(2):81–93

van der Aalst WMP, Donger B, van Herbst J, Maruster L, Schimm G, Weijters A (2003) Workflow mining: a survey of issues and approaches. Data Knowl Eng 47(2):237–267

WGARIA (working group "Accounting and Reporting of Intangible Assets" of the Schmalenbach Gesellschaft) (2005) Corporate Reporting on Intangibles – A Proposal from a German Background, in: Schmalenbach Business Review (2):65–100

Wang XZ (1999) Data mining and knowledge discovery for process monitoring and control. Springer, London

Yin RK (2008) Case study research – design and methods. Sage, Thousands Oaks, CA

# Process Classification Frameworks

**Chris Aitken, Christine Stephenson, and Ryan Brinkworth**

**Abstract** The consistent structuring and modeling of behavioral descriptions is a prerequisite to any successful Business Process Management (BPM) initiative. This chapter presents a simple practical framework for aligning various concepts and representations of organizational behavior, which assists identifying appropriate model types. The framework is presented as a means to improve process modeling within BPM initiatives and as a guide to the development and documentation of process architectures. A health sector based example is provided in which the framework is used to align descriptions of organizational behavior to produce useful integrated behavioral reference models. The framework is also used to analyze model and process architecture completeness. The chapter concludes by noting current limitations of the framework and issues to be addressed through its further refinement.

## 1 Introduction

The need for standardized methodologies and resources to guide process modeling and Business Process Management (BPM) initiatives has been documented previously (Larsen and Myers 1998; Murphy and Staples 1998; Amoroso 1998; Indulska et al. 2006; Stephenson and Bandara 2007). It is commonly assumed that core concepts such as business process, function, or service are defined and commonly agreed within the BPM community at large. However, it can be argued that this is often not evidenced in practice (van der Aalst et al. 2003).

The ability to readily compare models is fundamental to any BPM initiative concerned with process re-use, improvement, or integration. Business process

C. Aitken (✉)
QIC, Brisbane, QLD, Australia
e-mail: c.aitken@qic.com

J. vom Brocke and M. Rosemann (eds.), *Handbook on Business Process Management 2*, International Handbooks on Information Systems,
DOI 10.1007/978-3-642-01982-1_4, © Springer-Verlag Berlin Heidelberg 2010

modeling is often limited in its effectiveness by problems that hamper the ability to compare one process model with another, especially where the models have been developed within different organizations or within different contexts.[1] A common problem is that of establishing an appropriate level of decomposition for any description of organizational behavior. Although two models may have been developed to describe the same process, they may be different in scope and the level of detail they include. Combining or comparing such models often means that one of the models has to be revised in order to establish whether the scope of the individual models is compatible, and whether the same behavior is being represented. These problems can be further compounded where the level of abstraction differs between models.[2]

It is common for a hierarchy of business process models to be developed with a BPM initiative. Typically a "high level" model is developed to provide a context and frame of reference for "lower level" more detailed process models (Indulska et al. 2006; Brabänder et al. 2005). Although the development of process architecture is commonly touted as the means to achieve alignment between such models, there are few if any standardized approaches (Davis and Brabänder 2007; Stephenson and Bandara 2007). Without clear agreed definitions of the levels of abstraction and decomposition, it is difficult to establish whether lower level models within process architecture are aligned with those at higher a level of abstraction. This problem is partly due to the multiple levels at which organizational behavior might be understood, and that it is expressed as a continuum of activity and not discrete units. Although organizational behavior can be viewed at the macro level of the services provided, it can equally be viewed from the perspective of tasks and single executable steps within these. Moreover, organizational behavior can be understood in terms of the behaviors of groups of individual actors, as well as at the level of each individual. This multifaceted and fluid nature of organizational behavior means that there are few absolute points of reference upon which to structure and compare behavioral models. Consequently, there is a tendency for the term "Process" to be applied to behaviors that vary significantly in complexity and breadth. Furthermore, this lack of specificity may result in models of the same behavior that may bear little resemblance to one another. A further problem arises where process models include elements from differing levels of abstraction within the one model. Typical examples of this occur where for reasons of modeling expediency, implementation level details are mixed with logical or conceptual level descriptions. This limits the capacity for model re-use, and will inevitably mean that the model will need to be revised when there are changes made at the level of physical implementation.

Although the importance of developing process models which reflect the needs of relevant stakeholders is acknowledged (Becker et al. 2003), it is argued that the ability to reliably identify common levels of process decomposition, and modeling

[1]One approach to overcome this drawback is presented by Becker et al. (2010).

[2]Polyvyanyy et al. (2010) deal with this particular problem and propose an approach for consistent business model abstractions.

abstraction are equally important (Stephenson and Bandara 2007). This is particularly so in situations involving process architecture, where process integration and inter-operability are aims.

The approach presented in this chapter identifies a set of criteria that can be consistently applied to descriptions of behavior or activity to more reliably determine an appropriate level of behavior decomposition, level of abstraction, and modeling alternatives. In this way, the framework outlined in the following section provides a means to develop models of organizational behavior that are able to be more readily compared to identify genuine differences or similarities.

## 2 Framework Development

### *2.1 Background*

The need for a framework arose from a requirement to develop both function and service reference models within a large health sector agency in which an ehealth initiative was to be implemented. The ehealth initiative involved providing health services using information systems and technologies which enabled improved communication and collaboration between clinicians, as well as greater participation by patients in their own care. The aim in developing the reference models was to allow mapping of current and future state business processes and their supporting applications and technologies to better understand the scope of required changes. However, in the absence of recognized industry function and service reference models, the required models had to be derived by combining a number of existing models. Some of these models were specific to the health industry while others were more general descriptions of organizational behavior. The contributing models and their respective scopes are listed in Table 1.

The American Society for Testing and Materials (ASTM) has published a number of technical standards for the health care industry. Of particular interest to our modeling efforts was the Standard Specification for a Healthcare Conceptual Process Model (ASTM WK5068[3]). This is described as a conceptual level model

**Table 1** Contributing models and scope

| Model | Scope |
|---|---|
| ASTM standard specification for a health care conceptual process model | Health provider (Enterprise wide) |
| HL7 EHR system model | EHR application functions |
| ACHS functional requirements | Australian health service provider |
| APQC – process classification framework | Generic enterprise |

[3]At the time of writing, this document was still in draft form and unpublished.

and, in the absence of other standard process models in healthcare, has been drafted to standardize the development of solutions, models, products, and services to support healthcare delivery. The model is structured using the IDEF0 format (ANSI Publications 1320.1, 1998) and describes four levels of process decomposition, although not all levels are specified for all processes within the model.

The Health Level Seven (HL7) Electronic Health Records (EHR) System Model (ANSI 2007) also describes a conceptual level view of health functions. However, the EHR system model departs from the ASTM model by focusing on those functions necessary to support an EHR system. While this scope focuses on application functionality, the model has been developed to be independent of technology solution or implementation strategy. The model has four levels of decomposition; however, not all levels are specified for all functions specified in the model.

The Australian Council on Health Standards (ACHS) is an organization responsible for assessing, accrediting, and reviewing the performance of Australian health organizations in respect to their quality and safety. The Evaluation and Quality Improvement Program (EQuIP) was developed to support the ACHS. EQuIP was developed in 1996 and is now in its fourth version. The EQuIP requirements were used by the authors to identify a number of key process patterns. These patterns were then compiled into an overarching process model for health care treatment (Stephenson 2005).

The American Productivity and Quality Commission (APQC) has developed a comprehensive taxonomy of generic processes applicable in many industries. The APCQ model was the most comprehensive of the models referenced, with more than 1,000 processes and activities included. It provided a useful framework to describe and understand the nonclinical operations within the health agency. This model contains four levels of decomposition and is broadly structured according to the Porter Value Chain model (Porter 1996).

On inspection, it was apparent that the level of description and abstraction varied across the selected models. In order to successfully combine the various process and function descriptions contained within the models, it was necessary to develop a common frame of reference. The framework illustrated in Fig. 2 was developed for this purpose.

### *2.2 A Framework for Behavior Classification and Modeling*

This section describes a framework developed to categorize descriptions of organizational behavior. Although other models such as Process Architecture Framework (Davis 2006), Supply-Chain Operations Reference-model (Supply-Chain Council 2008) (SCOR), and Business Process Definition MetaModel Object Management Group (OMG) (2008) were considered, none was able to satisfy both the scope of concepts and levels of specificity required to develop the required reference models. Specifically, none of the alternative frameworks reviewed provided a list of criteria, which were able to be applied to a given behavior description or a model to unambiguously identify both description type and level of decomposition. Additionally, none of the alternative frameworks reviewed dealt with definitions of concepts relating to the environment in which an enterprise might operate (i.e., contextual level concepts; Aitken 2008). The framework needed to accommodate both process and functional perspectives, as well as provide clear criteria for distinguishing these concepts at differing levels of decomposition. Figure 1 illustrates a simplified representation of the distinction between the two independent perspectives of functions and services. The functional view provides a means to logically group processes within an organization, whereas a services oriented view describes the way in which processes are used. The wavy arrow lines in Fig. 1 could be considered to represent "compositions" or "arrangements" of processes.

To address the requirements of both sufficient scope and specificity of definition, the framework presented in this chapter uses levels of decreasing abstraction together with specific criteria to position representations of organizational behavior in relation to one another. The objectives of the framework were to clearly delineate types of behavioral description, define levels of decomposition, and identify appropriate model types for these.

The four levels of abstraction and their definitions are described in detail elsewhere (Aitken 2008; Stephenson and Bandara 2007). The framework presented in this chapter is an application of the Aitken (2008) general modeling framework within the specific context of business process modeling. Therefore, each level within the current framework is associated with a set of characteristics or criteria

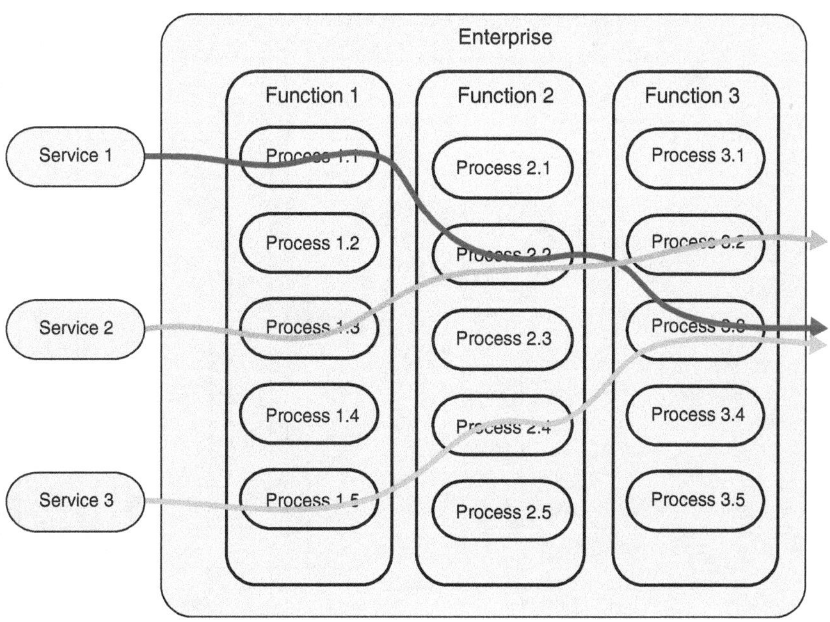


**Fig. 1** Service and functional perspectives

that apply to all representations within that level. Figure 2 provides a summary of the elements of the framework.

The framework defines the following concepts and their relationships: enterprise, service, function, process composition, process, task, and step. The framework draws on concepts and definitions within both ITU-T Rec. X.906|ISO/IEC

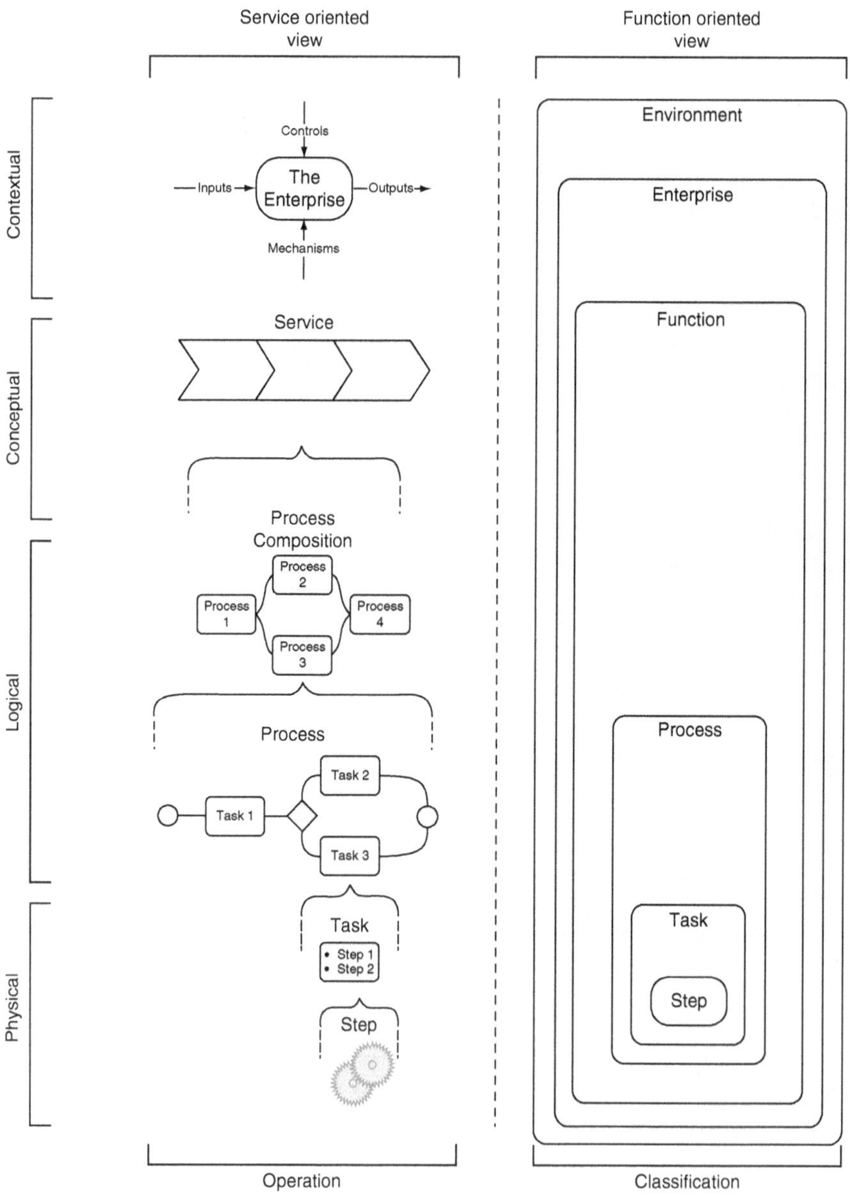


**Fig. 2** An organizational behavior classification and modeling framework

19793: Information technology – Open distributed processing – Use of Unified Modeling Language (UML) for Open Directory Project (ODP) system specification (2004), and the Business Process Modeling Notation, V1.1 OMG Available Specification (2008). The key definitions[4] within the framework are as follows:

- Environment: The context in which an enterprise operates, which includes external parties, their relationships to the enterprise, and the requirements of these relationships.
- Community: a group of *enterprise objects* which exhibit *behaviors* and fulfill *roles* to achieve a common purpose or aim.
- Enterprise: a type of *community*, as are the organizational units of which it is comprised, as well as other organizations the enterprise interacts with.
- Service: A sequence of *processes* initiated and terminated by a *client role*, delivered via an *interface role*, and controlled or constrained by a *contract*.
- Function: An enterprise capability represented by a normalized grouping of *processes* which share a common objective, aim, or goal.
- Process Composition: A sequence of *processes* which may implement all or part of a *service* and be undertaken by *actors* within one or more *communities*.
- Process: A sequence of *tasks* undertaken by *actors* within a single *community*.
- Task: A sequence of *steps* undertaken by an individual *actor* that results in the change in *state* of the *object* being acted upon.
- Step: *Activity* which results in a change to an attribute of an *object*.

These concepts form a hierarchy of behavioral decomposition in which subordinate concepts elaborate a parent concept. Figure 2 also illustrates the two alternative views of organizational behavior supported by the framework. The service oriented view is concerned with sequencing of behavior whereas the function oriented view provides a means for behavioral classification.

Although the levels of abstraction within the framework bear a superficial resemblance to those within other frameworks (e.g., The Zachman Framework, Zachman 2005), the terms "contextual," "conceptual," "logical," and "physical" have specific meanings that have been detailed elsewhere (Aitken 2008). The application of these levels to the behavioral concepts within the framework is now discussed.

The contextual level represents the highest level of abstraction within the framework. The concepts relevant to this level are the communities within the external environment of the enterprise or organization. The internal behavior of the organization is not described or represented by models at this level. However, the environment, external parties and customers, their relationships to the enterprise in question, and the requirements of these relationships are all legitimate behavioral components that might be represented within a contextual level behavioral model.

[4]Italicization indicates terms with specific meaning within the framework. Further definition of some terms used can be found in ITU-T Rec. X.906|ISO/IEC 19793: Information technology – Open distributed processing – Use of UML for ODP system specification (2004), and the Business Process Modelling Notation, V1.1 OMG Available Specification (2008).

The criteria for models at the contextual level are that they treat the enterprise of concern as a "black box," they model the roles and relationships between the enterprise and other entities in its environment, describe the requirements of these relationships, and identify the outcomes that are the result of enterprise activity. The IDEF0 Level 0 model might be used to represent some of these components, although other models such as the RM ODP Enterprise Specification model might equally be suitable candidates (see ITU-T Rec. X.906|ISO/IEC 19793: Information technology – Open distributed processing – Use of UML for ODP system specifications 2004). Such models are used within the framework to provide a frame of reference for, and identify the overall requirements that must be satisfied by the process compositions, and processes described in subsequent levels.

The second level of abstraction within the framework is represented by the conceptual level. This level is concerned with describing the internal behavioral constructs of the enterprise. The behavioral constructs at this level within the framework are represented by the concepts "service" and "function." These terms are considered conceptual level concepts in that they do not provide a description of the internal workings of the organization, but they do capture its defining behavioral characteristics. Both constructs can be considered concepts that describe "what" is done or needed to be achieved without specifying "how" this is done. Descriptions concerning "how" things are done (i.e., design) are covered at the logical level. In this sense, both the function and service views provide two separate perspectives on the same set of internal processes within an organization. The criteria for behavioral models at this level are as follows:

- The model only contains behavioral constructs and the relationships between these.
- A service might be modeled as being comprised of several "phases" or partitions of activity. For example, within the health sector, most services would conform to the following three broad phases; "receive the patient," "provide the required treatment," and "post-treatment follow-up." These logical segments of activity within a service will constitute separate process compositions to be modeled at the next level within the framework.
- The model does not contain processes, tasks, swim lanes, or logical gateways.

In accordance with these criteria, the Porter (1996) Value Chain would be an example of a conceptual behavioral model, as would be SCOR level 1 and 2 models.

The third level of the framework provides a logical view of the activities or behavior within an organization. A logical view depicts a particular design state and is composed of logical (i.e., implementation agnostic) components complied according to a set of identified design principles (Aitken 2008). Therefore, this level of the framework includes representations concerned with the composition of processes within an organization.

The concepts "process composition" and "process" are positioned most appropriately at the logical level within the framework. Given the requirements of logical level models (Aitken 2008) and the hierarchical structure of the framework, the following are the recommended criteria for process composition models:

- The model may include a pool where this represents the community in which the processes included in the process composition are performed. Most commonly, this is the organizational branch or division responsible for the service which the composition implements.
- The model includes lanes that may only represent sub-communities (i.e., organizational units or teams) and not individual actor roles as processes within a composition are likely to involve more than one actor. Actor level detail is provided within the associated subordinate process models.
- Process compositions include the initiating and terminating client role identified in the parent service model.
- May include alternative process flow pathways but do not include information about the logic gateways implicit in these. Gateways are described in the associated subordinate process models, as any gateway represented explicitly in a process composition would not be able to map to any element in any child process as it would lie outside the boundaries of any child process. This would mean that the gateway could not be described at the physical implementation level within the current framework.

The recommended criteria for process models are as follows:

- The model will include a pool that will correspond to one of the sub-communities within the parent process composition.
- The model includes logical actor roles as lanes.
- Tasks within the process do not bridge lanes (i.e., tasks are only performed by individual actors and therefore must remain within the lane of the actor role).
- The model will inherit initiating and terminating roles from the parent process composition.[5]

The fourth and final layer of the framework is the physical level. This level of description is concerned with actual implementation. The key terms in this level are task and step. SCOR level 4 process models would be examples of models appropriate to this level.

The various behavioral concepts within the framework, their definitions, and associated model types are summarized in Table 2.

## *2.3 Application of the Framework*

This section describes how the framework established in the previous section has been applied within a large health sector agency. The framework has been used as a means to integrate disparate behavioral models, and as a means to analyze and

[5]Note: the roles may not necessarily be the service initiating and terminating roles as this will depend on the scope of process composition in which the process is located.

**Table 2** Process Classification Framework Definitions

| Level | Term | Definition | Modeling criteria | Example |
|---|---|---|---|---|
| Contextual | Environment | The context in which the enterprise operates. This includes external parties, their relationships to the enterprise, and the requirements of these relationships. | The enterprise is represented as a "black box"<br>External parties, their relationships, and requirements are depicted or documented | IDEF0 – Level 0 Diagram |
| | Enterprise | A grouping of business objects with an identified objective | No depiction of the inner working of the organization | IDEF0 – Level 0 Diagram |
| Conceptual | Function | An enterprise capability represented by a normalized grouping of processes which share a common objective, aim, or goal. | Represents a group of processes. Identifies a common objective. Does not depict a sequence. | Value Chain |
| | Service | A sequence of processes initiated and terminated by a client role, delivered via an interface role, and controlled or constrained by a contract. | Represents a simple sequence with an identified initiating and terminating role, and a controlling or constraining contract or policy.<br>May depict service segments but, does not depict individual processes, alternative flows, gateways, or swim lanes. | Value Chain |
| Logical | Orchestration | A sequence of processes which may implement all or part of a service and be undertaken by actors within one or more communities. | Depicts a flow of processes. May depict alternative flows but does not depict gateways. May depict swim lanes where these are organizational units (i.e., not a single role) | BPMN Process model comprised of Collapsed Sub-processes only |
| | Process | A sequence of tasks undertaken by actors within a single community. | Depicts initiating and terminating events, decision gateways and tasks. | BPMN Process model comprised of Tasks only. |

(*continued*)

**Table 2** (continued)

| Level | Term | Definition | Modeling criteria | Example |
|---|---|---|---|---|
| | | | The swim lanes represent the logical role that undertakes a given Task. Does not include implementation detail. | UML Activity diagram |
| Physical | Task | A sequence of steps undertaken by an individual actor that results in the change in state of the object being acted upon. | Includes implementation level detail (i.e., the actual role within the organization that performs the task).<br>Depicts the steps necessary to complete the task, and the states of the object being acted upon. | UML Sequence diagram<br>UML State Machine |
| | Step | Activity which results in a change to an attribute of an object. | The actual instruction. | |

Note that some definitions draw on concepts defined in ITU-T Rec. X.906|ISO/IEC 19793: Information technology – Open distributed processing – Use of UML for ODP system specification (2004), and the Business Process Modeling Notation, V1.1 OMG Available Specification (2008)

structure process architecture models. Although the examples provided are set within the health industry, the framework is likely to have equal applicability in other industries.

### 2.3.1 Integration of Behavioral Descriptions

The framework outlined earlier in this chapter was used to develop both function and service reference models within a health sector agency. The framework was initially used to establish the level of abstraction required by both models. Through consultation with stakeholders, it was agreed that both reference models needed to be conceptual models. It was determined that it was not necessary to describe the implementation of individual processes, but rather to provide a means of categorizing processes according to the functions or services to which they belonged.

As described previously, several existing models of organizational behavior were selected as sources from which to compile the required reference models. The framework was then used to map the behavioral descriptions in each source model to the relevant behavior concept within the framework (i.e., service, function, process composition, process, etc.). Descriptions that met the framework criteria for the concepts "function" and "service" were selected for inclusion in the reference models. Descriptions that were similar and assessed to be of the same concept type and level of abstraction were combined. All function descriptions were then grouped according to their scope, such that functions with the widest scope were positioned as parent functions to those related child functions with narrower scope. The model contained 11 first level functional categories. Figure 3 depicts one of these, the Information and Communication Technology (ICT) and information management functional category including subcategories identifying the original models from which the descriptions were sourced (i.e., APQC and HL7).

A similar approach was used with service descriptions except that the scope of the client role associated with the service was used as the dimension for structuring service types. The services with the more generalized client role were positioned as parent services to those whose client role was more specialized.

The resultant functional reference model was then used as a taxonomy tool to uniquely classify and position the "as-is" processes within the organization. The function reference model was also used to classify and map the "to-be" processes within the newly proposed ehealth initiative to better understand the scope of impact of the proposed changes.

The service reference model was used to map both the "as-is" and "to-be" services, and then to identify those "to-be" processes which were common across services to be provided within the ehealth initiative. The model differed from the functional model in that processes could appear in more than one service type. These common processes were then candidates for further refinement and optimization.

### 2.4 *Process Architecture Analysis*

The ehealth initiative within the health agency included a number of priority areas in which to automate processes across the continuum of care for patients. The six priority areas were the following:

- Discharge Summary
- Clinical Notes
- Medications Management
- Orders Entry
- Results Reporting
- Scheduling

Challenges within this program included a lack of consistent terminology and limited understanding of the process boundaries between each of the six priority areas. The framework was used successfully to structure the six priority areas and to identify overlaps and gaps between them. The health initiative used a series of workshops with specialist staff from within the agency to develop an "as-is" and "to-be" process model for each priority area. However, due to the lack of a

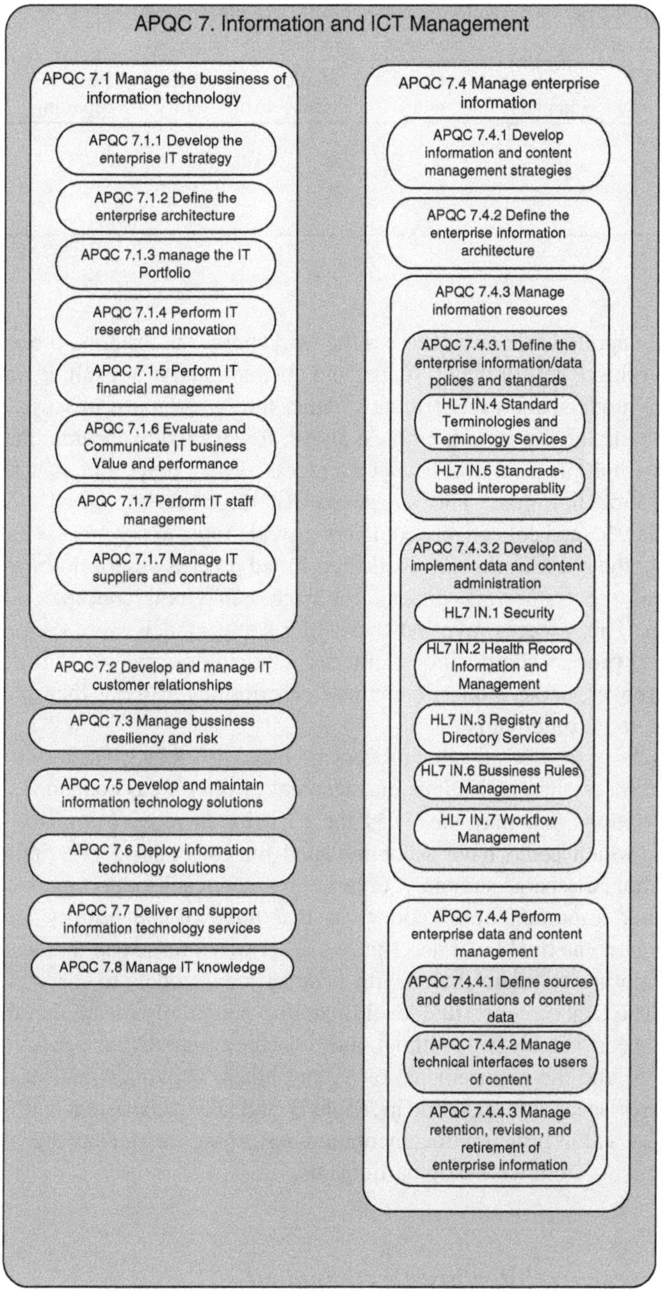


**Fig. 3** Example functional categories

**Table 3** Mapping between framework levels and ehealth priority areas

| Framework level | ehealth priority areas | | | | | |
|---|---|---|---|---|---|---|
| | Discharge summary | Clinical notes | Medication management | Order entry | Results reporting | Scheduling |
| Contextual | | | | | | |
| Conceptual | | X | X | | | |
| Logical | X | X | X | X | X | |
| Physical | | | | X | X | X |

consistently applied framework across the workshops, the resulting process models were of varying levels of detail, scope, and abstraction. As a result, it was difficult to compare models, and to determine whether they overlapped in scope.

By applying the framework outlined above, it was readily apparent that not only were there multiple overlaps between process descriptions, but that there were significant modeling gaps. This suggested that the workshop based models were seriously flawed, and collectively could not provide satisfactory process architecture.

To apply the framework, each workshop-based process description was analyzed in terms of the framework criteria for each behavioral concept and level of abstraction. This process revealed that while some models were concerned with services and process compositions, others contained descriptions of processes and tasks. Moreover, some models contained descriptions at more than one level of abstraction (e.g., order entry).

The results of the classification process are listed in Table 3. The results show that the clinical notes and medications management priority areas contained conceptual level descriptions that may have had the capacity to provide a conceptual level framework which could have accommodated the lower level descriptions within the scheduling, discharge summary, orders entry, and results reporting priority areas.

The other important observation was that none of the priority area models included any contextual level descriptions. This was a large gap that was apparent when attempting to relate the ehealth priority area models to the wider agency business. The lack of contextual level modeling potentially meant that the priority areas had been established without due consideration to the agency operating environment and the requirements of its key business partners and health consumers. These issues are apparent in Table 3 and were consistent with problems encountered within program documentation describing the priority areas and anecdotal comments from workshop participants.

## 2.5 Process Architecture Development

A series of model templates have been developed on the basis of the framework outlined earlier in the chapter. The templates can be used to document most levels of process architecture. The templates have been developed for the framework concepts: service, process composition, and process. Each template is presented and described below.

The service model template is illustrated in Fig. 4. The template identifies the enterprise, client, and interface roles and process compositions that make up the service. The interface role might be fulfilled by human, system, or community of actors. Each process composition identified in the service model may be modeled using the process composition template described next.

Figure 5 depicts the process composition model template. This template is comprised of Business Process Modeling Notation (BPMN) elements with the constraints that only collapsed subprocess elements can be used within the model,

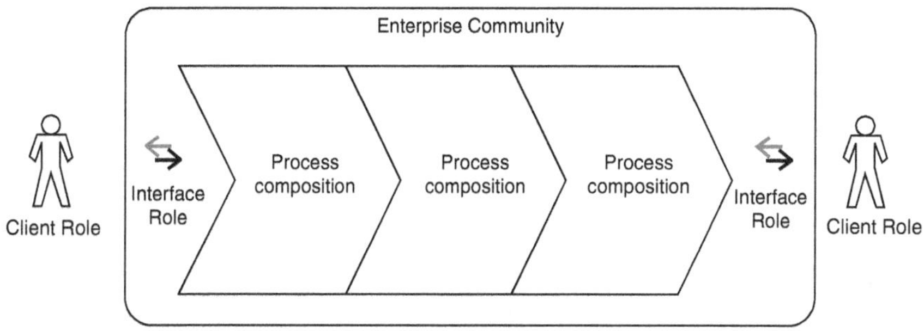


**Fig. 4** Service model template

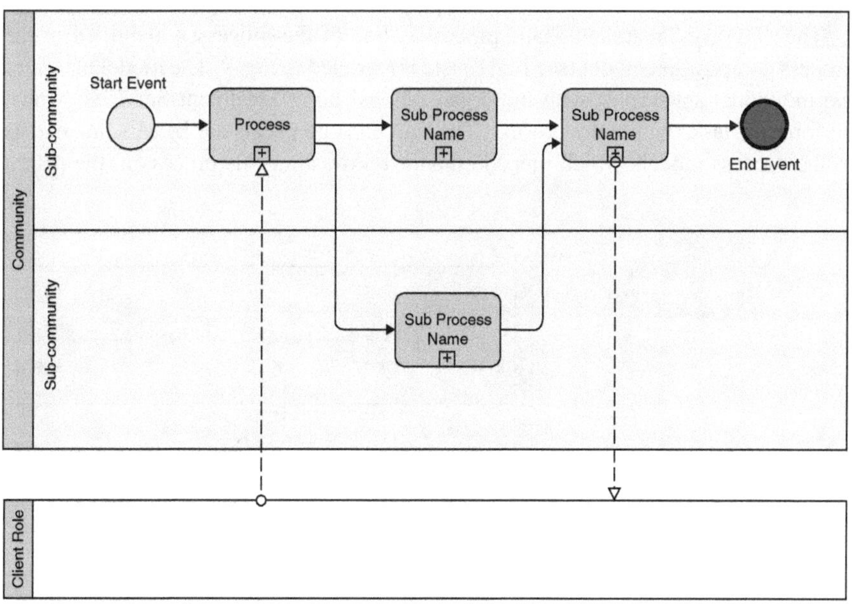


**Fig. 5** Process composition model template

and that lanes must represent organizational units (i.e., sub-communities) and not individual actor roles. Note that logical gateways are not included in the model. Although alternative pathways are represented in the process composition model, the decision gateway logic is detailed in a suitable child process model. Each process identified in the process composition may be modeled using the process template below. The process composition template also includes the client role specified in the parent service model. The specification of the interface role will depend on the requirements of the specific service and process composition. In some instances, the interface role will be fulfilled by individual actor roles, in others it may be fulfilled by an organizational unit (i.e., sub-community) within the enterprise.

The final template in the series is the process template. This template uses all BPMN elements with the constraints that only tasks can be used within the model, and that the lanes represent individual actor roles. The start and end events are commonly Business Process Modeling Notation link events unless they represent actual points at which the composition or service commences or terminates (Fig. 6).

The following health sector models were developed using the templates just described. The models were developed as an alternative to those developed within the ehealth workshops. The models demonstrate the way in which the templates help structure and align the behavioral descriptions across three levels of decomposition.

The health treatment service model is illustrated in Fig. 7. In this instance, it was decided to model the service as a single process composition and not to partition it into separate phases. The implementation of the service is shown in Fig. 8. The process composition references both the client (i.e., patient) and interface roles (i.e., patient administration) identified in the parent service model.

The "Prepare Treatment Plan" process is one of the processes identified in the process composition model (see Fig. 8) and is modeled in Fig. 9. The model identifies the individual actor roles with the organizational unit "Treatment Services" which perform the tasks within the process. The start and end events are BPMN link events to the process models which precede this or follow after this process in the parent

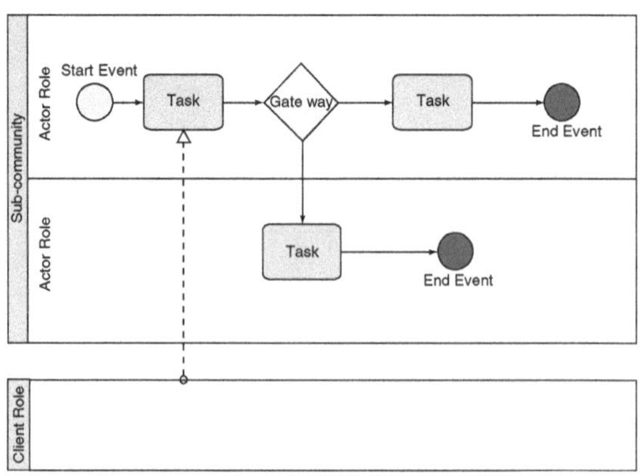


**Fig. 6** Process model template

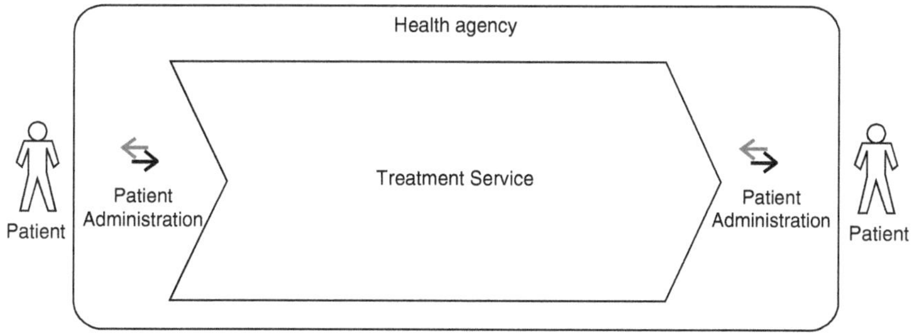


**Fig. 7** Health treatment service model

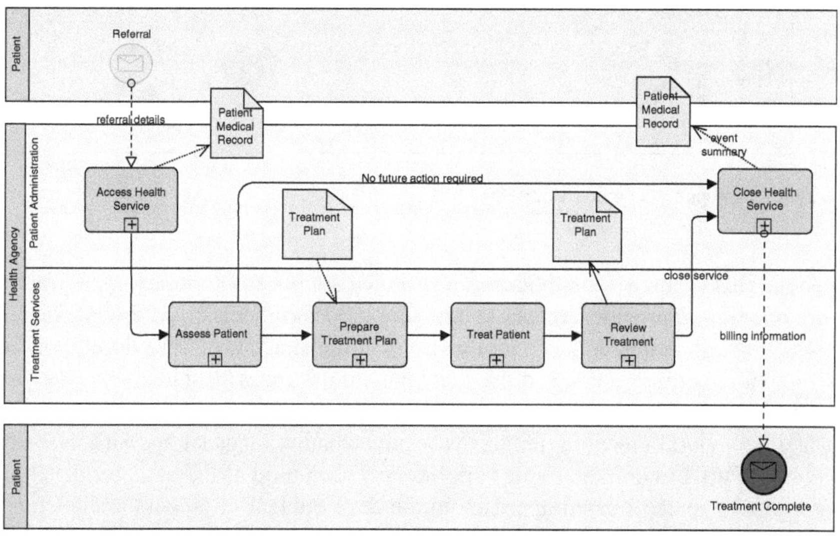


**Fig. 8** Health treatment process composition model

process composition. Process models were developed for each of the processes identified in the process composition model.

# 3 Conclusion and Future Work

This chapter has outlined a framework designed to promote greater consistency in the description and modeling of organizational behavior. The framework provides a means to position various behavioral descriptions in relation to one another, and to determine which model types might be best used to document them. The chapter has also described an initial application of the framework within a large health

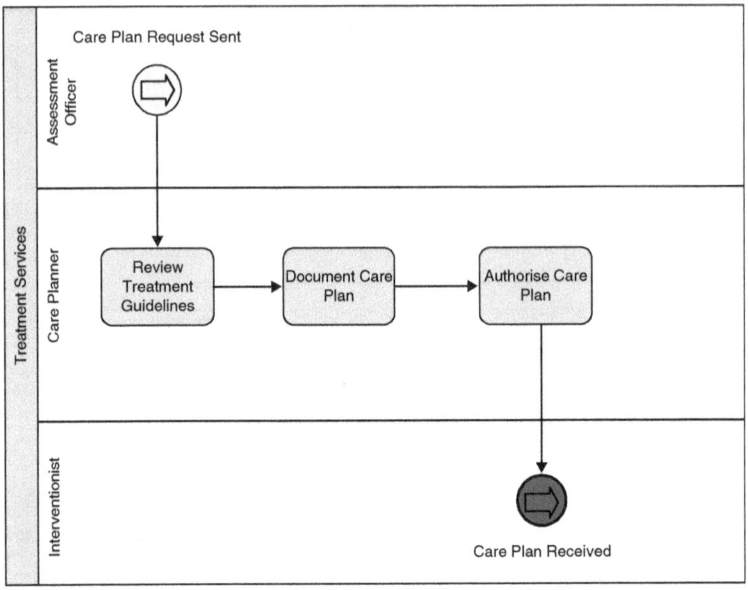


**Fig. 9** Prepare care plan process model

agency. This preliminary application has shown some early promise in the framework's ability to provide a means to structure process models of differing levels of abstraction and detail, and as a tool to assist in the analysis of behavioral models, architectural completeness, and the development of process architectures.

At the time of writing, the framework is being successfully used as the basis for further behavioral modeling initiatives within separate financial and airline sector agencies. Furthermore, the framework has also been used as the basis for developing a process pattern based approach to the development of process architectures (Stephenson and Bandara 2007). The ideas and concepts within the framework presented in this chapter are described in a meta-model available on request from the authors.

Despite this initial success, the framework requires further refinement with greater specificity and definition being provided for the concepts, levels, and associated model types. Although Table 2 provides an initial list of model types, further work is required to position additional model types such as Petri nets, and additional UML diagram types within the framework. A key model type for which a suitable candidate has yet to be identified is the contextual level model. The model also lacks any concept related to client outcome. However, the Enterprise Specification model within the UML Profile for ODP (see ITU-T Rec. X.906|ISO/IEC 19793, 2004) may provide the basis for the development of a model template for contextual models and provide the additional definitions for this level.

An additional shortcoming is that the scope of the framework is currently limited to process related descriptions. Other behavioral perspectives such as strategy and business rules or policy also suffer from a lack of modeling specificity and consistency. It is intended to extend the current framework to include these additional behavioral perspectives using concepts and definitions within the Business Motivation Model (BMM) (OMG 2006), Semantics of Business Vocabulary and Business Rules (SBVR) (OMG 2006), and ITU-T Rec. X.906|ISO/IEC 19793: Information technology – Open distributed processing – Use of UML for ODP system specification (2004).

## References


Aitken CJ (2008) Design integrity and EA governance. In: Saha P (ed) Advances in government enterprise architecture. Idea Group, Hershey, PA

Amoroso DL (1998) Developing a model to understand Reengineering project success. In: Proceedings of the Thirty-First Hawaii International Conference on System Sciences, vol. 6, pp 500–509

ANSI/HL7 EHR System Functional Model, Release 1 (2007)

ANSI Publications 1320.1-1998 IEEE standard for functional modeling language – syntax and semantics for IDEFO and 1320.2-1998 IEEE standard for conceptual modeling language – syntax and semantics for IDEF1X97 (IDEFobject)

Bandara W, Gable GG, Rosemann M (2005) Factors and measures of business process modeling: Model building through a multiple case study. Eur J Inform Syst 14:347–360

Becker J, Kugeler M, Rosemann M (2003) Process management: a guide for the design of business processes. Springer-Verlag, Berlin

Becker J, Pfeiffer D, Falk T, Räckers M (2010) Semantic business process management. In: vom Brocke J, Rosemann M (eds) Handbook on business process management, vol 1. Springer, Heidelberg

Davis R (2006) British telecom six level process hierarchy. In: Proceedings of the process days conference, Sydney, August 2224

Davis R, Brabänder E (2007) Aris design platform: getting started with BPM. Springer-Verlag, Berlin

Indulska M, Chong S, Bandara W, Sadiq S (2006) Major issues in business process management: an Australian perspective. In: Proceedings of the Australian Conference on Information Systems (ACIS 2006)

ITU-T Rec. X.906|ISO/IEC 19793: Information technology – Open distributed processing – Use of UML for ODP system specifications, 2004

Larsen MA, Myers MD (1998) BPR Success or failure? A business Process reengineering project in the financial services industry. Commun ACM, 367–381

Murphy F, Staples S (1998) Reengineering in Australia: Factors affecting success. In: Proceedings of the Australasian conference of information systems, Sydney, Australia

Object Management Group (OMG) (2006) Business Motivation Model (BMM) Specification – Adopted Specification, dtc/2006-08-03

Object Management Group (OMG) (2008) Business Process Definition Metamodel (BPDM). Retrieved 7/12/2008 from http://www.omg.org/spec/BPDM/1.0/

Polyvyanyy A, Smirnov S, Weske M (2010) Business process model abstraction. In: vom Brocke J, Rosemann M (eds) Handbook on business process management, vol 1. Springer, Heidelberg

Porter ME (1996) What is strategy? Harv Bus Rev, November–December, 61–78

Stephenson CP (2005) Health treatment pattern, unpublished manuscript

Stephenson CP, Brabänder W (2007) Enhancing best practices in public health: using process patterns for business process management. In Proceedings ECIS 2007 – The 15th European Conference on Information Systems. St. Gallen, Switzerland, pp. 2123–2134

Supply-Chain Council (2008) Supply-Chain Operations Reference-model (SCOR). Retrieved 7/12/2008 from http://www.supply-chain.org/cs/root/scor_tools_resources/scor_model/scor_model

van der Aalst WMP, ter Hofstede AHM, Weske M (2003) Business process management: a survey, in business process management. Springer, Berlin

Zachman JA (2005) The Zachman framework for enterprise architecture: a primer for enterprise engineering and manufacturing. Zachman International

# Taxonomy of Business Process Management Approaches

**Tobias Bucher and Robert Winter**

**Abstract** Both the design and the implementation of the Business Process Management (BPM) concept vary significantly from one organization to another. Organization-specific approaches to BPM are, among other things, influenced by organizational culture as well as by the maturity of the concept's adoption in the respective organization. This chapter reports on findings from an empirical study and is aimed at answering the question of precisely how organizations deal with the process-oriented management concept – today and in the near future. To address this issue, 38 medium-sized and large organizations from various industries were surveyed. Out of 18 variables used to characterize individual BPM approaches, four distinct design factors of BPM are identified: the degree of process performance measurement, the overall professionalism of process management, the impact of process managers, and the utilization of established methodology and standards. On the basis of these design factors, four generic approaches to BPM can be differentiated. Furthermore, these results are complemented by an interpolation of this classification into the near future, leading to the differentiation of five BPM project types. This part of the analysis shows that all surveyed organizations strive to achieve high BPM maturity. There are, however, significant differences with respect to the particular design of the aspired approaches to mature BPM. The presented results are particularly useful for the engineering and/or adaptation of situational methods in the field of BPM. The chapter therefore concludes with the exemplary adaptation of the "process innovation" method proposed by Davenport with respect to the identified five BPM project types. This adaptation also demonstrates the practical applicability of the presented findings.

R. Winter (✉)
Institute of Information Management, University of St. Gallen, St. Gallen, Switzerland
e-mail: robert.winter@unisg.ch

J. vom Brocke and M. Rosemann (eds.), *Handbook on Business Process Management 2*, International Handbooks on Information Systems,
DOI 10.1007/978-3-642-01982-1_5, 

## 1 Introduction and Motivation

"The story of the practical use of [b]usiness [p]rocess [m]anagement in different organizations is one of diversity and of effective outcomes" (Armistead et al. 1999). This statement highlights the fact that there is no "one-size-fits-all" approach to Business Process Management (BPM). Many academic authors argue that the progress toward organizational excellence through process-oriented management takes place in different stages, that different approaches or aspects thereof are predominant at different levels of organizational development, and that almost each and every organization has developed its own approach to BPM (Ho and Fung 1994; Armistead et al. 1999; Balzarova et al. 2004). Moreover, there is also evidence from corporate practice that real-world organizations adopt BPM in many different ways. However, research is scarce, which is explicitly directed at gaining insight into and understanding the nature of these situational aspects of BPM, or which aims at identifying, categorizing, and describing different BPM approaches.[1]

During the last 2 decades, a huge amount of methods to support BPM or particular stages thereof have been proposed. Two popular examples are methods for business process modeling (cf. e.g., Scholz-Reiter et al. 1999; List and Korherr 2006) and methods to support business process reengineering (cf. e.g., Davenport and Short 1990; Hammer 1990; Harrington 1991; Kaplan and Murdock 1991; Davenport 1993; Hammer and Champy 1993; Hammer and Stanton 1995; Harrington 1995; Imai and Heymans 1999). These proposals, however, are more or less generic, that is, they are aimed at supporting BPM or particular aspects thereof without taking into account situational aspects. Implicitly or even explicitly, almost universal validity is claimed.

In order to close this gap and to support the engineering of situation-specific methods, this chapter proposes taxonomy of BPM approaches. This taxonomy represents an essential basis for the situation-specific adaptation of generic methods and/or for the construction of new situational methods to support BPM within real-world organizations. Furthermore, the chapter is aimed at contributing to the current discussion about BPM maturity models (cf. e.g., DeToro and McCabe 1997; Pritchard and Armistead 1999; Maull et al. 2003; Rosemann and de Bruin 2005; Harmon 2006; de Bruin 2007; Hammer 2007).

The remainder of this chapter is structured as follows: Section 2 provides a detailed introduction to the principles of method construction and situational adaptation. Section 3 reports on empirical results of research targeted at the identification and systematization of BPM approaches as a basis for the engineering of situation-specific methods. These findings are largely on the basis of our previous work (Bucher and Winter 2006, 2008). Section 4 demonstrates the applicability of

---

[1]Rosemann and vom Brocke (2010) provide a framework to characterize BPM approaches according to six core elements.

those results by sketching situation-specific embodiments of Davenport's method for process redesign (Davenport and Short 1990; Davenport 1993). Section 5 summarizes the main findings and provides an outlook on further research.

# 2 Situational Method Engineering

This section is intended to familiarize the reader with the basic principles of method construction and situational adaptation. To this end, we first introduce design research for information systems as the fundamental research paradigm and outline the basics of method engineering. Two aspects of particular interest, namely the representation of situational characteristics as well as the definition of fragments as the essential building blocks of situational methods, are then discussed in detail.

## *2.1 Design Research for Information Systems*

The design research (DR) paradigm for information systems (IS) development has been discussed intensively in recent years. As opposed to behavioral research, DR for IS is not primarily aimed at discovering and justifying theories but rather at creating solutions to specific problems of practical relevance (March and Smith 1995; Hevner et al. 2004). Both design processes and design products play an important role in DR: "As a product, a design is 'a plan of something to be done or produced'; as a process, to design is 'to so plan and proportion the parts of a machine or structure that all requirements will be satisfied'" (Walls et al. 1992).

As for the process aspect, the current body of DR literature proposes a variety of IS research processes that are closely related to each other (cf. e.g., March and Smith 1995; Hevner et al. 2004). Niehaves (2006) summarizes these proposals and suggests the IS research cycle depicted in Fig. 1.

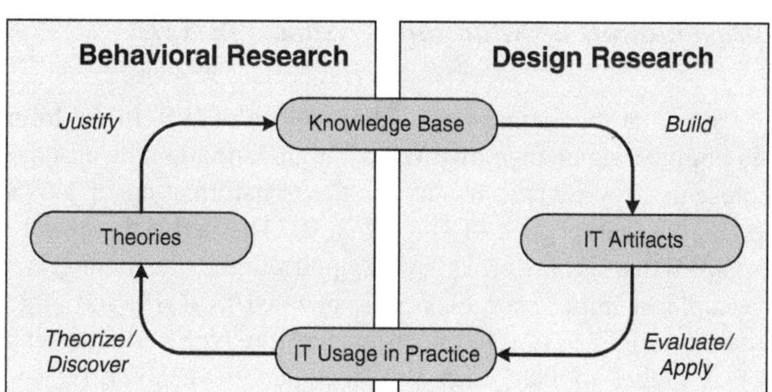


**Fig. 1** IS research cycle. Adapted from Niehaves (2006)

The outcome of the design process – the design product – is commonly referred to as "artifact," i.e., as human-made object of any kind (Simon 1996). In the context of DR for IS, artifacts are typically of four types, namely constructs, models, methods, and instantiations (Nunamaker et al. 1990; March and Smith 1995; Hevner et al. 2004). In the following, we will concentrate on methods as one particular type of DR artifacts. A method is "an approach to perform a systems development project, based on a specific way of thinking, consisting of directions and rules, structured in a systematic way in development activities with corresponding development products" (Brinkkemper 1996).

The discipline concerned with the design, construction, adaptation, and evaluation of methods is referred to as "method engineering" (ME). Most research in the field of ME originates from software engineering. For that reason, a lot of ME publications exhibit more or less explicit references to the domain of software engineering. In this chapter, we will argue that most of the underlying principles of ME can be applied to the business domain – namely Business Process Management – as well. The primary design object of the business domain is the so-called "IT-reliant work systems" (Alter 2003, 2006). A work system (WS) is defined as a "system in which human participants and/or machines perform work using information, technology, and other resources to produce products and/or services for internal or external customers" (Alter 2003). Consequently, methods pertaining to the business domain are targeted at the engineering and/or change of a WS.

In order to be applicable for IS development, methods need to be adapted to the specific characteristics of the so-called development situation or application situation. This approach is commonly referred to as "situational method engineering" (SME) (Kumar and Welke 1992; Harmsen et al. 1994; van Slooten and Hodes 1996; Harmsen 1997) and may be ascribed to the so-called "contingency model" proposed by Fiedler (1964). According to this scientific theory, there is no "best way" of organizing or leading an organization. On the contrary, there are various internal and external factors that influence organizational effectiveness, and therefore the organizational style must be contingent upon those factors.

## 2.2 *Representation of Situational Aspects in SME*

Methods are aimed at the engineering and/or change of WS. In the following, we will refer to engineering/change of a WS as "transformation." Consequentially, a method represents a systematic means for the transformation of a WS from an initial state (IS) to a target state (TS) (cf. Fig. 2). The part (i.e., the set of system elements) of a WS that is transformed by the application of the method is denoted as WSPT. The tuple of initial state of WSPT, denoted as PTIS, and target state of WSPT, denoted as PTTS, is referred to as "project type" (Bucher et al. 2007). However, as a matter of fact, each WSPT is part of a larger WS. All system elements that are not transformed by the application of the method (i.e., that are not part of WSPT) but that are part of the WS under consideration are referred to as

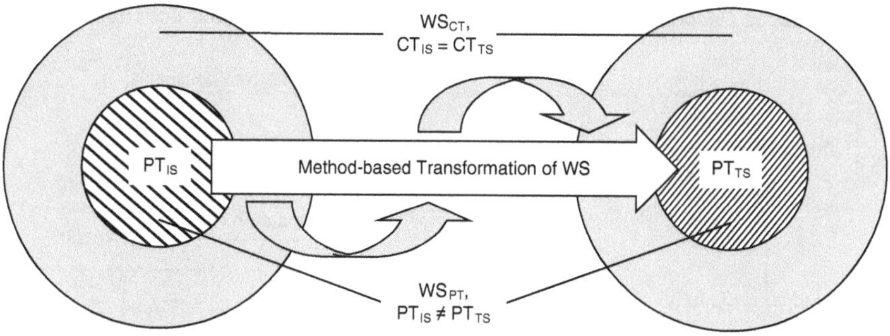


**Fig. 2** Method-based transformation of work systems. Bucher and Klesse (2006), Bucher et al. (2007)

environmental work system WSCT. The initial state CTIS of WSCT does not differ from its target state CTTS. Although WSCT is outside of the method's transformation scope, the state of its system elements (CTIS = CTTS, in the following denoted as "context type" (Bucher et al. 2007)) may influence the applicability, effectiveness, and efficiency of the method.

Context type (CT) therefore comprises all factors that do influence the IS development process but that themselves are not changed by the application of the method. In contrast to that, project type (PT) comprises all aspects of an IS development project that both influence the IS development process and that are at the same time changed/transformed through the method application.

Both CT and PT are relevant parameters that have to be considered in SME. They jointly constitute the so-called development situation. The development situation results from the combination of CT and PT. Both CT and PT are hierarchical constructs that can be refined/broken down into constituent CT factors and PT factors, respectively.

## 2.3 *Method Fragments as Building Blocks in SME*

The development situation – determined by CT and PT – influences the applicability of so-called method fragments.

Methods comprise specifications of both product and process aspects: A well-defined target/result is produced through specific activities and techniques (Avison and Fitzgerald 1988; Olle et al. 1988; Brinkkemper 1996; Harmsen 1997; Karlsson and Ågerfalk 2004; Karlsson and Wistrand 2006). In an analogous manner, we understand a method fragment as a combination of (one or multiple) design activities and (one or multiple) techniques that guide the creation of one particular design result (cf. Fig. 3). A method fragment therefore consists of a product description (i.e., the design result element) and a process description (i.e., the design activity and technique elements) (Cossentino et al. 2006; Agerfalk et al. 2007).

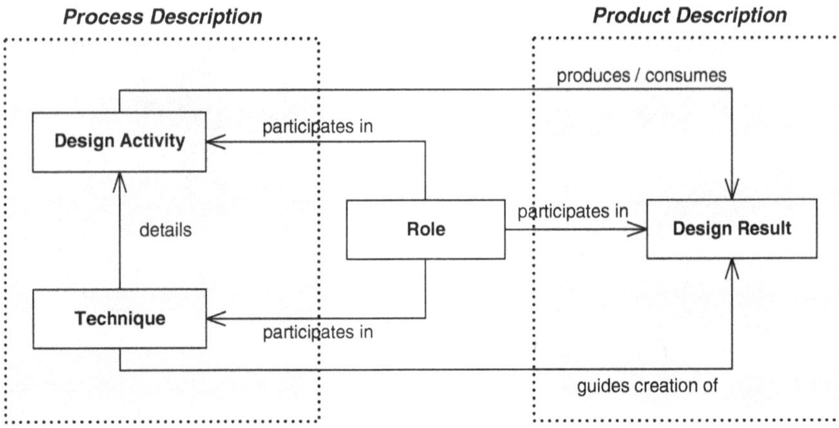


**Fig. 3** Elements of a method fragment. Adapted from Bucher (2008)

Each method fragment can be identified unambiguously by its design result. As a consequence, the design result of a particular method fragment must be invariant. Viewed from the outside, i.e., to support the aggregation of multiple method fragments into a situational method, the design result is the only element of interest – irrespective of the way it is created. On the contrary, viewed from the inside, one or multiple design activities and one or multiple techniques guide the creation of the design result. Viewed from the outside, a method fragment is characterized by three attributes (Bucher 2008): (1) the design result that is created, (2) the pre-conditions that have to be met for a method fragment to be applicable (i.e., other design results that have to be created beforehand), and (3) the specification of (one or multiple) development situations in which the design result (and therefore the method fragment) generally matters.

By the use of well-defined adaptation mechanisms, method fragments can be adapted and combined into a situational method (Becker et al. 2007a, b; Bucher et al. 2007). The application of a situational method is effected by the selection and aggregation of method fragments based on the development situation at hand as well as on the preconditions specified for each fragment.

The following section reports on empirical results that form the basis for the engineering of situational methods to support BPM. On the basis of these empirical insights, an exemplary adaptation of a well-known BPM method is then sketched. This adaptation builds upon the theoretical arguments about situational method engineering made in the previous section.

## 3 Empirical Study on Business Process Management Approaches

The section at hand presents results and implications of an empirical study on BPM approaches. First, the data set is characterized and the course of analysis is described. In the two subsections that follow, the results of the exploratory analysis are presented. We distinguish four BPM realization approaches, allowing for the differentiation of five PTs that characterize BPM development situations. In the remainder of this chapter, we focus explicitly on the identification and discussion of PTs while abstaining from contemplating CTs. This restriction is due to the nature of the underlying data set. In order to complete the proposed taxonomy of BPM approaches, complementary CTs need to be specified, too. However, this will be subject to further research.

### 3.1 Data Set and Course of Analysis

Data for the exploratory analysis were collected by means of a written questionnaire distributed at two BPM forums held in Germany and Switzerland in 2005. The forum participants were specialists and executive staff, primarily working in IT or operating departments concerned with organizational issues and process management.

The questionnaire was designed to assess both the current and the target state of BPM within the interviewed organizations. For this purpose, appropriate statements were formulated, and the respondents were asked to indicate both the current realization degree ("as-is value") as well as target values ("to-be values") of each variable in their organization on a five-tiered Likert scale. Before being used at the forum, experts revised the questionnaire in reference to its comprehensibility.

A total of 47 questionnaires were returned. After the elimination of questionnaires with missing values or other quality problems, 38 observations remained and were included in the analysis. Although the sample size is rather small, the data set is considered to constitute an adequate basis for an exploratory analysis.

The interviewed organizations are primarily large and medium-sized companies (71% have more than 1,000 employees, and another 20% have more than 200 employees) from the German-speaking countries. The sectors mainly represented were banking, finance, and insurance (32%); manufacturing and consumer goods (15%); public administration and healthcare (11%); information technology (9%); and utilities (9% as well).

In addition to demographic characteristics and information on the stage of maturity of BPM, the data set comprises 31 variables describing the design of BPM. These variables can be grouped into the five categories: (1) communication of process management, (2) role of process managers, (3) process design, (4) process performance measurement, and (5) other initiatives pertaining to BPM. The variables summarized in these categories allow for a detailed characterization of actual BPM realization approaches and, consequently, for a well-founded derivation of BPM PTs (Bucher and Winter 2006, 2008). The accurate communication of the BPM initiative itself, the design and the documentation of processes, and of underlying process activities are equally important as the implementation of adequate organizational structures to foster and support BPM as a whole. Furthermore, process monitoring and control as well as quality management are critical to the success of any BPM initiative.

Data analysis was conducted as follows:

- *Factor analysis*: To develop a deeper understanding of the current design factors of BPM, principal component analysis was conducted on the basis of the as-is values. Factor analysis can be applied to identify a small number of important and mutually independent factors from a multiplicity of contingent variables. As a result, four design factors of BPM were identified. BPM design factors summarize multiple variables (that have been included in the survey instrument) and can be used to characterize BPM realization approaches regarding specific thematic aspects of BPM.
- *Cluster analysis*: Consecutively, the 38 observations (each one representing a different organization) were clustered on the basis of as-is factor values calculated in the first step. The hierarchical Ward algorithm and the squared Euclidean distance were used as fusion algorithm and distance measure, respectively. As a result, four generic BPM realization approaches can be distinguished.
- *Regression analysis*: Finally, regression analysis was applied to calculate to-be factor values for each observation and each factor. On the basis of this information, target realization approaches could be determined for each organization surveyed. The comparison of the as-is and the to-be realization approaches yields five BPM PTs. Each PT represents a particular transformation path between two generic BPM approaches: one of the two BPM realization approaches that characterize a BPM PT serves as starting point, whereas the other realization approach represents the desired target state.

Comprehensive information and details of the statistical analysis can be found in our previous work (Bucher and Winter 2006, 2008).

## 3.2 BPM Design Factors

The factor analysis was conducted to gain insight into the dominant design factors of BPM. Principal component analysis (PCA) was chosen as extraction method. PCA is a technique for extracting a small number of mutually independent factors from a multiplicity of variables. It is aimed at answering the question of how to summarize the variables that load on a particular factor by the use of a collective term (Härdle and Simar 2003).

According to Dziuban and Shirkey (1974), a data set is appropriate for PCA if and only if the variables' anti-image covariance, that is the share of a variable's variance that is independent of the other variables, turns out as small as possible. Consequently, a set of variables qualifies for PCA if the proportion of nondiagonal elements in the anti-image covariance matrix that are different from zero accounts for 25% at the most. In the case at hand, this parameter value is about 17.6%. The measure of sampling adequacy (MSA, "Kaiser–Meyer–Olkin criterion") is about 0.753. The MSA indicates whether or not a factor analysis can reasonably be performed on a given data set. Kaiser and Rice (1974) appraise a value of 0.7 and more as "middling." Therefore, the data set is considered to be appropriate for applying PCA.

Four factors that jointly explain about 69.1% of the total variance were extracted by means of PCA (Eigenvalue >1.0; the scree plot heuristic points to this four factor solution as well). The component matrix was rotated using the Varimax method with Kaiser normalization to improve the interpretability of the variables' assignment to factors.

According to our analysis, there are four design factors of BPM.[2] These can be interpreted as follows:

- *Design factor 1: Degree of performance measurement.* A total of six variables were found to have a significant impact on the first factor. Our analysis results indicate that a high degree of performance measurement is characterized by (1.1) the usage of simulations for process design [e.g., van der Aalst et al. (2010)]; (1.2) the usage of surveys to assess the process customers' satisfaction with the processes [e.g., see the "integrated customer opinion service" presented in vom Brocke et al. (2010)]; (1.3) the measurement of process cycle times [e.g., zur Mühlen and Shapiro (2010)]; (1.4) the measurement of process outputs and performances; (1.5) the fact that performance measures are available without undesirable time lags; and (1.6) the fact that performance measurement is supported by a workflow management system.
- *Design factor 2: Professionalism of process management.* Four variables exhibit high loadings on the second factor. According to our analysis results, professional BPM is characterized by (2.1) the fact that the documentation of process performances and goals is common knowledge; (2.2) the fact that the documentation of non-financial measures is available to all employees without any restrictions [e.g., Hilti case in vom Brocke et al. (2010)]; (2.3) the existence of an organizational unit for strategic process management [e.g., Jesus et al. (2010)]; and (2.4) the existence of a dedicated education for process managers.
- *Design factor 3: Impact of process managers.* Likewise, four variables were found to have significant impact on the third factor. Our analysis results show that the impact of process managers is positively influenced by (3.1) the fact that process management is located at a sufficiently high level in organizational hierarchy [e.g., Hilti case in vom Brocke et al. (2010)]; (3.2) the fact that process managers enjoy high prestige in the organization; (3.3) the fact that process managers have sufficient decision-making power in order to influence process design and execution; and (3.4) the fact that process managers are actively engaged in change projects.

---

[2]Both volumes of this handbook together address all of the design factors and most of the related impact variables presented above.

- *Design factor 4: Usage of methodology and standards*. Finally, the fourth factor is made up of four variables as well. Corresponding to our analysis results, usage of methodology and standards is characterized by (4.1) the usage of procedure models for the design of performance management systems, (4.2) the usage of reference process models for process analysis and design [e.g., Burlton (2010) and Aitken et al. (2010)], (4.3) the fact that the organization is ISO-certified, and (4.4) the fact that the organization uses the European Foundation for Quality Management (EFQM) approach to quality management.

Comprehensive information and details of the statistical analysis can be found in our previous work (Bucher and Winter 2006, 2008).

## 3.3 BPM Realization Approaches

On the basis of these design factors, four clusters can be distinguished that represent four distinct realization approaches of BPM. Fig. 4 exhibits the standardized arithmetic means of each of the 18 variables' as-is values for each of the four clusters, grouped according to the four design factors.

These profile lines illustrate an obvious partitioning between two BPM approaches on the one hand, in the following referred to as "BPM freshman" (11 observations, i.e., 11 organizations) and "BPM intermediate" (seven observations), and the remaining two clusters on the other hand, subsequently labeled as "BPM collectivist" (nine observations) and "BPM individualist" (11 observations).

The first group (BPM freshman and BPM intermediate) is characterized by rather low realization degrees with respect to performance measurement, arrangements

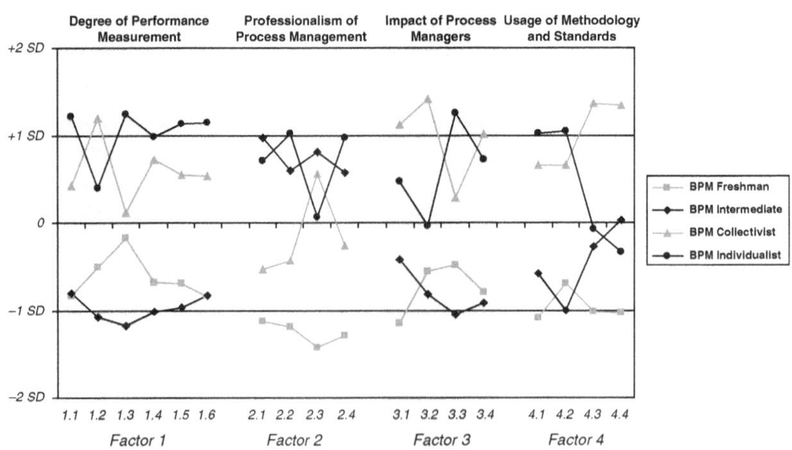


**Fig. 4** Profile lines of the four current realization approaches of Business Process Management. Bucher and Winter (2006)

supporting the work of process managers, and usage of methodology and standards (design factors 1, 3, and 4). Organizations clustered into the second group (BPM collectivist and BPM individualist), however, show significantly higher implementation degrees in terms of these factors. Thus, both the BPM collectivist and the BPM individualist approach can be characterized as mature approaches to process management. Accordingly, our findings suggest that the maturity level of BPM is determined by the variables summarized in design factors 1, 3, and 4.

The BPM freshman approach is branded by exceptionally low professionalism of process management (design factor 2). For that reason, the BPM freshman approach contrasts with the BPM intermediate stage. Although rather immature as well, organizations in the BPM intermediate stage have at least started to pay a certain amount of attention to the implementation of BPM, for example, by establishing an organizational unit for strategic process management and a dedicated education for process managers.

In contrast to this classification which relies on the degree of attention paid toward process management, the differentiation between the BPM collectivist and the BPM individualist approach is residing at the design level (cf. Fig. 5). The former approach is characterized by reliance on established standards as well as on procedure and reference models whereas organizations having adopted the last-mentioned approach to process management strive to implement a more tailor-made type of BPM. Thus, the main differences between these two highly mature realization approaches of BPM do exist with respect to the professionalism of process management and the usage of methodology and standards (design factors 2 and 4).

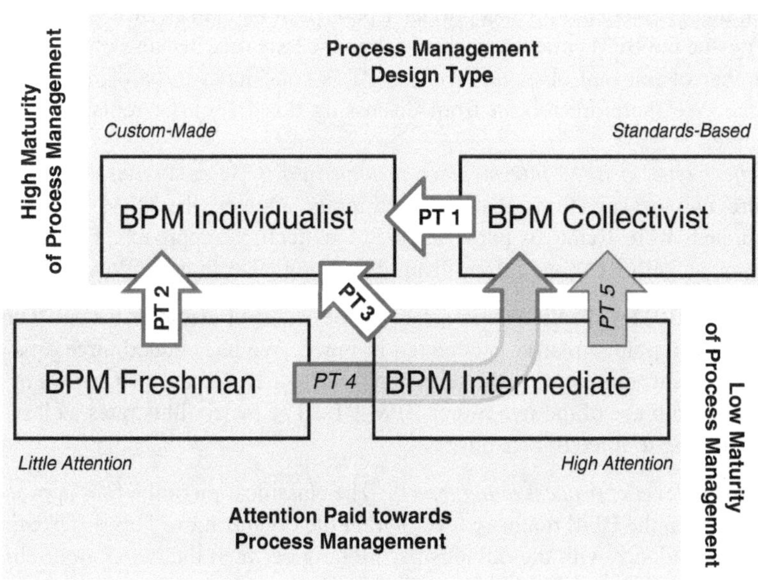


**Fig. 5** BPM typology matrix with project types. Adapted from Bucher and Winter (2006, 2008)

## 3.4 BPM Project Types

On the basis of the results of the regression analysis and a comparison of as-is and the to-be realization approaches, a total of five PTs for the engineering of situation-specific methods to support BPM can be identified. These PTs can be further subdivided into three of major importance (PTs 1–3, numerous cases in the data set) and two of minor importance (PTs 4 and 5, some isolated appearances):

- *Project type 1*: *BPM collectivist turning into BPM individualist*. Seven organizations that have currently adopted the BPM collectivist approach were found to pursue the BPM individualist approach. Both approaches are characterized by high maturity but differ with respect to the design type of process management.
- *Project type 2*: *BPM freshman turning into BPM individualist*. A total of ten organizations that have not yet begun or are at most about to deal with BPM were found to pursue the BPM individualist approach in the long run. This implies that those organizations need to improve the maturity of their BPM approach significantly and develop individual practices.
- *Project type 3*: *BPM intermediate turning into BPM individualist*. Five organizations that currently reside on the BPM intermediate stage, that is, that have started to pay a certain amount of attention to the implementation of BPM, were found to pursue the BPM individualist approach. Similar to PT 2, these organizations need to both improve the maturity of their BPM approach and develop independent procedures for BPM at the same time.
- *Project type 4*: *BPM freshman turning into BPM collectivist*. Just one organization that is branded with exceptionally poor professionalism of BPM was found to pursue the BPM collectivist approach in the long run. Because of the marginal number of relevant observations, this PT is considered to be of minor importance. We therefore refrain from discussing this PT in the remainder of this chapter.
- *Project type 5*: *BPM intermediate turning into BPM collectivist*. Similarly, a mere two organizations that have currently adopted the BPM intermediate approach were found to purse the BPM collectivist approach. For the same reason as with PT 4, we refrain from discussing PT 5 in the following.

The four BPM realization approaches can be arranged in matrix format. This so-called BPM typology matrix is depicted in Fig. 5. We have added three arrows in light gray color, representing the three major PTs of BPM, and two arrows in dark gray color, in place of the two minor BPM PTs. The matrix illustrates a classification according to three dimensions:

- *Maturity level of process management*: The classification of the four approaches depends on the BPM maturity level within the organization. This differentiation is in accordance with the obvious partitioning between the two bottom clusters (BPM freshman and BPM intermediate) on the one hand and the two top clusters (BPM collectivist and BPM individualist) on the other hand.

- *Attention paid toward process management*: If the maturity level is rather low, it is assumed that BPM has not played any significant role within the organization in the past. However, the BPM freshman and the BPM intermediate approach can be differentiated with respect to the amount of attention that is currently paid toward process management.
- *Process management design type*: On the contrary, if the maturity level of BPM is rather high (i.e., if the organization has dealt with the BPM concept for quite a long time), one can distinguish between two design types of process management. The BPM collectivist relies on established standards as well as on procedure models and reference models whereas the BPM individualist focuses on the adoption of a more tailor-made approach to BPM. For this purpose, the BPM individualist provides process managers with excellent education and far-reaching authority for decision-making with respect to process design and execution.

In our early work, we have argued that the BPM intermediate approach might be characterized as a transitional stage in an organization's shift toward process-oriented thinking (Bucher and Winter 2006). According to the results of subsequent research, this assumption does not hold completely true (Bucher and Winter 2008): PT 2 is made up of ten observations that develop directly from the BPM freshman approach to the BPM individualist approach.

The common ground of the three major PTs of BPM is that the target state in all cases is the BPM individualist approach. When compared to the other realization approaches, this particular approach is characterized by the highest implementation level with respect to 10 out of 18 variables that have been sampled and included into the analysis (cf. Fig. 4). This fact indicates areas that need to be explicitly addressed in BPM transformation projects. The assessment of relative distances of the BPM collectivist, BPM freshman, and BPM intermediate implementation levels from the BPM individualist implementation level with respect to the 18 variables covered in our analysis points toward the topics that are of particular importance in each one of the three PTs, for example, the collection of process customers' input regarding process design or the documentation of process performances and goals.

The section to follow will illustrate the exemplary adaptation of a well-known BPM method to account for the characteristics of the three major BPM project types that have been identified and discussed in the previous section.

# 4 Exemplary Adaptation of the "Process Innovation" Method

The following section demonstrates the applicability of the empirical results. We report on the exemplary adaptation of Davenport's "process innovation" method (Davenport 1993). After giving a brief overview of the (generic) method for process redesign, we will sketch situation-specific embodiments of the method that are based on the PTs identified in the previous section.

## 4.1 Overview of the Method

In the early 1990s, during the pioneer era of business process reengineering (BPR), many authors have proposed concepts and methods for process innovation and redesign. Recommendations were made by both academia (e.g., Davenport and Short 1990; Hammer 1990; Harrington 1991, 1995; Davenport 1993; Hammer and Champy 1993) and practitioners. For a compilation and comparison of different approaches, see Hess and Brecht (1996).

The "process innovation" method proposed by Davenport (1993) is a well-known example of such an early BPR method. It aims at the fundamental and radical examination, analysis, and redesign of existing business processes with the objective of improving performance with respect to quality, flexibility, time, and money.

Figure 6 depicts the method's procedure model as outlined by Davenport (1993). This method description is rather generic, that is, it is intended to be applicable to a variety of development situations. The procedure model of the generic method features 25 design activities grouped into five phases. To simplify matters, we will assume that one or multiple design activities described by Davenport (1993) yield one particular, common design result. We will furthermore abstain from discussing both roles and techniques in support of the design results' creation.

Figure 7 depicts the documentation model that has been deduced from the description of the "process innovation" method. The documentation model shows all design results that arise from the method's application as well as their mutual dependencies. In accordance with the terminology established in this chapter (cf. section "situational method engineering"), we refer to the combination of design activities and associated design results as method fragments. Each method fragment is characterized by (1) the design result that is created and (2) the preconditions that have to be met for the fragment to be applicable. The third attribute necessary for the complete description of a method fragment – the specification of development situations in which the design result matters – will be introduced in the subsequent section.

## 4.2 Situation-Specific Embodiments of the Method

For the engineering of situation-specific embodiments of Davenport's BPR method, we focus on the major PTs 1–3, that is, BPM collectivist, BPM freshman, and BPM intermediate turning into BPM individualist. Moreover, we concentrate on selected variables of the empirical analysis: variable 1.2 ("surveys are used to assess the process customers' satisfaction with the processes"), variable 1.4 ("process outputs and performances are measured"), variable 2.1 ("the documentation of process performances and goals is available without restriction to all employees"), variable 3.4 ("process managers are actively engaged in change projects"), variable 4.1 ("procedure models are used for the design of performance management systems"), variable 4.2 ("processes of competitors and/or reference processes are used for

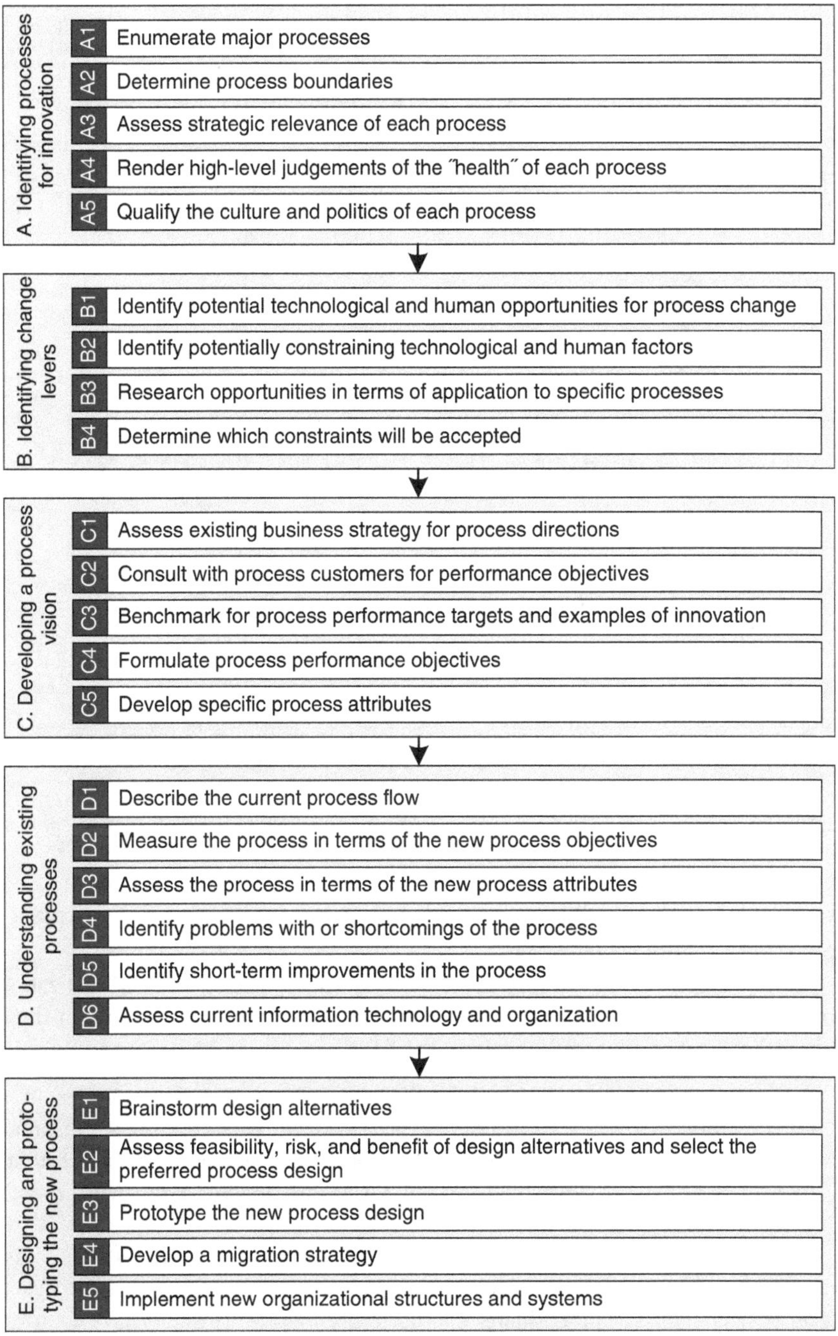


**Fig. 6** Procedure model of the "process innovation" method (on the basis of Davenport, 1993)

| Fragment | Activity | Design Result | Preconditions |
|---|---|---|---|
| Fragm. 01 | A1, A2 | Map of all business processes | No preconditions |
| Fragm. 02 | A3, A5 | Detailed characterization of all business processes | Fragment 01 completed |
| Fragm. 03 | A4 | List of advantages/disadvantages of current processes | Fragment 02 completed |
| Fragm. 04 | B1, B3 | Evaluated list of opportunities for process change | Fragment 03 completed |
| Fragm. 05 | B2, B4 | Evaluated list of constraints to process change | Fragment 03 completed |
| Fragm. 06 | C1, C2 | Process vision based on strategy and customers' input | Fragments 04, 05 completed |
| Fragm. 07 | C3 | "Best practice" examples and external benchmarks | Fragment 06 completed |
| Fragm. 08 | C4, C5 | List of quantitative and qualitative process objectives | Fragment 07 completed |
| Fragm. 09 | D1 | Detailed model of current business process | Fragment 03 completed |
| Fragm. 10 | D2, D3, D4 | Assessment of current process as to new objectives | Fragments 08, 09 completed |
| Fragm. 11 | D5 | Short-term process improvements | Fragment 10 completed |
| Fragm. 12 | D6 | Assessment of infrastructure in support of the process | Fragment 09 completed |
| Fragm. 13 | E1 | List of design alternatives | Fragments 11, 12 completed |
| Fragm. 14 | E2 | Assessment and ranking list of design alternatives | Fragment 13 completed |
| Fragm. 15 | E3 | Prototype of new process design | Fragment 14 completed |
| Fragm. 16 | E4 | Migration strategy for the implementation | Fragment 14 completed |
| Fragm. 17 | E5 | New organizational structures and systems in place | Fragments 15, 16 completed |

**Fig. 7** Documentation model and method fragments deduced from the description of the "process innovation" method

process analysis and design"), and variable 4.4 ("the organization uses the EFQM approach to quality management").

From the information depicted in the profile lines of the current BPM realization approaches (cf. Fig. 4), we can observe the following differences between these approaches (and consequently between the PTs):

- As for variable 1.2, the BPM individualist approach exhibits an implementation level slightly below the BPM collectivist approach. However, BPM freshman and BPM intermediate fall considerably short of this standard. The same holds true for variable 3.4. Variables 1.2 and 3.4 are particularly dealt with in conjunction with method fragment 6.
- As for variables 1.4, 4.1, and 4.2, the BPM individualist and the BPM collectivist approach exhibit implementation levels that are approximately equal to each other (with the BPM individualist approach scoring slightly higher). By contrast, the respective implementation levels of the BPM freshman and the BPM intermediate approach are significantly lower. Variable 1.4 is addressed by method fragment 10. Variables 4.1 and 4.2 relate to method fragment 07.

- As for variable 2.1, the BPM intermediate approach exhibits an implementation level that is approximately equal to the BPM individualist approach. The respective implementation levels of the BPM collectivist and the BPM freshman approach are considerably below this level. Variable 2.1 is not addressed by any of the fragments proposed by Davenport (1993). A new fragment therefore needs to be introduced to deal with this variable.
- As for variable 4.4, the BPM intermediate and the BPM individualist approach exhibit similar implementation levels that are significantly lower when compared to the BPM collectivist approach. When compared to the other three approaches, the BPM freshman approach scores lowest. The "process innovation" method does not explicitly address this variable. However, fragments 04 and 05 may be supported through the adoption of the EFQM approach.

Consequently, PT 1 (BPM collectivist turning into BPM individualist) needs to focus on the improvement of the implementation level with respect to variable 2.1 and might, at the same time, reduce the respective level of variable 4.4. PT 2 (BPM freshman turning into BPM individualist) needs to account for all of the aforementioned variables. PT 3 (BPM intermediate turning into BPM individualist) must focus on the improvement of variables 1.2, 1.4, 3.4, 4.1, and 4.2. From the fragment perspective, the new fragment introduced to deal with variable 2.1 (fragment 18; "documentation of process performances and goals") is of particular importance for PTs 1 and 2 but might be neglected in conjunction with PT 3. PT 1, by contrast, does not have to deal too much with fragments 6, 7, and 10. Those fragments are especially important to PTs 2 and 3. PT 3 might skip fragments 4 and 5.

Both Figs. 8 and 9 summarize these thoughts and propose a set of situation-specific embodiments of the "process innovation" method. The fragment list (cf. Fig. 8) depicts the fragments of the situational method. Changes with respect to Fig. 7 are marked with a diagonal shade. The network diagram (cf. Fig. 9) shows the generic method in continuous bold lines. Particular variations of this standard procedure that are valid for individual PTs alone are displayed in dashed lines (see figure key). To engineer a situational method that might be applied in real-world organizations, the required method fragments need to be selected and aggregated subject to the PT at hand.

## 5 Conclusion and Outlook

Our work is motivated by the conviction that no artifact (e.g., reference model or method) fits all development/application situations. On the one hand, a large range of development/application situations may be covered by an extremely generic artifact – but its generality makes it hard to concretely solve a specific problem. On the other hand, concrete problem situations may be addressed by a very specific artifact – but then, reuse potentials are very limited, and artifact development is hard to justify. Situational methods try to combine the best of both worlds: although such methods are designed as generic as possible, they can be adapted to fit a certain range of specific problem situations.

| Fragment | Design Result | Preconditions (if fragment is applicable) | Project Types |
|---|---|---|---|
| Fragm. 01 | Map of all business processes | No preconditions | PT1, PT2, PT3 |
| Fragm. 02 | Detailed characterization of all business processes | Fragment 01 completed | PT1, PT2, PT3 |
| Fragm. 03 | List of advantages/disadvantages of current processes | Fragment 02 completed | PT1, PT2, PT3 |
| Fragm. 04 | Evaluated list of opportunities for process change | Fragment 03 completed | PT1, PT2 |
| Fragm. 05 | Evaluated list of constraints to process change | Fragment 03 completed | PT1, PT2 |
| Fragm. 06 | Process vision based on strategy and customers'input | Fragments 03, 04, 05 completed | PT2, PT3 |
| Fragm. 07 | "Best practice" examples and external benchmarks | Fragment 06 completed | PT2, PT3 |
| Fragm. 08 | List of quantitative and qualitative process objectives | Fragments 04, 05, 07 completed | PT1, PT2, PT3 |
| Fragm. 09 | Detailed model of current business process | Fragment 03 completed | PT1, PT2, PT3 |
| Fragm. 10 | Assessment of current process as to new objectives | Fragments 08, 09 completed | PT2, PT3 |
| Fragm. 11 | Short-term process improvements | Fragments 08, 09, 10 completed | PT1, PT2, PT3 |
| Fragm. 12 | Assessment of infrastructure in support of the process | Fragment 09 completed | PT1, PT2, PT3 |
| Fragm. 13 | List of design alternatives | Fragments 11, 12 completed | PT1, PT2, PT3 |
| Fragm. 14 | Assessment and ranking list of design alternatives | Fragment 13 completed | PT1, PT2, PT3 |
| Fragm. 15 | Prototype of new process design | Fragment 14 completed | PT1, PT2, PT3 |
| Fragm. 16 | Migration strategy for the implementation | Fragment 14 completed | PT1, PT2, PT3 |
| Fragm. 17 | New organizational structures and systems in place | Fragments 15, 16 completed | PT1, PT2, PT3 |
| Fragm. 18 | Documentation of process performances and goals | Fragment 17 completed | PT1, PT2 |

**Fig. 8** Situation-specific embodiments of the "process innovation" method (fragment list)

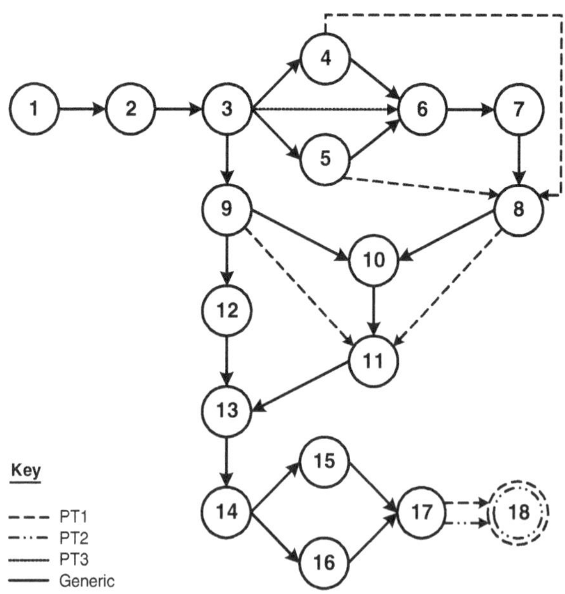


**Fig. 9** Situation-specific embodiments of the "process innovation" method (network diagram)

In order to engineer the generic method and appropriate adaptation mechanisms, a deep understanding of problem situations is needed. As our goal is to develop a situational approach to BPM, we therefore conducted a survey which, in a first step, identified four distinct design factors of BPM: (1) the degree of process performance measurement, (2) the overall professionalism of process management, (3) the impact of process managers, and (4) the utilization of established methodology and standards. On the basis of these design factors, four generic approaches to BPM were differentiated in a second step which we designated as (1) " BPM freshman," (2) "BPM intermediate," (3) "BPM collectivist," and (4) "BPM individualist." When interpolating the actual BPM approach with BPM plans in the near future, five BPM project types were differentiated in a third step: (1) BPM collectivist turning into BPM individualist, (2) BPM freshman turning into BPM individualist, (3) BPM intermediate turning into BPM individualist, (4) BPM freshmen turning into BPM collectivist (rare), and (5) BPM intermediate turning into BPM collectivist (rare). All surveyed organizations strive to achieve high BPM maturity. There are, however, significant differences with respect to the particular design of the aspired approaches to mature BPM.

The presented knowledge about design factors, generic approaches, and in particular PTs allows for developing a "customized" BPM method: The analysis of the relation of method fragments and fragment dependencies to PTs leads to a "core method," which can be systematically adapted by additional fragments and/or alternative fragment dependencies in order to fit certain PTs. The applicability of this approach to real-world BPM methods has been shown by using Davenport's "process innovation" method as a test case.

Future research is needed to further validate the empirical findings regarding BPM design factors, generic approaches to BPM, and BPM project types. On the basis of a growing common understanding of BPM situations, more case studies have to justify the usefulness of the proposed situational method engineering approach.

## References

Agerfalk PJ, Brinkkemper S, Gonzalez-Perez C, Henderson-Sellers B, Karlsson F, Karlsson F, Kelly S, Ralyté J (2007) Modularization constructs in method engineering – Towards common ground? In: Ralyté J, Brinkkemper S, Henderson-Sellers B (eds) Situational method engineering – Fundamentals and experiences (Proceedings of the IFIP WG8.1 Working Conference, 12–14 September 2007, Geneva, Switzerland), vol 244, International Federation for Information Processing. Springer, Boston, MA, pp 359–368

Aitken C, Stephenson C, Brinkworth R (2010) Process classification frameworks. In: vom Brocke J, Rosemann M (eds) Handbook on business process management, vol 2. Springer, Heidelberg

Alter S (2003) 18 reasons why IT-reliant work systems should replace "the IT artifact" as the core subject matter of the IS field. Commun Assoc Inf Syst 12(23):366–395

Alter S (2006) Work systems and IT artifacts – does the definition matter? Commun Assoc Inf Syst 17(14):299–313

Armistead C, Pritchard J-P, Machin S (1999) Strategic business process management for organizational effectiveness. Long Range Plann 32(1):96–106

Avison DE, Fitzgerald G (1988) Information systems development – methodologies, techniques and tools. Blackwell, Oxford
Balzarova MA, Bamber CJ, McCambridge S, Sharp JM (2004) Key success factors in implementation of process-based management – A UK housing association experience. Bus Process Manage J 10(4):387–399
Becker J, Janiesch C, Pfeiffer D (2007a) Reuse mechanisms in situational method engineering. In: Ralyté J, Brinkkemper S, Henderson-Sellers B (eds) Situational Method engineering – Fundamentals and Experiences (Proceedings of the IFIP WG8.1 Working Conference, 12-14 September 2007, Geneva, Switzerland, vol 244, International federation for information processing. Springer, Boston, pp 79–93
Becker J, Knackstedt R, Pfeiffer D, Janiesch C (2007) Configurative method engineering – on the applicability of reference modeling mechanisms in method engineering. In: Proceedings of the 13th Americas conference on information systems (AMCIS 2007) (13th Americas Conference on Information Systems (AMCIS 2007), Keystone, CO, pp 1–12
Brinkkemper S (1996) Method engineering – Engineering of information systems development methods and tools. Inf Softw Technol 38(4):275–280
Bucher T (2008) Ausrichtung der informationslogistik auf operative prozesse – Entwicklung und evaluation einer situativen Methode (in German language). Ph.D. Thesis, St. Gallen, University of St. Gallen (in press)
Bucher T, Klesse M (2006) Contextual method engineering. St. Gallen, Institute of Information Management, University of St. Gallen (Working Paper)
Bucher T, Winter R (2006) Classification of business process management approaches – an exploratory analysis. BIT Bank Inf Technol 7(3):9–20
Bucher T, Winter R (2008) Project types of business process management – Towards a scenario structure to enable situational method engineering for business process management. St. Gallen, University of St. Gallen (Working Paper).
Bucher T, Klesse M, Kurpjuweit S, Winter R (2007) Situational Method Engineering - On the Differentiation of "Context" and "Project Type". In: Ralyté J, Brinkkemper S, Henderson-Sellers B (eds) Situational method engineering – Fundamentals and experiences (Proceedings of the IFIP WG8.1 Working conference, 12–14 September 2007, Geneva, Switzerland), vol 244, International federation for information processing. Springer, Boston, pp 33–48
Burlton R (2010) Delivering business strategy through process management. In: vom Brocke J, Rosemann M (eds) Handbook on business process management, vol 2. Springer, Heidelberg
Cossentino M, Gaglio S, Henderson-Sellers B, Seidita V (2006) A Metamodelling-Based Approach for Method Fragment Comparison. In: Latour T, Petit M (eds) Proceedings of Workshops and Doctoral Consortium (The 18th International Conference on Advanced Information Systems Engineering - Trusted Information Systems (CAiSE'06), Luxembourg). Presses Universitaires de Namur, Namur, pp 419–432
Davenport TH (1993) Process innovation – Reengineering work through information technology. Harvard Business School, Boston, MA
Davenport TH, Short JE (1990) The new industrial engineering – information technology and business process redesign. Sloan Manage Rev 31(4):11–27
de Bruin T (2007) Insights into the evolution of BPM in organisations In: Proceedings of the 18th Australasian conference on information systems (ACIS 2007). University of Southern Queensland, Toowoomba, OLD
DeToro I, McCabe T (1997) How to stay flexible and elude fads. Qual Prog 30(3):55–60
Dziuban CD, Shirkey EC (1974) When is a correlation matrix appropriate for factor analysis? Psychol Bull 81(6):358–361
Fiedler FE (1964) A contingency model of leadership effectiveness. Adv Exp Soc Psychol 1:149–190
Hammer M (1990) Reengineering work – Don't automate, obliterate. Harv Bus Rev 68(4):104–112
Hammer M (2007) The process audit. Harv Bus Rev 85(4):111–123
Hammer M, Champy J (1993) Reengineering the corporation – A manifest for business revolution. Harper Collins, New York

Hammer M, Stanton SA (1995) The reengineering revolution – A handbook. Harper Business, New York
Härdle W, Simar L (2003) Applied multivariate statistical analysis. Springer, Berlin
Harmon P (2006). BPM methodologies and process maturity, retrieved 06.07.2006 from www.bpmtrends.com
Harmsen AF (1997) Situational method engineering. Moret Ernst and Young Management Consultants, Utrecht
Harmsen AF, Brinkkemper S, Oei H (1994) Situational method engineering for information system project approaches. In: Verrijn-Stuart AA, Olle TW (eds) Methods and associated tools for the information systems life cycle. North-Holland, Amsterdam, pp 169–194
Harrington HJ (1991) Business process improvement – The breakthrough strategy for total quality, productivity, and competitiveness. McGraw-Hill, New York
Harrington HJ (1995) Total improvement management – The next generation in performance improvement. McGraw-Hill, New York
Hess T, Brecht L (1996) State of the Art des Business Process Redesign – Darstellung und Vergleich bestehender Methoden (in German language). Wiesbaden, Gabler
Hevner AR, March ST, Park J, Ram S (2004) Design science in information systems research. MIS Quart 28(1):75–105
Ho SKM, Fung CKH (1994) Developing a TQM excellence model. TQM Mag 6(6):24–30
Imai M, Heymans B (1999) Gemba Kaizen. San Francisco, CA, Berrett-Koehler Communications
Jesus L, Macieira A, Karrer D, Caulliraux H (2010) BPM center of excellence. The case of a Brazilian company. In: vom Brocke J, Rosemann M (eds) Handbook on business process management, vol 2. Springer, Heidelberg
Kaiser HF, Rice J (1974) Little Jiffy, Mark IV. Educ Psychol Meas 34(1):111–117
Kaplan RB, Murdock L (1991) Rethinking the corporation – Core process redesign. McKinsey Quar 27(2):27–43
Karlsson F, Ågerfalk PJ (2004) Method configuration – adapting to situational characteristics while creating reusable assets. Inf Softw Technol 46(9):619–633
Karlsson F, Wistrand K (2006) Combining method engineering with activity theory - Theoretical grounding of the method component concept. Eur J Inf Syst 15(1):82–90
Kumar K, Welke RJ (1992) Methodology engineering - A proposal for situation-specific methodology construction. In: Cotterman WW, Senn JA (eds) Challenges and strategies for research in systems development. Wiley, Chichester, pp 257–269
List B, Korherr B (2006) An Evaluation of Conceptual Business Process Modelling Languages, Liebrock L (eds): Proceedings of the 21st Annual ACM Symposium on Applied Computing (SAC2006), ACM Press, New York, NY, USA, pp 1532–1539
March ST, Smith GF (1995) Design and natural science research on information technology. Decis Support Syst 15(4):251–266
Maull RS, Tranfield DR, Maull W (2003) Factors characterising the maturity of BPR programmes. Int J Oper Prod Manage 23(6):596–624
Niehaves B (2006) The reflective designer – Designing IT-consulting processes. Ph.D. Thesis, Münster, University of Münster
Nunamaker JF Jr, Chen M, Purdin TDM (1990) Systems development in information systems research. J Manage Inf Syst 7(3):89–106
Olle WT, Hagelstein J, Macdonald IG, Rolland C, Sol HG, van Assche FJM, Verrijn-Stuart AA (1988) Information systems methodologies – A framework for understanding. Addison-Wesley, Wokingham
Pritchard J-P, Armistead C (1999) Business process management – Lessons learned from European business. Bus Process Manage J 5(1):10–32
Rosemann M, de Bruin T (2005) Towards a business process management maturity model. In Bartmann D, Rajola F, Kallinikos J, Avison D, Winter R, Ein-Dor P, Becker J, Bodendorf F, Weinhardt C (eds) Proceedings of the Thirteenth European Conference On Information Systems (ECIS 2005), Regensburg

Rosemann M, vom Brocke J (2010) The six core elements of business process management. In: vom Brocke J, Rosemann M (eds) Handbook on business process management, vol 1. Springer, Heidelberg

Scholz-Reiter B, Stahlmann H-D, Nethe A (1999) Process modelling. Springer, Berlin

Simon HA (1996) The sciences of the artificial. MIT, Cambridge

van der Aalst WMP, Nakatumba J, Rozinat A, Russell N (2010) Business process simulation. In: vom Brocke J, Rosemann M (eds) Handbook on business process management, vol 1. Springer, Heidelberg

van Slooten K, Hodes B (1996) Characterizing IS development projects. In: Brinkkemper S, Lytinnen K, Welke RJ (eds) Method Engineering - Principles of Method Construction and Tool Support. Chapman & Hall, London, pp 29–44

vom Brocke J, Petry M, Sinnl T, Østerberg Kristensen B, Sonnenberg C (2010) Global processes and data: The cultural journey at the Hilti corporation. In: vom Brocke J, Rosemann M (eds) Handbook on business process management, vol 2. Springer, Heidelberg

Walls JG, Widmeyer GR, El Sawy OA (1992) Building an information system design theory for vigilant EIS. Inf Syst Res 3(1):36–59

zur Mühlen M, Shapiro R (2010) Business process analytics. In: vom Brocke J, Rosemann M (eds) Handbook on business process management, vol 2. Springer, Heidelberg

# Process Performance Management

**Diana Heckl and Jürgen Moormann**

**Abstract** The starting point for managing any process is the determination of the current performance. Thus, the process manager within a company has to permanently measure the process performance. In particular, he/she has to define criteria for determining the process performance. However, selecting the "right" criteria remains a difficult and highly debated topic, both in theory and practice. The objective of this chapter is to discuss different approaches for measuring process performance and to demonstrate how an individualized measurement system can be designed. Hence, process performance measurement will be discussed in relation to business performance measurement. In this context, relevant measurements and systems for determining process performance will be presented. The finding is that companies require a process performance measurement system that is tailored specifically to their business objectives and strategic success factors. On this basis, the authors suggest an approach to how a company-specific process performance measurement system can be set up.

## 1 Measurement as Part of Operational Process Controlling

In order to manage business processes, some authors suggest the implementation of an integrated concept of leadership, organization, and control (e.g., Davenport and Short 1990). The intention is to set up a target-oriented control system of business processes. The entire company should be aligned with the requirements of its clients and other stakeholders. Process targets should be defined for every single process within a well-designed business process control system. Every process manager's aim should be the successful, holistic control of the respective process.

J. Moormann (✉)
Frankfurt School of Finance & Management, Frankfurt/a.M., Germany
e-mail: j.moormann@frankfurt-school.de

J. vom Brocke and M. Rosemann (eds.), *Handbook on Business Process Management 2*, International Handbooks on Information Systems,
DOI 10.1007/978-3-642-01982-1_6, © Springer-Verlag Berlin Heidelberg 2010

Basically, the management of a process can be classified into the categories of normative, strategic, and operational process control:

- Process targets are the starting point. The targets have to be verified within a *normative control cycle* (Zairi and Sinclair 1995). First of all, the vision of the company has to be developed; it describes what the company wants to achieve in the long term (e.g., "We compete to be the leading global provider of financial solutions for demanding clients, creating exceptional value for our shareholders and people" [Deutsche Bank]). Based on the vision, business objectives for the whole company and for each strategic business unit (SBU) have to be derived.
- In terms of Double Loop Learning (Argyris 1999), the control of processes also refers to *strategic control aspects*. Hence, it may be necessary to reconsider and change the strategy with respect to the process architecture. If the target achievement appears to be out of reach, it would be necessary to develop a completely new or an improved process structure – in radical (Hammer and Champy 1993) as well as in evolutionary aspects (Andersson et al. 2006). There are numerous concepts available for improving processes (e.g., Business Process Redesign, Kaizen, and Six Sigma).
- Within the scope of *operational control*, the processes should be successfully managed to achieve the process targets. Therefore, the process manager permanently measures the current state of the process performance. In comparison with the process targets, he/she analyzes the level of target achievement. In case of a deviation beyond a defined bandwidth, the process manager searches for short-term improvements that immediately influence process performance results. These activities have to be aligned with the predetermined process strategy (see Sect. 3) which is also the basis for the company's operational and organizational structure (Kueng and Kawalek 1997).

This chapter focuses on operational control of processes.[1] In order to engage in operational controlling, process performance has to be defined. Process measurement, that is, the continuous measurement of predetermined performance indicators for the purpose of attaining process targets, represents an important task of operational process controlling. Although measuring a company's process performance is a topic that has been generally discussed in publications, precise definitions of performance measurement have been rarely provided. According to Neely et al. (2005, p. 1229) "... the level of performance a business attains [is] a function of the efficiency and effectiveness of the actions it undertakes." In their view, measurements are defined and established in order to define performance. A coordinated and aligned set of measurements (metrics) represents a measurement system that is suited to quantifying efficiency and effectiveness (performance).

---

[1] Burlton (2010) discusses this aspect within the broader scope of "delivering business strategy through process management" and positions the process performance management (including both strategic and operational control) within an "architect and align" phase when deriving and deploying a strategy compliant process architecture.

The objective of this chapter is to discuss different approaches to measuring process performance and to demonstrate how an individualized measurement system can be designed. In Sect. 2, process performance measurement will be discussed in relation to business performance measurement. Subsequently, basic terms related to performance measurement and concepts will be explained, and a number of measurements and measurement systems that have been offered in academic research will be introduced. This discussion will highlight that companies require a process performance measurement system that is tailored specifically to their business objectives and strategic success factors. In Sect. 3, an approach for developing a company-specific process performance measurement system will be outlined. Finally, Sect. 4 provides the conclusion of this chapter.

## 2 Approaches for Measuring Process Performance

In the following, cornerstones of process performance measurement will be discussed, starting with an overview of the current discussion related to the measurement of business performance. Subsequently, key terms of process performance analysis, measurements for determining process performance, and measurement systems will be presented.

### *2.1 Concepts for Performance Measurement*

In recent years, several approaches and methodologies for the determination of performance within a company have been developed. Each approach pursues different objectives, implies different characteristics, but shares certain elements with other approaches:

- *Balanced Scorecard*: Kaplan and Norton (1993) developed the Balanced Scorecard as an instrument in order to clarify and operationalize a company's vision and strategy on the basis of four perspectives (financial, customer, internal process, and learning and growth perspective). The instrument is used to track business performance, and the focus of tracking is geared toward the corporate level, SBUs, and further organizational units.
- *Self-Assessment*: On the basis of predetermined criteria and a defined framework, a business can undertake a self-assessment and analyze opportunities for improvement. Such frameworks have been developed and recommended by quality management associations (e.g., European Foundation of Quality Management, EFQM). A self-assessment of business performance offers a number of advantages: objective identification of the company's strengths and weaknesses, an analysis of the company's performance capabilities from a customer perspective, and the development of a strategic vision for continued performance improvement (Hakes 1996).

- *Traditional Controlling*: Traditional controlling entails directing, managing, and controlling the entire business. Key indicators to assess profitability, growth, and risk factors have to be defined and determined. Senior management can thus observe and coordinate profitability, growth, and risk objectives. Controlling therefore supports the management task of planning, initiating, coordinating, and controlling (Kueng 2000).
- *Process Performance Measurement Systems*: These systems serve to evaluate the performance of a single business process rather than the performance of the entire company. Using process objectives as a starting point, appropriate criteria for evaluating process results are established. The process manager is therefore in a position to assess process performance and to identify any corrective measures if required. Process deficiencies can thus be easily detected (Neely et al. 2000).
- *Workflow-based Monitoring*: Workflow systems allow for the automatic or semi-automatic analysis of process variations, the coordination of process activities, and communication between staff members involved in process provisioning (Kueng 2000). A by-product is the generation of a multitude of useful data, which can then be processed and analyzed automatically, resulting in valuable information pertaining to process costs, processing time, or process backlogs (zur Mühlen 2004). Quality-based metrics or evaluation of data relating to manually performed process activities is, however, not considered.
- *Statistical Process Control*: Juran and Gyrna (1993, p. 380) define this concept as "[...] the application of statistical methods to the measurement and analysis of variation in any process." The main objective pursued with statistical process control is the reduction in process variation in order to ensure stable processes that can be repeated. In other words, the process properties and output become predictable. This approach plays a vital role in product quality planning, as it allows for a prediction of whether or not customer requirements can be met.

For the purpose of this chapter, the focus and the scope of performance serve as the main dimensions when differentiating the approaches as shown in Fig. 1.

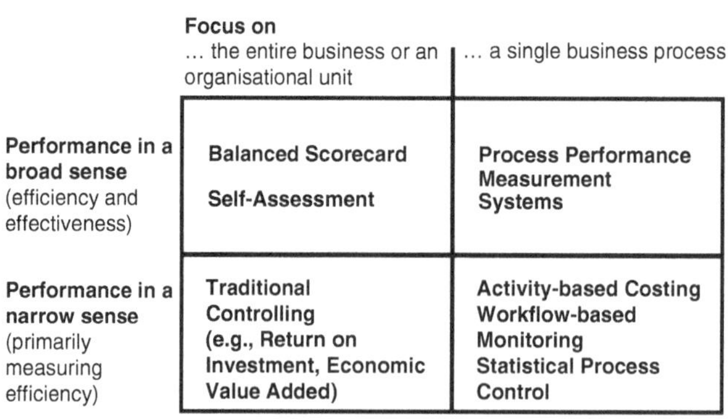


**Fig. 1** Positioning of process performance measurement systems

In summary, a process performance measurement system focuses on an individual business process, rather than on the entire company or an organizational unit. The Balanced Scorecard and self-assessment concepts are placed in the same box, because of their common focus on the whole company and their performance definition in a broad sense (efficiency and effectiveness) – although their approach to measuring performance is quite different. Statistical process control, activity-based costing, and workflow-based monitoring are usually used for measuring a single process focusing on efficiency aspects. Traditional controlling looks mostly on the company as a whole, focusing on efficiency.

The process-oriented view of a business serves therefore as the basis of a process performance measurement system. Moreover, the measurement system encompasses both efficiency metrics and effectiveness metrics to determine performance. The determination of measurements and/or development of the measurement system is, however, often based on traditional, existing approaches at a company level. The following discussion focuses in more detail on the determination of performance of business processes in a broad sense, i.e., focusing on efficiency and effectiveness.

## 2.2 *Process Performance Measurement Based on Indicators, Measures, and Figures*

Process controlling, as a part of Business Process Management and defined as measuring, analyzing, and improving processes, represents a loop that coordinates process execution (Kueng and Kawalek 1997), that is, transforming process inputs into process outputs. Process performance measurement entails capturing quantitative and qualitative information about the process. Measurements can be obtained either through continuous or periodic measuring. Subsequently, the measurements can be transformed into performance figures, which thus translate unfiltered data into information about process performance, enabling the process manager to deal with process controlling.

Different terms are used concerning the determination of process performance: performance indicators, performance measures, and performance figures. Definitions of these terms vary considerably, depending on the author. The following delineation of these terms according to Baker and Hart (1989) appears to be appropriate:

- *Performance Indicators*: In order to exactly determine process performance, indicators for the assessment of process performance have to be defined, and they have to be continuously monitored by the process manager. The definition of a performance indicator can be based on the company's strategy, business process objectives, and/or strategic success factors. For example, a financial services provider may state as a business process objective an increase in productivity by means of faster service provisioning. In order to determine the level of goal attainment, two performance indicators can be identified: time (as an input factor) and service quantity (as an output factor).

- *Performance Measures*: Measures represent the operationalization of each identified performance indicator. This entails determining precisely how the performance indicator will be measured, that is, questions related to what, how, when, by whom, and where of measurements for each performance indicator have to be addressed. For example, the performance indicator "time" might measure total cycle time, actual processing time etc., and the indicator "service quantity" might include the number of loan applications or the number of loan decisions that have been achieved.
- *Performance Figures*: Performance figures represent those measurements, for which the process manager has determined objectives. As a consequence, comparisons between targeted and actual performance are possible. Performance figures are normally included in management reports. Therefore, a performance figure can be the measure itself (e.g., cycle time) or a combination of different measures (e.g., throughput efficiency = number of loan decisions per hour of cycle time). Performance figures thus enable summarization and representation of large amounts of data in a condensed and precise manner. They serve the management team as a valuable source of comprehensive information on the company's objectives and results.

## 2.3 Measurements to Determine Process Performance

The beginning for measuring process performance is the identification of performance indicators that allow for a detailed specification of process performance. Therefore, numerous authors have suggested categories of indicators in order to facilitate a structured approach. Within the context of strategic production management, Leong et al. (1990) state that there are five groups of indicators suited to determining process performance: quality, delivery time, delivery reliability, costs, and flexibility. However, there is disagreement about which performance indicators (and subsequently which performance measures and performance figures) are included in these indicator groups. Wheelwright (1984) understands flexibility as the ability to change the production process, whereas Tunalv (1992) applies the term flexibility to the organizational capability of developing new products. Beamon (1999) favors clustering indicators into resource-based indicators, output-based indicators, and flexibility-related indicators. She thus adopts a process-based perspective, regarding resources as inputs, process results as outputs, and viewing flexibility as an inherent aspect of process execution. The majority of authors, such as Schonberger (1990), Stalk (1988), Garvin (1987), Gerwin (1987), and Slack (1987), have adopted a process-oriented view, resulting in the indicator groups quality, time, costs, and flexibility. These four indicator groups will be examined in the following.

In general, *quality* describes the degree to which the actual product attributes and properties conform to the underlying product specifications. In the past, indicators often included costs, for example, defect prevention, quality measurement costs, and costs related to failure rates (Campanella and Corcoran 1983). However, the emergence of quality improvement initiatives such as Total Quality Management has resulted in a new definition of the term quality. Nowadays, customer satisfaction serves as the yardstick for measuring the quality of a product or service. Consequently, methodologies such as Six Sigma define indicators on the basis of performance-related customer requirements (Andersson et al. 2006).

In the production point of view, *time* is considered to be an indicator of competitiveness and process performance. Yet, the time aspect can be looked at from different angles: Within a just-in-time production paradigm, for example, production and/or delivery of production outputs at a premature or belated point of time is considered to be a waste of time. Thus, the exact point of time is relevant, and an appropriate performance indicator would be the deviation from the targeted point of time. Within the field of research in optimized production technology (OPT), the main objective is seen in minimizing process time. Performance indicators and subsequent performance measures therefore include, for example, throughput time, actual processing time, waiting time, transportation time, and delivery time. In the time-based costing approach, time is viewed in yet a different way, namely in terms of production costs (Drucker 1990).

Research in the area of cost accounting provides the basis for the determination of *cost* indicators. A large number of academic contributions, for example, Johnson (1983), deal with the various cost aspects. Different cost factors provide the basis for cost indicators: labor costs, IT costs, production costs, product costs, service costs, failure costs, and so forth. A distinction can be made between fixed and variable costs. In addition, since the emergence of activity-based costing, indicators such as activity-based costs, sub-process-, or process-related costs are feasible.

Indicators to determine *flexibility* include, according to Slack (1987), the degree to which a production or service process can be modified, including the timeline and costs associated with the restructuring of a production or service process. A further indicator for flexibility relates to the number of product or service components that can be exchanged within a given time. Moreover, process flexibility may also be viewed as dealing with output volumes or resource utilization.

In summary, there are many indicators available that can be applied for the measurement of company-specific process performance. In the early 1980s, companies defined indicators that focused primarily on efficiency and to a lesser degree on effectiveness. Performance figures served to reduce costs rather than to improve profit-related issues. In order to avoid such misguided management, companies have to select indicators that are directly linked to their strategy, and they have to link the indicators to their business objectives and resources. This will then result in strategic performance figures that support senior management in navigating toward the desired strategic direction. Hence, the figures are highly dynamic, and the selection of strategically important performance indicators is related to the notion of "critical success factors" discussed by Rockart (1979). In order to be successful, each company has to determine performance indicators and, subsequently, performance measures and performance figures that are strategically relevant to its respective situation.

## 2.4 Frameworks for Measuring Process Performance

Due to the large number of potential indicators and the derived performance measures and performance figures, it becomes obvious that process performance is not anything absolute. The performance of a given process can differ significantly from other measurements of the same process. The company's vision and the stakeholder-related objectives serve as a basis for the determination of measurements for process performance. As the entire company should be aligned with the wishes and requirements of its clients and other stakeholders, the performance measures have to be aligned with the objectives of the stakeholders. Moreover, process performance is multi-dimensional, that is, process performance cannot be determined on the basis of a single indicator, such as productivity, but results from many different indicators, measures, and performance figures that cannot be simply summarized in one single number. In addition, process performance indicators are not independent from each other. Most process performance indicators exhibit a relationship with other indicators, that is, they complement one another or they conflict with each other (Gillies 1997).

As a result, performance measurement systems have been developed. They link individual performance figures that focus on an overarching objective, such as return on investment (ROI). Such systems offer three advantages: first, the system considers cause-and-effect relationships between individual performance figures; second, the system provides an opportunity to conduct more detailed analyses and comparisons; and third, the system allows for a simpler detection of conflicting objectives.

Researchers have therefore engaged themselves in the development of performance measurement systems (also referred to as measurement systems) for determining process performance, which take those three aspects of the performance definition into consideration. These measurement systems therefore regard process performance as multi-dimensional in itself and consequently provide recommendations for performance indicators. However, in most cases, the measurement systems do not identify specific performance measures, as process performance is not absolute. Instead, it is recommended that the individual performance measures should be determined on the basis of the performance indicators and the specific, individual objectives of the company. Therefore, one can refer to this as a framework for the development of an individualized measurement system. While researchers address the issue of interdependencies between process performance indicators, they do not offer any solution to the problem of the multi-dimensional performance definition. Examples of measurement systems will be presented and discussed in the following paragraphs.

In their literature reviews, Neely et al. (1995, 2000, 2005) have dedicated themselves to continuously presenting newly developed measurement systems and identifying research gaps. They clearly identify the Balanced Scorecard as one of the best-known frameworks for developing an individualized measurement system and for determining *business performance*. However, the Balanced Scorecard is only one out of many examples.

A multitude of other frameworks for determining a performance measurement system exists. Keegan, Eiler, and Jones introduced a *Performance Measurement Matrix* as an example for a classification system in 1989 (Fig. 2a). The framework developed by Fitzgerald et al. (1991) represents the insights gained from research in service industries. Their studies suggest that the competitiveness of a company is not merely a result of production costs and product price. The framework rather rests on the premise that performance indicators can be categorized into two different *Basic Types of Performance Indicators* (Fig. 2b): indicators that are related to and reflect process results (measurements assessing the competitive environment, such as market share or market growth, as well as financial measurements, such as costs and profits), and indicators that reflect the determinants of process success (measurements to determine quality, flexibility, resource utilization, and innovation). Yet another well-known framework for the determination of a measurement system is the *Performance Pyramid* (Lynch and Cross 1991, Fig. 2c). This framework stresses a hierarchical view of performance, that is, it considers the relationship between strategic performance (e.g., fulfilling the vision, market share, financial performance) and process performance (e.g., quality, cycle time, waste, or spoilage rate). The layer connecting the two hierarchical levels depicts those performance indicators that impact both levels (e.g., customer satisfaction, flexibility,

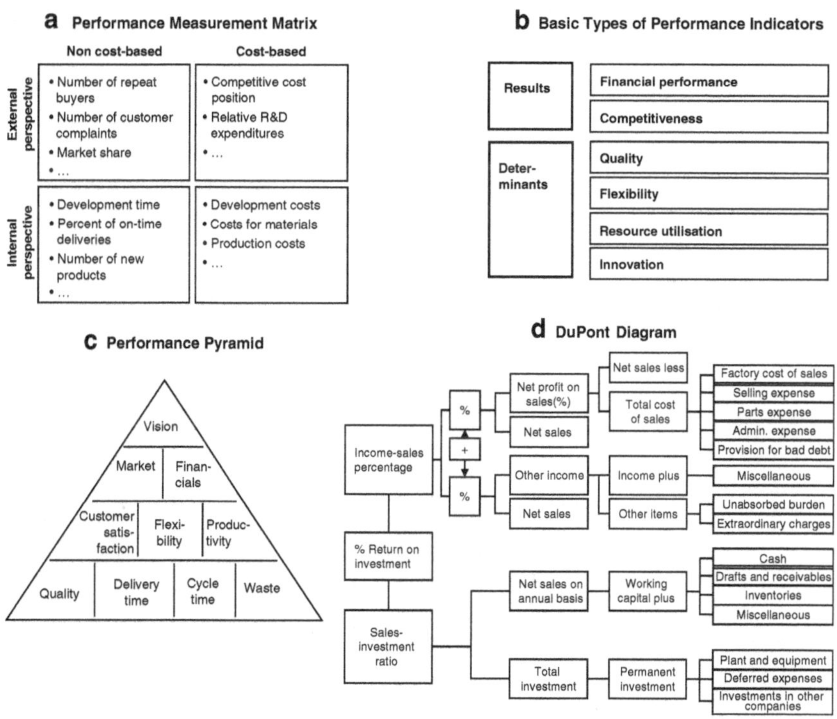


**Fig. 2** Frameworks for the development of performance measurement systems

and productivity). On the basis of a comprehensive literature review, The Institute of Chartered Accountants of Scotland (ICAS 1993) developed a framework that provides a list of possible financial and nonfinancial performance indicators. They arranged the identified indicators in a tree diagram in order to demonstrate the interdependencies and relationships between the indicators (Fig. 2d). The best-known example of a tree diagram is the *DuPont Diagram* (Chandler 1977) which, however, only considers financial performance indicators.

A stronger process perspective is emphasized by Brown (1996). His framework highlights the distinction between input, throughput, and output as he recommends determining performance indicators according to this classification (Fig. 3). Process input factors include, for example, employees, plant and equipment, as well as capital. The quality and quantity of these input factors can be a decisive factor in meeting customer requirements which themselves represent an additional input factor. During the throughput phase, input factors are utilized and combined. The output consists of a product, a service, and financial results. The *process performance* is therefore determined through a measurement system that encompasses performance measures for input, throughput, and output. In addition, performance measures related to meeting customer requirements (customer satisfaction) are included.

The review of the existing frameworks for developing a measurement system shows that only frameworks of high-level performance indicator groups have been considered so far. In most cases, there is no detailed specification of indicators available, as they are regarded as too specific for each individual company. Practice-based tests of the frameworks reveal that the individual performance measures and performance figures are dependent on the vision, mission, strategy, and the resulting business model of the respective company (Brignall and Ballantine 1996). In their analysis of service providers, Fitzgerald et al. (1991) identified three different business models that depend on the strategy: individualized service delivery, service shops, and mass delivery of services. The authors' analysis of service providers highlights that distinguishing on the basis of the business model is absolutely essential. Because of the dependence on the business

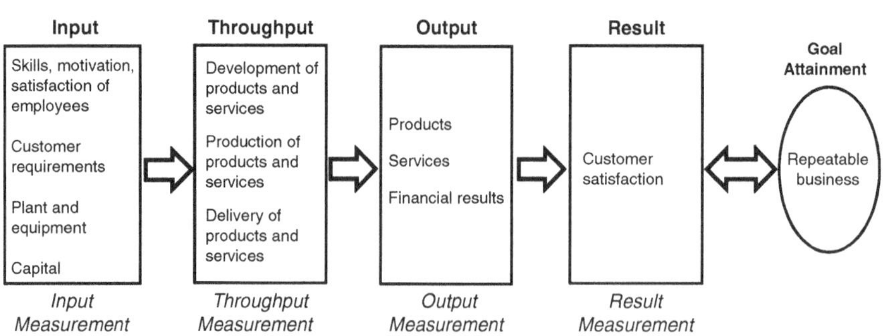


**Fig. 3** Framework for constructing a process-oriented performance measurement system (Brown 1996)

and process model, different performance indicators and different variations of indicators are required. For instance, a business model that focuses on mass delivery of services is likely to focus on minimizing customer contact time and the degree of service customization. However, a service provider specialized in highly individualized service delivery will be interested in the quality of the provided services, a longer customer contact time, and in customization of the service.

Since the publication by Fitzgerald et al. (1991), researchers have clearly pointed out that *Process Performance Measurement Systems* have to be tailored to the needs of each individual company. Brignall and Ballantine (1996), for example, conclude that, on the one hand, the specific company and its vision and strategy have to be considered. On the other hand, the internal organization, specifically the process model and its configuration, must also serve as the basis for a measurement system that aims to determine individual performance. The authors ascertain that these analysis requirements are comparable to Pettigrew's analysis variables "context, content, and process" (Pettigrew 1985).

In their first articles concerning the Balanced Scorecard, Kaplan and Norton (1992) focused only to a very limited extent on the determination of a specific measurement system. But then they quickly published eight steps, which they believe managers should follow in order to develop a measurement system in alignment with the Balanced Scorecard (Kaplan and Norton 1993): (1) prepare measurement system development, (2) conduct one-on-one interviews with senior managers (to elicit different vision and strategy approaches), (3) hold a first workshop with senior management (to agree on vision and strategy), (4) conduct extended interviews with senior management (to identify different indicators), (5) hold a second workshop with senior management (to determine performance indicators and target measures for each indicator), (6) conduct a third workshop with senior management (to define the Balanced Scorecard), (7) implement the measurement system, and (8) periodically review the measurement system. This procedure proposed by Kaplan and Norton highlights how the measurement system has to be aligned with vision, strategy, and strategic objectives. Keegan et al. (1989) observed as well that a dynamic framework (steps for developing a measurement system) is required in addition to a static framework (determination of performance indicator groups). They, too, view the definition of a vision and a strategy as the starting point. Vision and strategy serve as a basis for formulating strategic objectives and delineating senior management's scope of activities. Performance indicators, performance measures, and performance figures can then be determined resulting in a company-specific measurement system.

In summary, setting up a measurement system framework is a sensible undertaking. The outlined frameworks provide managers with guidance with respect to the development of an individualized measurement system. In doing so, emphasis should be placed on championing a methodology suited to developing a measurement system rather than prescribing a general "one-size-fits-all" measurement system. Brown (1996) provides an appropriate static framework for the measurement system, as he applies a process perspective in order to determine performance. In order to develop an individualized process performance measurement system, implementation steps have to be taken. These can be based on the recommendations by Brignall and Ballantine (1996), Fitzgerald et al. (1991), and/or Kaplan and Norton (1993). Subsequently, the external environment, the strategy, and the process model of the company have to be taken into consideration. An example of such a dynamic methodology is the framework delivered by Neely et al. (2000).

## 3 Development of a Company-Specific Process Performance Measurement System

Academic research distinguishes between two approaches to define and develop a process performance measurement system (Neely et al. 1995, 2000, 2005). The first approach utilizes existing generic performance indicators or performance measurement systems. This enables companies to build upon existing concepts and experiences rather than starting from scratch. The challenge, however, consists in selecting the appropriate indicators from an extensive list of potential indicators. Moreover, research indicates that there is not such a thing as "the one and only" accepted indicator list. The second approach entails selecting the performance indicators for a company on the basis of its business objectives and its success factors, resulting in performance indicators that are specific to the company. This procedure appears to be more closely aligned with the needs of the respective company.

The development of a process performance measurement system following the second approach can be accomplished according to the methodology depicted in Fig. 4. Initially, this methodology was designed for the definition of a performance

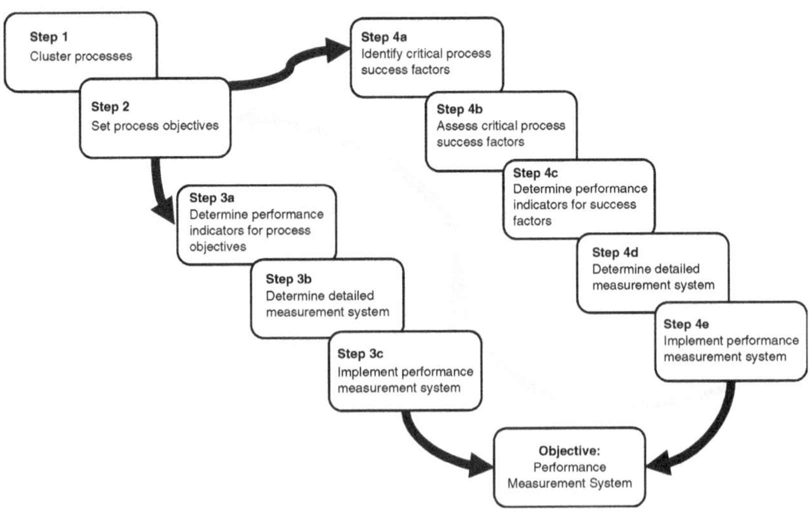


**Fig. 4** Steps for developing a company-specific process performance measurement system (based on Neely et al. 2000, p. 1139)

measurement system at corporate level (Neely et al. 2000). Here, we apply the methodology to a performance measurement system on business process level.

In a first step, processes have to be clustered depending on the architecture and objectives of the process (Fitzgerald et al. 1991). For each process cluster, both of the following steps are necessary: Process objectives have to be set and process success factors have to be assessed. In a next step, it is possible to derive the performance indicators and to develop and implement a measurement system for the process objectives as well as for the process success factors. However, the starting point is setting the objectives and identifying the success factors. Again, the objectives of the company's stakeholders provide the foundation for the subsequent steps of deriving process measures. The following sections outline how the process objectives can be determined and how the critical process success factors (CPSF) can be identified. Finally, performance indicators, performance measures, and performance figures will be derived.

## *3.1 Setting the Process Objectives*

A company's processes represent the arrangement of activities necessary for generating a specific output. The general objective of any process is the effective and efficient production of output. However, the particular definition of process efficiency and process effectiveness has to be derived from the business objectives which are articulated through the company's vision and strategy. The formulation of specific process objectives therefore depends on the presence of clearly defined business objectives. According to Simons (2000), a company's strategy is the result of a strategy development process:

1. At the outset, the company's situation has to be evaluated. Questions related to the positioning of the company within the entire business environment and concerning its *opportunities and threats* have to be addressed. The external environment can be analyzed using various tools. A PEST analysis, for example, serves to analyze the political, economic, socio-cultural and technological factors that influence the environment of a company. Similarly, Porter's "5 Forces" framework can be applied to analyze a company's position relative to the bargaining power of suppliers and customers, the threat of new market entrants, the threat of substitution, and the rivalry among existing competitors (Porter 1980, 2008).
2. Besides assessing opportunities and threats within the external environment, a company's *strengths and weaknesses* have to be analyzed. Suitable tools for such an internal exploration include resource-based analysis, core competency analysis, and value chain analysis. The resource-based view assumes a heterogeneous distribution of resources and potentials across companies. Consequently, a company's existing resources have to be evaluated with respect to their contribution toward enabling success in the current or future market. Resource-based analysis provides an answer to the question about which resources can deliver decisive

contributions to a company's success and which resources should therefore serve as the basis for the strategy that is to be developed. These resources can be considered as core competencies, if they contribute over-proportionately either to the delivery of customer benefits or to the efficiency of output production, or if they create a basis for a market entry (Hamel and Prahalad 1994).

3. On the basis of the company's vision, the identified opportunities and threats as well as the existing strengths and weaknesses, *strategic options* should be derived. The company's strategy represents the operationalization of the vision, as the strategy sets specific business objectives and determines courses of action to achieve these objectives. Porter (1980) states that a business acts in an optimal way, if it utilizes one of the generic competitive strategies: cost leadership strategy, differentiation strategy, or niche strategy. Other authors advocate that a combination of these generic competitive strategies is more likely to result in a competitive advantage. This approach requires developing an appropriate strategy for each business unit and even for each process cluster.
4. Once a competitive strategy has been selected, there are still several opportunities for expanding and enhancing the strategy. As a next step, all possible strategic options have to be *assessed and evaluated.* One can, for example, conduct a profitability analysis, a feasibility analysis, or an evaluation based on a key criteria catalog for each strategic option. Senior management then uses the results of the evaluation to decide on the final strategy for the company.
5. Moreover, *strategic programs* have to be developed that support and enable a consistent strategy implementation that addresses issues like process controlling as well as human and IT resources.

Companies have to engage repeatedly in strategy development, as the corporate strategy, business unit strategy, and/or process strategy have to be reviewed and adapted constantly. The frequency and depth of engaging in the strategy development process depend to a great extent on the industry and on the stage in the life cycle of a particular business.

Regardless of the selected strategy, long-term success will only occur if the strategy gets implemented via a strategic management process and if the strategy is pursued for the long-term. Strategy implementation encompasses aspects such as setting performance objectives for the entire company and for individual business processes. In addition, the entire organization and the processes have to be managed and directed with a strong focus on achieving the desired performance. The level of goal attainment, that is, the assessment whether the strategy implementation was successful, is determined through performance measurement and a comparison between targeted and actual performance.

In the following discussion, it is assumed that a company can only select one of Porter's (1980) generic competitive strategies. Thus, on the basis of the analysis of the external and internal environment, the company selects one of the strategies. Within the scope of defining appropriate strategic programs, the company's senior management has to set specific business objectives in order to measure the strategy implementation. Ideally, this is accomplished on the basis of Brown's (1996) model

**Table 1** Strategy process indicator matrix

| Process perspective | Generic strategy | | | | | | | | |
|---|---|---|---|---|---|---|---|---|---|
| | Cost leadership strategy | | | Differentiation strategy | | | Niche strategy | | |
| | $BO_1$ | ... | $BO_n$ | $BO_1$ | ... | $BO_n$ | $BO_1$ | ... | $BO_n$ |
| Input-related process indicators | $I_1$, $I_2$<br>$I_3$<br>... | | | | | | | | |
| Throughput-related process indicators | | | | | | | | | |
| Output-related process indicators | | | | | | | | | |
| Result-related process indicators | | | | | | | | | |

*BO* Business objective; *I* Indicator

for the determination of process objectives so that the business strategy can be operationalized in the form of process objectives and broken down into process indicators for input, throughput, output, and results. Table 1 exhibits the resulting template.

The selected strategy that emerges from the strategy development process, the company's business objectives, and the specific process objectives serves as the starting point for operational process controlling. Depending on the strategy, the individual input, throughput, output, or result indicators may be weighted differently. Hence, they represent the basis for the required process model and operational process controlling.

## 3.2 *Identifying Critical Process Success Factors*

In addition to process objectives, the process success factors serve as an important element for determining performance indicators. The notion of determining success factors for processes is based on the concept of success factors by Daniel (1961) and the concept of critical success factors by Rockart (1979). Both concepts address the impossibility of considering each single factor that might influence a company's success: "[...] a company's information system must be discriminating and selective. It should focus on ´success factors´. In most industries there are usually three to six factors that determine success; these key jobs must be done exceedingly well for a company to be successful" (Daniel 1961, p. 111). Hence, both authors assume that there are only a few factors and aspects that exert a significant influence on a company's success. These factors are referred to as "critical success factors." Thus, a company can only operate successfully, if it achieves satisfactory results in its critical success factors (Rockart 1979). The critical success factors within the industry and for the company therefore have to be defined and incorporated in the management and control system and then continuously measured.

Two approaches are utilized to determine critical success factors: The direct approach comprises asking individuals, such as managers, employees, customers, suppliers, and/or external experts for their opinion concerning success factors (Kueng 2000). The indirect approach involves identifying the success factors from a large pool of variables through intuition, experience, and statistical methods. The best-known direct approach is the critical success factors method developed by Rockart (1979), which can also be used to determine critical success factors at corporate level. According to Rockart, the following sources should be considered when identifying critical success factors:

- Industry structure
- Competitive strategy, position within the industry, and geographic location
- Environmental factors
- Temporary influences

In the past, the concept of critical success factors has been applied to industries or individual companies, but not to business processes. If a company is regarded as a value chain, and thus as a system of business processes, Rockart's model can be utilized to derive critical success factors for processes (CPSF). CPSF can therefore be represented either by parameters of the utilized process resources and capabilities (input), the process flow (throughput), or the end product or service (output). Obviously, they should only include those factors that have a decisive impact on the process success. CPSF therefore do not include objectives, areas of responsibility, or individual process steps, but always include process parameters, capabilities, or resources. In order to manage a process, it is essential to identify those factors that are important for all or at least for most processes, regardless of the processes' characteristics, which therefore have to be monitored continuously (*general CPSF*). At the same time, those success factors relevant for a specific process have to be identified (*specific CPSF*).

As customers expect delivery of a product or service at a certain point of time (i.e., availability), with certain attributes and characteristics (i.e., benefit), and at a reasonable price, processes can contribute to successfully meeting such customer expectations by generating the process output quickly, at the appropriate quality level, and at low costs. But different customer groups have different requirements. Therefore, processes have to be designed in such a way that they are flexible. Hence, the general CPSF are time, costs, quality, and flexibility. In publications on this topic, the following parameters, resources, and capabilities are regarded as general CPSF for the process flow: cycle time, defect rate, reliability, desired proximity to customers, information flow, manageability, efficiency, know-how, information systems, motivation, and ability to innovate (e.g., Kaplan and Norton 1993; Harrington 1991; Nagel 1988; Rockart 1979). However, an important question remains unanswered: How can senior management define general and specific CPSF?

Based on the approach described above, the process for deriving CPSF can be designed as follows:

1. In a first step, the CPSF concept and an analysis of potential sources for success factors should be introduced. This can be accomplished on the basis of an analytical and workshop-based discussion of the factors suggested by Rockart. After an evaluation and documentation of the results, this phase concludes with planning the next meetings and identifying participants for the subsequent phases.
2. The results of the first phase should be presented to the stakeholders of the examined process. Here, general as well as specific CPSF are elicited. Highly specific questions directed at the interviewee test whether all CPSF have been identified. Examples for such questions include the following: Which activities or tasks are currently decisive in your work? In which two or three areas would mistakes have the fastest and most critical impact? What would you need to know first upon returning to your office after a 2-week absence?
3. The derived CPSF have to be documented, analyzed, and then presented to all process stakeholders within a consolidation workshop. In this meeting, the CPSF are discussed, and then a maximum of six decisive CPSF are selected and, in a third step, prioritized. Ideally, a cause-and-effect diagram will be developed in order to show correlations between CPSF and the dependencies of the company and process success on the CPSF (Daniel 1961).
4. In the fourth step, CPSF programs have to be developed that support the consistent implementation of the CPSF with respect to the management of the processes. A CPSF program should for example enable monitoring of the CPSF, for example, the development of CPSF-oriented organizational structures, products, or services.

After defining the CPSF, it is necessary to determine indicators so that the CPSF can be continuously monitored and their impact on the company and process success can be analyzed. Table 2 shows an example for a performance matrix including the identified CPSF indicators. Indicators and figures for measuring general and specific CPSF are listed at the left. The matrix can be used to describe the current performance of the CPSF (dotted line) as well as the desired future performance of the CPSF (solid line). Moreover, the template allows to compare CPSF of different processes, sub-processes, or with competitors' CPSF. In addition to a simple appraisal of performance (from very high to very low), the specific actual and targeted performance figures should be added (e.g., cycle time: 6 days, standard deviation: 1.5 days).

## 3.3 Deriving Performance Indicators, Measures, and Figures

After developing the indicators with respect to the process objectives and the CPSF, the appropriate performance measures can be derived. The *performance indicators* fulfill several tasks. They serve to determine the level of process goal attainment, to assess the degree to which process success factors were successfully adhered to, and

**Table 2** Structure of a CPSF performance matrix

| CPSF indicators | Performance of CPSF | | | | |
|---|---|---|---|---|---|
| | Very high | High | Medium | Low | Very low |
| General CPSF indicators related to: | | | | | |
| – Time (e.g., cycle time, processing time, idle time) | | | | | |
| – Costs (e.g., production costs, productivity) | | | | | |
| – Quality (e.g., defect rate, complaint rate, quality costs) | | | | | |
| – Flexibility (e.g., process volumes, range of offer) | | | | | |
| Specific CPSF indicators related to: | | | | | |
| – Process input (e.g., employees, know-how) | | | | | |
| – Process throughput (e.g., flexible process design) | | | | | |
| – Process output (e.g., modular product design) | | | | | |
| – Process results (e.g., customer satisfaction) | | | | | |

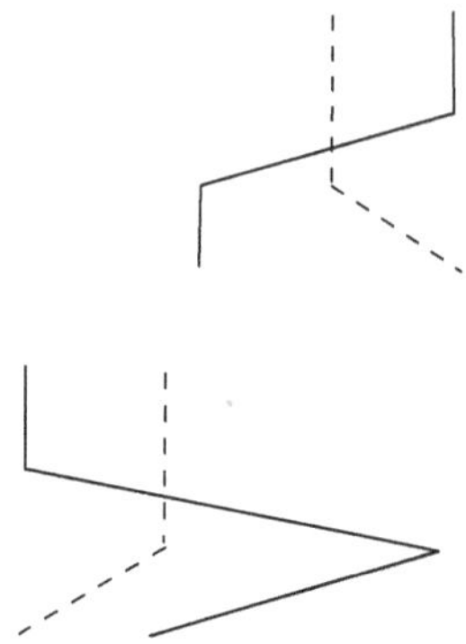

to determine which operational measures have to be identified and to which degree they have to be utilized in order to achieve the desired process objectives. The compilation of these indicators enables the definition of performance for a specific process. In other words, process performance is not measured on the basis of a single indicator, but rather is defined through multiple performance indicators that may even be in conflict with one another.

At least one performance indicator or measure has to be identified for each objective and each process success factor. Specific *performance measures* must be derived for each performance indicator (group), because they serve to measure the specific objectives and success factors. While determining the performance measure, the question of whether the performance indicator is measurable is answered indirectly as well. The performance measure has to meet two requirements, namely to concretize the performance indicator and to make the indicator measurable.

On the basis of *performance figures*, comparisons between targeted and actual achievements can be conducted for each performance indicator. At this point, day-to-day operational process controlling faces a critical question: What are the implications if the analysis points to significant performance deficits? Usually, further research into the causes for the performance deviation is required. One reason for performance deficits might be that employees did not stick to the formal methods and procedures of the respective process either because they were not familiar with them or lacked the ability to follow them, or because they were not willing to follow the methods and procedures. Furthermore, situation-specific factors and conditions may not have been taken sufficiently into account.

Depending on the findings of the deviation analysis, different performance measures have to be revised. Process objectives may have to be revised, or methods and procedures may have to be modified because of changes to the company's management and reward system in order to counter any dysfunctional behavior of the employees. Any subsequent changes and adjustments should be subject to organizational reviews in order to critically evaluate implementation feasibility and appropriateness. This will ensure the establishment of a continuous improvement process within the company.

## 4 Conclusion

If a process manager wants to assess opportunities for improving a given business process, he/she not only has to provide a formal depiction and description of the process. He/she also has to make a statement concerning the process performance. Hence, criteria to determine process performance (indicators, measures, figures) have to be defined beforehand. Selecting the "right" criteria, however, is a challenge, as there is no agreement in theory or practice on how to do this best.

In the beginning of this chapter, process performance measurement has been discussed in the context of operational process controlling. In a subsequent step, popular performance management concepts and terms have been outlined. Moreover, frequently discussed process performance measurements and measurement systems have been presented. The review has revealed that process managers are often challenged to develop a process performance measurement system which is tailored to their specific company. Following this finding, we have presented an approach for designing an individualized process performance controlling system based on company-specific process objectives and process success factors. It has also been shown how process performance indicators, measures, and figures can be derived. The approach presented here can be used as a starting point for determining process performance and ensuring capable operational process controlling.

## References

Andersson R, Eriksson H, Torstensson H (2006) Similarities and differences between TQM, six sigma and lean. TQM Mag 18(3):282–296

Argyris C (1999) On organizational learning, 2nd edn. Blackwell, Oxford

Baker MJ, Hart S (1989) Marketing and competitive success. Philip Allan, London

Beamon BM (1999) Measuring supply chain performance. Int J Oper Prod Manage 19(3/4):275–292

Brignall S, Ballantine J (1996) Performance measurement in service businesses revisited. Int J Serv Ind Manage 7(1):6–31

Brown M (1996) Keeping score: using the right metrics to drive world class performance. Quality Resources, New York

Burlton R (2010) Delivering business strategy through process management. In: vom Brocke J, Rosemann M (eds) Handbook on business process management, vol 2. Springer, Heidelberg

Campanella J, Corcoran FJ (1983) Principles of quality costs. Qual Prog 4(26):16–22

Chandler AD (1977) The visible hand: the managerial revolution in American business. Harvard University Press, Cambridge, MA
Daniel DR (1961) Management information crisis. Harv Bus Rev 39(5):111–121
Davenport TH, Short JE (1990) The new industrial engineering: information technology and business process redesign. Sloan Manage Rev 31(4):11–27
Drucker PF (1990) The emerging theory of manufacturing. Harv Bus Rev 68(3):94–102
Fitzgerald L, Johnston R, Brignall TJ, Silvestro R, Voss C (1991) Performance measurement in service businesses. CIMA, London
Garvin DA (1987) Competing on the eight dimensions of quality. Harv Bus Rev 65(6):101–109
Gerwin D (1987) An agenda of research on the flexibility of manufacturing processes. Int J Oper Prod Manage 7(1):38–49
Gillies A (1997) Software quality: theory and management, 2nd edn. Thomson Computer, London
Hakes C (1996) The corporate self assessment handbook, 3rd edn. Chapman & Hall, London
Hamel G, Prahalad CK (1994) Competing for the future. Harvard Business School, Boston, MA
Hammer M, Champy J (1993) Reengineering the corporation. A manifesto for business revolution. Harper Business, New York
Harrington HJ (1991) Business process improvement: the breakthrough strategy for total quality, productivity, and competitiveness. McGraw-Hill, New York
ICAS (1993) Measurement - the total picture. The Institute of Chartered Accountants of Scotland (ICAS), Edinburgh
Johnson HT (1983) The search for gain in markets and firms: a review of the historical emergence of management accounting systems. Account Org Soc 2(3):139–146
Juran JM, Gryna FM (1993) Quality planning and analysis: from product development through use. McGraw-Hill, New York
Kaplan RS, Norton DP (1992) The balanced scorecard – measures that drive performance. Harv Bus Rev 70(1):71–79
Kaplan RS, Norton DP (1993) Putting the balanced scorecard to work. Harv Bus Rev 71(5):134–147
Keegan DP, Eiler RG, Jones CR (1989) Are your performance measures obsolete? Manage Account 71(12):45–50
Kueng P (2000) Process performance measurement system – a tool to support process-based organizations. Total Qual Manage 11(1):67–86
Kueng P, Kawalek P (1997) Goal-based business process models – creation and evaluation. Bus Process Manage J 3(1):17–38
Leong GK, Snyder DL, Ward PT (1990) Research in the process and content of manufacturing strategy. OMEGA Int J Manage Sci 18(2):109–122
Lynch RL, Cross KF (1991) Measure up! Yardsticks for Continuous Improvement. Blackwell, Cambridge, MA
Nagel K (1988) Die 6 Erfolgsfaktoren des Unternehmens, 2nd edn. Landsberg am Lech, Moderne Industrie (in German)
Neely AD, Gregory M, Platts K (1995) Performance measurement system design. Int J Oper Prod Manage 15(4):80–116
Neely AD, Mills J, Platts K, Richards H, Gregory M, Bourne M, Kennerley M (2000) Performance measurement system design: developing and testing a process-based approach. Int J Oper Prod Manage 20(10):1119–1145
Neely AD, Gregory M, Platts K (2005) Performance measurement system design: a literature review and research agenda. Int J Oper Prod Manage 25(12):1228–1263
Pettigrew AM (1985) The awakening giant: Continuity and Change in ICI. Blackwell, Oxford
Porter ME (1980) Competitive strategy. Free Press, New York
Porter ME (2008) The five competitive forces that shape strategy. Harv Bus Rev 86(1):78–93
Rockart JF (1979) Chief executives define their own data needs. Harv Bus Rev 57(2):81–93
Schonberger RJ (1990) Creating a chain of customers. Guild, London
Simons R (2000) Performance measurement & control systems for implementing strategy. Prentice Hall, Upper Saddle River, NJ

Slack N (1987) The flexibility of manufacturing systems. Int J Oper Prod Manage 7(4):35–45
Stalk G (1988) Time – the next source of competitive advantage. Harv Bus Rev 66(4):41–51
Tunalv C (1992) Manufacturing strategy – plans and business performance. Int J Oper Prod Manage 12(3):4–24
Wheelwright SC (1984) Manufacturing strategy – defining the missing link. Strat Manage J 5(1):77–91
Zairi M, Sinclair D (1995) Business process reengineering and process improvement – a survey of current practice and future trends in integrated management. Manage Decis 33(3):3–16
zur Mühlen M (2004) Workflow-based process controlling. Foundation, design, and application of workflow-driven process information systems. Logos, Berlin

# Business Process Analytics

Michael zur Mühlen and Robert Shapiro

**Abstract** Business Process Management systems (BPMS) are a rich source of events that document the execution of processes and activities within these systems. Business Process Management analytics is the family of methods and tools that can be applied to these event streams in order to support decision making in organizations. The analysis of process events can focus on the behavior of completed processes, evaluate currently running process instances, or focus on predicting the behavior of process instances in the future. This chapter provides an overview of the different methods and technologies that can be employed in each of these three areas of process analytics. We discuss the underlying format and types of process events as the common source of analytics information, present techniques for the aggregation and composition of these events, and outline methods that support backward- and forward-looking process analytics.

## 1 Introduction

Business process analytics provides process participants, decision makers, and related stakeholders with insight about the efficiency and effectiveness of organizational processes. This insight can be motivated by performance or compliance considerations. From a *performance perspective*, the intent of process analytics is to shorten the reaction time of decision makers to events that may affect changes in process performance, and to allow a more immediate evaluation of the impact of process management decisions on process metrics. From a *compliance perspective*, the intent of process analytics is to establish the adherence of process execution with governing rules and regulations, and to ensure that contractual obligations and quality of service agreements are met.

M. zur Mühlen (✉)
Stevens Institute of Technology, Hoboken, NJ, USA
e-mail: mzurmühlen@stevens.edu

J. vom Brocke and M. Rosemann (eds.), *Handbook on Business Process Management 2*, International Handbooks on Information Systems,
DOI 10.1007/978-3-642-01982-1_7, 

There are three reasons why we might want to measure different aspects of business processes: To evaluate what has happened in the past, to understand what is happening at the moment, or to develop an understanding of what might happen in the future. The first area focuses on the *ex post* analysis of completed business processes, that is on *process controlling* (Schiefer et al. 2003; zur Muehlen 2004). This type of analysis may or may not be based on a pre-existing formal representation of the business process in question. If no documented process model exists or if the scope of the process under examination extends across multiple systems and process domains, such a model may be inductively generated through *process mining* approaches (van der Aalst et al. 2007). The second area focuses on the real-time monitoring of currently active business processes, that is, *business activity monitoring* (Grigori et al. 2004; Sayal et al. 2002). The third area uses business process data to forecast the future behavior of the organization through techniques such as scenario planning and simulation and is known as *process intelligence* (for example, Golfarelli et al. 2004).

Business Process Management systems (BPMS) usually include an analytics component for collecting and analyzing the events that occurred over the life of a process instance, either in real time or after the completion of process instances. While in the early days of workflow automation this facility was intended as a mechanism to debug the automated processes, it became clear early on that the resulting information could be used for more than just technical analysis. As a result, the demand for process dashboards (McLellan 1996) and process information cockpits (Sayal et al. 2002) has led BPMS vendors to offer this technology as an integral part of their products. Often, this is realized through the integration of open source platforms (such as Eclipse BIRT) or through the acquisition of specific technologies (e.g., Global 360s acquisition of CapeVisions, or TIBCO's acquisition of Spotfire). In addition to these reporting and analytics capabilities, an increasing number of BPMS includes a simulation component that allows the exploration of alternative process execution scenarios. In these scenarios, the resourcing, the processes themselves, and/or the workload are altered in order to discover ways to improve the overall performance of a business process.

In Sect. 2, we outline the concept of process analytics by first discussing the data from which analytics information, its sources, and raw formats can be generated. We also outline the basic metrics that can be gathered from raw BPMS events, and how an analyst can interpret these metrics. Furthermore, we discuss the three kinds of process analytics in detail: first historical analytics, then real-time analytics, and finally forward-looking analytics with a particular emphasis on using analytics information for process simulation purposes.

## 2 Sources for Process Analytics Data

Most process analyses are based on the aggregation, correlation, and evaluation of *events* that occur during the execution of a process. These events represent state changes of objects within the context of a business process. These objects may be activities, actors, data elements, information systems, or entire processes, among others. For example, activities can begin and end, actors can log on and off, the value of data elements may change, and many other events can occur over the typical lifespan of a process instance. The scope of events considered for analysis determines the context envelope of the analysis. In other words, a narrowly scoped process analysis might focus on a single activity by examining just those events that originated from this activity, its performers, and the resources that are input and output of the activity. In contrast, a more widely scoped process analysis might include events from multiple processes, involve data sources outside the organization and involve events from nonprocess-centric information systems.

Figure 1 shows the different stages of process analytics in context. The bottom of the picture depicts a typical heterogeneous IT infrastructure, comprising a BPMS, an electronic content management system, an enterprise resource planning (ERP) platform, and several other systems that are integrated using an enterprise application integration (EAI) solution. Each of these systems contains some capability to represent and execute processes, even if not all of these processes may be represented graphically. For instance, the process scripting language BPEL is a popular description format for system-to-system workflows within EAI platforms such as Oracle's BPEL Process Manager or ActiveEndpoints' ActiveVOS. Each component of the IT infrastructure can be a source of events. From a process management perspective, the events generated by dedicated workflow or BPMS constitute the most natural source of information for analysis. But systems such as an Electronic Content Management system may record events that can be used to detect business events prior to the initiation of a BPMS-supported process (e.g., the arrival of a fax), and transactional systems such as ERP platforms or legacy applications may record

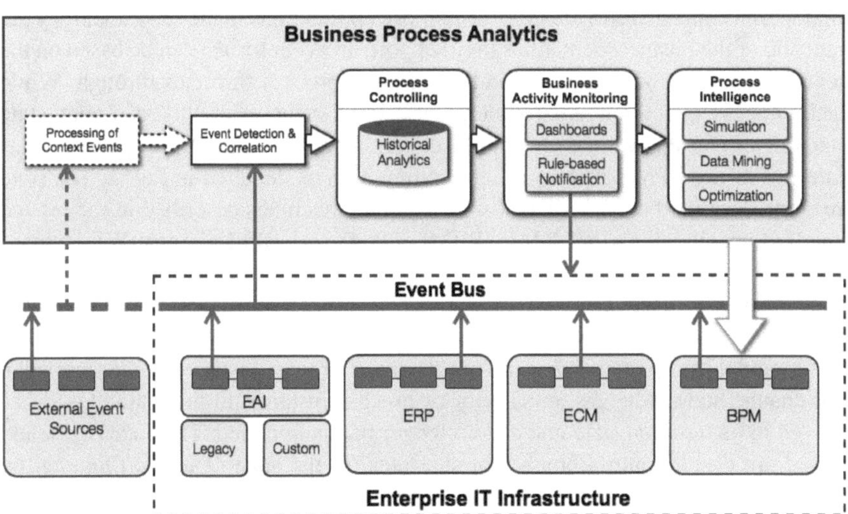


**Fig. 1** Business process analytics in context

the manipulation of business data that – taken together with the related process transactions – provides an in-depth picture of the operational state of an organization. EAI platforms may produce events related to the movement of data between legacy systems, and some vendors offer dedicated listening components that are designed to publish events if they detect changes in systems that are not designed to communicate these changes by default. For example, a popular application for these listeners is the surveillance of spreadsheets. If a cell in a spreadsheet changes, the listener sends out an event notification that can cause other systems to react to this event. Certain external systems can also be sources of events that are of interest in a process analytics application. For instance, the performance of an order fulfillment process may be affected by a traffic condition, which is not necessarily reflected in the internally generated events. The design of these open systems is sometimes summarized under the term *event-driven architecture* (EDA).

In order to make sense of process events, they are typically processed in an *event detection and correlation* stage. Event detection is used to uncover changes in operational systems that may not be published by default, for example, changes to a cell in a spreadsheet, as discussed above. Event correlation is used to link events that were generated by separate sources to a common process, for example, by tracing a common identifier such as an order number or a customer ID across multiple systems (zur Muehlen and Klein 2000). The resulting information can be used for historical analysis, real-time control, or predictive intelligence.

## 3 A Source Format for Process Events

In order to allow for the generic design of a process analytics system, an event format is required that is not specific to the semantics of the underlying process model. Since most BPMS are general-purpose applications in the sense that they are agnostic of the business semantics they support, an event format can be based on the general states a process activity and/or business process traverses through. While each process execution environment may implement a slightly different state machine, a consensus for a standardized state model for audit event purposes has emerged in the BPM software vendor community, as depicted in Fig. 2. The state machine described here is aligned with the state machines described in the related standard specifications Wf-XML (WfMC 2004) and BPEL4People/WS-HumanTask (OASIS 2008a, b).

A business process or a process activity will traverse through this state model over the lifetime of the respective process or activity instance. The two superstates of the model are *open* and *closed*. An activity or process instance in the state open can change state, whereas an activity or process instance in the state closed has arrived in its terminal state and can no longer be manipulated. The states open and closed are divided into a number of substates. In the state *Open.NotRunning*, no work is being performed on an activity or process instance, but the instance may be assigned to a multi-member role, or reserved by an individual process performer. In the state *Open.Running* a process or activity instance is actively being processed.

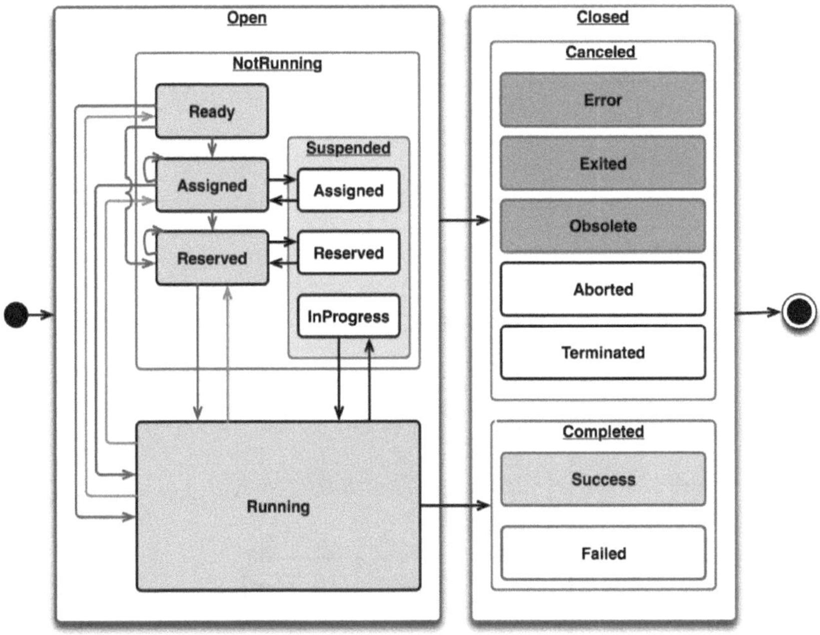


**Fig. 2** Process execution state model
*Source*: (WfMC 2009)

If a process or activity instance is forcefully terminated, it moves to the state *Closed.Canceled*. Some possible reasons for such termination may be a system error, the obsolescence of an activity (e.g., if a timeout or compensation activity occurs), or a manual cancelation. Processes and activities in this state have not achieved their objective. If a process or activity instance has been fully executed, it moves to the state *Closed.Completed*. Processes and activities in this state may or may not have achieved their objective, which a system can indicate through the states *Closed.Completed.Success* and *Closed.Completed.Failure*.

Individual process management products may support additional states beyond those represented in Fig. 2, and thus may produce additional runtime events. For example, a system could record that an activity was completed because a deadline expired. In this case, the system would record a final state of *Closed.Completed.TimeOut*. Alternatively, a process management system might only implement a subset of the states described in Fig. 2, thus reducing the different kinds of runtime events it can produce. For instance, a system might not allow for the suspension of activities, and thus it would not be able to produce audit events such as *Open.NotRunning.Suspended.InProgress*.

Events generated by a BPMS typically have a proprietary format, although there have been attempts at standardizing event formats (e.g., WfMC 1999; van Dongen and van der Aalst 2005). Figure 3 shows the structure of a process analytics event following the XML business process analytics format (BPAF) standard published

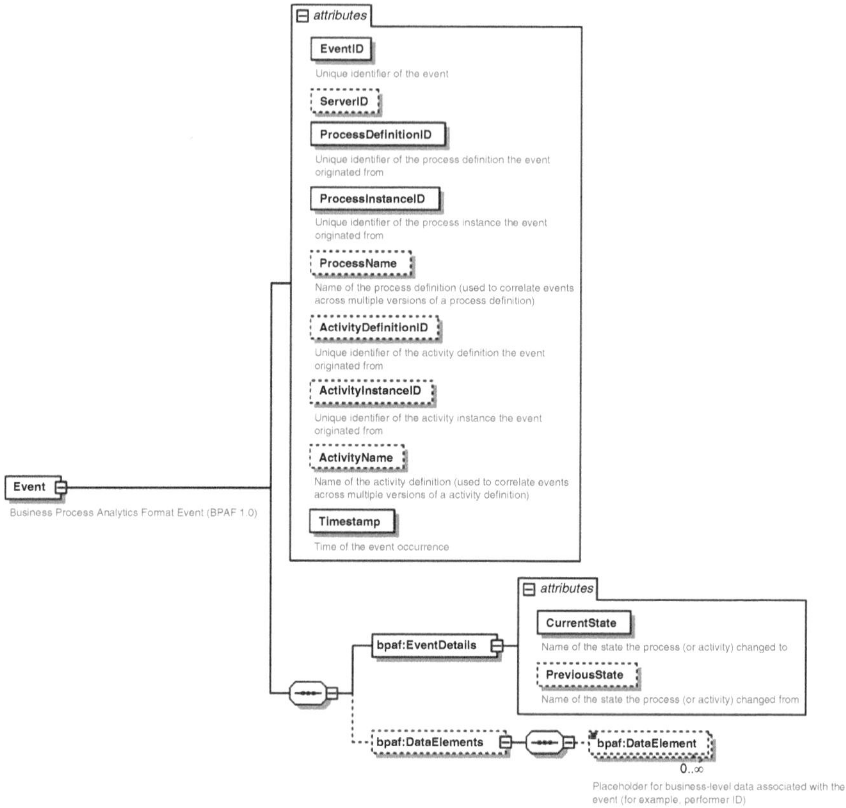


**Fig. 3** BPAF event format (WfMC 2009)

by the Workflow Management Coalition (WfMC 2009). An event contains at the minimum a unique identifier, the identifiers of the process definition and instance that it originated from, a time stamp, and information about the state of the process at the time of the event.

With this information, and the state model discussed above, a process analytics system will be able to deliver basic frequency and timing information to decision makers, such as the cycle times of processes, wait times, and counts of completed versus pending process instances. In order to deliver more detailed information, a number of optional data items can be included in the event format. An event may contain information about the server that generated the event, which is helpful in a distributed execution environment if an analyst is trying to isolate a location-specific problem. Furthermore, an event may contain the identifier of the activity it relates to, both for the activity definition and the activity instance, to allow for more fine-grained analysis. It may also contain the names of processes or activities to facilitate the aggregation of events across multiple versions of the same process or activity (since different versions of the same process will typically have different identifiers).

Arbitrary data elements may be enclosed in an event in order to preserve specific business-relevant data that was present at the time of event occurrence. A common use of this field would be the inclusion of the performer ID, in order to relate events to individual organization units, performers, or machines. Finally, an event may contain a description of the process/activity state prior to its occurrence in order to identify the specific state transition that is described by the event. This is useful in situations where a state can be reached from multiple other states, but through the use of timestamps this information can typically be recreated by stepping backward in time through the recorded events.

# 4 Process Metrics

The analytic figures that can be used to understand process performance range from absolute measurements, such as cycle times and wait times, to variance measurements, such as service-level variability, and qualitative measures, such as customer comments on a particular process. While the design of process performance measurements is discussed extensively in another chapter of this book (Heckl and Moormann 2010), this section focuses on the construction of elementary process metrics and their enhancement with line-of-business information.

The most elementary process metrics are obtained by analyzing the time stamps of several process-related events that belong to the same process or activity instance. The difference between these time stamps can provide an analyst with some basic insights into the behavior of a process instance.

At the most basic level, a process management system delivers frequency and temporal information to decision makers. Figure 4 shows the traversal of the state model described in Fig. 2 over the life cycle of a regular activity instance that involves a human performer. The Business Process Management system schedules the activity instance for execution when all of its preconditions are met. In the example, the system automatically places the activity instances on the work list of a role that may be shared by multiple performers (state *Open.Assigned*). One of these performers selects the work item (state change to *Open.Reserved*) and starts working on the activity instance (state change to *Open.Running.InProgress*). Some BPMS will move the activity instance into this state automatically upon selection of the work item, and thus will not record the *Open.Reserved* state. Later on, the user decides to take a break, and thus suspends and later resumes work on this activity instance (state changes to and from *Open.Running.Suspended*). When the user finally completes the activity instance, the BPMS changes the state of the instance to *Closed.Completed.Success*. Each state change in this life cycle will be recorded by the BPMS with the current time, the identifier of the related process instance, and – depending on the system configuration – additional data elements, such as the identifier of the user performing the activity instance, or workflow-relevant data that was available at the start of the activity instance.

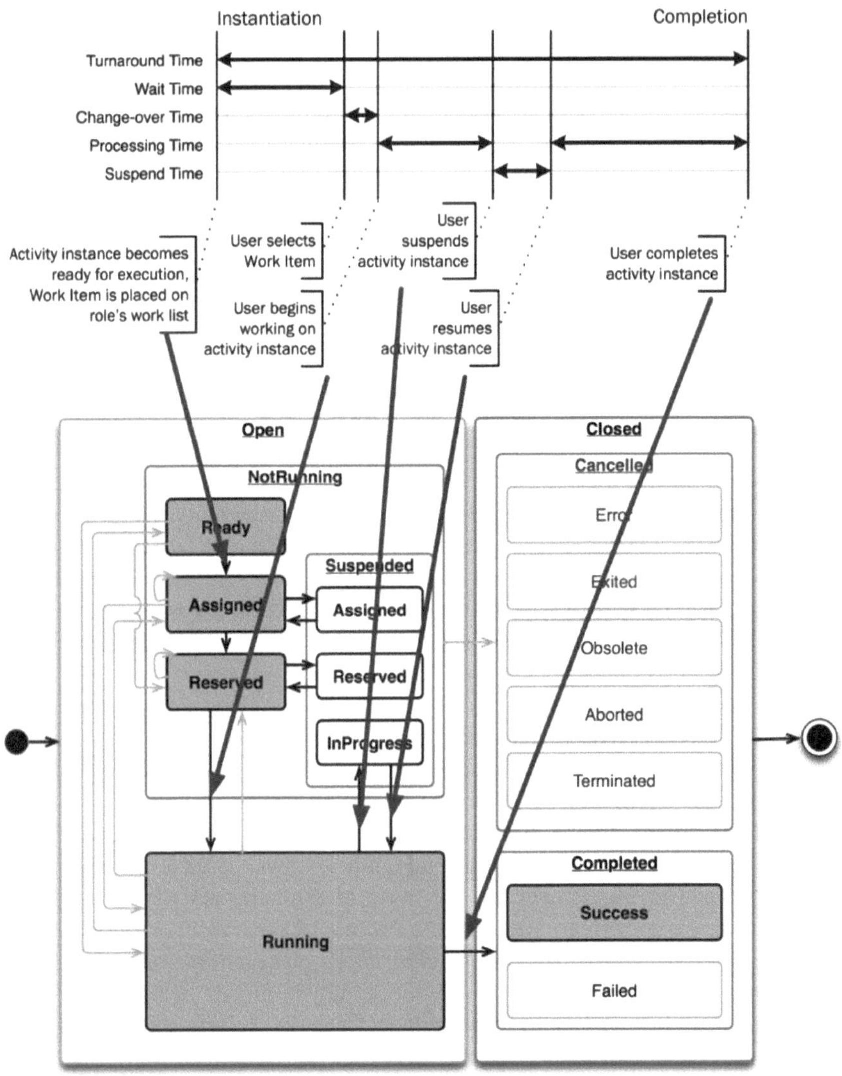


**Fig. 4** Activity instance metrics

Based on these events, an analyst can determine the wait time for each activity instance and type (i.e., the time elapsed before a user chose to select a particular work item). This may provide insight into user preferences or aversion toward certain types of tasks. The difference between work selection and the actual start of the activity instance represents the changeover time required to prepare for the activity instance. In industrial processes, this would be the time required to retool a workstation, and in office processes, this might be the time required to mentally adjust to a different task type. In multitasking environments, this mental adjustment can have a significant impact on overall performance (Burmistrov and Leonova 1996). If the previous task of the performing user is known, an analyst might be able to determine how compatible or conflicting two different task types are, and use this information to fine-tune the work assignment policies embedded in the process model or the BPMS. The time spent in the *Open.Running.InProgress* state provides the net processing time of the activity instance, while time spent in the *Open. Running.Suspended* state represents the suspend time of the activity. The difference between the first instantiation of the activity (arrival in the state *Open.NotRunning. Assigned*) and the final completion (arrival in the state *Closed.Completed.Success*) provides an analyst with the gross processing time of the activity. If permitted, an aggregation of these metrics across multiple activities of the same performer may give an analyst insight into learning effects and training effectiveness (Rosemann et al. 1996; zur Muehlen and Rosemann 2000).

Each of these fundamental metrics can be computed at the instance level and can be aggregated to an average model level metric. In addition, the execution frequency of activities and the traversal frequencies of certain control flow connections provide an analyst with the frequency distribution of alternative process pathways. Time stamps of process instantiation and activity instantiation can be used to determine the arrival distributions of individual process types, and the distribution of activity start times may provide insight into the work allocation on a daily basis. All of these metrics can be obtained from a BPMS automatically and at very little cost. However, they provide only limited insight into the underlying causes of process performance. To examine such causes, business-level information has to be integrated with the temporal and frequency information.

To this end, extended metrics add line of business attributes to key audit events. If, for instance, the customer ID or the order numbers are recorded in the process audit events, an analyst can correlate a process instance with the relevant business object that was being handled by this process instance. If this business information is available for retrieval in a data warehouse, an analyst may be able to analyze the behavior of process instances that share certain lines of business attributes (such as customer region or order amount). By using this technique in combination with OnLine Analytical Processing, an analyst may be able to determine those line-of-business attributes that affect the process performance or the choice of certain control flow paths.

## 5 Quality Criteria for Process Metrics

There are five key criteria for process metrics. They need to be accurate, cost effective to obtain, easy to understand, timely, and actionable.

The need for *accuracy* is self-evident: if the metrics do not correctly reflect reality, or if the inferred relationship between a metric and its underlying causes is incorrect, it is difficult for a decision maker to recommend changes that will have an impact on this metric. The distinction between cause and effect is important to note in this context. BPMS measure the effects of decisions, actions, and technical operations. They typically do not document the underlying causes for these effects.

Thus, just by looking at the automatically collected metrics a decision maker might want to infer causality when in fact there is no connection between two events. Only the combination of technical metrics with line-of-business attributes will provide a decision maker with the necessary context to draw such inferences.

The need for *cost-effective* measurement relates the expenses for a measurement infrastructure with the value derived from the availability of a particular metric. Internal metrics are generally cheaper to obtain than metrics that rely on external information sources such as markets, competitors, or customers. But the business value derived from decisions based on internal metrics often is lower than that of decisions based on an accurate understanding of the organization's ecosystem. Organizations that have a technical process management infrastructure in place will have an easier time gathering process metrics. However, these metrics mainly relate to internal operations such as resource scheduling, processing, and wait times for internal activities. Again, the integration of line-of-business attributes will increase the value of these process metrics, but at the same time this integration will increase the cost of measurement.

The need for an *easy-to-understand* presentation of process metrics relates to the cognitive effort required by decision makers to comprehend and act on analytics and intelligence information. If the cognitive effort to parse the presented information is high, more time will elapse before a decision maker will decide on an appropriate action. If the cognitive effort is too high, the information may be ignored and thus have no value at all to the decision maker. The presentation of metrics thus has a direct impact on decision latency.

The *timeliness* of analytics information is related to both the cost effectiveness, as faster information availability is typically more expensive than slower reporting of information, and to how actionable the information is, since delayed information availability may mean that a decision maker has no time to act anymore. Figure 5 shows the potential loss of business value that is caused by a delayed reaction to a business-relevant event. If a decision maker can react to a process disruption or disturbance in a timely fashion, it may be possible to mitigate the effects of the disturbance before it impacts the process customer. For instance, if it is apparent that a customer's luggage was not transferred to a connecting flight, an airline representative could greet the arriving customer at the gate and explain the situation, thus avoiding wait time and potential aggravation for the customer in the baggage claim area. If information about the misrouted luggage is reported too late, the customer will have waited in vain for his luggage and the resulting impression of the airline's service may result in a permanent loss of customer loyalty.

In most situations, there will be a delay between the occurrence of a business-relevant event and the initiation of remedial action. This delay can be decomposed into data, analysis, decision, and implementation latency.

- *Data latency* is the delay between the occurrence of a real-world event and the capturing of this event in an information system for further analysis. Contemporary information systems rely on publish/subscribe mechanisms that send events to a messaging bus from where they can be read by registered subscribers. The technical

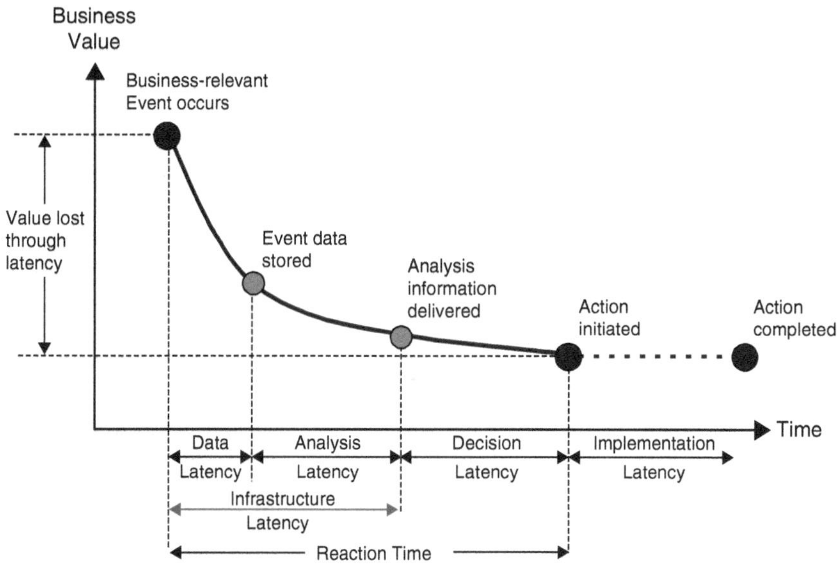


**Fig. 5** Latency types in process monitoring (cf. Hackathorn 2002)

delay is relatively low, but there may be a delay between the occurrence of an event in the real world (e.g., baggage is misplaced) and the creation of an electronic representation (e.g., a recognized mismatch of passenger and baggage on a flight).

- *Analysis latency* is the delay between the storage of event information in a repository and the subsequent transformation of this event information into an analyzable format, such as a notification, report, or indicator value. Traditional management accounting systems that rely on fixed cycles for the generation of reports create latency at this stage because report generation is not synchronized with event occurrence. The goal of real-time business intelligence systems is therefore the delivery of information whenever relevant events occur, not just in fixed cycles.
- *Decision latency* is the delay between the availability of a reported event and the initiation of remedial action. This latency results from the time it takes decision makers to read and comprehend the event report, to evaluate possible decision alternatives, to assess the consequences of their actions, and to ultimately initiate an activity.

Data and analysis latency directly correlate with the technical infrastructure used for the collection and representation of business-relevant events. Their sum can be treated as the infrastructure latency underlying the system. The use of BAM technology can reduce this latency through the shortening of the cycle time for capturing, storing, and visualizing business-relevant events. To a lesser extent, an adequate representation of business events based on the job requirements and decision privileges of decision makers can shorten the decision latency as well. Implementation latency is dependent on the responsiveness of the organization as well as the technical infrastructure available, and is outside of the scope of BAM systems.

*Implementation latency* is the delay between the decision of a stakeholder and the actual implementation of the action the stakeholder decided upon. In the context of a BPMS, this delay may be caused by the effort necessary to modify a given process. Some decisions, such as changes to staffing levels, can typically be deployed without modifying the process model, while other changes may require a redesign of a process model. While some systems (e.g., Fujitsu Interstage BPM) allow for the dynamic modification of running process instances, most BPMS do not allow for structural modifications (e.g., the introduction of new activities or gateways) once a process instance has been initiated. Any structural modifications in these systems require a fresh deployment of the modified process model, and consequently, the changes take effect only for new process instances.

Finally, process metrics need to be actionable in order to have value to decision makers. This means that there should be a clear relationship between actions of the decision maker and the observed metrics. If, for instance, a process analysis uncovers large variances in the processing time of a particular activity but the underlying causes are unknown, a decision maker will not be able to effectively decide on a course of action that will positively change this metric. In these cases, the use of simulation technology might help a decision maker understand better how a certain metric can be impacted. We discuss this in detail in the section on predictive analytics below.

## 6 Historical Process Analysis

The analysis of process metrics after the completion of processes is typically used when trends across multiple process instances or time periods (such as fiscal quarters or years) are of interest. It can also serve as a baseline, if process changes are imminent and an organization wants to understand if and how these changes will affect process metrics. This type of analysis is valuable as a first step to understand the actual process performance of an organization. The source data for historical process analysis can be found in the log files and event streams of workflow systems and other types of transaction processing software.

While the automated gathering and processing of this type of information is an easy and accurate way to determine process metrics, organizations that are just beginning to analyze their processes may not have the necessary infrastructure to obtain this type of data. In these cases, a manual measurement approach is often the only feasible way to obtain this information (zur Muehlen and Ho 2008).

Historical process information can be stored in data warehouse structures, following star or snowflake schemas of conventional data warehouses (Pau et al. 2007; zur Muehlen 2004; List et al. 2001). For the analysis of this information, OnLine Analytical Processing tools can be employed. If line of business data is captured with the elementary process metrics, the warehouse may contain a hypercube with many dimensions, as the warehouse structure of process audit data intersects with the warehouse structure of the line of business information. The selection of appropriate dimensions for analysis can thus require significant domain expertise.

# 7 Real-Time Process Analysis

Real-time process analytics focuses on the in-flight control of running process instances. Typically a business activity monitoring (BAM) system updates a set of key performance Indicators in real time (McCoy 2002). When a rules engine is applied to these indicators, a BAM system can generate alerts and actions, which inform managers of critical situations and may alter the behavior of the running processes. A typical example is the monitoring of workload in a BPMS. If the queue of pending work items for any users exceeds a certain threshold, the BAM system can automatically initiate the redistribution of excess work to other qualified performers. If no such performers are available, the system can then alert a manager to manually intervene. The purpose of BAM is to provide real-time control over currently active process instances.

The visualization of the analysis results commonly takes place in process dashboards that resemble a manufacturing control station. Figure 6 shows such a dashboard from a commercial Business Process Management system (Global 360). A properly designed dashboard allows an analyst to drill down into the process instances whose metrics are represented, in order to perform on-the-fly adjustments such as the reassignment of a work item.

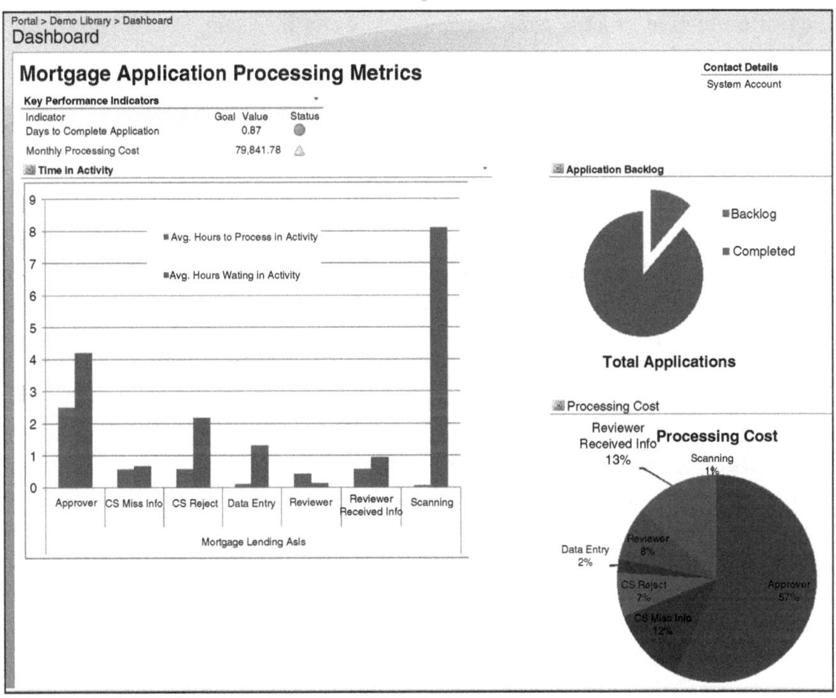


**Fig. 6** Process dashboard

An advanced variant of the BAM systems sends analytics events to an embedded rules engine that may trigger automated actions such as the automatic notification of decision makers or the automatic reprioritization of work. This configuration allows the automation of certain exception handling mechanisms and results in the implementation of a simple sense-and-respond environment. BAM systems have an advantage over traditional reporting systems (as well as historical process analytics) in that they reflect current operations that have not yet concluded. Their information is thus available in a more timely fashion than that of a warehouse-based system. However, the nature of the dashboard displays often limits the degree with which an analyst can combine the metrics with line-of-business attributes, since this relationship needs to be known during the design phase of the dashboard.

# 8 Predictive Process Analysis

Predictive process analysis aims at assessing the impact of process design changes on future instances of a business process. This type of analysis can take place during the initial design of a process model (build time), for example, to determine the performance trade-off between different process configurations, or after a process model has been deployed, for example, to determine whether a newly created process instance will complete within a given set of constraints. Three different kinds of predictive process analysis techniques can be distinguished: simulation, data mining, and optimization.

## *8.1 Simulation*[1]

Simulation models are typically used to perform what-if analyses of process designs before they are implemented. The use of simulation is distinct from animation features offered by some workflow products. While animation lets a developer step through the execution of a single process instance in order to detect potential model errors, simulation typically focuses on the execution of a number of process instances to determine resource and activity behavior under system load. Typical simulation scenarios focus on changes at the resource level (e.g., what if we bought a faster check sorter?), changes of the process structure (e.g., what if we allowed existing customers to skip the credit check activity?), or changes in the process context (e.g., what if the number of customer orders increased dramatically because of a marketing campaign?).

Simulation for new process models can be a useful tool to establish a baseline of expected performance that can be fed into BAM or process controlling platforms. In

[1]For a thorough discussion of common pitfalls of process simulation models we point the interested reader to van der Aalst et al. (2010).

some instances, it may be useful to develop a simulation model of an existing manual process in order to establish a contrast to an improved process design. Figure 7 shows the output of a BPMS simulation component (SunGard IPP) that annotates a process model with information about work queue length for the individual roles, processing times for the individual activities, and transition frequencies for the decision gateways.

The typical type of simulator for making predictions in a business process environment is a discrete event simulator. Most BPMS are well suited to serve as process simulators since they already contain an engine that advances process instances based on the occurrence of individual events. Instead of notifying potential process participants and invoking applications, a simulation engine will simulate the behavior of these resources according to parameters defined in a simulation scenario.

A process simulation scenario consists of the following:

*Process Definitions.* While many simulations focus on an individual process (e.g., to optimize the account opening process), resources typically participate in the execution of multiple processes. To accurately reflect these dependencies, it may be useful to include more than one process in the simulation scenario. The resulting process definitions provide, at a minimum, information about the activities performed, the routes taken, the rules impacting which routes and activities to perform, and the resources (human and automated) used to perform the activities.

*Incoming Work (Arrivals).* Each scenario must involve work to be processed. The scenario description includes information about when the work arrives, as well

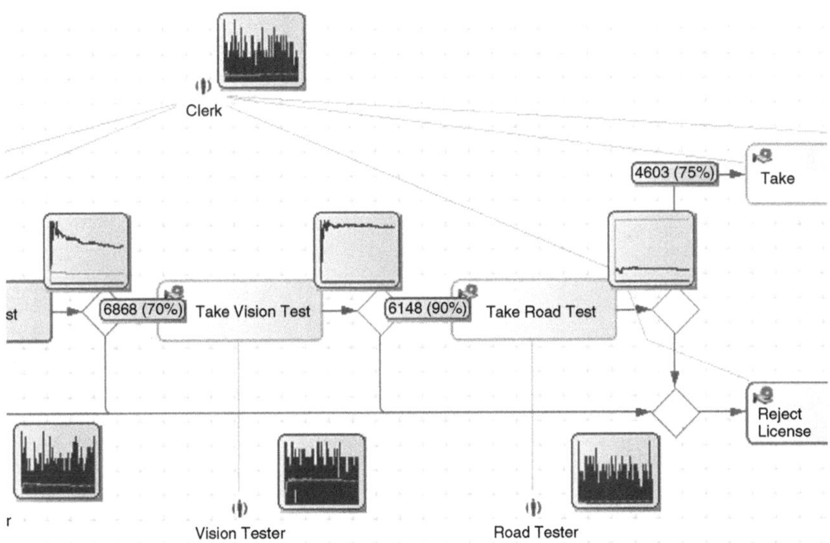


**Fig. 7** Process model with simulation data overlay

as all appropriate attributes of the work (e.g., region, amount, size) that may have an impact on processing and routing.

Figure 8 shows the arrival distribution editor of a simulation-enabled workflow system (SunGard IPP). The arrival rate indicates how many instances of the process in question are started on any given day. The business calendar is used to reflect weekends and holidays in the simulation scenario. Finally, the daily distribution area is used to approximate the creation of process instances at different times during a workday. The last aspect can have a significant impact on processing and wait times: for a process that is instantiated by the receipt of mail, the bulk of process instances might be created around the time of physical mail delivery, that is, once or twice a day, while the initiation of a process that is instantiated over the phone may be more evenly distributed throughout the day.

*Resources, Roles, and Work Shifts.* As work is routed to activities in a process, resources are required to perform each activity. Resources may be human resources; they may be pieces of equipment; or they might simply be application systems. Roles are often used to describe the function performed and the skill required to carry out these functions. Specific resources are then described as performing defined roles. The availability of resources and roles can also be controlled by using shift information and can be defined in a similar fashion to the arrival distribution of the process in question. If a resource participates in multiple processes, it is useful to assume less than 100% resource efficiency for simulation purposes; otherwise, the simulation results will assume that each resource devotes its entire availability to the simulated process.

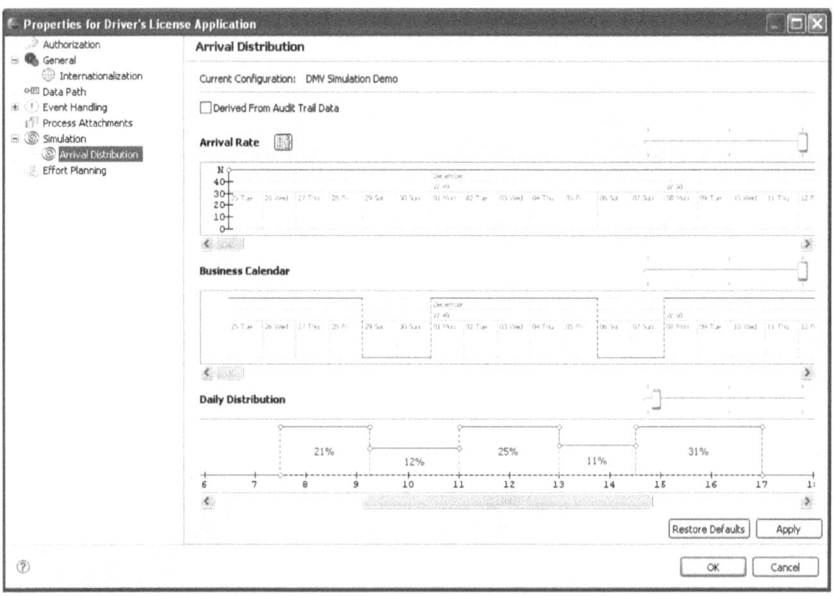


**Fig. 8** Defining the arrival distribution of a simulation scenario

*Activity Details*: In order for the simulator to reflect the real-world processing of a business process, additional information is often appended to the scenario. The duration of an activity is typically not defined in a workflow model, but is included in the scenario information (historical data collected by the analytics may be the source of this information). This and many other details can be expressed as a single integer or a complex expression involving the attributes of the work and/or the use of distribution functions for randomness. Figure 9 shows an example of a distribution duration editor for a process activity called *Perform Background Check*. In this example, the duration of each activity instance is governed by a Gaussian distribution with an expected value of 5 min and a standard deviation of 1.

If the simulation pertains to a new or significantly redesigned process, the duration information may not be known, and therefore estimates or probability distribution functions have to be employed. But if the simulation relates to an established process, it may be possible to derive this information and other scenario data from the historical log files of past process instances, which will lead to more accurate simulations. The integration of simulation components within business process management suites makes the implementation of such history-based forecasting mechanisms increasingly popular. The BPMS shown in Fig. 9 (SunGard Infinity Process Platform) allows the modeler to use historical process execution logs (Audit Trail Data) to automatically calculate the distribution based on historical data, which reduces the number of assumptions necessary to create the simulation model.

*Routing Information*. Simulation scenarios require additional information that is typically not part of a workflow model, in particular, routing information which tells the simulator under what conditions certain process paths are taken. Routing

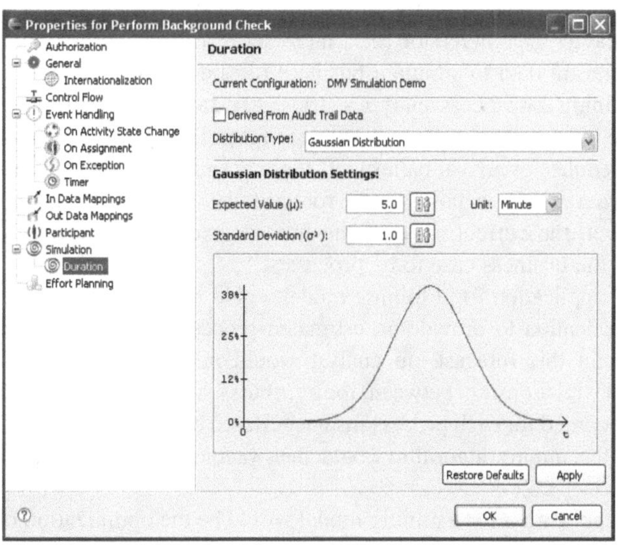


**Fig. 9** Duration distribution editor for a process activity (Source system: SunGard IPP)

information is typically based on rules that exist in the process definition, but it is often amended with percentages that reflect the likelihood of a certain outcome or path. In the simplest case, this routing information can be derived from historical data, or simply estimated by subject matter experts. A more accurate way to determine routings is for the simulation engine to perform the same type of evaluation of workflow-relevant data that a BPMS would perform during process execution. In such a scenario, the simulation engine would be supplied with (either actual or hypothetical) work attributes that characterize each process instance to be simulated. If this information can be derived from past execution, it enables the design of *replay* simulation scenarios, for example, a simulation of actual prior process instances within a potentially redesigned process and resource scenario.

A simulation run generates new data, which in turn can be used for analytics purposes, that is, the simulation results can be fed into a process controlling or BAM environment for reporting and visualization purposes, or to establish a baseline for a process design that has yet to be implemented.

## *8.2 Data Mining*

The behavior of business processes depends on many factors: the design of the process and its embedded rules, the arrival pattern of new process instances, the availability of resources and their skill level, the attributes of the business cases processed in each process instance, and other external business factors. Historical process analytics use business-relevant data to classify and navigate process instances and their related performance information. Simulation models are used to forecast the average behavior for a large set of process instances and may use workflow-relevant data to simulate business rules embedded in the process structure. Data mining for process analytics strives to establish correlations between key performance indicators and process-external factors, such as work item attributes, resource schedules, or arrival patterns. If these correlations can be established with sufficient accuracy, it is possible to forecast the behavior of a single process instance, given the current state of the process execution infrastructure and the attributes of the business case to be processed.

A typical application for a mining model would be the analysis of an incoming customer application to provide an estimated processing time to the customer. In order to obtain this forecast, an analyst would mine prior process instances to determine the relationship between the attributes of each business case and the cycle time recorded for each process instance. Based on the attributes of an incoming application, the mining algorithm could then predict the processing time for this specific case.

Another application for a mining model would be the optimization of branching rules in a process. Figure 10 shows a mining analysis of 600 instances of a credit approval process using Microsoft SQL Server. Of the overall set, 350 applications

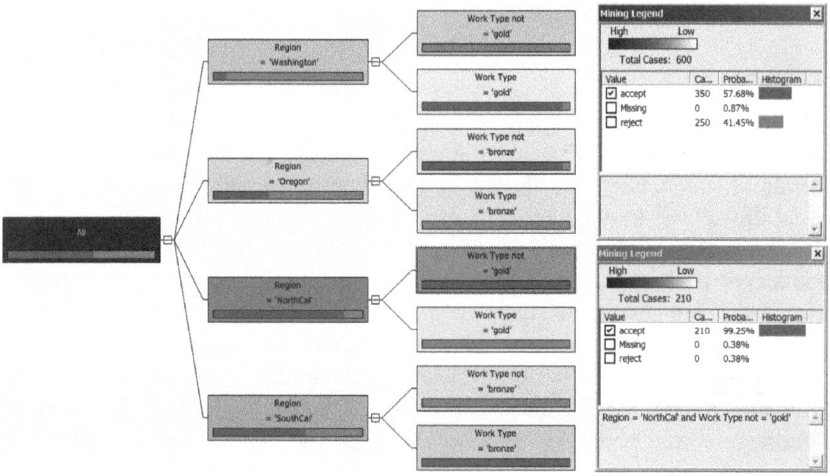


**Fig. 10** Data mining example for process optimization

were accepted, while 250 were rejected. In a general simulation scenario, an analyst might use this information to define the simulation scenario with a 58% acceptance probability and a 42% rejection probability. However, if we utilize data mining and analyze the attributes *region* and *work type*, we can determine that all 210 cases with the values "NorthCal" and "gold" have been accepted. Thus a process analyst could create a straight-through-processing rule that would allow cases with these attributes to be automatically accepted, rather than being routed through a manual review.

While the example above is based on just two parameters, most processes are affected by a significant number of business attributes. The design of an appropriate mining structure thus requires an analysis of historical data and subject matter expertise.

There are several differences between the simulation and the data mining approach to process analytics:

- A simulation model must be a sufficiently accurate representation of the collection of processes being executed. It can make predictions for situations not previously encountered so long as the underlying processes have not changed.
- Data mining predictions are based on a statistical analysis of process instances that have already been completed. A trained mining model assumes that these historical patterns are still valid.
- Simulation is computationally intensive. It takes significant time to obtain predictions, in particular if the simulation engine uses workflow-relevant data to enact each process instance in the simulation scenario.
- In data mining, the training is computationally intensive, but once a mining model is trained, predictions can be made at an extremely fast pace. However, periodic retraining may be required to keep the model accurate.

### 8.3 Process Optimization

Automatic process optimization represents the most advanced application of process intelligence and uses historical process analytics and process simulation to generate and evaluate proposals for achieving a set of goals. The analysis of the process structure in conjunction with historical data about processing delays and resource availability allows for the intelligent exploration of improvement strategies.

Optimization is a form of goal-seeking simulation. It uses process goals formulated as key performance indicators, analyzes historical process metrics, and proposes what changes are likely to help attain these goals. It can systematically evaluate the proposed changes, using the simulation tool as a forecasting mechanism. Optimization can be performed in a fully automated manner, with the analysis termination upon satisfying the goal or recognizing that no proposed change results in further improvement. A typical example for the application of optimization technology is the optimization of staff schedules while focusing on end-to-end cycle time and processing cost as key performance indicators. Process optimization technology is currently the domain of specialist providers, but the architecture of BPMS suggests that it will find its way into commercial BPMS over time.

## 9 Summary

Business process analytics leverages event traces generated by a BPMS infrastructure to generate metrics that feed historical reports, real-time dashboards, and predictive analytics instruments such as simulation and optimization tools. At the core of each of these instruments is a common understanding of the events generated by a process management platform as they follow a universal state model. While basic metrics such as cycle times, frequencies, and utilization can be obtained from the audit trail events alone, most decision makers will require the inclusion of some business-relevant data to place the process metrics in context.

Challenges for process analytics exist in the form of infrastructure systems that are not process aware, yet contribute to the completion of business processes, the sheer number of events generated, the heterogeneity of event formats, and the domain knowledge required to design analytical models, be they hypercubes that integrate process and business data, mining models that correlate business-relevant attributes with process behavior, or simulation and optimization models that correctly reflect the constraints of the real world.

## References

Burmistrov I, Leonova A (1996) Effects of interruptions on the computerised clerical task performance. Human-computer interaction: human aspects of business computing. Proc EWHCI 96:21–29

Golfarelli M, Rizzi S, Cella I (2004) Beyond data warehousing: what's next in business intelligence? In: Proceedings of the 7th ACM international workshop on Data warehousing and OLAP, pp 1–6
Grigori D et al. (2004) Business process intelligence. Comput Ind 53:321–343
Hackathorn R (2002) Minimizing action distance. DM Rev 12:22–23
Heckl D, Moormann J (2010) Process performance management. In: vom Brocke J, Rosemann M (eds) Handbook on business process management, vol 2. Springer Heidelberg
List B et al. (2001) Multidimensional business process analysis with the process warehouse. Kluwer International series in engineering and computer science, pp 211–228
McCoy D (2002) Business activity monitoring: Calm before the storm. Gartner Research Note LE-15-9727
McLellan M (1996) Workflow metrics – one of the great benefits of workflow management. In: Oesterle H, Vogler P (eds) Praxis des workflow-management. Vieweg, Braunschweig, pp 301–318
OASIS (2008a) Web services – Human task (WS-HumanTask) specification. 1.1 working draft, organization for the advancement of structured information standards
OASIS (2008b) WS-BPEL extension for people (BPEL4People) specification version 1.1. 1.1 working draft, organization for the advancement of structured information standards
Pau KC, Si YW, Dumas M (2007) Data Warehouse Model for Audit Trail Analysis in Workflows. In: Proceedings of the Student Workshop of 2007 IEEE International Conference on e-Business Engineering, (ICEBE)
Rosemann M, Denecke T, Puettmann M (1996) PISA – process information system with access. Design and realisation of an information system for process monitoring and controlling (German). Arbeitsberichte des Instituts fuer Wirtschaftsinformatik. Universitaet Münster, Germany
Sayal M et al. (2002) Business process cockpit. In: Proceedings of the 28th international conference on very large data bases. pp 880–883
Schiefer J, Jeng JJ, Bruckner RM (2003) Real-time workflow audit data integration into data warehouse systems. In: 11th European conference on information systems
van der WMP Aalst et al. (2007) Business process mining: an industrial application. Inf Syst 32:713–732
van der Aalst WMP, Nakatumba J, Rozinat A, Russell N (2010) Business process simulation. In: vom Brocke J, Rosemann M (eds) Handbook on business process management, vol 1. Springer, Heidelberg
van Dongen BF, van der Aalst WMP (2005) A meta model for process mining data. In: J. Casto, E. Teniente (Eds.), Proceedings of the CAiSE'05 Workshops (EMOI-INTEROP Workshop), FEUP, Porto, Portugal, vol. 2, pp 309–320
WfMC (1999) Audit data specification. Version 2. document number WFMC-TC-1015, available at www.wfmc.org
WfMC (2009) Business process analytics format – Draft specification. 1.0, Document number WFMC-TC-1015 available at www.wfmc.org
WfMC (2004) Wf-XML 2.0 – XML-based protocol for run-time integration of process engines. WfMC, Nov, WfMC-TC-1023, available at www.wfmc.org
zur Muehlen M (2004) Workflow-based process controlling. foundation, design, and implementation of workflow-driven process information systems. Logos, Berlin
zur Muehlen M, Klein F (2000) AFRICA: Workflow interoperability based on XML-messages. CAiSE 2000 International workshop on infrastructures for dynamic business-to-business service outsourcing
zur Muehlen M, Rosemann M (2000) Workflow-based process monitoring and controlling – technical and organizational issues. Proceedings of the 33rd Hawai'i International Conference on System Sciences, IEEE, Waikoloa, HI
zur Muehlen M, Ho DT (2008) Service Process Innovation: A Case Study of BPMN in Practice, Ralph Sprague, Jr., Proceedings of the 41st Hawai'i International Conference on System Sciences, IEEE, Waikoloa, HI

# Managing Regulatory Compliance in Business Processes

Shazia Sadiq and Guido Governatori

**Abstract** The ever-increasing obligations of regulatory compliance are presenting a new breed of challenges for organizations across several industry sectors. Aligning control objectives that stem from regulations and legislation with business objectives devised for improved business performance is a foremost challenge. The organizational as well as IT structures for the two classes of objectives are often distinct and potentially in conflict. In this chapter, we present an overarching methodology for aligning business and control objectives. The various phases of the methodology are then used as a basis for discussing state-of-the-art in compliance management. Contributions from research and academia as well as industry solutions are discussed. The chapter concludes with a discussion on the role of BPM as a driver for regulatory compliance and a presentation of open questions and challenges.

## 1 Introduction

Compliance is defined as ensuring that business processes, operations, and practice are in accordance with a prescribed and/or agreed set of norms. Compliance requirements may stem from legislature and regulatory bodies (e.g., Sarbanes-Oxley, Basel II, HIPAA), standards and codes of practice (e.g., SCOR, ISO9000), and also business partner contracts. The market value for compliance-related software and services was estimated as over $32 billion in 2008 (Hagerty et al. 2008). The boost in business investment is primarily a consequence of regulatory mandates that emerged as a result of events, which led to some of the largest scandals in corporate history such as Enron, WorldCom (USA), HIH (Australia),

S. Sadiq (✉)
School of Information Technology and Electrical Engineering, The University of Queensland, Brisbane, QLD, Australia
e-mail: shazia@itee.uq.edu.au

J. vom Brocke and M. Rosemann (eds.), *Handbook on Business Process Management 2*, International Handbooks on Information Systems,
DOI 10.1007/978-3-642-01982-1_8, © Springer-Verlag Berlin Heidelberg 2010

and Societe Generale (France). In spite of mandated deadlines, there is evidence that many organizations are still struggling with their compliance initiatives.

Compliance is historically viewed as a burden, although there are indications that businesses have started to see the regulations as an opportunity to improve their business processes and operations. Industry reports (BPM Forum 2006) indicate that up to 80% of companies expect to reap business benefits from improving their compliance regimens.

In general, a compliance regimen must include three interrelated but distinct perspectives on compliance, namely, corrective, detective, and preventative.

*Corrective* measures can be undertaken for a number of reasons, ranging from the introduction of a new regulation impacting upon the business, to breech reporting, to the organization coming under surveillance and scrutiny by a control authority, or, in the worst case, to an enforceable undertaking. Corrective measures undertaken in a proactive manner, position the organization favorably with regulators or other control authorities.

*Detective* measures are undertaken under two main approaches. First is *retrospective reporting*, wherein traditional audits are conducted for "after-the-fact" detection, through manual checks by consultants and/or through IT forensics and business intelligence (BI) tools. A second and more recent approach is to provide some level of automation through *automated detection*. The bulk of existing software solutions for compliance follow this approach. The proposed solutions hook into a variety of enterprise system components (e.g., SAP HR, LDAP Directory, Groupware, etc.) and generate audit reports against hard-coded checks performed on the requisite system. These solutions often specialize in certain class of checks, for example, the widely supported checks that relate to Segregation of Duty violations in role management systems. However, this approach still resides in the space of "after-the-fact" detection, although the assessment time is reduced and correspondingly the time to remediation and/or mitigation of control deficiencies is also improved.

A major issue with the above approaches (in varying degrees of impact) is the lack of sustainability. Even with automated detection facility, the hard-coded check repositories can quickly grow to a very large scale, making it extremely difficult to evolve and maintain them for changing legislatures and compliance requirements. In addition to external pressures, there is often a company internal push toward quality-of-service initiatives for process improvement, which have similar requirements.

In this chapter, we promote the use of sustainable approaches for compliance management, which we believe should fundamentally have a *preventative* focus, thus achieving *compliance by design* (Sadiq et al. 2007). That is, compliance should be embedded into the business practice, rather than be seen as a distinct activity. In particular, we argue that a compliance-by-design approach that capitalizes on Business Process Management (BPM) techniques has the potential to include also detective and corrective measures, leading to a holistic and effective compliance regimen.

The fundamental feature of the compliance-by-design approach is the ability to capture compliance requirements through a generic requirements modeling framework, and subsequently facilitate the propagation of these requirements into business process models and enterprise applications.

The biggest challenges in this regard is aligning control objectives that stem from regulations and legislation, with business objectives devised for improved business performance (KPMG 2005). The organizational as well as IT structures for the two classes of objectives are often distinct and potentially in conflict.

This chapter is dedicated to developing an understanding of the issues and challenges found in achieving the alignment between business and control objectives.

To this end, we will first introduce a guiding scenario in order to establish basic terms and concepts. We then present an overarching methodology for compliance management that focuses on aligning business and control objectives. The methodology demonstrates the use of Business Process Management and related technologies as a driver for managing compliance and is primarily intended to achieve compliance by design. Using the methodology as a basis for discussion, we will then provide a detailed discussion on state-of-the-art in compliance management services and solutions covering contributions from both academia as well as industry. The analysis of current solutions indicates that a process-driven approach to compliance management may be the most effective way to address this complex problem. The chapter concludes with a discussion on open questions and challenges toward effective compliance management.

## 2 Scenario and Background

Consider the following example. In 2006, a new legislative framework was put in place in Australia for anti-money laundering. The first phase of reforms for the Anti-Money Laundering and Counter-Terrorism Financing Act 2006 (AML/CTF) covers the financial sector including banks, credit unions, building societies, and trustees, and extends to casinos, wagering service providers, and bullion dealers. The AML/CTF act imposes a number of compliance obligations or *control objectives*, which include the following:

- Customer due diligence (identification, verification of identity, and ongoing monitoring of transactions)
- Reporting (suspicious matters, threshold transactions, and international funds transfer instructions)
- Record keeping
- Establishing and maintaining the AML/CTF program

AML/CTF is a *principles-based*[1] regulation, and hence, businesses need to determine the exact manner in which they will fulfill the obligations. This leads

[1] "The AML/CTF Act is a principles-based piece of legislation. It sets out broad obligations which reporting entities and others affected by the legislation must meet, but leaves the methods of meeting those obligations to be decided by those on whom the obligations fall" (AUSTRAC 2006).

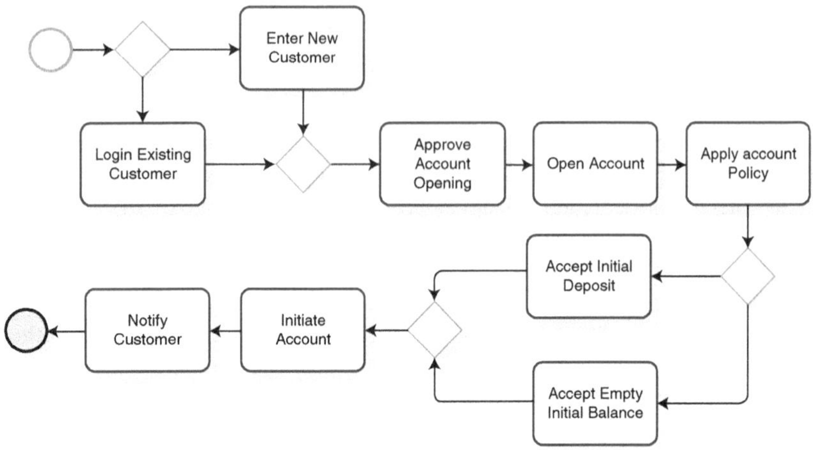


**Fig. 1** Example account-opening process

to the design of so-called internal controls[2] devised by a particular financial organization. For example, consider an account-opening process as depicted in Fig. 1. An internal control may mandate the "scanning of all new customer accounts against blocked entity datasets" in response to the obligation to provide customer due diligence during the account-opening process. This would require an additional check to be conducted after entering new customer information.

For a principles-based approach such as AML/CTF, the design of the internal controls typically reflects the *risk appetite* of the organization. Effective risk management begins with a clear understanding of an organization's appetite for risk and is essentially the process of identifying vulnerabilities and threats to the organization in achieving its business objectives. When establishing and implementing its system of risk management, a company will consider a number of risks such as financial reporting risks (the risk of a material error in the financial statements), operational, environmental, sustainability, strategic, external, ethical conduct, reputation or brand, technological, product or service quality, and human capital, as well as risks of noncompliance (ASX 2006).

In order to handle the risk, the organization may choose one or more well-known strategies such as *avoid risk*, for example, if possible, choose not to implement processes and/or remove the source of the risk; *mitigate risk*, for example, define and implement controls; *transfer risk*, for example, share or outsource risk (insurance); and/or *accept risk*, for example, formally acknowledge existence of risk and monitor it.

[2]"Internal control is broadly defined as a process effected by an entity's board of directors, management, and other personnel designed to provide reasonable assurance regarding the achievement of objectives in the following categories: effectiveness and efficiency of operations; reliability of financial reporting; and compliance with applicable laws and regulations" (COSO 1994).

The approach to risk management has a profound impact on how an organization would design and implement internal controls in response to compliance obligations. *Controls management* thus becomes a balancing act between compliance obligations, business objectives, and risks.

In the next section, we present a methodology for compliance management that aims to provide a means of aligning business and control objectives by using BPM and related technologies as drivers.

## 3 Methodology for Compliance Management

Previously, we have argued that *compliance by design* is a preferred approach for compliance management due to its preventative focus. In light of the heavy social, economic, and environmental costs of noncompliance, a priori embedding of requisite checks and triggers into the enterprise applications is clearly desirable but also extremely difficult, given that the business and technology landscape of today's organizations is disparate and distributed.

BPM is recognized as a means to enforce corporate policy. Regulatory mandates also provide policies and guidelines for business practice. One may argue why a separate requirements modeling facility is required to capture compliance requirements for business processes. We identify the following reasons against this argument:

Firstly, the source of these two objectives will be distinct, both from an ownership and governance perspective, as well as from a timeline perspective. Whereas businesses can be expected to have some form of business objectives, control objectives can be dictated by external sources and at different times.

Secondly, the two have differing concerns, namely, business objectives and control objectives. Thus, the use of business process languages to model control objectives may not provide a conceptually faithful representation. Compliance is in essence a normative notion, and thus control objectives are fundamentally descriptive, that is, indicating *what* needs to be done (in order to comply). Business process specifications are fundamentally prescriptive in nature, that is, detailing *how* business activity should take place. There is evidence of some developments toward descriptive approaches for BPM, but these works were predominantly focused on achieving flexibility in business process execution (e.g., Pesic and van der Aalst 2006; Sadiq et al. 2005).

Thirdly, there is likelihood of conflicts, inconsistencies, and redundancies within the two specifications. The intersection of the two, thus, needs to be carefully studied.

In summary, we present in Fig. 2, the interconnect between process management and controls management. The two are formulated by different stakeholders and have different lifecycles. The design of control will impact the way a business process is executed. On the other hand, a (re)design of a business process causes an update of the risk assessment, which may lead to a new/updated set of controls.

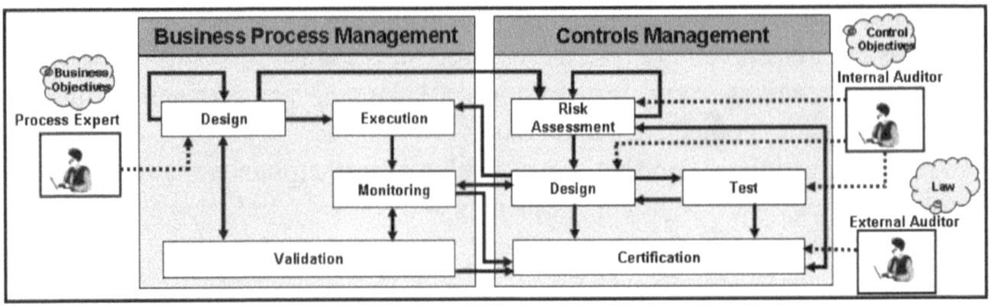


**Fig. 2** Interconnect of process management and controls management

Additionally, business process monitoring will assess the design of internal controls and serve as an input to internal controls certification.

Given the scale and diversity of compliance requirements and additionally given the fact that these requirements may frequently change, business process compliance is indeed a large and complex problem area with several challenges. Given further that business and control objectives are (or should be) designed separately, but must converge at some point, we present below a list of essential requirements and where relevant corresponding techniques and methods that need to be met/developed in order to tackle this overall problem.

## 3.1 Control Directory Management

Regulations and other compliance directives are complex and vague and require interpretation. Often in legalese, these mandates need to be translated by experts. For example, the COSO framework (COSO 1994) is recognized by regulatory bodies as a de facto standard for realizing controls for financial reporting. A company-specific interpretation results in the following (textual) information being created:

*<control objective, risk, internal control>*

| For example: | |
|---|---|
| Control objective: | *Prevent unauthorized use of purchase order process;* |
| Risk: | *Unauthorized creation of purchase orders and payments to nonexisting suppliers;* |
| Internal control: | *The creation and approval of purchase orders must be undertaken by two separate purchase officers.* |

The above example is typical of the well-known segregation-of-duty constraint (one individual does not participate in more than one key trading or operational function) mandated by Sarbanes-Oxley 404.

However, business will typically deal with a number of regulations/standards at one time. Thus there is a need to provide a structured means of managing the various interpretations within regional industry sector and organizational contexts.

We identify this as a need for a *controls directory*. Control directory management could be supported by database technology, and/or could present some interesting content management challenges, but will be an essential component in the overall solution. There is some evidence in industry reports that solution vendors are producing repositories of control objectives (and associated parameters) against the major regulations, see, for example, SAP GRC Repository and SAI Global GRC Knowledge and Information Services. Keeping abreast of frequently changing regulations is a clear challenge in the maintenance of such knowledge bases.

## 3.2 Ontological Alignment

Interpretation of regulations from legal /financial experts comes in the form of textual descriptions (see example in the previous section). Establishing an agreement on terms and usage between these descriptions and the business processes and constituent activities/transactions is a difficult but essential aspect of the overall methodology.

In Fig. 3, we present the relationships between the basic process modeling and control modeling concepts. Clearly, the relationship between process task and internal controls is much deeper than shown, as it would require alignment between embedded concepts, for example, task identification, particular data items, roles and performers, etc. However, it is evident that several controls may be applicable on a task, and one control may impact on multiple tasks as well. What tools and techniques are utilized to provide an effective alignment between the two conceptual spaces is not the focus of this paper but nonetheless an important question at hand.

## 3.3 Modeling Controls

The motivation to model controls is multifaceted. Firstly, a generic requirements modeling framework for compliance by design will provide a substantial improvement over current after-the-fact detection approaches. Secondly, it will allow for an analysis of compliance rules, thereby providing the ability to discover hidden dependencies, and view in holistic context, while maintaining a comprehensible

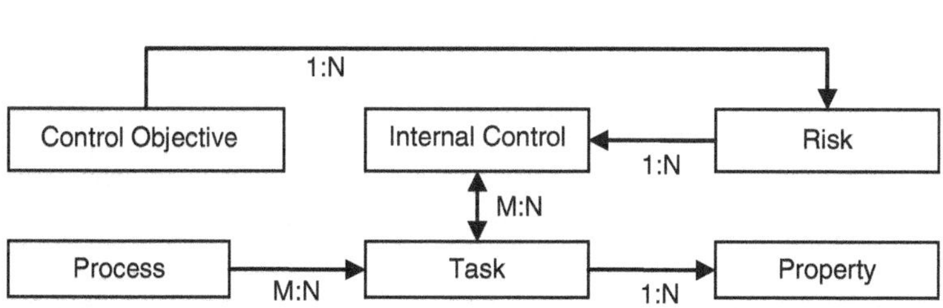


**Fig. 3** Relationships between process modeling and control modeling concepts

working space. Thirdly, a precise and unambiguous (formal) specification will facilitate the systematic enrichment of business processes with control objectives.

A fundamental question in this regard is the *appropriate formalism* to undertake the task. In the next section, we will deliberate further on this question and provide a discussion of complementary approaches in this regard.

Note, however, that modeling controls in a precise and unambiguous manner is a necessary first step, but cannot completely address compliance by design methodology. Process model enrichment as explained in the next section, constitutes a second essential step.

## 3.4 Process Model Enrichment

In this context, we use the term process model enrichment as the ability to enhance enterprise models (business processes) with compliance requirements. This can be provided as *process annotation*. Process annotations have been proposed by a number of researchers, for example, the notion of control tags (Sadiq et al. 2007), integrating risks on EPCs (zur Mühlen and Rosemann 2005), and semantic annotations (Governatori et al. 2008). The resultant visualization of controls on the process model facilitates a better understanding of the interaction between the two specifications for both stakeholders (process owners as well as compliance officers).

Consider, for example, the account-opening process presented in Fig. 1. An annotation at the activity "Enter New Customer" to indicate the need for "scanning of all new customer accounts against blocked entity data-sets" will assist in identifying the obligations relevant to AML/CTF. Figure 4 depicts a fragment of

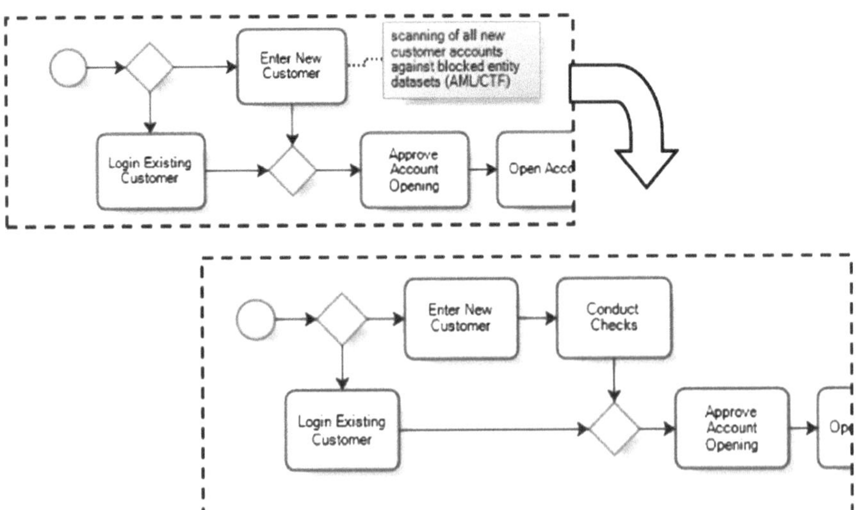


**Fig. 4** Process annotation and resultant redesign

the process model presented in Fig. 1 and shows an example of process annotation and resultant process redesign.

However, the visualization is only a first step. The new checks introduced within the process model can in turn be used to analyze the model for measures such as *compliance degree* (Lu et al. 2008), which can provide a quantification of the effort required to achieve a compliant process model. Eventually, process models may need to be modified to include the compliance requirements.

In large organizations, the process portfolio may consist of hundreds of process models that may span several business units. A diagnostic facility (Governatori et al. 2008) can empower the organizations to undertake a compliance assessment at a large scale, and then continue with compliance enforcement based on the measured compliance degree (or gap) and associated risks.

The methodology as presented so far can be summarized as in Fig. 5. Note however, that the Sects 3.1–3.4 as presented above are focused on providing *design time* support for compliance management. Although model-driven enforcement and monitoring is a main objective of the presented methodology, it is not always possible to achieve. Below, we present a brief summary of issues and techniques for *run time* support for compliance management.

### 3.5 Compliance Enforcement

Enforcement of controls is a key component in the overall methodology. Given that the technology landscape of today's organizations is highly diverse and disparate, translation of designed internal controls onto the IT infrastructure, and subsequently, into business transactions is clearly a significant challenge. A number of complementary technologies can be identified in this regard.

- Records management (e.g., incident logging, data retention systems, etc.)
- Integration technologies (e.g., enterprise application integration, master data management)
- Testing/simulation (e.g., what-if scenario analysis)
- Control automation (e.g., rule engines)

Model-driven business process execution (as envisaged in the ideal BPM vision) is of course a candidate in the above, and arguably provides the most effective means to enforcement of compliance-related controls. Unfortunately, the current state of enterprise systems does not reflect the ideal BPM vision, and hence, compliance enforcement is provided through a variety of tools and technologies.

### 3.6 Compliance Monitoring

The support provided in the design of compliant processes through process annotation and analysis and resultant process changes can eventually lead to a *model-*

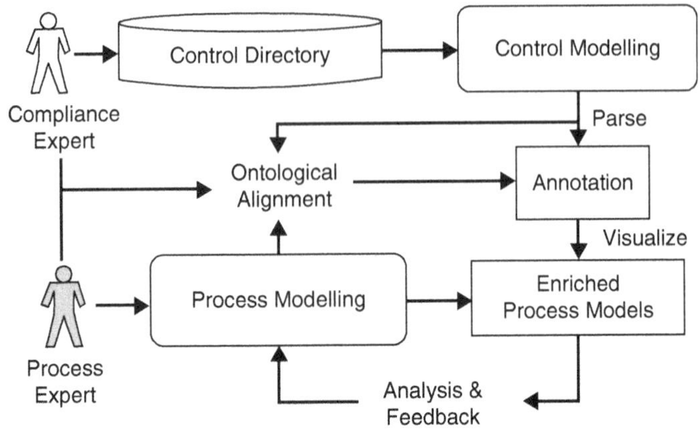


**Fig. 5** Summary of design time support in the methodology

*driven enforcement of compliance controls* (where process management systems are in place). However, it is naïve to assume that all organizations have the complete implementation of the BPM life cycle, and hence the process models and underlying applications may be disconnected. In this case, it is important to provide support for compliance through run-time monitoring. This has been the agenda for several vendors in this space targeting the so-called-automated detection, described earlier. In general, event monitoring is a well studied research topic (see, e.g., www.complexevents.com) and, although has not been widely/explicitly associated with the compliance issue, notably excepting Giblin et al. (2006), its usage in fraud detection and security is closely related.

Although, this chapter is primarily targeted at approaches conducive to achieving compliance by design by adopting a preventative approach facilitated by business process models, several works on formal modeling of control objectives (Governatori and Rotolo 2006) have taken into account the violations and resultant reparation policies that may surface at runtime.

## 4 State of the Art

Governance, risk, and compliance (GRC) is an emerging area of research that holds challenges for various communities including information systems; business software development; legal, cultural, and behavioral studies; and corporate governance.

In this chapter, we have focused on compliance management from an information systems perspective, in particular the modeling and analysis of compliance requirements. In this section, we report on the contributions from research and academia as well as industry solutions in the area of compliance management. The primary focus of the discussion is on preventative approaches to compliance or those that facilitate compliance by design, and hence the discussion is structured around *compliance modeling*, specifically issues relating to Sects 3.3–3.4.

## *4.1 Modeling Controls*

Both process modeling and modeling of normative requirements are well-studied fields independently, but until recently, the interactions between the two have been largely ignored (Desai et al. 2005; Padmanabhan et al. 2006). In particular, zur Mühlen et al. (2007) provide a valuable representational analysis to understand the synergies between process modeling and rule modeling.

It is obvious that the modeling of controls will be undertaken as rules, although the question of appropriate formalism is still understudied. A plethora of proposals exist both in the research community on formal modeling of rules and in the commercial arena through business rule management systems.

Historically, formal modeling of normative systems has focused on how to capture the logical properties of the notions of the normative concepts (e.g., obligations, prohibitions, permissions, violations, etc.) and how these relate to the entities in an organization and to the activities to be performed. Deontic logic is the branch of logic that studies normative concepts such as obligations, permissions, prohibitions, and related notions. Standard deontic logic (SDL) is the starting point for logical investigation of the basic normative notions and offers a very idealized and abstract conceptual representation of these notions, but at the same time, it suffers from several drawbacks, given its high level of abstraction (Sartor 2005). Over the years, many different deontic logics have been proposed to capture the different intuitions behind these normative notions and to overcome drawbacks and limitations of SDL. One of the main limitations in this context is its inability to reason with violations and the obligations arising in response to violations (Carmo and Jones 2002). Very often, normative statements pertinent to business processes, and in particular contracts, specify conditions about when other conditions in the document have not been fulfilled; that is, when some (contractual) clauses have been violated. Hence, any formal representation to be conceptually faithful has to be able to deal with these kinds of situations.

As we have discussed before, compliance is a relationship between two sets of specifications: the normative specifications that prescribe what a business has to do and the process modeling specification describing how a business performs its activities. Accordingly, to properly verify that a process/procedure complies with the norms regulating the particular business, one has to provide conceptually sound representations of the process on one side and the norms on the other, and then check the alignment of the formal specifications of the process and the formal specifications for the norms.

In the following paragarph, we present an account of the various proposals for formal modeling of controls. Governatori (2005) and Governatori and Milosevic (2006) have proposed FCL (formal contract language) as a candidate for control modeling, which has proved effective due to its ability to reason with violations. A rule in FCL is an expression of the form $r$: $A_1,\ldots, A_n \Rightarrow B$, where $r$ is the name of the rule (unique for each rule), $A_1,\ldots, A_n$ are the premises, (propositions in the logic), and $B$ is the conclusion of the rule (again $B$ is a proposition of the logic).

The propositions of the logic are built from a finite set of atomic propositions, and the following operators: $\neg$(negation), $O$(obligation), $P$(permission), $\otimes$(violation/reparation). The formation rules are as follows:

- Every atomic proposition is a proposition;
- If $p$ is an atomic proposition, then $\neg p$ is a proposition;
- If $p$ is a proposition, then $Op$ is an obligation proposition and $Pp$ is a permission proposition. Obligation propositions and permission propositions are deontic propositions;
- If $p_1,\ldots,p_n$ are obligation propositions and $q$ is a deontic proposition, then $p_1\otimes \ldots \otimes p_n \otimes q$ is a reparation chain.

A simple proposition corresponds to a factual statement. The deontic operators are then indexed by the subject of the normative position corresponding to the operator. Thus $O_s$ *Send Invoice* means that the supplier $s$ has the obligation to send the invoice to the purchaser, and $P_p$ *Charge Penalty* means that the purchaser $p$ is entitled (permitted) to charge a penalty to the supplier. A reparation chain, for example:

$$O_s \textit{ Provide Goods Timely} \otimes O_s \textit{ Offer Discout} \otimes P_p \textit{ Charge Penalty}$$

captures obligations and normative positions arising in response to violations of obligation. Thus the expression above means that the suppliers have the obligation to send the goods in a timely manner, but in case they do not comply with this (i.e., they violate the obligation do so) then they have the "secondary" obligation to offer a discount for the merchandise, and in case that they fail to fulfill this obligation (i. e., we have a violation of the possible reparation of the "primary" obligation), then, finally, the purchaser can charge the supplier with the penalty.

As usual in normative reasoning, there are two types of rules: definitional rules and normative rules. A definitional rule gives the conditions that assert a factual statement, while a normative rule allows us to conclude a normative position (i.e., an obligation, a permission, or a prohibition, where a prohibition is $O\neg$ or equivalently $\neg P$). According to the above distinction in definitional rules, the conclusion is a proposition, and in normative rules, the conclusion is either a deontic proposition or a reparation chain. In both cases, the premises are propositions and deontic propositions, but not reparation chains.

FCL offers two reasoning modules: (1) a normalizer to make explicit rules that can be derived from explicitly given rules by merging their normative conclusions, to remove redundancy and identify conflicts rules, and (2) an inference engine to derive conclusions given some propositions as input (Governatori 2005).

There have been some other notable contributions from research on the matter of control modeling. Goedertier and Vanthienen (2006) present a logical language

PENELOPE, which provides the ability to verify temporal constraints arising from compliance requirements on effected business processes. Kuster et al. (2007) provide a method to check compliance between object life cycles that provide reference models for data artifacts, for example, insurance claims and business process models. Giblin et al. (2006) provide temporal rule patterns for regulatory policies, although the objective of this work is to facilitate event monitoring rather than the usage of the patterns for support of design time activities. Furthermore, Agrawal et al. (2006) has presented a workflow architecture for supporting Sarbanes–Oxley internal controls, which includes functions such as workflow modeling, active enforcement, workflow auditing, as well as anomaly detection.

There has been some complementary work in the analysis of formal models representing normative notions. For example, Farrell et al. (2005) study the performance of business contract on the basis of their formal representation. Desai et al. (2008) seek to provide support for assessing the correctness of business contracts represented formally through a set of commitments. The reasoning is based on value of various states of commitment as perceived by cooperative agents. Research on closely related issues has also been carried out in the field of autonomous agents (Alberti et al. 2006).

## *4.2 Process Model Enrichment*

As discussed previously, modeling the controls is only the first step toward compliance by design. The second essential step is the enrichment of process models with compliance requirements (i.e., the modeled controls). Clearly, this cannot take place without a formal controls model (as proposed by above-mentioned works), or at least some machine-readable specification of the controls.

There have recently been some efforts toward support for business process modeling against compliance requirements. In particular, the works of zur Mühlen and Rosemann (2005) and Neiger et al. (2006) provide an appealing method for integrating risks in business processes. The proposed technique for "risk-aware" business process models is developed for EPCs (event process chains) using an extended notation. Sadiq et al. (2007) propose an approach based on control tags to visualize internal controls on process models. Liu et al. (2007) takes a similar approach of annotating and checking process models against compliance rules, although the visual rule language, namely BPSL, is general purpose and does not directly address the notions representing compliance requirements.

## *4.3 Summary*

Although this chapter has primarily focused on preventative approaches to compliance, it is important to identify the role of detective approaches as well, where a wide range of supporting technologies are present.

These include several commercial solutions such as business activity monitoring, BI, etc. Noteworthy in research literature with respect to compliance monitoring is the synergy with process mining techniques (van der Aalst et al. 2003; van Dongen et al. 2005) that provide the capability to discover run-time process behavior (and deviations) and can thereby assist in detection of compliance violations.

In terms of the compliance services and solutions, a number of compliance service/solution providers are currently available, including large consulting firms providing business services and advisory as well as software vendors. Software services are emerging from large corporations with products such as IBM Lotus workplace for business controls and reporting, Microsoft Office Solutions Accelerator for Sarbanes–Oxley, SAP GRC Solution, as well as niche vendors such as OpenPages, Paisley Consulting, Qumas Inc., and several others (Caldwell and Eid 2008).

Software solutions and tools for compliance are typically found under the umbrella of other technologies such as BI, business rules management, etc. As such, compliance vendors are not easily identified directly. Further, while many vendors provide sophisticated functionality of some aspect of the overall end-to-end methodology (as presented in Sect. 3), these solutions are of a piecemeal nature, for example, a business controls and reporting tool designed to help users manage processes, controls, and information, subject to Sarbanes–Oxley 404.

## 5 Discussion and Outlook

As the importance of GRC grows for various industries, there is an evident need to provide supporting tools and methods to enable organizations seeking corporate social responsibility to achieve their objectives. The challenges that reside in this topic warrant systematic approaches that motivate and empower business users to achieve a high degree of compliance with regulations, standards, and corporate policies.

One of the biggest challenges facing the compliance industry is the measurement of adequacy of controls (KPMG Advisory 2005), that is, achieving a balance between control and business objectives.

This has been a driver of the research presented in this chapter. The methodology presented in Sect. 3 provides a systematic means of aligning business and control objectives. However, several open issues still remain.

A number of proposals exist for *modeling controls* (see Sect. 4.1). Although several proposals provide a powerful and conceptually faithful means of capturing controls, it still remains to be studied how these formal models can be deployed in practice.

Effective framework for modeling controls is a necessary prerequisite to studying the alignment between business and control objectives. We have demonstrated how such models can provide a means of enriching and subsequently analyzing business process models, which in turn can be used for *model-driven compliance enforcement*.

*Enriched business process* models bring the added benefit of providing the *capability for diagnostics* (see Sect. 3.4): that is, provide a means of understanding as to what needs to be done in order to achieve (an acceptable degree of) compliance (Lu et al. 2008). This is a hard problem in general due to the semantically rich nature of the involved models.

A theoretically rigorous and practically feasible means of control modeling supported by a powerful analysis machinery that provides diagnostic support for comparing business and control objectives has the potential to create a holistic approach to compliance management, by providing not only preventative and detective techniques but also corrective recommendations.

Future research endeavors in this area should strive toward compliance management frameworks that provide a close integration of the three perspectives, namely, preventative, detective, and corrective. Such a framework can allow organizations to better respond to the changing regulatory demands and also reap the benefits of process improvement.

## References


Agrawal R, Johnson C, Kiernan J, Leymann F (2006) Taming compliance with sarbanes-oxley internal controls using database technology. In: Proceedings of the 22nd International conference on data engineering, 2006. Atlanta, GA, USA, IEEE Computer Society

Alberti M, Chesani F, Gavanelli M, Lamma E, Mello P, Torroni P (2006) Compliance verification of agent interaction: a logic based tool. Appl Artif Int 20(2–4):133–157

ASX (2006) Australian securities exchange principles of good governance, recommendation 7.1, Nov. 2006. www.asx.gov.au (last accesses June 01, 2008)

AUSTRAC (2006) Australian transaction reports and analysis centre supervisory framework. www.austrac.gov.au/files/supervisory_framework.pdf. Accessed 01 Jun 2008)

BPM Forum (2006) CEE: the future. Building the compliance enabled enterprise. Report produced by global fluency in partnership with: AXS-One, chief executive magazine and IT compliance institute

Caldwell F, Eid T (2007) Magic quadrant for finance governance, risk and compliance management software, 2007. Gartner RAS Core Research Note G00145150, 1 Feb 2007, RS196 0906 2007

Caldwell F, Eid T (2008) Magic quadrant for enterprise governance, risk and compliance platforms. ID. G00158295. June 2008. Gartner Research

Carmo J, Jones AJ (2002) Deontic logic and contrary to duties. In: Gabbay D, Guenther F (eds.) Handbook of Philosophical Logic, 2nd edn., vol. 8, pp 265–343

COSO –The committee of sponsoring organizations of the treadway commission (1994) Internal control – integrated framework. May 1994

Desai N, Mallya AU, Chopra AK, Singh MP (2005) Interaction protocols as design abstractions for business processes. IEEE Trans Softw Eng 31(12):1015–1027

Desai N, Nanjangud NC, Singh MP (2008) Checking correctness of business contracts via commitments. In: Padgham L, Parkes DC, Müller J, Parsons S (eds) Proceedings of 7th International conference on autonomous agents and multiagent systems (AAMAS2008), Estoril, Portugal, 12–16 May 2008

Farrell ADH, Sergot MJ, Sallé M, Bartolini C (2005) Using the event-calculus for tracking the normative state in contracts. Int J Coop Infor Syst 14(2–3):99–129

Giblin C, Muller S, Pfitzmann B (2006) From regulatory policies to event monitoring rules: towards model driven compliance automation. IBM Research Report. Zurich Research Laboratory

Goedertier S, Vanthienen J (2006) Designing compliant business processes with obligations and permissions. In Eder J, Dustdar S et al. (eds) Proceedings of workshop on business process design, Springer, Vienna, Austria, pp 5–14, LNCS 4103
Governatori G (2005) Representing business contracts in RuleML. Int J Coop Infor Syst 14 (2–3):181–216
Governatori G, Milosevic Z (2006) A formal analysis of a business contract language. Int J Coop Infor Syst 15(4):659–685
Governatori G, Rotolo A (2006) Logic of violations: a gentzen system for reasoning on contrary-to-duty obligations. Austral J Logic 4:193–215
Governatori G, Rotolo A, Sartor G (2005) Temporalised normative positions in defeasible logic. In: Gardner A (ed) Proceedings of the 10th International conference on artificial intelligence and law, ACM Press, pp 25–34
Governatori G, Milosevic Z, Sadiq S (2006) Compliance checking between business processes and business contracts. In: Proceedings of the 10th IEEE conference on enterprise distributed object computing, Hong Kong
Governatori G, Hoffmann J, Sadiq S, Weber, I (2008) Detecting regulatory compliance for business process models through semantic annotations. In: 4th International workshop on business process design (BPD'08). In conjunction with the 6th International Conference on Business Process Management, Milan, Italy. pp 1-4
Hagerty J, Hackbush J, Gaughan D, Jacobson S (2008) The governance, risk management, and compliance spending report, 2008–2009: Inside the $32B GRC Market. March 25, 2008. AMR Research, Boston USA
Kuster J, Ryndina K, Gall H (2007) Generation of business process models for object life cycle. In: Proceedings of the 5th International conference on business process management. Springer, Brisbane, Australia, pp 165–180
KPMG Advisory (2005) The compliance journey: balancing risk and controls with business improvement
Liu Y, Muller S, Xu K (2007) A static compliance checking framework for business process models. IBM Syst J 46:335–361
Lu R, Sadiq S, Governatori G (2008) Compliance aware business process design. Third International workshop on business process design (BPD'07). In: conjunction with the 5th International conference on business process management, 24–28 September 2007. Springer Berlin, LNCS Volume 4928/2008, pp 120–131
Neiger D, Churilov L, zur Mühlen M, Rosemann M (2006) Integrating risks in business process models with value focused process engineering. In: Proceedings of the 2006 European conference on information systems (ECIS 2006), Goteborg, Sweden, 12–14 June 2006
Padmanabhan V, Governatori G, Sadiq S, Colomb R, Rotolo A (2006) Process modeling: the deontic way. In Stumptner M, Hartmann S, Kiyoki Y (eds) Australia–Pacific conference on conceptual modeling, pp 75–84, CRPIT 53
Pesic M, van der Aalst WMP (2006) A declarative approach for flexible business processes. In: Eder J, Dustdar S (eds) Business process management workshops, workshop on dynamic process management (DPM 2006), volume 4103 of Lecture notes in computer science. Springer-Verlag, Berlin, pp 169–180
Sadiq S, Sadiq W, Orlowska M (2005) A framework for constraint specification and validation in flexible workflows. Inf Syst 30(5):349–378
Sadiq S, Governatori G, Naimiri K (2007) Modeling control objectives for business process compliance. In: Proceedings of the 5th International conference on business process management, Springer, Brisbane, Australia, pp 149–164
Sartor G (2005) Legal reasoning: a cognitive approach to the law. Springer, Berlin
van der Aalst WMP, van Dongen BF, Herbst J, Maruster L, Schimm G, Weijters AJMM (2003) Workflow mining: a survey of issues and approaches. Data Knowl Eng 47:237–267
van der Aalst WMP, Alves de Medeiros AK, Weijters AJMM (2006) Process equivalence: comparing two process models based on observed behavior. In: Proceedings of the 4th

International conference on business process management, Vienna, Austria, 2007. Springer, pp 129–144

van Dongen BF, de Medeiros AKA, Verbeek HMW, Weijters AJMM, van der Aalst WMP (2005) The ProM Framework: a new era in process mining tool support. In: Proceedings of 26th International conference applications and theory of petri nets, Springer, Miami, USA, pp 444–454

zur Mühlen M, Rosemann M (2005) Integrating risks in business process models. In: Proceedings of 16th Australasian conference on information systems. Sydney, Australia

zur Mühlen M, Indulska M, Kamp G (2007) Business process and business rule modelling languages for compliance management: a representational analysis. In: 26th International Conference on Conceptual Modelling - ER2007 –Tutorials, Posters, Panels and Industrial Contributions, Auckland, New Zealand

# Prioritizing Process Improvement: An Example from the Australian Financial Services Sector

**Wasana Bandara, Alain Guillemain, and Paul Coogans**

**Abstract** Process improvement has become a number one business priority, and more and more project requests are raised in organizations, seeking approval and resources for process-related projects. Realistically, the total of the requested funds exceeds the allocated budget, the number of projects is higher than the available bandwidth, and only some of these (very often only few) can be supported and most never see any light. Relevant resources are scarce, and correct decisions must be made to make sure that those projects that are of best value are implemented. How can decision makers make the right decision on the following: Which project(s) are to be approved and when to commence work on them? Which projects are most aligned with corporate strategy? How can the project's value to the business be calculated and explained? How can these decisions be made in a fair, justifiable manner that brings the best results to the company and its stakeholders? This chapter describes a business value scoring (BVS) model that was built, tested, and implemented by a leading financial institution in Australia to address these very questions. The chapter discusses the background and motivations for such an initiative and describes the tool in detail. All components and underlying concepts are explained, together with details on its application. This tool has been successfully implemented in the case organization. The chapter provides practical guidelines for organizations that wish to adopt this approach.

## 1 Introduction and Background

Recent Gartner studies (Blosch et al. 2005; McDonald and Nunno 2007; McDonald et al. 2006, 2008) have identified process improvement as the number one business priority of Chief Information Officers (CIOs). Choosing the correct projects is often

W. Bandara (✉)
Queensland University of Technology, Brisbane, QLD, Australia
e-mail: w.bandara@qut.edu.au

J. vom Brocke and M. Rosemann (eds.), *Handbook on Business Process Management 2*, International Handbooks on Information Systems,
DOI 10.1007/978-3-642-01982-1_9, 

identified as a critical factor for a successful business process model (BPM) (Olding and Rosser 2007) and one of the core BPM governance decisions (Harmon 2005; Kirchmer 2010)[1]. Managers often struggle to demonstrate the connection between costs and expected business benefits of BPM projects (Huxley 2003; Huxley and Stewart 2008; Thorp 1998). The founding fathers of BPM (i.e., Davenport 1993; Hammer and Champy 1993) explicitly state to make the selection of processes-to-improve transparent, and to provide a clear link between process objectives and organizational goals. However, "there is little in the literature that directs organizations towards this knowledge gap or region of complexity in process improvement" (Huxley 2003, Chap. 2, p. 5).

The guidelines available for practitioners are either of very high level and hence not of much assistance when attempting to implement BPM initiatives, or, on the contrary, are so detailed that it can take a significant effort to simply identify the critical processes. For example, Davenport (1993) states that organizations should "focus on the most important processes or those that conflict most with the business vision" and prioritize according to urgency. Hammer and Champy (1993) provide three criteria for selecting processes to improve, stating to base the selection upon (1) dysfunctional processes (those processes that are in the deepest trouble), (2) process importance (those processes that have the greatest impact on the company's customer), and (3) process feasibility (those processes that are most susceptible to successful redesign). Detailed guidelines on how to operationalize this assessment, however, are not provided. How could a practitioner determine the feasibility of a process, or those that are in dysfunction, or which ones are the most critical to business? Thus, while project selection is emphasized to be a critical part of BPM's success (Harmon 2005; Kirchmer 2010), it remains as a "mystery phase" in most available guidelines.

Huxley (2003) and Huxley and Stewart (2008) attempt to address this limitation by identifying "important" processes with a scoring method that has five criteria: (1) dependency (effect of failure of a process on the organization), (2) probability of failure of a process, (3) impact (relative contribution of a process on organizational objectives and goals), (4) cost/benefit of the process improvement project, and (5) probability of a successful process improvement project for that process. The authors' intensions were to provide a step-by-step guide for the identification of "important" processes and the selection of which of these processes should then be improved. Many tools/methods were made available to the practitioner for assessing the five factors of Huxley's (2003) process selection approach. While the authors claim to provide sufficient guidelines to successfully implement the methodology into organizations, the guidelines significantly lack (yet again) instructions on how to use these dimensions effectively within BPM initiatives. The tools and

[1]Burlton (2010) presents a methodological framework for implementing business strategies by means of process management. In this framework, the task of prioritizing processes is considered to be a vital step for maintaining effective and efficient process architectures and for keeping such architectures in sync with the strategic guidelines.

methods presented require many tasks to be completed, have few detailed guidelines on when and how to best apply them, and have no guidelines on how to adopt these to varying project and organizational specific contexts.

> "It's not worth trying to deploy a process selection method, if it takes equal or more time and resources to decide on what to do as it takes to actually do the work."
> *(Operations Strategy Manager, QIC, Personal Comm., 10.07.2008)*

In this chapter, the experiences of one of Australia's leading financial institutions, QIC, with BPM project selection are unfolded. It describes the current situation in the organization and how the need for a project selection approach emerged. A robust yet easy-to-use tool that supported transparency with regard to the projects that were selected and aligned with corporate goals was much needed. None of the methodologies and guidelines available suited the specific needs of the organization and hence two business process specialists were deployed to build, test, and implement one.

The remainder of this chapter first introduces the case organization. It then presents the tool, first with a high level overview followed by its detailed component descriptions. The validation process (and lessons learnt) of this tool is presented next. The chapter concludes with an overview of the adoptability and application of this tool.

## 2 Introducing the Case Organization

QIC[2] is the case organization that this study reports on. QIC is a leading institutional investment manager with $70 billion in funds under management as at present (2009). QIC (previously known as "Queensland Investment Corporation") is a Queensland Government-owned corporation that operates under the provision of the Government Owned Corporations Act 1993 and the Queensland Investment Corporation Act 1991. QIC operates as a fully commercial organization, charging fees for services and paying a dividend to the Queensland Government. It is registered under the Corporations Act 2001 as QIC Limited. QIC commenced investment operations in 1989 and was formally established in 1991. Since then, QIC has grown to be the largest institutional investment manager in Australia. QIC brings specialists from all major asset classes into one highly integrated organization, offering a broad range of solutions across equities, fixed interest, property, infrastructure, absolute return strategies, and capital and exposure management. QIC has over 80 institutional clients, who are located both nationally and internationally, including superannuation funds, government and statutory authorities, insurance organizations, charitable bodies, financial services companies, and educational institutions.

---

[2]The Org structure described here was correct as of Sept 09. For further details see http://www.qic.com/.

QIC's vision is to be a leading provider of professional and disciplined investment management services and to remain at the forefront of the industry best practice. QIC's corporate strategy is twofold: (1) to deliver investment performance, products, and services which exceed clients' expectations and ensure that the company remains the client's manager of choice; and (2) grow funds under management and client numbers by developing new business, where it adds value both to the existing business and to QIC's existing clients. In order to achieve these, it is essential that QIC operate on a fully commercial basis, continue to generate new sources of revenue while focusing on operational efficiency, and constantly innovate. The resultant savings and revenue base are used to first reinvest in QIC's people, teams, and infrastructure to ensure that they continue to deliver the best investment outcomes, products, and services; second, reduce clients' costs; and third, provide a return on equity to stakeholders.

> "We are client centric, not product centric" [...] "Our mission is to provide high quality investment management and consulting services to maximise investment returns for our clients, consistent with their expectations and risk tolerances."
>
> *(QIC Annual Report 2008)*

QIC's primary focus is to ensure that their clients meet set investment objectives. Thus, the client services team takes a proactive approach to managing relationships and continues to search for ways to improve client outcomes. The QIC operations division has experienced a significant level of structural change over the past year (see Appendix 1 for a QIC organizational chart and overview). This was driven by the requirement to ensure that the clients' needs are serviced in the most efficient, transparent, and cost-effective manner possible, while also enabling their investment divisions to focus on investment functions rather than administrative activities (QIC 2008, p. 14). One of the key changes was the introduction of operations relationship managers (ORMs). ORMs act as a central point of contact between operations and the other business areas of QIC; six new ORMs were appointed to represent the different business units. This has resulted in increased client alignment as well as more streamlined services. During 2008, a range of initiatives were introduced to improve overall task prioritization and ultimately increase transparency and client alignment. QIC plans to continue to consolidate and scale activities to ensure that the platforms they provide continue to deliver efficient, cost-effective solutions (QIC 2008, p. 14).

In order to cope with various external forces, QIC is continuously in a mode of reviewing and improving their processes. Such projects (also referred to as "improvement initiatives" in some parts of this chapter) within QIC are divided into three categories, mostly determined by the productive time and cost required to complete the task. These can broadly be categorized as follows:

- Low level: Costs less than Au $20,000.00 and requires approximately 20 person days or less to complete;
- Mid-range: Costs between Au $20,000.00–100,000.00, and requires approximately 20–100 person days to complete;
- High level: Costs more than Au $100,000.00, and requires more than 100 person days to complete.

Each project type has a separate governance structure and draws resources from overlapping resource pools. The tool presented here was designed to assist the prioritization of low- and mid-ranged projects only. High-ranged projects followed a different process, and hence are out of the scope of this chapter. The applications/process improvement team at QIC receives approximately 10 project requests every week (on an average, 10% of these are low-level projects and 90% are mid-range projects). In the past, this team was being utilized on a "first come first served" basis, meaning that improvement initiatives were actioned without an optimal prioritization or evaluation stage taking place. Furthermore, while many project requests still remained in the pipeline, new projects would be added to the queue and possibly actioned "out of turn", especially if the requester emphasized the perceived importance of the project, and depending on the pressure that a particular group of developers/process improvers were experiencing from an internal client. The company ran the risk of fewer things being completed on time as a result of having too much in the pipeline and having to address the disappointment from the various business areas (especially those who had their requests pushed for later, with the newer requests being accepted). The company did not have a transparent mechanism by which the actual business value for any of the requested projects was calculated, nor was there a record of which projects were pushed forward or backward and by whom. Furthermore, as a result of QIC's increasingly commercial focus, there are only limited resources available to work on requests at any one time, and more requests are received than the applications/process improvement team has the capacity to deliver. As a result, a call to review this process was made early in 2008 and a review commenced in April 2008.

A number of objectives that had to be addressed were raised very early:

1. All projects should be evaluated and ranked on the basis of a robust business value score (BVS[3]).
2. A complete view of risk, opportunity, and costs must be captured in determining the business value of the proposed project.
3. The scoring system must have balanced dimensions to capture the softer and harder aspects that are important to QIC's strategic direction when determining risk and opportunity.
4. The method should allow the risk and opportunity to be assessed by both the assenting ("by doing the project") and dissenting ("by not doing the project") views.
5. The overall scoring of a project to determine its business value should take minimal time.
6. The resulting BVS must be a genuine value; hence more than one person should be involved to score the cost and risk assessments.

[3]BVS is a comparative rating which will be used to rank and prioritize all requests for change (RFCs) submitted for development/delivery. It is a measure of the value of a change request, relative to its cost. See Fig. 1 for further details.

7. The resulting BVS must be simple enough to enable the comparison of different projects.
8. All related decisions must be made transparent to relevant stakeholders.

The goal was to derive a single numeric value that would be calculated with sufficient completeness (applying appropriate dimensions and accurate values and assessed by more than one person), so that it would be very clear what project choice is to be made just by simply comparing the numbers. The aim was to have a multidimensional, multilevel, multistakeholder approach in assessment, but collapse the result down to a single number.

# 3 Building the Business Value Scoring Tool

A number of options were investigated to see if a process selection method could be borrowed to fulfill the above-mentioned goals. Some examples included Kaplan and Norton's Balanced Scorecard (Kaplan and Norton, 1992); the Australian Business Excellence Framework (Australian Quality Council 2001); Critical process identification method (Huxley 2003; Huxley and Stewart 2008); the Australian/New Zealand Risk Management Guidelines AS/NZS 4360 (Standards Association of Australia & Standards New Zealand 1999); and an in-house-built method titled the "Process Filtering Model".[4] None of these was able to address the goals and requirements of the proposed process selection model. Hence a new tool/method was designed aiming to fulfill this.

## 3.1 *High Level Overview of the Business Value Scoring Tool*

The tool allows a requester, within approximately 5 min[5], to score a particular project to determine its business value. There are two main parts to it: (1) a risk and opportunity assessment (ROA, which has six dimensions that it works off) and (2) cost. The ROA[6] score is divided by the Cost to give a final BVS. Costing and risk

[4]This was designed to filter through a set of processes that QIC was looking to improve, which was designed and implemented to manage the prioritization of high ranged projects. In most cases it helped identify areas for improvement, but it did not equate to the available resources."*a list came back with 20 and we distilled that down to 10, but we really only had capability to work on 3, 2 or 3, 3 or 4, and so we had to objectively assess, well which 4 is it going to be*"(Operations Strategy Manager, QIC, Personal Comm.,10.07.2008).

[5]This time frame was only to fill the tool components. It was assumed that the requester would be intimate enough with the requested project to be able to enter the details into the tool without further investigation.

[6]ROA, or Risk and Opportunity Assessment, is a measure of a (requests for change) RFC's value to the business. It requires a critical assessment of the RFC and its value, either through delivery of a benefit or the mitigation of a risk.

**Fig. 1** Business value score calculation formula

*Simple concept:*

$$BVS = \frac{ROA}{Total\ costs}$$

*(a)Detailed formula:*

$$BVS = \frac{ROA \times 1000}{(\sqrt{Total\ costs})}$$

Where ROA is;

$$ROA = \sum_{All\ dimensions} (Outcome\ score \times dimension\ weight)$$

and opportunity scoring is done by two separate parties. The two tasks of calculating the costs and deriving the ROA are deliberately kept independent of each other, to avoid one value influencing the other. There are constants included in the calculation to manage the potential variations. See Fig. 1 for the overall formula for the BVS calculation. The following sections describe each of the main elements of the tool. Appendix 2 provides a summary of the BVS model (initial and revised versions).

## *3.2 Understanding the Components of the Tool*

### 3.2.1 Dimensions of Measurement

Six dimensions were identified as critical components to consider when assessing Risk and Opportunity for a project: namely, Reputation, Clients, Business Processes, Financial Opportunity, Regulation and Compliance, and Human Resources. Both tangible and intangible dimensions were included to maintain a balanced, complete measurement perspective (following Kaplan and Norton 1992). These were based on ideas generated from past literature (i.e., Australian Quality Council 2001; Kaplan and Norton 1992; Standards Association of Australia & Standards New Zealand 1999), workshops conducted with the developers and requesters, and one-to-one interviews that were conducted with the program managers (those who sponsored the approved projects). They were also evaluated and approved by the General Manager for the Division of Operations at QIC.

The primary criteria for the identification and adaption of these dimensions were based on corporate strategy. Each dimension had to contribute directly or indirectly to QIC's corporate strategy and each dimension was granted a relative weighting (see Table 1 and Column 1 in Fig. 3) to indicate how much each contributed to corporate strategy. These weighting values were derived on the basis of information collected from various strategy-related communications in the organization and was confirmed by the General Manager of Operations at QIC, through a series of face-to-face meetings. They were also presented at workshops to participating QIC employees (using the tool) for further feedback and validation.

**Table 1** Dimensions of the business value score tool and their relative weightings

| Dimension | Definition | Weights (as of date) |
|---|---|---|
| Reputation | The Reputation dimension was included to focus attention on the fact that requested changes should contribute to maintaining the good reputation of QIC | 16% |
| Clients | The Clients dimension was included to align with QIC's corporate strategy and recognize that QIC's mission is to provide high-quality investment management and consulting services to maximize investment returns for our clients, consistent with their expectations and risk tolerances | 22% |
| Business processes | The Business Process dimension was included, as QIC's ever increasing commercial focus demands that continual improvements be made to offer excellent service to clients while maximizing investment returns | 12% |
| Financial opportunity | The Financial Opportunity dimension was included to align with QIC's corporate strategy | 22% |
| Regulation and compliance | The Regulation and Compliance dimension was included as QIC's vision is to be a leading provider of professional and disciplined investment management services and to remain at the forefront of industry best practice | 16% |
| Human resources | The Human Resources dimension was included in recognition that people are what QIC's success is built on | 12% |

The senior management determines and controls the content and weightings of the dimensions. These dimension weightings are used as multipliers of the outcome scores when deriving the BVS score (see Fig. 1b and the Sect. 3.2.2).

### 3.2.2 Outcomes and Scores for Each Dimension

The outcome components were designed to capture the anticipated impact of the proposed project to QIC through simple quantitative means. The requester of the project had to score the project across each dimension. They had three main categories of options to select from (see Columns 2 and 3 in Fig. 3); (1) no impact, (2) anticipated impact when evaluating the project from the perspective of "doing" the project, and (3) anticipated impact when evaluating the project from the perspective of "not doing" the project (see Sect. 3.2.3 for further details on the *doing* and *not doing* options).

One would choose the *no impact* option if there was no justifiable impact from the requested project on a particular dimension. Each of the *doing* and *not doing* action categories have five outcomes to choose from (see Columns 2 and 3 in Fig. 3). The intention was to describe the outcome of the project in association with the dimension in a progressive way and in a simple and clear manner. It was decided to have only five options to describe possible outcomes to maintain simplicity (following scale development and psychometric literature). These outcome descriptors were derived from an iterative effort with multiple rounds, which were completed through a series of workshops. The final version (as depicted in Appendix 2) was validated by the company executives, who critically evaluated each description looking at their alignment with corporate strategy.

Each outcome descriptor had an outcome score (from 12 to 52) to align with the progressive way they were intended to relate to the dimension (see Column 4 in Fig. 3). The outcome scores were squared [12–52 (1, 4, 9, 16, 25) instead of leaving at 1, 2, 3, 4, 5] to create a greater separation in the final score, and give greater weight to those dimensions that scored highly.

It is acknowledged that there may be subjectivity on which outcome descriptor is used based on each individual who scores the project; from person to person, they might move up or down one level. But the idea is that once a person scores a project, he/she has to be able to stand by it and give good reasons why the things were scored the way they were, if asked to explain. Qualitative, descriptive information is not collected within the tool, as it defeats the "minimal time for entry" requirement. However, all assessors are asked to make sure that they can justify their selected options upon request by the company, and this information is closely audited through the overall change management process.

### 3.2.3 Choice of Evaluation Perspective

The tool was designed to allow the scoring around two action choices (perspectives): "by doing" and "by not doing" the proposed project (see Fig. 3, Column 2). This enabled the assessor to comment on either opportunity or risk for each dimension[7]. A "by doing" action states that the piece of work being assessed aims to pursue an opportunity for a given dimension. A "by not doing" action states that the piece of work being assessed aims to mitigate a risk for a given dimension. For example, one can either say "by doing a particular project, a particular gain is obtained" and "by not doing a particular thing (within a certain dimension), the company could stand to make a particular loss (i.e., loss of reputation, loss of financial opportunity, loss of staff, etc.)." The tool enables one to mix between "by doing" and "by not doing" actions across dimensions within the evaluation of a single proposed project. This was built in to support the fact that while some projects may aim to mitigate against a risk in a particular dimension, it may simultaneously seek to produce opportunity in another dimension.

During the initial roll out (see the Sect. 4 for a further update), all dimensions (except for the Regulation and Compliance dimension) had both choices; by doing and by not doing. For example, Financial Opportunity can make money (opportunity)

[7]To further elaborate, when 'by not doing' is chosen, it means the assessor wants to validate the importance of doing the project by depicting the negative impact to the company by not doing the project, hence gaining support for doing the project (arguing "don't not do it"). The tool is designed to score the outcomes showing how business value is obtained by mitigating against the negative impact.

or prevent losing money (risk mitigation); Reputation can boost the company reputation (opportunity) or can prevent losing the current status (risk mitigation). The Regulation and Compliance dimension only has the "by not doing" option, as compliance does not bring opportunity, rather it only mitigates risk. This dimension in the tool is related purely to the regulation compliance side of things, thus, with the law and regulation compliance, one only has to comply as there are hardly any new opportunities to reach.

The assessor can select either action (by doing *or* by not doing) for a particular dimension and select the outcome options that would best suit the project request (see details in Sect. 3.2.2 and in Fig. 3). Sometimes the choice between "by doing" and "by not doing" could result in quite different scores[8] (as one looks at it from an opportunity view and the other from a risk mitigation view). Thus, when either action ("by doing" and "not doing") could be an option, the assessor has the choice to select the best one (the one with the highest score for the dimension) to support their request.

> "So if 'by not doing' was going to get you a score of 1, but 'by doing' was going to get you a score of four squared, sixteen.., then that's the one you would choose, because ultimately you want your BVS high, because you want your piece of work to get done."
>
> *(BVS Tool Designer and Developer 1, QIC, Personal Comm., 25.11.2008)*

### 3.2.4 Cost Calculations

The cost calculations are not done as part of this tool. It is calculated separately using common cost estimation methods (e.g., Briand and Wieczorek 2002; Jorgensen 2004) and entered into the tool for the BVS calculation purposes. It is useful to note here that for the purpose of segregation of powers and to mediate any BVS score manipulations, the costing is done by a different person to the one requesting the project. The business representative requesting the project (most commonly the ORM for the business unit) will complete the ROA. The Project Manager or Developer actioning the change does the cost calculations, which is done separately for each project request, at a line-by-line level.

### 3.2.5 Formula Manipulation

The basic formula was manipulated (also see Fig. 1b) to yield best results for the purpose. The three main elements worthy of discussion are as follows: (1)

[8]See the Financial and HR dimensions outcome options in Fig. 3, for example. The Financial Dimension has the exact opposite, mirror image for both options, where as Human Resources dimension does not – hence potentially yielding different scores depending on which option was chosen.

calculation of dimension scores; (2) the square rooting of the costs; and (3) a constant of 1000 used as a multiplier for ROA. The BVS formula employs exponents in both the ROA calculation and the division by cost in order to achieve a realistic result of business value.

As mentioned earlier, in the ROA calculation, dimensions are scored in the form $d = z^x$, where $x$ is set to 2 and $z$ has a range between 1 and 5. The exponent $x = 2$ produces dispersion in the values of $d$ so as to avoid clumping (the values sitting too closely together), making it easier to discern between higher and lower values. Naturally, as $x$ grows large, values of $d$ disperse more widely. For QIC's purposes, $x$ set to 2 provided for ample dispersion. Other implementations of the BVS formula could set $x$ to any real value. However, for practical purposes, $1 \leq x \leq 3$ deems sensible as it produces a spread between values that is spaced widely enough but not excessively so.

It is reasoned that higher cost projects have less business value than lower cost projects with near or equal ROA values. To encapsulate this in the formula, the process of dividing ROA by cost is performed. However, due to existing dispersion in the dollar values of projects (moving in $1000 increments in the case of QIC), it was necessary to make a mathematical adjustment that would cluster the cost divisors, so as to produce sensible results. Dividing by nonclustered cost amounts resulted in projects with high cost achieving very low BVS values, which was not in line with company expectations of project value.

The cost divisor is denoted as $v = c^{1/y}$, where $c$ is cost and $y$ is set to 2 (thus, being equal to the square root of $c$). As $y$ grows large, values of $v$ cluster more closely. For QIC's purposes, $y$ set to 2 provided for acceptable clustering of cost divisors. Other implementations of the BVS formula could set $y$ to any real value. When $y$ was set to 1, BVS values produced by the formula were flawed; all high-cost projects achieved low BVS values and all low-cost projects achieved high BVS values. It is reasoned that such a result should not be the case across a diverse range of projects. When $y$ was set to 2, sensible BVS values were achieved (i.e., not all high cost projects are given low BVS values, which is not sensible).

The ROA values were multiplied by a constant (1000) in order to derive meaningful integer values for the resulting BVSs. It was found that without doing this, the resulting numbers were more difficult to understand for stakeholders, both for comparative and communicative purposes. This is a common practice in many mathematical formulas for business use, to make the resulting value easy to read and comprehensible by the users (e.g., DPO calculation used in Six Sigma projects (Breyfogle 2003; Chowdhury 2005)).

We acknowledge some limitations with this approach. In the current implementation of the BVS formula, both $x$ and $y$ are set to 2. While setting $x$ and $y$ to 2 produces excellent results for project prioritization of QIC's current project portfolio, it is not expected that setting $x$ and $y$ to 2 is optimal as a general case, especially for the variable y. It is expected that the value for $y$ would need to depend on the variability in project cost amounts. The expectation is that the higher the variability in cost amounts, the larger $y$ would need to be to produce sensible BVS values.

## 4 Testing and Implementing the Tool

The validation of the tool occurred in a few stages (see Table 2). Validation activities were built into the very early phases of the tool design. As mentioned earlier, the measurement dimensions and outcome descriptions were created with the interactive and iterative input from the tool users (the ORMs and Business Unit Representatives from QIC's different business units). The dimensions and their weights were also validated by senior management in the tool design phase.

A pilot phase was conducted prior to implementing the tool in the wider business, mainly to cater for user acceptance testing. For this, a random sample of 20 outstanding project requests was selected from the existing project request pool. Eighteen project requesters (mostly ORMs and/or Business Unit Representatives) responded, and they were asked to use the tool to derive a BVS value for the project request they represented. While they were aware of the tool and its functionality (by taking part in the tool design phase), a detailed workshop was conducted to orient them to the tool components and its purposes. All projects were scored after this workshop by the relevant ORM or Business Unit Representatives (who took part in the workshop). These results were then brought into a round table discussion facilitated by the two tool designers.

Inter-person variation with regard to differing BVS values was a critical observation made through this test. The round table session was conducted to investigate the cause for these variations. Projects were scored together by the participants "thinking out loud," which illustrated that the dimensions and outcomes can be interpreted by individuals in very diverse ways. Hence the need for very clear definitions and examples was identified. These were implemented for the next round (through enhanced documentation about the tool and the tool usage process).

The tool was also presented and approved by the executives prior to final implementation. These stages were undertaken to ensure that people within the company felt confident that they were actually using a tool that was in line with the company's strategic direction.

The final phase of validation was a 3-month post-implementation testing phase. The tool was made available through the change management process, and any project request that was made from mid-September 2008 had to present a BVS

**Table 2** Business value score tool validation phases

| Validation round | Time period | Involved stakeholders |
|---|---|---|
| Design phase | April–July 2008 | Operations relationship managers<br>Business unit members<br>Senior management |
| Pilot phase | August 2008 | Operations relationship managers<br>Business unit members<br>Senior management |
| Post-implementation testing | October–December 2008 | Operations relationship managers<br>Business unit members |

score with the request (with justification, if required). The goal was to see how the tool as a whole and its separate components (i.e., dimensions, outcome descriptors, weights, formulas, etc.) actually functioned when placed in a real-world business context.

Detailed resources in the form of step-by-step user guidelines and power-point slides (all made available on the corporate intranet) were derived and distributed to all tool users. Face-to-face training was conducted to orient the users to the tool and how best to use it. Four primary observations were made from this phase. These, together with the actions taken in response, are briefly described below.

1. *The terminology of the tool can have different meanings to different business units*: The tool was designed in a manner that was applicable to the entire business. However, this can at times cause confusion. For example, with the "Client" dimension, a business unit can have external clients (customers), internal clients (other employees of QIC), or both. Thus, depending on which client cohort one looks at, the scoring for the Clients section can vary. The tool-user guidelines were updated to assist interpretation in such situations.
2. *The mutual exclusivity of the dimensions was questioned*: Mutual exclusivity of the dimensions and if one can "double claim" the same aspect across two or more dimensions was another concern raised. For example, with certain change requests, a process change (i.e., increased efficiency) can be reached while at the same time reducing costs (i.e., changing from manual to automated operations, thereby reducing the required people costs). The user guidelines are updated to clarify whether the same aspect can be included in two or more dimensions if it genuinely brings different (disjoint) benefits and this can be justified.
3. *The Client dimension had to be adjusted*: During the implementation phase, the feedback received from the tool users pointed to the need to edit the Client dimension of the tool. It was recognized that client engagement at QIC were of two different types (namely; client reporting and interaction, and client service delivery) and that the QIC clientele could be clustered around three kinds of clients that they grouped as Gold, Platinum, and Diamond. These had to be represented in the revised outcome options. Further feedback also proved that the "by not doing" action option was not relevant to the client dimension. Thus, the overall Client dimension was changed (see Fig. 4) to address these observations made in the post-implementation testing phase.
4. *Sometimes the BVS score alone is not enough to determine which projects are to be addressed first*: While the BVS indicated the business value a project would bring to the company, this alone was at times not enough to decide upon which project to address first. Mapping the project characteristics (where the BVS played a significant role in determining priorities) to the available resources was a critical task that has to be done outside the BVS tool. For example, while completing a project with a high BVS score, it might also be feasible to merge the efforts with a lesser significant project (one with a lower BVS score) and let it piggyback the bigger one. Projects with a high BVS score might have to be assigned to experienced senior staff, while those with a lower BVS can be

assigned to a junior staff in training. These examples meant that projects with a lower BVS could be completed earlier than those with a higher BVS because of resource availability.

A forum takes place twice a week at QIC to support this mediation, where the project requesting party (represented by the ORMs and/or Business Unit Representatives) and the Change Managers get together to discuss the final decisions on the ranked projects. This is when the actual resource allocations for the projects and any proposed changes to the prioritization list, generated by the tool, are discussed. The decisions made within these forums are carefully captured and archived for trend analysis and auditing purposes. The concept of a "Notional BVS" (see next section for details) was also formalized to allow for and manage such intervention to the BVS.

The limitations identified in these validation efforts have been addressed, and the tool has been deployed at QIC since December 2008.

# 5 Tool Adoptability and Application

The core components of the BVS tool (the dimensions, the action options, the outcomes and scores, etc.) and the overall validation of its components were presented in the sections above. The goal was to build a feasible, transparent project selection method. While the sections above described the tool as it currently stands, it can be edited and changed to suit changing organizational circumstances. For example, the dimensions can be edited or new dimensions introduced in response to emerging strategic directions. Furthermore, the weights assigned to each dimension can also change (even without any of the dimensions themselves changing) to respond to changes in strategic focus. These changes will only be allowed in long-term intervals (encouraged only every 12 months to reflect changed business directions) with appropriate validations and approval from the senior management.

While the tool will automatically produce a report of the projects, from highest business value to the lowest, this ranking is mediated and the requests' ranking can still be adjusted manually (via discussions at the forum mentioned earlier) – but only with evidence to justify why the requested change was made. All such change requests are recorded and periodically evaluated to identify potential patterns.

> "3 months, 6 months, 12 months down the track, we can print off a report that says okay, what was moved from which rank to which rank. Who motioned for it to be moved and does this person keep moving things all the time."... "It will also help to see what reviews or changes the tool requires as time passes with its application in the company."
> *(BVS Tool Designer and Developer 1, QIC, Personal Comm., 25.11.2008)*

The concept of a "Notional BVS" was developed to allow for human intervention in the final derived BVS. This was in acknowledgement of the fact that owing to the wide variety of project request types received, it may not always be possible for a single model to adequately capture all dimensions of all requests. For example, short-term market conditions may necessitate rapid development and/or modification to existing processes of a business. Urgency is not a dimension included in the BVS model, as urgency does not necessarily imply importance. However, should this need be reflected in the final BVS, a notional BVS can be applied. Following discussion with all involved stakeholders, should it be decided to increase the priority of a requested project, this can be done by overwriting the existing BVS. The possibility for manual intervention increases the flexibility of the system overall. It is important to note that this stage is also fully transparent and auditable, with any notional BVS being suffixed with the letter "n" in the records residing with the tool. It is also necessary for the person who has successfully requested that a notional BVS be applied to register not only their name but also the reason for the application of the notional score. Other situations in which notional BVS would be assigned to a project request include the following:

- A small, simple piece of work which could be packaged with a larger work item (requiring the same skill set) to realize operational efficiency;
- A relatively simple piece of work which may be used to upskill a staff member on a particular skill set.

The BVS tool explained here is very flexible, allowing the company to adjust the tool to address varying environmental and organizational changes. However, it is recommended to review such changes only in longitudinal intervals (i.e., annually) because if the BVS tool's underlying model changes too often, it could invalidate the tool in the eyes of stakeholders. In any case, once bedded into an organization, it is thought that changes to such a tool would only be made to reflect changes in a company's strategic outlook which, in reality, change over timescales measured in years, not months or weeks. QIC's model was built with this in mind, allowing any changes applied to the model to be retrospectively applied to all outstanding change requests in the pipeline, allowing a consistent "apples with apples" comparison between both new and queued requests.

This tool has enabled QIC to achieve its goals. All projects are ranked on the basis of a BVS using a tool, which takes minimal time to complete. This assessment captures the risk, opportunity, and costs, with a balanced set of dimensions (that captured softer and harder aspects that are important to QIC's strategic direction) and the method allows the project to be assessed from both assenting and dissenting views. Different people are involved in the scoring process to maintain genuine results, and the ultimate values (BVSs) are simple to interpret and compare against different projects. All related decisions about what projects are funded and in what order they are completed are transparent to all relevant stakeholders.

> In a nutshell, transparency is what we are looking for; transparency into what is valuable, transparency into who is requesting things, transparency into what is the demand, what is the supply.
>
> *(Operations Strategy Manager, QIC, Personal Comm., 10.07. 2008)*

The tool also enables QIC to conduct and maintain justifiable, transparent business decisions, not only for current project selection but also for long-term planning.

> The application of the tool enables us to analyze what types of projects are requested and what kinds of skills are sought for... Which of these QIC has and which ones QIC should further develop or seek externally for.
>
> *(Business Process Manager, QIC, Personal Comm., 10.07.2008)*

# 6 Conclusion

This chapter described a BVS model that can be used to assist with project selection decisions for business improvements. It described the current status of project selection challenges for process improvement and introduced the case organization (QIC) which this chapter is based upon. QIC, like most other organizations also was facing these common challenges of project selection. *How does one know which project to commence work on? How is the project's value to the business justified and explained? How can these decisions be made in a fair, justifiable manner that brings the best results to QIC and its stakeholders?* These are just some of the questions that QIC's decision makers were faced with in early 2008.

Every organization is striving for the means to identify only the most value-adding, feasible projects, while stakeholders demand that all decisions made are transparent and justifiable. QIC designed and tested a simple yet robust tool to address this challenge. All details of the tool, i.e., its fundamental concepts, all its elements, the design, validation, and application process, were presented in this chapter in detail. The BVS tool presented here can be adopted and applied within any organization, in particular to support the decision making of small to medium scale process improvement requests.

The tool presented here has a few limitations. For example, the resource planning aspect is not automated as part of the tool. There is also no facility within the tool to account for "project health"; i.e., to take into account what other contextual factors might constitute the success of a project. Arguably, however, this is not something that should be considered when looking solely at project value. Future adopters may use the tool presented here as a basis and add these enhanced features with additional research. Furthermore, we acknowledge some limitations with the calculations related to the tool. In the current implementation of the BVS formula, as explained in Sect. 3.2.5, the ROA is multiplied by a constant 1000, and the square root of the cost is used instead of the direct cost in the formula. While these settings produced suitable results for project prioritization of QIC's current project portfolio, it is not expected that this is optimal as a general case. This is especially true when manipulating the cost variable, and there is need to make this decision on the variability of the costs for the project that this tool will be used for. The chapter explains the rationale behind these manipulations that the future tool adopters can consider when adopting the associated formulas. Further research would propose that a mathematical link be made in the formula between the cost divisor and the variability of cost amounts in the project portfolio.

There are no current plans to further amend the tool at QIC because it is already being used companywide, and constant changing of dimensions and weightings would invalidate the tool. Only major changes in strategic direction should cause the need for significant modification to the tool.

## Appendix 1: QIC Organizational Chart

Figure 2 depicts the QIC organizational chart after the structural changes conducted in 2008. One of the key changes was the introduction of ORMs. ORMs act as a central point of contact between Operations and the other business areas of QIC. Thus, six new ORMs and an ORM manager were appointed to represent the different business units. Divisions without an ORM have a named Business Unit Representative who fulfills the same interface function between their area and Operations.

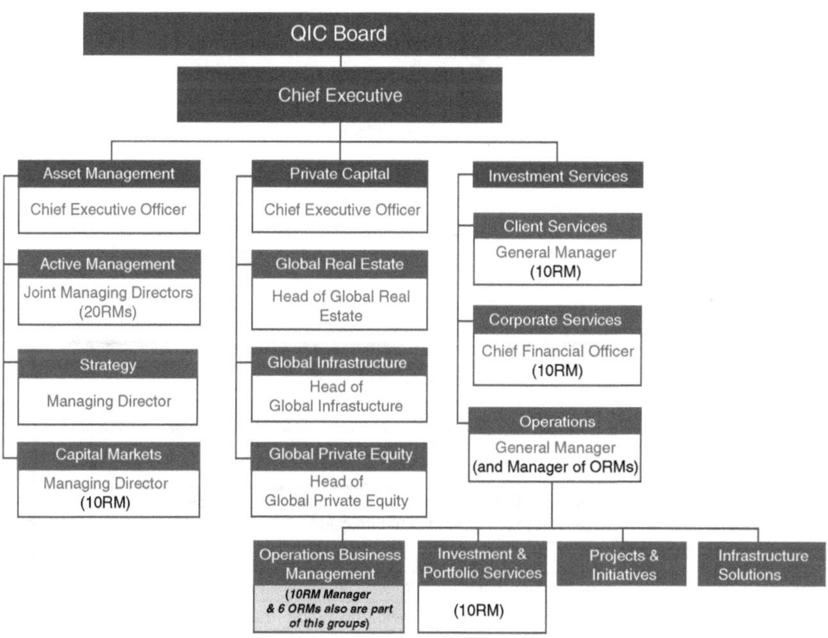


Fig. 2 QIC organizational chart

# Appendix 2: Business Value Score Tool Elements

See Figs. 3 and 4.

| *Col 1* | *Col 2* | *Col 3* | *Col 4* |
|---|---|---|---|
| Dimension and relative weight | Selected action | Outcome | Outcome score |
| FINANCIAL OPPORTUNITY (22%) | ***No Impact*** | No impact on financial opportunity | 0 |
| | ***By Doing*** | Will result in a financial gain of $10k | 1 |
| | | Will result in a financial gain of $100k | 4 |
| | | Will result in a financial gain of $250k | 9 |
| | | Will result in a financial gain of $1m | 16 |
| | | Will result in a financial gain of $5m | 25 |
| | ***By Not Doing*** | Will result in a financial loss of $10k | 1 |
| | | Will result in a financial loss of $100k | 4 |
| | | Will result in a financial loss of $250k | 9 |
| | | Will result in a financial loss of $1m | 16 |
| | | Will result in a financial loss of $5m | 25 |
| REGULATION & COMPLIANCE (16%) | ***No Impact*** | No impact on regulation or compliance | 0 |
| | ***By Not Doing*** | Will be in breach of QIC policy | 1 |
| | | Likely to be in breach of industry regulation | 4 |
| | | Sure to be in breach of industry regulation | 9 |
| | | Likely to be in breach of statutory or case law | 16 |
| | | Sure to be in breach of statutory or case law | 25 |
| HUMAN RESOURCES (12%) | ***No Impact*** | No impact on human resources | 0 |
| | ***By Doing*** | Like to cause a slight upturn in staff morale | 1 |
| | | Likely to have a positive impact on staff morale | 4 |
| | | Likely to aid retention of key staff | 9 |
| | | Sure to aid retention of key staff | 16 |
| | | Contributes and aligns with strategic HR objectives | 25 |
| | ***By Not Doing*** | Likely to cause a slight downturn in staff morale | 1 |
| | | Likely to have a negative impact on staff morale | 4 |
| | | Likely to cause >25% staff turnover at department level within 6 months | 9 |
| | | Likely to cause >50% staff turnover at department level within 6 months | 16 |
| | | Likely to cause >50% staff turnover at division level within 6 months | 25 |

**Fig. 3** Summary of the initial business value score tool

| | ***Selected Action*** | ***Outcome*** | ***Score*** |
|---|---|---|---|
| CLIENTS (22%) | | No impact on client relationship | 0 |
| | By doing | will bring about a Client Reporting and Interaction/ Client Service Delivery benefit to a gold client | 1 |
| | | will bring about a Client Reporting and Interaction/ Client Service Delivery benefit to a diamond/platinum client | 4 |
| | | will improve a gold client's investment performance | 9 |
| | | will improve a platinum client's investment performance | 16 |
| | | will improve a diamond client's investment performance | 25 |

**Fig. 4** Summary of the revised business value score tool

## References


Australian Quality Council (2001) Australian business excellence framework, Australian Quality Council, Sydney

Blosch M, McDonald MP, Stevens S (2005) Delivering it's contribution: the 2005 CIO agenda, Gartner EXP Premier Reports, Gartner

Breyfogle FW (ed) (2003) Implementing six sigma: smarter solutions using statistical methods, 2nd edn. Wiley, Hoboken, NJ

Briand LC, Wieczorek I (eds) (2002) Resource estimation in software engineering. Wiley, New York

Burlton R (2010) Delivering business strategy through process management. In: vom Brocke J, Rosemann M (eds) Handbook on business process management, vol 2. Springer, Heidelberg

Chowdhury S (ed) (2005) Design for six sigma: the revolutionary process for achieving extraordinary profits. Dearborn Trade, Chicago, IL

Davenport T (1993) Process Innovation: re-engineering work through information technology. Harvard Business School, Cambridge, MA

Hammer M, Champy J (1993) Reengineering the corporation: A manifesto for business revolution. HarperCollins, New York

Harmon P (2005) BPM Governance. BPTrends E-Mail Advisor, 3(3), February 8, 2005. Retrieved from http://www.bptrends.com/publicationfiles/bptemailadvisor020805.pdf

Huxley C (2003) An improved method to identify critical processes. Queensland University of Technology, Brisbane

Huxley C, Stewart G (eds) (2008) Reducing the Odds: A Practioners Guide to Identifying Critical Processes: VDM Verlag Dr. Muller Aktiengesellschaft & Co. KG, Saarbrucken, Germany

Jorgensen M (2004) A review of studies on expert estimation of software development effort. J Syst Softw 70(1–2):37–60

Kaplan RS, Norton DP (eds) (1992) The Balanced Scorecard: Measures that Drive Performance, 1 edition Vol. 70. Harv Bus Rev

Kirchmer M (ed) (2009) High Performance Through Process Excellence – From Strategy to Operations, Berlin Heidelberg: Springer-Verlag

Kirchmer M (2010) Management of process excellence. In: vom Brocke J, Rosemann M (eds) Handbook on business process management, vol 2. Springer, Heidelberg

McDonald MP, Nunno T (2007) Creating enterprise leverage: the 2007 CIO agenda, Gartner EXP Premier Reports, Gartner

McDonald MP, Blosch M, Jaffarian T, Mok L, Stevens S (2006) Growing it's contribution: the 2006 CIO agenda, Gartner EXP Premier Reports, Gartner

McDonald MP, Nunno T, Aron D (2008) Making the difference: the 2008 CIO agenda, Gartner EXP Premier Reports, Gartner

Olding E, Rosser B (2007) Getting started With BPM, Part 3: understanding critical success factors, Gartner Research 4 October 2007 ID Number: G00151762, Gartner Inc

QIC (2008) QIC Annual Report, Brisbane, QLD

Standards Association of Australia, & Standards New Zealand (1999) Risk management standards, Strathfield, NSW

Thorp J (ed) (1998) The information paradox. Realizing the business benefits of information technology. McGraw-Hill, New York

# Part II
# Governance

## Governance

The often dominating focus on the managerial challenges of process-related initiatives has to be embedded in guiding principles that clearly define roles and responsibilities and decision making for BPM, both on a program and on a project management level. This area is captured by the notion of BPM Governance. It is dedicated to questions such as: Who is responsible for which process? What decision rights rest with a process owner? What are the reporting structures in an organization that aims toward increased process orientation? How can we set incentives in order to enable an efficient performance of processes? What responsibilities are assigned to a central BPM Center of Excellence?

At least two dimensions of BPM Governance can be differentiated: (a) the governance of processes, and (b) the governance of process management itself. These two dimensions form part of the following opening chapters: In the first chapter, M. Lynne Markus and Dax D. Jacobson give an introduction to the domain of governing processes. They point out various mechanisms when designing a cost-effective governance structure. The authors ensure a better understanding of the specific advantages and challenges of these mechanisms by granting practical insight into highly informative cases, that is, Texas Instruments and Procter and Gamble. In the second chapter, Andrew Spanyi takes the perspective of governing the management of business processes. He reflects on how successful companies are able to sustain and optimize performance improvements. Presenting specific principles and practices for BPM Governance, he provides sound guidelines for the practical deployment and a valuable point of reference for the remainder of the section.

After these two introductory articles, specific facets of BPM Governance are considered. First, August-Wilhelm Scheer and Eric Brabänder focus on the process of BPM. The authors take a holistic, organization-wide perspective and identify phases, roles, and responsibilities that are required along the entire process of process management. As a major element, the widely adopted concept of a so-called BPM

Center of Excellence (CoE) is then described in detail by Michael Rosemann. He concentrates on the typical set of services that is provided by such an organizational unit, elaborates on the idea of service portfolio management and discusses the outcomes of an empirical study that shows the popularity of different CoE services. The next chapter builds well on this discussion by showcasing the specific setup of such a BPM Center of Excellence in the case of a Brazilian organization. This chapter by Leandro Jesus, André Macieira, Daniel Karrer, and Heitor Caulliraux explains also how the role of the CoE might change over time.

Against this background, we then address major challenges in BPM Governance. We first take a look at the balancing act between global and local BPM. The chapter of Roger Tregear on Business Process Standardization discusses these issues which are most relevant for all companies operating on a global scale. A global BPM framework is described, which is meant to facilitate the management of the conflicting demands of both global efficiency and local effectiveness. As another current topic of global interest, the growing field of Business Process Outsourcing (BPO) is examined. In addition to decision making on outsourcing, the management of outsourcing relations is an essential element for future BPM Governance. This is the focus of the chapter by Jyoti M. Bhat, Jude Fernancez, Manish Kumar, and Sukriti Goel. The authors present a framework for BPM analysis and also report on case studies from Infosys BPO as a global offshore BPO provider.

We close this section with two practical cases on Business Process Governance in which the various issues mentioned earlier are tackled in an integrated manner. First, the case of ThyssenKruppPresta, presented by Stefan Novotny and Nicholas Rohmann, report from results in implementing a global Process Management System. Second, a chapter on experiences from implementing BPM in the public administration presented by Jörg Zwicker, Peter Fettke and Peter Loos elaborates on the role of BPM Maturity management.

# Business Process Governance

**M. Lynne Markus and Dax D. Jacobson**

**Abstract** Good business process governance is necessary for the success of business processes, which in turn are essential for business success. The term business process governance refers to the direction, coordination, and control of individuals, groups, or organizations that are at least to some extent autonomous: that is, not directly subject to the same hierarchical authority. Business process governance comprises a variety of mechanisms that may be impersonal (e.g., laws or rules) or personal (i.e., administered by individuals who may or may not have formally designated responsibility or accountability for governance). All governance mechanisms have pros and cons; some mechanisms are more effective (and more costly) than others. The challenge is to design a cost-effective governance structure, which usually consists of several mechanisms working in combination. This chapter describes various governance mechanisms, identifies their advantages and disadvantages, and provides examples that reveal how governance mechanisms contribute to business process success.

## 1 Introduction

Loosely speaking, governance means direction, coordination, and control. Good governance is necessary for the success of business processes, which in turn, contribute to business success (Rosemann and de Bruin 2005). Whether business processes are inter-organizational or intra-organizational in scope, they need governance at all stages of their life cycles – when they are first designed (or are significantly redesigned), when they are operating under "business-as-usual"

M.L. Markus (✉)
Bentley University, Waltham, MA, USA
e-mail: mlmarkus@bentley.edu

J. vom Brocke and M. Rosemann (eds.), *Handbook on Business Process Management 2*, International Handbooks on Information Systems,
DOI 10.1007/978-3-642-01982-1_10, 

conditions, and when they need either minor adjustments for changing circumstances or ongoing performance improvements.

The term governance is generally used in situations wherein the individuals, groups, or organizations that need direction, coordination, and control are partially or entirely autonomous of each other. That is, they are approximately peers rather than linked in hierarchical authority relations (Lynn et al. 2001). Put differently, governance comes into play when none of the parties involved in a situation requiring coordination have the formal hierarchical authority to command others to behave in certain ways. This condition applies most obviously in the case of inter-organizational business processes, such as the business-to-business sales and purchasing processes. But the condition also characterizes many core business processes inside organizations, such as new product development or human resource management, which cut across multiple organizational functions such as marketing, manufacturing, and engineering. It may appear that vertical or hierarchical managerial authority could accomplish the direction and control of intra-organizational organization business processes, but, in fact, business process success generally requires considerable lateral coordination across units, just as inter-organizational processes do.

Many people use the term governance to refer mainly to *impersonal* or institutional mechanisms: that is, to the laws, regulations, standards, and contracts by which relationships among citizens and legal entities are arranged. Such impersonal forms of governance are essential when business processes cross the boundaries of legal entities, but, in the form of rules and procedures, impersonal governance mechanisms are common in intra-organizational business processes too.

At the same time, impersonal governance mechanisms are rarely effective unless they operate in conjunction with *personal* governance mechanisms, in which individuals act to direct, coordinate, and control a process, even though they may lack the vertical or hierarchical managerial authority to do so. For instance, in inter-organizational business processes, monitoring and the imposition of fines by the buyer are often needed to ensure that suppliers honor the terms of sales contracts. Similarly, in intra-organizational processes, personal governance may be needed to augment impersonal mechanisms such as service level agreements. Personal governance can be informal, that is, not explicitly assigned as a responsibility to particular individuals or organizations, or it may be formal. And, if personal governance is formal, it can take various forms, such as liaison roles, standing committees, coordination units, or process organizations, each of which has pros and cons.

In short, business process governance comprises several different kinds of mechanisms, each of which has advantages and disadvantages. The purpose of this chapter is to identify and describe the mechanisms, to articulate their pros and cons, and to provide examples of the mechanisms in use in real organizations – often in combinations.

The challenges of post-design process governance vary considerably with the organizational scope of the business process, that is, with the number of functional units and legal entities crossed by the process. Therefore, this chapter examines governance strategies for business processes both within and across the boundaries of legal organizational entities. However, the chapter has a more limited temporal scope. Much has been written about the governance of business process design projects (Becker et al. 2003; Kettinger and Grover 1995), such as about the need for project sponsorship, project team management, participation of stakeholders on the design team, etc. But when a process has been redesigned, the role of the project team ends. Without a careful plan for transitioning the new process into a workable governance framework, the need for effective process operation and continuous improvement is likely to conflict with management priorities in the existing authority structure, and process results will suffer. Therefore, this chapter focuses primarily on business process governance during the important, but neglected, post-design phases of the business process lifecycle.

The first major section of this chapter (1) reviews the basics of business process governance in relation to organizational structures and vertical or hierarchical authority relationships, and (2) discusses the general trade-offs in the choice of horizontal or lateral governance mechanisms for business processes. Subsequent sections provide examples – for (1) intra-organizational and (2) inter-organizational business processes – of governance mechanisms used in several well-known cases and analyze the mechanisms in these cases according to the trade-offs framework developed below.

## 2 The Management of Organizational Structures and Business Process Governance

Business process governance is challenging in intra-organizational contexts because it cannot easily be disentangled from the management of the people, functions, and organizations that perform the activities making up a business process. In this section, which draws heavily on Galbraith (1994), we explain how organizational structures and management hierarchies parallel each other, why lateral relations are needed to govern across organizational units, and how there are always trade-offs involved in the design of business process governance.

### *2.1 Management Hierarchies and Business Processes*

Intra-organizational business processes are frequently depicted as cutting horizontally across functionally structured companies or business units (see Fig. 1). In this functional organizational structure, each specialized unit, such as engineering, manufacturing, and marketing, has a manager whose goals and priorities have been set by the organization's general manager. Often, these goals and priorities have more to do with the activities of the functional units, for example, reducing the

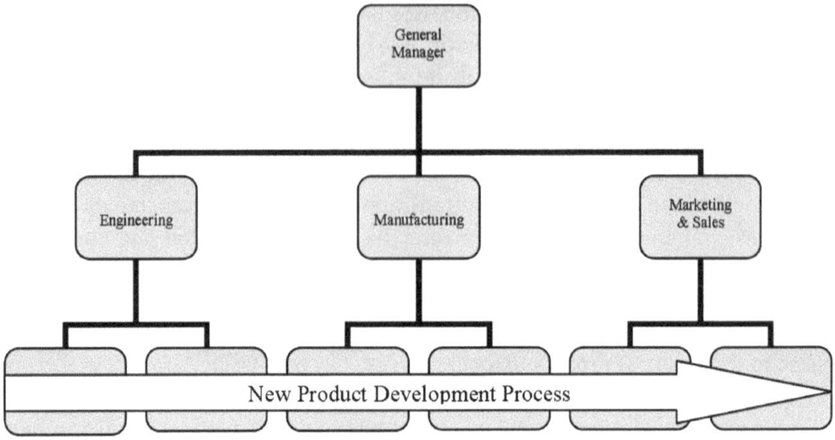


**Fig. 1** The new product development process in a functional organization

manufacturing "box" cost, than with cross-cutting process priorities such as achieving faster delivery of products to the customer. Each functional unit manager, in turn, sets goals and priorities for people within the specialized unit, assigns work to them, and measures and rewards their performance. Because no one person (at operational levels of the hierarchy) is responsible for whole cross-cutting processes, decisions made in the specialized functional units may actually worsen business process performance. As a result, many functionally organized enterprises have poorly performing process and experience the need for process redesign.

The problem is, of course, that if a redesigned process is grafted back into an existing functional organizational structure *with no other changes*, the prevailing managerial emphasis on functional concerns will continue, and process performance will eventually suffer again. To understand what other changes are needed to ensure the smooth operation and continuous improvement of redesigned business processes, one needs to understand the advantages as well as the disadvantages of various organizational structures and what can be lost as well as gained by structuring organizations differently.

Any organization that grows in size beyond a large team creates a hierarchy of business units, because otherwise the supervisory and decision-making demands on the general manager become too great. The hierarchy may be flat or tall, but it exists, and the reason is to break up the people and activities of the organization into units that can each report to the general manager as a single entity, thus reducing the manager's span of control. The hierarchy is a crucial aspect of organizational design, because it sets the action execution framework for the organization; it defines the organization's most important activity groupings (also called the bases of organization); and it identifies the individuals responsible for getting these activities done – usually people with the authority to allocate resources to activities and to monitor and reward process workers' performance.

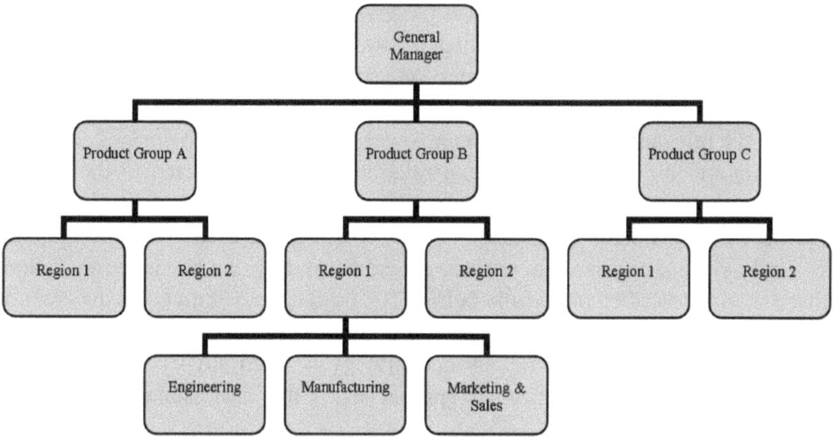


**Fig. 2** A multinational organization design

Specialized business functions (e.g., accounting and marketing) represent one basis by which people and activities can be grouped into organizational units. Organizations can also be structured around products or services, customers or geographies, and indeed around business processes. Organizations frequently need to manage multiple bases of organization simultaneously, but effective execution usually demands deciding which is *the* most important basis of organization – units of this type report directly to the general manager – and subordinating the other bases of organization to the most important one. Thus, in multidivisional organizations, the top level of the hierarchy may be organized around product groups; each product group may have customer-oriented subunits; and each customer unit may be functionally organized (see Fig. 2).

Regardless of how the organization is structured, there will always be issues that cut across units. In a product-structured organization, there may be opportunities to attract new customers with a "product solution" involving products from several different units or opportunities to develop entirely new products that require the technical experience found in two or more units. In a customer-focused enterprise, there may be opportunities to create standardized product offerings that are more efficient to produce or the need to develop shared business services to lower administrative costs. In a functionally organized business unit, the process of new product development may require expertise from marketing, engineering, and manufacturing units. Because there are always cross-cutting issues in organizations, there will always be need for governance across units.

There are three basic ways to handle cross-cutting issues in organizations: (1) referral up the *hierarchy*, (2) *lateral relations*, and (3) creation of one or more *new organizational units*. The first approach is for the issue to be referred up in the hierarchy to the next managerial level. For example, a new product development project could be led by the general manager in conjunction with functional unit heads. Naturally, this approach is unavailable for processes that involve multiple legal entities. Furthermore, it is not a preferred approach, even within organizations, because it diverts general managers' attention from their own key priorities (often facing outward toward customers and financial markets) and reflects poorly on subordinates' ability to manage their responsibilities. Thus, the second approach, in which the relevant decisions are made lower in the hierarchy by means of what is called a lateral organization or lateral relations is often preferred to the upward referral approach. Examples of lateral relations include both *formal* personal governance mechanisms (e.g., liaison roles, coordination units, standing committees) and *informal* personal governance mechanisms, (e.g., ad hoc meetings, phone calls, e-mails) described more fully below. The third approach involves the creation of new activity units around the cross-cutting issue, thus making the process a primary basis of organization. This last strategy is often advocated by business process experts, but, like the other approaches, it has disadvantages as well as benefits, as discussed below.

In a different language, cross-cutting issues are "business processes" such as new product development. The lateral relations approach is the most common strategy for "business process governance." And creating an organizational unit to operate a business process is an instance of what is called "process organization." We now examine the lateral relations and process organization approaches for governing business processes in more detail.

## 2.2 Lateral Relations and Process Organization Mechanisms of Business Process Governance

The lateral relations needed to govern business processes across organizational units may occur spontaneously and informally, without official recognition by the organization. Alternatively, lateral relations may be explicitly set up as formal organizational responsibilities and accountabilities. Formal mechanisms can vary in their requirements for organizational commitment – that is, in the level of resources necessary to fund their operation. Finally, organizations can entirely restructure along process lines.

At the *informal* end of the governance spectrum, people in different units who are mutually involved in a cross-cutting business process may call ad hoc meetings, place phone calls, or send e-mails when they experience a situation that needs coordination. For example, an engineer working on a new product design may call a colleague in manufacturing to ask whether the proposed design would be expensive to build or difficult to maintain. The most important drawbacks of informal relations as a strategy for business process governance is that they are not certain to happen, because the responsibility and accountability for these lateral relations have not been explicitly assigned. After all, if people do not liaise well informally, they cannot really be accused of not doing their jobs.

Furthermore, if problems arise during informal coordination that cannot be resolved by the parties involved, the conflicts must be escalated up at least two levels of hierarchy (to the manager of the managers of the units in which the coordinators work) in order to be resolved effectively. In practice, such escalation rarely happens, and processes fraught with informal conflicts usually remain ungoverned.

Finally, although informal liaison can work adequately for the ongoing operation of a process, it generally fails when the process needs to be improved or redesigned. The reason is that process improvement and redesign generally require the allocation of resources (e.g., people's time to work on the redesign team, funds for new software or equipment), and informal coordinators often lack the authority to make these resource commitments. In general, if the process is at all important to the organization, it requires some level of *formal* lateral governance.

At the lowest level of formal process governance, an organization can designate a *liaison role*, assigning to someone the responsibility for coordinating across organizational lines (see Fig. 3.) At greater expense, the organization may set up a *standing committee*, often staffed with relatively senior managers from the affected units, to oversee the operation and improvement of a cross-cutting business process. Such a group would typically identify appropriate process metrics, track them, and recommend improvement actions. But the group would have no authority to allocate resources (other than their own budgets, if any) or to compel the execution of its recommendations, so the group members would have to negotiate with other leaders to ensure that changes are made. An even more expensive lateral relations strategy is for the organization to create a separate organizational unit charged with responsibility to coordinate a business process, while the activities that make up the process continue to be executed in operating business units.

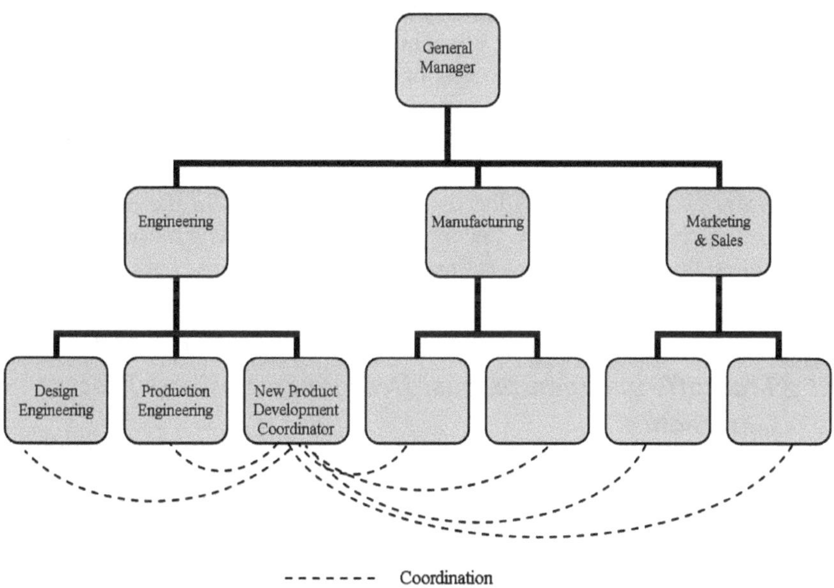


**Fig. 3** A new product development liaison role

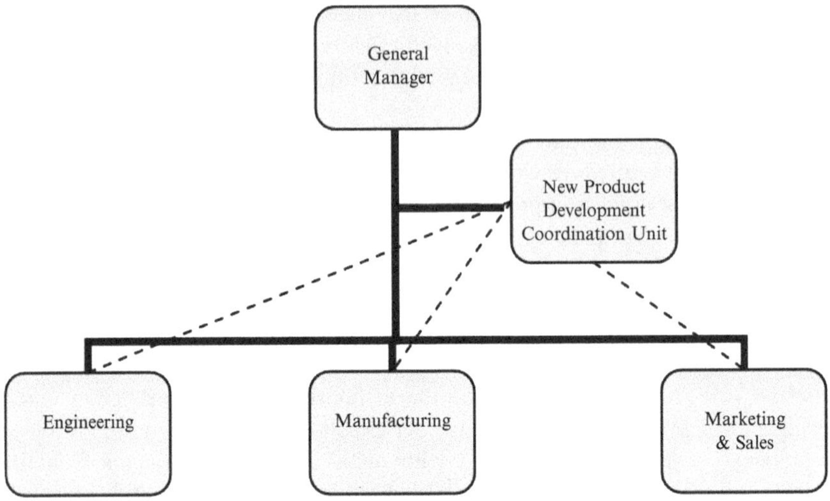


**Fig. 4** A new product development coordination unit

This *process coordination unit* (often called a "process owner") would generally have only a small staff and would be responsible for such activities as process design, setting process performance targets and budgets, providing training, "purchasing" products or services from operating units, and so forth. This unit would not, however, actually "manage" process workers and activities (see Fig. 4).

Moving beyond these purely coordinative strategies, the organization could restructure around processes – that is, change the basis by which activities are combined into units and hierarchically managed. In the *process unit* version of this strategy, the organization sets up a new operating unit to perform many activities associated with a business process, such as new product development (see Fig. 5). This new product development unit differs from the product development *coordination* unit in Fig. 4 in that the development unit actually performs the product development activities whereas the coordination does not. In the most extreme version of restructuring strategy, the organization is completely reorganized along process lines, thus creating a *process organization* (see Fig. 6).

## 2.3 *Tradeoffs in Organizational Design and Business Process Governance*

Clearly, restructuring an organization to create a new operating unit for a particularly important process or restructuring entirely along process lines focuses the strongest levels of managerial attention on business processes, maximizing the chances that the processes will perform well. Why, then, would an organization even consider lower levels of process governance (e.g., lateral relations)? The short

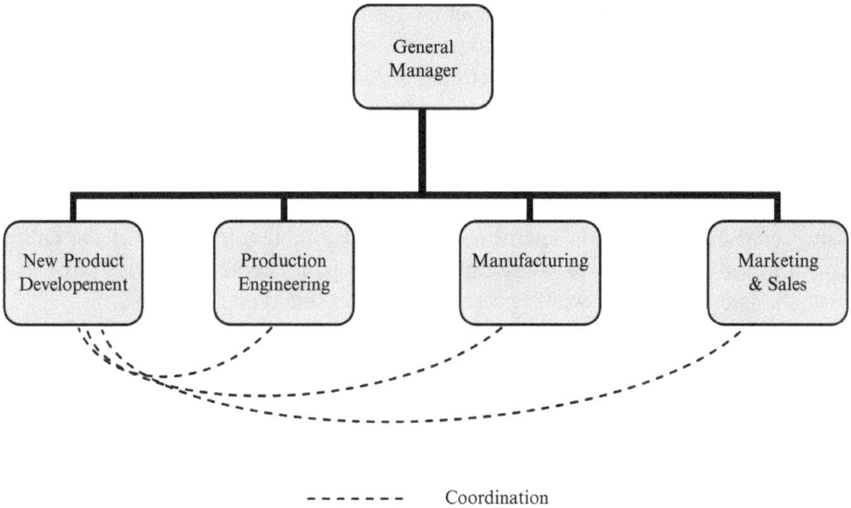


**Fig. 5** A new product development process organizational unit

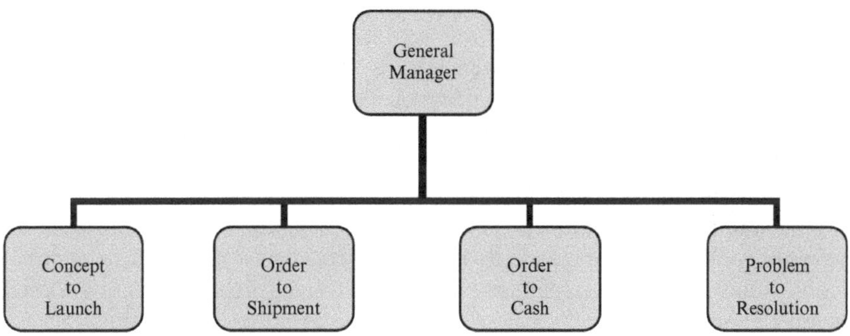


**Fig. 6** An organization structured entirely along process lines

answer is that restructuring the activity units of an organization is always more expensive than creating lateral coordination or governance mechanisms. Furthermore, emphasizing processes to such an extent means de-emphasizing other bases of organization, and organizational executives must be absolutely convinced that the merits of reorganization will outweigh its great costs.

To be more specific, setting up a process unit or process organization involves moving people, organizationally and often physically as well, from functional units to process units. In the course of restructuring, employees get new bosses and new co-workers – a very stressful situation for everyone. In addition, the organization's reporting, budgeting, and control processes must all be redesigned, which may require a substantial investment in information systems or services. On top of that, the new unit still needs to coordinate with other operating units, thus new lateral relations must be developed or encouraged to emerge. For instance, consider an organization that sets up a new unit to perform new product development, not just to coordinate development across functional departments, as shown in Fig. 5. Every time the new department creates a new product, responsibility for that product must be transitioned to the operational units responsible for selling it, manufacturing it, servicing it, etc., along with information about how it is to be built, sold to customers, maintained, etc. Lateral relations must to be created to govern these transitional activities. New lateral relations would be required even if the entire organization were restructured along process lines, as depicted in Fig. 6. In this case, the lateral relations would probably focus on functional expertise.

The sad truth is that every way of structuring and managing organizations and every way of designing and governing business processes has pros and cons. (See Table 1 for a summary.) Every design choice involves trading off some costs to achieve some benefits. For example, completely reorganizing from a functional structure into a process-based one does not eliminate the need for a lateral organization to coordinate across units. It merely changes the kind of lateral coordination that is needed. In a functional organization, business processes need to be coordinated laterally across functional units; in a process organization, functional expertise and efficiency need to be coordinated across process units.

The functional organizational structure may appear deficient when viewed from a process perspective, but it is efficient, because it reduces the need to replicate functional specialists in many different units. The functional organization also enables the organization to develop depth of specialized expertise in areas such as mechanical engineering, electronics or hydraulic technology, marketing research, software development, etc. Thus, the decision to reorganize an enterprise or business unit on the basis of processes is a business decision that processes are more important to manage than functions are, and therefore, that the functions either do not need to be explicitly managed (in other words, they can be left to informal coordination) or that the functions should be governed lightly through a formal lateral organization.

The same holds true for any basis of organization, for example, for product and customer bases of organization, in addition to process and function. The decision to elevate one basis of organization, say customers, in importance is a decision to de-emphasize another basis of organization, for example products. Occasionally, two bases of organization are believed to be nearly equal in importance, and complex "matrix" structures are set up to coordinate them. But these structures can be extraordinarily expensive to maintain, because they involve parallel management systems for goal setting, budgeting and scheduling, performance evaluation, and financial control.

In general, organizations large enough and complex enough to have multiple product lines and multiple customer segments are organized primarily by one or both of those bases; functions such as manufacturing and operational business processes such as new product development are generally subordinated to customer and/or product units. (In other words, the customer or product units report higher in the management hierarchy than the functions or processes do.) Naturally, it follows from our earlier discussion that there will still be issues that cut across the product

**Table 1** The pros and cons of different types of governance mechanisms

| Governance Concept | Definition | Pros | Cons | When to use |
|---|---|---|---|---|
| Impersonal governance | Governance achieved when individuals and organizations adhere to norms of behavior or documented rules promulgated by institutional actors, such as governments, standards bodies, industry associations, etc.; Includes laws, rules, procedures, contracts, budgets, SLAs, pricing plans | Can clearly specify roles and responsibilities, compliance requirements, and penalties for non-compliance; If norms are internalized, the costs of governance can be low; Can avoid some of the conflicts associated with personal governance | Impossible to pre-specify every contingency; May be ineffective without expensive monitoring and enforcement | When certain levels of service are required and can be monitored; When coordination is needed across organizations |
| Personal governance | Governance exercised directly by people regardless of authority or responsibility; Includes vertical (hierarchical) authority, horizontal or lateral relations, and organizational restructuring along process lines | Flexible; Has the ability to respond to unforeseen circumstances | May provoke more conflicts than impersonal governance; May result in less consistent application than documented rules | Always required in some form, for instance, needed to create impersonal rules |
| Vertical (hierarchical) authority | Direction or control exerted by superiors in a managerial hierarchy | Effective for activities that occur entirely under the direct authority of a line manager; Can help generate commitment to business process changes within organizations | Not sufficient for business processes, because they cross intra- or inter-organizational lines | |
| Horizontal or lateral relations | Coordination across boundaries within or across organizations; includes informal and formal governance; Excludes organizational restructuring along process lines | | | Always required for business processes, because they cross organizational lines |
| Informal governance | Governance negotiated informally by people with responsibility for various tasks or resources; Includes ad hoc | Execution requires informal governance – this is how work gets done; Facilitates | No way to ensure that informal coordination will happen; No formal method | Always required; Should be encouraged in addition to other governance |

*(continued)*

**Table 1** (continued)

| Governance Concept | Definition | Pros | Cons | When to use |
|---|---|---|---|---|
| | meetings, phone calls, e-mails, hallway discussions, etc. | development of shared understanding; Can compensate for gaps in structure or governance | to resolve issues, leading to escalation up the hierarchy; Ineffective for process redesign | mechanisms; Not recommended as the sole form of business process governance in complex organizations |
| Formal governance | Governance administered or negotiated by people working in formally assigned coordination roles; Includes liaison roles, standing committees, and process coordination units | Ensures that functions and organizations are represented; Problem ownership and resolution are clearly identified | Often expensive | Especially important when coordination involves the allocation of resources |
| Liaison roles | Formal assignment of responsibility for coordinating a business process to a designated person (see Fig. 3) | Relatively low cost formal mechanism, because the liaison role may be an additional assignment to an existing role | No authority to allocate resources or compel execution of recommendations | When business process governance requirements are relatively "light" |
| Standing committees | Creation of a permanent group of people, representing the different organizational units involved in a business process, with formally designated responsibility for governing a business process | Ensures that the organizational units involved in a process are represented in process governance, signaling and reinforcing attention and commitment | More costly than the liaison role because such committees are often staffed by relatively senior people; No authority to allocate resources or compel execution of recommendations | When the business process is important enough to require high-level visibility and commitment from multiple organizational units |
| Process coordination units, the "process owner" strategy | Creation of an organizational unit to coordinate (but not execute) a business process (see Fig. 4) | More effective than liaison roles and standing committees, because such units often have budgets to purchase services from operating units and thus have a say in the operating units' performance evaluations | More costly than liaison roles, because new jobs are created and staffed; More costly than the standing committee, because the process coordination unit and a standing governance committee are often used in combination | When the organization is prepared to manage the process formally – that is, to set goals and metrics, to draw up budgets, and to evaluate and reward performance |

| | | | | |
|---|---|---|---|---|
| Organizational restructuring | Change in the basis for organizing activities and their reporting relationships; Includes process organizational units and process organizational structures | Powerfully directs managerial attention to one or more key business processes | Always more expensive than lateral relations | When the organization is prepared to make very significant resource commitments |
| Process organizational unit | Creation of an organizational unit to execute a business process (see Fig. 5) | Gives the business process considerable autonomy to pursue its own goals and objectives | Requires the creation of new governance arrangements, because the new unit will need to liaise with the existing operating units | When the process is vitally important to the health of the organization, the process has underperformed under previous governance regimes, and the organization is unwilling to completely restructure |
| The process organizational structure | Complete reorganization of the enterprise, changing the primary basis of organization from function, product, or geography to process (see Fig. 6) | Gives major managerial attention and visibility to end-to-end customer facing processes | Extraordinarily expensive, because it completely reassigns people, authority, and responsibility; Requires creation of new management systems and governance arrangements; May result in significant erosion of functional, product, or geographic capability | When the organization is convinced that process is the most important basis of organization and is willing to incur the extraordinary expense of complete reorganization |

or customer units. A prime example is decision making about enterprise IT systems and shared business services (e.g., human resource management and accounting). Some of these cross-cutting issues may be thought important enough to be formally governed by means of the strategies described above.

In short, business process governance cannot be designed in a vacuum. Business process governance needs to be designed in conjunction with an enterprise's primary organizational design decisions, which are strategic business decisions. Whether or not a "process owner" should be named or a process organization structure set up is not a black or white question, and no one solution is best in every situation. Trade-offs must always be made. That said, let us now examine some governance choices that have been made in actual situations.

## 3 Process Governance Within Organizations

Redesigning business processes to make them more efficient and customer-focused is not enough to ensure process success. Numerous companies have found that attempting to introduce redesigned business processes to an existing organizational structure is a recipe for process failure:

> That was the theory. But it didn't work out that way. The first pilot teams ... barely managed to operate at all. They were, in effect, sabotaged by the existing organization. Functional departments were unwilling to cede people, space, or responsibility to the teams. ... The problem was not in the design of the process. The problem was that power continued to lie in the old functional departments.
>
> *(Hammer and Stanton 1999), p. 110.*

This, and many other experiences suggest that relying on informal lateral coordination, whether by functional unit managers or by process workers, to ensure the smooth operation and ongoing improvement of critical business processes does not work. Some degree of formal structural change seems to be necessary. The question is what kind of change is required. The two primary options are (1) the establishment of formal lateral relations, whether by liaison roles, coordination committees, or a process coordination unit (also known as the "process owner" strategy) and (2) the creation of new operating units responsible for executing a business process. Both strategies have been successfully used. In the following paragraphs, we analyze familiar examples of three formal mechanisms – the process coordination unit, the process organization, and the process unit – in terms of the analytic framework we developed earlier.

### *3.1 Process Coordination Units: The Example of Duke Power*

Before process redesign, the Customer Operations unit at Duke Power – the unit responsible for delivering electricity to customers – was primarily structured along geographical market lines (Hammer and Stanton 1999). Four regional vice presidents reported to the head of Customer Operations. The geographic basis of organization makes good business sense for an electricity provider, the operations of which require deploying large numbers of people efficiently across large areas. The major disadvantage of this structure is that business processes such as marketing, acquiring new customers, and service delivery must be laterally coordinated across the geographic regions. At Duke Power, those processes were not as efficiently and effectively coordinated as they needed to be.

In a process redesign project, five important processes were identified: developing market strategies, acquiring and maintaining customers, delivering products and services, providing reliability and integrity (maintenance), and calculating and collecting revenues. A new organizational unit was created to coordinate each process. The leaders of the new units reported directly to the head of Customer Operations, *along with* the four vice presidents of regional operating units. Thus, the general manager's direct span of control more than doubled as a result of this change.

In the new structure, the regions for the most part managed the people and activities, and the process units governed the money. Most of the personnel in Duke Power remained in the regional units to be managed by the regional vice presidents. The process unit leaders, who had only small staffs, were responsible for designing business processes, setting performance targets for processes, and establishing budgets (impersonal governance mechanisms) that covered not just what it would take to operate the processes, but also what would be needed for process improvement activities such as redesigning warehouse operations and introducing a new scheduling system. Then the process unit leaders allocated budgets to the regions. Each regional vice president had to manage to the goals and budgets that were set in large part by the five process unit leaders. (The vice presidents may also have had additional goals and other sources of funding for their activities.) Within their units, the regional vice presidents had the authority to allocate resources that they saw fit to achieve their targets.

In the terms used earlier in this chapter, Duke Power employed an expensive strategy of formal lateral relations to govern its processes – the creation of separate units to coordinate each key process across the regional operating units. This strategy was expensive, not only because it involved five new (though small) units each with high-level leaders but also because it introduced a new budgeting process, and because it required close informal coordination (and negotiation!) between process unit leaders and regional vice presidents to make sure that budgets were fair and that process decisions were sound. The advantages were much greater effectiveness and accountability for the outcomes of importance to Duke Power's customers.

It should be noted that the lateral organization strategy employed by Duke Power was probably not the only way the company could have achieved its goals. One alternative would have been to pull the people working on certain business processes – say marketing – out of the regional operating units and to combine them into functionally organized units reporting to the head of Customer Operations. This solution may have been more efficient than keeping these specialists in the regional operating units. On the other hand, it is likely to have encountered resistance from the regional managers, who would have lost resources and power, and it would have required much lateral coordination with the operating units to avoid reducing responsiveness to local customer needs.

The point is that *all* ways of structuring activities and governing processes have pros and cons; organizations need to design the best solution given their unique circumstances, including the level of change management required. For example, the new process organization at Duke Power did not work well until the regional vice presidents and process leaders got together and developed a document specifying (1) who would be responsible for making each key decision, (2) who had to be consulted before each key decision was made, and (3) who had to be informed after each key decision was made. This meeting not only created an impersonal mechanism of governance – the framework, it also created the shared understanding that ensured that the vice presidents would comply with the framework.

An alternative to the coordinating unit strategy is the even more expensive strategy of creating one or more process organizational units. At Texas Instruments, the entire operational organization was restructured along process lines – as reflected in a series of product development units. At Procter & Gamble, a single new process unit was set up with managerial authority for shared processes related to employees and to business activities.

## 3.2 Process Organization: The Example of Texas Instruments

Texas Instruments was originally structured on a functional basis. Managers in the company believed that the product development process needed improvement and created a process redesign in which cross-functional teams of people from various specialties (engineering, marketing, etc.) were assembled in the samc location (Hammer and Stanton 1999). Each team was supposed to be responsible for the "concept to launch" process for a new product, which involved setting advertizing strategies, producing product documentation, creating training materials, and so forth. But the existing functional organizational structure was not changed. Not surprisingly, the process redesign project team learned that the new teams could not operate effectively in the old organizational structure.

The result was a decision to restructure the enterprise completely into product development units. Budgets that had been set up for functional departments were now created for the product development units instead. Since the old functional departments were no longer responsible for performing activities related to product development, they were reincarnated as formal lateral coordinating units. Their purpose became ensuring the preservation of functional expertise and quality standards across the product developments units by means of training, methods improvements, etc.

In short, Texas Instruments' governance strategy was almost the reverse of that used at Duke Power. Whereas Duke Power added process coordination units and a new budgeting process to a functional operating structure, Texas Instruments created functional coordination units for a new process operating structure. But Texas Instrument had far more work to do to implement its change. Duke Power created a new governance strategy for an existing organizational design; Texas Instruments had to completely redesign its structure (changed its fundamental basis of organization) and also develop a new governance approach.

## 3.3 *Process Unit: The Example of Shared Services at Procter and Gamble*

An increasingly popular organizational redesign involves the creation of "shared services" business units to perform certain support activities for all other organizational operating units, which are otherwise left intact. An example is Procter & Gamble, which began setting up its worldwide shared services organization in 1999 (Weill et al. 2007). Although only a single new operating unit was created, in contrast to Texas Instruments' complete process reorganization, the scope of P&G's new Global Business Services (GBS) unit was enormous, comprising human resources and facilities management, information services, accounting, marketing research, demand planning, packaging development, and more. The new organizational design evolved over a matter of years. In 2007, GBS employed 6,500 people.

Like other operating units, shared services units can have huge budgets and large staffs. But they differ from other organizational operating units in one key respect. Shared services units are focused inside the organization: most of their services are provided to other operating units[1]. The other operating units, by contrast, are externally focused: they produce products and services for external customers. Because shared services units operate certain processes on behalf of multiple other operating units, lateral governance mechanisms must be created to link them to their internal clients.

The governance mechanisms associated with shared services units are many and complex, involving both impersonal and personal governance forms (Davis 2005; Grant et al. 2007). The impersonal mechanisms include service level agreements (SLAs) and pricing plans. For example, P&G set prices, which varied by region, for each service offered by its GBS unit. Operating units were required to use about 70% of the services offered, but 30% were optional, and operating unit managers could influence their costs by choosing a level of service and how much of each service they consumed. In addition, because some of the shared services were provided by external partners (including three IT service providers), there were

[1]Naturally there are important exceptions to this statement. Some other operating units primarily support internal customers, e.g., a manufacturing unit that "sells" its output to product units that transact with external customers. Some shared services units are operated for the client organization by another company. Some shared services units support external customers as well as internal ones.

also inter-organizational outsourcing contracts (Weill et al. 2007). The charges that GBS recouped from its client units comprised the budget that GBS managers had to manage within, and the SLAs outlined the process performance metrics they had to meet and that were used in evaluating their performance.

The rewards for such careful business process governance can be considerable. P&G's GBS unit was able to guarantee its clients an upfront 10–30% reduction in the cost of the shared services, as well as annual cost reductions (Weill et al. 2007). Another organization sought to achieve 30–40% reductions in costs by means of shared services (Davis 2005). It is important to understand, however, that achieving such benefits requires substantial ongoing outlays for business process governance.

Not described for P&G's shared services, but a prominent feature of many shared services designs, is a complex structure of formal lateral governance relations – personal governance – in addition to the impersonal mechanisms of prices and service level agreements. Many organizations put in place a hierarchy of committees staffed with representatives from the shared services unit, its client operating units, and its external services providers (if any) (Grant et al. 2007). Some governance committee hierarchies have two levels – an operating committee and executive steering committee; some have three levels – technical, managerial, and executive. In complex multinationals, the shared services governance committee hierarchy may essentially parallel the overall organizational structure, with standing governance committees for each country, each region, and each product group. *In addition* to the committee hierarchy, shared services governance may also include liaison roles within the shared services organization to coordinate with client operating units and possibly also liaison roles within the operating units to coordinate with the shared services unit.

All-in-all, a shared services process organization can be part of a company's strategy for governing certain business processes, such as information services, human resources management, accounting, etc. However, the benefits of process organizational units must be balanced against the costs of governing them. Shared services units require impersonal governance mechanisms such as contracts, budgets, and SLAs, and personal lateral governance mechanisms such as liaison roles and a governance committee hierarchy. Whenever external providers deliver some of the shared services, governance mechanisms are also needed for external coordination.

As costly as such inter-organizational business process governance can be, the demands of external process governance are in many ways greater. We discuss inter-organizational business process governance in the next section.

## 4 Governing Processes that Cross Organizational Lines

Intra-organizational processes have governance advantages that inter-organizational processes do not. Although hierarchical authority cannot suffice to govern intra-organizational business processes, it can help with governance by facilitating the creation of formal lateral relations or process organizations and by supporting a control framework that can be aligned with process objectives. In addition, among organizational units reporting to a common authority, there may be cultural conditions that support effective informal coordination. Most of these factors are absent when business processes cross the boundaries of legal entities.

Distinct legal entities that conduct business transactions may differ greatly in their relative power and influence, but legal autonomy means that inter-organizational process governance strategies are more limited than those available within organizations (Huiskonen and Pirttila 2002). As a result, inter-organizational processes must rely more on impersonal mechanisms of governance. And, if personal governance strategies are used, they are more palatable when they are enacted by "neutral third parties" such as outsourcers, professional services firms, industry associations, and trade facilitators. Below, we consider two examples of inter-organizational business processes – emergency medical services (EMS) provision in San Mateo County, California, and the supply chain management process.

## *4.1 Multiple Mechanisms for Inter-Organizational Process Governance: The Example of San Mateo County EMS*

The provision of EMS in the United States is an inter-organizational process involving both governmental agencies and private businesses – police and fire services, hospitals, ambulance services, etc. The process entails numerous handoffs, and no vertical (hierarchical) authority can command efficient and effective process performance (Horan and Schooley 2007). Officials in the EMS Agency of San Mateo County, California, took responsibility for leading process improvement, and, after a 4-year redesign activity with the participation of paramedics, nurses, physicians, hospitals, fire agencies, and a private ambulance provider (American Medical Response or AMR), EMS catalyzed an innovative public–private partnership that addressed the end-to-end emergency medical services process (Schooley and Horan 2007).

Central to the redesigned inter-organizational process was an impersonal governance mechanism – a master contract with AMR for ambulance and paramedic first response services. This award-winning "performance-based" contract specified target response times that varied with responder type and emergency location and required at least 90% compliance with the targets.

The master contract, however, covered only one part of the EMS process. Other key parts included the response of police and fire services and patient treatment in hospitals. To ensure that collaboration among all parties remained effective, the San Mateo County EMS Agency convened a monthly standing committee. The focus of committee meetings was to evaluate the performance of the end-to-end process and to manage its continuous improvement. In addition, the Agency developed standards for process worker training, record keeping, and communication. Thus, the success of the EMS process in San Mateo County depended on a combination of impersonal governance mechanisms (e.g., the master contract) and personal governance mechanisms (e.g., the standing committee and ongoing informal interactions).

## 4.2 *Multiple Mechanisms for Inter-Organizational Process Governance: The Supply Chain Management Example*

As another common example, the inter-organizational processes connecting an organizational buyer with its suppliers often need improvement. Formal purchasing contracts are rarely enough to address every contingency, particularly since suppliers often depend on *their* suppliers to ensure timely and accurate deliveries (Hammer 2001). Volumes have been written about strategies for improving supply chain processes – strategies that usually combine a variety of personal governance mechanisms. Examples of such personal mechanisms include the following:

- Informal relations, bolstered by co-location of the buyer and supplier companies (Huiskonen and Pirttila 2002)
- Liaison roles, frequently mirrored in the partner organizations (Danese et al. 2004), and sometimes demanded by third parties that perform some part of an inter-organizational process (Huiskonen and Pirttila 2002)
- Standing committees, such as steering committees and process improvement teams (Huiskonen and Pirttila 2002)
- Coordination units and process organizations internal to one or multiple partners (Danese et al. 2004)
- External coordination units and process organizations, often in the form of third or fourth party logistics providers (Huiskonen and Pirttila 2002)

Successful supply chain management generally depends on impersonal governance mechanisms to complement personal mechanisms. Examples of the impersonal mechanisms used in the supply chain management process include the following:

- Trading partner agreements, distinct from purchasing contracts, that specify goals, procedures, tools and/or metrics for business process improvement (Danese et al. 2004)
- Information systems, many times developed by the customer organization to provide visibility into the supply chain (Cartwright et al. 2005; Leser et al. 2005), occasionally coupled with process redesigns in which the customer organization takes over the process of ordering from second tier suppliers the products that will be used by first tier suppliers (Hammer 2001)
- Data and process standards designed to specify business-to-business communication requirements and to streamline and standardize business transactions (Markus et al. 2006)
- Formalized business practice guidelines, created by industry associations, such as Collaborative Planning, Forecasting and Replenishment (Danese et al. 2004;

Davenport 2005; Markus and Gelinas 2006), which may include references to impersonal governance mechanisms, such as trading partner agreements and the use of particular information systems or standards.

When inter-organizational processes become larger in scope, encompassing more organizations or more organizational types, the need for complex combinations of personal and impersonal governance mechanisms increases. In addition, third parties such as industry associations and trade facilitators are usually pressed to take on more substantial roles. For instance, when the barcode was introduced to facilitate inter-organizational commerce, it became necessary to establish a permanent governance organization to administer the barcode and to test for compliance with technical standards and guidelines (Brown 1997). More recently, organizations such as GS1 are working with industry participants to craft a suitable governance model to spur the adoption and administer the use of radio-frequency identification (RFID). As yet, however, diffusion of RFID standards appears to be hindered by one important element of inter-organizational governance – the pricing of participation in the standards consortium.

## 5 Concluding Remarks

Business processes need governance to ensure their smooth operation and continuous improvement, not just to coordinate their initial design or re-engineering. Business process governance mechanisms can be impersonal or personal, informal or formal. Each governance mechanism has pros and cons. In general, more powerful governance mechanisms are more expensive in money, time, and good will to deploy and maintain. Thus, executives must be aware of the trade-offs in governance design and the benefits of designing a cost-effective governance solution. Often, the most effective approach is to use multiple "light weight" governance mechanisms in combination (e.g., a combination of impersonal mechanisms and formal lateral relations) rather than one powerful intervention (e.g., organizational structure change to create a process organization). Governance becomes both more necessary and more challenging to do well when the scope of business processes increases, particularly when processes cross the boundaries of autonomous legal entities. Although effective business process governance can be challenging to design and expensive to deploy, it is as important for the success of business processes as business process redesign.

## References

Becker J, Kugeler M, Rosemann M (2003) Process management: a guide for the design of business processes. Springer, Berlin

Brown SA (1997) Revolution at the checkout counter. Harvard Business School, Boston, MA

Cartwright J, Hahn-Steichen J, He J, Miller T (2005) Rosettanet for Intel's trading entity automation. Intel Technol J 9(3):239–246
Danese P, Romano P, Vinelli A (2004) Managing business processes across supply networks: the role of coordination mechanisms. J Purch Supply Manage 10:165–177
Davenport TH (2005) The coming commoditization of processes. Harv Bus Rev (June):101–108
Davis TR (2005) Integrating shared services with the strategy and operations of MNEs. J Gen Manage 31(2):1–17
Galbraith JR (1994) Competing with flexible lateral organizations, 2nd edn. Addison-Wesley, Reading, MA
Grant G, McKnight S, Uruthirapathy A, Brown A (2007) Designing governance for shared services organizations in the public service. Gov Inf Q 24(3):522–538
Hammer M (2001) The superefficient company. Harv Bus Rev (September):82–91
Hammer M, Stanton S (1999) How process enterprises really work. Harv Bus Rev (November–December):108–118
Horan TA, Schooley BL (2007) Time-critical information services. Commun ACM 50(3):73–78
Huiskonen J, Pirttila T (2002) Lateral coordination in a logistics outsourcing relationship. Int J Prod Econ 78:177–185
Kettinger WJ, Grover V (1995) Special section: toward a theory of business process change management. J Manage Inf Syst 12(1):9–30
Leser F, Alt R, Österle H (2005) Implementing collaborative process management-the case of net-tech. Int J Cases Electron Commer 1(4):1–18
Lynn J, Laurence E, Heinrich CJ, Hill CJ (2001) Improving governance: a new logic for empirical research. Georgetown University Press, Washington, DC
Markus ML, Gelinas JUJ (2006) Comparing the standards lens with other perspectives on is innovations: the case of CPFR. J IT Stand Standard Res 4(1):24–42
Markus ML, Steinfield CW, Wigand RT, Minton G (2006) Industry-wide is standardization as collective action: the case of the US residential mortgage industry. MIS Q 30(Special Issue):439–465
Rosemann M, de Bruin T (2005) Towards a business process management maturity model. In: 13th European conference on information systems, Regensburg, Germany
Schooley BL, Horan TA (2007) Towards end-to-end government performance management: Case study of interorganizational information integration in emergency medical services (EMS). Gov Inf Q 24:755–784
Weill P, Soh C, Sia SK (2007) Governance of global shared solutions at procter & gamble, research briefing. MIT Sloan School of Management, Center for Information Systems Research, Cambridge, MA

# Business Process Management Governance

**Andrew Spanyi**

**Abstract** Most executives, if not all, are concerned about improving operational performance. While this may be obvious, what is not nearly as apparent is precisely how the most successful firms are able to sustain and optimize operational performance improvements. Whereas most firms are becoming increasingly adept at executing improvements to their operations in projects of small scope, many firms continue to struggle when it comes to projects of larger scope requiring broad cross-functional collaboration. More importantly, they often do not put in place the subtle, yet critical, elements of BPM governance, including the refinements to organization structure, executive roles and responsibilities, and measurement discipline that are needed to sustain and optimize operational performance improvements. This chapter examines the management practices of BPM governance that enable achieving sustainable, consistent, and flawless execution.

## 1 Introduction

Let us agree on a basic premise. A company creates value for customers and shareholders via the effectiveness and efficiency of activities or work that flows across traditional organization boundaries – often referred to as the firm's complex, cross-functional business processes (Spanyi 2006).

In order to optimize and sustain improvements to operational performance, it is essential to overlay some form of governance that creates the right structures, metrics, roles, and responsibilities to measure and manage the performance of a firm's end-to-end business processes. This is called BPM governance.

Most firms are becoming increasingly adept at executing improvements to their operations in projects of small scope, and yet many firms continue to struggle when

A. Spanyi
Spanyi International Inc., Oakville, ON, Canada
e-mail: andrew@spanyi.com

J. vom Brocke and M. Rosemann (eds.), *Handbook on Business Process Management 2*, International Handbooks on Information Systems,
DOI 10.1007/978-3-642-01982-1_11, 

it comes to projects of larger scope requiring broad cross-functional collaboration. Why have many organizations become more proficient in executing projects of small scope? The principal reason is that the various methods of process improvement, such as Lean, Six Sigma, Lean-Six Sigma, and Continuous Process Improvement, have become codified over the past decade. As these projects are often defined within the boundaries of one department or unit, the needed governance is in place due to the existing organization design.

But that is not the case when it comes to projects of larger scope requiring broad cross-functional collaboration. Indeed, the success rate for such larger projects remains disappointing. It has been widely reported that 50 to 70% of reengineering projects fail, and IT projects over the past decade have not fared much better. The Standish Group has been conducting a survey on the performance of IT projects since 1995, and even though project success has increased from 16.2% in 1995 to 35% in 2006, around two-thirds of IT projects are still considered failures (The Standish Group 2009). This statistic would be more dismal if the survey had been limited to large projects requiring cross-functional collaboration.

Why do companies continue to struggle when it comes to executing larger operational improvement projects and sustaining results? There are at least three reasons:

- Lack of a robust framework. While business literature emphasizes the importance of improving and managing key end-to-end business processes, there is a deficit of information on precisely how to do it (Davenport 1993; Hammer 2001a, b, 2007; Hammer and Stanton 1999; Harmon 2003; Rummler and Brache 1995).
- Lack of codification of management practices. The codification of process improvement methods does not sufficiently emphasize the need for the type of leadership behavior that is intrinsic to BPM governance.
- Resistance to change. The majority of companies continue to be organized along traditional lines, and the traditional financial metrics continue to dominate executive thinking and behavior (Herbold 2004). There is resistance to the subtle, yet important, changes in measurement and management practices that are needed for BPM governance to sustain improvements to operational performance.

This chapter will begin with an overview of the results of research on what organizations need to do to effectively execute and sustain improvements to operational performance. Next, a more thorough discussion of the impediments to effectively execute and sustain improvements to operational performance will be presented. Then, the final section of this chapter will examine the role of BPM governance in how to effectively execute and sustain improvements to operational performance.[1]

---

[1]Markus and Jacobson (2010) additionally describe various governance mechanisms, identify their advantages and disadvantages, and provide examples that reveal how governance mechanisms contribute to business process success.

## 2 Research

There is a gap in the literature when it comes to leadership mindset and behavior needed for BPM governance. This author's work on the Mindset Study was one appraisal that did examine this topic (Spanyi 2005, 2006). The Mindset Study, conducted in collaboration with the Babson College Process Management Center, was a qualitative survey of the management practices of 18 firms, which had professed advanced levels of process orientation. The research took the form of a qualitative survey, and interviews were conducted with respondents from businesses who were considered to be concerned with improving operational performance and had advanced levels of process orientation. This was supplemented with Internet-based secondary research. Air Products and Chemicals, Caterpillar, Infosys, Nokia, and Xerox were just a few of the companies in this survey.

Two of the primary insights derived from this qualitative research were thought provoking. (1) There is increasing interest and skill in improving operational performance when it involves a single business process of limited scope. (2) The traditional mindset of leaders continues to be one of the major obstacles in taking process management principles and practices to the next level via BPM governance, where there is sustainable focus on the improvement and management of the firm's large, end-to-end business processes.

The research set out to identify the set of leadership behaviors that organizations need in order to effectively improve operational performance via process management. The hypothesis was that the leading firms would have made progress in all three of the following areas:

- The leadership team would have monitored key performance metrics from a customer's point of view, and attempted to link these to the key financial metrics.
- The leadership team would have developed an enterprise view of the business in process terms, a schematic or map, for example.
- They would have appointed business process owners or stewards for some of the firm's large cross-functional business processes.

The findings were revealing. Six of the respondents were observed to have made some progress in each of the three areas, while the other 12 respondents had not. In what follows, the group of firms that had made some progress in each of three areas of models, metrics, and accountability will be called "leading firms" and the other group will be referred to as "typical firms." There were three common characteristics and three common behaviors practiced by these leading companies that characterized their success in establishing a governance framework for their improvement efforts, that is, BPM governance. Following were the three common company characteristics:

- Passion about performing for customers. In fact, the respondents from the leading companies talked about customer satisfaction twice as often as respondents from typical firms. In these companies, there was a dual purpose for executing process improvement efforts – increasing customer satisfaction and reducing operating costs.

- A compelling business threat. All of the respondents from leading companies expressed concern with a perceived imminent competitive threat and/or flattening growth.
- A receptive culture. Each of the leading companies had a long history of improving operational performance. In most cases, this dated back to before the birth of methods such as reengineering and Six Sigma. Further, in each of the leading companies, the CEO was a vocal proponent.

In addition to these three common characteristics, the leading companies also practiced several common behaviors with respect to the process models, metrics, and accountability needed for BPM governance. First, they broadly communicated the enterprise process model or schematic, and the appointment of process owners throughout the corporation. This was done primarily via their Intranet, and reinforced through "town hall" meetings, executive presentations, memos, and e-mail. Next, they placed increasing focus on monitoring key performance metrics from a customer's point of view. Two of the commonly observed metrics were company performance in delivering "perfect orders" and responsiveness in resolving customer inquiries and complaints. Then, these companies appointed some process owners for end-to-end processes that crossed traditional organizational boundaries and set up a small group of subject matter experts in a center of excellence type of structure.

Do those firms that have established the needed behaviors for BPM governance, that is, the leading firms, have better financial performance than typical firms? The answer to this question appears to be a resounding YES. Five of the six leading firms were publicly traded companies in the USA. Four of the five consistently beat the Dow Jones Average over the period 2004–2008. In contrast, in examining the typical firms, five of which were also publicly traded companies in the US, it was found that four of the five typical firms failed to beat the DJI over the same period. Of course, there is much more to financial performance than a process orientation, yet these findings are thought provoking.

The respondents from the group of typical firms laid the blame for their relative lack of progress in the areas of models, metrics, and accountability on two primary factors: a traditional, functional mindset, and a narrow view of process. Even the respondents from leading firms continued to struggle with these two obstacles. The prevalence of a traditional, functional mindset was emphasized by respondents in several ways. The COO of a major health care institution said, "In health care – the org chart gets in the way of care delivery." And it was not just in health care, the majority of respondent expressed concern about leaders' perception of the organization as a group of functional entities. The VP Operations for a technology company said the following with respect to the common mental attitude of leaders at his company, "I think there's some understanding ... but I think it still reverts back to the siloed concept at various levels. When you get to the upper levels, the executive levels of the company, it's like OK – so that's what happens inside this operational financial space, so if I'm in Engineering, I don't really have to worry about that. And you may choose to do that, and that's an initiative you're spending time on, well –we've got other initiatives that we're working on."

An unduly narrow view of process was the other broadly perceived obstacle to progress. A VP from a major chemical company stated that "Most of the time I'm pleased with the existence of processes. Sporadically, I loathe them. You are more apt to hear that the process doesn't allow something as opposed to hearing that sure – we can handle that special request easily" (Spanyi 2005). Clearly, this respondent's view of process was at a tactical, procedural level as opposed to being at the level of an end-to-end, value creating set of activities. The COO of a major health care institution expressed concern about the fact that management tends to view processes as being solely within their own functional areas and said that a move needs to be made such that leaders understand the following, "In health care – we all have a responsibility for the whole process – no matter where we sit in the process... I think leaders have to be looking at the whole system and not just the pieces – it's back to this institutional approach. Breaking down silos. Turning tables. Working together." (Spanyi 2005)

The combined impact of a traditional, functional view of business and an unduly narrow view of process is significant. It serves to limit process improvement efforts to cost reduction and stands in the way of developing the key, needed elements of BPM governance. The following section explores some of the underlying reasons for the persistence of these obstacles.

## 3 Obstacles

It is somewhat puzzling why leaders continue to cling to a traditional, functional view of business and an unduly narrow view of process (Herbold 2004). For nearly two decades, thought leaders have emphasized the need for cross-functional collaboration and for viewing business in the context of an organization's end-to-end business processes (Davenport 1993; Hammer 2007; Harmon 2003; Rummler and Brache 1995; Spanyi 2006). Yet, the pace of progress in influencing the mindset of executives has been slow. Some of the blame must be placed squarely at the feet of academia. Most universities have relegated the study of process improvement and management to the confines of their courses on operations and information systems. Essential process concepts are rarely part of MBA courses on leadership (which is precisely where they belong). Given the resistance to change in the academic world, this is not likely to change in the near future.

So let us turn our attention to other underlying reasons that stand in the way of viewing business from the customers' point of view and establishing the needed elements for BPM governance. There are at least three important areas to consider in this respect:

- The prominent process reference models do not sufficiently address the need for customer focus and cross-functional collaboration.

- The codification of process improvement methods, Six Sigma in particular, does not sufficiently emphasize the need for the type of leadership behavior that is intrinsic to BPM governance.
- When the governance needed for sustainable operational performance improvement is addressed, it is often related to "process maturity models" and appears complex and perceived as "just too hard" to do.

## *3.1 Reference Models Lack Cross-Functionality*

The Massachusetts Institute of Technology (MIT) business activity model and American Productivity & Quality Center's (APQC)'s process classification framework are two of the more widely known process reference models. The work on the MIT process handbook dates back to 1991, and the foundation for the APQC process classification framework (PCF) also began in the early 1990s (Malone et al. 2003; APQC 2009). Both models offer a wealth of information to organizations interested in increasing their level of process orientation. Yet, the highest-level process definitions for both models do not go far enough in acknowledging the importance of cross-functional collaboration. Instead, it is all too easy for companies to interpret these process reference models solely in accordance with traditional functional lines. Figure 1 depicts the MIT business activity model. Note how the key activity areas are closely aligned with the traditional functional departments of R&D, Procurement, and Sales/Marketing.

We observe a similar phenomenon with the APQC PCF which is depicted in Fig. 2. While the APQC PCF provides more detail on both operating and enabling business processes, the nomenclature employed is such that again these are closely aligned with traditional functional departments.

This is also an issue with industry specific process model such as eTOM (tmforum 2009) which serves the needs of the telecommunications industry, and Association for Cooperative Research and Development (ACORD) (2009), which is targeted at the insurance industry. Accordingly, it is not uncommon to see

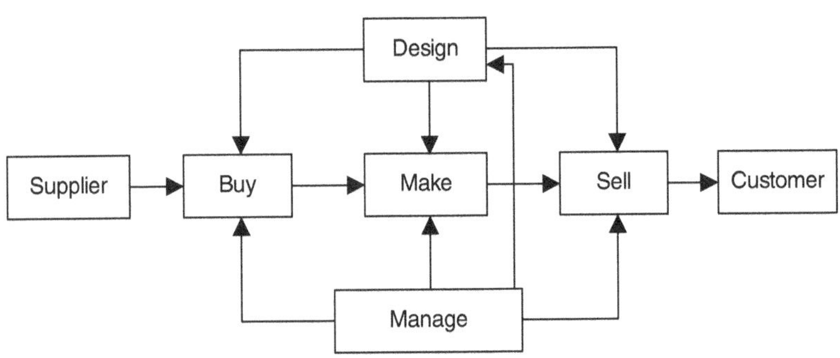


**Fig. 1** The MIT business activity model (Malone et al. 2003)

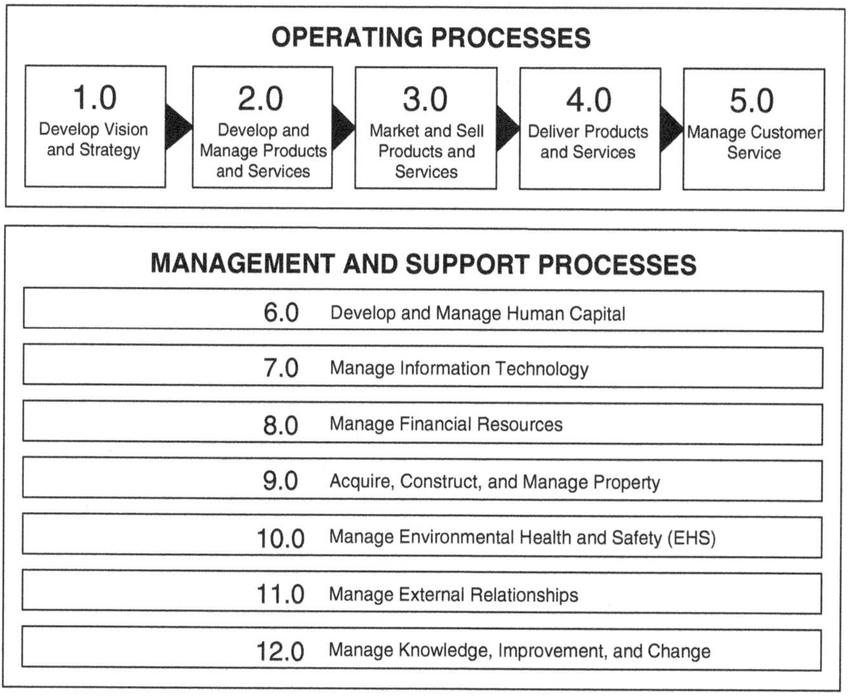


**Fig. 2** The APQC PCF (APQC 2009)[2]

organizations define their own enterprise process models in the context of their organization chart versus the end-to-end processes that truly create value for customers and shareholders.

## *3.2 Improvement Method Deployment*

The way in which process improvement methods are deployed is the second major underlying reason for why leaders continue to adopt a traditional, functional view of business and an un-duly narrow view of process. Six Sigma is the undisputed leading methodology used to improve and manage processes. In theory, Six Sigma is indeed a robust method. In practice, it has some flaws. In theory, Six Sigma should be deployed to meet customer needs and strategic improvement objectives. In theory, it is focused first and foremost on improving the customer experience through defect reduction. In practice, Six Sigma is often deployed as the means to cut costs, even though lip service is paid to improving the customer experience.

[2]The APQC PCF is also discussed by Aitken et al. (2010).

A surprising number of firms simply do not get beyond the phase of deploying Six Sigma for cost containment and never reach its true potential. Simply stated, Six Sigma is frequently deployed along functional or departmental lines simply because that is the predominant mental model of leadership. Whenever Six Sigma is deployed on a departmental basis, it is observed that Black Belts are trained and assigned to the functional departments. They are then typically tasked with completing four to six projects per annum, where each project delivers around $250,000.00 of cost savings. In many instances, Black Belts receive bonuses for bringing in the targeted cost savings. This naturally leads to a narrower definition of projects, as that tends to improve the likelihood of completing projects on time and reaching the targeted goals. In other words, while the rhetoric may emphasize customer centricity, the action is focused on cost reduction, and when it comes to actual projects, there is a very high degree of reliance on the Black Belt.

This method of deployment understandably leads to a large number of relatively small projects, which in turn drives a certain degree of duplication of effort. Given the predominant practice of launching many smaller projects, it is not surprising that most projects are not very cross-functional in nature. Accordingly, some of the largest opportunities for improvement, which have to do with managing cross-functional handoffs in a different and novel way, are not addressed.

There are three key points to note here. First, as some of the largest opportunities for improvement are found at cross-functional handoffs, the firm that fails to tackle the end-to-end, cross-functional processes sub-optimizes the opportunity for performance improvement. Then, due to the high reliance of the Black Belt role, the Six Sigma methodology has done far less to codify the needed leadership behaviors. Instead of using well-defined steering teams, reliance is placed on so called stakeholders, where roles and responsibilities are not as well defined as they could be and certainly not executed consistently. Finally, whenever dozens or even hundreds of small Six Sigma projects are launched to fix the problems in one large process, there is a need for an overarching process framework to integrate results and exercise control. In the absence of such a framework, the longer-term benefits of the improvements can, and frequently are, compromised.

## *3.3 Process Maturity*

The third area that stands in the way of further progress in the development of BPM governance is that it simply seems too hard to do. There exists an extensive body of literature on business process maturity models that attempts to define key activity areas. Invariably, governance is one of these key activity areas needed for increased process maturity (see Rosemann, vom Brocke 2010). The degree of complexity inherent in such business process maturity models is daunting (Table 1). Figure 1 depicts the framework for one such model.

The daunting level of complexity is not limited to work emanating from academia. Dr. Michael Hammer, considered by many to be the *principal proselytizer* for

**Table 1** Dephi study: process management maturity (de Bruin 2005)[3]

| Strategic alignment | Governance | Methods | Information technology | People | Culture & leadership |
|---|---|---|---|---|---|
| Process improvement plan | Process management decision-making | Process design & modeling | Process design & modeling | Process skills & expertise | Responsiveness to process change |
| Strategy & process capability linkage | Process Roles & responsibilities | Process implementation & execution | Process implementation & execution | Process management knowledge | Process values & beliefs |
| Process architecture | Process metrics & performance linkage | Process control & measurement | process control & measurement | Process education & learning | Process attitudes & behaviors |
| Process output measurement | Process management standards | Process improvement & innovation | Process improvement & innovation | Process collaboration & communication | Leadership attention to process |
| Process customers & stakeholders | Process management controls | Process project & program mgmt | Process project & program mgmt | Process management leaders | Process management social networks |

[3]For a more detailed discussion on process management maturity and its relations to the topics by Rosemann and vom Brocke (2010). To see how the process maturity model is applied in practice, refer to de Bruin and Doebeli (2010).

process orientation, released his version of a business process maturity model called Process and Enterprise Maturity Model (PEMM) (Hammer 2007). This model includes one assessment instrument for enterprise maturity and a second for process maturity. The key factors in the PEMM are outlined in Table 2.

There are two issues with these complex maturity models. The first is that they are indeed complex, all encompassing, and perceived as hard to do. The second is that there is simply not a strong enough link to operational performance. The size of the prize is un-clear and hence the effort involved in taking action is difficult to justify for the leaders of most organizations.

A combination of three factors – lack of useable models, shortcomings in the codification of the needed leadership behaviors, and the perception that it is "too hard to do"– is a substantial obstacle. Yet, some companies have made progress in installing the needed elements for BPM governance, and the next section addresses some of the relevant critical success factors in this respect.

## 4 BPM Governance Principles and Practices

Based on the mindset study research, it is clear that models, metrics, and management accountability for end-to-end process performance are a few of the critical success factors in establishing the type of BPM governance needed for sustainable improvements to operational performance. While there is no shortage of guidance on why companies should increase their focus on end-to-end business processes and generally on what they should do, there is little guidance on how to do it. That is the topic of this section.

The topic of BPM governance is only germane once the leadership team is committed to employing a process focus to improve performance for both

**Table 2** The components of Dr. Hammer's PEMM. Adapted from Hammer (2007)

| How mature is the | Enterprise? | How mature are the | Processes? |
|---|---|---|---|
| Leadership | Awareness<br>Alignment<br>Behavior<br>Style | Design | Purpose<br>Context<br>Documentation |
| Culture | Teamwork<br>Customer Focus<br>Responsibility<br>Attitude to Change | Performers | Knowledge<br>Skill<br>Behavior |
| Expertise | People<br>Methodology | Owners | Identity<br>Activities<br>Authority |
| Governance | Process Model<br>Accountability<br>Integration | Infrastructure | IT Systems<br>HR Systems |
| | | Metric | Definition<br>Uses |

customers and shareholders. So, let us assume that this intent is in place. Then, there are the following fundamental principles, essential for BPM governance, to consider:

- The highest-level process model for the enterprise must explicitly address the need for cross-functional collaboration and management accountability for the firm's end-to-end business processes.
- Operational performance must be measured from both the customer's and the company's point of view.
- The organization needs to have a plan in place that outlines the top priorities for the improvement of operational performance.
- Enabling information technology (IT) is one of the most powerful catalysts.

A number of management practices need to be put in place so as to convert these guiding principles into action.

## 5 Management Accountability

Any organization dedicated to the use of process thinking for sustainable improvements to operational performance will see the need to develop a high-level process model. The terms used to define end-to-end processes in this respect are important. There are three common conventions for naming processes in such models: one word (MIT, Supply Chain Operations Reference Model (SCOR)), phrase (APQC), and "from-to" (Malone et al. 2003; Spanyi 2005; Supply-Chain Council 2009). The major drawback of only using the one word or the phrase naming convention is that the process names can easily be mistaken for traditional departments. The benefit of the "from-to" naming convention is that it explicitly addresses the boundaries of the business process. Further, it lends itself to catchy memorable expressions that capture the need for cross-functional collaboration. While the exact nature of a firm's high-level process model varies understandably from one company to the next, Table 3 illustrates the value of combining the "from-to" naming convention for some of the typical, major enterprise processes.

By indicating which functions are involved, the table illustrates the fundamental cross-functional nature of each end-to-end process. There are two alternatives to assigning accountability for the performance of these large cross-functional processes. Some companies have chosen to appoint a well respected department head (who sometimes manages most of the resources in the process and has the most to gain or lose based on process performance) as the process owner. In this instance, the process owner wears two hats – one for the function or department and the other for the process. Other organizations have chosen to appoint a full-time senior staff member as the process owner. In this latter case, the role of the process owner is to encourage collaboration among the functional leaders involved in the process. Achieving a shared understanding of the definition of the full set of end-to-end business processes is a fundamental requirement for BPM governance (Spanyi 2006).

Table 3 End-to-end processes

| Process Name | From-To | Abbreviation (Nickname) | Output | Functions Involved |
|---|---|---|---|---|
| Sales | Promotion to order | P2O | Order | Sales<br>Marketing<br>Call center |
| Delivery | Order to delivery | O2D | Delivery | Operations<br>Call center |
| Development | Concept to customer | C2C | Product or service | Sales<br>R&D<br>Operations |
| Procurement | Requisition to receipt | R2R | Product or service | Purchasing<br>Operations<br>Others |
| Inquiries/Complaints | Inquiry to resolution | I2R | Solution | Call center<br>Others |

The executive process owner often recognizes the need to assemble a group of managers from various departments to work on a part-time basis as a standing process management team. It is this team that expands the degree of detail in the definition of the end-to-end process, monitors the relevant performance measures, and provides support to the executive process owner in terms of the identification and execution of process improvement opportunities. Any discussion of accountability is meaningless in the absence of performance measures. That is the topic of the next section.

## 6 Measuring Performance

Most executives would readily agree with the principle that operational performance needs to be measured from the customer's as well as the company's point of view. It is well known that customers want and expect to receive what they ordered, when they asked for it, complete and error free. The supply chain council calls this metric a "perfect order." Customers also want and expect their problems resolved and their inquiries handled right the first time. Yet, according to the Mindset Study, the senior leadership team monitored these two metrics in only about a third of the companies surveyed. A further complication is that some of the performance indicators that customers care about are in the middle of the end-to-end processes. For example, customers want and expect timely and complete proposals. On the other hand, most companies are typically quite clear on the major metrics of company performance. Indeed, when a leadership team selects the 5–8 key metrics to monitor week in and week out, the performance measures that are important to the company seem to dominate. Table 4 gives a comparison of the customer view and the company view for selected end-to-end processes.

**Table 4** The customer view versus the company view

| Process Name | From-To | Output | Metrics – Customer View | Metrics – Company View |
|---|---|---|---|---|
| Sales | Promotion to order | Order | Orders | Sales |
| | | | Accurate & Complete Proposals, Timely and Complete | Revenues |
| Delivery | Order to delivery | Delivery | Perfect Order | Cost/Order |
| Development | Concept to customer | Product or service | Available when promised | On budget, on time |
| Procurement | Requisition to receipt | Product or service | Available when promised | On budget, on time |
| Inquiries/ Complaints | Inquiry to resolution | Solution | First Time Right | Cost/Inquiry |

Monitoring what's important to customers as well as the company is simply the beginning of the needed discipline for BPM governance. Executive process owners in a process oriented firm will task their process management team to identify the set of performance measures for each sub-process in the relevant end-to-end process. For example, for the end-to-end delivery process, it is important to identify the relevant metrics for the sub-processes of order entry, credit check, scheduling, packing, and delivery. Then, the process-oriented firm will also recognize the importance of the following:

- Including customer centric metrics in monthly operating reviews
- Establishing a keen focus on the top 4–7 enterprise-level metrics
- Developing the means to cascade metrics to the next level for rapid diagnosis
- Using the principal performance metrics as the foundation for recognition and reward systems
- Expressing the impact of improving process performance in financial terms

This set of management practices also equips the leadership team to estimate the size of the gap between current performance and desired performance which is valuable in terms of identifying the high potential process improvement projects.

## 7 Process Management Plan

Once the leadership team has a shared understanding of the definition of the firm's enterprise-level business processes and its current performance, the company can define a plan that will improve and manage the firm's large, cross-functional business processes. This plan needs to answer two fundamental questions: Which of our business processes need to be improved, and by how much, in order to achieve our strategic objectives? Who will be held accountable for this planned improvement and performance management?

The role of BPM governance also involves certain management practices that will increase the likelihood of success in deploying the process management plan. This includes the development of an effective communication plan, on which processes will be improved in what priority and why, establishing and maintaining a permanent, part-time process management team for each end-to-end business process, and assembling a small group of subject matter experts with deep skills on the various aspects of process improvement. This latter group is often referred to as a "center of excellence."

The process management plan becomes the reference point for the process-oriented organization as it proceeds on the journey to improve and manage key end-to-end processes. It should be noted that the focus of improvement efforts is not always on the full end-to-end process. Instead, some targeted improvement efforts may be on a specific sub-process within the end-to-end process. Table 5 provides a partial process improvement and management plan for a manufacturing company.

While improvement methods such as the Define-Measure-Analyze-Improve-Control (DMAIC) approach in Six Sigma may be useful to address incremental improvement of certain business processes, invariably there are one or two end-to-end processes that call for more radical change. That is why organizations that emphasize the development of various integrated methods of process improvement appear to have greater success sustaining a process orientation. A joint study between Babson College and The Queensland University of Technology found that "methods," as defined by "the approaches and techniques that support and enable consistent process actions and outcomes," was one of six critical success factors in the assessment of the degree of process management maturity of an enterprise (de Bruin 2009).

In addition, the effective use of influence is surely one of the critical success factors in the improvement and management of end-to-end business processes. The ability to influence peers is an essential skill set for process managers at all levels and particularly for process owners. This has to do with the fact that the end-to-end business processes are typically too large for any one individual to have absolute control. Similarly, the enabling role of IT, as one of the primary catalysts of change is crucial, partly due to the sheer size of end-to-end processes.

**Table 5** Process improvement and management plan

| End-to-end process | Process owner | Process improvement focus | Goal | Scope of improvement needed |
|---|---|---|---|---|
| Promote to Order | VP Sales | Responding to RFPs | 98% on time, complete | Incremental |
| Order to delivery | VP Operations | Perfect orders | 97% perfect order delivery | Moderate |
| Concept to customer | VP R&D | Product launch | 100% on promised date | Significant |
| Inquiry to resolution | VP Customer Service | Complaint resolution | 95% first time right | Moderate |

## 8 Deploying Information Technology

The role of IT is fundamentally to enable the performance of an organization's business processes in creating value for customers and shareholders. In this day and age, practically any broad-based improvement effort relies extensively on IT. An essential role of BPM governance is to assure that IT investments are closely linked to the company's business strategy, and that the payoff from IT investments is directly derived from the specific improvements in business process performance. This will minimize the chances that technology is implemented for its own sake, and should positively impact the relationship between business users of IT and IT practitioners. The potential for IT to act as the primary catalyst for change increases in proportion to the size of the process under consideration. That is one of the reasons why improvement methods that employ dozens and even hundreds of projects of small scope find it difficult to engage IT in the improvement program.

Those organizations that recognize the potential enabling role of IT will emphasize the following as part of their management practices:

- Process improvement-related IT projects are close to the top of the IT agenda (right after compliance-related items).
- IT subject matter experts are involved early in all major process improvement efforts.
- IT subject matter experts play a role on each permanent, part-time process management team.
- IT subject matter experts are represented in the organizations' "center of excellence" for process management.

## 9 Summary

This chapter began with an overview of the results of research on what organizations need to do to effectively execute and sustain improvements to operational performance. Then, a discussion of the impediments to being able to effectively execute and sustain improvements to operational performance was presented. The final section of this chapter examined some of the management practices intrinsic to BPM governance that enable the effective execution and sustainment of improvements to operational performance. The four areas of management practice discussed in the last section are needed for BPM governance effectiveness.

## References

ACORD – Association for Cooperative Operations Research and Development (2009) "Governing documents". http://www.acord.org/about/governing_docs.aspx. Accessed 16 January 2009

APQC (2009) Global benchmarking and metrics: APQC'S PCF. http://www.apqc.org/portal/apqc/site/?path=/research/pcf/index.html. Accessed 16 January 2009

Aitken C et al. (2010) Process classification frameworks. In: vom Brocke J, Rosemann M (eds) Handbook on business process management, vol 2. Springer, Heidelberg
Davenport TH (1993) Process innovation. Harvard Business School, Boston, MA
de Bruin T (2009) Business Process Management: Theory on Progression and Maturity. PhD Thesis. Queensland University of Technology. Brisbane, Australia
de Bruin T, Doebeli G (2010) An organizational approach to BPM: the experience of an Australian transport provider. In: vom Brocke J, Rosemann M (eds) Handbook on business process management, vol 2. Springer, Heidelberg
Hammer M (2001a) The superefficient company. Harv Bus Rev (September):82–92
Hammer M (2001b) The agenda. Crown Business, New York
Hammer M (2007) The process audit. Harv Bus Rev (April):111–123
Hammer M, Stanton S (1999) How process enterprises really work. Harv Bus Rev (November-–December):108–118
Harmon P (2003) Business process change. Morgan Kaufmann, San Francisco, CA
Herbold RJ (2004) The Fiefdom syndrome. Doubleday, New York
Malone TW, Crowston K, Herman GA (2003) Organizing business knowledge: the MIT process handbook. MIT, Cambridge, MA
Markus ML, Jacobson DD (2010) Business process goverance. In: vom Brocke J, Rosemann M (eds) Handbook on business process management, vol 2. Springer, Heidelberg
Rosemann M, vom Brocke J (2010) The six core elements of business process management. In: vom Brocke J, Rosemann M (eds) Handbook on business process management, vol 2. Springer, Heidelberg
Rummler GA, Brache A (1995) Improving performance: how to manage the white space on the organization chart. Jossey-Bass, Sanfranciso, CA
Spanyi A (2005) Process management and the central role of executive mindset. Babson College Process Management Research Report
Spanyi A (2006) More for less: the power of process management. Meghan-Kiffer Press, London
Supply-Chain Council (2009) Supply-chain operations reference-model. http://www.supply-chain.org/galleries/public-gallery/SCOR%209.0%20Overview%20Booklet.pdf. Accessed 16 January 2009
The Standish Group (2009) http://www.standishgroup.com/. Accessed 16 January 2009
tmforum (2009) NGOSS business process frame-work (eTOM). http://www.tmforum.org/browse.aspx?catID=1648. Accessed 16 January 2009

# The Process of Business Process Management

**August-Wilhelm Scheer and Eric Brabänder**

**Abstract** This chapter provides an overview of the process of Business Process Management (BPM) and the elements needed to establish a holistic, organization-wide BPM approach. The objective of this chapter is to describe the optimal organizational infrastructure for achieving a holistic BPM approach and to identify the processes, roles, and responsibilities that need to be put in place. The chapter starts with an introduction into the necessity for a holistic, organization-wide BPM approach and typical misinterpretations of the meaning of BPM within that context. Based on an analysis of the process of BPM itself, the main elements of a holistic BPM approach are then identified and described in more detail. Special attention is paid to a detailed description of the Center of Excellence for BPM, its services and responsibilities within a company, and the resulting roles needed for a company's BPM structures. The chapter ends with a summary and a best practice example that shows what steps should be taken to implement holistic, enterprise-wide organizational structures to support BPM.

## 1 Introduction

Today, managers are facing a fast-moving business environment with changing customer needs and expectations, fast-evolving technologies and product life-cycles, strong globalization effects, accelerating innovation, and increasing digitization of products. Within this environment, managers need to ensure long-term business success for their company. In a growing market, it is important to respond by investing in innovative new products, sales channels, and marketing strategies. Organizations operating in a tough economic environment, on the other hand, need

A.-W. Scheer (✉)
Institute for Information Systems (IWi) at the German Research Center for Artificial Intelligence, Saarbrücken, Germany
e-mail: scheer@iwi.uni-sb.de

J. vom Brocke and M. Rosemann (eds.), *Handbook on Business Process Management 2*, International Handbooks on Information Systems,
DOI 10.1007/978-3-642-01982-1_12, 

to focus on optimizing costs, timescales, and product resources in order to boost efficiency.

Long-term business success is all about the ability of an organization to respond quickly to the changing market conditions, adapting their business model, and bringing their market strategy to operational execution through appropriate business processes, people, and technologies.

Business Process Management (BPM) is essential to ensure long-term business success based on flexible, market-responsive structures that simultaneously promote efficiency. But what is BPM and what is the right way to set up BPM structures that work within a company? What are the main elements of an effective BPM approach and which roles should be defined? What are good examples and best practices? This chapter is dedicated to showing some examples and structures of how to establish efficient BPM structures.

A *business process* is a continuous series of enterprise tasks, undertaken for the purpose of creating output. The starting point and final product of the business process is the output requested and utilized by corporate or external "customers" (Scheer 1999). Business processes enable the value chain of the enterprise, as well as focusing on the customer when the output is created (Hammer and Champy 1993). All companies have business processes, regardless of size or industry. A company's internal and inter-company processes are comparable to a body's nervous system. When maintained and optimized, they will ensure competitiveness and survival in the marketplace. In a nutshell: "Processes are not just something your business does; processes are your business" (Brabänder and Davis 2007).

Often, there are different reasons for a company to launch a business process-related initiative. One of the main reasons is to boost operational efficiency and reduce costs. Based on process analysis, it is possible to make the right decisions, significantly improve product and service quality, boost efficiency, and cut costs. Hence, it provides insights into weaknesses in important corporate processes and reduces the cost associated with daily workflows.

CosmosDirekt, Germany's biggest direct insurer, leveraged BPM to slash wait times by half when processing life insurance applications, reduce the number of cases where additional information or clarification was needed by 28%, and cut complaints by 60%. Collectively, these measures delivered cost savings of 20% (Ströbele 2008). Other projects also demonstrate the efficiency of actively managing a company's BPM activities. BMW Financial Services was able to streamline and significantly shorten credit and leasing processes and cut processing times in the Dealer Service Center (DSC) by 69%. The BPM initiative slashed process costs by 58% and staff requirements by 67% (IS Report 2005).

But there are also other triggers for launching BPM initiatives within a company:

- Implementing IT systems and business applications such as ERP, CRM, and SRM systems or
- Executing processes based on workflow management systems or BPM execution engines
- Establishing quality management systems for ISO certification or

- Initiating Six Sigma projects
- Implementing standardization frameworks, such as Zachman, TOGAF, etc.
- Introducing process-based requirement analysis for software engineering and software development processes
- Adopting legislation-based compliance management approaches that focus on business processes, e.g., Sarbanes-Oxley Act, KonTraG, etc.

Although all these different use cases can trigger a BPM initiative and are related to business process analysis, this is not always BPM per se.

BPM is a structured approach employing methods, policies, metrics, management practices, and software tools to coordinate and continuously optimize an organization's activities and processes. Its objective is to control and improve an organization's business through active, coordinated governance of all aspects of the specification, design, implementation, operation, measurement, analysis, and optimization of business processes in order to effectively and efficiently deliver business objectives (Brabänder and Davis 2007).

Hence BPM is a management discipline itself (Melenovsky 2006), but research into the "State of Business Process Management" in 2008 found that only 40% of 274 participating companies regard BPM as a "management discipline to organize, manage, and measure an organization based on the organization's core processes" (Harmon and Wolf 2006). All other participants saw BPM as a kind of business process improvement project (29%), cost-saving initiative (13%), and the use of technologies to manage IT (9%), or other activity (8%).

All activities performed by businesses to optimize and adapt their processes are part of BPM. To fulfill the requirement of adapting business processes to an ever-changing environment, the BPM process itself is structured like a continuous improvement lifecycle (Scheer and Jost 2006). This is the basic difference between a holistic BPM approach and business process analysis as an isolated initiative for process improvement or as part of an ERP implementation or BPR project (Hegedus 2008). BPM itself is a process that must be implemented and executed inside an organization. Doing this requires that process steps are clearly described and defined and the corresponding roles and responsibilities within the company must be identified and embedded in organizational structures. It is thus important to examine the BPM process in detail in order to better understand the associated roles, tasks, and responsibilities.

## 2 The Process of Business Process Management

The BPM lifecycle required to manage operational business processes consists of four major phases, as described in Fig. 1:

- Business process strategy
- Business process design
- Business process implementation
- Business process controlling

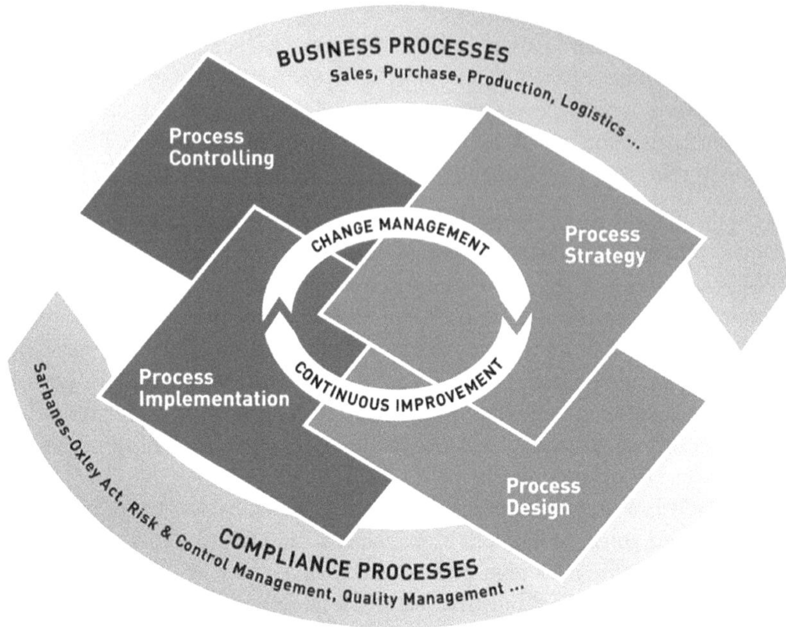


**Fig. 1** The BPM lifecycle Scheer and Jost (2006)

A typical BPM process follows the four phases and every phase consists of many typical work steps or activities related to the expected outcome and result of each phase. However, depending on the objective and the complexity of the organization, the focus area, and the problems to be solved with BPM, certain activities within the phases will always be implemented, while others can be optional or may be adapted to the needs of the organization.

## 2.1 Business Process Strategy Phase

Only those organizations that define and regularly modify targets can work toward them and be successful in the marketplace. The core business processes enable organizational solutions to optimally support the chosen strategy. Therefore, the business process strategy phase forms the foundation for aligning business processes with general corporate strategy.[1] Depending on the business model and market environment, organizations often adjust their strategies within very short time periods.

[1]Burlton (2010) is dedicated to present a methodological framework for realizing business strategy through process management. Process governance is regarded a vital prerequisite to establish a sustainable process architecture which is aligned with the business strategy.

These changes in strategy need to be reflected in business processes. Thus, with every strategy change, a company must pay careful attention to the underlying business process strategy and the changes to business processes. Key success factors in introducing a business process strategy are the commitment of top management and the involvement of employees through appropriate communication activity. Knowledge of the company's strategy and business objectives is essential to align this with the appropriate business processes. Additionally, an "enterprise process map" provides a high-level entry point into the organization's enterprise architecture and processes (Chhabra 2007). A process map represents a bird's eye view of the organization's core processes. Figure 2 shows a typical enterprise process map defined for a company in the automotive industry. An enterprise process map can be created from scratch or – much faster and simpler – by leveraging an industry-specific reference model. These models contain predefined process content, which can be selected according to specific criteria (Hilt 2008).

The following questions are a good starting point for key success factor analysis and the creation of an enterprise process map during the strategy phase (Hilt 2008):

- What products/services are offered to which markets?
- How important are the different business segments for the achievement of the overall strategy?
- What are the critical success factors that define the business objectives we wish to achieve?

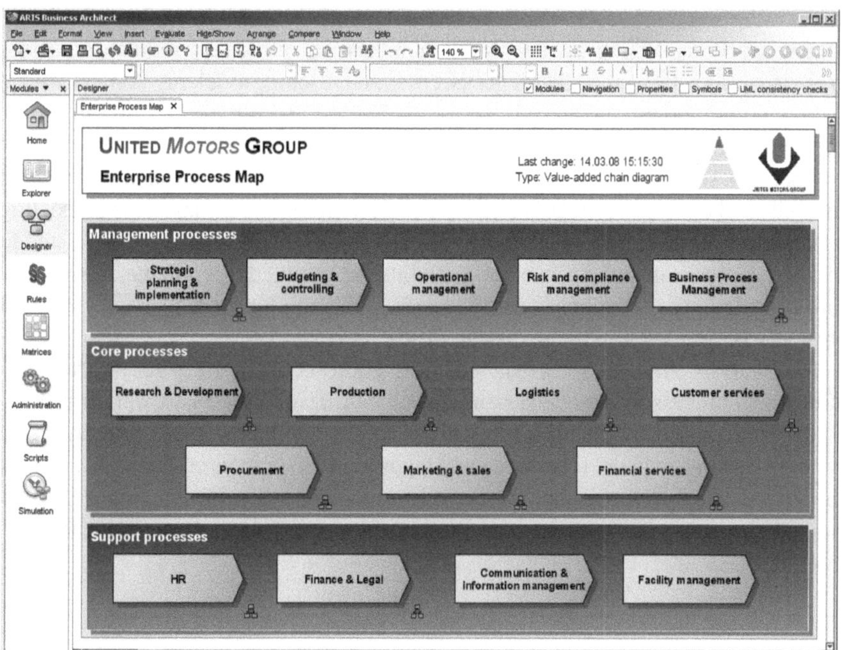


**Fig. 2** Enterprise process map of an automotive company

- Which members of the organization are key to achieving the business objectives?
- What is the company's high-level process structure, organizational structure, and IT structure?
- Which process areas and which processes are related to the business objectives and what are the related processes KPIs (key performance indicators)?
- Which activities are required in order to achieve the business objectives?
- What is the organization's overall BPM strategy?

## 2.2 *Business Process Design Phase*

The major goal of the business process design phase is the alignment of a company's processes with the needs and requirements of the market, including the design, analysis, and optimization of the processes as part of a continuous improvement cycle. The function of the design phase is to provide transparency of the current "as-is" process flow, to analyze the process flow, and to optimize it by creating a more efficient "to-be" process flow with higher quality.

This requires a method-based approach and a unified, structured, and understandable description language (Scheer 1994). The design phase answers the questions: "Who does what, in what sequence, what services or products are produced, and what software systems and data are used to support the process?"

As part of the process analysis, organizational, structural, and technological weak points in the processes are revealed and improvement potential is identified. This can be done solely by visualizing a business process, but it is also possible to simulate processes to uncover more detail about bottlenecks, costs, and resource problems. A standardized and common modeling notation, such as the Event-Driven Process Chain in Fig. 3, ensures that BPM design phase results can be compared across the organization.

The first step toward professional BPM involves the related areas of design, analysis, and optimization. Design consists of recording the actual status of existing ("as-is") processes (see Fig. 3). Processes can only be made visible and subjected to detailed analysis after the consolidation of all the knowledge available about them. This knowledge exists primarily in the heads of the employees who are in charge of or otherwise involved in the operation of the processes.

The analysis phase provides detailed information about the structure and efficiency of business processes. Cost center and resource utilization levels, as well as process bottlenecks caused by changes in medium and discontinuity in the underlying IT systems, become evident. Evaluation and reporting (i.e., process cost analysis, what-if analyzes, or process simulation) provide organizations with important process indicators regarding processing and wait times, utilization of resources, and costs (see Fig. 4).[2]

[2]For a detailed discussion refer to van der Aalst et al. (2010). The chapter by zur Mühlen and Shapiro (2010) is dedicated to the overall field of process analysis and provides a comprehensive overview of analysis methods, such as process mining and process simulation.

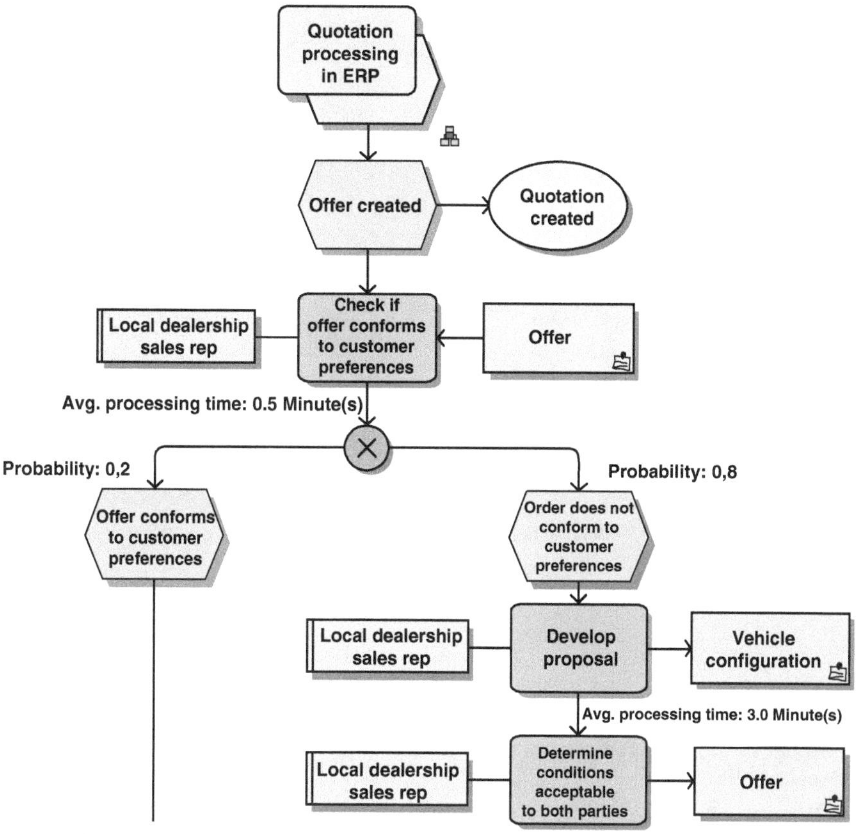


**Fig. 3** Contract process in an automotive company based on an Event-Driven Process Chain in ARIS Business Designer

The results of the analysis, combined with corporate goals, are used to derive and define target or "to-be" processes (i.e., processes that will help the company to create better value in the future).

During the business process design phase, different roles and skills are needed to get the best results. There is a need for people with project and/or process responsibility to drive the BPM process itself. But BPM methodology experts are also necessary to help the people in charge of the business express their knowledge about the workflow they already have in their heads. The roles involved in this phase are not only project leaders, BPM methodology experts, and department managers, but also business users or employees who are responsible for daily operations within the area affected by the BPM analysis.

Within the design phase, the following questions need to be answered:

- What is the detailed process architecture in the relevant main processes?
- What is the "as-is" process flow, including the related roles, data, and IT systems?

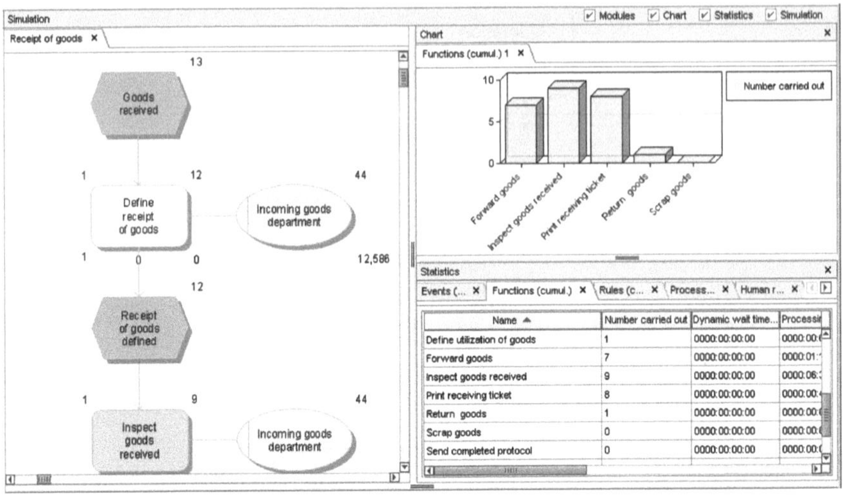


**Fig. 4** Dynamic process simulation to identify bottlenecks in a goods receiving process, based on an EPC model

- What are the dynamic resource requirements and the end-to-end processing time?
- What is the resource-related process time and what are the costs for the processes?
- What weaknesses do the processes display, and how can we overcome them?
- How can we restructure the processes at a high level and in detail? What are the implications?
- Which changes do we have to implement in order to successfully optimize the process and what does the newly designed "to-be" process flow look like?
- Which process areas can be optimized using new technologies (e.g., SOA)?
- Which processes need high flexibility and where do we need to service-enable our existing software systems?
- How can we ensure process-based and non-disruptive support via IT systems that meet the requirements of individual business departments?

## 2.3 *Business Process Implementation Phase*

BPM does not end with modeling and analysis of the improvement potential of business processes. The process changes must be implemented in practice by way of a transformation and change management process. Besides changing the workflow itself, process changes often impact a company's organizational structure and IT systems. The information technology to support, implement, and improve company processes is assuming ever greater importance. Increasingly, IT departments are taking on the role of business process innovators through the implementation of evolving IT technology. As information technology becomes more and more commoditized, standardized, and more flexible, the role of IT and the CIO is changing from a technology-oriented focus toward a business-oriented focus and is becoming responsible for the overall enterprise process architecture and company-wide BPM approach (Jost 2004).

The business process implementation phase focuses on the transformation of the daily process flow itself, the associated change in employee roles and responsibilities, and the seamless mapping of business processes and business requirements into operating application software with minimum information loss (Scheer et al. 2005). An organization must first focus on the business processes to be implemented and, only then, on actual implementation and IT systems. When processes have been modeled as "to-be" processes and the operational requirements are clearly understood, implementation through technology can commence. A variety of technologies can be used:

- Implementation of standardized ERP systems (i.e., SAP, Oracle, etc.)
- Establishing a service-oriented architecture (SOA)
- Implementation of workflow systems
- Classic software engineering and custom software development

In addition to IT-related implementation, communication and training concepts also need to be developed and executed to support employees affected by the new process and organizational changes. Process participants must be informed about the changes and take ownership of them (Hilt 2008). The process implementation phase requires not only IT experts and process methodology experts, but also people with good skills in internal communication and training in the context of change projects.

Typical questions in this phase are:

- Who will be affected by the process changes and organizational changes?
- Which roles and responsibilities will change within the organization?
- How can the defined automation requirements in the "to-be" processes be realized?
- Where can components and functionalities delivered by standard software be used?
- Which business activities require custom development work?
- What new employee tasks are created and which new IT functionalities do users need training for?
- How will the communication and training process be handled?
- How should process changes and role changes be communicated and which tools should be used?

## 2.4 Business Process Controlling Phase

If it cannot be measured, it cannot be managed. The business process controlling phase enables qualitative and quantitative measures to be compared against targets, thus revealing areas with potential for improvement and greater productivity. The business process controlling phase involves measurement of the efficiency of the business processes implemented with the help of IT systems and the implementation of internal control systems to monitor compliance with a wide range of regulations. The basic target of process controlling is to ensure the implemented business processes are running as they were defined during the design phase and that all process control steps are in place and working.

Furthermore, process efficiency is measured and analyzed against targets defined for the key performance indicators (KPIs) in order to identify opportunities to make changes that close the BPM optimization loop. This improvement potential can be analyzed on the basis of actual data, such as process throughput times, return frequencies, and deadline reliability.

Complete control of operational processes allows companies to introduce proactive BPM. Strategic corporate goals are monitored by installing a process performance management system that continuously monitors each "as-is" process instance against a set of "to-be" targets defined during the process design phase. This can provide prompt warning of deviations from planned figures and allow appropriate countermeasures to be taken.[3] Continuous monitoring of actual business processes bridges the gap between corporate strategy and its operational implementation and helps measure and control business performance (Jost 2008).

The following questions should be answered during the controlling phase:

- How is the organization performing? Do bottlenecks still exist?
- Is the performance of the processes as planned? How can we improve them?
- Are the processes being executed as modeled during the design phase? Where are the differences and why are the processes running differently?
- How are the transformed applications and systems performing? Are service level agreements being met?
- Are the defined roles and responsibilities working as defined?
- Is the process improvement and feedback cycle up and running?
- Are the processes compliant with the defined frameworks?
- How can we continuously improve and manage the processes and quickly react to required changes?
- Have we installed a process release cycle management system?

[3]Heckl and Moormann (2010) comprehensively discuss related problems and methods.

## 3 Main Elements of a Holistic BPM Approach

The process of BPM as a holistic management practice described in the previous section is an ideal-world model. Organization-wide implementation of the BPM process is a non-trivial and challenging task. In enterprise reality, the organization-wide adoption of BPM typically goes through *multiple stages* (Rosemann 2010):

- *Become aware of the benefits and methodologies of BPM*: During this stage, a deeper understanding of the methodologies and benefits of BPM as a management discipline has to be developed, based on detailed information and training.
- *Convert awareness into the desire to adopt BPM*: Based on a business-related driver (e.g., mergers, IT system implementations, new business segments, cost reduction activities, etc.), the desire to adopt a BPM approach within the organization grows (Harmon and Wolf 2006). Often, the existence of a BPM champion within the enterprise, an individual with a passion for the idea of BPM, is a major success factor in driving this awareness and desire. During this stage, BPM champions can be found within different layers of the organization (e.g., IT managers, line of business managers, chief executives, etc.).
- *Set up, execute, and monitor individual BPM projects*: BPM credibility and its capabilities are built up within the organization. BPM projects are often executed to achieve quick win situations and to market the idea of BPM across the organization.
- *Convert from multiple BPM projects to a governing and more centralized BPM program*: If several BPM projects were successful, organizations seek to capitalize on the BPM idea. They convert from multiple BPM projects to a more centralized and governing BPM approach. In this stage, BPM becomes a management discipline that supports the BPM process, as described below. An overall and organization-wide BPM methodology needs to be designed. Methods, techniques, and tools have to be specified, documented, installed, communicated, and maintained. During this stage, a BPM strategy must be developed. An enterprise-wide process architecture and a process hierarchy, as well as BPM guidelines, standards, and conventions, must be established. In this stage, the use of a BPM maturity model can help develop a BPM roadmap for the organization.
- *Productize BPM through a BPM Center of Excellence*: In this stage of the BPM adoption process, a BPM group is formed within the organization. This department or group is sometimes called a "BPM Center of Excellence," a "Global Process Office," or a "BPM Support Office." The main goal of this stage is to productize BPM, i.e., to consciously identify the BPM-related services on offer by such a BPM Center of Excellence. A BPM service portfolio for the BPM Center of Excellence is defined, and the services are offered to the stakeholders within the organization, e.g., to business departments, the IT department, etc.

Ultimately, the different stages of BPM adoption converge toward a single goal: To run the process of BPM efficiently and beneficially for the whole organization.

To reach this goal of a holistic BPM approach, the same elements must be in place that are necessary to run any process efficiently:

- The definition and clear understanding of the process of BPM itself
- *Clear objectives* regarding the outcome and benefits of BPM activities
- A *BPM organization and a BPM Center of Excellence* with appropriate knowledge, roles, and responsibilities
- *A defined, organization-wide BPM methodology*, BPM standards, and BPM service offerings
- *A mature BPM technology and tools* that optimally support an efficient BPM approach across the organization

If these elements are in place, the process of BPM can be run efficiently within an organization. A Gartner research note states that 80% of enterprise companies conducting BPM projects will experience a return on investment greater than 15%. The survey looked at responses from 20 companies that had completed 154 BPM projects and 95% of the companies experienced more than a 90% success rate among their BPM projects. All successful projects had a return on investment greater than 10%, Gartner found. Seventy-eight percent of the respondents had ROI rates greater than 15% (Dubie 2004).

Organizations with an identified BPM Center of Excellence can achieve a five times greater ROI over those with no Center of Excellence or dedicated process team (Palmer 2007). Similarly, those with a dedicated business process team in place reported nearly twice the ROI of those without any dedicated team in place (Palmer 2007).

In a survey from BPM Trends covering 74 companies worldwide, only 15% had successfully implemented a BPM Center of Excellence (Palmer 2007). As shown in Fig. 5, about 46% of the participants have identified and defined an internal team tasked with business process services. 16% are planning to create a BPM Center of Excellence, and 23% have not identified or defined specific process teams. The survey shows a clear positive correlation between BPM project success and the leverage of a dedicated process team or establishment of a Center of Excellence. Companies with neither of these in place were significantly more likely to face problems or lack of success with BPM programs. On the other hand, the only organizations reporting very successful BPM were those with a Center of Excellence or business process team in place.

A similar situation is revealed by another BPM study from BPTrends (Harmon and Wolf 2006), where about a third of the respondents (269, in total) say they do not have a BPM group or a Center of Excellence. Of those having a BPM group, about equal numbers have the group located at the executive level, at the departmental level, or at the divisional level and in IT. Only 20% of the respondents from large companies said they did not have a BPM group, while 47% of those from small or medium-sized companies reported that they lack a formal BPM group.

This shows that the installation of a *BPM Center of Excellence* within an organization is crucial for the success and efficiency of an organization's BPM activities. But many companies have still not achieved this organizational implementation

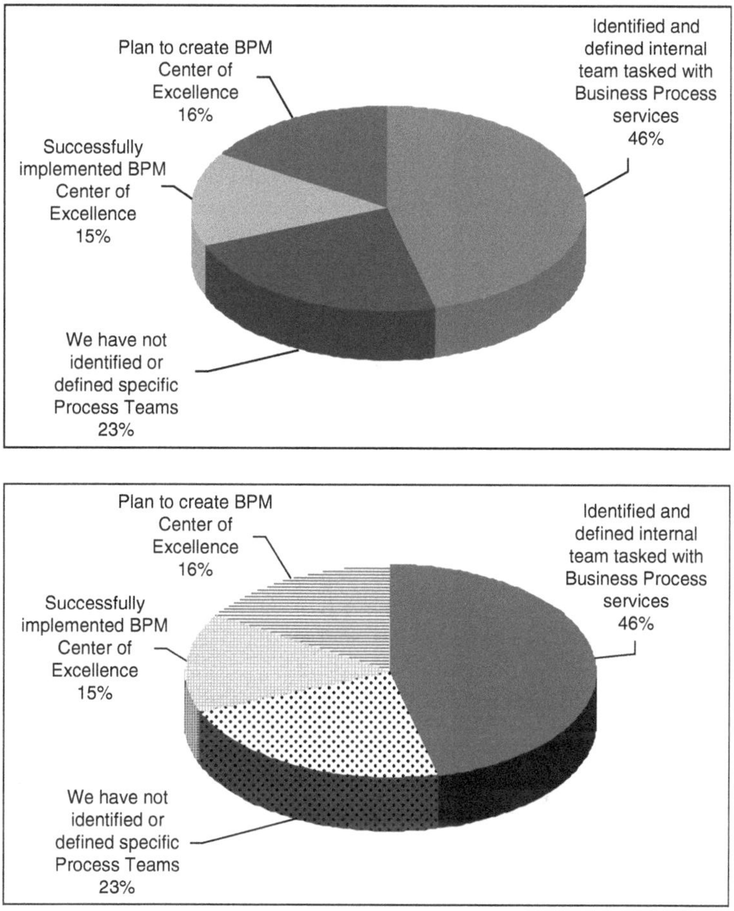


**Fig. 5** Status of business process initiatives [Palmer (2007)]

of BPM. The main tasks of a BPM Center of Excellence are to provide BPM governance and additional BPM services for the company, as well as to establish appropriate roles and responsibilities for an efficient BPM organization.

# 4 Services and Responsibilities of a BPM Center of Excellence

In order to implement a BPM Center of Excellence within an organization to support a holistic BPM approach, specific service offerings for stakeholders should be defined, along with internal roles and responsibilities. A service offering is a combination of methodology, tools, and communication activities that together address a strategic BPM target field of the organization. The organization's BPM target fields should be analyzed and prioritized first to identify the necessary BPM service offerings. Every target field (e.g., strategic decision support, ITIL implementation and review, IT system implementation, cost reduction initiatives, or the market launch of new products and services, etc.) must be identified and described. Current projects in the context of every target field should be analyzed. Additionally, the strategic and operational importance of every target field should be evaluated. Based on this prioritization, the necessary service offerings can be defined as a combination of BPM methodologies, tools, and communication activities.

Rosemann proposes analyzing and managing the BPM services portfolio offered by the BPM Center of Excellence based on the two dimensions of demand and capability (Rosemann 2010). Demand reflects the current organizational needs and appetite for a specific BPM service that can also be derived from the above-mentioned BPM target field analysis. The capabilities describe the readiness of the BPM Center of Excellence to provide a certain service. This dimension reflects the accumulated knowledge, skills, and experience of the BPM Center of Excellence, as well as the technological capacities to successfully deliver the defined BPM service. Four quadrants can be differentiated in this portfolio analysis:

- *The Perfect Match*: It exists if high demand meets high capability.
- *Over-Engineering*: If the BPM Center of Excellence provides a set of capabilities without there being a corresponding demand for them.
- *Vacuum*: If the demand for a specific BPM service is high, but the BPM Center of Excellence lacks the capabilities to deliver.
- *No-Action Zone*: This indicates a lack of both demand and capability.

Every BPM service offered and/or provided by a centralized BPM Center of Excellence can now be analyzed within this portfolio framework. Based on the quadrant, appropriate strategies can then be implemented to provide the relevant services.

When it comes to producing and delivering the required services, five main responsibilities of a centralized and enterprise-wide BPM Center of Excellence organization can be identified:

- BPM leadership
- Regulatory framework
- Project support
- Training and communication
- Process controlling

## 4.1 BPM Leadership

The area of BPM Leadership summarizes activities, such as the identification of the BPM stakeholders, the evaluation of BPM maturity, and the definition of a BPM vision and a BPM strategy for the company, as well as the internal marketing and communication of the value of BPM (see Fig. 6). Based on the BPM strategy, a master plan and a BPM roadmap need to be defined in a 2–3 year plan that provides

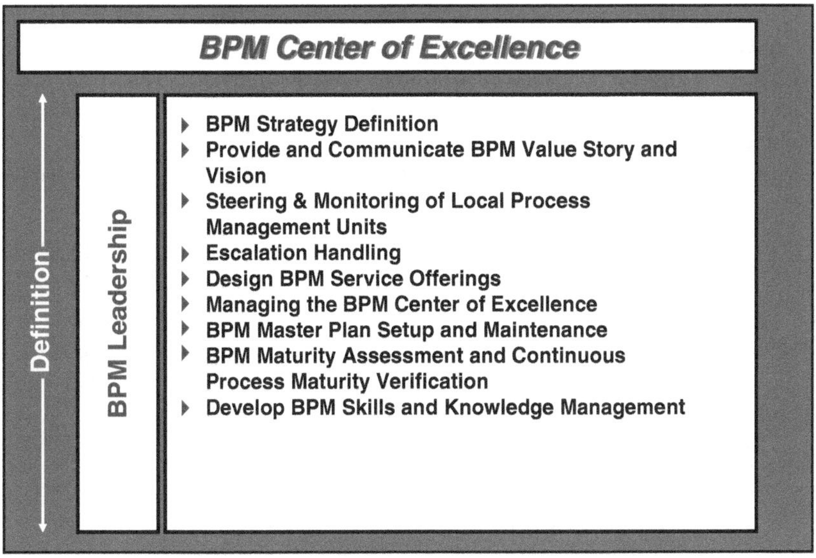


**Fig. 6** Main elements of the BPM Leadership

a preliminary assessment of the topics that the internal resources will have to be focused on and the timeframe in which specific milestones can be achieved within the BPM target fields. The design of the BPM offerings, the development of the necessary BPM skills, and the setting up of a BPM knowledge management system are typical BPM leadership activities.

The identification of the BPM stakeholders is an important part of BPM leadership. After identification of the BPM stakeholders, it is important to understand their current influence and in what ways they can be influenced in the future. Stakeholders are analyzed from a level, structure, culture, power, and trust point of view. A "stakeholder influence map" can help analyze the stakeholders with regard to their influence in the organization. The influence map assists in identifying stakeholders' interests, making it possible to understand their main needs and requirements. Each stakeholder or stakeholder group is analyzed based on their interest in the organization. A list is created that includes their needs and requirements and, consequently, their expectations with regard to the BPM organization.

A fundamental service within BPM leadership is the ongoing assessment of the BPM maturity of different parts of the organization. The evaluation of "as-is" BPM maturity is an important starting point for the definition of a BPM vision and strategy and a further BPM roadmap. During the BPM maturity assessment, the maturity level for each phase of the process of BPM is determined. Five stages of BPM maturity can be differentiated within the area of analysis:

- *Stage 1*: *Initial*: No structured activities in the area of analysis.
- *Stage 2*: *Awareness*: Awareness for the subject exists within the area of analysis. Planning activities have begun.

- *Stage 3*: *Defined*: The subject is clearly defined within the area of analysis. Implementation has not yet begun or is ongoing.
- *Stage 4*: *Managed*: The subject is implemented and managed within the area of analysis (i.e., people and roles are assigned; communication to relevant roles is taking place, etc.).
- *Stage 5*: *Excellence*: The subject has been implemented enterprise-wide, and an ongoing review and improvement process is in place.

Every phase of the BPM lifecycle within an organization can be evaluated and assessed in terms of these five maturity levels to identify weak points and improvement potential and to create a BPM strategy and BPM roadmap for the organization. A BPM maturity assessment should analyze every phase of the BPM process in detail. Typical questions derived from a number of BPM projects to deliver a quick overview of BPM maturity are listed in Table 1.

**Table 1** Overview of BPM maturity questions IDS Scheer Maturity Check (2008)

| BPM strategy maturity | BPM design maturity | BPM implementation maturity | BPM controlling maturity |
|---|---|---|---|
| BPM Strategy Alignment: How are your BPM strategy and objectives aligned with the business strategy? | Business Process Transparency: How transparent are your business processes? | Process Change Management: How are the required changes in the processes managed? | Process Performance Management: How are the implemented processes measured? |
| BPM Organizational Aptitude: What is your organizational readiness for BPM? | Business Process Analysis: To what extent have the organizational structures required for analysis of the business processes identified been put in place? | Organization Change Management: How much did the process improvements affect the organizational structure of the company? | Controlling BPM Achievements: How well is a target system for the BPM objectives defined? |
| BPM Organization: How is the BPM organization managed? | Business Process Evaluation: What level of qualitative process evaluation is implemented? | IT Change Management: How much did the process improvements affect the supporting IT system? | BPM Development Management: How is the implementa-tion of BPM knowledge and communication of BPM achieve-ments managed? |
| BPM Tools and Methods: Are BPM tools and methods defined as standards for BPM initiatives? | Business Process Optimization: What is being done in terms of process improvements? | BPM Knowledge Management: How are the business processes communicated and how is BPM knowledge managed? | Continuous Improvement Management: How are suggestions for improvements and related process changes managed? |

## 4.2 Regulatory Framework

The regulatory framework provided by the BPM Center of Excellence ensures a BPM approach that is consistent across the enterprise, reusable, and efficient (see Fig. 7). The development and maintenance of policy, conventions, and standards for an enterprise-wide BPM approach are the main tasks of the BPM Center of Excellence. The BPM standards cover the definition of the roles within the BPM organization, the definition of a process framework (enterprise reference processes), process conventions, and an enterprise-wide process architecture.

The enterprise-wide process architecture is a hierarchical structure of process description levels and directly related views covering the whole organization from a business process point of view (Brabänder and Davis 2007). It starts with high-level process maps representing a conceptual business view down to the detailed process flow descriptions describing specific tasks and their relation to roles, organization, data, and IT systems (see Fig. 8). The business process architecture and the related modeling conventions help structure the BPM landscape within an organization. The architecture describes how to structure the business process models horizontally by segmenting models into manageable chunks, which link together, and how to structure them vertically in a hierarchical structure that decomposes each model into increasing levels of detail.

Typically, the business process architecture consists of between four and six levels of process models. Besides the structure of process models, the architecture

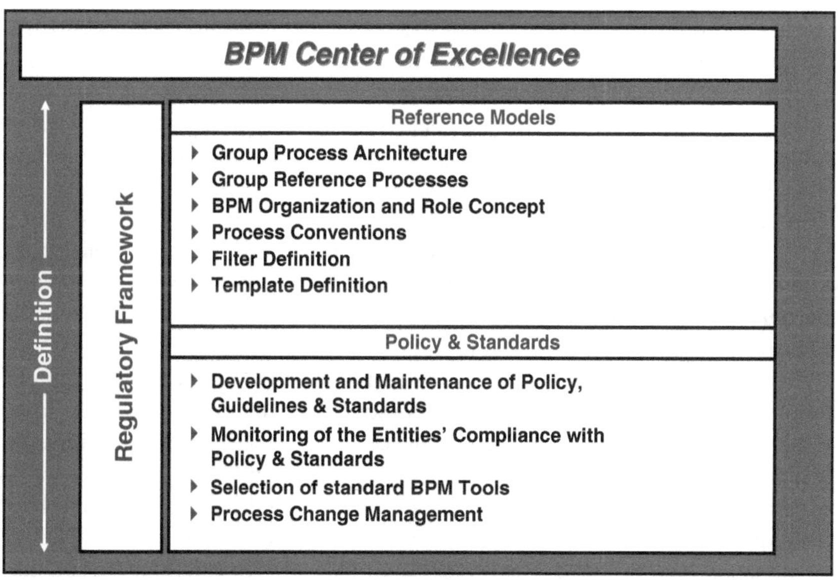


**Fig. 7** Main elements of the regulatory framework

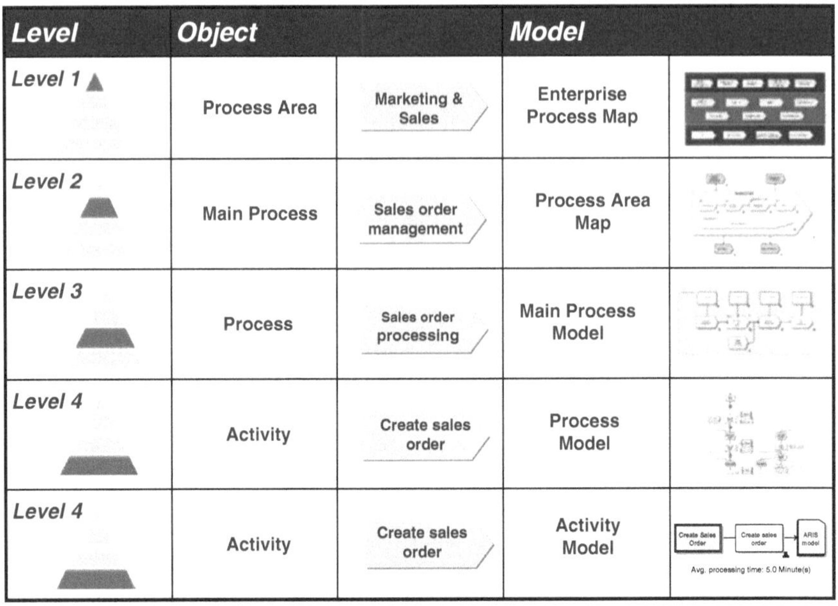


**Fig. 8** Process view and process architecture levels in ARIS

will also include other views (e.g., organizational diagrams, data models, objectives diagrams, IT landscape models, etc.). Once the process architecture is in place, it becomes a useful tool for everyone in the organization because it helps them to orientate what they do in the process structure and identify potential improvements. Figure 9 shows the process hierarchy at British Telecommunications (BT) as an example of a six-level process architecture including role diagrams, system application model, and other views in addition to the process hierarchy (Brabänder and Davis 2007).

Based on the process architecture, an enterprise-wide reference process structure and the related basic building blocks can be derived for every element of the process architecture that describes reusable parts within the process modeling environment. These elements will be managed by the BPM Center of Excellence and provided within a central BPM repository, such as ARIS.

The process architecture and the BPM standards are described and communicated by means of process conventions. A process convention handbook developed by the BPM Center of Excellence is the basis for all BPM projects within the organization and describes the process architecture and all related BPM elements and procedures. The process convention handbook provides the BPM policies and standards for the process of BPM and process modeling. It is regularly reviewed and updated by the BPM Center of Excellence based on new stakeholder requirements or project experience.

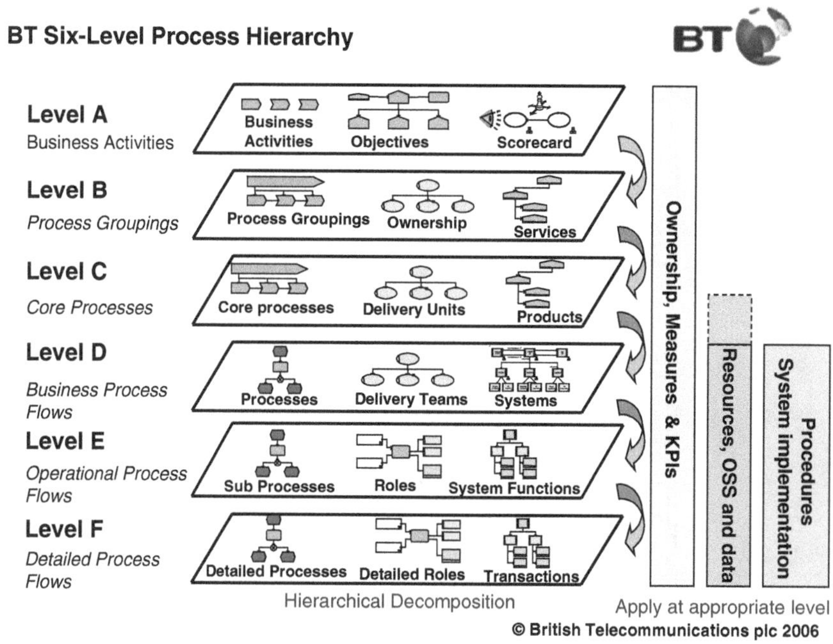


**Fig. 9** Six-level process hierarchy at British telecommunications (Brabänder and Davis 2007)

## 4.3 *Project Support*

Project support for BPM projects is one of the main services provided by the BPM Center of Excellence (see Fig. 10). The BPM methodology and process management experts of the BPM Center of Excellence provide support throughout all the phases of the BPM project, from strategy phase to design phase, implementation phase, and controlling phase. Throughout all phases, the BPM experts will help ensure that all necessary project steps during the process of BPM are realized and the requirements of stakeholders are met. In addition to project support and execution, this also includes project review and a final status report detailing project benefits and lessons learnt. Newly developed knowledge about process management methodologies or BPM project management is gathered within the feedback pool and knowledge management system of the BPM Center of Excellence.

To support all the phases of a BPM project, the BPM Center of Excellence team needs to have in-depth knowledge of BPM methodologies, as well as good skills in project management. During a project, they need to stick to their policies and conventions, but they also have to be open to improvement proposals and new stakeholder requirements. That means they also need very good soft skills in working together with a large number of individuals from other departments. During the course of the different projects, the BPM standards are rolled out into the organization.

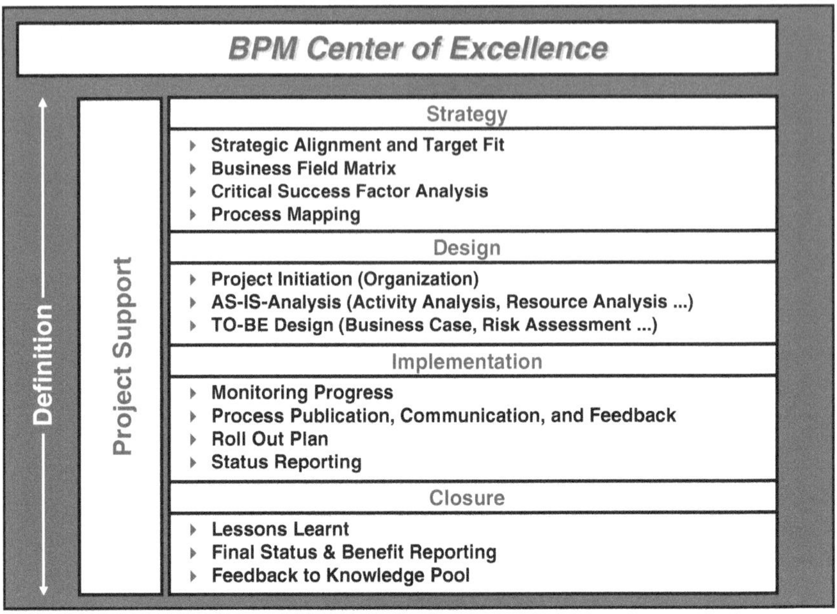


**Fig. 10** Main elements of the project support

### 4.4 *Training, Communication, and Process Controlling*

The training and communication responsibilities include all activities relating to installation, license management, and first-level user support for the internal BPM software and tools, such as ARIS (see Fig. 11). The provision and maintenance of BPM software, including the associated administration services, are also part of this area of responsibility.

Furthermore, training programs are developed to cover enterprise-wide BPM methodology and to train people to use the BPM technology and software chosen for the enterprise-wide BPM approach by the BPM Center of Excellence.

The communication activities target both change management measures within the company and internal marketing activities to promote the BPM concept and BPM Center of Excellence within the organization.

## 5 Roles Within a BPM Organization

Setting up a BPM Center of Excellence and identifying the appropriate services to support the process of BPM within an organization are important steps toward establishing a holistic BPM approach. However, based on the main services and the

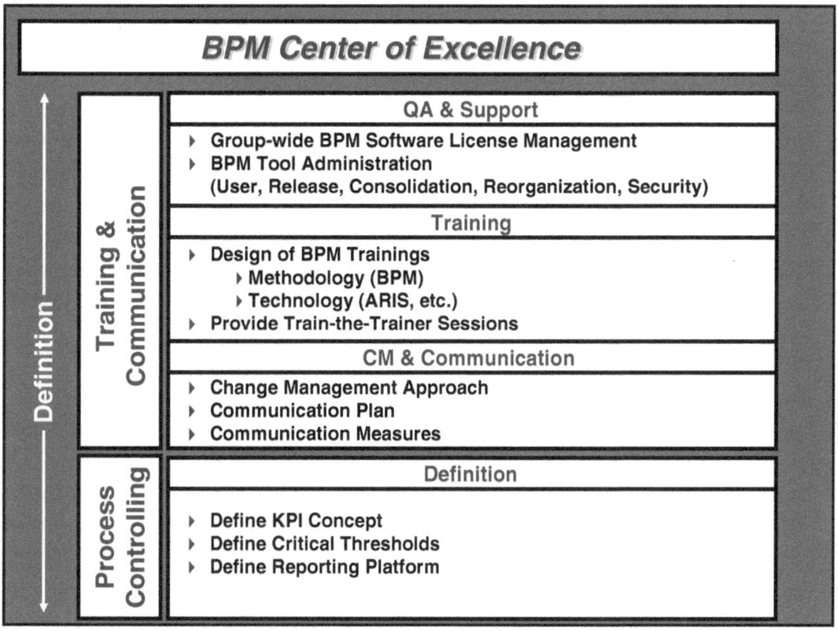


**Fig. 11** Main elements of training, communication and process controlling

responsibilities, it is also important to understand the roles that are necessary within that BPM structure.

The BPM governance process defines the accountability framework for creating a decision-making process that determines the services, architecture, standards, and policies for continuous management of business processes. It ensures that a management process is in place for setting goals and establishing policies, practices, procedures, organizational structure, roles, and responsibilities to ensure that enterprise goals will be achieved. A major part in this BPM governance process is played by the BPM Center of Excellence and its related roles. In the following paragraph, the roles within organizational BPM structures will be analyzed in more detail.

- *The BPM Sponsor*
  Before a BPM Center of Excellence can be established, the commitment of the top management to the concept of BPM has to be ensured. This means that a "BPM Sponsor" is needed at the executive board level, who is willing to initiate, fund, and drive this important topic from a senior management perspective. The BPM Sponsor must understand the importance of BPM for the organization. He or she also needs to understand that setting up a BPM Center of Excellence and establishing the process of BPM in the organization can have a significant impact on the organization's business performance and requires organizational change. He or she should be aware that BPM is not a separate function or activity, but that it is inextricably linked with the business.

The BPM Sponsor must also agree that people responsible for the operational business processes need the support of business process experts from the BPM Center of Excellence who understand BPM methodologies and concepts. The BPM Sponsor is a member of the organization's BPM Steering Committee.
If the company already has a strong business process culture, the role of the BPM Sponsor can be enhanced to become the Chief Process Officer, who is responsible for BPM initiatives within the organization at the executive management level (Jost 2004). Without a BPM Sponsor at the executive level who is committed to internally marketing all BPM initiatives, BMP awareness and status will not be strong enough. If there is no such BPM Sponsor, the holistic BPM approach could fail.

- *The Head of BPM*
  The Head of BPM supervises and manages all process management activities at a group or regional/local level and manages a team of organization-wide business process experts gathered together in the BPM Center of Excellence. The Head of BPM should be experienced in BPM and be well accepted by the individual business departments. He or she should have detailed process knowledge, strong knowledge regarding methodologies, coupled with well developed negotiation and communication skills, so that his or her authority will be accepted by the organization's senior management. The Head of BPM should also have excellent personal and social skills as he or she is often the mediator between different business units and also between the business units and the BPM Center of Excellence.

  While the BPM Sponsor stresses the importance of BPM and markets it at the executive level, the Head of BPM is responsible for organization-wide implementation and structuring of BPM activities. He or she is tasked with establishing a BPM Center of Excellence, proving that BPM efforts and projects within the organization are efficient and that they help improve business performance.

  Typical tasks of the Head of BPM are:
  - Defining the organization's BPM strategy
  - Managing and coordinating organization-wide BPM efforts
  - Defining the enterprise process map
  - Operating process working groups
  - Designing the BPM services offered by the BPM Center of Excellence
  - Suggesting process-related KPIs and building a consensus to support them
  - Developing and managing a BPM master plan and the associated implementation work
  - Steering and monitoring regional or local BPM managers and process coordinators
  - Joint leadership of the BPM Steering Committee

    Depending on the size of the organization, there may be a need for multilevel BPM structures. Large organizations with regional and local entities can implement a Head of BPM at the group level and also at the regional level. These individuals will have similar responsibilities but with a different regional or local focus.

- *The BPM Steering Committee*
  The BPM Steering Committee is responsible for setting, monitoring, and directing the BPM strategy of the business (Olding and Rosser 2008). The committee is chaired by the Head of BPM and is attended by the BPM Sponsor. The steering committee is also attended by the regional Heads of BPM (in a large organization) and specific business process experts as required, based on current BPM activities and projects.
  The main responsibility of the BPM Steering Committee is to oversee and monitor all BPM-related activities and projects within the organization and to align these activities to achieve higher efficiency. In the event of escalation or uncertainty, the BPM Steering Committee will be asked to make a decision.
- *The BPM Center of Excellence*
  The BPM Center of Excellence is led by the Head of BPM and comprises business process experts from throughout the enterprise. The responsibilities of the BPM Center of Excellence are BPM leadership, implementing a regulatory framework for BPM, offering project support, providing training and communication, and process controlling and governance. The BPM Center of Excellence offers internal process management consultants for group-wide business projects and is in charge of methodological excellence.
- *Business Process Experts*
  The Business Process Experts work as internal process management consultants for organization-wide business projects and are in charge of methodological excellence and the rollout of BPM knowledge into all projects. They are attached to the BPM Center of Excellence and are led by the Head of BPM. They have profound knowledge regarding BPM methodologies and process management tools, as well as project management skills.
- *The Process Owner*
  Process Owners own a dedicated core process (e.g., generic processes like sales order processes, procurement processes, and also industry core competences, such as retail loan processes, central credit processes, etc.) and are responsible for the operating performance and continuous process improvement of their process. They can be located at the group level or at the local/regional level, depending on the size of the organization. Process Owners should have a good knowledge of the enterprise and of the process areas under their supervision. They should also have an understanding of the business process architecture and the IT systems used in their business area. Furthermore, they should have some expertise in process management and the use and management of process key performance indicators (KPIs).
  Typical responsibilities and activities of Process Owners are:
  - Monitoring and managing business process performance (meeting KPIs)
  - Process improvement
  - Ensuring customer satisfaction
  - Identification of process interfaces and integration into the business process architecture

  - Defining process KPIs in compliance with the organization's process KPI structure
  - Recording and publishing process KPIs (e.g., time, cost, and quality)
  - Communication with process participants and process coordinators
- *The Process Coordinator*
  Process Coordinator is a special and extended role of a Process Owner. They own a dedicated business process area or a core process (i.e., retail loan processes, etc.) at the global/group-wide level and are responsible for standardization of these process areas and coordination of interfaces to other process areas. They should have a good knowledge of their business area and processes under their supervision and should understand the business process architecture of the organization. The Process Coordinator needs to understand the enterprise process map and the systems in use.

  They work together with other process coordinators and members of the BPM organization to establish transparent, measurable, comparable, and well-standardized processes for their area. They lead and coordinate the activities of all process owners in their process area and try to find the most practicable routes toward process standardization (see Fig. 12).

  The work of Process Coordinators can help achieve high efficiency in process standardization and positive cost effects throughout the organization. The SCALE project at Coca-Cola offers an example of a high degree of standardization based on the roles of Process Owners and Process Coordinators. Coca-Cola's largest bottling companies have established uniformity in all their

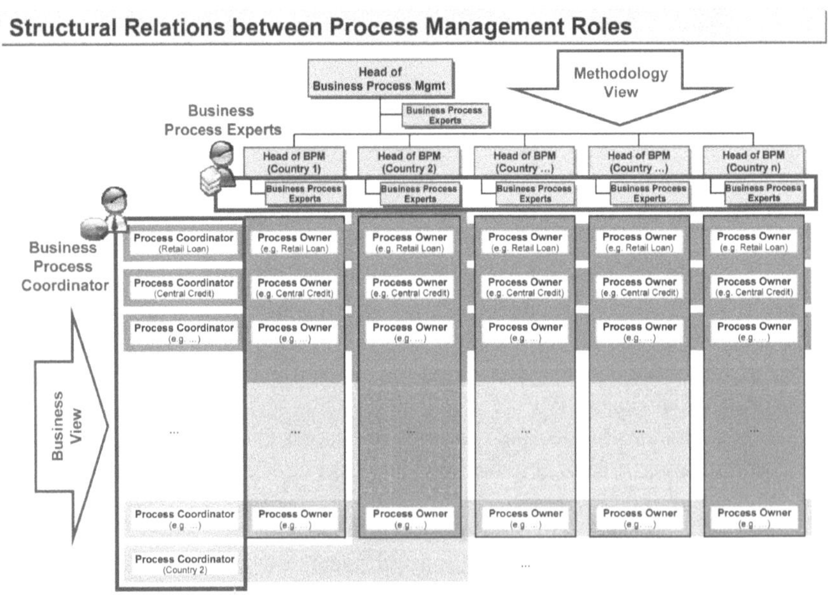


**Fig. 12** Structural relationships between BPM roles within a large organization (project example)

processes using a process-oriented approach for the harmonization of their IT systems. Within the SCALE project, they established roles for group-wide coordination of BPM activities, plus roles for the regional coordination, standardization, and realignment of business processes (named "Process Leads"), which are comparable with the role of Process Coordinators and Process Owners. When Process Coordinators from the various business areas started to analyze the standard business processes, they found that the degree of alignment was extremely high, but human resources and bookkeeping areas showed significant country-specific differences that couldn't be included in, the global standardized process architecture without some adjustment. The market-to-cash process met up to 94% of the requirements, forecast-to-deploy came in at 99%, and procure-to-pay was 100% identical. Beyond the main process lines, 94% of the processes were ranked as easy to standardize and another 5% could get there with justifiable cost and effort. Only 1%, were classified as highly specific (SCHEER Magazine 2008).

- *The Process Modeler*
  An important role needed for a business process design project and for a BPM organization is that of the Process Modelers. They are located in the local business organization and are responsible for business process modeling and process verification in compliance with the defined BPM modeling standards. Typically, they will also be responsible for promoting BPM and modeling tool knowledge. Some experienced Process Modelers may take on more responsibility in their teams by offering technical services, such as method filter configuration, database administration, creating and maintaining modeling libraries, or publishing models. They are often trained and supported by Business Process Experts.

## 6 Conclusion: How to Establish a Holistic BPM Approach Within an Organization

Based on the main elements of a holistic BPM approach, the methodology and procedural model shown in Fig. 13 describe the proposed steps that are necessary to install the process of BPM, the BPM Center of Excellence, and the necessary roles and responsibilities within an organization. The approach comprises four phases: strategy, design, implementation, and controlling.

The procedural model summarizes the different steps needed to establish enterprise-wide BPM with the main elements as described in the previous paragraphs. To achieve this goal, the company and its corporate culture as a whole must be examined. Maturity and process orientation are strictly evaluated during the strategy phase. In addition, relevant persons (stakeholders) are identified to persuade them, of the value of BPM as a solution for the company's most urgent issues. The core tasks in the design phase include defining BPM roles and responsibilities on the organizational side, as well as specifying architecture standards and frameworks

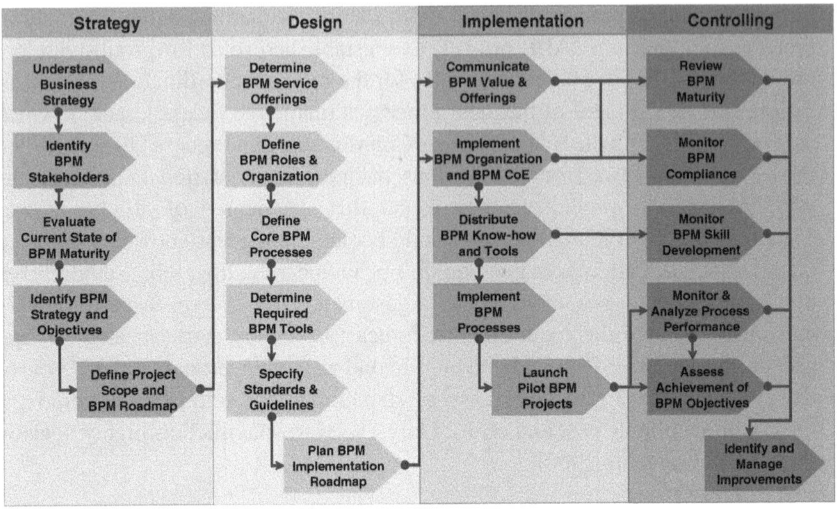


**Fig. 13** Procedural model to establish a holistic BPM approach within an organization

for technical implementation. Finally, in the design phase a BPM framework that fully describes all tasks, responsibilities, tool support, and methods, is created. In the implementation phase, this framework is gradually established within the corporate organization, while training sessions and project monitoring make successful implementation and controlling easier.

The chapter describes a best practice approach for enabling organizations to handle BPM far more efficiently. By installing the process of BPM, defining the appropriate roles and responsibilities, and setting up a defined organizational unit responsible for driving the efficiency of BPM (BPM Center of Excellence), the impact and value of BPM can be made much more visible to both divisional managers and the executive management team. Successful project examples underline the value of BPM.

## References

Brabänder E, Davis R (2007) ARIS design platform – getting started with BPM. Springer, London

Burlton R (2010) Delivering business strategy thorugh process management. In: vom Brocke J, Rosemann M (eds) Handbook on business process management, vol 2. Springer, Heidelberg

Chhabra S (2007) Enterprise process maps: a picture paints a thousand words. ARIS Expert Paper, http://www.ids-scheer.com/set/6473/ARIS_Expert_Paper-EBPM-Enterprise_Process_Maps_Chhabra_2007-11_en.pdf. Accessed 11 Dec 2008

Dubie D (2004) BPM and ROI. NetworkWorld.com, http://www.networkworld.com/weblogs/management/005640.html. Accessed 03 June 2008

Hammer and Champy (1993) Reengineering the corporation: a manifesto for business revolution. HarperBusiness, New York

Harmon P, Wolf C (2006) The state of Business Process Management, BPTrends 2008, February 2008
Heckl D, Moormann J (2010) Process performance management. In: vom Brocke J, Rosemann M (eds) Handbook on business process management, vol 2. Springer, Heidelberg
Hegedus I (2008) BPM & PI, Business Performance Partners (Part 2), BPTrends, March 2008
Hilt B (2008) The art of sustained process improvement – a practical guide, ARIS Expert Paper, http://www.ids-scheer.com/set/6473/EBPM – Hilt – Process Improvement – AEP en.pdf. Accessed 11 Dec 2008
IDS Scheer Maturity Check (2008) The Business Process Management (BPM) Maturity Check – How mature is your organization when it comes to managing its business proc-esses?, http://www.bpmmaturity.com. Accessed 15 Dec 2008
IS Report (2005) Konkrete Ergebnisse mit Prozessmethode. is report. doi: 7+8/2005, 9. Jahrgang. www.oxygon.de
Jost W (2004) Vom CIO zum CPO. Havard Business Manager. doi: September 2004, manager magazin Verlag, Hamburg
Jost W (2008) Geschäftsprozessmanagement steuert Business Performance. Information Management and Consulting. doi: Heft 2/2008
Melenovsky MJ (2006) Business process management as a discipline. doi: 1 August 2006. ID Number: G00139856. Gartner Research
Olding E, Rosser B (2008) Laying the Groundwork for Your BPM Initiative. doi: 23 May 2008. ID Number: G00158302. Gartner Research
Palmer N (2007) A survey of business process initiatives – a BPT report. BPTrends. doi: January 2007. www.bptrends.com
Rosemann M (2010) The service portfolio of a BPM center of excellence. In: vom Brocke J, Rosemann M (eds) Handbook on business process management, vol 2. Springer, Heidelberg
Scheer AW (1994) Business process engineering: reference models for industrial enterprises, 2nd edn. Springer, Berlin
Scheer AW (1999) ARIS – Business Process Frameworks, 3rd edn. Springer, Berlin
Scheer AW, Jost W (2006) From process documentation to corporate performance management. In: Scheer AW, Jost W, Heß H, Kronz A (eds) Corporate performance management – ARIS in practice. Berlin, Springer
Scheer AW, Adam O, Erbach F (2005) Next generation business process management. In: Scheer AW, Jost W, Wagner K (eds) Von Prozessmodellen zu lauffähigen Anwendungssystemen – ARIS in der Praxis. Springer, Berlin
SCHEER Magazine (2008) The IDS Scheer management magazine for business process excellence; International issue 1.2008, www.ids-scheer.com/scheermagazine
Ströbele E (2008) Mit Prozessmanagement die Spitzenposition behaupten – Business Process Management bei der CosmosDirekt. versicherungsbetriebe. doi: 4/2008
van der Aalst WMP, Nakatumba J, Rozinat A, Russell N (2010) Business process simulation. In: vom Brocke J, Rosemann M (eds) Handbook on business process management, vol 1. Springer, Heidelberg
zur Mühlen M, Shapiro R (2010) Business process analytics. In: vom Brocke J, Rosemann M (eds) Handbook on business process management, vol 2. Springer, Heidelberg

# The Service Portfolio of a BPM Center of Excellence

**Michael Rosemann**

**Abstract** A key concept for the centralized provision of Business Process Management (BPM) is the Center of Excellence (CoE). Organizations establish a CoE (aka BPM Support Office) as their BPM maturity increases in order to ensure a consistent and cost-effective way of offering BPM services. The definition of the offerings of such a center and the allocation of roles and responsibilities play an important role within BPM Governance. In order to plan the role of such a BPM CoE, this chapter proposes the productization of BPM leading to a set of fifteen distinct BPM services. A portfolio management approach is suggested to position these services. The approach allows identifying specific normative strategies for each BPM service, such as further training or BPM communication and marketing. A public sector case study provides further insights into how this approach has been used in practice. Empirical evidence from a survey with 15 organizations confirms the coverage of this set of BPM services and shows typical profiles for such BPM Centers of Excellence.

## 1 Typical Stages of Business Process Management Adoption

The enterprise-wide adoption of Business Process Management (BPM) in organizations tends to go through multiple stages.

First, an *awareness* of the benefits and methodologies of BPM has to occur. In many cases, we see a limited adoption of BPM simply because of a lack of a deeper understanding of BPM. This might be explained by an existing high activity level of an organization, by its previous commitment to another methodology for organizational engineering or by the absence of a demand for change and improvement.

---

M. Rosemann
Queensland University of Technology, Brisbane, QLD, Australia
e-mail: m.rosemann@qut.edu.au

J. vom Brocke and M. Rosemann (eds.), *Handbook on Business Process Management 2*, International Handbooks on Information Systems,
DOI 10.1007/978-3-642-01982-1_13, 

The initiating BPM proponents may also lack the required comprehensive appreciation of the methodologies, merits, and challenges of BPM or how these could be utilized within the specific context of an organization. Overall, an inhibiting lack of awareness is often due to lack of training, which, once conducted, is the most promising means of creating, increasing, and maintaining BPM awareness.

Second, this awareness and understanding of BPM has to convert into a *desire to adopt*. This is a critical stage and requires a business driver, that is, a sense of urgency, (e.g., a large system implementation or a corporate merger) and a champion, that is, at least one individual with passion for the idea of BPM. Such drivers and champions can be found in various parts and on alternative layers of the organization. In some cases, IT managers build the business cases for BPM. This is typically based on the impact that IT capabilities can have on business processes. In this context, Davenport and Short differentiate among other transactional, geographical, automational, analytical, informational, and sequential IT capabilities (Davenport and Short 1990). In other cases, the desire to adopt BPM is triggered by business improvement teams, HR departments, or business stakeholders such as line managers or senior executives. It remains, in any case and without a doubt, an ongoing challenge for the community that BPM has no classical home in an organization.

Third, assuming that the business case was successful, individual *BPM projects* have to be set up, executed, and monitored, often with the desire to achieve quick-win situations that can then be used to market and expand the BPM ideas across an organization. This is typically the phase in which organizations build up BPM capabilities and credibility. It also often means that individuals develop a fascination with BPM, see potential career paths in its development, and take (often unofficial) BPM ownership.

Fourth, assuming that individual BPM projects have been successful, organizations seek a wider capitalization on the BPM idea and convert multiple, but potentially isolated BPM projects into a governing and typically more centralized *BPM program*. In this stage, an overall BPM methodology needs to be designed. Methods, techniques, and tools have to be specified, documented, installed, communicated, and maintained. A main challenge in this phase is the design of a BPM strategy that has at its core a roadmap that specifies the planned BPM-related activities over the next 3–5 years. We recommend for this exercise the use of a BPM maturity model centered on the factors strategic alignment, governance, methods, process-aware information systems (PAIS), people, and culture (Rosemann and de Bruin 2006; Rosemann and vom Brocke 2010). A high number of organizations globally adopted this approach and have specified roadmaps that describe how and in what sequence they plan to increase the maturity in each of these six factors (de Bruin and Doebeli 2010). Once this type of momentum is gained, accountabilities have been assigned, and a roadmap is agreed on, a more specific definition of the deliverables and the overall benefit realization of BPM is required.

This fifth phase of a BPM adoption is the focus of this chapter. The typical scenario at this stage is that a centralized BPM Center of Excellence (CoE) is established in order to consolidate all BPM-related activities and ensure consistency and cost-effectiveness in their delivery. In addition to the activity-focused view of a maturity-driven BPM roadmap, it is now required to *productize BPM*, that is, to consciously identify the BPM-related services offered by such a central BPM Group. In this chapter, we will not discuss how the set of these services varies over time with increased BPM maturity as this would lead to highly contextualized recommendations.

## 2 The Business Process Management Service Portfolio

The following overview of typical, as well as emerging and rather visionary, BPM services has been derived through a series of workshops with organizations from the public and private sector. These workshops took place as part of engagements that were aimed toward the design and organizational setup of a BPM CoE. This set of services enables managers in charge of the BPM journey to start productizing their portfolio of current and future BPM services. The conceptual idea behind this framework is the design of a BPM service portfolio (Fig. 1); that is, all services offered by the BPM CoE are positioned in a portfolio with the two dimensions of demand and capability. Each of these represents a continuum and not just a simple dichotomy of high and low. *Demand* reflects the current organizational appetite for

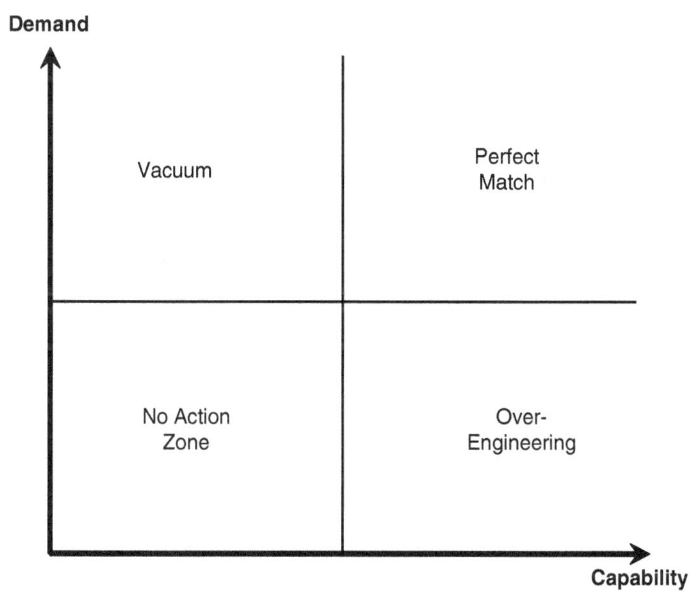


**Fig. 1** The demand-capability-portfolio

a BPM service. Like all demands, the demand for BPM services can be influenced through appropriate marketing and communication strategies. The given demand is a good, first indicator for the prioritization of the current suite of BPM services, especially when the CoE is project funded. *Capabilities* describe the readiness of the BPM CoE to provide a certain service. These capabilities reflect the accumulated knowledge, skills, and experience of the BPM CoE as well as available technological capacities to successfully deliver the individual BPM service.

In this portfolio, four quadrants can be differentiated (Fig. 1).

The *perfect match* exists, when high demand for a service and high capability to deliver it meet. Organizational requests for a BPM service can be satisfied assuming the BPM CoE has a sufficient bandwidth to deliver and a funding model that supports growth with increasing demand. Being able to comply with service level agreements and providing skilled resources will be key challenges. A typical strategy for sustainable and scalable service delivery is to progressively transfer accountabilities from the BPM CoE under the banner of "BPM self services" into the lines of business. This can be typically observed for services such as process modeling or process improvement.

It is more critical when the BPM CoE possesses a set of capabilities without corresponding demand for it. This could indicate capabilities that, at least at this moment in time, are *over-engineered*. The BPM CoE might have undertaken training in process simulation, in the conversion of conceptual to logical process models, or in the implementation of BPM Systems for process execution. However, the organization may not (yet) see the demand for such services. There are two possible pathways from here. Either the service will be retired, or the BPM CoE is convinced of the importance and benefits of the service. Assuming that the capabilities are of sufficient quality, the CoE will then invest in a stakeholder-specific communication and marketing plan for this service in order to increase the awareness for the potential future benefits of the service.

A very different challenge exists when the demand for the BPM service is high but the BPM CoE lacks the capabilities to deliver. This scenario is, in fact, most often the case for newly established BPM initiatives. Awareness and the desire to adopt exist, but there is no corresponding investment in BPM training and education programs. This obvious *vacuum* is often filled, in the short term, with external resources. The internal BPM CoE has to carefully consider whether or not to build up the required capabilities internally. Funding such a capability development and the sustainability of the demand will be the main challenges and require sound business cases based on a long-term BPM strategy. In some cases, this might be simply a very specific or temporary demand (e.g., Enterprise Systems upgrade or support for a corporate merger).

The *no-action zone* indicates a lack of demand *and* capability. However, ongoing monitoring for emerging BPM services (e.g., process forensics or process portfolio management) is advisable. A continuous assessment (e.g., by using surveys or focus groups) is required in order to evaluate the demand for further capability building.

As with all portfolio management approaches (e.g., Jeffery and Leliveld 2004), a BPM manager would seek a natural balance between the BPM services. In a charge-per-service environment, certain services like process modeling might become cash cows that can be used to subsidize the development of entire new services (e.g., process forensics or process portfolio management). Also, existing capabilities and skills should be carefully screened in order to identify potential for further growth.

BPM services might be differentiated into three types. First, essential 'keep the lights on services' (e.g., library management) are managed in a cost center (service) fashion. They provide a supportive capability to the organization but have limited impact on the current or future business model, customer experiences or overall revenue. Funding for such services will require a central, nonproject-specific budget to ensure the sustainability of the delivery. Second, some services will be critical for the quality of the interaction with external stakeholders. An example for such a service could be process improvement. These services could be seen as a 'profit services'. Funding could come from specific projects and the consuming side within the business will have a high level of interest in being involved in these services. Third and finally, there is a class of 'innovative services' (e.g., process portfolio management). A specific innovation fund needs to be allocated to develop these services even when the business case for this development cannot be clearly articulated.

# 3 A Proposed List of Business Process Management Services

The introduced portfolio can now be populated with specific BPM services. While the list (and labels) of these services will vary from organization to organization and by no means claims to be complete, the reference list provided in the following serves at least as a starting point for the identification of BPM services. We focus on those services that potentially could be offered by a centralized BPM CoE. However, it is acknowledged that many of these, and additional services, could (and should) be offered by other departments (e.g., IT, Corporate Governance, Business Improvement, Compliance Management, Project Management, Human Capital Management, external providers) and that the service ownership might vary over time. An appropriate funding model (e.g., budget and cost recovery) and service governance models are important. These issues are out of scope for the purpose of this chapter.

## *3.1 Business Process Management Maturity Assessment*

As indicated above, we see the ongoing assessment of the BPM maturity of different parts of the organization as a fundamental service. Nowadays, a number of BPM maturity models are available (Hammer 2007; OMG 2008; Rosemann et al. 2006). While these models differ, among others, in their understanding of BPM, their scope, their depth, the richness of the supporting methodology, or their empirical or theoretical foundation, they have in common that they are designed around a number of perceived critical factors. Following the BPM maturity model by (Rosemann et al. 2006) the evaluation of the six central organizational capabilities – strategic alignment, governance, methods, PAIS, people, and culture – provides a starting point for the identification of BPM priorities and a corresponding roadmap for BPM implementation and evolution (Rosemann and vom Brocke 2010). Such a BPM maturity assessment service could be offered in different packages, ranging from interviews with senior executives and workshops with multiple stakeholders to comprehensive surveys. It could also focus on a subset of the factors within the maturity model, e.g., strategic alignment only. The key contribution of this service is the triangulation of different sources of information to a rich, valid and reliable picture about the current status of the organizational BPM capabilities and the design of a way forward that considers organizational context factors such as executive buy-in, organizational disposition, or relevant external factors (de Bruin 2009).

## 3.2 Strategic Alignment

Before any BPM activities (e.g., process documentation or process improvement) are initiated, a dedicated service should target the assessment of a process under consideration, or of BPM overall, in terms of its alignment to corporate strategy and mission (de Bruin 2008). The value proposition of this service is twofold. First, it will help allocating priorities to processes based on their strategic alignment. Second, it will ensure that all process-related work will contribute to the corporate agenda. This service is based on a solid understanding of the organizational strategy and the way it can be operationalized for various processes. Strategic tools such as Strategy Maps can be utilized for this purpose (Kaplan and Norton 2004). It also requires the capability to regularly collect relevant process performance data in order to quantify the alignment without making this data collection a large project on its own. The deliverables of this service most notably feed into potential business cases and also operationalize objectives and constraints for BPM activities such as process documentation or process re-redesign.

## 3.3 Process Modeling

The advanced graphical and repository-based documentation of business processes in the form of process models can be broken down into two sub-services. First, it includes the methodology for model lifecycle management itself. For this purpose, the BPM CoE should host the BPM methodologist and the process modeling tool competence. Related services can then include training in this methodology and supportive tools, model governance, development of procedural models, methodological upgrades, and the provision of conventions and advanced practices. It will also facilitate the adaptation of this methodology to emerging requirements (e.g., process-based compliance or risk management). Second, process modeling as a narrowly defined service covers the actual capture and documentation of a current or intended future business process. This service could be offered on different levels of granularity and may cover modeling high level enterprise-wide processes, cross-departmental value chains, and detailed and more transactional business processes. It could also require attending related workshops and interviews, and providing process modeling support, facilitation and coaching services as part of these events (Sharp and McDermott 2008). Process modeling is often the "bread-and-butter service" of a BPM CoE, and it demands substantial scalability and expertise. Junior process analysts with limited domain and process improvement knowledge, but a deep knowledge of underlying methods, tools, architectures, and modeling conventions, can provide this service especially for more transactional processes. However, it is important to stress that the required skills go beyond mastering the modeling tools and techniques as multiple pitfalls are related to process modeling (Rosemann 2006a). The more process modeling is about enterprise-wide processes or the design of a process architecture (Aitken et al. 2010), the higher will be the requirements in terms of the qualification and domain experiences of the process analyst. It will be important for the BPM CoE to define a clear strategy how the fast increasing number of process models can be managed in terms of integration, update, change management, communication, and simple scale ("modeling in the large"). Moreover, it has to be defined when process model ownership will be transferred to the business. Otherwise, a further ongoing process model maintenance service could be offered.

## *3.4 Library Management*

In addition to modeling and managing business processes, a number of related artifacts have to be maintained. These artifacts can, for instance, be complementary conceptual models of data, knowledge, risks, services, and applications, as well as conventions, policies, business rule descriptions, best practices, etc., that provide a wider context for the business process models. A BPM CoE will typically outsource the management of at least parts of these models to other groups (e.g., IT or Human Capital Management), and provide some sort of methodological constraints to these groups to ensure the overall integration. The BPM CoE, however, might also decide to maintain at least a subset of these artifacts itself (e.g., organizational charts, knowledge maps) and potentially charge other departments for the service of bringing essential artifacts to a higher conceptual and more integrated level. In any case, this service will require close alignment with the design and ongoing management of the Enterprise Architecture. Furthermore, the Library Management service could include managing a process-related knowledge repository, covering, for example, emerging social network solutions such as communities of practices (e.g., http://bpm-collaboration.com), discussion groups, and the entire management of process issues and process improvement ideas.

## 3.5 *Process Improvement*

Process improvement as a BPM service goes beyond simple process modeling, and concentrates on deriving an improved version of a process. The involved process analysts should be more senior than those involved in basic reflective process modeling. A certain understanding of the domain and a wide set of skills, including creativity management and organizational improvement skills, but also financial analysis or risk and compliance assessments are essential. The capability to improve a process requires expertise in process analysis (e.g., Pareto, bottleneck, viewpoint or root-cause analysis), process enhancement (e.g., the transfer of as-is into to-be models using techniques such as TRIZ or process improvement (best practice) patterns (Mansar and Reijers 2007), process utilization (e.g., a resource-driven approach towards process improvement such as positive deviance), process derivation (e.g., use of external reference models and benchmarks), and process innovation (e.g., the design of entire new solutions and processes via brainstorming, de Bono's Six Hats or other lateral think skills). Further capabilities related to moderation, presentation, change, and conflict management are also essential. Process improvement is a high-value add activity of the BPM CoE and may be its most important profit service. The related service specification has to be clear about the final delivery, which will often be a set of (to-be) process models, issue registers, and improvement proposals. A concluding business case is, often out of scope and in the hands of a project manager outside the BPM CoE.

## 3.6 *Designing Process-Aware Information Systems*

In many cases, improving the business process will, at least in parts, demand process automation or support through existing or future IT infrastructure (Davenport and Short 1990). Detailed process design captures all services related to the development of models that build on the process analysis and convert these conceptual models into requirements that inform the design and configuration of PAIS (Dumas et al. 2005) or even entire service-oriented architectures or web service ecosystems. This service will require very specialized resources, deep knowledge of BPM systems, close affiliation with related vendors and standards and training to ensure a high level of awareness with current technologies. The service provides the critical glue in the overall aim of process-oriented business-IT alignment.

## 3.7 *Process Automation*

Further from the process design, a BPM service could exist that is dedicated to the actual implementation and execution of a business process. This will be typical system development work that tends to be located in the IT department or an external service provider. Process automation is a fast developing BPM service that requires staying on top of topics such as Service-Oriented Architectures and various other types of middleware, Web 2.0, social software, etc. It also covers the evaluation, selection, and implementation of PAIS.

## 3.8 *Process Change Management*

In addition to the IT-related implementation challenges, change management will be required to ensure a smooth transition of all organizational issues, procedures, policies, reporting structures, forms, cultural values, etc. This rich service covers organizational re-design, cultural assessments, personal and organizational profiling, job ranking, recruiting, policy and document revisions, etc. While it is the core act in the transformation to an improved process, a centralized BPM Group tends to have a rather secondary role in this service. Its involvement focuses on ensuring consistency with the conceptual process blueprints, required revisions, and extensions of it, and also the provision of support services for the change manager. In any case, it is important to integrate existing BPM and Change Management approaches within the organization.

## 3.9 *Management of Business Process Management Projects*

In addition to services related to the individual steps of a BPM initiative (e.g., process modeling, process improvement, process analysis), a service might also be dedicated to the task of managing the project. A process-minded project manager will ensure a strong focus on business processes during the entire project. Strong BPM skills have to be complemented with deep knowledge of the enterprise-specific project management methodology (e.g., PRINCE2, PMBOK). A BPM CoE that provides project management as a service will take over a more significant influence in projects leading to a higher opportunity to stress the critical role of process design. Merging process management, project management, and also change management methodologies will be a main challenge in this context.

### 3.10 Process Governance

Services related to the set-up of appropriate process governance structures will often stretch beyond the initial competencies of Enterprise Architects and Business Analysts. Nevertheless, it is an essential capability, and should be part of the initial BPM service catalog. Governance covers roles (e.g., process owner, process manager, and process analyst), responsibilities, duties, and decision-making processes (Spanyi 2010). While the governance of BPM itself is a more internal activity in the setup of the BPM CoE (e.g., who nominates process owners, who signs off on a new BPM methodology, etc.), a core BPM service can evolve around the governance of specific business processes. This service includes advice on the responsibilities of a process owner, the implementation of corresponding decision-making authorities and procedures, and the institutionalization of process-related tasks in a line of business. It will typically involve a close collaboration with Human Capital Management.

### 3.11 Process Compliance

The design of not only high performing, but also compliant, processes has become an area of substantial interest (Sadiq and Governatori 2010). Organizations increasingly acknowledge the role of business processes and business process models in their transfer to more compliant entities. The related challenges for the BPM CoE will be to build up a sufficient level of knowledge about relevant compliance standards (e.g., BASEL2, SOX) in order to customize the BPM methods, tools, and techniques. This will typically mean collaboration with (external) compliance experts and auditors. The contributions of a central BPM CoE tend to be limited to the design of compliant process models (i.e., does a process model comply with a mandated standard?). However, this service could also include support services related to ongoing compliance monitoring (i.e., does the organization work in a way compliant to the specified process model?). Again, the BPM Group will be challenged by issues related to scalability when a high number of compliance standards in various regions of the world matter, as this not only requires dealing with a high number of standards but also deep knowledge in each of these.

### 3.12 Process Performance Measurement

Measuring the performance of a business process is another potential high-value service of a BPM Group (Heckl and Moormann 2010). Many organizations show a high interest in, but only a limited uptake of, process-based performance management or process analytics (zur Mühlen and Shapiro 2010). The BPM CoE will have to possess, or have access to, solid skills related to techniques such as activity-based costing (ABC), economic value added (EVA), selected Six Sigma techniques (Conger 2010), forecasting, process simulation or process/data mining. Process performance measures will have to be derived from available documents such as Balanced Scorecards and Strategy Maps (Kaplan and Norton 2004). Appropriate and cost-effective ways of collecting and analyzing the identified measures have to be established. The identification, collection, and collation of process performance data is another high-value but also highly specialized service. The BPM CoE requires not only substantial skills within the group, but also high maturity in the line of business demanding this service, as well as in the IT-based implementation and application of these measurement concepts. Advanced BPM suites already offer a wide range of technological services to support the measurement of process performance.

## 3.13 Process Forensics

Process forensics is dedicated to the objective of identifying the reasons for process failures. While thorough process governance will strive for the avoidance of such a situation, it can never be completely excluded. Process forensics as a service is a clear statement that an organization is committed to uncover the causes of past errors in the execution of business processes. This service will require close collaboration with other (e.g., financial) forensic activities in an organization, and naturally will be triggered by insufficient process performance or compliance. It may even be envisaged that process forensics can be integrated with other ex-post analysis approaches such as incident and problem management.

## 3.14 Process (Management) Education/Training

Educating the organization on BPM will be an ongoing BPM service and is key to warranting sustained BPM success. Demand will increase when an enterprise-wide roll-out of BPM is the ultimate goal. While many organizations utilize external offerings from professional or academic BPM training partners, some organizations start to internalize this service, for instance, by adopting train-the-trainer education methodologies. In addition to providing process management skills (e.g., process improvement skills, process methodologies), the BPM CoE could also create a service related to process education, i.e., teaching the specifics of a certain process. Such a service could be, for example, consumed by the Human Capital Management department as part of an induction process for a new cohort of employees.

### *3.15 Process Portfolio Management*

In higher stages of BPM maturity, an organization will convert from a reactive approach, in which the BPM CoE responds to specific needs for process improvement articulated by the lines of business, to a more proactive approach in which the BPM Group uses process portfolios to identify relevant processes (Rosemann 2006b). Process portfolio analysis requires an Enterprise Process Architecture and is used to identify those business processes that are of the highest priority for initiatives, such as compliance management, process improvement, or the upcoming roll-out of an Enterprise System. As such, process portfolio management can provide a BPM service of high interest for senior executives in an organization as it helps to condense the high volume of process (model) information, and it has the potential to become a substantial base for decision-making processes.

## 4 Case Study

A brief case study provides some insights into an organization from the public sector that adopted the BPM service portfolio management approach described in this chapter. Four former Business Analysts in this organization had been assigned the responsibility to establish and populate BPM within a specific line of business of this Australian organization comprising approximately 200 employees.

The four analysts undertook a 6-day BPM training with the BPM Research Group of the Queensland University of Technology (www.bpm-training.com). While 5 days were dedicated to establishing essential skills in process modeling, improvement, analysis, and BPM evolution, the additional day six of the program was dedicated to customizing the contents of the previous days for the specific purposes of the organization. Based on the fifteen potential BPM services above, a portfolio was designed that clearly positioned each of these services in the demand-capability-diagram shown in Fig. 1. For each of the 15 above-mentioned services, the organization also differentiated the intended ownership model (BPM CoE or line of business). Each service was evaluated in terms of demand and capability by each of the four analysts. The resulting portfolio (Fig. 2), is now used for the design of the wider BPM roll-out and specifies upcoming BPM training needs (i.e., to increase BPM capabilities). It also helps with the BPM communication and marketing plan targeted toward increasing the organizational appetite for some of the low-demand services (i.e., to increase BPM demand).

Process modeling and improvement are the clear and expected mainstream services in this portfolio. BPM education will be another main target for the near future, even though it is envisaged that Human Resource Management and individual business managers will be in charge of process education. The BPM CoE of this organization is committed to invest in further training related to the design of PAIS. Due to the specific expertise required, process compliance and process automation will only be secondary priorities for the BPM CoE. Specific communication and

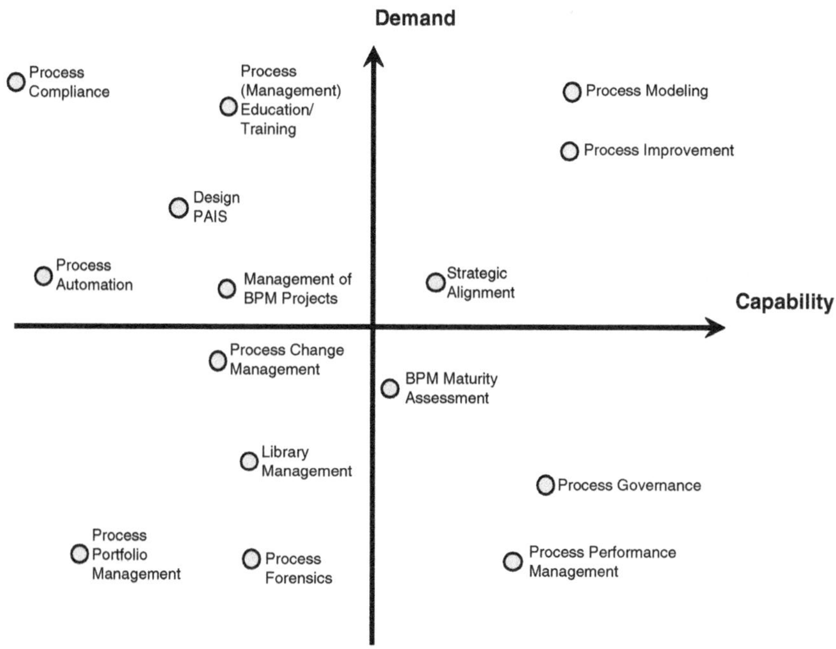


**Fig. 2** The demand-capability-portfolio in the case of a public sector organization

marketing strategies are planned for process governance and process performance management as the BPM CoE is convinced that the low demand can be explained by a lack of awareness more than by a lack of importance. Process change management and library management will be approached when internal resources become available while process portfolio management and process forensics are seen as interesting and relevant services in the future. However, at this stage, both the line of business and the BPM CoE lack the required maturity.

## 5 Patterns in Business Process Management Center of Excellence Service Portfolios

In order to generalize beyond the findings from a specific case study and to gain insights into typical patterns in the configuration of the service portfolio of a CoE, a brief survey was conducted in May 2008. All participating organizations are active members of the Australian BPM Community of Practice (http://bpm-collaboration.com). They belong to a variety of industries (among others aviation, retail, banking, energy, consulting, state government). Most of these organizations are part of Australia's Fortune 100. The survey instrument was sent to 38 members of this community of practice. Membership is individualized and by invitation only. It is restricted to the manager in charge for BPM within the organization. At its core, the instrument asked for a ranking of the perceived capability and the perceived internal demand for each of the 15 listed services above on a 1–5 Likert scale with 1 meaning very low and 5 meaning very high. The managers were also asked to name any further services that their BPM CoE provides beyond the set of 15 services listed in the instrument.

In total, 15 valid responses (39% response rate) were received. The following four additional services were all mentioned only once indicating a high level of completeness of the identified set of services.

- Process documentation (policies, procedures, work instructions)
- Business process analyst resource pool management
- Business analysis
- Balanced Scorecard reporting and analysis

It was interesting to note that when asked for the name of the central BPM entity, a long list of names came back as responses, indicating a lack of common branding in the BPM community. Here are the titles as reported by the survey participants:

- Process Support and Improvement Group
- Business Excellence
- Business Process and Systems
- Process Capability
- Business Process Services
- Corporate Development
- BPM Team
- BPM Support Office
- Business Improvement Group
- BPM Group
- Architecture and Liaison Office
- BPM CoE

In a similar way, it was astonishing to note the high diversity of reporting structures in which the BPM Group is integrated. Explicitly, we asked the question 'Who does the Head of the central BPM Group report to?' The following list of responses indicates the severe problem of a 'default home' for a BPM CoE.

- Chief Financial Officer (CFO)
- Chief Information Officer (CIO)
- Chief Technology Officer (CTO)
- General Manager Shared Business Services
- Global Director Business Process and Applications
- Manager Employee Relations and Development
- General Manager Operations
- Director Business Performance and Improvement
- Director Project Support Office

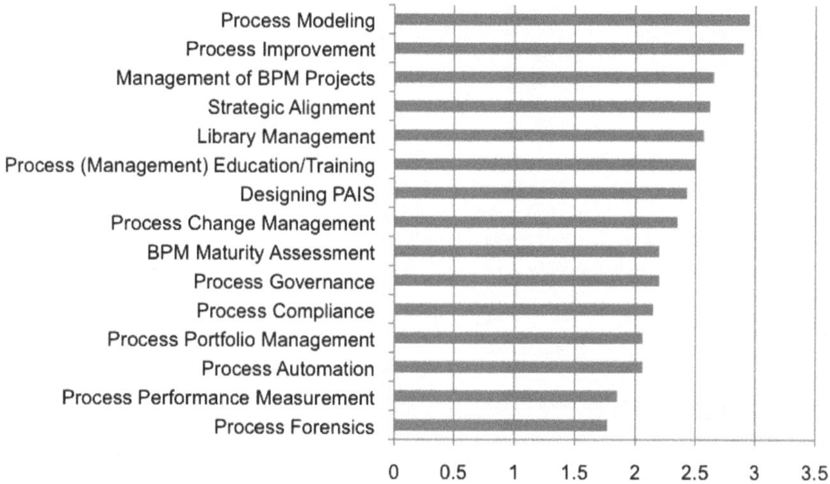


**Fig. 3** The perceived capability to deliver BPM services

- Executive Director, Division of IT
- Manager Enterprise Solutions (IT)
- President of Customer Services

When asked how the individual managers rank the perceived quality to deliver the individual services on a Likert scale from 1 to 5 with 5 being the highest, the two 'mainstream services' process modeling and process improvement clearly stood out (see Fig. 3 with the average values, per service).

In a similar way, the next Fig. 4 reports, using the same 1–5 scale, on the perceived internal demand for each of the 15 services. Again, process improvement and process modeling were the highest ranked services.

An interesting analysis is now to calculate the perceived gap between demand and capability, that is, where do the demands for certain BPM services exceed the internal capability, and vice versa. Figure 5 shows the result when calculating perceived capability–perceived demand. Strong negative values indicate that the organizational demand exceeds the perceived BPM CoE capabilities. This is, in particular, evident for the following services: process automation, process performance management, and process change management. However, also the two mainstream services, process improvement and process modeling appear in this list. On the opposite site, it is interesting to note that the three services that appear to have a capability that exceeds the demand can all be regarded as belonging largely to BPM program management, and less to the set of services required for an individual process re-design initiative. This can and may be seen as an indicator that the high demand of organizational departments is indeed with the specifics of process re-design, and that the development of a wider BPM capability is less appreciated (at this stage).

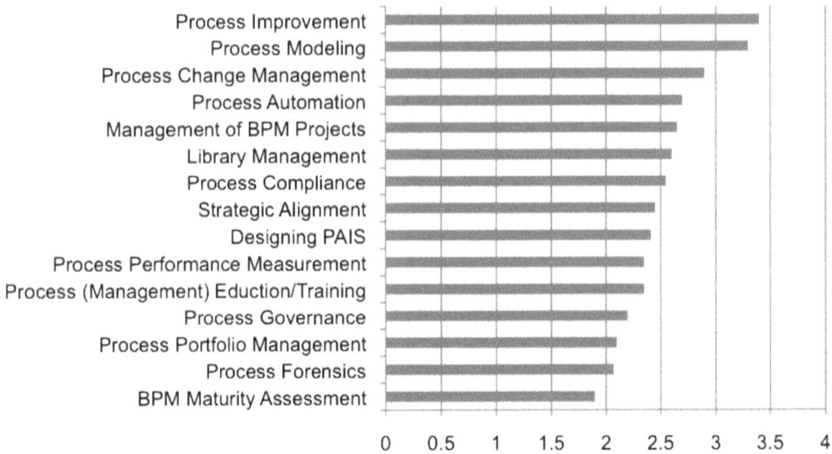


**Fig. 4** The perceived internal demand for BPM services

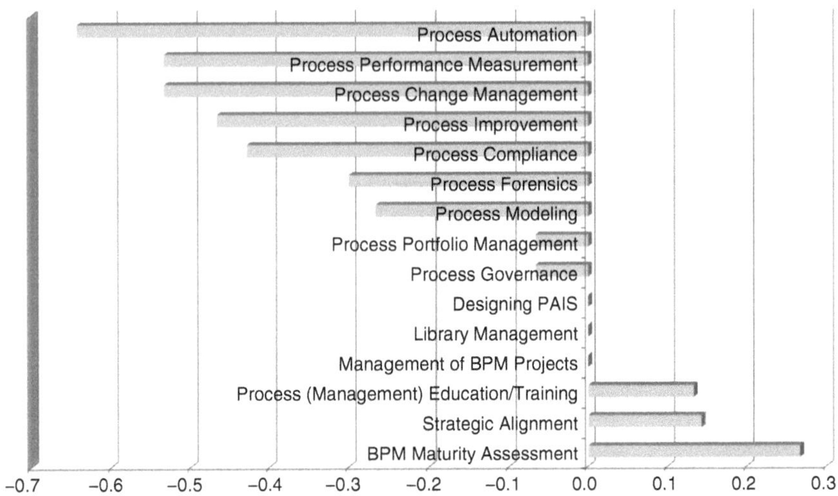


**Fig. 5** The difference between perceived capability and perceived demand for BPM services

It is important to be clear about some of the *limitations* of this study. First and foremost, the study reports on the perceptions of BPM managers. As such, there are constraints with regards to the validity and reliability of the data. There might also be a bias within the group of respondents. We also did not seek multiple responses from within one organization due to the individualized membership. Second, the notions of capability and demand do not necessarily equal actual activity levels per service and cannot reflect any future developments. Third, we are very much aware that a set of 15 respondents is too small to derive statistically significant data.

However, we are convinced that the data presented in this chapter shows at least important trends. Fourth, while we added definitions per service to the survey instrument, we cannot exclude differences in the interpretation of the meanings. This potentially compromises the comparability of the responses. Fifth, the comparability of the demand and capability scores (see also Fig. 5) is not guaranteed so that this last diagram can only show rough directions.

## 6 Conclusion

While the academic and practical BPM literature comprehensively covers BPM methods, techniques, and tools, there is a shortage of advice on BPM strategy design and BPM adoption and evolution models. Previously, we proposed a BPM maturity model (Rosemann et al. 2006) for the design of a BPM strategy roadmap. This chapter ventures to complement this work and provides some guidance on the actual specification of the portfolio of BPM services for an emerging BPM CoE as a cornerstone of organizational BPM Governance. A set of 15 BPM services has been defined that gives organizations, with an interest in institutionalizing a BPM program a, guideline for how they can specify and improve the services of such a group. Insights from a public sector case study provide an example for such a populated service portfolio. Results from a survey with 15 large Australian organizations across multiple industries provide an impression for common patterns in the set-up of such BPM CoEs.

Further challenges are related to the exact specification of the two fundamental dimensions of demand and capability (supply), related service level agreement and funding models, the contents of related training programs, and how BPM communication and marketing plans can help increase the organizational demands for BPM. Moreover, a closer alignment of this set of services with the proposed BPM maturity model will be required to ensure consistency between these two models (de Bruin 2009). It can also be observed that some BPM CoEs started considering the commercialization of their services beyond the narrow boundaries of their organization. This will lead to new business models and requires deeper investigation.

While applied research in these areas is currently undertaken, we believe that the proposed model, even in its current form, will be beneficial for stakeholders in charge of BPM and its governance.

## References

Aitken C et al. (2010) Process classification frameworks. In: vom Brocke J, Rosemann M (eds) Handbook on business process management, vol 2. Springer, Heidelberg

Conger S (2010) Six sigma and business process management. In: vom Brocke J, Rosemann M (eds) Handbook on business process management, vol 1. Springer, Heidelberg

Davenport T, Short JE (1990) The new industrial engineering: information technology and business process redesign. Sloan Manage Rev 31(4):11–27 de Bruin, T (2008) Strategies to increase executive commitment to business process management. In: Proceedings of the 16th European conference on information systems (ECIS), Galway, Ireland, 9–11 June

de Bruin T (2009) BPM maturity – a formative maturity model and a theory on progression, QUT, Faculty of Science and Technology, PhD Thesis, Brisbane

de Bruin T, Doebeli G (2010) An organizational approach to BPM: the experience of an Australian transport provider. In: vom Brocke J, Rosemann M (eds) Handbook on business process management, vol 2. Springer, Heidelberg

Dumas M, van der Aalst WM, ter Hofstede AH (2005) Process-aware information systems. Bridging people and software through process technology. Wiley-Interscience, New York

Hammer M (2007) The process audit. Harv Bus Rev 85:111–123

Heckl D, Moormann J (2010) Process performance management. In: vom Brocke J, Rosemann M (eds) Handbook on business process management, vol 2. Springer, Heidelberg

Jeffery M, Leliveld I (2004) Best practices in IT portfolio management. MIT Sloan Manage Rev 45(3):41–49

Kaplan RS, Norton DN (2004) Strategy maps: converting intangible assets into tangible outcomes. Harvard Business Press, Boston

Mansar SL, Reijers HA (2007) Best practices in business process redesign: use and impact. Bus Process Manage J 13(2):193–213

OMG (2008) Business Process Maturity Model (BPMM), Version 1.0. OMG

Rosemann M, de Bruin T, Power B (2006) BPM Maturity. In: Business Process Management. Practical Guidelines to Successful Implementations. Jeston J, Nelis J (eds). Elsevier 2006, 299–315.

Rosemann M (2006a) Potential pitfalls of process modelling. Bus Process Manage J 12(2/3): 249–254, 377–384

Rosemann M (2006b) Process portfolio management. BPTrends

Rosemann M, vom Brocke J (2010) The six core elements of business process management. In: vom Brocke J, Rosemann M (eds) Handbook on business process management, vol 2. Springer, Heidelberg

Sadiq S, Governatori G (2010) Managing regulatory compliance in business processes. In: vom Brocke J, Rosemann M (eds) Handbook on business process management, vol 2. Springer, Heidelberg

Sharp A, McDermott P (2008) Workflow modeling: tools for process improvement and application development, 2nd edn. Artech House, Norwood, MA, USA

Spanyi A (2010) Business process management governance. In: vom Brocke J, Rosemann M (eds) Handbook on business process management, vol 2. Springer, Heidelberg

zur Mühlen M, Shapiro R (2010) Business process analytics. In: vom Brocke J, Rosemann M (eds) Handbook on business process management, vol 2. Springer, Heidelberg

# BPM Center of Excellence: The Case of a Brazilian Company

**Leandro Jesus, André Macieira, Daniel Karrer, and Heitor Caulliraux**

**Abstract** The BPM Center of Excellence (CoE) has been widely adopted in organizations that believe in BPM's potential as a tool to promote an organizational environment that is technically and culturally prone to innovation and change. This chapter shows the relevance of a BPM CoE in order to implement an effective BPM Governance that generates synergy, efficiency, and collaboration within all types of existent BPM initiatives inside an organization. It also discusses lessons learnt related to the implementation of a BPM CoE by presenting a real case in a Brazilian company.

## 1 Introduction

The world of management has never been more complex and competition has never been fiercer. Research shows that the average time a company spends in the Standard & Poor's 500 List has declined by 80%, from 75 years in the late 1930s to 15 years in 2000 (Hagel and Brown 2005). Moreover, managers are increasingly facing a fast-moving business environment with changing customer needs and expectations, fast-evolving technologies and product lifecycles, strong globalization effects, accelerating innovation, and increasing digitization of products (Scheer and Brabänder 2010).

This context has led modern enterprises to continually invest in new management techniques, and one of the most relevant of these techniques has been Business Process Management (BPM). Hence, in recent years, several organizations have made significant investments in a multitude of BPM initiatives. In Brazil, as well as in South America as a whole, there are numerous examples where BPM projects lead to significant transformations inside organizations, such as process automation,

L. Jesus (✉)
Federal University of Rio de Janeiro, Rio de Janeiro, Brazil
e-mail: leandro.jesus@elogroup.com.br

J. vom Brocke and M. Rosemann (eds.), *Handbook on Business Process Management 2*, International Handbooks on Information Systems,
DOI 10.1007/978-3-642-01982-1_14, 

performance monitoring enhancement, organization's structure redesign, and implementation of reference models.

This scenario shows that BPM is widely recognized as a powerful instrument to improve and modify an organization's operation, with the potential of being a starting point to several improvement initiatives that affect the overall way of doing business.

However, a key characteristic that all these BPM initiatives seem to share is that most of the time they are conducted in an isolated way inside an organization, leading to a waste of resources and diminished return on investment. In this context, conceptual research as found at (Jeston and Nelis 2008; Richardson 2006; Vollmer et al. 2008) shows that managers face serious issues, as follows:

- "I have mapped my organization's processes. What do I do next?" One of the big challenges in the BPM adoption is assuring sustainability from the executed actions, and effectively maximizing the return on investment.
- "How do I turn BPM into a technique that is legitimated and used as an improvement tool throughout my entire organization?" Value from BPM initiatives range from modest to substantial, accordingly to its purpose, degree of synergy with other continuous improvement initiatives, and degree of BPM cultural adoption.

These two main motivations are driving the necessity for creating a formal BPM group usually called BPM Center of Excellence (BPM CoE) or BPM Office. A BPM CoE is an important organizational mechanism that has been adopted by many enterprises aiming at institutionalizing BPM initiatives and perpetuating its benefits throughout the years. An effective BPM CoE empowers process vision as a central axis in an innovative and systemized way of thinking of an enterprise's operations.

This chapter will be based on this main idea having the following objectives: (1) discuss the main roles that should be assumed by a BPM CoE; (2) describe a BPM CoE implementation case detailing the major steps done; (3) present practical insights on the difficulties and obstacles faced when conducting this effort; (4) discuss the value gradually obtained when implementing a BPM CoE, as an evolutionary effort that is highly linked with the organization's management maturity and its strategic needs.

In the next section, we provide a brief description of the three capabilities of a BPM CoE. After that, in Sect. 3, a case study on the implementation of a BPM CoE in a Brazilian company is given. Finally, in Sect. 4, we present our final conclusions and observe some trends in the BPM field that will impact organizations and BPM CoE initiatives in the future.

## 2 The BPM CoE's Three Main Capabilities

In Sect. 1, we have already discussed that the BPM CoE is an important instrument to institutionalize business processes based initiatives inside an organization. In order to achieve these objectives, the BPM CoE must execute three main capabilities that should be gradually developed (Table 1):

**Table 1** The BPM CoE three main capabilities

| Capability | Description |
|---|---|
| Diffusion of BPM Culture | Establish a common understanding that BPM is about creating a cultural and technical environment that is prone to a continuous and qualified discussion of how things are done. BPM should be thought of as the organizational engine to continuous change and performance improvement through a collaborative, empowered and sustainable way. |
| Creation of Convergence among BPM Initiatives | Promote the alignment, governance, and convergence of all BPM-related initiatives, increasing its synergy, efficiency and return on investment. This helps strengthen the adoption of BPM-based initiatives as a management best practice within the organization. |
| Internal Consulting Orientation | Implement and maintain a service orientation approach for each BPM-based initiative putting the organizational strategy and the business units as important clients that demands productivity increase, managerial visibility enhancement and innovation promotion. |

During the remainder of this section, we will present a detailed analysis of these three main capabilities based on practical experiences in implementing BPM CoE in Brazil as well as on conceptual research on BPM literature (Harmon 2007; Jeston and Nelis 2008; Richardson 2006; Rosemann 2010; Snabe et al. 2009; Spanyi 2009; Spanyi et al. 2008; Vollmer et al. 2008). These capabilities will serve as the basis upon which we will draw our understanding of the case study presented in Sect. 3.

## 2.1 *Diffusion of BPM Culture*

Some of the main questions that arise in the early phases of a BPM CoE implementation are as follows: how can we convince businesses areas that they have to map their processes? What is the best way to convince top management that business process practices will actually bring value to an organization? How do we ensure that process documentation will not end up stuck in somebody's drawer? All these questions represent the anxieties of professionals who are trying to materialize the value of BPM into an organization that does not have BPM culture oriented to performance improvement (see also the Hilti case in vom Brocke et al. 2010).

To answer these questions, first of all, it is important to change the corporate mindset about what BPM is all about. An effective BPM philosophy should be based on three central principles:

- To manage business processes of an organization is to continually change the way this organization executes its activities (Scheer and Brabänder 2010), aiming at significant performance improvements such as: operational excellence strengthening, managerial visibility enhancement and innovation promotion

- BPM value comes from constructing an ideal environment to rethink the way an organization executes its activities. This environment should be collaborative, culturally sustainable, and supported by appropriate methods and tools
- Process models are not a BPM final result, but an intermediary tool. Thus, the key question to be asked to a manager should not be only "are there any processes left to be mapped?", but "are there any opportunities to reduce cost, improve business areas interfaces, and optimize decision making inside my organization?"

Hence, the BPM adoption starts with a cultural change. Organizations need to understand and disseminate internally the idea that BPM is about organizational performance improvement.

In this context, BPM CoE must be thought of as the organizational gatekeeper of the BPM Brand, and consequently the formal responsible for BPM Marketing activities inside the organization. This means that the CoE itself must create an image of competence and professionalism, and disseminate throughout the organization the importance of BPM as best practices management tools to leverage organizational performance.

According to this, a BPM CoE has to make sure that all stakeholders are continuously aware of the benefits of each BPM-based solution, and how these benefits can be obtained. This helps decision makers get comfortable using BPM-based solutions as a legitimate mean to: (1) strengthen operational excellence, (2) enhance managerial visibility, and (3) promote organizational innovation.

The BPM Marketing and BPM Brand concepts also create the need to provide proof and evidence that the BPM initiatives are actually bringing value to the organization, as well as institutionalizing the BPM culture. This means that the BPM CoE must carefully plan its strategy to strike the right balance between process quick wins and long term improvements.

## 2.2 Creation of Convergence Among BPM Initiatives

Processes are at the center of today's and tomorrow's competition. Organizations have to come to the conclusion that efficiency as well as quality and customer experience, are to be delivered by business processes. Due to this tendency, Business Process Management came to light as an attractive bundle of management solutions that address a variety of organizational problems (Willaert et al. 2007).

Therefore, BPM has emerged as a robust portfolio of management solutions that attend to a series of heterogeneous problems, challenges and opportunities. Initiatives like Enterprise Architecture definition, six sigma adoption, compliance management, performance monitoring, risk analysis, and competencies management are all examples of business process-based initiatives. These initiatives have been used throughout the years to support the achievement of a myriad of organizational objectives, such as: cost reduction, expertise retention, client's satisfaction enhancement, and product differentiation.

The key common element in all these BPM-related initiatives is the idea of synthesizing the reality and the complexity of an enterprise operation into process models ruled by notation standards and specific taxonomies. In all these BPM-based initiatives, business process models are used as fundamental tools to guarantee a coherent and consistent understanding of the organization, and consequently, an intelligent and effective intervention. Consequently, the BPM concept could be positioned at the center of all these approaches to improve operations performance.

However, these BPM initiatives tend to emerge in organizations for different reasons, sponsored by different actors and with different scopes. This leads to several problems: process model documents being underutilized, difficulties to consolidate different modeling techniques, different areas demanding the same information from other business areas, redundant actions plans, inefficient intervention, focusing on consequences beside root causes, misalignment with enterprise strategy, among others.

In this context, generating convergence among the many BPM-related initiatives is an important managerial attention point and a fundamental cornerstone of the BPM CoE. This implies that the BPM CoE should propel an organization to enhance its BPM governance, helping organizations to migrate from isolated BPM initiatives to integrated and synergic ones.

But what process governance is really about? Getting back to BPM literature we could find out some important definitions:

- "Process Governance is the organization of management. It refers to goals, principles and organizational charts that define who can make what decisions, as well as the policies and the rules that define what managers can do" (Harmon 2007).
- "Governance in the context of BPM establishes relevant and transparent accountability, decision making and reward process to guide actions" (Richardson 2006).
- "In order to optimize and sustain business process improvements it's essential to overlay some form of governance that creates the right structure, metrics, roles and responsibilities to measure, improve and manage the performance of a firm's end-to-end business processes" (Spanyi 2007).
- "In order to optimize and sustain improvements to operational performance it is essential to overlay some form of governance that creates the right structures, metrics, roles, and responsibilities to measure and manage the performance of a firm's end-to-end business processes. This is called BPM Governance" (Spanyi 2010).

Based on that, some examples of a BPM CoE's attributions are:

- To manage business area demands for BPM-related initiatives, improving organizational performance while conciliating its heterogeneous purpose, timing, and scopes
- To support the delimitation of roles and responsibilities for each actor somehow involved in BPM initiatives

- To ensure that all BPM initiatives are not only methodologically aligned, but that they are built on convergent foundations and aligned with organizations strategic priorities
- To map the information inputs and outputs associated with each BPM initiative assuring that the same information will not be demanded for a business area more than once
- To create a collaborative planning approach in order to optimize the best possible way to execute all BPM-based initiatives minimizing redundancies
- To promote convergence to all action plans generated by each BPM initiative, helping to create a unified "management agenda" and avoiding the duplication of efforts

Finally, it is very important to point out that putting the BPM CoE as the governance center of all BPM initiatives by no means implies that it must be responsible for the direct execution of all BPM iniatives. The success of a BPM CoE depends on its ability to recognize and interact with the particular organizational political and power contexts associated with those BPM initiatives that occur within.

## 2.3 *Internal Consulting Orientation*

If the previous capability focused at increasing the synergy and efficiency of how BPM initiatives are done, this third and final capability discuss how to significantly increase the value created to areas that benefits from each BPM initiative.

The BPM CoE should study and analyze the current portfolio of BPM initiatives and formulate how to redesign it as a portfolio of BPM-based services to be offered to business areas. The conceptual idea is to design a BPM portfolio that is both honed to the organization's demand for process management services as it is to the organizations strategic priorities. This logic of work allows the BPM Center of Excellence to align its activities with the organizations strategic objectives and consequently its appetite for BPM services.

One clear point should be made here: this is not just a simple change of terms. This means that the traditional approach of BPM initiatives should be updated by a new paradigm that puts business areas as clients of a portfolio of BPM-based services.

A BPM service should be understood as a customized and flexible product of performance improvement delivered to business areas according to its specifics issues and problems: high cost, lack of visibility, high rate of errors, interface gaps between areas, competence gap, excess of manual inputs, etc.

To mature from BPM initiatives to BPM services means that a BPM CoE has to understand existing demands in each business area and customize a proper management solution combining the available BPM services and consequently linking the available BPM tools, techniques, and methods. Also, with this new client orientation to BPM Initiatives emerges the necessities:

- To improve process prioritization methods as in (Bandara et al. 2010) to better understand the nature and business impact of areas' demands. A better identification of the improvement opportunity will be fundamental to determine the proper BPM services to be delivered.
- To increase usage of BPM Maturity Models as in (Hammer 2007; de Bruin 2009; de Bruin and Doebeli 2010) to better understand the whole scope of possible BPM actions. Seeing the whole picture of BPM in a consistent framework will be very important to plan BPM development strategy – service by service – during the years.

Finally, the next section will describe the case of a BPM CoE detailing all the steps, highlights, challenges, and findings perceived during this implementation.

## 3 Implementing a BPM CoE in a Brazilian Company

In this section, we will provide a rational reconstruction of the history of the implementation of a BPM CoE in a Brazilian Company, placing special emphasis on the practical insights, learning points, difficulties, pitfalls, and landmarks of this process. Also, throughout the case, we will show the evolution of the roles assigned to the BPM CoE and to discuss whether it has delivered value to the organization through time.

This section will be divided as follows: first, it will present a brief contextualization of the organization and an inventory of BPM actions that were conducted. Second, it will present a detailed explanation of the initial cycle of the design and implementation of the BPM CoE, with the main lessons learnt. Third, the CoE's evolution as a coordination mechanism and service provider to the organization, characterized by the inclusion of more strategic services to it, will be shown. Finally, we will discuss some of the tendencies related to its future roles and services, perceived by an analysis of its evolutionary path.

### *3.1 Organization's Main Characteristics and its History of BPM Initiatives*

The organization in question is a business unit of a Brazilian Oil & Gas company. From now on, we shall refer to the business unit as just "organization," since it will constitute our main unit of analysis in this case study.

This organization has more than 1,500 employees (800 direct employees, and more than 700 third-party employees) and provides internal support services such as: maintenance of infrastructure and equipments, engineering services, supply procurement and general logistics, janitorial and linen services, internal transportation, and patrimonial security.

Due to the nature of these services, the organization has strong managerial guidelines that focus on procedures and process standardization and emphasize the effort for efficiency and agility in internal process execution through the utilization of an Enterprise Resource Planning (ERP). The main focus of the organization is to achieve the desired level of excellence in its internal services provisioning.

The organization's relationship with the BPM concept and initiatives started during the year of 2005, with a first pilot initiative of process redesign that focused in the *service desk* and its processes. These processes deal with the relationship of the organization with its clients. At the time, there was a perception by the Top Management that the modeling and redesign of these business processes was crucial to optimize utilization of the ERP system, as well as to improve the interfaces that existed between different business areas. At this point, the organization sought help from an external consulting group for executing this initiative.

Throughout the year of 2005, this process redesign initiative turned into a broader management concern, when the Top Management decided to join the Brazilian National Quality Award. This decision performed a shift of focus in the BPM initiative, concentrating its efforts in the redesign of all of the organization's processes and procedures. This decision also broadened the conceptual focus of the initiative that by this time included not only the redesign of processes itself but also themes such as KPI's definition, workforce competence revision, re-structuring of all IT systems and infrastructure to support processes, and organization's structure redesign.

With this major shift of focus, during the year of 2006, all the organization's processes were modeled and redesigned. To accomplish that task, the organization created several specific collaborative workgroups that were centered in specific themes. These workgroups had full sponsorship from the Top Management to propose improvements to their processes and were composed of several employees from the organization's internal areas.

The implementation of the proposed improvements and solutions led to the need of institutionalization of BPM practices and tools, through the transferring of knowledge related to BPM's best practices and solutions that are utilized in the BPM market, from the consulting team to the organization. In this context, the continuous maintenance and improvement of process models and its building blocks (by-products such as the knowledge architecture, strategic indicators map, etc.) became a cornerstone to the success and the sustainability of all managerial actions. Therefore, some employees started to be trained in best practices and BPM solutions that would latter constitute the basic knowledge to the BPM CoE.

Besides, this, a strong idea of an area that would be responsible for continuously promoting a process-aware culture emerged. This activity was perceived by the Top Management as a crucial point to enable the effectiveness of all actions presented in the management agenda, enhancing productivity and leveraging organizational performance. Since the organization was committed to performing well at the Brazilian National Quality Award, BPM's best practices and techniques were seen as the main bridge needed to support the introduction of innovative managerial practices that would conduct them to a new level of excellence.

## 3.2 The BPM CoE Initial Design and Implementation

For the initial design and implementation of any BPM CoE, six main decisions must be made. These decisions will be represented from letters A to F in this subsection and referred to: (a) Insertion in the Organizational Structure; (b) BPM Services and Governance Design; (c) Internal routines, methods and tools design; (d) Design of the relationship with organizational Areas; (e) Resource Base Design; and (f) Implementation design.

For the case study, the rational reconstruction of this first design and implementation round will follow each basic step, punctuating the main lessons that were learned regarding each decision that was made.

### 3.2.1 CoE's Insertion in the Organizational Structure

The first step that was taken to create and effectively implement the BPM CoE was to define its position in the organizational structure, as well as its roles and goals.

The BPM CoE itself started becoming a reality in the organization in the beginning of 2007, when several improvements and solutions that emerged from the diagnosis phase were still being implemented. The Top Management concluded that the most adequate position for the BPM CoE in the organization was within an internal area called Integrated Planning – a managerial area created to work as a lateral coordination mechanism to integrate and enhance the collaboration among all other business areas of the organization. This decision reinforces the ideas discussed in the Sect. 2 – the BPM CoE acts as an area that supports managerial work with BPM-related best practices and solutions, aiming to leverage organizational performance and address business strategic needs.

Hence, some roles originally attributed to the BPM CoE were:

- To be the guardian/gatekeeper of all BPM best practices, solutions and methodologies that would support management and help leverage organizational performance
- To coordinate the several process improvement and other BPM-related initiatives; working closely with all the organization's business areas
- To perform a continuous and rigorous analysis of all business processes and to report to the Top Management, process improvement needs

### 3.2.2 BPM Services and Governance Design

Once all macro-roles related to the BPM CoE were designed, further details of BPM Services that were going to be provided to the Organization were needed. Also, it was clear that a proper governance structure, including a clear definition of roles and responsibilities around these BPM services, was a critical success factor for the initiative, due to the existence of several organizational stakeholders that strongly interacted with them. This was also important to ensure the maximum synergy among BPM initiatives, and to guarantee that all BPM-related initiatives were supporting the organization's strategic objectives and actually leveraging the organization's performance (as mentioned in Sect. 2.2).

The table below describes the services that were originally conceived for the BPM CoE at that point in time. For each service, a list of details is pointed out: a brief description, the service to client logic and the main stakeholder (Table 2):

The execution of all services was the direct responsibility of the BPM CoE. However, most of them involved approvals and/or collaboration of other organizational actors. The way these several organizational actors interacted can be illustrated by a RACI chart as displayed below. This RACI chart states the responsibilities and accountabilities of each relevant organizational actor for each BPM Service through the following terminology: (R) means "is responsible for"; (A) means "approves"; (C) means "contributes to" and (I) means "is informed about" (Table 3).

**Table 2** BPM services portfolio for the case study – initial phase

| BPM service | Details |
|---|---|
| Process modeling | *Description*: Modeling and publishing processes in the organization's intranet, through specific interviewing techniques.<br>*Service to client logic*: on demand or triggered by the CoE's perception of updates and improvements in specific processes.<br>*Main stakeholders*: business areas. |
| Process analysis and redesign | *Description*: Identification and analysis of problems and improvement opportunities in the modeled processes.<br>*Service to client logic*: provided upon request through the conduction of thematic workgroups composed of CoE's members and the organization's workforce.<br>*Main stakeholders*: Top Management and business managers. |
| Improvement implementation monitoring | *Description*: Monitoring and reporting the implementation status of all prioritized improvements in the processes.<br>*Service to client logic*: provided upon request through the conduction of thematic workgroups composed of CoE's members and the organization's workforce.<br>*Main stakeholder*: Top Management and business managers. |
| Procedures design and maintenance | *Description*: elaboration, maintenance, revision, publishing and communication of internal procedures based on the designed processes.<br>*Service to client logic*: on demand or triggered by the CoE's perception.<br>*Main stakeholders*: business areas. |
| Process audit and compliance | *Description*: Verification of the adherence of the process models to reality.<br>*Service to client logic*: Bi-annual interviews with the workforce and unobtrusive observations.<br>*Main stakeholders*: business managers. |
| Process-based competence modeling | *Description*: Process-based competence (knowledge, ability, and attitude) modeling for each position.<br>*Service to client logic*: annual interviews with the workforce.<br>*Main stakeholders*: Human Resources area and business managers. |

**Table 3** RACI chart for the BPM services – year 1

| BPM service | Top management | Business areas | BPM CoE | IT area | HR area |
|---|---|---|---|---|---|
| Process modeling | | C, A | R | C | |
| Process analysis and redesign | A | C | R | C | |
| Improvement implementation monitoring | I | C | R | | |
| Procedures design and maintenance | | C, A | R | | |
| Process audit and compliance | | I | R | | |
| Process-based competence modeling | | I | R | | I |

### 3.2.3 CoE's Internal Routines, Methods and Tools Design

Based on the previous decisions, it was time to design the CoE internal work routines, methods, and tools that would effectively enable the CoE's operational execution. First, we would like to point out two important tools that were designed to support the initial structuring of the BPM CoE.

One of them is the "service request form." This tool should be used by any member of the organization that had a demand for the execution of a BPM Service or had the need to improve some performance variable that could be leveraged through the provision of a BPM Service. This tool's main goal was to organize and prioritize all of the CoE's staff workload, as well as position the CoE as a Service provider of BPM Services within the organization. This tool also served to create an image of the CoE as facilitator that would work hand in hand with the organization's business areas to improve their managerial practices, levering their performance through the application of BPM-related best-practices and solutions.

The "service request form" was communicated to the entire organization so that all areas could effectively demand BPM Service to the CoE at any time through e-mail. Only e-mails with fulfilled requests were accepted by the CoE as legitimate demands.

The second tool that was created in this first year of implementation and design was the process compliance check (PCC). Its purpose was to provide to the organization and to the CoE's staff a systematic routine of verifying adherence of process models and procedures, to a reality check. By interviewing workforce and observing executed processes, CoE's staff could check out if there were any nonconformities in execution and/or if process models needed to be updated. This meant that, while the service request forms were a part of a reactive and on demand way of providing the BPM Services to the Organization, the PCC represented a more proactive way of work of the BPM CoE.

Besides these tools, the BPM CoE also assimilated from the external consultant group more traditional BPM related methods:

- A method of process design and redesign
- A process modeling notation standard that should be followed by all initiatives
- Templates for the documentation of improvement opportunities
- The systematic of constituting thematic workgroups

### 3.2.4 Design of the CoE's Relationship with Other Organizational Areas

No service level agreements between the BPM CoE and the other organizational areas were agreed on the first year of implementation. However, there was a tacit understanding that, as the BPM CoE matured, the internal expectation's level would rise, and with that, the definition of performance parameters through service level agreements would be important to mediate the CoE's relationship with other organizational areas.

Although the organization had chosen that the BPM CoE would relate with its business areas through a service to client orientation, the CoE's budget and financial resource allocation did not follow the same direction. In other words, the CoE's budget was not estimated on the average cost of each service and allocated to the area that benefited from the service. Instead, the CoE's budget was a fixed one in a defined cost center inside the "Integrated Planning" cost structure.

This was due to two specific factors: the first one was a lack of historical data to create a baseline on how each BPM Service would cost. This made the budgeting exercise less precise. Also, to allocate the CoE's cost to the business areas that actually benefited from them would demand a huge maturity leap that the organization was not ready to perform at the moment.

### 3.2.5 CoE's Resources Design

BPM CoE's team was constituted of three employees from the organization and two external consultants. All of the employees' profiles were constituted of industrial engineers and/or business degrees.

This initial arrangement meant that a mixed team of internal employees and external consultants aimed at transferring the accumulated knowledge that was generated through the consulting project to the organization. It is necessary to point out that a formal specialization and division of labor was not agreed upon – all of the BPM CoE resources were included in all tasks, which facilitated the knowledge sharing process, but also made it inefficient.

Technological resources that were estimated to support the work at the CoE included the allocation of a Business Process Modeling and Analysis tool to each of the CoE workers. Processes publication in the intranet was performed with the support of Information Technology area.

### 3.2.6 Implementation Design

Aiming to implement all the definitions given above, the organization performed an effort of communication and dissemination of BPM CoE's concept to each area of the organization. All business managers were directly involved in initial presentations that were performed to disclose the BPM Services Portfolio, in order to increase the legitimacy and the institutionalization of BPM CoE within the organization.

The initial structuring and implementation effort of the BPM CoE lasted throughout the year of 2007. One the main lessons learnt is to highlight the internal resistance from all the organization's employees in relation to the process culture instead of a more functional one. This was highly due to the fact that the concept of BPM itself had a low level of maturity within the organization, and that in the beginning most of the knowledge related to BPM practices resided in the external consulting group.

Despite that, the results that were achieved in the first year of implementation were quite satisfactory, although still with a strong focus on efficiency and productivity improvement. In this sense, there were obtained significant reductions in process execution lead-times in two important organizational processes, which served as an important quick win to reinforce the role of the BPM CoE as a producer of managerial and operational benefits to the organization. A certain level of better visibility to support decision making was also already perceived by the organization, since the CoE allowed the organization to better integrate its BPM-related initiatives. However, the BPM's best practices and solutions still did not in fact enable decision making in the organization.

## 3.3 *The Transition to a more Strategic Role of the BPM CoE*

At the end of 2007 and through the beginning of 2008, it could be observed that the initial obstacles faced by the BPM CoE began to be fully surpassed. The internal routines and practices of BPM CoE became more mature and the organization's maturity as a whole in terms of incorporating Business Process Management as an enabler of continuous improvement also increased.

The rational reconstruction of this second design and implementation round can be told using the same structure as the first one, to allow comparability.

### 3.3.1 CoE's Insertion in the Organizational Structure

The decision to establish the CoE within the Integrated Planning Area is regarded by the organization as one of the critical success factors for the CoE's implementation, and that did not change in the first year. However, the organization felt the need to approximate the CoE's work to the organization's performance drivers and decision making needs. To achieve this purpose, two new roles were incorporated into the BPM CoE:

- Support all decision making processes in the organization
- Communicate and reinforce a process-aware culture in the organization

### 3.3.2 BPM Services and Governance Design

In order to fulfill these two new roles, some new services were incorporated into the original BPM Services Portfolio. A first service was the monitoring and revision of all key performance indicators (KPIs) related to the business processes. A second service was BPM-related training and dissemination of a process-aware culture in the organization. A third service was the periodical process-based operational risk analysis.

These new BPM Services reinforced the link between the BPM CoE's work, the organizations strategy, and the Top Management interests. This symbolized the effort to move away from a strictly productivity and efficiency improvement benefits in the direction to better visibility to support decision-making. In this context, the CoE started to be perceived as an important actor supporting the organization's strategic planning and goals revision. This also created a positive pressure that all process improvements started to be conceived connected to the organization's strategic goals and targets.

All other services that were presented on the previous year's portfolio remained unaltered. The table below shows all new services that were incorporated into the BPM Services portfolio, on top of the old ones (that were still maintained) (Table 4):

The execution of all services still remained as BPM CoE's direct responsibility. However, most of them involved the approval or collaboration of other

**Table 4** New BPM services portfolio for the case study

| BPM service | Details |
|---|---|
| Key Performance Indicators Monitoring | *Description*: support in the definition of the most adequate KPIs related to internal processes and in their monitoring. Also includes the structuring and maintenance of BAM performance dashboards that enable decision making.<br>*Service to client logic*: monthly.<br>*Main stakeholder*: managers. |
| Process-based training | *Description*: training in process methods, tools, and practices and road shows to disseminate a process-aware culture.<br>*Service to client logic*: on demand or triggered by the CoE's perception<br>*Main stakeholder*: business areas. |
| Process-based operational risk analysis | *Description*: analysis of the most relevant operational risks in each process and proposal of internal controls to mitigate those risks.<br>*Service to client logic*: Bi-annually, through a specific interviewing technique with employees.<br>*Main stakeholder*: Top Management. |

**Table 5** RACI chart for the BPM services – year 2

| BPM service | Top management | Business areas | BPM CoE | Communication area |
|---|---|---|---|---|
| Key performance indicators monitoring | I | A, C | R | |
| Process-based training | I, A | | R | A, C |
| Process-based operational risk analysis | I | A, C | R | |

organizational actors, especially Top Management since the added services had a more strategic flavor. Responsibilities and accountabilities associated to these services can be seen below (Table 5).

### 3.3.3 CoE's Internal Routines, Methods, and Tools Design

The three services that were added required new methods and tools to support them. The "Key Performance Indicators Monitoring" service required that some KPIs dashboards were created, in a first effort to constitute a Business Activity Monitoring (BAM). These dashboards could be monitored by several different employees and managers, and allowed effective decision making.

For the process-based training, several educational videos and messages were created with the help of the Communication area, in order to disseminate the process-aware culture in the organization.

Finally, for the process-based operational risk analysis, several tools were created, to better enable decision making based on the organization's risk profile. Such tools were:

- The risk and control strategic matrix
- Process prioritization's and risk rating matrix
- Symptoms table

### 3.3.4 Design of the CoE's Relationship with Other Organizational Areas

The perception on business managers was that the organization had not yet matured to develop service level agreements that regulated the relationship between the CoE and other organizational areas. Hence, this item was the one that changed less throughout the whole project.

### 3.3.5 CoE's Resources Design

The fact that the current portfolio had a more interesting mix of operational and strategic services suggested that a more formal division of labor should be adopted, segregating workers that would attend to operational demands and workers that would coach managers and attend to more strategic demands. However, such division of labor did not occur.

### 3.3.6 Implementation Design

With this need of enabling decision making throughout the entire organization, a second wave of awareness efforts was performed, but this time with a stronger focus on the managerial and top management levels.

These levels appeared to offer more resistance to change, and this awareness efforts are not completed yet. Results remain to be seen on this matter.

## 3.4 BPM CoE's Implementation Analysis

The implementation path that was undertaken by the BPM CoE in both cycles can be compared as below:

The Fig. 1, estimates the organizational perception of value added on each one of the six decisions presented, based on selected project team members' point of view. There is no formal scale to measure the value added by each decision. The used method was a roundtable between selected project members, where a discussion would be made regarding the value of each decision in relation to the others. This method was utilized since the main variable that the chart wishes to highlight is the differential importance of each decision (the relative importance of each decision in comparison to the set of decisions), and not the absolute value of each decision.

Based on the result of this exercise, we can conclude that the first round of the CoE's design and implementation has resulted in a low value perception, basically associated with efficiency benefits in the processes redesign. The CoE was seen essentially as an operational area. The second round improved this value perception, mainly because of the creation of new BPM services that contributed to organizational strategic management.

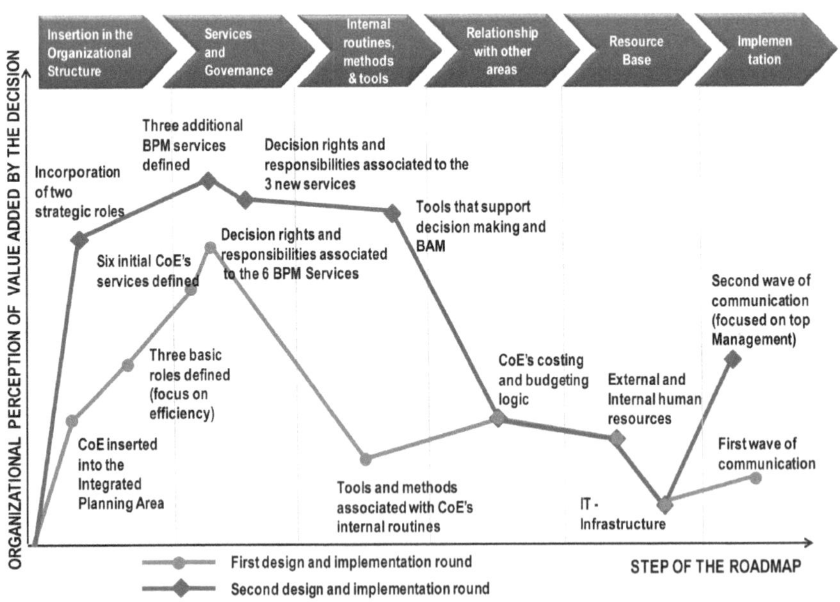


Fig. 1 Implementation path for the BPM CoE

**Table 6** BPM CoE vision main goals applied to the case study

| Capabilities | Description |
|---|---|
| Diffusion of BPM Culture | There were several established action plans to disseminate a process aware culture, focusing on the fact that BPM constitutes on a set of best practices and solutions that can help managers leverage their organizational performance. All mapped processes are published in the organizations Intranet to stimulate their use as an effective managerial instrument. The link between processes and KPIs has provided an important bridge between operation execution and decision making at a tactic/strategic level. |
| Creation of Convergence among BPM Initiatives | All BPM related initiatives must have the involvement of the BPM CoE, mitigating the risk of misalignment BPM-related actions. Besides that, the BPM CoE strives to provide effective support to managers and top managers of the execution of such processes. This is mainly done through the Key Performance indicators strategic maps. There is not, however, a systematic methodology of evaluation the Return on Investment on BPM-initiatives. |
| Internal Consulting Orientation | The BPM CoE is legitimately recognized as an internal service provider. As time passes, new services are being added to its portfolio of BPM services, in an effort to align its line of action with the organization's strategic priorities. Besides that, the CoE has recently began to take part in scientific events and communities of practice in order to guarantee excellence in its services and deliver state of the art best practices and BPM solutions to its clients. |

In spite of that, we believe there are still many value improvement opportunities, for example, developing SLA's with its clients and formalizing a labor division within its internal staff.

We can also analyze CoE's maturity in the organization by comparing it to the three capability levels defined in Sect. 2 (Table 6):

## 3.5 Synthesis of Lessons Learnt and Tendencies of Evolution

We believe that there are some important lessons that could be learned from this case study. The following table synthesizes, in the authors point of view, some of the major success factors and pitfalls related to the BPM CoE implementation.

Furthermore, we believe the current design of the BPM CoE signals some tendencies regarding its future evolutionary path. Some of these tendencies include:

1. The decentralization to process owners of activities and responsibilities of process design and redesign under the methodological orientation of the BPM CoE. The BPM CoE would then gradually start to act as a gatekeeper of knowledge and process standards.
2. A deeper analysis of the return on investment that is obtained from the BPM Services, with the creation of a formal ROI evaluation method.

3. The establishment of formal service level agreements that could regulate the delivery of BPM services and balance the expectations regarding the provision of services, both on the costs and benefits dimensions.
4. A deeper level of specialization and segregation of roles among the BPM CoE staff, with the establishment of specific focal points for each of the organization's process.
5. An increasing demand for organizational innovation supported by the process culture, with the incorporation of new attributions to the BPM CoE related to the best practices of benchmarking and prospection of new managerial solutions for the organization.
6. The development of a financial methodology to fund the BPM CoE operation with specific rules to charge for each BPM services according to its local impact to the demanding area and total impact to the business.

## 4 Final Conclusions

Once presented and exemplified the strategic roles of a BPM CoE, it is important to finish this chapter stressing two points we believe are crucial to any CoE implementation. First, a BPM CoE should act inside an organization in order to change the mindset and the way BPM is faced, as follows:

- From process models as main products to process models as management improvement understanding platforms
- From punctual improvements to continuous improvements
- From isolated BPM initiatives to systematic BPM services and strengthened culture
- From a competitive advantage based on efficiency to one based on flexibility and innovation

In the second place, it is important to highlight that an organization should gradually implement the three roles proposed in this article, in the order they were exposed. As discussed in Table 7, it takes time for an organization to be able to absorb and internalize the idea proposed in each role.

The following, in Fig. 2, illustrates an organization's trajectory passing through the three strategic roles described in this article:

A BPM CoE in the first stage does not yet add significant value with BPM actions. This type of BPM CoE usually has several improvement opportunities, but is not yet mature enough to implement the strategic roles and change the way BPM is dealt with internally.

Once passed this stage, an organization and its BPM CoE advance toward promoting operational excellence. Several BPM initiatives have started to proliferate aiming at eliminating many organizational problems. At that point, BPM starts to be perceived as a solution to eliminating existing pains. The first strategic role of a BPM CoE is now activated.

**Table 7** List of challenges, success factors, and pitfalls related to the case study

| Key success factors | Pitfalls |
|---|---|
| *Top Management's sponsorship*: since the beginning of the journey, Top Management commitment was clear to all stakeholders involved. This commitment remains the same and helps evidence the strategic role of BPM and its Center of Excellence | *No previous conscience of the need of a BPM CoE during first BPM initiatives*: BPM CoE emerged when it became clear to the organization that it needed to internalize BPM methods and tools. If it was planned since the beginning of the consulting work, results obtained could have been better and transfer of knowledge could have been easier. |
| *Gradual implementation of BPM services*: there was a previous conscience that BPM services needed to be introduced in the organization gradually. This means the BPM CoE would not be as robust as desired at first implementation cycle, but instead would become more mature throughout the years | *No planned composition of CoE's team*: we believe the CoE's team could have been formed as a mix of people with distinct competencies, including interpersonal abilities, previous knowledge of organization's internal processes and/or BPM-related knowledge. This was not possible since there was not enough time to recruit and select the adequate employees. CoE was created with a team of similar competencies. |
| *Strong communication*: there was always a strong effort of communication of BPM CoE's role to the organization, in order to disseminate process-oriented culture and avoid any misunderstandings and possible resistance. | *No defined metrics to evaluate the success of BPM CoE*: as there were no previous metrics defined, it's still difficult to prove BPM CoE implementation's success and tangible results. A better emphasis at BPM CoE ROI should have been given since the beginning. |
| *Service to client orientation*: BPM CoE was always placed as an internal service provider. This showed business areas that the CoE's team wanted to help them improve their processes and activities and therefore could be seen as a partner. | |

Within this second stage, some of the perceived benefits are systematic optimization about the way work is executed throughput multiple areas to deliver products and/or services to the client; Reduction of losses, better use of raw material and labor hours, smaller lead times and failures.

In advancing to the third stage, the organization starts to look for convergence among diverse initiatives, until then disintegrated, through the BPM CoE. This way, managerial visibility for decision making increases through BPM initiatives. The second role of the BPM CoE is also now implanted.

Within this third stage some of the perceived benefits are general coordination capacity and decision making improvement throughout the organization; clear visibility and accountability about what's happening day by day; better and faster information for decision making.

Finally, at the fourth stage, the BPM CoE itself starts to adopt a service orientation to other areas. Such services are integrated to the organization's strategy in order to promote flexibility and innovation. It is at this point that the third and last BPM CoE's role has been achieved.

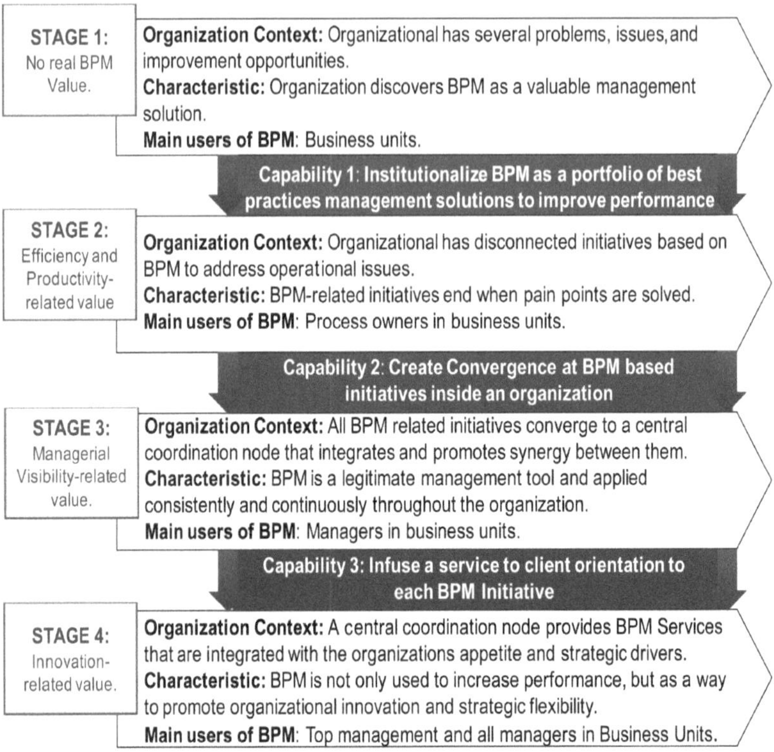


**Fig. 2** BPM CoE strategic roles adoption stages

Within this fourth stage, some of the perceived benefits are gaining of flexibility and adaptability to quickly detect and explore opportunities that are aligned with the organization's strategy; high success rate of change, ability to explore new opportunities; high synergy between actions at different areas; collaborative discussions, that lead to new ways of doing business.

Under a practical perspective, we studied the case of the BPM CoE implementation in an Oil & Gas company in Brazil. As it is always important to point out, this process takes a long time until it reaches a point in which the BPM CoE starts to really add value to the organization.

In that case, it was not different. BPM initiatives began very timidly in 2005 with a few process design initiatives. But it was not until the Top Management started to realize the great potential value behind these initiatives that the BPM culture and implementation started to take off in the organization.

Once implemented a massive BPM initiative in which the whole organization was analyzed and improved, the BPM CoE came as a natural solution to be formalized. The organization as a whole had already perceived a great deal of improvement gained from BPM, so it was a smart decision to internalize and institutionalize this capability in order to maintain a continuous improvement throughout the following years. The way of doing this was creating a new area accountable for this role, the BPM CoE.

This BPM CoE implementation was made in a structured six step way:

- CoE's insertion in the Organizational Structure
- BPM Services and Governance Design
- CoE's Internal routines, methods, and tools design
- Design of the CoE's relationship with other organizational areas
- CoE's resources design
- Implementation design

After the BPM CoE implementation, it started to rethink itself in order to encounter ways of adding more value to the organization. The way of doing this was revisiting the same six steps taken in the implementation in order to find possible changes to be made that could improve the job made by the BPM CoE.

After almost 4 years from the first contacts with BPM, this organization's BPM CoE has made its way through the three value stages and is today a fundamental piece that institutionalizes a portfolio of best practices management solutions that promotes the convergence of BPM based initiatives and provides excellence to the organization in a service to client orientation.

However, this has not stopped this BPM CoE as well as the whole organization to keep looking for new and better ways to execute their jobs and delivering services to their customers.

## References


Bandara W, Guillemain A, Coogans P (2010) Prioritizing process improvement: an example from the Australian financial services sector. In: vom Brocke J, Rosemann M (eds) Handbook on business process management, vol 2. Springer, Heidelberg

de Bruin T (2009) Business Process Management: Theory on Progression and Maturity. QUT, PhD thesis. Brisbane

de Bruin T, Doebeli G (2010) An organizational approach to BPM: the experience of an Australian transport provider. In: vom Brocke J, Rosemann M (eds) Handbook on business process management, vol 2. Springer, Heidelberg

Hagel J III, Brown J (2005) The only sustainable edge. Harvard Business School Press, Boston, MA

Hammer M (2007) The process audit. Harv Bus Rev (April):111–123

Harmon P (2007) Business process change – a guide for business managers and BPM and six sigma professionals. Morgan Kaufmann, Massachusetts, USA

Jeston J, Nelis J (2008) Business process management: practical guidelines to sucessful implementations. Elsevier, Hungary

Richardson C (2006) Process governance best practices: building a BPM center of excellence BPTrends. April 2006

Rosemann M (2010) The service portfolio of a BPM center of excellence. In: vom Brocke J, Rosemann M (eds) Handbook on business process management, vol 2, Springer, Heidelberg

Scheer A-W, Brabänder E (2010) The process of bussiness process management. In: vom Brocke J, Rosemann M (eds) Handbook on business process management, vol 2. Springer, Heidelberg

Snabe J, Rosenberg A, Moller C, Scavillo M (2009) Business process management – the SAP roadmap. Galileo Press Inc, Boston, MA

Spanyi A (2007) Governance is key to BPM success. BPInstitute, BPM Strategy Magazine
Spanyi A, Rose A, Dwyer T (2008) Best practices for building BPM and SOA centers of excellence. BPM Institute.org Presentation
Spanyi A (2010) Business process management governance. In: vom Brocke J, Rosemann M (eds) Handbook on business process management, vol 2. Springer, Heidelberg
Vollmer K, Leganza G, Pilecki M, Smillie K (2008) The EA View: BPM has become mainstream: BPM centers of excellence provide the catalyst for success. Forrester
vom Brocke J, Petry M, Sinnl T, Østerberg Kristensen B, Sonnenberg C (2010) Global processes and data: The cultural journey at the Hilti corporation. In: vom Brocke J, Rosemann M (eds) Handbook on business process management, vol 2. Springer, Heidelberg
Willaert P, Van de Berg J, Willems J, Deschoolmeester D (2007) The process-oriented organisation: a holistic view. In: Alonso G, Dadam P, Rosemann M (eds) Business process management – proceedings of the 5th International conference, BPM2007. Brisbane, Autralia

# Business Process Standardization

**Roger Tregear**

**Abstract** Across its own functional and geographic structures, every organization has many processes with the same, or similar outputs and inputs. These processes comprise comparable activities, are constrained by similar rules, and are supported by like resources. They are common processes. They could be identical processes; multiple instances of the same process. Consider the corporate process, Purchase Goods, based on a global standard to use a single contracted supplier. At the same time, credible arguments can be made for local variations on these common processes to meet local requirements. Should a local variation of Purchase Goods be allowed in a location where the sole supplier has no office? In planning the implementation of a large software application for use in 30 countries, to what extent should local practice be allowed to customize the corporate application, potentially creating 30 different instances of the application? Is 30 too many? How about 10? 20? How many is too many? At what point does the cost-benefit balance shift away from global standardization to favor local relevance?

In this chapter, we address complex issues about process standardization. A Global BPM Framework is described that facilitates management of the conflicting demands of standardization for global efficiency versus variation for local effectiveness.

## 1 Standardization Dilemma

Every organization would like to avoid uncoordinated business process activity with isolated business units constantly re-inventing the wheel. The arguments for standardization are compelling. So are those for variation in response to particular

---

R. Tregear
Leonardo Consulting, Canberra, Australia
e-mail: r.tregear@leonardo.com.au

J. vom Brocke and M. Rosemann (eds.), *Handbook on Business Process Management 2*, International Handbooks on Information Systems,
DOI 10.1007/978-3-642-01982-1_15, 

local requirements. This is true on any scale within and across state, province, or national borders[1].

In this context, process standardization means the development of a standard or best-practice process to be used as a template for all instances of the process throughout the organization. Our emphasis here is on the organization development and culture issues that relate to BPM governance.

The development and use of technical standards, e.g. BPEL and BPMN, for the development of BPM systems are not part of our considerations. These issues are covered by Leymann et al. (2010).

Neither does this chapter address the technical management of process model variants. These issues are covered by Hallerbach et al. (2010).

Questions about the effective standardization of business processes go to the heart of process governance. They can drive or limit process change. They bring into sharper focus questions of process performance accountability. They shape organizational culture.

Harmon (2007) states the case for standardization plainly "... if a company is doing the same activity in many different locations, it should consider doing them in the same way."

Any organization seeking to develop a process-centric culture must find ways to reconcile the tension between standardization and local variation, between centralized control and distributed autonomy. Can we achieve business process change with a predisposition toward standardization and still support critical local differences?

Hammer (2010) discusses seven axiomatic principles of process management. One of these principles is that "One process version is better than many" and he says "Standardizing processes across all parts of an enterprise presents a single face to customers and suppliers, yields profound economies in support services such as training and IT systems, allows the redeployment of people from one business unit to another, and yields a host of other benefits. These payoffs must be balanced against the intrinsically different needs of different units and their customers, but our bias should be in favor of standardization."

Standardization actually involves two related questions: How should standards be developed and how should compliance be managed. Should process best practice be determined centrally or can the wisdom of the crowd of process participants be harvested to inform best practice decisions?

We discuss a two-tier approach that can deliver business processes that work at both the global and the local levels. We describe a Global BPM Framework that facilitates the execution of a Global BPM Strategy, which delivers a process view that is globally consistent and locally relevant.

Drawing on the Object Management Group's definition of strategy from its Business Motivation Model (BMM) (Object Management Group 2009) we define

[1]For a real case on the challenge of globalization and localization in BPM see the Hilti case in vom Brocke et al. (2010).

a Global BPM Strategy as the essential course of action required to achieve the goal of process-based management. The case for committing to process-based management is made elsewhere in this handbook, for example, in Hammer (2010) and de Bruin and Doebeli (2010). In this chapter, we assume that general commitment and suggest how it might be operationalized with a particular emphasis on the question of standardizing common processes across the organization.

The Global BPM Framework is a set of concepts, principles, constraints, and relationships that provide the basis for the development and execution of the Global BPM Strategy.

The more general aspects of BPM governance are discussed in detail by Markus and Jacobson (2010) and Spanyi (2010). Baumöl (2010) and vom Brocke et al. (2010) also cover cultural aspects of BPM.

Many of the concepts discussed in this chapter have been developed and refined in working with a leading international financial services provider. Given both the sensitivities that surround their business environment and their significant internal change in management opportunities and challenges, we are unable to identify the company[2].

## 1.1 Defining Variation

Before we discuss options for reducing and managing business process variation, we should be clear about what we mean by such variation.

The simplest process diagram (Burlton 2001; Harmon 2007) is a single box showing inputs, outputs, guides and enablers (see Fig. 1.). The process is a sequence

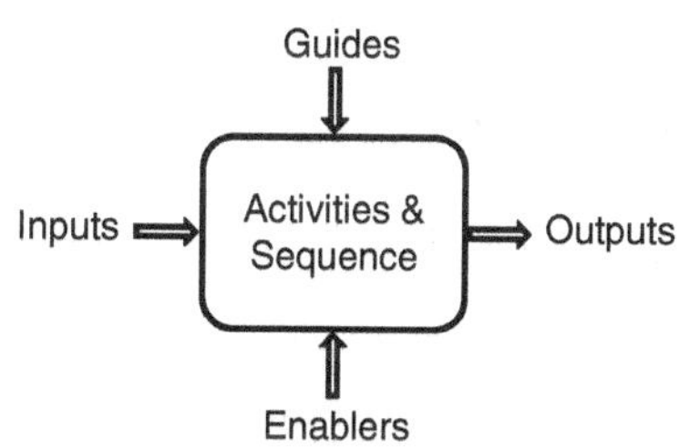


**Fig. 1** Simple process diagram

[2]Operating in 30 countries with 6,000 staff, its banking, finance and leasing services are essentially the same in most places. The company is a major player in each of its markets. Total operating income is €1 billion and the company is profitable with excellent credit ratings. Global efficiency objectives and the desire for common systems make global standardization attractive. The contrary attraction for local specialization is driven by local customer demands and regulatory requirements. These are ongoing discussions. The ultimate choices are not just financially and operationally significant, they are mission critical.

of activities that transforms inputs into outputs using the enablers and informed and constrained by the guides. The key focus is on the outputs and this must include the customer(s) for whom the process output represents some form of value. The impact on other stakeholders such as suppliers and partners must also be considered. Variations occur with one or more of the inputs, guides, enablers or sequence of activities transforming inputs into outputs. Deriving the same outputs based on different suppliers (inputs), or different regulations or policies (guides), or by using different IT systems (enablers), gives rise to the potential for standardization.

## 2 Globally Consistent or Locally Relevant

As in many of life's dilemmas, the question is one of balance. The idea of the "one true process" executed consistently throughout the organization is persuasive. The conflicting argument for a primary focus on particular needs at the customer interface is compelling.

### *2.1 Attraction of the Global*

In a perfect (process) world, an organization would have many standardized processes throughout its operations. Whether it is a single site operation or spread across a country or spread across many countries, the same process would be executed exactly the same way in each place. Common processes would be documented, executed, managed and measured in the same way in every instance. The "one true process" would be maintained and enforced, if not by cultural norms, then by a central authority.

Training would be uniform. People and work would move seamlessly between locations. Customers would always have the same experience of the same process irrespective of location. Partners would have an optimized and well understood role in the supply chain. IT development, implementation and maintenance costs would be greatly reduced. Other elements of the infrastructure of common process execution would also be consistent across the organization. Economies of scale would be significant. Opportunities for consolidation, outsourcing and offshoring would be more readily and accurately identified, and consequently, more effectively managed.

Quality assurance would be consistent and more manageable across the organization. Compliance management generally would be greatly enhanced, leading to better understanding and management of risk.

In this environment, it would be possible to have comparable performance measures between locations (process instances) and process improvements would be redesigned once for immediate implementation across the organization, giving the added benefit of economies of scale. Management of the organization and its processes would also be standardized.

The opportunity to create common standardized process does not arise only where an organization operates across national borders. An organization working from a single location will also have common processes. These processes could be executed by different parts of the same organization in the same building or across the world. The case for standardization will be just as strong, and its achievement may be just as difficult, in this single location as in a global diverse organization.

There are many benefits to be gained from the standardization of processes. Surely the arguments are compelling. The conclusion must be that every organization should document its process architecture, model its processes to at least two levels, assign process owners, seek out variation, determine its "best process" and standardize. Next stop, Nirvana.

## 2.2 *Attraction of the Local*

In reality, most organizations working across a range of geographies, cultures and operating environments do not achieve this level of standardization. Indeed many do not even want to try.

For them, the arguments for local variation are just as compelling. Each location or business unit is best left to run with reasonable autonomy. Global management is not done by micromanaging from afar in the Head Office. Local requirements require process differences in each location. Having the various business units only loosely coupled to the Head Office, and each other, makes them much easier to sell or reorganize when required. Establishing and maintaining the degree of rigor required for effective centralized control is difficult and distracting. The traditional arguments against enforced standardization are that it is too hard, takes too long and can be disruptively confrontational.

## 2.3 *Balancing Act*

Let us consider this global/local balancing act in general terms before we return to a more detailed analysis of the drivers and costs of local variation.

The polar opposites of centralized control and loosely-coupled association have given rise to many debates in the lives of individuals and communities.

How can we resolve the tension between the competing cases for standardized global processes versus locally tailored processes? Should organizational energy be expended in enforcing compliance with global standards or in managing the variability that is inevitable in complex organizations? Do we achieve standardization at the expense of agility or do common processes increase the ability to safely and quickly achieve meaningful change?

A further aspect of the balancing act involves choices about the degree of authoritarianism involved. How do we determine what the standard processes should be? Should a central unit work out what is best and issue instructions? Perhaps a central unit's primary role should be to relentlessly capture and disseminate examples of good practice and thereby facilitate the evolution of standard processes?

Once a standard has been set, how will its use be enforced? Careful choices are required in limiting local autonomy. The culture of the organization and it's customary approach to policing compliance will play a large role. No organization allows business units to design their own accounting systems. Such rigor may not be so strictly applied to the management of processes. For a multinational operation, differences in national cultures will be important. Hofstede (2001) reminds us that "culture is more often a source of conflict than synergy".

The problem also changes at different process depths. At the highest levels of the processes' architectural view of an organization, there are many seemingly common, or at least similar, processes. A common process that might be described in any public or private sector organization of any size and in any country is Hire-to-Retire. Such a process would describe all of the activities, policies and rules involved in HR management. You can easily imagine a level one process sequence such as Define Role, Recruit Employee, Manage Employment, and Finalize Employment. At this level, such a sequence could be common throughout an organization, indeed perhaps common between different organizations. The further we drill down into the subprocesses, the more variation we might find. One example of variation would be that recruitment might be done via public advertising or via an agency. Reference frameworks such as the Supply–Chain Councils process reference model, Supply–Chain Operations Reference (SCOR)[3] and the APQC's Process Classification Framework[4] also illustrate the levels of abstraction issue. The SCOR model's highest level defines five processes that describe any supply chain across a wide variety of organizations: Plan, Source, Make Deliver, and Return.

Another consideration will be whether it might be appropriate to maintain standardized "back office" processes at a particular business unit location while having customized "front office" processes. Even if a customer segment genuinely requires customization of customer-facing processes, that may not mean that the changes need to be deep. Variation may need to go no further than the customer's limited field of view.

Whatever standardization approaches are adopted in an organization, there will need to be some flexibility in their application. Some business units and locations will be able to successfully introduce much better local variations. Others will lack the maturity to be allowed to vary far from the global standards.

[3]Supply Chain Council, http://www.supply-chain.org/.

[4]http://www.apqc.org/portal/apqc/site.

There will be genuine reasons for some process variations from location to location, from business unit to business unit. Clearly identifying similarities and differences in business processes allows us to validate the cost-benefits and re-use best practice for business optimization and change.

The intent is not to create robotic organizations all working in the same way in every aspect. Henry Ford's phenomenal success was built largely on standardization of the components and construction processes of the Model T, the "Car of the Century" (Brooke 2008). Even so, he was keen to point out that "The eventuality of industry is not a standardized, automatic world in which people will not need brains. The eventuality is a world in which people will have a chance to use their brains ..." (Ford 1926). This idea is reflected in the Toyota concept of "autonomation" meaning "automation with a human touch" (Ohno 1988, pp. 6; Shigeo, 1989, pp. 59).

Given the current condition of the automotive manufacturing industry, there is some irony in comparing the beginnings of the Ford and Toyota companies. The Toyoa family studied the work of Henry Ford very carefully and for some years before establishing their Toyota company in 1936. By this time the Ford Motor Company was well established. The manufacturing and marketing phenomenon that was the Model T had been over for nearly a decade. Taiichi Ohno, the architect of the Toyota Production System was "in awe of (Henry) Ford's greatness" (Ohno 1988, pp. 97). Today, the Toyota Motor Corporation in Japan receives some 600,000 improvement suggestions each year from staff. A staggering 99% of these suggestions are implemented (Magee 2007). That is almost one successful improvement per month per employee. Katsuaki Watanabe, the then President of Toyota Motor Corporation, said in 2007 that "There's no genius in our company. We just do whatever we believe is right, trying every day to improve every little bit and piece. But when 70 years of very small improvements accumulate, they become a revolution" (Stewart and Raman 2007).

What if every organization had a way of collecting successful process improvements made across its locations and business units and standardizing processes based on that knowledge? Over time, would a complete set of standardized processes evolve?

## 3 Local Variation

Inevitably there will be local variations on common processes. These variations will arise for many reasons. Each variation imposes a cost on its host organization.

### *3.1 Reasons for Variations*

Despite the compelling arguments for standardization, there are many reasons why common processes are designed and executed differently in different locations. Some of these reasons, for example, legislative requirements, make variations inevitable. Other causes are less proscriptive. Some seem to result from personal whims. To understand the validity of a variation and the cost of supporting it, it is necessary to understand why the variation exists in the first place.

Various reasons for business process variations can be described.

- *Legislative requirements*: These are mandatory and unavoidable variations that come from differences in financial regulations, taxation regimes, import/export regulations and employment practices.
- *Local market imperatives*: Although these changes can be harder to define, they are more common and have a significant effect. They are caused by differences in national or regional culture, customer expectations, market maturity, competitive landscape or local market conditions.
- *Personal preference*: Some differences are more to do with the personal preference of an individual with authority to make, stop, or change.
- *Knowledge is power*: Related to the effect of personal preferences, but less benign, some see the sharing of knowledge about how a process works as a loss of control and power.
- *Drift*: Processes can change for no obvious reasons. Over time they drift away from the standard by the accretion of many tiny variations.
- *Resource constraints*: What works in one location may not be possible in another if the necessary resources are not available or affordable.
- *Product/service variations*: Differences in product and services may require variation in the processes that create, deliver and maintain them.
- *Mergers & Acquisitions*: When organizations join there are usually at least two versions of notionally common processes. In theory, this problem would be resolved and a single process selected, but old processes sometimes die hard.
- *IT driven*: IT systems, particularly legacy systems, may force variations in business processes.
- *Unstructured, unmeasured and unrepeatable* (Davenport 2005): Knowledge work is often said to be impossible to document and model as a process.

There are many reasons why variation from a global standard for a particular business process might occur. Some of the variations are inevitable and organizations need to manage that diversity. Others have no such compelling purpose.

It is common for people and business units to express the view that what they do is "special" and "different" and cannot be seen to be standard. Sometimes this is true. Mostly, it is less so. We rarely hear people successfully argue that financial management or project management should be handled in a special way for their business unit. Should process management be different? Resolution of this tension is a complex and important aspect of global management.

## 3.2 Costs of Variation

There is a cost for variation. Such costs are not always apparent as they seldom appear as line items in financial reports. They are no less real. Continued support for unnecessary process variations is a lost opportunity for performance improvement. "Opportunity losses" are seldom recognized, let alone reported.

Across a large organization, and even in some smaller ones, there can be many processes in play that could be standardized but this opportunity is not recognized because nobody is looking. Expressing a fundamental premise of what we would come to know as Lean Management, Shigeo Shingo (1988) wrote in 1981 that "We cannot find and eliminate waste if we are not looking for it".

The costs of variation take many forms.

- *Customer dissatisfaction*: Customers expect the consistent outcomes that result from consistent processes when they deal with an organization. Customer dissatisfaction leads to loss of sales and/or resources wasted in dealing with complaints.
- *Inefficiency*: The performance of most processes can be made more efficient. There can be a significant cost in not removing inefficiency.
- *Ineffectiveness*: No matter how efficient a process is made, it is entirely wasted if it is the wrong process.
- *Training*: Multiple versions of a process can impact on training material incurring additional development and maintenance costs.
- *Documentation*: Process variation means multiple versions of documentation are being maintained (or should be).
- *Lack of information*: There is a potential opportunity cost in decision making not informed by the best consistent and comparable information.
- *Loss of "best process"*: Without a system to identify and standardize "best process" across an organization, it is inevitable that some parts of the organization will be operating in a suboptimal way.
- *Increased complexity*: Organizational complexity is increased by process variations. Complexity adds cost and risk to management.
- *Re-inventing wheels*: Uncoordinated business process activity by isolated entities re-inventing solutions is clearly wasted.
- *Losing competitive advantage*: Failure to reduce costs, improve customer satisfaction, reduce time to market and reduced quality decision making must result in the loss of competitive advantage.
- *IT development & support*: Process variations will often require variations in IT systems to support them, creating additional development and maintenance costs.
- *Staff impacts*: For almost all organizations, staffing costs are significant. In many cases they are the largest single cost. Suboptimal processes waste and disrespect these important and expensive resources.

There are many ways in which the existence of, unnecessary process variations impose costs on an organization. In large and complex organizations, these costs could amount to many millions of dollars, perhaps annually.

Each organization needs to assess the trade- off between the cost of standardization and the costs of nonstandardization. In doing so, most organizations will find that the financial costs of standardization are reducing. The availability of better global information and knowledge management tools, reducing communication costs and improving technology, and globalization of thinking and operations are weakening financial arguments against standardization. This trend will continue.

Variations in process may have both costs and benefits. A variation that might seem beneficial at one level of cost may seem extravagant at another. The common circumstance is that this cost-benefit is neither calculated nor challenged.

## 4 Resolving the Dilemma

A two tier approach is proposed to deliver business processes that will help balance the demands of standardization and local variation. There are two integrated and closely coupled activity streams. One involves the development and maintenance of a Global BPM Framework[5]. The Framework includes models, templates, and general guidance. The second stream entails the use of the Framework in the execution of the Global BPM Strategy. Both streams are continuous and enduring.

The Global BPM Strategy is realized via the following artifacts:

- A *Global BPM Framework* supports ongoing development and management of globally consistent and locally relevant processes.
- A *BPM Governance Scheme* provides policies, principles, and conventions for coordinated process development and management.
- A *Global Process Council* is the custodian of the global policy aspects of the Global BPM Framework.
- A *Global Process Office* conducts day-to-day operations, analysis, and reporting on the global usage of the Global BPM Framework and supports the execution of the Global BPM Strategy.
- *Local Process Councils* in each location/country are the custodians of the local policy aspects of the Global BPM Framework.
- *Local Process Offices* conduct day-to-day operations, analysis, and reporting on the local usage of the Global BPM Framework and support the execution of the local aspects of the Global BPM Strategy.
- A *BPM Knowledge Exchange* captures and disseminates learnings from across the organization about BPM's best practice.
- A *BPM Capability Development Plan* provides a common method for developing BPM implementation and management capabilities.

Guiding the operation of the Global BPM Framework is a tri-state definition of levels of process standardization (see also Fig. 2) The three levels provide a trajectory for development of processes towards a global standard. The three states are:

[5]Some aspects of the Global BPM Framework are derived from the published models and training material of BPTrends Associates. http://www.bptrends.com and Harmon (2007).

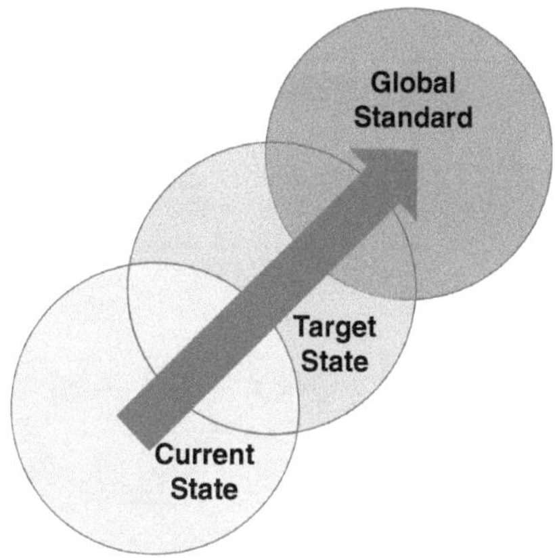


**Fig. 2** Levels of process standardization

- *Global Standard*. This is the notional global standard representing the ideal state for all business units everywhere from a standardized process perspective. The global standard may be one of the available process reference models such as SCOR or it may be an internally designed reference.
- *Current State*. This is the current state of the process in the particular business unit. Where complete standardization of the process has been achieved, this would be the same as the Global Standard. Where local variation is accepted as a necessary process may never move further toward the Global Standard.
- *Target State*. This is the current target for the process in a particular business unit. It represents improvement from the Current State. Although the trajectory from Current State to Target State would ultimately reach the Global Standard, the Target State may be short of the Global Standard. Where local variations have been accepted as valid, the Target State and Current State are coincidental.

The Global Standard is maintained by the Global Process Office with the authority of the Global Process Council. Current and Target States for business units are managed by the Local Process Offices and Councils.

## 4.1 Global BPM Framework

The Global BPM Framework allows all business units to develop coherent approaches to BPM. Standardization is encouraged and necessary local variation is supported.

The Global BPM Framework is shown in Fig. 3. Its most obvious characteristic is the integration of global and local perspectives. The Global BPM Strategy is developed and managed by the Global Process Council assisted by the Global

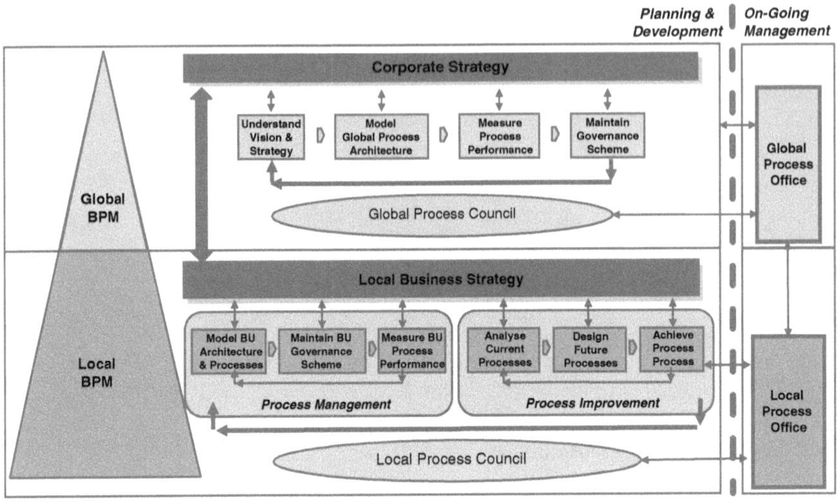


**Fig. 3** Global BPM framework

Process Office. The Local Process Councils are accountable for the implementation of the Global BPM Framework adjusted for local conditions. The Local Process Office supports the management, measurement, and reporting of local process performance and the coordination of process improvement activities.

Global BPM activities are driven by, and fed back to, corporate strategy. Similarly, local business strategies are closely coupled with local BPM activities.

The Process Councils are responsible for BPM policy. Process Offices are responsible for day-to-day management, logistics, coordination and support of process improvement and management activities.

Local Process Offices and the Global Process Offices, work together to provide global and local support for BPM.

## 4.2 *Development and Management*

The Global BPM Framework, (Fig. 3,) provides the basis for the execution of the Global BPM Strategy.

An important distinction is made between development and maintenance of the Strategy and its ongoing execution. The thick dotted vertical line in the schematic shows the relationship between these closely coupled aspects. Planning and development of the Strategy involves its initial creation and subsequent maintenance. The other side of the vertical line represents day-to-day process execution and management. These separate but integrated aspects create a process management environment that is consistent yet responsive to changing organizational needs.

### 4.3 Balancing Global and Local

Some aspects of the Global BPM Framework must be managed and controlled on a global level. These elements need to have a single owner and be used in identical ways in all business units.

Apart from the Framework itself, such global aspects include:

- BPM Knowledge Exchange
- Global Standards (for common process)
- BPM Capability Development Plan
- Global and Local Process Council Charters
- Global and Local Process Office Charters
- Process Architecture
- Global analysis and reporting specifications
- Global process modeling and management tools
- Process modeling conventions and standards.

The global-local balance must be maintained in a dynamic environment. It is not a matter of designing systems and achieving balance just once. Rather the requirement is to maintain equilibrium despite changes at both the global and local levels. The Global Standard, Current State, and Target State are all able to change as an organization's circumstances change.

Global standards should change over time. As Henry Ford said "If you think of standardization as the best, that you know today, but which is improved tomorrow – you get somewhere. But if you think of standards as confining, then you stop." (Ford 1926) Interestingly, Taiichi Ohno, the creator of the Toyota Production System and progenitor of Lean Management, makes a very similar point "... standards should be changing constantly. Instead, if you think of the standard as the best you can do, it's all over. The standard is only a baseline for doing further kaizen." (Ohno 2007) Change control requires input from all stakeholders. Change requests are considered, in consultation with local Process Councils and Process Offices, to determine whether (1) a change should be made on a global basis, (2) a localized change should be made or (3) no change should be made at all. Such decisions would be made on a case-by-case basis. Some general questions can be applied. Can the local variation be justified; do the benefits of variation out way the initial and ongoing costs? Is the local variation really necessary; what is the business impact of not having the variation? If the local variation is justified, is the same variation applicable in other local environments? Is the variation so widely applicable that it should become the new global standard?

Changes will also occur at the local level as an organization responds to changes in customer demand, competitive pressures, new product developments, economic conditions and other external factors.

Harmonization of activities is managed by the Global and Local Process Councils (policy) and the Global and Local Process Offices (operations).

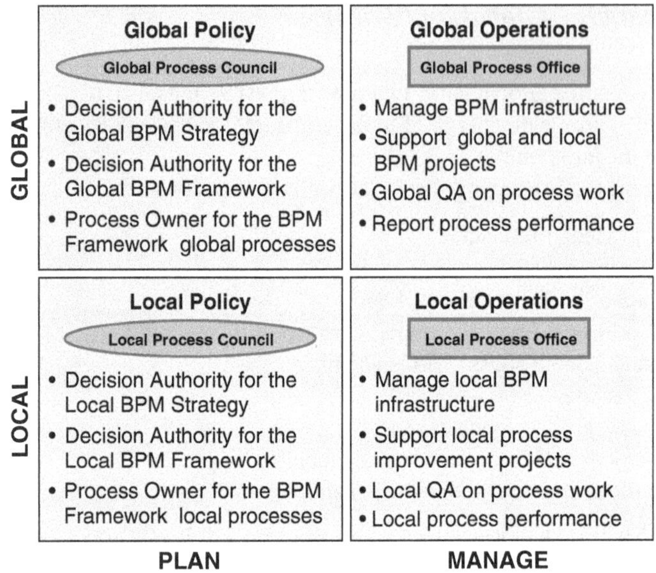


**Fig. 4** Harmonization matrix

While global consistency is important, it is equally important to ensure that global requirements do not adversely affect local business operations. Fig. 4, illustrates the four integrated harmonization activities:

1. global planning and development
2. local planning and development
3. global day-to-day management
4. local day-to-day management.

Global Standards are established from reference models, other best practice sources, or personal experience. These set the nominal target for all parts of the business using the common processes. Local requirements are considered and, if a case can be made, local variations to the Global Standard are approved and implemented. Local variations are also assessed for more general applicability. Where local variations can be usefully applied globally, they are used to challenge and change the Global Standard. In this way, a bias toward global standardization is harmonized with requirements for localization.

The Framework separates, but leaves closely coupled, the activities undertaken as part of the Global BPM and Local BPM.

## 4.4 Global BPM

At the global level, the process management focus is on creating a global approach that supports local business requirements. The key purpose of the Global BPM Strategy is to enable the coordinated management and continuous improvement of local business processes.

| GLOBAL BPM | | | |
|---|---|---|---|
| | Global BPM Key Activities | | |
| Process | Global Lead Activities | Local Involvement | Outcomes |
| Understand Vision & Strategy | • Develop and maintain BPM Global Framework<br>• Develop change control mechanisms<br>• Communicate vision and strategy to stakeholders | • Advise Global Process Council | Shared understanding of how the concepts of BPM are applied |
| Model Global Process Architecture | • Create/maintain global reference model<br>• Develop change control mechanisms<br>• Communicate with stakeholders | • Review for local applicability issues<br>• Submit change requests | Agreed model describing major processes and their relationships and dependencies |
| Measure Process Performance | • Define global process performance measures<br>• Establish measurement methods<br>• Set targets for measures<br>• Establish current performance levels<br>• Review/maintain measurement architecture | • Advise Global Process Council<br>• Localize process performance schemes | Agreed description of measures, targets, measurement methods and current values for major process. |
| Maintain Governance Scheme | • Define global governance<br>• Establish Process Ownership | • Integrate global governance in local Governance Scheme | Agreed accountability for process performance. |

**Fig. 5** Global BPM activities

As illustrated in Fig. 3, BPM planning and development is based on four subprocesses that are closely coupled to corporate strategy. Each step draws on, and provides feedback to, the corporate strategy. Together they articulate a vision for global BPM, describe the organization and its business performance in process terms, and create mechanisms for the management of these processes. These activities are undertaken by the Global Process Office, in consultation with Local Process Offices and the Global Process Council. Figure 5 shows, for each subprocess, the key activities at the global level, how the local business collaborates, in these activities and the shared target outcome. Beyond some initial one-off setup requirements, these activities are enduring.

## *4.5 Local BPM*

Figure 3 shows how, at the local level, process activity has two focal points, Process Management and Process Improvement.

Local Process Management involves the establishment of levels of BPM capability and planning to close identified process performance gaps within a localized process architecture and governance scheme.

Local Process Improvement involves the running of process redesign projects to improve processes selected by local management with the advice of the Local Process Office.

The six subprocesses are described in Fig. 6.

# 5 Managing The Dilemma

At the outset we described the "standardization dilemma" as follows: "Can we achieve business process change with a predisposition towards standardization and still support critical local differences?" In theory, all common processes would be standardized everywhere giving consistent interfaces for customers, suppliers and other external stakeholders as well as cost savings in IT, training and documentation management, with work and people moving freely across organizational and geographic boundaries. In practice, local variation in business processes is inevitable and necessary. Local variation must be constrained by cost-benefit considerations. Such constraint must not be allowed to stifle genuine business needs and aspirations.

The Global BPM Framework presented in Fig. 3, provides a coherent environment to manage the global versus local balancing act. It provides a pragmatic division of labor between global and local process management via Process Councils and Process Offices. The BPM Knowledge Exchange facilitates the dissemination of the emerging best practices and the details of current global standards across the process architecture. Since all of this must be achieved in a dynamic environment, the task is to manage the dilemma rather than resolve it. There can be no static resolution in a changing system. A quasi-stationary equilibrium is maintained in local management autonomy versus centralized control, global efficiency versus local effectiveness and centralized process design versus organic evolution of best practice.

The Framework is a big picture view of managing the conflicting demands of standardization for global efficiency versus variation for local effectiveness. Practical use of the Framework will need to be informed by a range of variables resulting in different timetables and degrees of change. Key issues may include: The level of BPM maturity of the organization, internal and national cultural variation across the organization, current practices regarding centralization versus local autonomy, the sense of urgency (Kotter 2008) perceived by middle management and their teams, motivations for the change, and the more pragmatic issues such as resources, funding, and executive support.

## *5.1 Achieving Standardization*

A key issue requires further consideration. How can process standardization be introduced across an organization while nurturing and sustaining a culture of

| LOCAL BPM | | | | |
|---|---|---|---|---|
| | | Local BPM Key Activities | | |
| | Process | Local Business Lead | Global Involvement | Outcomes |
| Local Process Management | Model BU Architecture & Processes | • Create/maintain a local process architecture consistent with the global architecture<br>• Develop local change control mechanisms<br>• Communicate with local stakeholders | • Review/advise<br>• Provide support to develop and maintain<br>• Make local architectures available | Agreed local model describing processes, their interrelationships and variations from the Global Standard and local Target State |
| Local Process Management | Maintain BU Governance Scheme | • Define local process governance<br>• Establish local process ownership<br>• Report outcomes | • Review and advise on local governance<br>• Capture best practice | Clear under-standing of BPM governance in each business area |
| Local Process Management | Measure BU Process Performance | • Define local process performance measures<br>• Establish measurement methods<br>• Set targets for measures<br>• Establish current performance levels<br>• Maintain measurement architecture | • Review and advise on local measurement approaches<br>• Capture and disseminate best practice | Agreed descrip-tion of local measures, tar-gets,measure-ment methods and current values for major processes |
| Local Process Improvement | Analyze Current Processes | • Priorities processes<br>• Model processes and collect related data<br>• Document process issues and impacts<br>• Consult BPM Knowledge Exchange | • Collect, collate local issues into BPM Knowledge Exchange<br>• Support local activities | Thorough under-standing of curr-ent processes, problems and scope for improvement |
| Local Process Improvement | Design Future Processes | • Redesign processes to improve performance<br>• Assess impacts/risks<br>• Review process measurement system changes<br>• Communicate change<br>• Prepare Business Cases<br>• Plan Change Management<br>• Prepare Projects Plan(s) | • Assess change proposals<br>• Approve global variations<br>• Update Knowledge Exchange<br>• Update global process measurement arrangements | Continuous lo-calized process improvement in a controlled, risk managed and constructive environment |
| Local Process Improvement | Achieve Process Changes | • Initiate and manage process change projects<br>• Measure performance and ensure changes effective | • Post Implemen-tation Reviews<br>• Assess global process change requirements | Forecast changes achieved; learnings gathered for future projects |

**Fig. 6** Local BPM activities

innovation, creativity, and resourcefulness? Michael Hammer suggested that "business units are no longer independent, but merely executors of centrally designed processes" (Raman 2008). Will the McDonaldization (Ritzer 2007) of global business mean the end of local business units?

The Toyota Motor Corporation is the world's most successful manufacturing company. Not immune to the current difficult economic conditions, it is still in the order of magnitude more successful on most measures than its competitors, and most other companies. Toyota is widely known for having extremely detailed work instructions and extensive training programs for its workers to ensure that all work is done precisely and consistently. Toyota managers are considered to be fanatical about the close adherence to detailed work instructions. Toyota workers are seen to be well crafted (and willing) cogs in superefficient factories that are entirely micromanaged in fine detail. This is to misunderstand the Toyota Way.

Standardized work is a cornerstone of the Toyota Production System. However, not all work is standardized to the same degree. Toyota determines the most critical parts of the work and requires those parts to be executed flawlessly. They document these critical processes in significant detail and train the workers relentlessly to achieve perfection. Other parts of the work are completed with less control. By focusing on the critical processes and being relatively relaxed about the other parts, Toyota consistently produces extraordinary results (Liker and Meier 2007).

In developing global standards, it is sensible to think carefully about the degree of standardization to which common processes should be subjected.

A recent book, "Extreme Toyota" (Oson et al. 2008), written by Japanese speaking authors with unprecedented access inside the company, sheds light on the local variation versus standardization question within Toyota. The book gives a more nuanced view of how this dichotomy is managed. It identifies six balancing forces that drive constant renewal characterized by both continuous and discontinuous change.

One of the six forces is *local customization*, which sees Toyota customizing "products and operations to incorporate the sophistication and diversity of local markets around the world". The instructive twist in the tail here is that the process starts with customizing to suit the local market and then collecting and collating those innovations into a global repository. Bottom-up much more than top-down. Global standards and proven variations are developed from the experiments and experience of local business units. Toyota culture actively encourages a high level of controlled and purposeful experimentation and insists on the institutionalizing of successful practice via an extensive ecosystem of information sharing. The intent of the Toyota information nerve system is to allow everybody to know everything, based as much on personal human contact as on accessing digital information. IT enabled knowledge sharing is not seen as a substitute for social networks based on personal human interaction.

Other organizations can learn a lot from this. Standardization and centralized control are not the same idea. The intent of globalization of common processes is to capture and make available the "best process" outcomes from throughout the organization. Implemented properly, global process standardization is less like a police action and more like a collaborative information sharing exercise. Good ideas for process improvement bubble up from the workplace. They are collected, collated, and disseminated. With echoes of Darwinian theory, standardized, best processes evolve based on many choices made in the organizational ecosystem.

**Table 1** Coercive and enabling systems

| Coercive systems & procedures | Enabling systems & procedures |
|---|---|
| Systems focus on performance standard so as to highlight poor performance. | Focus on best practice methods: information on performance standards is not much use without information on best practices for achieving them. |
| Standardize the systems to minimize game playing and monitoring costs. | Systems should allow customization to different levels of skill/experience and should guide flexible improvisation. |
| Systems should be designed so as to keep employees out of the control loop. | Systems should help people control their own work: help them form mental models of the system by "glass box" design. |
| Systems are instructions to be followed, not challenged. | Systems are best practice templates to be improved. |

Jeffrey Liker (2004) draws on Paul Adler's analysis of Toyota's organizational practices to further understand the balancing act between highly proscriptive environments where rules are rigidly enforced and organic environments where flexibility, empowerment, and initiative are the valued attributes.

Adler (1999) contrasts "coercive" and "enabling" bureaucracies. Coercive bureaucracy seeks to control people via standards. Enabling bureaucracy uses standards to help people control their work. In Table 1, he summarizes how a coercive approach looks for something wrong and the enabling approach looks for something right (Adler 1999).

In global process standardization initiatives our efforts will be much better rewarded if we create enabling rather than coercive systems. We should first carefully decide which processes will give an appropriate return from standardization investments. We must also strike a balance between standardization being based on process design originating from the Head Office and a proactive system of collecting global best practice and making it available to all.

# 6 Summary

The arguments for the standardization of common processes across an organization are compelling. Customers and suppliers have a consistent interface. There are economies of scale in training, IT development and operation, document control, process improvement, change management, performance measurement, and quality assurance.

Are these benefits enough to sacrifice local variations that respond to local needs? The arguments for allowing, indeed promoting, local variation in common processes are also persuasive.

The dilemma faced by an organization moving to process-based management is where to strike the balance between global efficiency and local effectiveness. Issues of central control versus local autonomy often arise in developing process governance policies. These tensions must be resolved if process management is to be adopted as the core management philosophy.

Should organizational energy be expended in enforcing compliance or used to encourage diversity? Do we develop standard processes centrally and promulgate them as mandatory decrees or can the wisdom of the crowd be used to inform best process decisions? Do variations need to be deep or just within the customer's field of view? Will compliance with the standards be achieved by forceful policing or empowering encouragement? At what level of the process architecture will standardization be required?

The need to balance centralized control and loosely-coupled association is enduring. As circumstances change, so do the balance points.

We have described a Global BPM Framework comprising a set of concepts, principles, constraints, and relationships that provide the basis for execution of a Global BPM Strategy, the essential course of action required to achieve the goal of process-based management.

Global Standards are established by the Global Process Council. This is achieved via reference models, other best practice sources, and personal experience. The Global Standards set the nominal target for the common processes. Local requirements are considered by the Local Process Councils and, if a case can be made, local variations to the Global Standard are approved and implemented. Local variations are continuously assessed for more general applicability. Where local variations can be usefully applied globally, they are used to change the Global Standard. In this way, a bias toward global standardization is harmonized with genuine requirements for localization. The flow is circular; both bottom-up and top-down.

This approach separates, but leaves closely coupled, the activities undertaken as part of Global BPM and Local BPM. The dilemma is not so much resolved as managed, since the global-local balance must be maintained in a dynamic environment. There can be no static resolution in a changing system.

The BPM Framework provides a solid basis for modeling, communicating, analyzing, testing, proving, controlling, and managing the costs and benefits of global consistency versus local relevance.

## References


Adler P (1999) Building better bureaucracies. Acad Manage Exec 13(4):36–47

Baumöl U (2010) Cultural change in process management. In: vom Brocke J, Rosemann M (eds) Handbook on business process management, vol 2. Springer, Heidelberg

Brooke L (2008) Ford model T: The car that put the world on wheels. Motorbooks, Minneapolis

Burlton RT (2001) Business process management: Profiting from process. Sams Publishing, Indiana

Davenport TH (2005) Thinking for a living: How to get better performance and results from knowledge workers. Harvard Business School Press, Boston, MA

de Bruin T, Doebeli G (2010) An organizational approach to BPM: the experience of an Australian transport provider. In: vom Brocke J, Rosemann M (eds) Handbook on business process management, vol 2. Springer, Heidelberg

Ford H (1926) Today and tomorrow. Doubleday Page & Company, New York
Hallerbach (2010) Configuration and management of process variants. In: vom Brocke J, Rosemann M (eds) Handbook on business process management, vol 1. Springer, Heidelberg
Hammer M (2010) What is business process management? In: vom Brocke J, Rosemann M (eds) Handbook on business process management, vol 1. Springer, Heidelberg
Harmon P (2007) Business process change: A guide for managers and BPM and six sigma professionals. Morgan Kaufmann, San Francisco
Hofstede G (2001) Culture's consequences: Comparing values, Behaviours, institutions and organizations across nations. Sage Publications, CA
Kotter JP (2008) A sense of urgency. Harvard Business Press, Boston
Leymann F et al. (2010) Business process management standards. In: vom Brocke J, Rosemann M (eds) Handbook on business process management, vol 1. Springer, Heidelberg
Liker JK (2004) The Toyota way: 14 management principles from the world's greatest manufacturer. McGraw-Hill, New York
Liker JK, Meier A (2007) Toyota talent: Developing your people the Toyota way. McGraw-Hill, New York
Magee D (2007) How Toyota became #1: Leadership lessons from the world's greatest car company. Portfolio, New York
Markus ML, Jacobson DD (2010) Business process goverance. In: vom Brocke J, Rosemann M (eds) Handbook on business process management, vol 2. Springer, Heidelberg
Object management group (2009) Business motivation model Ver 1.0. http://www.omg.org/docs/formal/08-08-02.pdf. Accessed 8 February 2009
Ohno T (1988) Toyota production system: Beyond large scale production. Productivity Press, New York
Ohno T (2007) Workplace management. Gemba Press. ISBN 0-9786387-5-1
Oson E, Shimizu N, Tekeuchi H (2008) Extreme toyota: Radical contradictions that drive success at the world's best manufacturer. Wiley, New Jersey
Raman A (2008) Michael Hammer: A tribute to the guru of operations. harvard business publishing. HBR Editors' Blog, http://discussionleader.hbsp.com/hbreditors/2008/09/michael_hammer_a_tribute.html. Accessed 28 May 2009
Ritzer G (2007) The McDonaldization of society, 2nd edn. Pine Forge Press, Thousand Oaks. http://www.amazon.com/McDonadization-Society-George-Ritzer/dp/0761988122#noop
Shigeo S (1989) A study of the toyota production system. Productivity Press, New York
Stewart TA, Raman AP (2007) Lessons from toyota's long drive: A conversation with Katsuaki Watanabe. Harv Bus Rev, Harvard, July 2007
Spanyi A (2010) Business process management governance. In: vom Brocke J, Rosemann M (eds) Handbook on business process management, vol 2. Springer, Heidelberg
vom Brocke J, Petry M, Sinnl T, Østerberg Kristensen B, Sonnenberg C (2010) Global processes and data: The cultural journey at the Hilti Corporation. In: vom Brocke J, Rosemann M (eds) Handbook on business management, vol 2. Springer, Heidelberg

# BPO through the BPM Lens: A Case Study

**Jyoti M. Bhat, Jude Fernandez, Manish Kumar, and Sukriti Goel**

**Abstract** Process outsourcing industry, a multibillion dollar market, is a highly competitive area with intense competition among companies across outsourcing destinations. After the initial cost advantages, Business Process Outsourcing (BPO) clients increasingly expect innovation and improved performance, which acts as a driver for BPO providers to adopt different aspects of Business Process Management (BPM). Most of the literature on BPO and BPM focuses on the outsourcing organization's point of view. While BPOs use Six Sigma techniques and IT for improving their performance, the adoption of BPM by a BPO has not been analyzed from a holistic perspective. In this chapter, the authors analyze the various BPM lifecycle activities and supporting elements as applied to a BPO provider–client relationship and the benefits derived using a BPM framework. This chapter uses case studies from an Indian BPO provider and is based on the considerable experience of the authors in BPM and BPM implementations in a BPO service provider.

## 1 Introduction

Business Process Outsourcing (BPO) has slowly gained popularity from the initial experiments to a must-have item in the organization strategy in the last few years. BPO involves contracting specific business processes and tasks to a third-party service provider. The processes being outsourced are typically important functions, but classified as noncore (Namasivayam 2004). BPO, according to Scholl (2003), includes the outsourcing of entire functions such as supply (moving, storing, making, and buying of goods and services) and demand (customer selection, acquisition, retention, etc.) management, and some enterprise-related areas for

J.M. Bhat (✉)
BPM Research Group, SETLabs, Infosys Technologies Limited, Bangalore, India
e-mail: JYOTIMB@infosys.com

J. vom Brocke and M. Rosemann (eds.), *Handbook on Business Process Management 2*, International Handbooks on Information Systems,
DOI 10.1007/978-3-642-01982-1_16, 

example, HR, finance, IT, and facilities management and customer-related processes such as marketing and support.

From a focus on leveraging the cost efficiencies of outsourcing noncore processes to external service providers with skilled resources, organizations are exploring process outsourcing options to take advantage of process optimization, flexibility, and scalability of resources (number, types of skills, etc.), skills and technologies. Typically, the initial expectations of the outsourcing company cover cost arbitrage and availability of skilled resources. Over time, client expectations mature and focus on innovation, performance improvements, and parameters such as speed and flexibility (Kaka et al. 2006). Today, increased competition in the BPO market is putting pressure on the rates the BPO organizations can charge their clients. Additional challenges are the increased costs of resources (due to manpower salary rises) and that of retaining valuable employees in an industry environment where high attrition is common. BPO vendors face a strong imperative to constantly innovate and improve their performance to remain competitive while meeting the rising customer expectations.

The success of the relationship between the BPO service provider and the client depends on how the entire lifecycle of the outsourcing relationship is handled in a holistic manner covering management processes, governance structures, technology usage, monitoring, service level agreements, and commitment from all stakeholders. Given this, Business Process Management (BPM) provides an appropriate framework for BPO vendors to meet their objectives and address the challenges of the outsourcing relationship. The BPM term has expanded considerably from its initial narrow focus and is today understood to cover a holistic approach to managing processes using appropriate methods, standards, and technology, together with the right supporting elements of governance, people aspects, infrastructure, etc. (Bhat and Fernandez 2008). The outsourcing relationship between the BPO and the client, post deal finalization, usually follows a pattern: discovery phase (process identification, analysis, etc.), transition of the process from the existing client environment to the BPO vendor environment, stabilization at the BPO vendor, and finally the steady state. In a steady-state mode, the BPO vendor usually aims to continuously improve and transform the process, based on client expectations and the vendor's motivation to remain competitive. In addition, a closer analysis of the relationship will reveal that there are the governing elements of SLAs, audits, reporting, etc.

The applicability of BPM to the BPO landscape can be analyzed from different dimensions. The first dimension is how the organizations exploring process outsourcing can leverage BPM principles for success of their BPO strategy, which has been studied by many and is available in literature (Martin et al. 2008; Mattig 2008). Second, BPM as applied to managing the BPO service provider would be a case similar to the BPM adoption strategy by any business organization. But applying BPM principles to the BPO relationships of the provider and analyzing the various activities and elements of BPM governance is not a well-researched item.

We will examine the BPM elements and its adoption by the BPO providers in managing the outsourcing relationship with their clients. To analyze how BPM principles can support the BPO relationship objectives, it is useful to bring in a suitable BPM framework that covers the BPM lifecycle elements on both process and technology along with the supporting elements including governance. In this chapter, the various aspects of a BPO relationship are examined from a BPM point of view using three outsourcing relationship case studies (at different levels of maturity) from a global BPO organization. The analysis covers the adoption of process management methods, BPM technology adoption, success factors, and benefits to the client and the BPO provider.

## 2 Business Process Outsourcing: A Closer Look

Organizations exploring BPO usually look at IT-enabled processes or using IT to enable the outsourcing exercise, which has led to common BPO definitions having an IT flavor.

Halvey and Melby (2000) give two definitions:

> The management of one or more specific business processes or functions (e.g., procurement, accounting, human resources, asset or property management) by a third party, together with the information technology (IT) that supports the process or functions.

and

> The delegation of one or more IT-intensive business processes to an external provider who, in turn, administers and manages the selection processes based upon defined and measurable performance metrics.

Rouse and Corbitt (2006) have explored the various definitions of BPO and the types of outsourcing, including offshore outsourcing. Their investigation into the previous research on BPO reveals that academic research on BPO has yet to catch up with the popularity of BPO. An offshoot of BPO is knowledge process outsourcing (KPO), which includes those activities that require greater skill, knowledge, education and expertise to handle for example, valuation research, investment research, patent filing, etc. (Sen and Shiel 2006).

The BPO space has seen tremendous growth and considerable changes over the last few years. The BPO market worldwide grew from $19 billion in 2004 to an estimated $146 billion in 2008. The global BPO market is forecast to hit $450 billion by 2012 (NelsonHall 2008). Mehta et al. (2006) attribute the phenomenal growth to technological advancements, (e.g., Internet) which have brought down communication costs and enabled the internationalization of business processes and services. The BPO industry has multiple categories, for example, horizontal process domains such as HR, logistics, or finance, or vertical specializations for example, medical transcription (health sector) and check processing and imaging (banking sector). Some vendors focus only on a single process for example, accounts payable in banking; others are more comprehensive and support multiple business processes within a single support area for example, finance. The more complex BPOs offer services to clients in multiple domains for example, a vendor may be responsible for HR, core processes in finance, and accounting, as well as customer relations for clients across different verticals. Another variation in the BPO relationship is the location from which they deliver the services to the client – same country, near-shore (like Canada and Mexico for US clients and Eastern Europe for Central European countries) and offshore locations (India, China, Philippines, Israel, etc.). While the choice of location for the BPO service is primarily driven by cost, resource availability, and client comfort, the lifecycle activities, governance mechanisms and technology usage in the BPO provider and client relationship are similar, irrespective of the location.

Feeny et al. (2005) portray three competencies that BPO vendors possess, regardless of the domain and type of services they offer. *Delivery competency* – it is a measure of how well the supplier responds to the client's day-to-day operational requirements; *Transformational competency* – this represents how well the vendor is able to improve the outsourced services on dimensions of cost, quality, performance, etc.; and finally, *Relationship competency* – the extent to which the vendor is willing to invest in building a win–win relationship aligning client and supplier goals and incentives over the longer run. Feeny et al. (2005) also talk about the BPO vendor capabilities, which are critical for a successful relationship like business management, technology exploitation, process re-engineering, governance, program management, organizational structure, etc. Click and Duening (2004), while discussing the BPO relationship success factors, mention project management, IT integration, cultural integration, client involvement and commitment, governance, and goal alignment as some of the factors that need focus.

BPO vendors are developing and maturing their capabilities by adopting frameworks, best practices, and technology that have been proven in other industries. Defined processes and various IT architectures for delivering process outsourcing are being employed by BPO providers. The outsourcing process has defined stages such as feasibility study, transition, and execution to ensure the smooth transfer of the business process from the client organization to the BPO, and ongoing improvement on the process. Process outsourcing services are offered on different delivery architectures, from advanced offerings such as software as a service (SaaS), BPM platform-based process offerings, standardized processes using packaged applications, web-based collaborative process executions, etc., to basic process automation and even manual processing. The delivery architecture depends on the type of process being outsourced such as simple data entry, decision-making based on business policies and rules, or knowledge-based services. BPO initiatives are typically led by the business units in the client organizations, while the IT group is involved to identify data and system interfaces and integration with the BPO provider's systems. The partnership between client's IT group and the BPO's IT group is a required aspect of governance. While the dependency is high during the transition phase, it is also required on an ongoing basis to support and sustain operations, as well as the process improvements being brought in.

A BPO relationship passes through various lifecycle activities before it reaches a steady state, during which aspects related to process methods and technologies, process performance, organization structure, management, reporting, escalations, training, and governance are addressed. Given these characteristics of a BPO relationship and its apparent similarities to the BPM paradigm, we use a suitable

BPM framework, which encompasses the aspects of process lifecycle activities, technology implementation, governance requirements, critical success factors, etc., to examine the BPO relationship through the BPM lens. Though handling cultural differences and governance mechanisms are critical to the BPO relationship, we do not examine these aspects in this chapter.

## 3 Business Process Management Framework for Analysis

A BPO relationship goes through various BPM lifecycle activities around the business process being outsourced and the technology used to implement the process along with other program management and change management issues related to training, client and vendor commitments, organization structure, roadmap definition, etc. An analysis of the BPM frameworks available today shows that they can be classified into two groups: Firstly, the maturity models and assessment tools and secondly, BPM lifecycle methodologies. The BPM maturity models provide a comprehensive view into the various elements of process management maturity and technology implementation, including governance and strategy. Notable examples of these are the BPM maturity model developed by the Queensland University of Technology (Rosemann et al. 2004),[1] OMG's Business Process Maturity Model (OMG 2008), Michael Hammer's Process and Enterprise Maturity Model (Hammer 2007), and Gartner's BPM Maturity and Adoption Model (Melenovsky and Sinur 2006). These models are quite comprehensive and detailed and appear to address the needs of assessing process management maturity. A BPO relationship starts with activities that are associated with the early stages of a typical BPM journey and hence they are not ready for such elaborate and rigorous assessments (Bhat and Fernandez 2008). The BPM lifecycle views cover the various stages of the lifecycle of implementing BPM and show the linkages between different elements and the iterative nature of the lifecycle (zur Mühlen 2004). However, they do not address the supporting elements, such as governance, people aspects, etc.

To analyze the BPO relationship from a BPM viewpoint, we use BizPAD – *Bus*iness *P*rocess Management *Ad*option Framework (Bhat and Fernandez 2008) as it integrates the lifecycle model and the elements of the BPM maturity model covering process management and technology implementation. It covers measurements, monitoring, analysis and the feedback loop back to process planning. The framework facilitates identification of gaps to realize the promise of BPM. The granularity of the framework elements is designed to bring business and IT groups on the same page so that the activities and interfaces between IT and business are made visible. Organizations can extend and define the next level of granularity of the framework

[1]Rosemann and vom Brocke (2010) provide a detailed discussion of the six core elements of the BPM maturity model. de Bruin and Doebeli (2010) demonstrate the application of the BPM maturity model in practice.

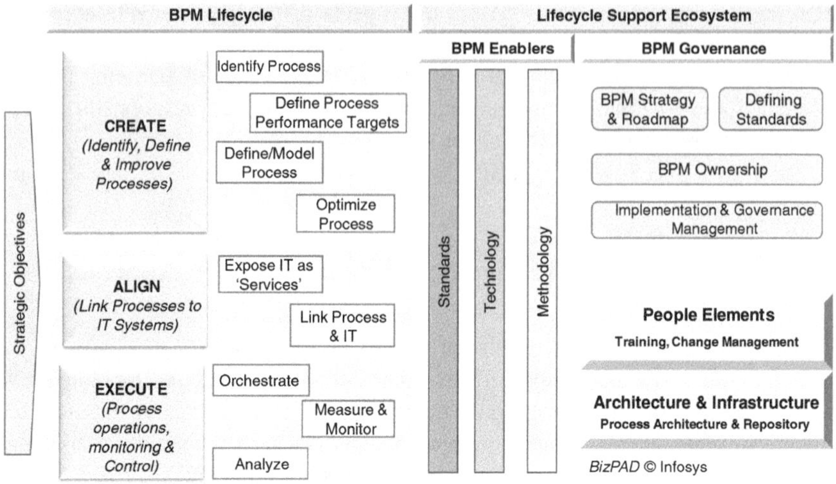


**Fig. 1** BizPAD: The BPM adoption framework

by linking it to methods, methodologies, tools, and standards for the different elements of the framework and publish it as the standard for their organization.

The BizPAD framework (Fig. 1) depicts the BPM lifecycle elements grouped under phases on one dimension and the lifecycle support ecosystem which covers the enablers for the lifecycle elements (standards, technology and methodology) along with BPM governance, people, and infrastructure as the other dimensions. The process lifecycle is separated into high-level phases, namely, *Create*, *Align,* and *Execute*. These phases and activities have been created to ensure segregation of activities related to business process design, IT design and implementation activities, and the operations and control type of activities. The governance aspects that support the BPM life cycle cover the BPM strategy and roadmap, role clarity in BPM, and ensuring consistency. The people elements cover change management, training, etc, while Infrastructure elements include process architecture, repository, architecture elements, technology library, and building blocks, etc. BizPAD helps blend the various individual elements of BPM into a harmonized entity.

We will use BizPAD to analyze the three BPO relationship case studies to understand all the BPM elements that are relevant in a BPO relationship: the BPM lifecycle activities, the BPM enablers, and other success factors, which form the ecosystem supporting BPM.

## 4 Case Study

Infosys BPO (IBPO) (http://www.infosys.com/bpo) is one of the highly rated offshore BPO providers with an employee strength of about 17,000 and revenues of $215 million (April–December 2008). IBPO has 11 delivery centers across India,

China, Philippines, Mexico, Poland, Thailand, and Czech Republic. IBPO, which started in 2002, has had a rapid organic growth with a focus on continuous process improvements along with an integrated process and IT approach and leading people management practices. The organization has adopted different frameworks to meet its improvement objectives for example, the Six Sigma process framework, ISO 9001:2001, eSCM level 4 amongst others. IBPO provides outsourcing with a focus on end-to-end business processes and functions and partners with clients to move from "operating" their business processes to "transforming" the business process through innovation, process re-engineering, and the use of technology.

In the following sections, we describe three outsourcing relationships of IBPO, which are at different levels of engagement maturity to bring out the variations and the relevance of BPM principles in maturing a BPO relationship.

## *4.1 Business Process Outsourcing Relationship 1: Maturing from Cost-Effective to Optimized*

The client company, Alpha's core business is to provide aggregated financial information, with a focus on accuracy and timeliness, to professionals and enterprises to help them in their businesses. In the process under study, Alpha aggregates data from various analysts and provides a consensus view to its clients on the expectations on each company. The outsourced segment of the process involves aggregating analysts' estimates of company performance and share price forecast processing, consolidating the data, and sending it back to Alpha for further analysis. Earlier, Alpha used to purchase the aggregated data from a third party data provider, which was discontinued because of data, quality issues related to inaccurate data aggregation and summarization like incorrect averages, numbers' mismatch, etc. Alpha then decided to manage the information aggregation process themselves by partnering with IBPO.

### 4.1.1 Process Details

Alpha receives data from different investment analysts and sources in various forms: e-mails, spread sheets, and documented reports like balance sheets. The outsourced process handled by IBPO focuses on the documented reports available in pdf and HTML formats. The process activities (Fig. 2) involve receiving the files, reading the textual data in the document, analyzing it, and entering relevant data into a database; essentially converting the data from an unstructured to a structured format. The data extraction falls under three categories, namely, earnings estimate, profiles data for key personnel in the companies, and analyst recommendations from all the major financial markets. Subsequently, the data is normalized for consistency in the usage of business terms and sent back to Alpha as an XML file.

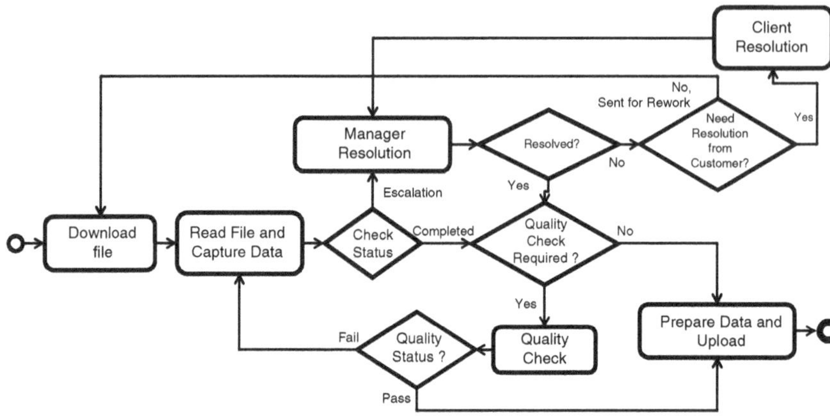


**Fig. 2** Alpha's data aggregation process model

About 848,000 files per annum across 14 different languages (English, four Asian, and nine European languages) are received for processing. The volumes for the process peak in the month following a financial quarter end because of the various earning reports and company announcements being made.

### 4.1.2 Challenges/Interesting Aspects

Alpha did not have the in-house process as it used to purchase the data from a provider. IBPO did not receive any process knowledge from Alpha, apart from some business rules, and consequently, the process hand-offs and other process details were not clear. Knowledge of applicable tools and methods was also not available. This meant that IBPO had to recreate the process from the desired end output specified by the client (which was an "XML" file).

In this regard, Alpha partnered effectively, by taking the responsibility of creating and maintaining detailed process documentation. It also handled the responsibility of ongoing training and maintenance of a knowledge management repository.

To handle the work in multiple languages, IBPO had to execute the process from three locations (India for English, Czech Republic for European, and China for Asian Languages). The process is executed 24 × 5 with employees working shifts across all the locations.

Alpha set aggressive tiered turnaround times (TAT) based on the importance of the company covered in the research report, starting from 4 h (Tier 1) and 12 h (Tier 2) to 24 h (Tier 3). Quality of deliverables was a critical aspect (99.5% accuracy for the extracted data) so as to avoid the data integrity issues of the previous data provider.

Alpha is an integral part of the process execution as IBPO can escalate specific items to Alpha for clarifications. IBPO was, in some cases, asked by Alpha for the exact source location of the extracted data point. Alpha also requested many process changes as it was learning along with IBPO on this process.

#### 4.1.3 Process Requirements

The tasks were related to varying complexities and languages with different SLAs, which could be handled by specific resource pools across geographies. This required focus on task allocation, queuing, and SLA tracking. Some of the task durations were more than the shift hours (8 h) with TATs less than a day and hence there was a need for coordination mechanisms to ensure that the work gets reallocated at the end of the shift to agents of the next shift. Task reallocation and support was another requirement.

Audits were introduced to meet the quality objectives. The customer, Alpha, audited the process only from the outcomes perspective and was not involved in the in-process details. For auditing and customer visibility, the traceability between the input file and the extracted data had to be maintained. There was also the requirement to be able to include the customer in a specific process instance.

#### 4.1.4 Technology Usage

IBPO realized that the existing mechanisms of work allocation, tracking, data extraction, and consolidation which was facilitated using spreadsheets would not scale up to meet the needs of the process. The financial data aggregation process needed to be superimposed with the workflow and project management processes. Hence, the data aggregation process workflow was set up on a third-party BPM product to handle the task allocation and process handoffs between the various participants across geographies, namely, the manager, the agents, quality auditors and the client. This ensured allocation of work to different geographies based on skill and prioritization based on TAT and reallocation during shift change. In addition, the tasks allocated to each employee was prioritized and presented based on the time left to meet the TAT. The visibility provided by the BPM platform helped manage the TAT and quality requirements and added scalability and productivity improvements. Issue resolution was also handled by including an escalation mechanism in the workflow through the BPM platform, wherever customer input and feedback were required for completing the task. On completion of the task by the employee, tasks were assigned to the quality auditors for verifying the quality of work. The process was further automated by integrating and storing the inputs and outputs of the task as part of the BPM platform. This facilitated smooth transfer of a task between employees during shift change as the next shift picked up the task and started filling in data from the point where the employee from the previous shift had left.

#### 4.1.5 Process Improvement

IBPO had committed on continuous process improvement to Alpha at the beginning of the contract. While Alpha provided continuous feedback based on its domain and process knowledge to improve the process, IBPO team used Six Sigma techniques and technology solutions for process optimization. These focused on reduction of defects, efforts, etc., and productivity. Given below are a few examples:

- Initially, IBPO spent a lot of effort in review. To minimize review effort and yet maintain quality levels, instead of auditing every file, a quality control algorithm was developed based on employee performance and learning theory. This enabled the planning of an optimal number of audits based on the need so as to ensure quality levels. Once all the anomalies were corrected, the file was packaged as an XML output file, validated for good form, encrypted and posted back to the client.
- Knowledge Management was introduced by storing the inputs and feedback received from Alpha on various escalations in a knowledge repository for reference at a later date. This improved the productivity, TAT, and reduced the customer involvement required going forward.
- As process knowledge was not strong initially within the IBPO, there were a lot of escalations to the client. Later, IBPO found that 50% escalations were solved by the customer by referring to data from their terminals. IBPO requested access to the customer terminals and integrated it with the process flow, further reducing the need for customer involvement.
- Utilization levels were improved by training the employees on multiple languages and allocating primary and secondary languages, tiers, and priorities to them. Task allocation and queuing on the BPM platform was leveraged to support this. IBPO was able to transfer all the work from Czech Republic to the China center as the Chinese employees learnt three languages and were able to handle all the European language requirements. Currently, this process operates out of India (110 people) and China (125 people).
- Many technology solutions were integrated with the workflow setup on the BPM product to improve the process.
- Automatic case creation and allocation to employees based on the input pdf file and the language tag of the file picked up directly from Alpha's servers replaced the manual download and task allocation by the IBPO managers.
- Use of *Poka Yoke* (Mistake-proofing): Important data and figures in the unstructured data were highlighted and color coded using text mining and knowledge engineering technologies to ensure that the employee did not miss it.
- Reducing waste of motion: two screens to provided the employee to eliminate the switching between windows.
- Improved Data capture through the use of a "point and shoot" solution: instead of copying data from document to the data entry screen, the point-and-shoot application replicated the selected data to the desired field in the data entry screen.
- Auto population of data based on business rules.
- Regular update to Alpha was done usually through daily, weekly, and monthly reports. Now, a dashboard is being developed on the BPM platform to provide real-time visibility to Alpha.

- Initially, IBPO could not contest the SLAs and TAT set by Alpha because of lack of historical data. At times, IBPO found it difficult to meet the stringent TAT while maintaining quality. But, once IBPO was able to demonstrate predictable and improving process performance through the application of various methods and technologies, Alpha was able to appreciate the need to revise the SLAs. Subsequently, Alpha and IBPO worked together to baseline suitable SLAs for the outsourced process which could meet the requirements of both Alpha and IBPO.

### 4.1.6 Critical Success Factors

Many of the success factors for a BPO relationship are visible in the IBPO–Alpha relationship such as process ownership, organization structure, usage of technology, client commitment and involvement, program management, and goal alignment. IBPO's organization structure had a dedicated operations team (Ops), which handled the execution of Alpha's process, and a central Transformation Solutions Group (TSG), which provided the technology solutions and support. The effective synergy between Ops and TSG had been one of the core foundations for success. While Ops identified process improvements based on process execution data, TSG looked at improvements through technology implementation. The Ops team owned the process and hence took complete ownership of the application with detailed involvement and provided the requirements for the BPM technology implementation. The Ops team established an effective feedback mechanism on process changes which resulted in new feature requirements on the technology. The BPM platform enabled TSG to adopt an iterative development methodology and provided frequent releases of the application instead of a big bang approach. The use of BPM technology enabled the TSG team to measure and analyze the process KPIs and report improvement in the process against the process KPIs. Though the decisions on process design and technology architecture were taken by IBPO, Alpha was involved in reviewing and providing feedback. Alpha's commitment and involvement could also be seen from the ownership it took for training, process documentation, and knowledge management. IBPO's process execution framework established interfaces with Alpha's people (escalation resolution) and technology (direct access to customer terminals and file upload/download). IBPO's strong program management capabilities were supported on the BPM product and regular reporting to Alpha was another factor contributing to the success of the relationship. The joint fine-tuning of IBPO's goals and deliverables to Alpha ensured that both Alpha and IBPO met their business objectives.

### 4.1.7 Impact of the Business Process Management Initiative

IBPO was able to scale its process volumes and increase productivity because of the process changes and the technology architecture used. The increased productivity

(50% improvement in TAT) of IBPO resulted in a capacity creation within IBPO for Alpha. Alpha was able to scale rapidly and introduce new product lines to their customers much faster at no additional cost. The outsourcing relationship which started with an objective of cheaper and better data 5 years ago matured to provide newer capabilities to Alpha. This resulted in additional processes being planned for outsourcing. Apart from the business benefits, IBPO also benefited from increased employee morale.

## *4.2 Business Process Outsourcing Relationship 2: Eliminating the Work*

Beta is a financial services organization operating in the US and Europe offering credit cards and a variety of loans and savings products. The outsourced operation is a part of the process which handles credit card application processing at Beta. The credit card application process can originate through three different channels in Beta. The applicant calls up Beta and the Beta representative enters information about the applicant (caller) into the origination system, and a form along with terms and conditions is mailed across for signatures and any modification (if required) by the applicant. Alternatively, the applicant can fill in a physical form and send it to Beta or the form can be filled online through the internet by the applicant. The first two scenarios result in physical forms. The process work outsourced to IBPO involves the data extraction from these physical forms and creation of structured data to be fed into the origination system. The origination system then does the credit verification with the various bureaus before making a decision. This process, "keying-in process" given in Fig. 3, was transitioned from an existing vendor to IBPO.

### 4.2.1 Process Details

Beta scans the physical credit card application forms, creates batches of a maximum of 25 applications and sends it to IBPO through a secure channel. IBPO employees

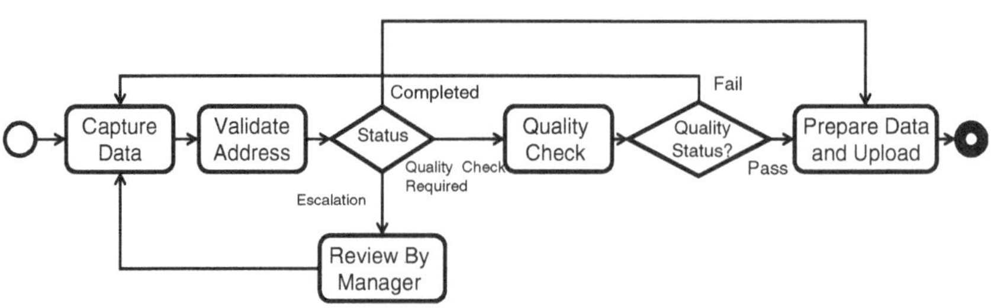


**Fig. 3** Beta's keying-in process model

read the data from the scanned image and key it into specific formats. A prespecified format is provided by Beta to IBPO for different application form templates (initially there were 25 forms). The data in the prespecified format is sent back to Beta by the batches received. The volumes for the process ranged from 2,000 to 6,000 credit card applications per month. The scope also includes “Managing Exceptions” which focuses on addressing errors found in the keying-in process. IBPO employed 19 people to handle the two processes.

### 4.2.2 Challenges/Interesting Aspects

This process was earlier serviced by another vendor. On analysis of the process, IBPO decided that the existing vendor’s processes and tools for managing the process execution were not very suitable and decided to recreate the process and the supporting tools. As part of the transition process which lasted 3 months, the IBPO team studied the process and created a detailed process manual right down to the key stroke level. As Beta had expectations of 90% compliance to the prespecified format and data quality, IBPO built in checks and counterchecks into the process to enable mistake-proofing.

Beta introduced new credit card application forms based on business needs, to the existing 25 different forms. This introduced new prespecified formats for IBPO to key into, requiring changes in task steps and technology. Illegible writing in the scans received from Beta and typos by IBPO employees introduced errors in the output file. TAT SLA agreed with Beta was 12 h for 70% of the batches with the remaining 30% to be completed in 24 h.

### 4.2.3 Process Requirements

The TAT is applied to each batch received from Beta; hence, the task allocation had to be done such that a batch could be split and handed over to different employees for parallel processing of individual applications. Here, there was a need to split a batch and consolidate the work back into a single output file before sending it back to Beta. On analysis, IBPO realized that processing a batch sequentially took 75 min, whereas if it could be split up, the time could be brought down to 3 min. For this, the batch needed to be split up into separate cases, each with a unique identifier, so as to enable consolidation postprocessing. This step to handle batch splitting had to be integrated with the keying-in processes. Shift support was another requirement, as the TAT was greater than the shift duration.

The process was heavy on key strokes, with 25 different types of application forms with an average of 299 fields in each form. Hence, reducing keystrokes was essential for increasing the productivity and reducing errors. In addition, the process had to incorporate the stringent quality audits to ensure compliance.

### 4.2.4 Technology Usage

TSG built an application, "keying-in application," on a third party net-based BPM platform using the detailed process manual created by the Ops team. The keying-in application is used for work flow management, allocation of work, work prioritization, queue management, escalation, monitoring, and audit. The IBPO team leader can allocate and reallocate work items to the employees who can directly fetch the work items from the system and key the data into the forms. Forms are built into the system with built-in data validation checks. New forms can be designed quickly based on new credit card application templates of the customer. The system saves the data from specific forms into the designated prespecified file formats. Form-specific quality audit checks are facilitated by the keying-in application by linking the relevant audit checklists. The "keying-in application" is integrated with Beta's software through file uploads to ensure transfer of input batches from Beta and output files from IBPO.

### 4.2.5 Process Improvements

The main objective of process improvements was to extract the data from an image and key it into a form in the least time with zero errors. The Ops group studied the process execution to create a key stroke level process model and made the operating procedures more robust using methods such as Failure Mode and Effect Analysis (FMEA), leading to better process control. Some of the process improvements done were: Identifying critical and noncritical fields in the form, because for the noncritical fields, the cost of validation was more than cost of error. New processes were defined as in the case of similar names of prospective customers, for which rules were defined to identify whether it was a name change application or a new applicant. This was codified as business rules on the system to auto-update fields and disable edits by the key-in on certain fields.

TSG provided innovative technical solutions to improve key stroke level performance; such as multiple page images to reduce waste in motion, double keying for critical data fields, highlighting missing mandatory fields, auto-update of some fields based on business rules, etc. IBPO studied the credit card application and suggested changes in the template to Beta to reduce the data entry effort and errors. This in turn helped Beta improve its web-based origination application. The suggested changes also include implementing Optical Character Recognition (OCR) for the process. This will reduce work in keying and is expected to result in 30% productivity improvement.

The errors in entering the address fields because of illegible scan or typos has been reduced by integrating the application with the postal system's address database for carrying out address validation. This also reduced the number of fields to be typed in. The reduction in the errors in the data entry in turn reduced the workload on the downstream process of Manage Exceptions (also handled by IBPO) which used to handle the errors and other exceptions discovered during quality checks.

#### 4.2.6 Critical Success Factors

Process re-engineering supported by technology was one of the factors that contributed to successful transition of the process to IBPO. During the transition phase, IBPO analyzed the process, redesigned it, and implemented it on a BPM platform before taking over the process from Beta's existing vendor. The role clarity and ownership of the Ops and TSG team in process redesign and process improvements exercise was another factor. Further, process integration with third-party data providers and technology usage provided improved process performance. Client commitment and involvement was an important contributor as Beta was involved in all the key stages of the process and application design and validated it at all stages. Beta even invested into the building of the application by IBPO.

#### 4.2.7 Impact of the Business Process Management Initiative

IBPO has been able to increase the acceptance of the applications by 30%, which has reduced the need for Beta to go back to the credit card applicant for further validation. The team also achieved a reduction in the number of exceptions to be managed, bringing it down from 30 to 5% currently. Since this process was charged to Beta on a per transaction basis, the cost of the process to Beta has reduced considerably. Further, the new enhancements implemented have resulted in productivity benefits to the tune of 30% (at peak volumes). Other suggestions by IBPO, such as form redesign and improvements in its web-based application, when implemented, can drastically reduce/eliminate the need for the keying in.

The process improvements carried out by IBPO reduced the number of people required to handle the processes. While the improvements were done at IBPO's initiative, its revenues went down because of reduced billing. Such situations typically create a conflict of interest for the BPO vendor in pursuing improvements. Mature client–BPO relationships will look at the bigger picture of reducing overall cost and resource requirement so that more processes can be outsourced. In this case, IBPO has been able to win other process outsourcing contracts from Beta based on the benefits delivered through process excellence.

### *4.3 Business Process Outsourcing Relationship 3: Stabilizing for Predictability*

A global bank, Gamma, with employees across different geographies outsourced its HR support processes to IBPO. The outsourced process here is to provide first and second level support for all HR process areas in the bank, and covers the following areas: HR Helpdesk, Payroll second level support, people and positions related. The HR Helpdesk provides voice / e-mail support to employees on all HR-related matters with average calls per month handled in the range of 10,000 whereas the e-mails responded to are in the range of 4,000 per month. The Payroll support covers running defined payroll-related reports and correcting errors. The SLA for this process is completion of the daily defined tasks (certain set of reports each day of the month) by 6 pm, with an accuracy of 100%. Pay roll run is done at 6 pm on Friday on a fortnightly basis.

The people and positions support pertains to the areas of organization structure, new code creation, letter of offers, etc.

### 4.3.1 Process Details

IBPO executes this process from a single location. The calls are routed to IBPO through an IVR through which the IBPO employee responds to Gamma's employee queries and requests. The e-mail support is handled by responding to the e-mails on Gamma's mail system. IBPO employs 27 people to handle the HR helpdesk. The payroll processing is done on Gamma's SAP system, which is accessed remotely by IBPO.

### 4.3.2 Challenges/Interesting Aspects

Gamma was new to process outsourcing and was not able to appreciate the need for a proper "discovery" phase before the process was transferred, owing to which this phase was shortened significantly. While Gamma did not invest enough resources into transitioning the process, IBPO on the other hand underestimated the complexity and variability in understanding the HR processes and policies. Further, the staffing of the IBPO Discovery and Transitioning team also was not of the right skillets. As a consequence, IBPO's understanding of the HR Helpdesk process was not complete and this increased the time taken to transition and stabilize the voice support process. These issues were subsequently addressed through proper training involving both Gamma and IBPO.

As most of the processes can be executed only on Gamma's systems, the task allocation, tracking, and reporting happens in a disjointed manner on IBPO's application. The process flow and the project management processes are currently not executed in an integrated manner.

### 4.3.3 Process Requirements

Knowledge management and training were identified as a critical aspect of this process as the process tasks were complex and knowledge-intensive. The payroll processing support, which has an accuracy requirement of 100% with a 6-pm deadline everyday, has stringent audit requirements. In view of the stringent quality requirements, a comprehensive auditing plan was introduced. The auditor is either drawn from the peer group or the team leader; this group is supplemented by auditors from the Quality Group. The audits are carried out based on sample transactions chosen. The e-mail support for the HR Helpdesk before outsourcing operated from 8 am to 5 pm. After the process was transitioned to IBPO, they suggested to the client on having three shifts in India to ensure more complete coverage and also to complete the daily work backlog. This has helped improve performance as well as customer satisfaction.

### 4.3.4 Technology Usage

In the initial stages for this client, IBPO used an excel-based tracking mechanism which was supplemented by an MS-Access tool for tracking SLAs and productivity. Subsequently, the Ops and the TSG groups partnered to build a new tool, the Operations Excellence Management system (OEMS) to facilitate the SLA and operations data reporting and tracking. IBPO has recommended a set of enhancements to Gamma's SAP system to help in improving the process. These recommendations are currently being taken up for implementation.

### 4.3.5 Process Improvement

The splitting of the HR Helpdesk workforce from one shift (as planned initially) to three shifts helped improve the process performance significantly. The HR Helpdesk is intended to address six streams of HR areas as per Gamma's requirement. To ensure better resource utilization, IBPO initially organized the helpdesk as a single resource pool, which was expected to be well-versed with the processes and policies of all the six HR streams. This was difficult to manage both from training and work allocation perspective. Subsequently, IBPO found it better to split the helpdesk such that each HR stream is supported by two dedicated groups who received specific training. This helped in better performance because of the specialization of the workforce along different tracks.

A Wiki has been planned to capture the knowledge of the IBPO team as it learns the process.

### 4.3.6 Critical Success Factors

This relationship is fairly new and as such the emphasis has been more on stabilizing the processes transitioned. IBPO and Gamma faced some initial challenges as they did not focus on certain critical factors such as client involvement, goal alignment, and process knowledge. These were later addressed through focused analysis of the process and appropriate training to suit the client's specific contexts. BPM technology implementation to integrate the process workflow with the program management processes is another factor which could not be leveraged here as the clients systems are not yet integrated with the IBPO systems.

### 4.3.7 Impact of the Business Process Management Initiative

This relationship took some time to stabilize because of the factors mentioned above. Today, the client appreciates the process improvements made by IBPO as the turnaround time and the quality of the HR Helpdesk improved considerably from the pre-outsourcing levels. IBPO has the challenge and the opportunity now to deepen this relationship by bringing in more aspects of BPM for example, a BPM-based workflow to integrate IBPO tracking systems with the client's systems.

## *4.4 Case Study Analysis*

The three outsourcing relationships described in the previous section exhibit different levels of BPM adoption and BPO relationship maturity. We analyze the BPM applicability in the three cases by exploring the usage of various BPM principles and lifecycle activities using BizPAD.

### 4.4.1 Strategic Objectives

IBPO's strategic objective is about reducing the resource cost per transaction in addition to increasing customer satisfaction and revenue growth. Most of the process improvements across all the cases studied detail IBPO's efforts toward meeting these objectives. The IBPO's client objectives are also met as the SLA and commitments on improvement defined at the beginning of the transition are driven by the clients. Alpha's objective was to improve the quality of financial analysis and estimates and the process design, which focused on reduction of error in data consolidation, was geared to achieve this. Beta's objective of reducing cycle time for processing the applications was achieved by reducing the exceptions and the need to go back to the applicant for more details. Goal alignment, which is one of the critical success factors of a BPO relationship, is about ensuring that both the BPO vendor and the client are able to decide on mutually agreeable targets in line with the organizational needs of each party. The BPO should be able to balance the SLA's set by the client and its own business objectives.

### 4.4.2 Business Process Management Lifecycle

The BPM lifecycle covers all process and technology activities starting from process identification to analysis of the results.

Create (Identify, Define and Improve Processes)

The process selection in an outsourcing relationship is usually done by the client organization with defined process performance measures in the form of SLAs, with the BPO being involved in some of these cases. The process outsourced is usually a segment of the end-to-end business process of the client, but could also be the entire process. The outsourced processes execution involves the task of execution, quality check, escalation, consolidation, and communication. The process re-engineering capability of the BPO along with technology exploitation and integration is a critical requirement for the success of the outsourced process execution.

The BPO organization does its own assessment of the SLAs and process scope during the discovery and transition phase, and this helps to identify the exact start and end points of the process along with the process details and the commitments that can be made to the client. It is also critical for setting up the delivery architecture and technology infrastructure. As in the case of Alpha and Beta, the process starts at the point at which the files had to be accessed from the client location, which required access to client servers and infrastructure for secure transfer. The Ops group in IBPO also looks at process optimization before transitioning the work; this could involve redesign of the process as in the case of Beta where the batches were restructured before processing. The TSG group looks at process optimization using technology which involves using BPM platforms, automation, and usage of specific technology capabilities such as OCR, etc. The Ops and TSG need to work together along with the client to ensure an optimized process. The shortened process discovery phase which did not allow for proper understanding of the process by IBPO in the Gamma case hindered the efficient transition of the process to IBPO. The BPO organization needs to superimpose the project management activities like case creation, task allocation, shift handling, and quality checks on the outsourced process flow. A typical BPO process to handle an outsourced process is given is Fig. 4. All these activities are supported by a workflow or BPM engine.

IBPO accepted the targets imposed by the client on resource utilization, turnaround times and throughput based on the experience of the people involved in transition. IBPO could have contested the very stringent TATs Alpha expected right at the beginning by using simulation. Similarly, the reallocation of the European

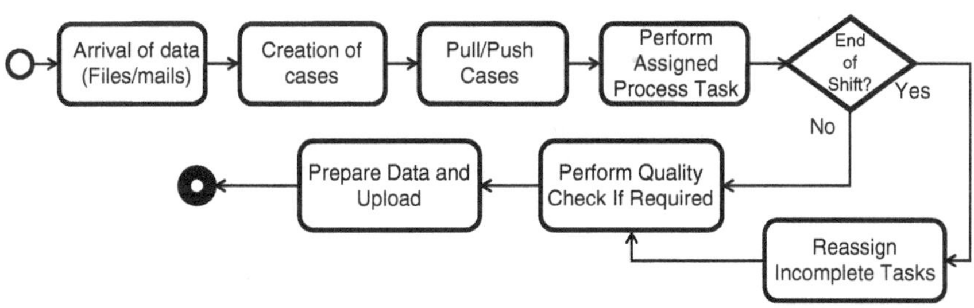


**Fig. 4** A typical BPO process

language work to China and improving resource utilization could have been verified for performance requirements using process simulation. In the case of Gamma, the resource allocation for the voice-based helpdesk and the splitting of work into six streams could also have been verified using this approach. While most of the BPO processes are human centric, the sequencing of tasks, usage of technology, scheduling, and allocation of resources can be simulated to verify the outcomes before making any commitments. BPOs can use process simulation and what–if analysis for identifying process bottlenecks, deciding on capacity planning and process redesign decisions, which will help in negotiating the SLAs in the initial stages of the outsourcing relationship.

While IBPO uses Six Sigma principles, we find that other process improvement and optimization methods like lean principles (Womack and Jones 2003), application of process patterns (Reijers and Mansar 2005) are also visible in the three case studies. We have tried to identify some of the important process improvement patterns that are visible in the case studies. The KM solution implemented in Alpha and Gamma cases reducing the need to contact the customers is a case of "*contact reduction*" pattern. In the Beta relationship, getting the data from the postal system address database for validating the address fields is a typical example of *"trusted party"* pattern. The *"Integral Business Process Technology,"* *"Flexible allocation,"* and *"task automation"* are patterns which are used in all the three cases. In Gamma the *Specialization–Generalization* pattern is visible where IBPO initially tried generalization to improve the HR Helpdesk utilization. On realizing that the effort required to sustain quality with generalized resources was extremely high, they switched back to regular ways, still managing some generalization by training candidates in at least two streams. In the Beta relationship, data validations were introduced at the time of data entry into the field, unlike most web-based forms where validation happens at the time of submitting the form. This is an example of the usage of the Lean principle wherein checks should be as near as possible to the occurrence of error, in space and time. Bringing address validation from the Manage Exceptions stage to the keying-in stage is another example of the usage of Lean Principles. Eliminating the switching between windows, thus reducing some motion, which was used in Alpha and Beta, is another example of Jidoka, one of the Lean principles.

### Align (Link Processes to IT Systems)

The linkage between process and IT is very strong in BPO executions. IBPO has interfaced wherever possible with the client's IT systems and external data providers to leverage the services offered (access to Alpha's terminals to resolve escalations, data from postal systems in the case of Beta) and also integrated technology-based process improvements into its BPM platform. But a strong example of BPO technology platform using business services and functionality available on the client's systems is not showcased in the above cases. Such a possibility exists in the Gamma relationship; if IBPO can seamlessly integrate the

OEMS, their operations management system with Gamma's mail system and SAP system, this would enable IBPO to execute the entire process on the OEMS while invoking the business and technical services on Gamma's systems.

Execute (Process Operations, Monitoring and Control)

The BPM platform-based applications in Alpha and Beta ensure that process orchestration happens through the BPM engine using features such as automatic task creation and allocation, handoffs, issue escalations, etc. The measurements and monitoring of critical performance parameters such as TAT, SLAs, throughput, defects, cycle time, etc., are handled by the same applications. The dashboards being built by TSG provides real-time visibility even to the clients on various process parameters. The process data captured by the BPM platforms is used by Ops to analyze the process further and identify improvement opportunities.

### 4.4.3 Business Process Management Enablers

The BPM lifecycle activities are enabled by following established standards, methodologies, and technologies within the organization. These form a part of the ecosystem that supports the BPM lifecycle.

IBPO has established the standards, methodologies, and technologies to be used for managing its outsourcing relationships. The Ops group has defined the four-stage outsourcing methodology with standards and guidelines for different activities. Six Sigma techniques are used for process improvements. Process modeling guidelines and modeling tools are decided by Ops. TSG sets the standards for the technologies and the technology architecture to be used, including the security requirements. For example, the BPM platform along with most of the other applications within IBPO are .net based and hence technical resource availability will not be an issue.

### 4.4.4 Business Process Management Governance, People, and Infrastructure

Another critical part of the BPM lifecycle support ecosystem is the BPM governance covering roadmap, governance structure, ownership, and implementation.[2]

[2]For a general introduction into BPM governance, refer Markus and Jacobson (2010), Spanyi (2010) and Rosemann (2010).

### Business Process Management Roadmap and Strategy

IBPO has a roadmap and strategy for technology deployment for each BPO relationship as can be seen from the Alpha relationship. While there has been some evidence seen, there is an opportunity for a deeper, joint partnering between IBPO and the client (including business and IT groups) to create a long-term BPM strategy spanning the relationship and not just a single process. This would call for long-term commitments from the client organizations with incentives to IBPO to offset the reduced billing due to the improvements.

### Business Process Management Ownership

Most of the outsourcing relationships are led by the business in the client organizations. The involvement of the IT group in the transition phase is critical for defining the SLAs and improvement objectives of the business process (Tornbohm and Kyte 2008). As can be seen in all the three cases, IBPO requires the data and interface to the client's IT systems to bring in the efficiencies and innovation required in the processes. Hence, the client's business and IT group need to be involved in the governance of the relationship. The process ownership was clearly distributed between Ops and TSG in IBPO and both groups worked on ensuring success of the relationship by focusing on their core competencies. Each relationship has a defined team structure with team leads, process executors, auditors, and managers which ensures the implementation of the defined processes and standards. The client commitment and involvement was also clearly visible in the cases of Alpha and Beta.

### People Aspects

The transition and parallel-run stages of the outsourcing methodology provides for handling the training and change management aspects for the IBPO employees in the outsourcing relationship. Many of the process improvements by IBPO resulted in reducing/removing the mechanical tasks of the employees and improving the job content, thus improving motivation. This contributes to reducing attrition which is a challenge for most BPOs.

### Process and Technology Infrastructure

The technology and process infrastructure forms the backbone of the entire BPO relationship and needs special focus. The TSG and Ops group work with other departments within the BPO to provide and enable this infrastructure.

The critical success factors of a BPO relationship are addressed through the various elements under BPM. Table 1 provides a summary of the critical success

**Table 1** Comparison of the critical success factors across the cases

| BPO relationship critical success factors | Covered under the BizPAD framework element | Alpha | Beta | Gamma |
|---|---|---|---|---|
| Process re-engineering | Create | Strong | Strong | Good |
| Technology exploitation/IT integration | Align | Good | Good | Weak |
| Project/Program management | Implementation and governance management/change management | Strong | Strong | Good |
| Client involvement and commitment | BPM ownership | Strong | Strong | Weak |
| Goal alignment | Strategic objectives/BPM strategy and roadmap | Weak (initially) Good (later) | Weak (initially) Good (later) | Not visible |
| Governance | Defining standards/ governance management | Not analyzed | Not analyzed | Not analyzed |
| Organization structure | BPM ownership | Strong | Strong | Good |
| Cultural integration | People elements | Not analyzed | Not analyzed | Not analyzed |

factors of a BPO relationship, the BPM framework element that covers them and a comparison[3] of the three IBPO cases.

Another dimension of analysis of the three relationships can be from the maturity of the BPO relationship. Carnegie Mellon University has developed eSCM-SP, a best practices model for service providers in IT-enabled sourcing and eSCM-CL, for client organizations seeking to improve their sourcing capabilities and relationships (CMU 2006). While the eSCM can be used to assess the maturity of BPO vendors on their IT-based process services capabilities, it is not suited for assessing the maturity of the BPO relationship. From the three cases, we find that the relationships are at differing levels of BPO relationship maturity based on the value proposition of the relationship to the client. While the value proposition may also depend on the type of outsourcing relationship (single process, multiple process or multiple functions and domains), the BPO vendor capabilities and BPO success factors play an important role in the BPO relationship maturity. A BPO relationship maturity model can be developed based on the value proposition of the relationship and the type of outsourcing relationship. We propose a BPO relationship maturity model in Fig. 5 based on our experience and analysis of the

[3]For rating the relationships we use the following scale: Strong, Good, Fair, Weak, Absent/Not Visible/Not Analyzed.

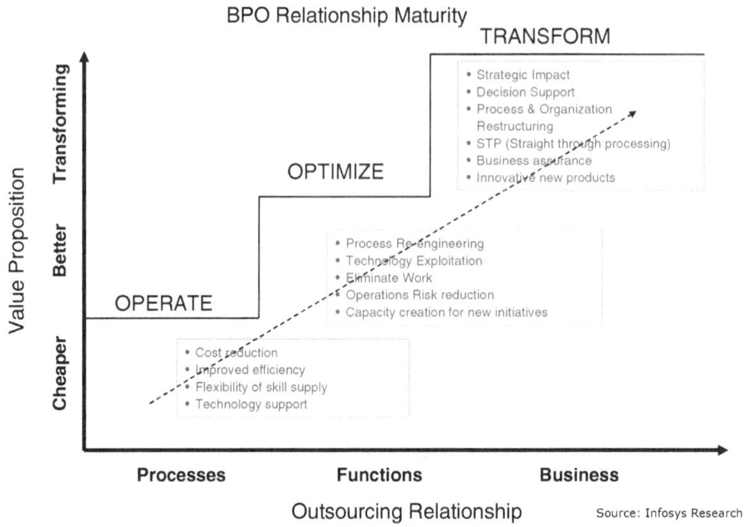


**Fig. 5** Proposed BPO relationship maturity model

BPO relationships we studied. The critical success factors discussed above, along with the BPO vendor capabilities and the client's commitment to the outsourcing relationship, determine the maturity of the BPO relationship. These parameters can be mapped to the maturity levels to create a detailed maturity model. BPM maturity models would also serve as a good input to create such a model as BPO relationships' critical success factors can be mapped on to a BPM Framework.

The Alpha relationship began at the "Operate" level and has subsequently matured into a substantially higher level in the "Optimize" space and currently provides newer capabilities to the client. Similarly, Beta relationship started at Operate level and has matured into a level comparable to Alpha. The Gamma relationship is fairly new and, after initial hiccups, is stabilizing at the Operate level.

We have analyzed BPO relationships from the different requirements of BPM covering the BPM lifecycle activities and elements of governance. We find that adoption of the different BPM elements will help BPO vendors and clients mature their BPO relationship to provide higher value proposition.

## 5 Conclusions

BPO providers can take their relationships with clients to a higher level of maturity, improve their value proposition and enable further growth by adopting BPM principles. BPOs apply process improvements and technology solutions based on an individual's experience and expertise and achieve reasonable benefits, but a structured approach using BPM will provide for transformational benefits and impact. The process modeling, optimization, and simulation methods of BPM act as enablers for BPO. The critical needs of BPO are related to agility and flexibility, process routing, multi-site execution, human centric workflows, process visibility, etc. which have a good fit with the promise of BPM technology. While BPOs enable the process execution through BPM technologies, the full benefit is not realized until the BPM platform is completely integrated into the client's systems. A seamless integration would provide client managers with higher visibility into the details of the process execution and alerts and escalation on noncompliance to policies and performance requirements. The governance structure and ownership with involvement from all stakeholders is critical for the success of the BPO relationship. We found that the BPO relationship's critical success factors can be mapped on to the various BPM requirements. While we analyzed BPOs from a BPM point of view, further research and analysis needs to be done on the specific needs of BPO providers from BPM methodologies and frameworks. Our research indicates that the BPO can uncover significant insights for improving the way it approaches its relationships. We encountered a relative vacuum in terms of academic literature in the BPO space from the viewpoint of the service provider. Specifically, we see considerable value in further research on how the BPM Framework can be leveraged to take the BPO relationship to higher levels of maturity. We also propose a BPO relationship maturity model that can be developed with inputs from existing BPM maturity models.

**Acknowledgments** We would like to thank Satish Nair, Bipin Nambiar, Alex Joseph, Sudhir Chandran and Yogesh Jagga of Infosys BPO for providing the required information and data on the different case studies. We also thank Shivi Mithal from the BPM Research Group at Infosys for his inputs and comments.

## References

Bhat JM, Fernandez J (2008) A holistic adoption framework for long term success of BPM. In: Fisher L (ed) BPM and workflow handbook digital edition v2, http://store.futstrat.com/servlet/Detail?no=42

Click RL, Duening TN (2004) Business process outsourcing: the competitive advantage. Wiley, New York, pp 154–171

CMU (2006) eSourcing capability model for service providers v2, http://itsqc.cmu.edu/

de Bruin T, Doebeli G (2010) An organizational approach to BPM: the experience of an Australian transport provider. In: vom Brocke J, Rosemann M (eds) Handbook on business process management, vol 2. Springer, Heidelberg

Feeny D, Lacity M, Willcocks LP (2005) Taking the measure of outsourcing partners. MIT Sloan Manage Rev 46(3):41–48

Halvey JK, Melby BM (2000) Business process outsourcing: process, strategies and contracts. John Wiley, New York

Hammer M (2007) The process audit. Harv Bus Rev (April):111–123

Kaka NF, Kekre SS, Sarangan S (2006) Benchmarking India's business process outsourcers. The McKinsey Quarterly, July 2006

Markus ML, Jacobson DD (2010) Business process goverance. In: vom Brocke J, Rosemann M (eds) Handbook on business process management, vol 2. Springer, Heidelberg

Martin SF, Beimborn D, Parikh MA, Weitzel T (2008) Organizational readiness for business process outsourcing: a model of determinants and impact on outsourcing success. In: Proceedings of the 41st Hawaii international conference on system sciences, 7–10 January 2008; doi: 10.1109/HICSS.2008.340
Mattig A (2008) Modes of governance in business process outsourcing: executive versus market's perspective. In: Proceedings of the 41st Hawaii international conference on system sciences – 2008, 7–10 January 2008; doi: 10.1109/HICSS.2008.321
Mehta A, Armenakis A, Mehta N, Irani F (2006) Challenges and opportunities in business process outsourcing in India. J Labor Res, 27(3), 323–338
Melenovsky MJ, Sinur J (2006) BPM maturity model identifies six phases for successful BPM adoption. Gartner Research. http://www.gartner.com/DisplayDocument?id=497289. Accessed 15 Dec 2008
Namasivayam S (2004) Profiting from business process outsourcing, IT Pro. http://doi.ieeecomputersociety.org/10.1109/MITP.2004.1265537
NelsonHall (2008) Global BPO market forecast: 2008 – 2012, market assessment, June 2008. http://www.nelson-hall.com/service-line-programs/bpo-market-development/?avpage-views=article&id=62422&fv=1
OMG (2008) Business Process Maturity Model (BPMM) version 1.0, OMG. http://www.omg.org/spec/BPMM/1.0/PDF. Accessed 15 Dec 2008
Reijers HA, Mansar SL (2005) Best practices in business process redesign: an overview and qualitative evaluation of successful redesign heuristics, Omega, 33(4), 283–306.
Rosemann M (2010) The service portfolio of a BPM center of excellence. In: vom Brocke J, Rosemann M (eds) Handbook on business process management, vol 2. Springer, Heidelberg
Rosemann M, vom Brocke J (2010) The six core elements of business process management. In: vom Brocke J, Rosemann M (eds) Handbook on business process management, vol 1. Springer, Heidelberg
Rosemann M, de Bruin T, Hueffner T (2004) A model for business process management maturity. In: ACIS 2004 Proceedings
Rouse AC, Corbitt BJ (2006) Business process outsourcing: the hysterisis effect and other lessons. In: Hirschheim RA, Heinzl A, Dibbern J (eds) Information systems outsourcing, 2nd edn. Springer, Berlin, Heidelberg
Scholl RS (2003) BPO validated: verticalization and aggregation accelerate, Gartner Dataquest Report. ID Number: ITOU-WW-MT-0107
Sen F, Shiel M (2006), From business process outsourcing (BPO) to knowledge process outsourcing (KPO): some issues. Hum Syst Manage 25:145–155; IOS Press
Spanyi A (2010) Business process management governance. In: vom Brocke J, Rosemann M (eds) Handbook on business process management, vol 2. Springer, Heidelberg
Tornbohm C, Kyte A (2008) Ten critical IT steps CIOs must take to ensure success in BPO endeavors. Gartner ID Number: G00161194, www.gartner.com. Accessed on 15 Dec 2008
Womack JP, Jones DT (2003) Lean thinking: banish waste and create wealth in your corporation. Simon & Schuster, New York
zur Mühlen M (2004) Workflow-based process controlling: foundation, design and application of workflow-driven process information systems. Logos, Berlin

# Toward a Global Process Management System: The ThyssenKrupp Presta Case

**Stefan Novotny and Nicholas Rohmann**

**Abstract** This case provides experiences from ThyssenKrupp Presta, an automotive supplier company that provides steering systems for carmakers worldwide. Process orientation has been a focus for years and has had influence on the organizational structure already about 15 years ago. In 2005, the formation of a BPM organization was targeted to realize process harmonization in post-merger projects, canalize the application of IT systems for process automation and take process orientation to a higher grade of maturity using state-of-the art process modeling systems. This chapter presents a summary of experiences out of the work of this BPM organization, which leads process harmonization and process improvement projects worldwide within Presta. Our experiences show that process management needs a good organizational, structural and technical (BPM-tool) foundation, and also relies on the involvement of the affected people and a process organization that consists of the key players in the operation devices of the company. At Presta, a sustainable process definition, process implementation, and continuous improvement had to be supported and governed by the corporate BPM organization. Presta considers the most important role to be the process owner who – across all locations – releases a process and decides on the necessity and size of changes and improvements.

## 1 Introduction

Automotive supplier companies today are faced with intensive external pressure of providing new, energy-saving technologies and at the same time outdoing their competitors pricewise in new projects as well as providing annual rationales for their customers on running products. In recent years, the focus in ThyssenKrupp Presta – as in many others of the branch – often lay on the optimization of processes

S. Novotny (✉)
Divison Manager Quality and Processes, ThyssenKrupp Presta AG, Eschen, Liechtenstein
e-mail: Stefan.novotny@thyssenkrupp.com

J. vom Brocke and M. Rosemann (eds.), *Handbook on Business Process Management 2*, International Handbooks on Information Systems,
DOI 10.1007/978-3-642-01982-1_17, 

in production and close to production to bring down the costs and master these market challenges. In the meanwhile, production processes are very near to maximized optimization while there are still high potentials to be realized in the business processes of development and other indirect business areas.

## 2 The Case Organization ThyssenKrupp Presta

The authors have gained experiences in global BPM projects at ThyssenKrupp Presta, an automotive supplier company that provides steering systems for carmakers worldwide. With over 4,000 employees in 16 locations worldwide, Presta produces steering shafts, steering columns as well as hydraulically or electrically power-assisted steering gears generating a turnover of close to 1,000 Mio €. Customers are many of the big passenger car OEMs, including the Volkswagen Group, Ford Group and others. Presta has their own strong technology and R&D departments providing the latest steering technology to OEMs worldwide. Product development is done in customer-driven projects often including complete platforms. While most part of the development work is done in the headquarters in Eschen, Principality of Liechtenstein, there are development sites in Germany, Hungary, USA and China, creating the need for international collaboration in R&D projects. Business processes have to provide continuous and flawless collaboration and information flow through these development sites as well as to and from the production sites.

In 2005, a global initiative was started, founded on a team of 5–10 people, involving 11 of the 16 locations worldwide in the first step (making for approximately 70% of the more than 4,000 employees) and targeting on, including all locations, toward 2015. The key objectives for the involved projects were

- Post-merger integration of an acquired OEM division
- Clarification and optimization of interfaces across divisions and locations
- Reduction of involved IT systems and establishment of common databases
- Setup of a global process landscape and management system

In the following, lessons learnt from these projects are reported. While the source of knowledge mainly stems from internal experiences complemented by talks to experts from both academia and business, the authors are convinced that these findings may well be transferable to other settings.

## 3 Strategic Alignment of the Business-Driven Approach

The main objective of the automotive supplier company ThyssenKrupp Presta is to focus on their business excellence in the indirect processes to strengthen its success factors (Fig. 1) identified as synergy, transparency, quality, speed and sustainability.

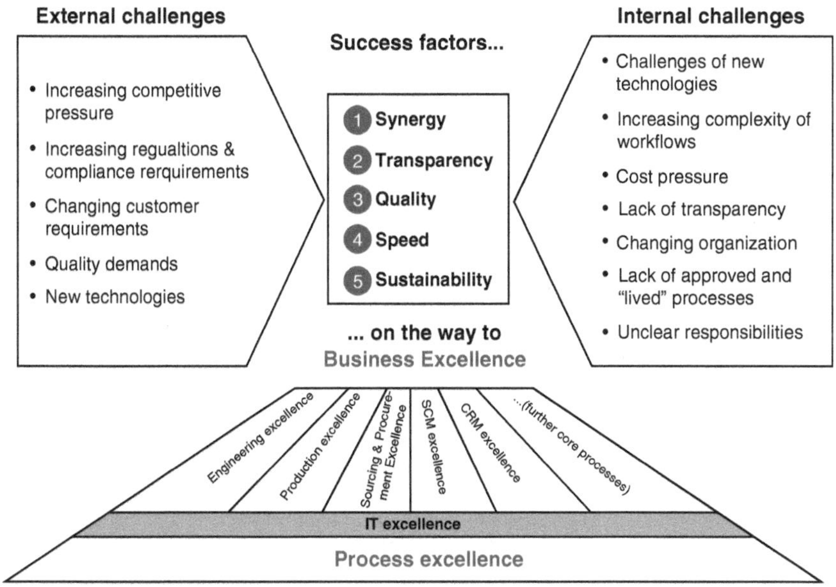


**Fig. 1** Internal and external challenges require worldwide acting companies to have a strong process orientation and a continuous corporate management system

Other challenges are

- Still rising levels of quality are required from the start of production on
- Rising demands for compliance to international standards (ISO 16949, etc.) vda qmc (2002)
- Rising governmental and customer restrictions to be considered in new projects
- More complex products due to higher functionality in modules and systems and due to more electronics and software in products

For the Presta, this means to concentrate on the effectiveness and efficiency of indirectly productive processes – the ones that "are manufacturing information" instead of touchable products. To improve these processes and their performance is the motivation and objective of our corporate process management system (PMS).

Derived from the company vision, the vision of process management in the considered company was to bring the whole organization to a higher level of maturity by driving

- Process definition and standardization
- Process documentation (sustainable knowledge management)
- Process (and sometimes IT system) governance
- Process culture and sustainable implementation of a process improvement organization within the operation divisions (Fig. 2)

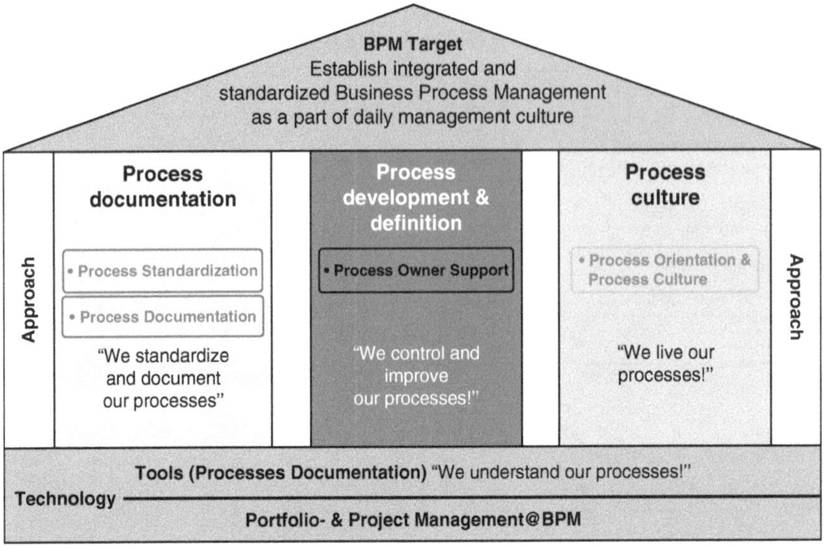


**Fig. 2** The vision of Business Process Management means development, definition and implementation of processes and the respective culture

To initiate and drive such a vision, a Business Process Management (BPM) has been established in Presta. This BPM organization was successfully targeted on a vision explicitly broader than mere fulfillment of compliances such as ISO 9001 or ISO 15504. In the author's view, these standards are good references for process management basics; however, there is a high risk of artificially copying them into the company instead of using the processes grown on the company's strengths and step by step altering their maturity.

Depending on the maturity level of the organization, the authors consider the responsibilities of the BPM organization as

- Implementation of the process documentation system including the respective system governance. Presta decided to use a combination of the document management system "Xeri" by Plato and the graphic process modeling tool "Income" by Synlogic
- Building up a process culture
- Building up a process organization
- Supporting the process definition in the line organizations
- Describe requirements for the IT system that shall be used for the process
- Drive process improvement in the line organizations
- Provide services like process modeling or template layout

Even though the BPM organization at Presta has proven to be needed for initiation and strategic process management (see Fig. 3), it was the strategic goal to implement process management roles in the operating divisions of the company as soon as possible (Figs. 3 and 4). As the term "process management" already

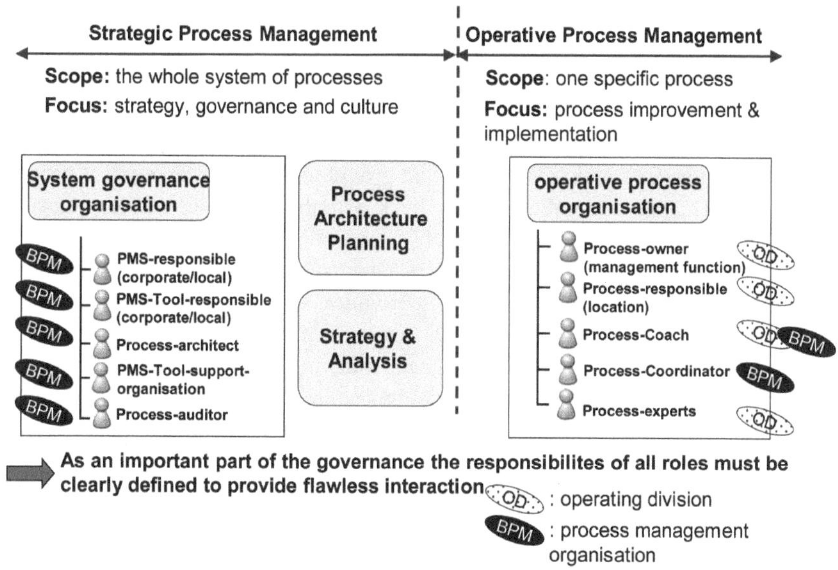


**Fig. 3** Process organization comprises roles with strategic responsibility for the whole system as well as roles for operative process improvement, located in both the BPM organization and the operating divisions (OD)

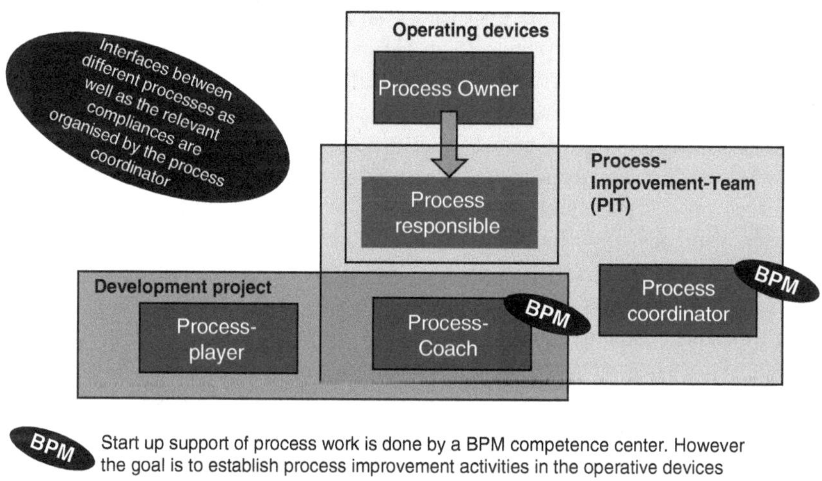


**Fig. 4** Different roles are defined for process work and cooperate in the functionally oriented process organization. It has proven to be good to have only few of them located in the central BPM organization

suggests, design, implementation and improvement must be one of the most important responsibilities of each person in a management function.

For better understanding of the different responsibilities and activities, roles in strategic and operative process management were defined. According to Presta's definition, strategic process management is needed to implement and run the PMS corporate-wide as well as locally in each plant/location of a worldwide distributed group. This means to control and structure the contents of the management system (done by the PMS-responsible) but also provide the infrastructure of the PMS-tool. A process architect was needed to define the rules of process structuring, especially in the chosen graphic modeling system that provide language-independent process information. The process auditor has to check both the adherence of the respective devices to the defined processes as well as the compliance of the implemented processes to the applicable standards, laws and other requirements. With these roles, the strategic process management provides a well-defined framework for the process culture and sustainably drives process improvement by setting targets for the process owners, and measuring and tracking the implementation status, maturity and improvement potentials of all processes. The roles of strategic process management have been successfully implemented in the central BPM division at Presta.

While strategic process management focuses on governance of the whole system of processes, the operative process management comprises the actions and responsibilities targeting at one specific process or process group. At ThyssenKrupp Presta, it has been proven to be efficient for good process implementation to take the roles of the operative process management organization as much as possible by operative business (operative devices). By this, process definition was no longer considered the responsibility of the BPM organization but the duty of operative business and especially the process owners. At Presta, the process owner's responsibility for a process is corporate-wide. He has to make sure that the process is defined, released and published, implemented, measured and controlled. In the Presta Group, this role is taken by 40–50 people, mostly from upper management functions. These process owners typically delegate most of the operative work involved to the process team (process responsibles, experts, coaches) but keep to themselves the management part of setting the goals, controlling the business relevance of process descriptions, and releasing the process and driving its implementation. To complement the global role of the process owner, the process responsible is installed to manage the process locally or in a branch of the company. Taken from daily local experience the process responsible suggests improvements and localisations of the process to the owner. Process coaches are needed especially when major changes to a process are done or several new processes have to be implemented e.g. due to major technology changes. They may be from the process improvement team or may as well come from operative business and help the "process players" to live the defined process by face-to-face training. Having coaching functions means additional resource effort, but considerably shortens the time for the change of the organization from old to new processes. In Presta, it was possible to jump up one "SPICE-Level" (according to ISO 15504) (Hörmann et al. 2006) in process maturity in just one year by installing coaches for the concerned processes. Process coaches may first be installed in the BPM organization but soon should move to operative business. The authors are of the opinion that the right place or time for the organizational switch depends on the process culture of the company, e.g. measured by process maturity models, e.g. (http://www.sei.cmu.edu/cmmi, http://www.omg.org/spec/BPMM/), etc.

The process coordinator in Presta functions as moderator for process improvement workshops and provides the project management for improvement projects. He has to make sure that applicable standards are available and respected for the respective process and also takes care that processes are defined lean and not too detailed. Even though this is no more than a support role, experience at Presta shows that the coordinator role is just as important as the process owner's. This role controls the effectiveness of process management by managing workshops, coaching process orientations and explaining targets and steps of process definition as well as its efficiency by keeping the focus on a beneficial level of detail in the process descriptions and on the business orientation of used process names and other terms. This role of operative process management at Presta is mostly provided by the BPM organization. Process experts are taken from the operating division to provide their expertise and experience for the to-be-defined processes.

# 4 Technical and Organizational Issues Involved in Using a Corporate Process Modeling and Documentation System

Operative optimization of single processes using the operative process management organization as described earlier at ThyssenKrupp Presta:

- Sampling the business demands arising from internal or external audits, from enhanced or new compliance requirements, from company strategy or from process player feedbacks and deriving the improvement goals (preparation phase)
- Driving the process improvement by obtaining the process owner's project order, setting up the team and timeline, inviting and moderating workshops, etc. (process improvement phase)
- Getting the process released by all relevant stakeholders, especially by the process owner and support in the implementation by piloting and rollout, enhancement of the involved IT-tools, training and coaching (rollout phase)

Taking these steps of operative process management at Presta led to better solutions for the affected processes, and thereby saved cost. Examples of projects carried out according to this scheme in the considered company are

- Process and IT-system harmonization in an acquired part of the company (four additional locations with approximately 2,000 employees). Using a budget of more than 2 Mio € within 15 months, this harmonization has reduced the IT landscape by three larger IT systems (PLM, ERP and BPM software) including several interfaces with high maintenance costs. It enabled certification at production plants, including their interfaces to the development sites as well as their inclusion in the group-wide management reporting. The savings in personnel costs by reducing process interfaces, enabling reuse of articles and

synchronizing the product industrialization process with the rest of the company are not possible to measure (the measurement of these, often indirect, savings seems to be a general problem of company-wide process improvement). However, it can be estimated that with 500 engineering and production planning people involved, the savings are in the range of 10,000 person days per year.
- Realization of a company-wide change management process for technical changes, providing clear responsibilities and a workflow system for electronic information flow and feasibility documentation. Information quality in product version information was roughly doubled (measured by the number of products with information slacks between engineering and production). However, this project also showed that electronic workflows on the one hand make information flow and documentation easier, but on the other hand tend to reduce the direct personal contact between the affected workers in engineering, purchasing, quality, production planning, and manufacturing. These shortcomings had to be reduced by additional training and "process player" support.
- Systematization and transparency for the project lifecycle in engineering, building the backbone of most processes in an automotive supplier company that exclusively provides customer-specific high-volume products. In a 10-month activity, the definitions of project classes, project status and rough resource allocations were developed. The corresponding processes were supported by a simple database solution that now serves as the basis for reporting, detailed project planning, and budgeting as well as resource planning in manufacturing and the prototype and testing shops.
- Building up of a group-wide process modeling system enabling all locations to use the same information base for process documentation. The benefits of this still ongoing projects are the global availability of process information, providing the different retrieval paths as shown in Fig. 6. Local IT systems were replaced by one web-based tool using a company license. Compliance requirements asking for group-wide responsibility charts are possible to cover. The main benefit, however, is seen in the building of a group-wide "process corporate identity" driving a continuous process culture and providing a standardization and improvement platform. With growing process standardization as well, the respective certification audits can now be reduced, saving internal as well as external efforts.

The latter mentioned project was targeted to have all other process improvement actions embedded into a company-wide framework, thus providing sustainability and company-wide process availability and reuse. By this, the PMS (sometimes still called "quality management system") for Presta is the central tool of knowledge management. This framework as the singe "source of truth" is available in all locations of the company (Fig. 5). In Presta, as a worldwide operating automotive supplier company, the variety of locations and processes involved made this system grow very soon to a size of thousands of process artifacts (templates, guidelines, descriptions, etc.). A state-of-the-art database and model-based solution was the choice of the system since mere document-based systems tend to be hard to manage

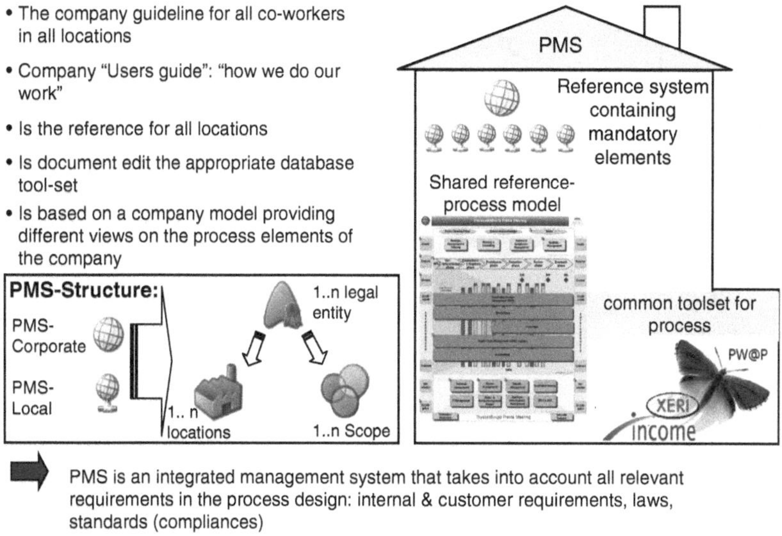


**Fig. 5** The model-based process management system (PMS) is targeted to be the process-oriented knowledge platform for all coworkers worldwide

and also bear the risk that the contained information gets inconsistent in interfaces and contains redundant information. Keyword-based search functions may be a help to find relevant information but reach their limits if the terminology is not standardized company-wide.

Strategic process management in the globally active Presta group therefore provides a manageable process information and management system PMS as a database- and web-based system and tool. Besides basic document management functions (storing, releasing, versioning, etc.), it provides the process information as structured as possible [petri net logic (Baumgarten 1996)]. In Presta, it was found that this is best supported by graphical structuring in a hierarchical process map. Consistency and nonredundancy can be provided if the system is model based. The model requires consistent interfaces between processes by using so-called "work products" that are exchanged between the processes. It also means that process information can be looked at and retrieved from different starting points, for example, the process view as well as the role-based view (see Fig. 6).

## 5 Governmental Issues of Setting the Right Structures

In Presta, the PMS had to be set up by a specialized BPM group providing the theoretical foundation and services such as tool evaluation and implementation, trainings, and role definitions. However, Presta management found it mandatory that the operative process organization be involved as much as possible in the

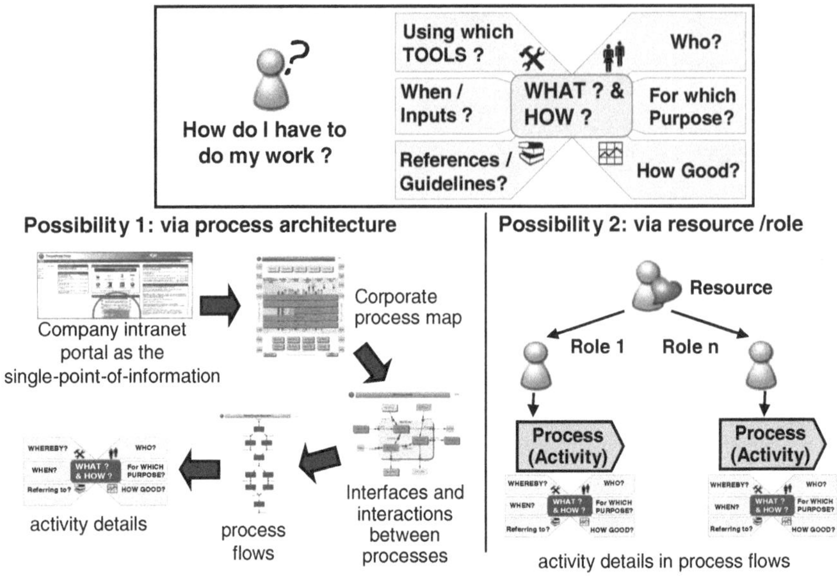


**Fig. 6** Storing process information in a database model provides the opportunity to retrieve the needed information on how to do the work on different paths

architecture definition of the process model. Therefore, most if not all members of the company's management have a role as a process owner and they must be the ones to name and define their processes from a management point of view (sometimes called "the eagle's view"). It is tempting to have this definition rather done by "process specialists" and reduce the involvement of the process owners to confirmation and release. However, this requires a high level of process maturity and a thorough understanding of the process owner's role which was not present in Presta from start. Earlier, process definition projects had their shortfalls, especially in the area of management involvement, and suffered a lack of sustainability afterward. Therefore, asking the process owners to define their processes themselves seemed the only sustainable way at Presta to define a PMS that is meant to be a real management tool after definition.

To support the structure of Presta's worldwide distributed company, it seemed helpful to define a corresponding system structure of the PMS. Therefore, process modeling at Presta first meant building up a layered structure of all company processes starting from the process map. This was started as a corporate approach but still leaves room for enhancements as locations join the process step by step. Processes defined in the corporate process map are "inherited" into the locations, especially on the upper layers of the process pyramid (Fig. 7). Locations may add processes they use to this corporate map in accordance with the (corporate) process owners. On the more detailed levels of the process structure, local enhancements or adaptations must be allowed because of local requirements for example by law or culture.

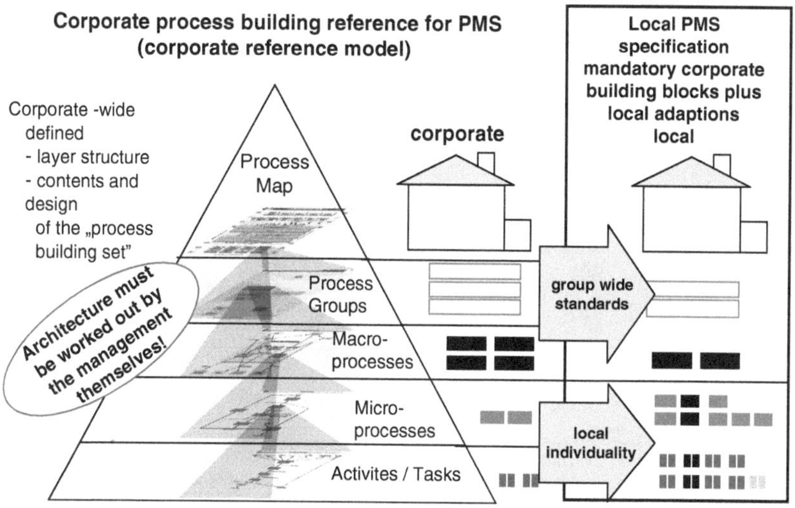


**Fig. 7** The reference process model is the corporate building set from which all local process management systems can be built up

## 6 Finding a Stepwise Approach to Process Improvement

At ThyssenKrupp Presta, it was defined that process implementation should follow a stepwise approach, mainly due to two reasons: first, the organizational level of process orientation (process culture) needed to follow the degree of process implementation. Changes in culture are time-dependent processes which suggested a step-by-step approach. Secondly, the organization was not (yet) organized according to the processes but mostly according to functions (sometimes called "silos"). Therefore, the changes in processes at a certain maturity level (step) had to be accompanied by changes in the organizational structure as well as in the culture of the company.

At Presta, the stepwise approach shown in Fig. 8 was chosen, starting from building up the BPM organization and framework. It was and still is one of the major challenges to prevent process documentation from being carried out too detailed once it gets done. Especially from the management perspective, it was helpful to focus on the process structure (process map and its layers) as well as the inputs, outputs, goals, and responsibilities of all processes. It proved to be of less importance to describe the steps of the process flow in too much detail (which we found is one of the potential pitfalls of process documentation, often leading to a high consumption of resources and hence must be avoided by the process coordinator). Process documentation, however, at Presta was the important precondition to sustainable process monitoring and it provides the required transparency on processes needed by the business.

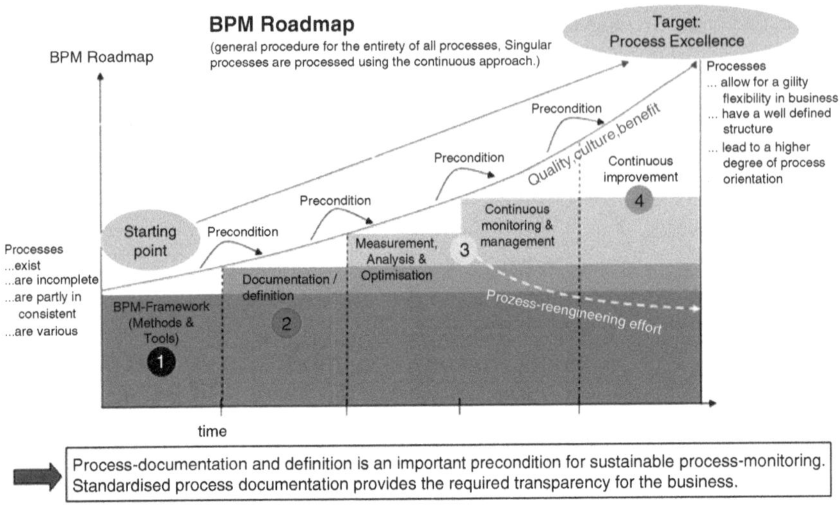


**Fig. 8** The BPM roadmap provided an idea of our stepwise approach, starting at the very base of process definition and documentation to "speak the same language"

One major prerequisite for the sustainable and successful implementation of process management in the Presta organization is the strong request by and the full support of the top management. In our case, it was helpful that at least one member of the company board had a deep understanding and a full commitment for process orientation and process management. Presta management was convinced that it is definitely not enough to do it "because others do it also." Constant attention to the process improvement program is secured by planning and achieving step-by-step benefits ("low-hanging fruits") which should be as far as possible measurable in cash-like cost improvements or higher possible turnover with the same effort. However, the measurement of the benefits of process improvement at Presta seems to be one of the major challenges in this field, since process costs are seldom measured correctly and the effects of strategic process management such as more transparency and a common understanding of processes and interfaces are basic but hard-to-measure values of a company.

At the beginning of the projects, the Presta organization tended to underestimate the effort needed to communicate the vision, objectives, and benefits of process definition, process documentation, and process management. It has proven to be beneficial that as many as possible persons in Presta should understand why all this effort is being done to gain acceptance of the reached solutions and high degree of implementation of the defined processes.

Today, Presta emphasizes that the process specialists in the organization involved in the process definition and modeling always must be aware that the main objective of the process modeling system is to provide fast, easy, and understandable information to the process "players" (the people that shall "live" the processes). Even though it should provide information on the sometimes very complex interaction of processes, the BPM tool must not be just the tool for the expert in Presta. Otherwise, the effort needed for bringing the process information into the tool, especially for the ongoing actualization, will not match the benefits for the organization. The people that know the processes and their interaction in detail will not give this information away without having a benefit for themselves and/or their coworkers.

## 7 Summary and Outlook

ThyssenKrupp Presta has experienced that a process-oriented company considerably raises its cost efficiency and especially uses the still-existing big cost-saving potentials of the business processes. This benefit relies on an appropriate process organization targeting on the strategic aspects of process improvement as well as on the operational ones. Process work at Presta must not be done for and by process specialists. It also must not focus more than absolutely necessary on "technical aspects of process management," such as process models, BPM tool features, or the "theoretically optimal process." In Presta, BPM must support the needs of all members of the company and build a common process culture by involving as many of the affected persons as possible. Especially, the members of Presta's company management have to get into the driver's seat and must not only actively define the processes but also be examples for employees as well as define process objectives for their staff (reward process improvement work and process adherence).

It was helpful to have measurable benefits alongside the company goals of defined and used processes must be identified and constantly communicated throughout the organization. At Presta, the communication effort may consume as much as 40% of a process improvement program. A stepwise process management approach that is strongly supported and exemplified by upper management for Presta was mandatory for beneficial model-based process management in the globally acting company.

## References

Baumgarten P (1996) Petri Netze. Spektrum Akademischer Verlag, Heidelberg

Hörmann K, Dittmann L, Hindel B, Müller M (2006) SPICE in der Praxis. dpunkt.verlag, Heidelberg

http://www.sei.cmu.edu/cmmi

http://www.omg.org/spec/BPMM/

vda qmc (2002) Qualitätsmanagementsysteme, Besondere Anforderungen bei Anwendung von ISO 9001:2000 für die Serien- und Ersatzteil-Produktion in der Automobilindustrie, ISO/TS 16949, Oberursel

# Business Process Maturity in Public Administrations

Jörg Zwicker, Peter Fettke, and Peter Loos

**Abstract** Business Process Management (BPM) increasingly provides an important contribution to public administration modernization. Besides providing the potentials for the improvement of efficiency and effectiveness of public administration, BPM approaches also enable the improvement of service orientation. One building block of service orientation is the response time of public authorities between the application of a public service and the provision of service result. Based on specifics of the public administration domain, in this chapter, a domain-specific BPM maturity model for the fulfillment of a 48-h-service promise is proposed. Using the maturity model, a BPM for government processes can be established realizing a response time of 48 h for public authorities. The model is based on and adapts existing BPM maturity models. The chapter outlines the features and describes the evaluation of the model.

## 1 Challenges of Public Administration Modernization

### *1.1 Problem Identification and Motivation*

In the last few years, public administration had to experience national and international transformation processes. There arose new requirements out of internal and external challenges. Increasing service orientation is one of the major aims of public administration to align government actions with the desires of the public administration customers. This shall contribute to the satisfaction of stakeholders from

J. Zwicker (✉)
German Research Center for Artificial Intelligence (DFKI), Institute for Information Systems (IWi), Saarbrücken, Germany
e-mail: joerg.zwicker@iwi.dfki.de

J. vom Brocke and M. Rosemann (eds.), *Handbook on Business Process Management 2*, International Handbooks on Information Systems,
DOI 10.1007/978-3-642-01982-1_18, 

politics, public administration, citizenship, and enterprises. For efforts such as, for example, the reduction of the response time of public authorities between the application of a public service and the provision of service results, approaches, and experiences from the private sector can be applied. However, these can only be successful within the public sector if they are adapted to the domain-specific requirements.

Several of these service improvement efforts and modernization approaches influence the organizational structure and the government process within public authorities. Assuming that successful processes will be reflected in higher public administration success, the government processes have to be improved. Moreover, for improving the service orientation in public administration through improving the processes, certain means for the management and improvement of the government processes are required. In this regard, an increasingly important contribution to public administration modernization is to be made by applying private sector BPM approaches [e.g. (Becker et al. 2007; Hunziker 1999)]. Besides the contribution to the improvement of efficiency and effectiveness of public administration, BPM approaches also enable the improvement of service orientation. However, experiences regarding BPM within the private sector have shown that a global answer concerning the process orientation of a company is not reasonable: it is rather meaningful to distinguish several maturity levels regarding process orientation. Such an approach in terms of a maturity model provides various potentials in the respective public administration (Rosemann et al. 2006):

- *Descriptive view*: It is possible to determine differentiated strengths and weaknesses of public administration regarding BPM.
- *Prescriptive view*: It is possible to provide information for improving the administration's capability to manage processes.
- *Comparative view*: It is possible to compare the capabilities of different public authorities.

Besides the general importance of BPM for the design and implementation of public administration as well as service orientation, the systematic improvement of all activities of BPM is important. Maturity models for BPM support, at the same time, the improvement of BPM. However, known maturity models do not consider the particularities of public administration. Therefore, it is necessary to design and evaluate a domain-specific maturity model before applying it in the area of public administration (OMG 2008, p. 69).

Based on the specifics of the public administration domain, in this chapter, a domain-specific BPM maturity model for the fulfillment of a 48-h-service promise in the public administration domain is proposed. Using this maturity model, a BPM for government processes can be established realizing a response time of 48 h for public authorities. By introducing this 48-h-service promise, incoming requests or applications to public authorities shall be responded within 48 h by a confirmation of receipt or an official notification, at the latest. Herewith, the customers of the respective public authorities shall be provided with reliable first information about the state of their application or request without a high expense.

In summary, the main objective of this chapter is three-folded:

1. The application of BPM maturity models for the fulfillment of a 48-h-service promise in public administrations is being motivated.
2. Based on prior maturity models, a domain-specific BPM maturity model for the fulfillment of a 48-h-service promise in public administrations is being developed.
3. Using a descriptive evaluation and a case study approach, the developed BPM maturity model is being demonstrated and validated.

## *1.2 Design Science as the Overall Approach of Research*

Our research, the design and evaluation of the maturity model, is based on a design science approach. Design science is to be seen as a complement to the behavioral science approach that dominates the field of Information Systems research. It "focuses on creating and evaluating innovative IT artifacts that enable organizations to address important information-related tasks" (Hevner et al. 2004, p. 98). The ultimate goal of this research is to design a BPM maturity model which is useful for developing and implementing BPM in public administrations.

Our understanding of design science is very broad because the design artifact proposed in this chapter is not part of a software system but of an organizational system. The developed maturity model can be seen as an organizational tool, which can be used for BPM in public administrations. In other words, our idea of design science is not only to develop software systems but also to design organizations.

Figure 1 depicts the design science research process proposed by Peffers et al. (2007) which was obeyed by our research.

Based on this methodology, this chapter unfolds as presented in Table 1. In addition, an overview of the results of the research process is already provided in the table.

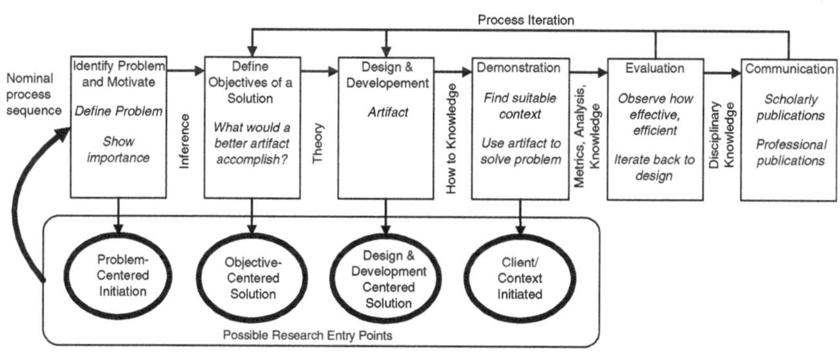


**Fig. 1** Research life-cycle; based on Peffers et al. (2007)

**Table 1** Structure of this chapter and results of the research process

| Step | Activity | Results | Section |
|---|---|---|---|
| 1 | Identify problem and motivate | - Problem description | #1 |
| 2 | Define objectives of a solution | - Description of objectives | #2 and #3 |
| 3 | Design & development | - Maturity model | #4 |
| 4 | Demonstration & evaluation | - Results obtained by descriptive evaluation<br>- Results obtained by case study | #5 |
| 5 | Communication | - This chapter | #1 to #6 |

# 2 Define Objectives of a Solution

## *2.1 Preliminary Considerations*

Improving the service orientation in public administrations can be addressed by several, different objectives and be realized by different actions. In regard to the context described in Sect. 1, the implementation of a 48-h-service promise within public authorities, actions are necessary for the following:

1. *Built-time of the 48-h-service promise*: actions for the planning, design, organization, and implementation of the 48-h-service promise within a public authority including actions for the organizational and technological implementation,
2. *Run-time of the 48-h-service promise*: actions for managing (plan, organize, monitor, and control) the 48-h-service promise as well as actions for the operational execution of the 48-h-service promise.

Considering the aforementioned actions, a comprehensive management approach is necessary which enables and implements the planning, organization, execution, monitoring, and control of the 48-h-service promise within public authorities. Further, based on the application context, the public administration domain, the management approach has to consider the following requirements:

- The approach has to be applicable for the public administration domain. That is, the approach has to consider requirements which arise from this domain.
- Because of the high amount of different public services which are provided by public administrations, the approach has to be applicable and valid for the different public services.
- The heterogeneity of the numerous internal and external stakeholders of the public administration including their different objectives in regard to the 48-h-service promise has to be considered by the approach.

Considering all the named requirements, BPM as a comprehensive management approach is proposed in the following. This is to be justified in Sect. 2.2 based on an example of producing a public service. Using the means of BPM, an appropriate solution for the implementation and realization of the 48-h-service promise can be provided.

## 2.2 BPM in the Context of the 48-h-Service Promise

Subjects of the administrative work are public services executed by public authorities. The execution in terms of the production and provision of a public service can be realized by several administrative units or positions within a public authority. Despite the shared service execution, the administrative tasks for producing and providing the service constitute one or several sequences of activities. Thus, the entirety of activities can be considered as a government process. Hence, performing a public service can be comprehended as realizing a government process. Following this thought, introduction and implementation of the 48-h-service promise through sending a confirmation of receipt or by official notification have to be realized by changing activities within the process or by changing the whole process.

In order to fulfill the 48-h-service promise respecting the 48-h-service deadline, three alternatives exist. Table 2 depicts these alternatives and their influence on the government process.

In the majority of public services and their processes, the fulfillment of the 48-h-service promise will exclusively be reached through alternative three. The reason is that the most government processes overrun 48 h, and the optimization of the processes (alternative two) achieves processing times less than 48 h in few cases only. Nevertheless, the optimization is still necessary to achieve the objectives of modernization efforts in public administrations. Moreover, also in the case of

**Table 2** Alternatives for the fulfillment of the 48-h-service promise

| # | Alternative | Application condition | Influence on the government process |
|---|---|---|---|
| 1 | No change | - If the processing time of the whole government process for the public service is already under 48 h | - No influence |
| 2 | Reduction of processing time of the government process under 48 h | - If the processing time of the whole government process for the public service overruns 48 h<br>- If the processing time of the whole process can be reduced under 48 h | - Reorganization of whole operational government process<br>- Implementation or reorganization of management processes<br>- Employees have to adapt to new processes<br>- etc. |
| 3 | Sending a confirmation of receipt within 48 h after the incoming of the application | - If the processing time of the whole government process for the public service overruns 48 h | - Extending – sometimes reorganizing – the government process with activities for creating and sending the confirmation of receipt<br>- Implementation or reorganization of corresponding management processes<br>- Employees have to adapt to new processes<br>- etc. |

alternative three, the revision of government processes is necessary which can, at the same time, be analyzed and optimized. Due to the limited amount of space in this chapter, alternative three is focused in the following, but alternative two is further on considered within the context of realizing the third alternative.

Based on a basic process management model after Rummler and Brache (Rummler and Brache 1995), according to Harmon (2004), Fig. 2 exemplarily illustrates a section of producing a public service, namely a severely handicapped pass. The production of the public service, starting from the incoming of an application until the sending of an official notification, is realized through a multitude of sequential activities confirming a government process. The incoming application for the severely handicapped pass initiates the application processing within the public authority. The process consists of several, sequential sub-processes, which are operated by different employees. The process and each of its sub-processes are managed by different process owners or process managers (i.e., by different heads of division or heads of department). The planning, organizing, implementing as well as the controlling tasks of the process owner or process manager can be divided into two classes of management processes. The persons in charge are responsible for setting plans and resources, planning the processing or activities, providing personal and technical resources, and controlling the results.

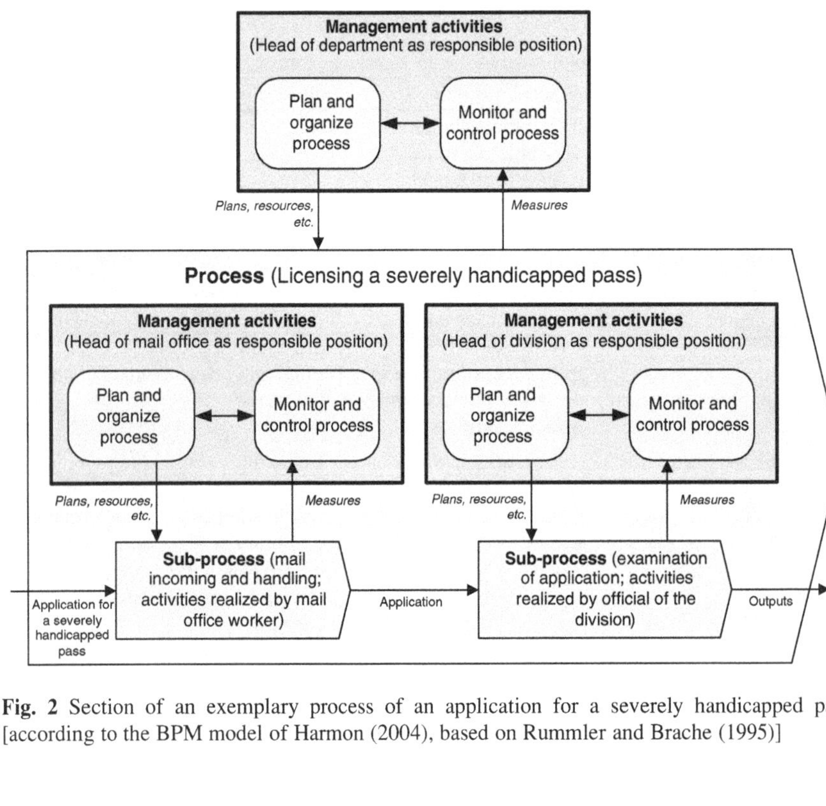


**Fig. 2** Section of an exemplary process of an application for a severely handicapped pass [according to the BPM model of Harmon (2004), based on Rummler and Brache (1995)]

In order to introduce and implement the 48-h-service promise through sending a confirmation of receipt for an application, it has to be defined during which sub-process and at which time the confirmation has to be created and sent. Moreover, the responsible persons/positions for managing the 48-h-service promise as well as the persons/positions in charge of creating and sending the confirmation have to be defined.

A simplified illustration of the process architecture of Figs. 2 and 3 shows the transmission of an application (incoming object) of a public administration customer (sender) to an organizational unit within the public authority (addressee). The sender uses a communication channel (incoming communication channel) for the transmission of the application. The incoming application initiates a process within the public authority. During the processes or at the end of one of the sub-processes, a response in terms of a confirmation of receipt (outgoing object) will be transmitted from the addressee to the sender. The addressee also uses a special communication channel (outgoing communication channel).

The introduction and the fulfillment of the 48-h-service promise depend on the elements of the depicted interaction of Fig. 3. For the 48-h-service promise, the elements can be variously configured. Based on this consideration, the following aspects have to be fulfilled for realizing the 48-h-service promise, among other things:

- Activating conditions for the release of a 48-h-service promise measurement have to be specified (form of application, kind of incoming communication channel, etc.).
- Conditions which enable a sufficient response in terms of the 48-h-service promise have to be specified (content of the response, outgoing communication channel, etc.).

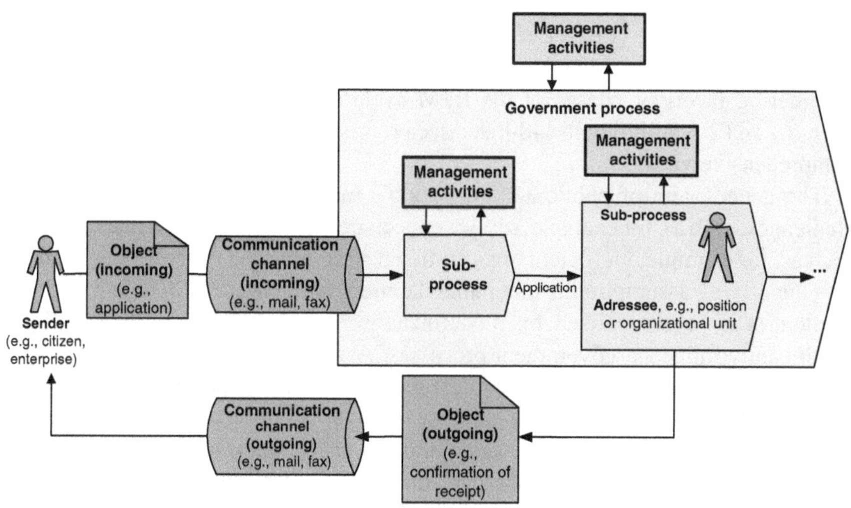


**Fig. 3** Communication scenario

- To create and transmit the notification or the confirmation of receipt, specific actions have to be defined and realized.
- The process, sub-processes, and their relationships among each other must be known and transparent.
- Processes for planning, organizing, implementing, and controlling the 48-h-service promise have to be established and the 48-h-service deadline to be determined.
- Roles and responsibilities for the management and the execution of the 48-h-service promise have to be determined.
- Process measures for examining the adherence to the 48-h-service deadline have to be defined and carried out.

In summary, the aforementioned example reveals that realizing a 48-h-service promise during the application processing within the public authority requires adequate management and implementation of the government processes as well as the 48-h-service promise. BPM, as the established and integrated approach of managing, organizing, implementing, controlling, and improving business processes, shall therefore be applied realizing the 48-h-service promise.

## 2.3 BPM Maturity for the Fulfillment of the 48-h-Service Promise

It has been broadly established that BPM comprises several activities which can exemplarily be classified into a cycle of phases: business process planning, business process design, business process implementation, and business process controlling. Numerous means, such as, for example, methods, modeling languages, or tools for implementing and supporting the several BPM activities are proposed from research and practice (Becker et al. 2003). They can be divided into two types of means: means with a comprehensive support of the whole BPM cycle and means considering facets or phases of the BPM cycle. Based on the considerations of Sect. 2.1 and 2.2, fulfilling the 48-h-service promise necessitates BPM means with a comprehensive view.

The generic aim of public administration's modernization is to meet external challenges, such as, for example, service expectations, as well as internal challenges, such as, for example, inefficient organizational structures and process organization. The underlying assumption is that public administration success in regard to these challenges is to be realized by modernization efforts. Several of those efforts significantly influence government processes. Assuming that successful processes in terms of mature processes will be reflected in higher public administration success, means for improving the maturity of government processes are necessary. Moreover, improving the service orientation in public administration through the 48-h-service promise, certain means for the fulfillment of the service promise are required. By reason that the success and maturity of processes depend on the management of these processes, a further assumption is that a higher maturity of

BPM will be reflected in higher process maturity. The BPM has simultaneously a positive impact on the fulfillment of the 48-h-service promise. Figure 4 shows the underlying assumptions regarding the dependencies between BPM maturity and public administration success. See for analogous considerations (Rosemann and de Bruin 2005; Rosemann et al. 2006; Rosemann, vom Brocke 2010).

As described in Sect. 2.1, introduction and implementation of the 48-h-service promise have to be realized by changing activities within the process or by changing the whole process. In other words, the fulfillment of the 48-h-service promise or service improvement in general can be seen as part of process maturity which is influenced by the BPM maturity. Hence, the 48-h-service promise is also impacted by process maturity and vice versa. However, they are separately depicted in Fig. 4 for a better illustration of the relationship between BPM maturity and process maturity.

Means for the assessment and improvement of BPM maturity can be subsumed under several terms, such as process-oriented quality management, Total Quality Management (TQM), process benchmarking, and process audit. A comprehensive approach which explicitly addresses the assessment and improvement of the whole BPM is proposed by BPM maturity models. A BPM maturity model describes different maturity levels for the assessment of BPM regarding the fulfillment of defined BPM requirements. Each maturity level is defined as an amount of attributes BPM has to fulfill as well as an amount of actions necessary to achieve that level. Numerous maturity models for BPM have been proposed.

Despite the multitude of means, maturity models are considered in the following as the instrument for implementing and realizing the 48-h-service promise. Considering the requirements for a 48-h-service promise solution from Sect. 2.1, the question arises whether using a generic BPM maturity model is reasonable. Most of the existing models seem to be designed for the use in private sector organizations. Therefore, the differences of BPM between public and private sector are discussed in the following section before the existing maturity models are analyzed.

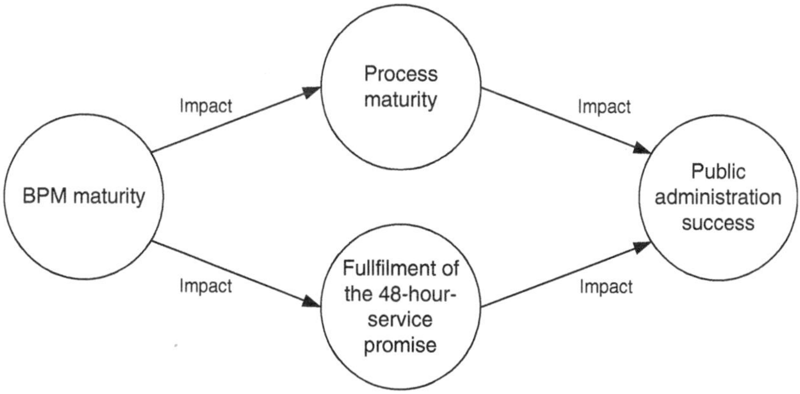


**Fig. 4** Underlying assumptions

## 2.4 Specifics of Business Process Management in Public Administration

The main difference between the public administrations and private sector are the bureaucratic principles of administrative actions (Becker et al. 2007; Güngöz 2007) which directly affect government processes. Table 3 shows a selection of those principles and several further characteristics of the public sector in comparison to the private sector.

The principles and characteristics which are valid for the public sector constitute special conditions for task fulfillment in public authorities in comparison to private sector organizations (Lenk et al. 2002). Thus, an economically inefficient action cannot be seen as a deficit of the task fulfillment or the management within the public authorities because the public services and actions are defined by binding political aims and are legally regulated. Moreover, for recommendations for the implementation or improvement of the production and provision of public services, the government processes need to consider the binding of actions to specific intents, laws, and welfare. In summary, the several specifics in public administrations (cp. Table 3) seem to influence the implementation of BPM within public authorities. Hence, these specifics are discussed in the following based on the six core elements of BPM (Rosemann and vom Brocke (2010) provide a comprehensive discussion of these elements). Figure 5 summarizes important influencing factors on the core elements of BPM. In addition, the figure depicts that other domains such as manufacturing and commerce reveal further domain-specific influencing factors on BPM.

**Table 3** Differences between organizations operating in private sector and public sector; partly based on (Becker et al. 2007; Gisler 2001)

| | Private sector | Public sector |
|---|---|---|
| Aim | Profit maximization | Public task fulfillment (binding to welfare and economic principles) |
| Lawfulness of actions | Actions are primarily unbounded but aligned to the organization's visions and objectives | Actions are primarily bound to laws and regulations (principle of lawfulness) |
| Control | Economical market organization | Political legitimization |
| Market position | Competitive environment | No competition (monopoly character) |
| Organization structure | No established structure; individual to the organization | Strict hierarchical structure possessing clear line of authority |
| Documentation requirements | No explicit documentation requirements | All decisions and occurrences have to be documented for control purposes |
| Customer segment | Mostly heterogeneous | Heterogeneous |
| Product range | Mostly heterogeneous | Heterogeneous |

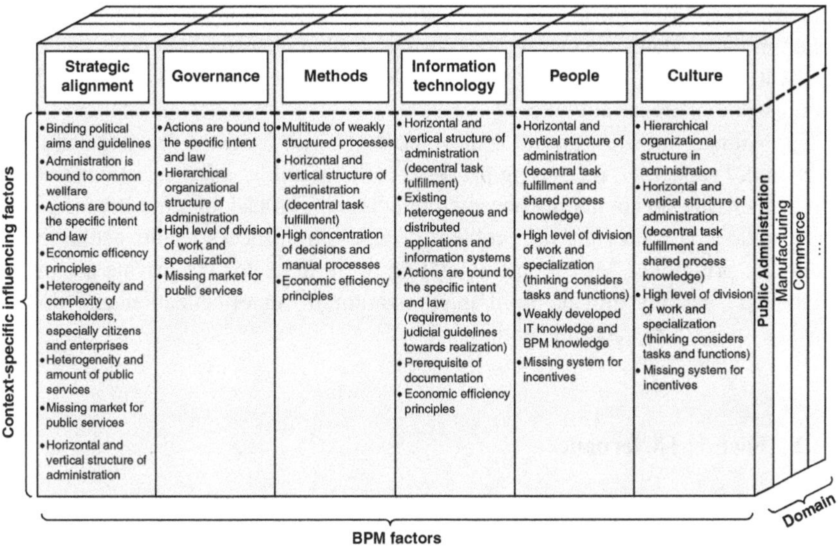


**Fig. 5** Context-specific influencing factors on BPM

The general, domain-neutral description of the six core elements in the following is based on publications of Rosemann et al. (Rosemann and de Bruin 2005; Rosemann et al. 2006; Rosemann, vom Brocke 2010).

### 2.4.1 Factor: Strategic Alignment

Strategic alignment establishes a relation between the strategy of an organization and the business processes. It supports the operative alignment of government processes toward strategic objectives of the administration. Thus, the strategic alignment is especially influenced by political aims and the binding of actions to specific intents, laws, and welfare. Strategies and objectives in public administration are deductions of political aims and, at the same time, bound to common welfare. The definition of processes needs to be in line with politically legitimated guidelines and needs to follow the laws, instructions, and regulations of the administration.

As a reason of the increasing pursuit of service orientation, legal regulations as well as the multitude and heterogeneous stakeholders of administrations, especially citizens and enterprises with their different interests, need to be considered during the process design. In addition, the heterogeneity of the service portfolio and the fact that an organization is horizontally and vertically segmented require a case-by-case alignment of the processes toward the aims, as all services and organizational units cannot be analyzed or grasped by a single general approach.

Furthermore, guidelines are occasionally provided for the design of strategies. The European Union service directive (directive 2006/123/EC) (Fontelles and

Pekkarinen 2006), for instance, defines some special requirements for the European Union member states concerning the design of administrative processes and management. But state authorities can also determine some propositions for local administrations in certain fields.

To evaluate the strategy and achievement of objectives, the results need to be measured. Frequently, measuring process results in public administrations is difficult as there are no commonly accepted indicators. The lack of a market for public services does not alleviate the problem of assessing process results according to economic principles. Measurements as they were done for the private sector are inadequate, as they aim at profit maximization of an organization and do not consider to welfare maximization.

### 2.4.2 Factor: Governance

Governance means a systematic leadership and control of BPM through established and relevant decision guidance and processes. As a result of the legal guidelines and the hierarchical structure of the public administration, this factor possesses exceptionally high requirements. Assigning roles and responsibilities often follows clear guidelines due to legal rules and suppresses a wide flexibility. For example, there are special regulations in Germany for data privacy in the social sector, which allows only responsible officials to access certain personal data. Hence, changes in the organization of the BPM are problematic.

To provide standards for the BPM, administrative rules have to be considered. The monitoring of the abidance to rules in BPM by responsible persons is a challenge. Identifying suitable metrics is often a problem. They have to ensure a measurement of BPM capability according to BPM standards, and, furthermore, they have to value the abidance to rules and further conditions.

Decisions for a systematic leadership and control of the BPM need to be bound to central roles and responsible persons in the government hierarchy. On the one hand, this is necessary because of the hierarchy, while on the other hand, there exists a decentralized organization of task fulfillment as a reason of the high level of division of work. Accordingly, super-ordinate instances for systematic leadership and control are necessary.

### 2.4.3 Factor: Methods

The literature describes a multitude of methods for realizing and supporting BPM in general. Nevertheless, several methods are especially aligned to public administration or e-Government. During the conception of a process, legal rules can easily be used to reason design decisions. Likewise, the high complexity of government processes and organizational structures in public administrations necessitates special methods and tools for modeling the processes (Palkovits and Wimmer 2003).

Methods for the transfer of process concepts to electronic implementations in the case of e-Government have to consider infrastructural conditions (cp. information technology). The high concentration of decisions in public administration requires the continuance of manual processes. An electronic implementation of the processes often has to be reduced to an electronic support of manual processes. Furthermore, the necessity of documentation of all decisions and occurrences (principle of documentation requirements) during the process implementation through corresponding techniques and systems has to be considered.

### 2.4.4 Factor: Information Technology

Information technology is necessary to realize the approaches of BPM. In the context of public administration, there result several particularities as the information technology frequently presents itself as heterogeneous and outdated. Accordingly, there result special requirements on information technologies which have a high importance concerning the maturity measurement.

Besides, particularities result from fragmented infrastructures because of the separation of administrative authorities in federal states. The current administration and the accompanying decentralized organization are not motivated by information technological causes, but solely result from the historical development. Therefore, special information technological requirements arise for the management of processes, which have to be executed across the states, administrative levels, and authorities.

Furthermore, there results a multitude of information technological requirements from political requirements or legal guidelines. This is exemplified by the German DOMEA approach (DOMEA: document management and electronical archiving in IT-supported business processes) (KBSt -Koordinierungs- und Beratungsstelle der Bundesregierung für Informationstechnik in der Bundesverwaltung 2005). This standard raises requirements for the implementation of tools and systems for BPM like, for instance, content or document management system.

### 2.4.5 Factor: People

People represent an important component when realizing an efficient BPM. In public administration, there often exists a high level of division of work and specialization, so that process knowledge is often concentrated in just a few employees. This implies the following consequences: First, approaches to survey the process knowledge require a significantly higher involvement of employees in order to determine the process steps in detail; otherwise, real "as-is" processes in administration can hardly be determined. Second, actions for reorganization are often strictly limited or require special coaching because of a lack of necessary competencies. New "to-be" processes cannot be successfully implemented. Third, it is often difficult to identify appropriate responsible persons for such processes, which is due to the decentralized organization in public administration.

Because of the structures in public administration so far, the knowledge of methods and technologies for BPM is hardly developed. Hence, in comparison to the private sector, intensive methods for developing necessary knowledge regarding BPM have to be introduced. The implementation of a process organization in public administration is complicated by the fact that the responsible persons have to be convinced that a higher level of process orientation would be useful.

### 2.4.6 Factor: Culture

This factor comprises the responsiveness to process changes, process values, and beliefs, as well as the strength of leadership in respect of BPM. Regarding this aspect, there are hardly any particularities in the public sector in comparison to the private sector.

However, the organizational culture is seen as a whole: organizational culture is considered as an amount of assumptions shared by a group of people, which has been invented, detected, or developed by them for solving problems based on the division of work (Schein 1984). Accordingly, hierarchy culture, market culture, clan culture, and adhocracy culture can be distinguished. The organizational culture in public administration is especially affected by a hierarchy culture. Because of the hierarchical organizational structure, it can be assumed that the maturity of the organizational culture in public administration is generally rather low, in this respect. Hence, methods for improving the process maturity as far as the organizational culture is concerned should be considered notably (see vom Brocke et al. 2010).

BPM maturity models were considered as means for implementing and realizing the 48-h-service promise in public administration. For this purpose, they have to consider the requirements for a 48-h-service promise solution. According to the high amount of specifics of BPM in public administration, they have additionally to consider the particular requirements which arise from the public administration domain (OMG 2008, p. 69). However, most of the existing BPM maturity models seem to be proposed for the application within the private sector. Therefore, Sect. 3 analyzes known maturity models for BPM and public administration.

## 3 Known Maturity Models for BPM and Public Administration

Numerous maturity models for BPM have been proposed which can be divided into two types of models: models with a comprehensive view on BPM [e.g., (OMG, 2008)] and models considering facets of BPM [e.g., (Luftman, 2000)] [cp. here and in the following also (Rosemann and de Bruin 2005; Rosemann et al. 2006)]. The majority of these models are provided as instruments for the assessment of the capability of BPM. Recommendations shall contribute to an improvement of the maturity of BPM and, accordingly, to a higher quality of processes. The main target is to raise the company's success by an improvement of business processes.

A common basis of various BPM maturity models is the *Capability Maturity Model* (CMM) (Paulk et al. 1993; Rosemann and de Bruin 2005). It is based on the assumption that the maturity level of software development within an organization can be valued at assessed development processes. The CMM defines five sequent maturity levels. Based on these maturity levels, Harmon (Harmon 2004) proposes a more elementary maturity model. More effort was necessary for designing the *Business Process Maturity Model* (OMG, 2008) of the *Object Management Group* (OMG). Currently, it represents the largest CMM-based BPM maturity model. Fisher (Fisher 2004) also proposes a model with five maturity levels. However, he defined different levels as used by CMM and combined his levels with five BPM-critical success factors. A promising approach is the *Business Process Management Maturity Model* of Rosemann and de Bruin (Rosemann and de Bruin 2005). They enlarge the CMM model to three dimensions and consider the six core factors of BPM (Rosemann and vom Brocke 2010). Hereby, the current state of knowledge about crucial factors shall be regarded to a greater extent than in existing models. A more popular model is the *Process and Enterprise Maturity Model* of Hammer (Hammer 2007). His BPM maturity model consists of two parts, one for assessing process enablers and the other for assessing enterprise capabilities.

A comparison of the mentioned BPM maturity models is provided in Table 4. The definition of the five comparison criteria is based on Hüffner (Hüffner 2004):

- The *scope* criterion distinguishes the application of the maturity model on whole organizations, a business unit or a process.
- The specialization of the model is captured by the *focus* criterion. Therewith, it is being stated that the application of the maturity model can be either general or focused on a specific domain, like, e.g., the public administration.
- Regarding the *comprehensiveness* criterion, it is being distinguished whether the maturity model is designed to measure the "as-is" situation, to determine a "to-be" maturity level, or to recommend actions for achieving a "to-be" level.
- The criterion *maturity level representation* distinguishes between a staged and a continuous representation of the maturity levels. The former describes the fact that only one organization-wide or process-wide maturity level can be estimated using the model. For the continuous representation, in contrast, a number of maturity levels can be calculated by independently assessing different maturity model factors.

Table 4 shows that BPM maturity models are primarily designed for BPM in general. Domain specifics or particular application contexts are hardly considered. Furthermore, only few models exist which comprise recommendations for the improvement. However, there exist special maturity models for the public administration without a foundation on the CMM model or BPM maturity models. They do not focus on BPM, but on the assessment and improvement of electronic public

**Table 4** Comparison of BPM maturity models

| | (Hammer 2007) | (Rosemann and de Bruin, 2005); (Rosemann et al. 2006) | (OMG 2008) | (Fisher 2004) | (Harmon 2004) |
|---|---|---|---|---|---|
| Scope | Processes, organization | Organization, business units | Processes, organization | Organization | Process, organization |
| Focus | General | General | General | General | General |
| Comprehensive-ness | Measure | Measure | Measure, improve | Measure | Measure |
| Maturity level representation | Continuous | Staged, continuous | Staged | Staged | Staged |

services. Because of the concentration on technological aid, those models are known as e-Government maturity models or e-Government stage models.

E-Government maturity models can be divided into models with an academic background [e.g., (Esteves and Joseph 2008; Lam 2004; Stamoulis et al. 2001)] and models developed in practice [e.g., (United Nations and ASPA 2002)]. Most of them present themselves as tools for the improvement of electronic public services. They distinguish several maturity levels of access to these services via electronic media (Shackleton et al. 2004). For example, Layne and Lee (2001) differentiate four maturity stages starting with a simple Internet presence of an administration (catalog), through online-based services and forms as well as assistance for transaction (transaction), to vertical Integrated information systems (vertical integration) and overall cross-functional integrated systems (horizontal integration). The majority of the models concentrate on the evaluation of the electronic interface between administration and external stakeholders (focus on interfaces and front end). In most of the cases, to identify a maturity level, the level of technological assistance during the provision of public services has to be valued (focus on technology). Advice and recommendations for raising the maturity level are limited to aspects like the depth of transaction or integration. There are approaches which try to avoid that strong focus on technology, for example, the model of Anderson and Henriksen (Andersen and Henriksen 2006), but they hardly expand their focus.

In summary, regardless of the multitude of maturity models, the authors do not mention a use case of a BPM maturity model which is adapted to the needs of public administrations in general and the case of 48-h-service promise in particular. However, e-Government maturity models consider the particularities of the public administration domain. Nevertheless, they do not address the BPM within public authorities. Therefore, the following sections introduce a domain-specific BPM maturity model that eliminates the lack of process orientation in existing e-Government maturity models and that considers the particularities of public administration as well as the 48-h-service promise.

## 4 Design and Development

Based on the mentioned prior work on maturity models, we developed a BPM maturity model for the fulfillment of the 48-h-serivce promise. This maturity model consists of five maturity levels which reflect the degree of fulfillment of the 48-h-service promise (cp. Fig. 6):

- *Level 1*: "incomplete 48-h-service promise"; no particular actions are defined to fulfill the 48-h-service promise.
- *Level 2*: "managed 48-h-service promise"; some basic actions for the fulfillment of the 48-h-service promise are established.
- *Level 3*: "defined 48-h-service promise"; all necessary actions for the fulfillment of the 48-h-service promise are defined.

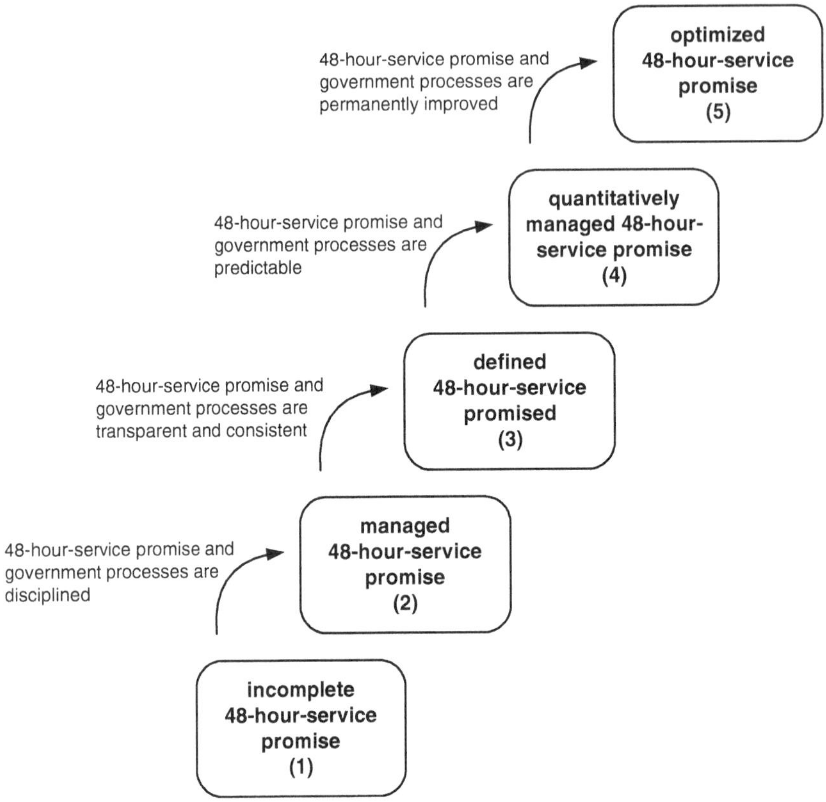


**Fig. 6** Maturity levels for the 48-h-service promise

- *Level 4*: "quantitatively managed 48-h-service promise"; actions for the fulfillment of the 48-service promise are quantitatively planned, controlled, and monitored.
- *Level 5*: "optimized 48-h-service promise"; all actions for the fulfillment of the 48-h-service promise are permanently and systematically improved.

In order to measure the maturity of a 48-h-service promise of an organization, the proposed maturity model contains five main factors which cover relevant actions and characteristics of the 48-h-service promise:

- *Main factor "Strategy of the 48-h-service promise"*: This main factor consists of aspects which are relevant for a long term plan of action designed to achieve the 48-h-service promise.
- *Main factor "Design of the 48-h-service promise"*: All aspects relevant for the definition and documentation of the implementation of the 48-h-service promise are grouped by this factor.
- *Main factor "Implementation of the 48-h-service promise"*: This factor addresses the realization of the 48-h-service promise.

- *Main factor "Controlling of the 48-h-service promise"*: This main factor includes setting standards, measuring actual performance, and taking corrective action for the implementation of the 48-h-service promise.
- *Main factor "People and culture"*: The people's knowledge, competency, and willingness for implementing the 48-h-service promise are addressed by this factor.

The utilization of these five factors is based on design decisions during the development process of the maturity model (cp. Sect. 5). The five main factors are further operationalized by 18 factors. Table 5 explains these factors in more detail.

The maturity model defines different objectives, which have to be attained to achieve a particular maturity level for all the factors. By definition, every organization has reached maturity level 1. Table 6 introduces the particular objectives, which have to be achieved to reach maturity level 2.

For each factor, several actions are proposed for implementation, which improves the 48-h-service promise of an organization. For example, the main factor "Design of the 48-h-service promise" contains the factor "Definition of roles and responsibilities". To achieve the second maturity level of this factor, the objective says that the roles and responsibilities of the management and the implementation of the 48-h-service promise must be defined. The maturity model proposes two actions to achieve this objective:

1. The organizational units responsible for the management of the 48-h-service promise must be defined within the relevant government process.
2. The leading organizational units responsible for the execution of necessary actions to fulfill the 48-h-service promise must be defined.

Additionally, the description of the maturity model contains a deeper explanation for why it is necessary to define the roles and responsibilities of different organizational units for the management and implementation of the 48-h-service promise.

To assess the maturity of a public authority, each factor of the maturity model has to be measured. The first maturity level of each factor is achieved by definition. To achieve the second maturity level of a factor, the first maturity level of this factor has to be achieved and all objectives assigned to this factor on the second maturity level have to be accomplished and so forth.

Typically, a radar chart can be used to visualize the results of a maturity assessment. Such a radar chart consists of 18 axes each representing one factor of the maturity model. Figure 7 depicts an exemplary radar chart visualizing the results of a fictitious maturity assessment.

Please note, because of space limitations, this chapter just overviews some important parts of the maturity model as an example. It is planned to publish the complete maturity model on the Web page http://www.e-government-cc.org/. In the meantime, please contact the first author to obtain a copy of the complete maturity model.

**Table 5** Factors of the maturity model

| Main factor | Factor | Explanation |
|---|---|---|
| Strategy of the 48-h-service promise | Definition of objective | Definition and communication of the 48-h-service promise as a strategic objective |
| | Definition of objective values | Definition and communication of measures for the 48-h-service promise |
| Design of the 48-h-service promise | Process documentation | Process survey and documentation of relevant government processes |
| | Definition of basic parameters | Identification and definition of relevant basic parameters for the implementation of the 48-h-service promise |
| | Definition of actions | Definition of operational actions for the fulfillment of the 48-h-service promise |
| | Definition of roles and responsibilities | Definition of responsible and operational organizational units for the 48-h-service promise |
| | Information systems for design | Use of information systems for the design of the 48-h-service promise |
| Implementation of the 48-h-service promise | Resource planning and allocation | Planning and allocation of all necessary employees and material resources for the 48-h-service promise |
| | Management enforcement | Responsible organizational units enforce necessary managements actions |
| | Implementation of actions | Responsible organizational units implement all defined actions to fulfill 48-h-service promise |
| | Implementation of cooperation and communication | Cooperation and communication between all organizational units involved in the implementation of the 48-h-service promise |
| | Information systems for implementation | Use of information systems for the implementation of the 48-h-service promise |
| Controlling of the 48-h-service promise | Definition of measures | Definition of measures for the implementation of 48-h-service promise |
| | Use of measures | Use of measures for the implementation of the 48-h-service promise |
| | Information systems for controlling | Use of information systems for the controlling of the 48-h-service promise |
| People and culture | Knowledge and competencies of operational organizational units | Guarantee that operational organizational units responsible for the implementation of the 48-h-service promise possess necessary knowledge and competencies |
| | Knowledge and competencies of responsible organizational units | Guarantee that organizational units responsible for the management of the 48-h-service promise possess necessary knowledge and competencies |
| | Willingness to implement 48-h-service promise | Guarantee that all organizational units accept and adopt the 48-h-service promise |

**Table 6** Overview of objectives of maturity level 2

| Main factor | Factor | Objectives |
|---|---|---|
| Strategy of the 48-h-service promise | Definition of objective | 48-h-service promise is defined as a strategic objective |
| | Definition of objective values | Measures for the 48-h-service promise are defined |
| Design of the 48-h-service promise | Process documentation | Sub-processes of the relevant administration process are identified |
| | Definition of basic arameters | Relevant basic parameters for the implementation of the 48-h-service promise are identified |
| | Definition of actions | Rough operational actions for the fulfillment of the 48-h-service promise are established |
| | Definition of roles and responsibilities | Responsible and operational organizational units for the 48-h-service promise are appointed |
| | Information systems for design | – |
| Implementation of the 48-h-service promise | Resource planning and allocation | – |
| | Management enforcement | Responsible organizational units submit proposals for the enforcement of necessary managements actions |
| | Implementation of actions | Rough operational actions for the fulfillment of 48-h-service promise are implemented in at least 80% of all cases |
| | Implementation of cooperation and communication | – |
| | Information systems for implementation | – |
| Controlling of the 48-h-service promise | Definition of measures | – |
| | Use of measures | – |
| | Information systems or controlling | – |
| People and culture | Knowledge and competencies of operational organizational units | Organizational units responsible for the implementation of the 48-h-service promise understand defined objectives and actions and obtain necessary knowledge and competencies for the implementation |
| | Knowledge and competencies of responsible organizational units | Organizational units responsible for the management of the 48-h-service promise possess basic knowledge of BPM |
| | Willingness to implement 48-h-service promise | – |

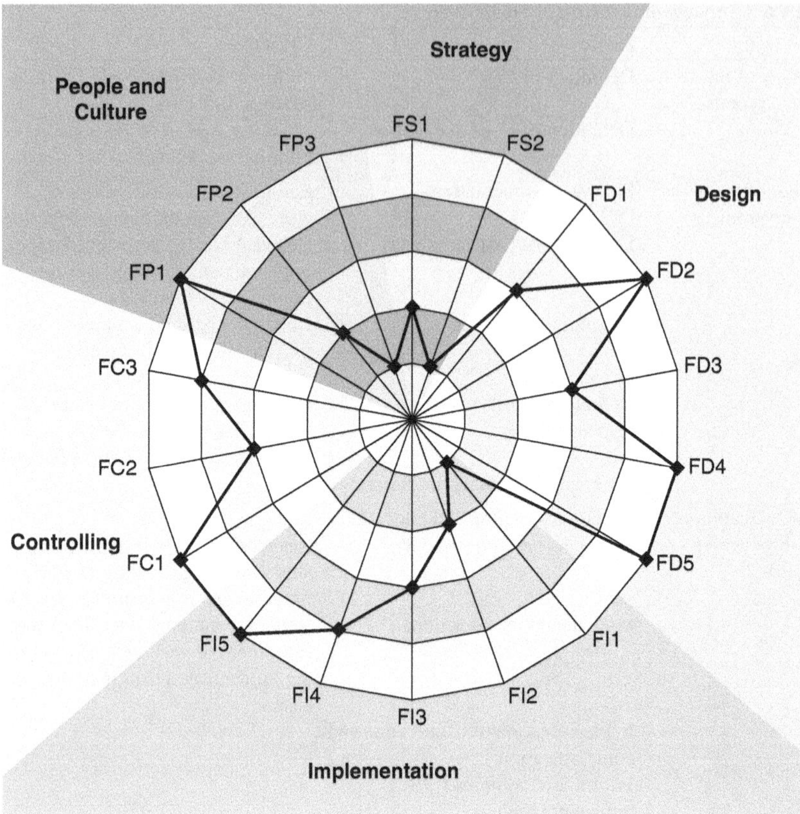


**Fig. 7** Exemplary results of an assessment

Compared to known BPM maturity models, our proposed maturity model can be characterized by some important features:

- *Public administration focus*: The proposed model explicitly focuses on the need for BPM in the area of public administration.
- *Purpose-oriented*: The proposed model defines some particular actions and levels for BPM in the context of the purpose of the fulfillment of the 48-h-service promise.

Because of these aspects, we characterize the proposed maturity model as a domain-specific BPM maturity model.

# 5 Demonstration and Evaluation

After developing the proposed maturity model, the usability and quality of the maturity model have to be demonstrated via well-known evaluation methods. The public administration environment described in Sect. 2 establishes the requirements which the maturity model must be tested against. Thus, the evaluation comprises the application of the maturity model within the environment offered by public authorities.

Hevner et al. (Hevner et al. 2004) distinguish five different design evaluation methods, namely observational, analytical, experimental, testing, and descriptive. We used observational and descriptive evaluation methods for the demonstration of the usability and quality of the proposed maturity model.

A descriptive evaluation is typically less rigorous but can be applied during all phases of the development cycle of a research artifact. We used a descriptive evaluation method during the development phase of the maturity model. The designing of innovative artifacts in general and a maturity model in particular is an inherently iterative process (Fig. 8). During this process, we developed several design alternatives and tested these alternatives against the requirements mentioned in Sect. 2.

During the development process, we used two approaches in particular:

- *Expert feedback*: We discussed developed design alternatives with several experts from the domain of BPM as well as practitioners responsible for the modernization of public administration processes and fulfillment of 48-h-service promise.
- *Scenario development*: The aim of the scenario development was the analysis of selected real-world public services in a German state administration in order to estimate the state of the art of fulfilling the 48-h-service promise and to acquire possible means and activities for realizing the service promise. For this purpose, a special public authority that provides social services for citizens of the German state was selected. Within this authority, four of the most requested services were selected for surveying their production and provision processes. The processes were documented in survey forms and event-driven process chains (EPC). The analysis of the processes identified several necessary activities and

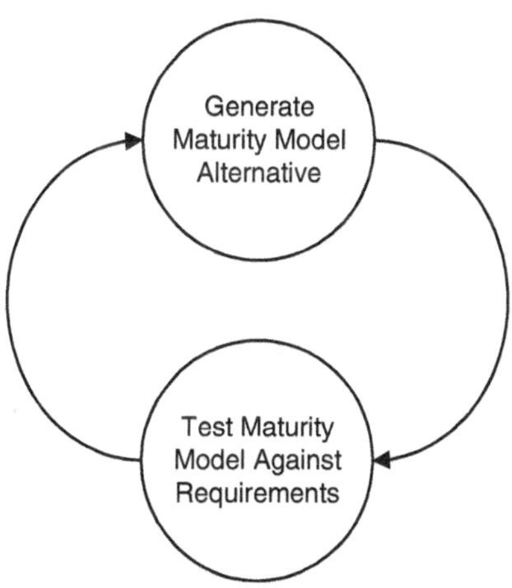


**Fig. 8** Generate and test cycle; based on Simon (1996) and Hevner et al. (2004)

resources for the implementation and fulfillment of the 48-h-service promise which were analyzed according to the background of the maturity model.

The described evaluation approaches were already applied during the development of the BPM maturity model. Such a "Design to Quality" approach significantly supports the usability and quality of the developed maturity model. However, to further assure and assess the usefulness, we employed a case study as an observational evaluation method.

The already presented maturity model was applied in the context of a project which was to increase the service orientation in a German state administration. This state administration has been continuously improving the quality of their services for citizens and enterprises. One building block is a faster communication between applicants and public authorities. The aim of the project is to improve the customer orientation as well as service orientation by introducing a 48-h-service promise. Figure 9 unfolds the procedure and the main phases of the project. Main activities of the first phase were concentrated on the conceptualization of the 48-h-service promise. For this purpose, the configuration parameter for a response in terms of a 48-h-service promise was specified. Moreover, while defining the time frame for the 48-h-service deadline influencing factors for releasing the start-event and end-event were specified. Therefore, several activating conditions for the release of a 48-h-service promise measurement as well as conditions which fulfill a sufficient response in terms of the 48-h-service promise were determined and specified during this project phase.

The aim of the second project phase was the analysis of selected real-world public services in the German state administration in order to estimate the state of the art of fulfilling the 48-h-service promise and to acquire possible means and activities for realizing the service promise based on real-world scenarios. This analysis was based on the developed BPM maturity model for 48-h-service promise.

The results of the preceding two project phases were used in the third phase for specifying an implementation concept for the service promise. Based on the consideration that public services and their processes as well as their activities can be managed using the BPM approach, the 48-h-service promise as a new part with special means and activities within these processes can be realized by an adequate BPM. For the purpose of introducing, managing, and improving the 48-h-service promise for the public services of the German state administration, the proposed maturity model was used. Therefore, the maturity model was applied and typical areas for process improvements were identified.

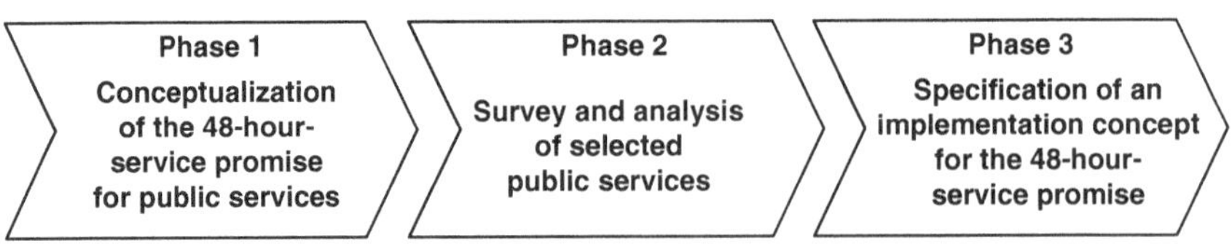


**Fig. 9** Project phases

Our experience in using the maturity model shows the following advantages:

- The maturity model helps bridge the gap between domain expert's view of BPM and its implementation.
- It is suited for communication with users in the domain.
- Because of a focused scope, the application of the maturity model is less challenging.
- The maturity model provides a better support for one particular BPM purpose, namely the fulfillment of the 48-h-service promise in public administrations.

To conclude, according to our findings, a domain-specific BPM maturity model has major advantages compared to domain-neutral BPM maturity models. These experiences are similar to experiences acquired in the context of domain specific modeling (France and Rumpe 2005, p. 1).

In general, it might be argued that the domain-specific development of the proposed maturity model does not make sense because this model might be useful only in one particular organization. However, this argumentation ignores the fact that the developed maturity model is based on requirements gathered at all authorities of a German state. Hence, the model is useful for BPM not only in one particular authority but also in a large class of authorities.

Because of the development process of the maturity model, it can be argued that the model can effectively and efficiently applied by authorities of a German state. According to our experiences and knowledge of particularities of the public administration system in Germany, it will not be difficult to adapt the proposed maturity model to requirements of authorities of other states in Germany. However, today, it is not sure to what extent the developed model can be generalized to the needs of authorities in other countries. From the perspective of BPM, the proposed model does not introduce some particular actions which are typically for Germany. But there may be some national laws in other countries which must be taken into account if the application domain of the proposed maturity model is to be extended.

## 6 Summary and Outlook

BPM has gained tremendous importance in many industries. In the last few years, public administrations have successfully adopted the idea of BPM as a means for modernization. BPM approaches have much potential for the improvement of efficiency and effectiveness as well as the service orientation of public administrations. One important aspect of service orientation is a 48-h-service promise which was particularly focused in this chapter.

Against this background, there is a need for a maturity model for BPM in public administrations which take into account the fulfillment of a 48-h-service promise. In this chapter, we first analyzed particularities of the domain "public administration" compared to the private sector. Because of important differences between the private sector and public administrations, we proposed that existing maturity models for BPM need to be adapted appropriately to the need of the fulfillment of a 48-h-service promise in the public administration domain. A new proposal was developed which takes into account the fulfillment of a 48-h-service promise in public administrations. Furthermore, the utilization of the model was tested in the context of a project within a particular German state whose authorities want to improve their service orientation in general and to introduce a 48-h-service promise in particular.

We characterize our proposed maturity model as domain-specific because it is adapted to the particular requirements of the fulfillment of a 48-h-service promise in public administrations. Our experiences in applying the domain-oriented maturity model are very promising. For example, we realized that the domain-specific model helps bridge the gap between domain expert's view of BPM and its implementation and is suited for better communication with users in the domain.

Even though the experiences of the application are very encouraging, there are further questions that have to be answered by future research:

- Experiences concerning the utilization of the maturity model in public administration by authorities of one particular German state are available so far. In the context of further applications, additional experiences need to be collected to improve the utilization and practicability of the model.
- As in the case of other known maturity models, the proposed model is based on the assumption that an improvement of the maturity degree is fundamentally positive for success. Hence, in the future, it is necessary to intensively investigate whether a higher maturity level always results in a better success of a public administration or whether there are some circumstances, which, in this respect, have a negative impact on success.
- The developed maturity model addresses the fulfillment of a 48-h-service promise in public administrations. A 48-h-service promise is one aspect of a general service promise that today's public administrations wish to achieve. Therefore, it will be necessary to extend the proposed maturity model accordingly.

**Acknowledgment** This paper presents results from the research project "Prozessorientiertes Verwaltungshandeln durch innovative E-Government-Lösungen" (innoGov, "Using innovative E-Government solutions for process-oriented public administrations") funded by the European Union (EFRE), Ministerium für Wirtschaft und Wissenschaft des Saarlandes ("Saarland Ministry for Economic and Science") and the IT-Innovationszentrum Saarland ("Saarland IT Innovation Center").

## References

Andersen KV, Henriksen HZ (2006) *E-Government maturity models*: Extension of the Layne and Lee model. Gov Inf Q 23(2):236–248

Becker J, Algermissen L, Falk T (2007) Prozessorientierte Verwaltungsmodernisierung: Prozessmanagement im Zeitalter von E-Government und New Public Management. Springer, Berlin

Becker J, Kugeler M, Rosemann M (eds) (2003) Process management. Springer, Berlin

Esteves J, Joseph RC (2008) A comprehensive framework for the assessment of eGovernment projects. Gov Inf Q 25(1):118–132

Fisher DM (2004) The business process maturity model – a practical approach for identifying opportunities for optimization [Electronic Version]. Business Process Trends. Retrieved 2008-07-23 from http://www.bptrends.com/publicationfiles/10%2D04%20ART%20BP%20Maturity%20Model%20%2D%20Fisher%2Epdf

Fontelles JB, Pekkarinen M (2006) Directive 2006/123/EC of the European Parliament and of the Council of 12 December 2006 on services in the internal market. 2006/123/EC, European Union, L 376

France RB, Rumpe B (2005) Domain specific modeling. Softw Syst Model 4(1):1–3

Gisler M (2001) Einführung in die Begriffswelt des E-Government. In: Gisler M, Spahni D (eds) eGovernment: Eine Standortbestimmung. Bern, Haupt pp 13–30

Güngöz Ö (2007) Modellgestütztes Rahmenwerk für das Management von komplexen und schwach-strukturierten Verwaltungsprozessen. Lohmar, Eul

Hammer M (2007) The Process Audit. Harv Bus Rev 85(4):124–131

Harmon P (2004) Evaluating an organization's business process maturity [Electronic Version]. *Business Process Trends, 2*. Retrieved 2008-7-23 from http://www.bptrends.com/publicationfiles/03-04%20NL%20Eval%20BP%20Maturity%20-%20Harmon.pdf

Hevner AR, March ST, Park J, Ram S (2004) Design science in information systems research. MIS Q 28(1):75–105

Hüffner T (2004) The BPM maturity model – towards a framework for assessing the business process management maturity of organisations. GRIN, München, Ravensburg

Hunziker AW (1999) Prozessorganisation in der öffentlichen Verwaltung: New Public Management und Business Reengineering in der schweizerischen Bundesverwaltung. HBLB Karlsruhe, Bern

KBSt -Koordinierungs- und Beratungsstelle der Bundesregierung für Informationstechnik in der Bundesverwaltung. (2005) Domea Concept, Organisational Concept 2.0, Document Management and Electronic Archiving in Electronic Courses of Business (No. 74). Berlin, Bundesministerium des Innern

Lam W (2004) Integration challenges towards increasing E-Government maturity. J E-Gov 1(2):45–59

Layne K, Lee J (2001) Developing fully functional E-government: a four stage model. Gov Inf Q 18(2):122–136

Lenk K, Traunmüller R, Wimmer MA (2002). The significance of law and knowledge for electronic Government. In: Grönlund Å (ed) Electronic government: design, application & management. Hershey et al.: Idea Group, pp 61–77

Luftman J (2000) Assessing Business-IT alignment maturity. Communications of the AIS, 4(Article 14)

OMG (2008) Business Process Maturity Model (BPMM) Version 1.0 (No. formal/2008-06-01). Object Management Group, Needham, MA

Palkovits S, Wimmer MA (2003) Processes in E-Government – a holistic framework for modelling electronic public services. In: Traunmüller R (ed) Electronic government: Second International Conference, EGOV 2003, Prague, Czech Republic, September 1–5, 2003, Proceedings, Vol. LNCS. Springer, Berlin, pp 213–219

Paulk MC, Curtis B, Chrissis MB, Weber CV (1993) Capability Maturity Model for Software, Version 1.1 (No. CMU/SEI-93-TR-024). Software Engineering Institute, Carnegie Mellon University, Pittsburgh, PA

Peffers K, Tuunanen T, Rothenberger MA, Chatterjee S (2007) A design science research methodology for information systems research. J Manage Inf Syst 24(3):45–77

Rosemann M, de Bruin T (2005) Towards a business process management maturity model. In: Bartmann D, Rajola F, Kallinikos J, Avison D, Winter R, Ein-Dor P, Becker J, Bodendorf F, Weinhardt C (eds) Proceedings of the thirteenth European conference on information systems. Regensburg, Germany, pp 521–532

Rosemann M, vom Brocke J (2010) The six core elements of business process management. In: vom Brocke J, Rosemann M (eds) Handbook on business process management, vol 1. Springer, Heidelberg

Rosemann M, de Bruin T, Power B (2006) BPM Maturity. In: Jeston J, Nelis J (eds) Business Process Management Practical Guidelines to Successful Implementations 2nd edn. Butterworth Heinemann, pp 299–315

Rummler GA, Brache AP (1995) Improving performance: how to manage the white space on the organization chart, 2nd edn. Jossey-Bass, San Francisco

Schein EH (1984) Coming to a new awareness of organizational culture. Sloan Manage Rev 25(2):3–16

Shackleton P, Fisher J, Dawson L (2004) Evolution of local government E-Services: the applicability of e-Business maturity models. In: Proceedings of the 37th Hawaii International Conference on System Sciences (HICSS'04) – Track 5 – Volume 5. IEEE Computer Society, Washington, DC, p. 50120b

Simon HA (1996) The science of the artificial, 3rd edn. MIT Press, Cambridge, MA

Stamoulis D, Gouscos D, Georgiadis P, Martakos D (2001) Revisiting public information management for effective E-government services. Inform Manage Comput Secur 9(4):146–153

United Nations, & ASPA (2002) Benchmarking E-government: a global perspective – assessing the progress of the UN member states. United Nations, ASPA, New York

vom Brocke J, Petry M, Sinni T, Østerberg Kristensen B, Sonnenberg C (2010) Global processes and data: The cultural journey at the Hilti corporation. In: vom Brocke J, Rosemann M (eds) Handbook on business process management, vol 2. Springer, Heidelberg

# Part III
# People and Culture

## People and Culture

While information technology is very often the driver for process change, the success of Business Process Management initiatives is very much dependent on the human factor. The section "People and Culture" divides this factor into (a) the experience and skills in terms of processes and process management (people), and in (b) the overall leadership and organizational and individual acceptance of BPM (culture).

In this context, questions arise such as: How can we make sure that people proactively drive process change and accept process changes? What is the BPM body of knowledge? What is needed on the human side to make such a process change happen in the most effective and efficient manner? What leadership skills are required to make sure that culture becomes an enabler and not an inhibitor of process change? The following part of the BPM Handbook revolves around questions like these and explores the impact of the human factor on Business Process Management from different viewpoints.

As an introduction, we first included two chapters on the various competences required when introducing BPM in an organization. In the first chapter, Alexandra Kokkonen and Wasana Bandara present a so-called BPM expertise model. Drawing from theories, related work and case study findings, the authors contrast different areas of BPM expertise and derive corresponding fields of literature contributing to a map of required BPM knowledge. In the second chapter, Yvonne Lederer-Antonucci then takes a closer look into the design of BPM course curricula. Since many organizations have assigned the process transformation leadership to the existing business analysts, she reviews the role of a business analyst within the context of BPM practice and suggests a curriculum designed to cultivate skills for the emerging role of the business process analyst.

When managing change in business processes, various factors resulting from the human perspective have to be taken into consideration. These factors are considered in the next set of chapters. First, an introduction is given by Keith Harrison-Broninski in his chapter on dealing with human-driven processes. He presents an approach of analyzing and describing processes with a focus on human interactions. The approach intends to facilitate the management of teams, communication, knowledge, time, and plans. The focus lies on how to take into account the role of human collaboration in Business Process Management.

In the chapter by Dimitris Karagiannis and Robert Woitsch, the role of "knowledge" as a part of Business Process Management forms the main focus. Their work contributes to the increasingly important domain of knowledge-sensitive BPM. The two authors show how Knowledge Engineering can be incorporated in BPM with a particular focus on frameworks, management methods, and deployment initiatives. Apart from knowledge, culture is a major aspect brought about by the human factor in BPM. This aspect is the core of the chapter by Ulrike Baumöl. Her contribution on cultural change in BPM provides an engineering perspective on how to organize change in an organization. Both elements, knowledge and culture, contribute to the creativity in an organization. This phenomenon of growing competitive relevance to BPM is discussed by Stefan Seidel, Katherine Shortland, David Court, and Didier Elzinga. Drawing from observations at one of the leading postproduction studios, Rising Sun Pictures, the authors present a deep understanding of how creativity impacts business processes. They derive guidelines on the management of creativity-intensive processes that are of major importance to a wide range of industries today.

We round up the section with two case studies on the role of people and culture in BPM. First, the case study of the Hilti Corporation gives practical insights in a global BPM change project. Jan vom Brocke, Theresa Sinnl, and Christian Sonnenberg report on findings derived from a set of interviews conducted at Hilti Global IT. Together with their co-authors from the Hilti Corporation, Martin Petry and Bo Østerberg Kristensen, they give insight into the role of culture when introducing global processes and data. Second, an Australian transport provider serves as a case study in order to demonstrate the various interdependences between the six core components of a BPM maturity model. Tonia de Bruin and Gaby Doebeli give illustrative examples once more highlighting the importance of understanding BPM as an organizational approach.

6. Managing Creativity-intensive Processes:
   Learning from Film and Visual Effects Production
   by Stefan Seidel, Katherine Shortland, David Court, and Didier Elzinga
7. Global Processes and Data:
   The Cultural Journey at the Hilti Corporation
   by Jan vom Brocke, Martin Petry, Theresa Sinnl, Bo Østerberg Kristensen, and Christian Sonnenberg
8. An Organizational Approach to BPM:
   The Experience of an Australian Transport Provider
   by Tonia de Bruin and Gaby Doebeli

# Expertise in Business Process Management

**Alexandra Kokkonen and Wasana Bandara**

**Abstract** As organizations attempt to become more business process-oriented, existing role descriptions are revised and entire new business process-related roles emerge. A lot of attention is often being paid to the technological aspect of Business Process Management (BPM), but relatively little work has been done concerning the people factor of BPM and the specification of BPM expertise in particular. This study tries to close this gap by proposing a comprehensive BPM expertise model, which consolidates existing theories and related work. This model describes the key attributes characterizing "BPM expertise" and outlines their structure, dynamics, and interrelationships. Understanding BPM expertise is a predecessor to being able to develop and apply it effectively. This is the cornerstone of human capital and talent management in BPM.

## 1 Introduction and Background

> "Business Process Management skills are a hot commodity these day [. . .] But what exactly is the skill set of a BPM expert?"
>
> (*zur Mühlen 2008*)

With the rapidly growing emphasis and focus on process improvement activities across the globe, many organizations ask the following questions: What do we

A. Kokkonen (✉)
BPM Group, Faculty of Science and Technology, Queensland University of Technology, Brisbane, QLD, Australia
e-mail: akokkone@yahoo.com.au

J. vom Brocke and M. Rosemann (eds.), *Handbook on Business Process Management 2*, International Handbooks on Information Systems,
DOI 10.1007/978-3-642-01982-1_19, 

know about the expertise of Business Process Management (BPM) ? What does our understanding (or lack of understanding) of BPM expertise mean to the BPM arena?

BPM has emerged in recent years as a management philosophy and discipline centered around business processes, and is continuing to rapidly evolve (Gartner 2008). Preceding related disciplines included Total Quality Management (TQM) in the 1980s, followed by Business Process Reengineering (BPR) in the early 1990s, and in the mid and later 1990s Enterprise Resource Planning (ERP) (Koch 2001; Jeston and Nelis 2008). In essence, BPM is an old discipline (Verner 2004).

"BPM is considered as an organizational management philosophy; a holistic approach which focuses on the organizational (BPM) capability required to optimize process management practices within the organization" (Rosemann and de Bruin 2005). As such, this approach encompasses the integration, coordination, and management of BPM practices as they are applied across and within key end-to-end processes and the lower level processes that go to support them (Rosemann and de Bruin 2005). Thus, BPM goes beyond mere automation of business processes, or solving business problems; BPM creates value through competitive advantage by responding to consumer changes, market(s), and regulatory requirements faster and more effectively or efficiently than competitors respond.

As BPM has evolved and organizations are becoming more business process oriented, the need for BPM expertise and experience has increased. Roles, which recognize this requirement, are being introduced in organizations [such as; Business process director; Business process consultant; Business process architect; Business process analyst (Melenovsky and Hill 2006) to name a few]. While great attention is being paid by the BPM community to the technological aspect of BPM [such as van der Aalst et al. (2003)], relatively little research or work has been done concerning the people factor (Rosemann and de Bruin 2005), and expertise and experience component of BPM (BPM Basics 2007; Harris 2007).

The dynamic, complex, and interdependent nature of the business process environment means that business process roles require a breadth of various expertise and experience, ranging from the business itself to the technology concerned. These roles are sometimes referred to as business process expert roles; however, there is little common understanding of what such roles are. The deficit in focus and research on the people component of BPM (Rosemann et al. 2005, 2007) has resulted in poor understanding of what the term "business process expertise" means in practice, its manifestation and application within organizations, or in the implications of the manifestation and application.

The people element, defined as "the individuals and groups who continually enhance and apply their process skills and knowledge to improve business performance" (following Rosemann et al. 2005), is considered a key factor of BPM; as evidenced by the many BPM critical success factor studies (e.g., Raymond et al. 1995; Amoroso 1998; Grover et al. 1998) that specifically state the role of people for the success and failure of BPM. One of the few BPM studies that discuss the people factor in BPM in detail is the de Bruin's (2005, 2008) model of Business Process Management Maturity (BPMM). The "people factor" refers to one of the six key components identified by de Bruin (2008) in the (BPMM) model.[1] A deficit in any one of the six component areas will affect other areas of BPM to some extent, as none of the components operate in isolation. Thus, any deficit in the people factor will invariably affect the other BPM components to a greater or lesser extent. Other BPM-related models that emphasize the people component are Zachman's Enterprise Architecture framework (Zachman 2007) and the Enterprise Business Process Architecture model (BPMEnterprise.com).[2]

While it is widely agreed that BPM expertise and experience are required at different organizational levels, from operational to executive management levels, there is no common framework in existence, describing the fundamental elements characterizing BPM expertise. This has resulted in a poor understanding of what BPM expertise is, or of what the implications of the dynamics and interrelationships of BPM expertise elements may bring forth to the organization. This knowledge deficit has contributed to the void in the understanding and managing the implications of business process expertise in different organizational areas, and its development. Attempting to address business process issues through technology, architecture, data, and processes alone, independent of (or ignoring) the people involved and their expertise, is like "doctors trying to treat humans by only looking at their feet" (Vestey 2006, p. 60 )

> Even if the organization has their structure optimized, people are the ones who execute the processes and make things happen. Without them you have nothing.
>
> (*Jeston and Nelis 2006, p. 169*)

BPM guidelines for success often provide advice such as: "Establish a robust governance framework that identifies process ownership," "Appoint a business process analyst to work on each major business process," "Create a BPM center of excellence," "Select an experienced person to head the BPM center of excellence (e.g., Hill et al. 2006; Olding and Rosser 2007)." People cannot be appointed to fulfill BPM expertise roles successfully, or create governance around the deployment and management of BPM expertise, or establish a center of excellence consolidating BPM expertise, without first knowing what BPM expertise is meant to be.

This study aims to develop a deeper understanding of what BPM expertise is, and what the key attributes and dynamics characterizing business process expertise are. The focus of this study is BPM expertise as a holistic concept. This is different

---

[1]The other components are Strategic Alignment, Governance, Technology, Methods and Culture (Rosemann et al. 2007).

[2]Whilst these are enterprise architecture (EA) models, BPM plays a central role in EA (Pieterse 2005); the two fields may even merge in future (Zsambok and Klein 1997; Stevens 2007). Zachman's framework considers people to be the "who" component of enterprise architecture, while organizational aspects – people, roles, and functions are one of the seven components of the Enterprise Business Process Architecture model (BPM Enterprise.com).

in scope from "process expertise" or a "business process expert"; each of these is considered a subset of BPM expertise. Thus, the term "BPM expertise" encompasses all forms of knowledge and experience relating to business processes, including the management and architecture of business processes, characteristics of the person(s) involved in the expertise, the level of expertise, and the context in which the BPM expertise is situated.

## 2 Business Process Management Expertise Model

A deductive approach (referred to informally as a "top-down" approach) was used to derive the BPM Expertise Model, as an a-priori attempt. An a-priori is defined as "prior to or independent of experience; contrasted with 'a posteriori' (empirical)". (Audi 2001, p. 35). A priori approach marks a distinct epistemic justification and derivative approach as well as a kind of proposition, knowledge, and argument, that is, the way the concept is acquired (Audi 2001). The initial topic of interest was identified based on the research topic (i.e., the experience, knowledge, abilities, and aptitude required in BPM). Theories, frameworks, and models related to the research topic were searched across analogous domains, and those that were related were borrowed and adapted in the derivation of the BPM expertise model presented in this paper. The primary literature disciplines chosen as representative of the core aspects of a-priori model-building are as per Table 1.

**Table 1** Mapping of literature domains to model constructs

| BPM expertise model construct | BPM expertise primary sub-construct | Corresponding literature domain |
|---|---|---|
| Living system | Living system-person (l-PER) | Autopoiesis |
| | Living system-organization (l-ORG) | Autopoiesis organizationational management |
| Knowledge | Explicit knowledge | Experience and expertise |
| | Tacit knowledge | Experience and expertise |
| Behavioral characteristics | Mind | Applied social science (counceling) experience and expertise |
| | Behavioral system | Applied social science (counceling) experience and expertise |
| | Spirit | Applied social science (counceling) Naturalistic decision making |
| Context | Context of the person (l-PER-C) | Developmental management |
| | Context of the organization (l-ORG-C) | BPM organizational management |
| Decision making | Situation awareness | Naturalistic decision making |
| | Decision | |
| | Action | |
| | Feedback | |

The literature domains, and why they were selected, are briefly described below. The constructs these descriptions refer to are introduced and described in the next section.

Autopoiesis: "This body of theory concerns the dynamics of living systems, purporting to answer the question "what is the characteristic organization of living systems?" The process of Autopoiesis lies at the heart of the answer" (Department of Computer Science University College London 2008). Autopoiesis was selected as it was considered to describe the living system construct, which was designed to capture the living nature of BPM expertise comprehensively; there is no other comparable theory.

Developmental Management: This domain covers literature relating to developmental management, which was chosen for the creation of the context of the individual person (I-PER-C) primary sub-construct as this provided a comprehensive view of the complete context of the person in a contextual setting. The context of the person cannot be separated from his/her professional context (BPM); therefore, this was a critical area to cover.

Organizational Management: this domain covers literature relating to organizational management, and was chosen to develop the external context of the organization (I-ORG-EC) secondary sub-construct, plus the Living System – Organization primary sub-construct. BPM cannot be separated from the organizational context in which it resides in, hence this is a critical area to include.

Experience and Expertise: this domain covers literature pertaining to experience and expertise, and was selected as expertise is at the core of the research problem, that is, to characterize BPM expertise.

Applied Social Science (Counseling): this domain covers literature relating to applied social science in the counseling field. The "contextualization of self" material was selected to develop the behavioral characteristics construct, as this was considered the most comprehensive approach to this part of the BPM expertise model.

Naturalistic Decision-Making (NDM): This domain covers material related to NDM, including situation awareness and mental model-building. This domain was chosen to develop the decision-making construct of the model, as it reflects the real world nature of decision making in the BPM environment.

BPM: this domain covers literature pertaining specifically to the context of BPM, and was selected because BPM is at the core of the research problem, that is, to characterize BPM expertise, and was used to develop the context of the organization (I-ORG-C) construct.

These key literature domains themselves were established upon identification of the research focus, and through review of associated literature areas. Hence, each element within the BPM expertise model originated from established theory from related disciplines, where they were iteratively integrated into the model, the goal being to build a BPM expertise model that was as complete and justifiable as possible.

The next sections present the elements of the BPM expertise model. The derived BPM expertise model is complex in nature, having a number of elements, which are

| Construct | Living System | Knowledge | Behavioural Characteristics | Context |
|---|---|---|---|---|
| Primary Sub-constructs | Organisation (I-ORG) | Explicit Knowledge | Mind | Context of the Organisation |
| | | | Behavioural System | |
| | Person (I-PER) | Tacit Knowledge | Spirit | Context of the Person |

**Fig. 1** Summary of model constructs and primary sub-constructs

represented and discussed throughout the remainder of this paper. First, it is important to introduce the terms used to depict these different model elements. The main elements (see Fig. 1) are referred to as "constructs." The secondary elements relating to the constructs are referred to as sub-constructs; these decompose the main constructs. A construct is a variable in a theory (adopted from Analytic Technologies 2008), a "higher-level abstraction from things that cannot be observed or illustrated by specific objects or events" (Ohio State University 2008). It is defined as "an abstract or general idea inferred or derived from specific instances" (Webster's Revised Unabridged Dictionary 1913; Princeton University 2008c). A sub-construct in this a-priori model is defined as "a part of the referenced construct" (Webster's Revised Unabridged Dictionary 1913).

## 2.1 *Constructs of the Model*

The Business Process Management Expertise model is depicted in Fig. 1 and its primary elements, the living system, knowledge, behavioral characteristics and context are presented below. Figure 1 depicts the model constructs, and their respective primary sub-constructs [for example, the primary sub-constructs of the living system construct, are the organization (I-ORG) and person (I-PER]. BPM expertise exists throughout the organization and goes beyond technical or functional IT knowledge, or just business knowledge; knowledge itself is only one part of the concept; thus it is a multi-dimensional concept.

### 2.1.1 Living System Construct

The living system is considered self-organizing, having the special characteristics of life and interacting with its environment (Miller 2008). It is defined in this context as "a composite unity whose organization can be described as a closed network of productions of components that through their interactions constitute the network of productions that produce them, and specify the networks extension by constituting boundaries in their domain of existence" (Maula 2006, p. 229). It is considered to be an autopoietic entity, and is a special case of organizationally closed autonomous systems. The living system construct is made up of two primary subconstructs; the individual person (I-PER) and individual organization (I-ORG).

BPM expertise exists at both the individual person and individual organization level. The concept of collective BPM expertise, as it relates to the organization, is akin to that of "collective mind" (Hakkarainen et al. 2004). Collective mind is "an approach that emphasizes how highly trained and experienced teams function as if of one single mind. This kind of collective mind has systemic characteristics that cannot be reduced to the sum of individual minds". (Hakkarainen et al. 2004, p. 242). Likewise collective BPM expertise cannot be reduced to the sum of individual minds and must be recognized at the organizational, as well as personal level.

The Living System – Person (I-PER) primary subconstruct represents the individual person as the entity where expertise resides. Expertise resides in people (Bereiter and Scardamalia 1993a, b), each person being an autopoietic entity (Maturana et al. 1992; Maula 2006).

The Living System – Organization (I-ORG) primary subconstruct represents the individual organization deploying BPM. The organization is also considered to be an autopoietic entity (Maula 2006), though it consists of many individual people which are also autopoietic entities in their own right. The organizational qualities arise or emerge as a result of the ongoing autopoiesis of the living system's biological components (people) of the organization (Department of Computer Science University College London 2008).

The living system concept is important to BPM expertise as it reflects aspects of the holistic entity deploying a BPM philosophy. An example is the ability of the organization to sense its surrounding environment and be aware of change in relevant contextual areas such as the task, industry, and macro environment (including economic, technical and social) aspects affecting BPM. Task environment items may include changes in the customer base and activities the specific organization carries out. Interactive processes and communication with the surrounding environment, both internal and external are crucial to disseminate BPM strategy and ensure that governance is occurring and effective, and that processes are optimal. Internal standards are important for BPM governance to be effective. Other aspects concerned with the living system entity from an organizational perspective include experimentation often necessary in BPM to develop new processes and ways of doing things, and information and communication systems. The living system also reflects the individual person working in the BPM environment; examples of individual people in BPM include employees, contractors, vendors, or customers. Prior relevant BPM experience in areas such as technology, process, governance, industry, and functional area are necessary to varying extents and are also reflected in the living system construct along with personal history relevant to BPM; it is considered to take 10 years on an average to become an expert in any domain. How the person functions overall as a living system affects his/her ability to function in the BPM environment; experience and knowing affect knowledge, interactions affect behavior as do behavioral domains, and language affects communication: an important aspect of BPM given positioning between the business and IT; these aspects are also reflected via the living system construct.

### 2.1.2 Knowledge Construct

Knowledge is defined in this context as "a blend of experience, values, information in context, and insight that forms a basis on which to build new experiences and information, or to achieve specific goals. It refers to the process of comprehending, comparing, judging, remembering, and reasoning. . . . is the uniquely human capability of interpreting and extracting meaning" (quantumiii 2008). Knowledge plays a central role in expertise (Bereiter and Scardamalia 1993a, b), regardless of the specific domain of expertise (Charness 1991; Bereiter and Scardamalia 1993a, b; Selinger and Crease 2006; Chi 2007). Knowledge is considered a key characteristic for two main reasons. Firstly, many other factors may contribute to BPM expertise but are not essential. Secondly, the behavioral characteristics only explain in part, how knowledge is acquired. "Knowledge is about beliefs and commitment, action, and meaning. Information and knowledge are context-specific and relational; they depend on situations and are created dynamically in social interaction among people" (Maula 2006, p. 66*).* "The conventional view of knowledge is not only limited as to what knowledge includes but it is also limited in its conception of how knowledge is acquired and how it works" (Bereiter and Scardamalia 1993a, b, p. 45). The knowledge construct of the a-priori model is considered to comprise two primary subconstructs, explicit knowledge and tacit knowledge (Audi 2001) as depicted in Fig. 1.

Within each of these primary subconstructs are secondary subconstructs. Explicit knowledge is considered to be made up of the three secondary subconstructs of declarative knowledge (Bereiter and Scardamalia, 1993a, b) which is concerned with "knowing about," explanatory knowledge (Kim 1994) which is concerned with "knowing why," and procedural knowledge (Cianciolo et al. 2007) which is concerned with "knowing how" (Bereiter and Scardamalia 1993a, b).

Declarative examples include formal knowledge considered to be "negotiable" knowledge in the sense that it arises through processes similar to negotiation, is something people can negotiate about, and "is negotiable in the sense that it can be transferred, exchanged, even purchased for money" (Bereiter and Scardamalia 1993a, b), plus "domain knowledge" which is the content of a particular field of knowledge.

Examples relating to procedural knowledge are skills and habit. Skills are the "ability to do something well, usually gained through training or experience," or "something that requires training and experience to do well, e.g., an art or trade" (Encarta.msn.com 2008c). Habit refers to a regularly repeated behavior pattern "an action or pattern of behavior that is repeated so often that it becomes typical of somebody, although he or she may be unaware of it." (Encarta.msn.com 2008a, 2008b, 2008c). In the BPM domain, these may be technical or process management skills and habits.

Explanatory knowledge is essentially metaphysics or science according to Aristotle, and is defined as "knowledge of why things are as they are" (Politis 2004, p. 33). It is concerned with "knowing why" (KRII 2008).

Explanatory knowledge samples include the work-domain knowledge type, which is necessary to understand increasingly complex phenomena in the background of modern society, to provide "a scientific understanding of the world (Beckham 1999)... It appears to constitute the core of work-domain knowledge (Vicente 1999) that has an essential role in mastering complex sociotechnical systems." (Hakkarainen et al. 2004, p. 21). It is knowledge that pertains directly to performing primary work such as a design engineers engineering knowledge, knowledge of systems, and procedures for performing design work.

Tacit knowledge is considered to be made up of informal knowledge (Bereiter and Scardamalia 1993a, b) such as common sense and promisingness, impressionistic knowledge such as judgement, trust (Platts and Leong 2006), and intuition (Bereiter and Scardamalia 1993a, b), and self regulatory knowledge such as self-knowledge, beliefs (Zimmerman 2007), and values.

Samples related to informal knowledge are common sense, which refers to "sound and prudent judgment based on a simple perception of the situation or facts" (Merriam Webster 2008a, b, c, d), and promisingness which refers to "a kind of judgement" (Bereiter and Scardamalia 1993a, b, p. 58), and depends on impressionistic knowledge, distinguishing creative from non-creative expertise (Bereiter and Scardamalia 1993a, b). According to Bereiter and Scardamalia (1993a, b), knowledge of promisingness can only come from "deep and long immersion in progressive problem solving within a domain" (Bereiter and Scardamalia 1993a, b, p. 235). Impressionistic knowledge samples are "judgement," which refers to a knowledgeable opinion (Merriam Webster 2008a, b, c, d), trust, which is concerned with reliance "based on past experience" and faith (wordreference.com 2008), and finally intuition, which is defined as "quick and ready insight; the power or faculty of attaining to direct knowledge or cognition without evident rational thought or inference" (Merriam Webster 2008c).

Self-knowledge refers to "knowledge of one's self, or of one's own character, powers, limitations" (selfknowledge.com 2008). A belief is considered to be a known in the subconscious, hence the relationship between belief and knowledge is subtle (wikipedia.org 2008) and is defined as "any cognitive content held as true" (Princeton 2008a, 2008b, 2008c, 2008d, 2008e). While believers in a claim often state they "know" something, philosophers distinguish between belief and knowledge. Values refers to "beliefs of a person or social group in which they have an emotional investment (either for or against something)" (Princeton 2008a, 2008b, 2008c, 2008d, 2008e), while "self-efficacy" refers *to* "perceptions about ones capabilities to organize and implement actions necessary to attain designated performance of skill for specific tasks."(Zimmerman 1989, p. 2)

Explicit knowledge of the internal and external context of the organization, as well as the individual people, in BPM is both essential and broad because of the inherent complexity of the BPM domain. Hence, explicit knowledge of many areas is required to varying extents. Explicit knowledge of the organization includes, but is not limited to the business itself (what is does) and includes geography, industry, company, all aspects of governance (including compliance and regulatory frameworks and procedures), business processes, associated technology such as ERP and BI systems, various business strategies plus the alignment and integration of those strategies, industry strategic direction, functional strategic direction such as key direction in the supply chain/logistics environment, plus the people that constitute the organization. Explicit knowledge of relevant external influences such as political, economic, technical, and socio-cultural is also necessary, as these have a direct bearing on the organization and the people working in the BPM environment. Explicit knowledge alone, however, does not make an expert; tacit knowledge is key to expertise in any domain delineating experts from nonexperts, and hence tacit knowledge of all the afore-mentioned areas is also necessary to varying extents in BPM expertise. Each type of explicit knowledge has a role to play in BPM expertise; declarative knowledge is concerned with knowing about aspects of BPM such as specific processes, governance, or associated technology. Explanatory knowledge is concerned with knowing why certain external organizational events are occurring, such as changes in economic circumstances, and how they will impact various aspects of the business and strategy. Procedural knowledge is concerned with knowing how, for example how specific technology works and the benefits it can yield for the business through process improvement. All aspects of tacit knowledge also have a role to play in BPM expertise. Informal knowledge of BPM areas such as processes and technology are no less important than formal knowledge of such areas. Impressions can be a valuable source of knowledge concerning less tangible aspects of BPM such as process attitudes, or values and beliefs. Self-regulatory knowledge is essential for anyone in the BPM field to manage themselves and therefore contribute in an optimal way to the organization and BPM field.

### 2.1.3 Behavioral Characteristics Construct

Behavior, is defined as "action or reaction of something under specified circumstances, the way a person behaves toward other people, the aggregate of the responses or reactions or movements made by an organism in any situation and [the] manner of acting or controlling yourself" (Princeton University 2008a, 2008b, 2008c, 2008d, 2008e) in this context. It too plays a central role in expertise regardless of the domain of expertise (Chi 2007; Feltovich et al. 2007; Hunt 2007). Expertise cannot be explained by knowledge alone. The behavioral characteristics component of expertise is key to understanding the utilization of knowledge and interaction with the environment in which the expertise occurs.

Thinking ability, practical sense (Cianciolo et al. 2007), and intuition (Haldin-Herrgard 2004) are key components of expertise (Bereiter and Scardamalia 1993a, b), and must therefore be acknowledged and reflected in a model of expertise. Given the importance of the people factor in BPM (Rosemann et al. 2005), which is the context of the a-priori model, behavior is undoubtedly considered a key aspect of BPM expertise, due to the behavioral characteristics of each person involved in BPM expertise. The behavioral characteristics construct of the a-priori model is made up of three primary sub-constructs. These are mind, the behavioral system, and spirit (Huitt 2003a, b).

The Mind is "the functioning of the brain to process information and control action in a flexible and adaptive manner" (Farthing 1992, p. 5). The mind is not a filing cabinet; it is impossible to understand the criticality of knowledge to expertise if this "filing cabinet" view is retained, akin to a cook having a well-stocked pantry; it does not say anything about how the cook actually cooks; the pantry is not the cook, and likewise the filing cabinet is not the expert (Bereiter and Scardamalia 1993a, b). The primary subconstruct mind is made up of the cognitive, conative, and affective secondary subconstructs (Huitt 2001). Examples of the cognitive secondary subconstruct include thinking, knowing, understanding, problem solving, mental resources, and reasoning (Huitt 2006). Examples of the cognitive secondary subconstruct include volition, will, intention, reason, and persistence (Huitt 1999), while examples of the affective secondary subconstruct include attitude, emotion, predisposition, and feelings (Huitt 2003a, b).

Behavioral System refers to *the* "Overt action of organism (output of the individual)" (Huitt 2003a, b). The output of the behavioral system is action and displayed behavior. Behavioral system theory recognizes that there is a feedback loop between overt responses (or "behavior") and resulting stimuli from the environment (Huitt 2003a, b).

Spirit is concerned with "How we approach the unknowns of life, how we define and relate to the sacred" (Huitt 2003a, b). One's view of spirituality has an important influence on one's values and self-concept (Huitt 2000).

An understanding of the various aspects of BPM such as the business, business processes, industry, company, governance, technology, and external factors, such as political, economic, socio-cultural environment, and technical environment, in relation to the organization and people within it is essential to BPM expertise. Thinking and problem-solving abilities are also required to deal with BPM challenges such as process design and implementation, or an appropriate governance approach and strategy for regulatory and compliance requirements such as SOX, IFRS, and GAAP. Ability and mental resources for problem solving are essential in the BPM, given the inherent problemsolving involved in many BPM activities. Sufficient cognitive complexity to handle problems and issues in the BPM domain is also necessary because of the complex and dynamic nature of the domain. Examples are changes to business processes to accommodate internal management reporting, overlaid with technical system, funding, and time constraints; changes to governance requirements can be complex, requiring implementation in a specific and often short timeframe. In BPM, there are often significant changes occurring in parallel in multiple areas, for example, changes to strategy in different functions (invoice to cash, record to report, or procure to pay) which are not always congruent; at the same time, complex governance changes may need to be addressed and therefore have to be understood in relation to the respective strategies and associated technology and processes. Persistence, a further behavioral characteristic, with problem-solving can be difficult in BPM because of ongoing complexity. BPM can require diplomacy because of the "dual" role between IT and the business, hence the need for professionalism. The ability to reason is also essential as many issues in BPM are not straight forward, requiring strong reasoning ability, particularly where conflicts in strategy, technical approach, funding, or timing occur.

Affective elements of behavior are also very important (emotion, attitude, disposition) because of the need to interface with many people in many different business areas, internally and externally, often with varying levels of knowledge and understanding, conflicting views, and priorities in the BPM field. Learning facilitates self-regulation, and is an important aspect of being "expert." It is crucial in BPM, even at nonexpert levels because of the constant change and new challenges and problems to be addressed, particularly in technology areas, and is therefore reflected in BPM expertise. Spirit is concerned with how unknowns of life are approached, and is important in BPM expertise as people working in BPM are constantly faced with unknowns and new situations; spirit relates to how these situations are approached. A person's view of spirituality has an important effect on his/her values and self-concept, which in turn affects how the person aligns with the BPM values of process and action orientation.

### 2.1.4 Context Construct

Context, is derived from the Latin term "contextere" meaning "weave together" (Brown 1993, p. 493; Encarta.msn.com, 2008a) and refers to "ambient conditions; a set of circumstances" (Brown 1993, p. 493), and is concerned with the surrounding facts, situation, and structure (Merriam Webster 2008a) as determining behavior. It is defined in this study as "the circumstances or events that form the environment within which something exists or takes place" (Encarta.msn.com 2008a) including interrelated conditions (Merriam Webster 2008b), and is identified as an important aspect of expertise due to the context dependency of expertise (Bereiter and Scardamalia 1993a, b; Chi 2007; Mieg 2007; Ward et al. 2007), along with other elements of expertise such as knowledge, behavioral characteristics, and the living system. These interrelated conditions, facts, and circumstances in which the expertise exists have a direct influence on the nature of the expertise. Hence explaining the context of the expertise (i.e., BPM) is crucial to the characterization of BPM expertise, as it is the circumstance and condition, (i.e., context), of the expertise being characterized.

Contextualism is also a necessary consideration in the development of the model due to the context-dependent nature of expertise; expertise is domain specific (Feltovich et al. 1997; LaFrance 1997; Sonnentag et al. 2007) and the influence of the BPM context. Context is concerned with the relationship between the entity, subject to the context, and the context itself. In the BPM expertise model, this "entity" is referred to, and represented by the living system construct, which resides in the BPM context. In order to understand the relationship between the living system and the context, it is first necessary to outline the context. For this purpose, the BPM context is described from two perspectives. The context construct is made up of two primary sub-constructs, the context of the organization and the context of the person, each of which is further divided into two secondary sub-constructs; the internal context of the organization (I-ORG-IC), the external context of the organization (I-ORG-EC), the internal context of the person (I-PER-IC), and the external context of the person (I-PER-EC).

The internal context of the living system describes the internal conditions, circumstances, and factors affecting the living system. In general, these factors are considered to be at least partially controllable by the living system itself as they are within the boundary of the living system, that is, the boundary of the organization (I-ORG) and the boundary of the person (I-PER). Different internal context factors are applicable to the Individual – Organization (I-ORG) and Individual – Person (I-PER), which describe the domain specific aspects of BPM for the organization and person respectively. Examples of factors affecting the internal context of the organization are strategic alignment, governance, technology, process methods, people, and culture (Rosemann et al. 2007). Examples of factors affecting the internal context of the person deployed in BPM include his/her consciousness, neurosensory system, mind, body, and emotion (Parikh 1999).

The external context describes the external factors affecting the living system. These factors are considered to be largely beyond the control of the living system, and are outside of the living system boundary. As with the internal context, different external context factors are applicable to the Individual – Organization (I-ORG) and Individual – Person (I-PER). Examples of factors affecting the external context of the organization include the task, industry, and macro environments (Morrison 1992) such as political factors, changes to the economy such as interest, taxation, and inflation rates, all of which affect BPM strategy. The external context of the person is affected by the external factors in which he is immersed, such as, the BPM organizational environment, societal, managerial, such as how the persons role is structured and position within the BPM organization, personal, and existential (Parikh 1999) factors.

## 2.2 Dynamic Nature of the Model

The recognition of the dynamic nature of the constructs of the BPM expertise model is important in characterizing BPM expertise, due to the inherently dynamic nature of expertise itself (Bereiter and Scardamalia 1993a, b), (Gasson 2005). The dynamic nature of each construct and its reciprocal interaction with the other constructs are also acknowledged. This study does not aim to complete an exhaustive study of the interactions between every combination of constructs; however, it does provide an overview of the dynamic nature of the constructs and their interactions, plus a discussion of two key cycles identified in BPM expertise: (1) knowledge flows (sensing and memory) (Maula 2006) and (2) learning. These cycles are also in constant motion, resulting in a continually changed state of BPM expertise.

### 2.2.1 Knowledge Flows

Through knowledge, we relate to ourselves and to our context. There is no "self" existing separate from our knowledge. "Past experience has made you what you are, and knowledge is an aspect of who you are." (Bereiter and Scardamalia 1993a, b, pp. 45–46). In recognizing expertise as a process, there is recognition of transactional activity and movement involved. Knowledge flows are applicable to both the person (I-PER) and organization (I-ORG). As a person draws on his/her sensing and perception of his/her environment plus his/her memory to draw knowledge and bring it to the person's decision making process, so does an organization through the collective sensing and memory of its constituent people.

In BPM, sensing helps the living system, whether an organization or person, to acquire, create, and improve knowledge in relevant areas such as process management and governance, and coordinates the person or organization (living system) with their internal and external environment. For example, sensing aids the coordination of the organization and its external economic factors such as exchange rate fluctuations or changes in industry direction. Both the individual person and organization have memory, comprising shared beliefs and norms affecting the BPM culture, memory of procedures such as BPM methods and processes, plus routines, scripts, and artifacts.

### 2.2.2 Learning

Learning refers to "the cognitive process of acquiring skill or knowledge" (Princeton University 2008d); "(1) the process of acquiring knowledge, attitudes, or skills from study, instruction, or experience. (2) the knowledge, attitudes, or skills acquired" (Australian Government; Department of Education 2008), and can be defined as "a change in the state of knowledge" (Maula 2006, p. 14) of either a person or an organization. It is based on the codification and diffusion of knowledge about objective reality, and is dependent on the continuous creation of conflicts between old and new knowledge (Maula 2006). The emphasis in BPM expertise is on knowledge and a change of state of that knowledge. As the knowledge construct interacts with the other model constructs, change is considered to occur in each of the other constructs resulting in a change in the overall state of BPM expertise.

Management and innovation literature considers learning to be an attempt to retain and improve competitiveness, productivity, and innovativeness. Overall learning for organizations is an integrative concept unifying various organizational levels of analysis: individual, group, and corporate (Maula 2006). "Learning is a dynamic concept that emphasizes the continually changing nature of organizations" (Maula 2006, p. 13). For both the person and the organization, learning can be regarded as a cyclic action starting from experience, and continuing through reflective observation, abstract conceptualization, and experimentation. However, the learning process itself is different at the individual person and organization levels (Maula 2006), as an organization is made up of several individual people each person undergoing his/her own learning process.

Each of the model constructs identified (living system, knowledge, behavioral characteristics, and context) are constantly changing; they are in motion to some degree and are not at any point completely static. The constructs also all interact with each other continually, thus compounding the overall degree of change in BPM expertise occurring.

# 3 Model Applicability

The primary applications of the BPM expertise model are professional education and development, human capital and talent management, business integration, and leadership and business decision making. In the field of professional education and development, the model can assist with developing an alternative understanding of learning in BPM. It can assist to understand what knowledge is required at certain BPM scenarios; by applying the detailed description of the knowledge construct (as per the BPM model presented). This provides both a high-level manageable view and a detailed, granular view of the actual knowledge required. The model can also be used to develop a greater understanding of what people do in their roles through explicit characterization of the BPM expertise involved and required. The approach to professional development in BPM must be continuous and integrated ongoing, opposed to ad hoc isolated training events. BPM expertise is a form of human capital and therefore of real value to the organization. It is an asset and must be managed as such; this can be achieved significantly more effectively through detailed characterization and management of the BPM expertise components required. The characterization of BPM expertise is also directly applicable to recruitment, employee placement, succession planning, and organizational restructuring where a deeper understanding of BPM expertise is required to manage these functions and processes effectively. Business integration, as in the case of mergers and acquisitions, involves the coming together of two or more organizations, and the combination of the BPM expertise of those organizations. In order to manage the transitional process, a deep understanding of the BPM expertise of the organizations pre- and postintegration is required, to develop transitional strategies and roadmaps. Business integration can occur internally too with the same detailed understanding of BPM expertise required, for example where companies are globalizing and merging organizations internally. Business integration, whether internal, or external through mergers and acquisitions, has horizontal as well as vertical structural implications, as the boundaries of operational, tactical, and strategic management layers are shifted in the formation of the end state BPM organization.

## 4 Summary

No known or published work has been done to establish the attributes characterizing Business Process Management expertise. This study's aim is to understand how the attributes of BPM expertise are described and defined, and to show how such details can be applied in practice for better BPM skills development, deployment, and overall BPM project success.

This chapter presents an a-priori BPM expertise model, which is the first attempt to characterize the concept of BPM Expertise. This a-priori model consists of four primary elements, namely living system, knowledge, behavioral characteristics, and context and is a first step toward defining and understanding expertise in a BPM context at both organizational and individual levels.

The presented a-priori model is not without its limitations. The study domain is essentially new, and primarily theory based. Research in BPM expertise is particularly immature; hence, there is not much to build on, but to borrow from analogous domains. This does not mean the study has no theoretical foundation; to the contrary it has a large theoretical foundation and has used a range of established frameworks, to derive and support the presented model. This study aims to characterize BPM expertise and validate that characterization, drawing heavily on referent domains to establish the initial set of candidate attributes and the dynamics and interrelationships thereof. The primary data collection, analysis, and synthesis were conducted by a single researcher, which can be prone to researcher bias. One of the potential limitations is the researcher's search for all possible pieces of literature related to the research focus. This can easily be influenced by the researchers' prior preconception and background. The range and volume of available literature available are vast and constantly changing. A review of literature of this nature can only be deemed complete, at a given point in time.

A number of further research tasks has already been planned to address these limitations and to extend the current research results. As explained earlier, this chapter is the preliminary results of the first phase, among a study design of three phases. This literature based a-priori model will be extended with further theories and concepts that capture the multilayered, dynamic nature of BPM expertise. The second phase of the study will validate the model with empirical evidence from case organizations, further re-specifying the model. In the final phase, detailed guidelines will be derived on how to apply the demystified concept of BPM expertise for the progress of BPM projects and tasks in organizations.

Practitioners can apply the study results across many contexts: professional education and development in BPM, human capital and talent management in BPM (and also for human resource strategy change), business discipline and governance development and deployment, and business integration, to name a few. Academia can apply this a-priori model for future research related to BPM expertise and expertise in general. The overall study outcomes can help derive a detailed research agenda for future research on BPM expertise which can assist in addressing some of the current gaps in the discipline. Further operationalizing the BPM expertise model; testing the relationships between the different constructs in the BPM expertise model and how they interact; testing the causality with other constructs and BPM expertise [as an independent variable (i.e., the relationship with BPM success) and a dependent variable (i.e., the relationship with constructs like effective training, employee motivation, and self-regulation)]; and deriving means of achieving BPM expertise are some examples of further research that can occur using the results of this study.

## References

Amoroso DL (1998) Developing a model to understand reengineering project success. IEEE, Los Alamitos, CA

Analytic Technologies (2008) Construct definition. Research Glossary Retrieved 20 November 2008, from http://www.analytictech.com/mb313/glossary.htm

Audi R (ed) (2001) The Cambridge dictionary of philosophy. Cambridge University Press, Cambridge

Australian Government; Department of Education, E. a. W. R. (2008) Learning definition. Retrieved 22 October, 2008, from http://www.dest.gov.au/sectors/training_skills/policy_issues_reviews/key_issues/nts/glo/ftol.htm#Glossary_-_L

Beckham TJ (1999) The current state of knowledge management. Knowledge management: Handbook. J. Leibowitz. Boca Raton, CRC. 1: pp 1–22

BPM Basics (2007) BPM toolkit. Retrieved 5 October, 2007, from http://www.bpmbasics.com/pdfs/bpmkit.pdf

Bereiter C, Scardamalia M (1993a) Surpassing ourselves; an inquiry into the nature and implications of expertise. Open Court Publishing Company, Chicago IL

Bereiter C, Scardamalia M (1993b) Surpassing ourselves: an inquiry into the nature and implications of expertise. Open Court, Chicago, IL

BPMEnterprise.com. Defining an enterprise business process architecture. Retrieved 14 January, 2008, from http://www.bpmenterprise.com/content/c070806a.asp

Brown L (ed) (1993) The new shorter Oxford English dictionary, vol 1. Oxford, Clarendon Press

Charness N (1991) Expertise in chess: the balance between knowledge and search. In: Ericsson KA, Smith J (eds) Toward a general theory of expertise. Cambridge University Press, Cambridge

Chi MTH (2007) Part I: Introduction and perspective, Chapter 2: Two approaches to the study of experts' characteristics. In: Ericsson KA, Charness N, Feltovich PJ, Hoffman RR (eds)

The Cambridge handbook of expertise and expert performance. Cambridge University Press, Cambridge
Cianciolo AT, Matthew C et al. (2007) Part VI: Generizable mechanisms mediating expertise and general issues, Chapter 35: Tacit knowledge, practical intelligence, and expertise. In: Ericsson KA, Charness N, Feltovich PJ, Hoffman RR (eds) The Cambridge handbook of expertise and expert performance. Cambridge University Press, Cambridge
Department of Computer Science University College London (2008) Autopoiesis. Retrieved 6 June, 2008, from http://www.cs.ucl.ac.uk/staff/t.quick/autopoiesis.html#related
de Bruin T (2008) BPM maturity. Queensland University of Technology, Brisbane, QLD
Encarta.msn.com (2008a) Context definition. Retrieved 28 November, 2008, from http://encarta.msn.com/dictionary_1861599909/context.html
Encarta.msn.com (2008b) Habit definition. Retrieved 11 June, 2008, from http://encarta.msn.com/dictionary_1861616026/habit.html
Encarta.msn.com. (2008c). Skill definition. Retrieved 10 June, 2008, from http://encarta.msn.com/dictionary_/skill.html
Eventful Management (2008) Masering SAP technologies 2009. Retrieved 20 December, 2008, from http://www.masteringsap.com/tech/features.php
Farthing GW (1992) The Pschology of Consciousness. Englewood Cliff, New Jersey, Apprentice Hall
Feltovich PJ, Ford KM et al. (eds) (1997) Expertise in context: human and machine. AAAI Press/The MIT Press, Menlo Park CA/Cambridge MA
Feltovich PJ, Prietula MJ et al. (2007) Part II: Overview of approaches to the study of expertise – brief historical accounts of theories and methods, Chapter 4: Studies of expertise from psychological perspectives. In: Ericsson KA, Charness N, Feltovich PJ, Hoffman RR (eds) The Cambridge handbook of expertise and expert performance. Cambridge University Press, Cambridge
Gartner (2008) Making the difference: The 2008 CIO agenda. EXPPremier Report Volume
Gasson S (2005) The dynamics of sensemaking, knowledge, and expertise in collaborative, boundary-spanning design. J Comput-Mediat Commun 10(4)
Grover V, Teng J et al. (1998) The influence of information technology diffusion and business process change on perceived productivity: The IS executive's perspective. Inf Manage 34:141–159
Hakkarainen KPJ, Palonen T et al. (eds) (2004) Communities of networked expertise: professional and educational perspectives (Advances in learning and instruction). Helsinki, Elsevier
Haldin-Herrgard T (2004) Diving under the surface of tacit knowledge. Department of Management and Organization, Swedish School of Economics and Business Administration, Vasa, Finland, p 21
Harris J (2007) Why is the exploration of the challenge of creating Business Process Experts important? Auckland University press, Auckland
Hill JB, Sinur J et al. (2006) Gartner's position on Business Process Management. Gartner Research reports, Gartner
Huitt W (1999) Conation as an important factor of mind. Retrieved 28 November, 2008, from http://chiron.valdosta.edu/whuitt/col/regsys/conation.html
Huitt W (2000) The spiritual nature of a human being. Retrieved 21 May, 2008, from http://chiron.valdosta.edu/whuitt/col/spiritual/spirit.html
Huitt W (2001). The mind. Retrieved 21 May, 2008, from http://chiron.valdosta.edu/whuitt/col/summary/mind.html
Huitt W (2003a) The affective system. Retrieved 21 May, 2008, from http://chiron.valdosta.edu/whuitt/col/affsys/affsys.html
Huitt W (2003b) A systems model of human behaviour. Retrieved 27 April, 2008, from http://chiron.valdosta.edu/whuitt/materials/sysmdlo.html
Huitt W (2006) The cognitive system. Retrieved 21 May, 2008, from http://chiron.valdosta.edu/whuitt/col/cogsys/cogsys.html

Hunt E (2007) Part I: Introduction and perspective, Chapter 3: Expertise, talent, and social encouragement. In: Ericsson KA, Charness N, Feltovich PJ, Hoffman RR (eds) The Cambridge handbook of expertise and expert performance. Cambridge, Cambridge University Press

Jeston J, Nelis J (2006) Business process management: practical guidelines to successful implementations. Butterworth-Heinemann, Oxford

Jeston J, Nelis J (2008) Business process management: practical guidelines to successful implementation. Butterworth-Heinemann, Oxford

Kim J (1994) Explnatory knowlege and metaphysical dependence. Philos Issues 5:51–69

Koch C (2001) BPR and ERP: realizing a vision of process with IT. Bus Process Manage J 7(3):258–265

KRII (2008) Work-domain definition. Retrieved 11 June, 2008, from http://www.krii.com/downloads/KM_glossary.pdf

LaFrance M (1997) Section II. Expertise in context, Chapter 7. Metaphors for expertise: how knowledge engineers picture human expertise. In: Feltovich PJ, Ford KM, Hoffman RR (eds) Expertise in context. MIT, Cambridge MA

Maturana P, Humberto R, Varela P, Francisco J (1992) The tree of knowledge. Shambhala, Boston, MA

Maula M (2006) Organizations as learning systems: "living composition" as an enabling infrastructure (Advanced series in management). Elsevier, Helsinki

Melenovsky MJ, Hill JB (2006) Role definition and organizational structure: business process improvement. G. R. Reports, Gartner

Merriam Webster Dictionary (2008a) Common sense definition. Retrieved 11 June, 2008, from http://mw1.m-w.com/dictionary/common%20sense

Merriam Webster Dictionary (2008b) Context definition. Retrieved 21 June, 2008, from http://www.merriam-webster.com/dictionary/context

Merriam Webster Dictionary (2008c) Intuition definition. Retrieved 11 June, 2008, from http://www.merriam-webster.com/dictionary/intuition

Merriam Webster Dictionary (2008d) Judgement definition. Retrieved 11 June, 2008, from http://www.merriam-webster.com/dictionary/judgment

Mieg HA (2007) Part VI: Generizable mechanisms mediating expertise and general issues, Chapter 41: Social and sociological factors in the development of expertise. In: Ericsson KA, Charness N, Feltovich PJ, Hoffman RR (eds) The Cambridge handbook of expertise and expert performance. Cambridge University Press, Cambridge

Miller JG (2008) The living systems theory. Retrieved 28 November, 2008, from http://www.newciv.org/ISSS_Primer/asem14ep.html

Morrison JL (1992) Environmental scanning. In: Whitely MA, Porter JD, Fenske RH (eds) A primer for new institutional researchers. The Association for Institutional Research, Tallahassee, FL, pp 86–99

Ohio State University (2008) Construct definition. Retrieved 20 November, 2008, from http://www.ag.ohio-state.edu/~aged885/Glossary/GLOSSARY.htm

Olding E, Rosser B (2007) Getting started With BPM, Part 3: Understanding critical success factors. G. R. Reports, Gartner

Parikh J (1999) Managing your self: management by detached involvement. Blackwell, Oxford

Pieterse J (2005) Enterprise design strategy: aligning IT & business practices. Retrieved 19 November, 2008, from http://it.toolbox.com/blogs/enterprise-design/will-bpm-be-the-backbone-of-enterprise-architecture-2926

Platts J, Leong YY (2006) Bio-manufacturing networks: linking creativity and trust. University of Cambridge, Cambridge, p 13

Politis V (2004) Chapter 2: Metaphysics as the ultimate explanations of all things Routledge Philosophy guidebook to aristotle and the metaphysics. New York, Routledge, pp 23–63

Princeton University (2008a) Behaviour definition. Retrieved 22 June, 2008, from http://wordnet.princeton.edu/perl/webwn?s=behaviour

Princeton University (2008b) Belief definition. Retrieved 19 December, 2008, from http://wordnetweb.princeton.edu/perl/webwn?s=belief
Princeton University (2008c) Construct definition. Retrieved 28 November, 2008, from http://wordnet.princeton.edu/perl/webwn?s=construct
Princeton University (2008d) Learning definition. Retrieved 22 October, 2008, from http://wordnet.princeton.edu/perl/webwn?s=learning
Princeton University (2008e) Values definition. Retrieved 9 December, 2008, from http://wordnet.princeton.edu/perl/webwn?s=values
quantumiii (2008) Knowledge definition. Retrieved 20 November, 2008, from http://www.quantum3.co.za/CI%20Glossary.htm
Raymond EM, Coleman HJ Jr et al. (1995) Key to success in cooperate redesign. Calif Manage Rev 37:128–145
Rosemann M, de Bruin T et al. (2005) A model to measure business process management maturity and improve performance. In: 13th European conference on information systems (ECIS 2005), Regensburg
Rosemann M, de Bruin T et al. (2007) Part III: BPM and the organizaiton, Chapter 27: BPM maturity. In: Jeston J, Nelis J (eds) Business process managment: practical guidelines to successful implementations. Butterworth-Heinemann, Oxford, pp 299–315
SAP (2008) SAP TechEd '08. Retrieved 20 December, 2008, from http://www.sapteched.com/usa/
selfknowledge.com (2008) Self-knowledge definition. Retrieved 11 June, 2008, from http://www.selfknowledge.com/86359.htm
Selinger E, Crease RP (2006) Part II: Expertise and practical knowledge, Chapter 7. Dreyfus on Expertise: the limits of phenomenological analysis. In: Selinger E, Crease RP (eds) The philosophy of expertise. Columbia University Press, New York
Sonnentag S, Niessen C et al. (2007) Part V: Professional domains, Part V.A: Professional domains, Chapter 21: Expertise in software design. In: Ericsson KA, Charness N, Feltovich PJ, Hoffman RR (eds) The Cambridge handbook of expertise and expert performance. Cambridge University Press, Cambridge
Stevens D (2007) Live from Gartner symposium ITxpo –The new business architecture: enterprise architecture and BPM Retrieved 19 November, 2008, from http://www.edmblog.com/weblog/2006/10/live_from_gartn_5.html
van der Aalst WMP, ter Hofstede AHM et al. (2003) Business process management: a survey. In: 1st International conference of business process management Eindhoven, the Netherlands
Verner L (2004) BPM: the promise and the challenge. DSP 2(1)
Vestey J (2006) Faces of exploration. Andre Deutsch, London
Vicente KJ (1999) Cognitive work analysis: Toward safe, productive, and healthy computer-based work. Mahwah, NJ Erlbaum
Ward P, Williams AM et al. (2007) Part III: Methods for studying the structure of expertise, Chapter 14: Simulation for performance and training. In: Ericsson KA, Charness N, Feltovich PJ, Hoffman RR (eds) The Cambridge handbook of expertise and expert performance. Cambridge University Press, Cambridge
Webster's Revised Unabridged Dictionary (1913) Construct definition. Retrieved 4 June, 2008, from http://dictionary.die.net/construct
Webster's Revised Unabridged Dictionary (1913) Subconstruct definition. Retrieved 4 June, 2008, from http://dictionary.die.net/sub
wikipedia.org (2008) Belief definition. Retrieved 11 June, 2008, from http://en.wikipedia.org/wiki/Beliefs
wordreference.com (2008) Trust definition. Retrieved 11 June, 2008, from http://www.wordreference.com/definition/trust
Zachman J (2007) The Zachman framework. Retrieved 14 January, 2008, from http://www.zifa.com/
Zimmerman BJ (1989) a social cognitive view of self-regulated academic learning. J Educ Psychol 81(3):23

Zimmerman BJ (2007) Part VI: Generizable mechanisms mediating expertise and general issues, Chapter 39: Development and adaptation of expertise: the role of self-regulatory processes and beliefs. In: Ericsson KA, Charness N, Feltovich PJ, Hoffman RR (eds) The Cambridge handbook of expertise and expert performance. Cambridge University Press, Cambridge
Zsambok CE, Klein G (eds) (1997) Naturalistic decision making. expertise: research and applications. Mahwah, NJ, Lawrence Erlbaum Associates, Publishers
zur Mühlen M (2008) Class notes: BPM research and education. BPTrends

# Business Process Management Curriculum

**Yvonne Lederer Antonucci**

**Abstract** As organizations continue to focus on improving and managing business processes, the ability to acquire and cultivate the appropriate skilled workforce has remained a challenge. While Business Process Management (BPM) was once defined in terms of tools and technologies, it has recently emerged as a discipline encompassing a broad spectrum of organizational practices. As a result, the skill-sets for BPM endeavors of today's organizations have gone beyond the automation of processes to encompass a wide variety of strategic, technical, and people skills that are difficult to find in today's professionals. Many organizations have assigned the process transformation leadership to existing business analysts who find that they require additional training and education. This chapter reviews the role of a business analyst within the context of BPM practice and suggests a curriculum designed to cultivate skills for the emerging business process (BP) analyst.

## 1 Introduction

Business Process Management (BPM) practices continue to gain attention and adoption by organizations worldwide. The focus on well-defined processes across entire value chains marks the beginning of organizational success. However, the key to sustaining that success lies in the ability to create value through effectively managing, orchestrating, communicating, and transforming business processes across the organization. These efforts require a plethora of skills and abilities that many organizations find difficult to fill and cultivate (Antonucci 2006; Hadfield

Y.L. Antonucci
SAP/IDS Scheer Business Process Innovation Center of Excellence, School of Business, Widener University, Chester, PA, USA
e-mail: yantonucci@widener.edu

J. vom Brocke and M. Rosemann (eds.), *Handbook on Business Process Management 2*, International Handbooks on Information Systems,
DOI 10.1007/978-3-642-01982-1_20, 

2007; Hill et al. 2006). This has given rise to interest in and need for a BPM curriculum that addresses the cultivation of the business process (BP) professional.

In response to the shortage of BPM training and education, several professional organizations, such as ABPMP, BPTrends, and BPMInstitute, along with a few companies, such as SAP AG, have introduced BPM certifications (sap.bpx.com; abpmp.org; bptrends.org, bpmi.org). In the year 2008, ABPMP introduced a general model curriculum for BPM professionals representing the first attempt to define comprehensive education requirements for the BPM practice (ABPMP Education 2008). As the BP discipline continues to change, the need for effective BP professionals has intensified. Consequently, in an effort to respond to industry interests and needs, an increase in BPM corporate training and university education programs has emerged with variations of business and information technology (IT) focus and coverage. While BPM was once defined in terms of tools and technologies, it has recently emerged as a discipline encompassing a broad spectrum of organizational practices (Hill et al. 2006). The current practices of BPM have broadened in scope from the business process reengineering (BPR) initial goals of achieving performance breakthroughs through eliminating nonvalue-added operational process steps (Khalil 1997) to integrating both IT and business practices (Hill et al. 2006). A global effort to define BPM certification requirements based on these current practices of BPM has emerged with joint efforts and partnerships between industry professional groups and universities. Several of these efforts have resulted in the deployment of a common BPM training (BPTrends.org, butrain.com, BPMInstitute.org), providing some direction toward BPM certification and education. Several universities have included BPM content in a limited number of courses, with others merely adding process topics to existing information systems courses or attempting to cover many BPM topics in one course. Very few universities offer a comprehensive curriculum coverage of BPM practices from both the business and IT perspectives that embody the wide variety of strategic, technical, and people skills required for BPM success (Fingar 2006). A majority of the current BPM training and education offerings are on-site or are deployed using a blend of online methods with prearranged "face-to-face" meetings either on-site or via online meetings.

As organizations continue to focus on improving and managing business processes, the ability to acquire and cultivate the appropriate skilled workforce has remained a challenge.

Consequently, several organizations have assigned the process transformation leadership to existing business analysts expecting that these analysts would have the required BPM knowledge[1] (Bandara et al. 2007). This chapter reviews the role of a business analyst within the context of BPM practice and outlines a curriculum designed to cultivate skills for the emerging BP analyst. The objective for this curriculum is to provide a guideline for both individuals interested in furthering

---

[1]Kokkonen and Bandara (2010) delve into this topic by exploring what it takes to develop BPM expertise.

their BPM knowledge, and for program designers to develop a basic common body of knowledge for BPM. This curriculum is based on industry practices and skill needs of BPM professionals (Melenovsky and Hill 2006), the efforts of ABPMP (ABPMP Education 2008), and several current offerings of BPM curriculum by both industry (BPMInstitute.org; BPTrends.org) and universities (howe.stevens.edu; QUT.edu.au; widener.edu). Individuals may use this to help them identify appropriate BPM training and education offerings. This will also benefit educational institutions and industry training programs by providing a standard for developing their own curriculum.

The required skill-set for BPM practice includes a wide variety of strategic, technical, and people skills that encompasses both business and IT knowledge. Before an organization can obtain or develop a skilled BP workforce, they must understand the required activities for BPM success, followed by the identification and alignment of appropriate roles and positions. The next section identifies the current tasks associated with BP analysts engaged in BPM practice. Using these identified tasks, a curriculum for BP analysts is presented.

## 2 Understanding the Role of Business Process Analyst in Current Business Process Management Practice

There have been many attempts to categorize the tasks associated with BPM practices (Paim et al. 2008). Most of these studies are based on the activities and transformation practices required in BPM practice. Several recognized variations of BPM practice life-cycles exist with a majority including (1) process planning and strategy used to direct (2) analysis, design, and modeling of business processes, that drives the (3) configuration of business processes, leading to the implementation of processes and (4) process execution, creating processes instances that can then be (5) monitored and controlled, providing (6) feedback for process refinement and continued process performance analysis, leading to additional (7) analysis, design, modeling, and so forth as depicted in Fig. 1. In addition, studies have identified

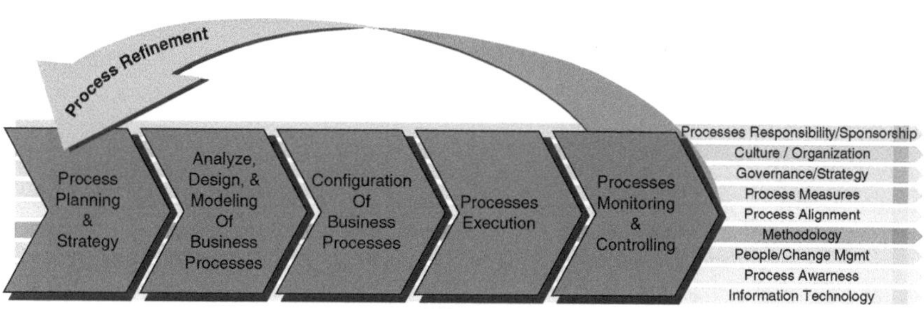


**Fig. 1** BPM practice life-cycle and threaded success factors

successful BPM practices that need to be supported by simultaneous management activities throughout the life-cycle while maintaining balance and integration of process initiatives between business and IT (DeFee and Harmon 2004; Dreiling et al. 2005; Fisher 2004; Hammer 2007; Rummler and Brache 2004). Figure 1 illustrates some of these management activities such as establishing appropriate process responsibility, sponsorship, governance, and process measures.[2] Appropriately defined BP positions are needed to correspond to these interacting practices and activities.

The most comprehensive effort at identifying BP positions and tasks has been led by practitioners. Melenovsky and Hill (2006) defined BP positions and their associated tasks for both business and IT. Based on the best industrial practices of four leading organizations, they defined four key BP positions: (1) BP director; (2) BP consultant; (3) BP architect; and (4) BP analyst. Each of these positions was further described and associated with primary tasks and titles (roles) (Melenovsky and Hill 2006). The validity of these role definitions and reported activities of each role are in question as the study only involved four organizations. A recent study was able to validate these tasks and positions, finding significant agreement from 111 BP professionals in addition to verifying that the reported activities were assigned to the appropriate positions (Antonucci and Goeke 2009). While there still needs to be further studies to identify and verify the appropriate activities for BP positions, these roles and activities are used as a basis for the proposed curriculum.

According to Melenovsky and Hill (2006), the BP director, BP architect, and BP consultant are higher-level positions primarily supporting strategic activities, whereas the BP analyst has an operational focus relating closely to the daily support of BPM practices. Table 1 summarizes this BP analyst position description and activities, listing the current titles in columns 1 and 2 as noted by Melenovsky and Hill (2006). Further analysis of the BP analyst position description and activities identified in process maturity studies (Hammer 2007) revealed skills and knowledge areas required for each activity as indicated in column 3 of Table 1.

These activities indicate that the BP analyst does in fact require a plethora of skills. These skills involve both management and IT knowledge as they relate to business processes with significant communication ability. As a result, the following section suggests a BPM curriculum designed to cultivate an effective BP analyst for the twenty-first century.

[2]Hammer (2010) provides a general discussion on what Business Process Management is about and what BPM activities should be generally considered. Burlton (2010) provides a methodological framework and demonstrates how these high-level activities should be broken down into more fine-grained BPM activities in order to successfully implement business strategies by means of BPM. To account for the governance aspects of BPM, Markus and Jacobson (2010) and Spanyi (2010) provide a general introduction into governance in BPM.

**Table 1** BP analyst position required skills and knowledge areas summary

| | Business process analyst | Knowledge area indicates need: |
|---|---|---|
| Position description | • Deals with tactical day-to-day aspects of discovering, validating, documenting, and communicating business process-related knowledge through modeling, simulating, and analyzing current and future states; | • To understand business<br>• To communicate to both business and IT -level personnel<br>• To model end-to-end processes<br>• To communicate end-to-end processes<br>• To analyze business processes<br>• To be able to assign appropriate measures to processes |
| | • Ensures that changes to process environment are carried out; | • To work with IT to ensure that technology infrastructure is aligned for process changes [technical knowledge]<br>• To communicate with business and IT areas of organization the process changes and reasons for the change[relationship management, communication]<br>• To help business process participants understand and accept changes<br>• To understand how to deploy effective change management and change implementation methods |
| | • Reports to process owner and IT development department. | • For communication skills<br>• For IT knowledge<br>• To understand business relationships<br>• To understand the integration of IT and business |
| Activities | • Document business processes through modeling; | • To understand process modeling techniques<br>• To have ability to document end-to-end processes |
| | • Demonstrate to process owner the opportunities for best in class process orchestration and control; | • To understand end-to-end process integration<br>• To identify potential improvements to business processes<br>• To identify and design process controls<br>• For communication ability of process and technical knowledge to both technical and nontechnical managers |
| | • Liaison or relationship manager between business community and departments; | • For collaboration and negotiation ability concerning the communication of business process potential and operations across the organization |

(*continued*)

Table 1 (continued)

| | Business process analyst | Knowledge area indicates need: |
|---|---|---|
| | | • To be able to work in and with teams |
| | • Perform continuous reviews to align process orchestration with changing business conditions; | • For understanding of end-to-end business processes<br>• To monitor, control, and change business processes<br>• For ability to identify when processes need changing and propose improvements |
| | • Maintain and share process knowledge; | • To understand how to maintain a process repository<br>• To understand how to communicate business processes across the organization<br>• To understand how to make business processes visible across the organization<br>• To cultivate and maintain a shared vision and understanding of business processes across the organization. |
| | • Show process stakeholders how to identify and solve process challenges, analyze performance metrics; | • To understand how to measure and analyze business processes<br>• To identify key metrics of processes for performance analysis<br>• To transform business processes using process performance techniques |
| | • Ensure coordination between IT organization and process owners. | • To understand how to model and communicate various views of business processes to include both business and IT views.<br>• To understand the integration of IT and business within a business process. |
| Current titles | • Business analyst<br>• Process and data manager<br>• Analyst<br>• Systems analyst<br>• Process engineer<br>• Process developer<br>• Process analyst<br>• Lead analyst<br>• Senior advisor<br>• Process designer | |

## 3 Business Process Analyst Curriculum Description

The following proposed curriculum is designed to cultivate the skills and activities required of BP analysts during BPM practice as depicted in Fig. 1. While the model BPM curriculum efforts of ABPMP (ABPMP Education 2008) provided an initial framework for this curriculum, industry research findings of BP analyst roles and positions along with several current offerings of BPM curriculum by both industry and universities were used to identify the resulting curriculum. This curriculum provides assistance to organizations in developing an educated staff that understands the holistic nature of BPM for successful BP transformation. Individuals from both business and technical areas of the organization can use this curriculum to identify skills needed to strengthen their knowledge of BPM practices. Colleges and universities have a consistent challenge of remaining competitive in light of business practice changes; this curriculum serves as a framework to help develop comprehensive BPM programs.

Figure 2 represents a depiction of the general courses and a suggested sequence. The first course in the curriculum, BPM foundations (BP00), is recommended for all participants whether they are in an industry training program or college course. Regardless of the program scope, this first course should be a prerequisite for all other courses. The next level of courses represents the primary practices of the BPM life-cycle; this includes process planning, strategy, and governance (BP01); process analysis (BP03); process modeling (BP02); process design (BP04); process

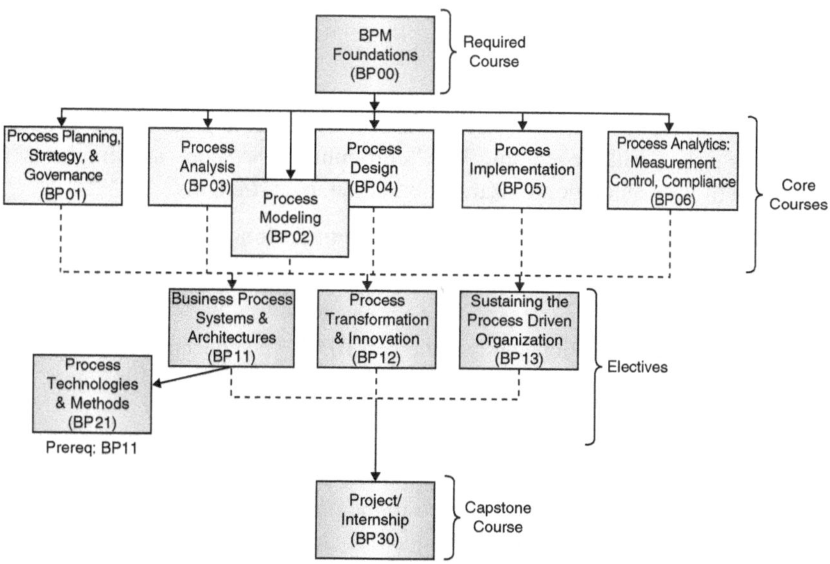


**Fig. 2** General BPM course sequence

implementation (BP05); and process analytics, measurement, control, and compliance (BP06). BP01 is included as a core course due to its importance for BPM practice success. The recent emphasis on process analytics throughout the BPM life-cycle is the primary reason for a core course on BP06. It is recommended that the BP analyst understands how to accomplish and manage the activities of this life-cycle. For this reason, these courses are recommended as core courses for the BPM curriculum. The third level of courses described in Fig. 2 represents advanced topics for both IT and management related to the deployment and management of BPM. These courses include business process systems and architectures (BP11); process transformation and innovation (BP12); and sustaining the process-driven organization (BP13). While these three courses involve activities typically carried out by higher-level BP positions (as in BP12 and BP13) or more technical positions (as in BP11), it is recommended that the BP analysts further their knowledge in these areas. For this reason, these courses are recommended as electives. Similar to the ABPMP BPM model curriculum, the project or internship course (BP30) is recommended as a capstone course to allow the participants opportunity to apply their newly obtained knowledge of BPM practice. There are several other advanced courses that can be added to the list of electives such as the one depicted in Fig. 2, that is, process technologies and methods (BP21). These advanced courses can be a continuation of other courses listed such as advanced process modeling. The following section provides a detailed list of these courses, their descriptions, learning objectives, and suggested topics.

The integration of business and IT practices that are embedded into this proposed curriculum has merit for enhancing existing MBA programs. Several of these courses could be extracted to create a BPM track with the existing MBA.

## 3.1 Course Descriptions

The course descriptions in this section are intended as a guide to be used by individuals tasked with developing BPM curriculum. The scope and emphasis of coverage will vary among organizations based on their strengths.

**BP00 – Business Process Management Foundations: General Overview and Principles**

*Description*:
This course is an introduction and overview of BPM. The concepts, fundamentals, methods, and strategies required for managing holistic end-to-end business processes are introduced.
*Intended Audience*:
This course is recommended for all BP roles. This course is a foundation for concepts, terminology, and issues related to the practice and sustainment of BPM, providing a common language for subsequent courses. It is recommended for those who are new to BPM or have had little exposure to BPM practices in recent years.

*Learning Objectives*:

- Understand the principles of a process and various process types
- Understand the basic concepts and issues of BPM
- Understand the criticality and centrality of BPs as a value driver
- Understand a distinction between process-oriented, process-centric, and process-driven organizations
- Understand the roles process management, strategy, change management, process analysis, process redesign, process improvement, process architectures, and BPM systems in BPM practices
- Understand BPM best practices and methodologies
- Understand the principles of process management
- Understand the BPM maturity factors and levels
- Understand basic BPM management and measurement techniques
- Understand the issues, risks, and success factors of BPM practices

*Suggested Topics*:

- Introduction and overview of BPM: Understanding BPM topics, terms, and issues
  - What is a process? Process versus function
  - What is a BP?
  - What is BPM?
  - What is the value of BPM to an organization? Benefits?
  - What is a BPM system?
  - Who are the BPM players in the market?
  - What is meant by "a Process-Centric Organization"?
  - What is business process automation?
  - What are business rules?
  - What are the management issues and success factors involved with BPM?
  - Examination of process performance controls and metrics
- Introduction to BPM practices and success factors
  - Where Do You Start? Understanding the BPM practice
  - Identifying end-to-end processes in an organization
  - Levels of BPM maturity and factors
  - What is a process audit and how is it used?
- Principles of Process Management
  - What is involved in developing a BPM strategy – an overview
  - Identifying stakeholders and process owners
  - The role of a process governance system
  - The importance of change management in BPM – people issues
  - Process management and project management
- Process Implementation Issues
  - Risk factors in BPM
  - Standards
  - Developing frameworks for BPM
  - Introduction to systems, architectures, tools, and trends

- Implementation Issues
- Overview of organizational roles and responsibilities involved in BPM

## BP01 – Process Planning, Strategy, and Governance

*Description*:
Organizations strive to create value for its customers through optimal performance of end-to-end business processes. These processes determine how the organization designs, makes, sells, delivers, and services its products and services. This course overviews strategies and methods of managing and governing business processes.
*Intended Audience*:
The BP director, BP consultant, and BP architect are highly recommended to take this course as their primary activity is supporting strategic activities. The BP analyst should have the knowledge of the topics in this course in order to effectively design and deploy processes within the strategic framework of the organization.
*Learning Objectives*:

- Understand the process-driven organization; strategy, leadership, management, and governance structure
- Identify how the strategy, structure, culture, governance system, human resource management system, and the IT need to be aligned.
- Understand how to align processes with corporate strategy
- Identify and understand the need for a BPM Governance Board to oversee the process transition
- Understand the fundamental differences between managing functions and managing processes
- Develop the process vision
- Align business and IT goals
- Fundamentals of team building and leadership for process teams. Specific communication, coordination, and collaboration issues are addressed.
- Identify and deploy appropriate project management methods for managing process initiatives
- Understand the organizational issues in BPM
- Understand the customer focused process
- Understand how to link corporate strategy to business processes
- Understand how to develop a business case for BPM deployment.

*Suggested Topics*:

- Overview of BPM strategic issues
- Understanding process management value
- Understanding and developing a process-centric organization; formulating a process vision
- Business process strategy formulation
- Considerations of a process-based approach to BP change management
- Strategic, tactical, and operational considerations in a BPM framework
- How to plan for cross-organization acceptance and implementation

- Process management frameworks
- Partnerships and business process outsourcing
- The process-oriented organization
- Process ownership and stewardship
- Process-oriented roles and responsibilities
  - Leadership and communication skills for the process manager
- Strategic planning for process change
- Understanding process improvement
- Six Sigma, Scorecard, and other techniques
- Understanding and planning for BPM Key Performance Indicator (KPIs) (knowing what and where to measure)

### 3.1.1 Business Process Modeling, Analysis, and Design

The development of successful end-to-end business processes involves techniques analyzing and designing processes supported by BP modeling methods. As such, the following three courses can be combined into one or two courses depending on the focus of the desired program. If the courses are combined, it is recommended that an advanced process analysis, modeling, and design course be added to the curriculum to dive deeper into the techniques.

**GP02 – Process Modeling**

*Description*:
Process modeling should occur at various stages of the BPM practice cycle and also at various levels of detail. This course introduces current BP modeling methods and techniques practiced today. Models for both the business and IT professional are presented and explained. There is an emphasis on graphical models to document existing and renewed processes. Several popular modeling techniques are explained and used including Business Process Modeling Notation (BPMN).
*Intended Audience*:
This course is recommended for the BP analyst, BP architect, and BP consultant. It is recommended for anyone desiring to model and/or document business processes.
*Learning Objectives*:

- Recognize the importance and benefits of process modeling
- Understand how to develop a common language for describing business processes
- How to model business processes using BPMN notation for analyzing current processes and designing an improved process
- Understand other process modeling methods such as Swimlanes and Event Driven Process Chains (EPC)
- Understand how to model the Enterprise Business Architecture using methods of process decomposition and mapping to include several sub-process levels and various organizational views, including the business, process, technology, and data models

*Suggested Topics*:

- What is BP modeling?
- What is a model? What are the benefits to modeling?
- What Does It Represent?
- Physical/logical/essential models
- Process modeling techniques and methods
  - BPMN
  - Swimlanes
  - EPC
- Developing a common language throughout the organization
- Types of process model views: Business, IT, and data
- levels of process models
- Process decomposition and process mapping

**BP03 – Process Analysis**

*Description*:

This course is an introduction to the skills and techniques required to analyze current business processes and identify improvement potentials for effective and efficient processes. There is an emphasis on the process analysis techniques and tools required to improve process performance. This involves the documentation of the current process in order to identify opportunities for process change and utilize measurement techniques for evaluating outcomes. This course overviews various process analysis methods for all levels of the organization. Appropriate process modeling techniques are explained and aligned with process analyses.

*Intended Audience*:

This course is recommended for all BP roles. It is recommended for those who want to learn how to analyze and discover organizational processes.

*Learning Objectives*:

- Recognize the importance and benefits of process modeling
- Understand to identify how related business activities are classified as processes
- Understand and utilize process analysis methods and activities that evaluate end-to-end enterprise processes
- Understand and utilize available best practices for identifying processes along with understanding the value of reference models as process blueprints for assisting with a process definition
- Build a business case
- Develop the ability to analyze business processes

*Suggested Topics*:

- Process and project scoping
- Process efficiency and effectiveness
- Role of process metrics in process analysis
- Process thinking and reengineering
- Mapping existing process understanding
- Understanding process modeling techniques for analysis

- Concept of decomposition models
- Architecting your processes and aligning them to organizational strategy
- Designing the AS-IS process model for analysis
- Building a business case for process improvement

## BP04 – Process Design

*Description*:
This course is an introduction to the skills and techniques required to design new processes or to redesign and improve existing processes. There is an emphasis on BP design techniques and methods required to improve performance. Modeling methods are used to scope and document the renewed process.
*Intended Audience*:
This course is recommended for the BP analyst, BP architect, and BP consultant.
*Learning Objectives*:
- Design and model the renewed process
- Develop an improved process model to implementation level that includes all views of the enterprise architecture
- Consider the integration of business rules with the renewed process

*Suggested Topics*:
- Understanding various process modeling tools and techniques in the market
- Benchmarking processes
- Understanding process modeling techniques for design and implementation
- Designing and modeling the renewed process (TO-BE)

## BP05 – Process Implementation

*Description*:
BP implementation is the bridge between design and execution. This course is designed to help the participant understand the issues and procedures necessary to implement a renewed process design into a set of documented, tested, and operational sub-processes and workflows. Various enabling technologies for BPM are introduced along with the techniques for process automation. Management issues associated with process automation are examined such as change management.
*Intended Audience*:
This course is recommended for the BP analyst and BP consultant.
*Learning Objectives*:
- Understand the basic information systems and technologies required to enable a BPM implementation
- Understand the process automation techniques and practices
- Develop knowledge regarding process automation
- Understand how to link a process design to process execution
- Utilize a workflow management system or BPM system to implement the renewed process
- Understand the management issues associated with process automation

*Suggested Topics*:
- Understanding the implementation phase
- Deploying BPM
- Process automation
- Understand BPM best practices and methodologies
- BPM reporting and monitoring
- Preparing for business testing
- Developing rollout plans
- Implementing changes
- Managing BP change

**BP06 – Process Analytics: Measurement, Control, and Compliance**

*Description*:
The monitoring, controlling, and compliance of automated processes are critical to process improvement. In addition, the appropriate use and understanding of real-time analytics can significantly improve and dynamically manage business processes. This course explores performance monitoring and analyzes methods of business processes in order to uncover potential problems, making continuous process improvement and regulatory compliance possible. The goals of adaptability and agility can only be attained if processes and products are measured, monitored, and analyzed. Various types and methods of analytics are emphasized.
*Intended Audience*:
This course is recommended for all BP roles.

*Learning Objectives*:
- Identify types of process metrics
- Understand and deploy the alignment of process metrics with process strategy and models
- Understand methods of metrics analysis
- Identify relevant reference models
- Understand balanced scorecards
- Understand business activity monitoring (BAM) techniques
- Understand methods of measuring process maturity
- Design and utilize dashboards and mash-ups as reporting tools
- Understand how to use business intelligence as the basis for reporting and analysis of business processes
- Understand methods of process control
- Understand the role of process monitoring in compliance with regulations

*Suggested Topics*:
- Overview of the importance of process performance measurement in formulating and attaining operational and strategic goals
- Deploying a process improvement strategy

- Performance measurement and management techniques
  - Use of reference models for best practices and KPIs: Supply Chain Operation Reference-Modell (SCOR), American Productivity & Quality Center (APQC), Capability Maturity Model Integration (CMMI)
- Measuring process maturity – the process audit
- Types of quantitative and statistical techniques in business intelligence, simulation, and forecasting
- Operational metrics for business processes
- The link to strategic key performance indicators
- Issues involved in measuring, monitoring, and controlling inter-organizational processes
- Measuring performance and designing of a performance management system
- Designing and implementing BPM key performance indicators
- Process managing and monitoring
- Understanding and developing balanced scorecards
- BAM
- Measurement, diagnosis, and improvement
- Technologies for process analytics
  - Dash boards and mash-ups
- Types of analytics:
  - Reporting or business analytics – utilization of historical information for reporting
  - Data mining analytics – data trend analysis
  - Predictive analytics – determining future decisions and actions based on trend analysis
- Business rules and process analytics

## BP11 – Business Process Systems and Architectures

*Description*:
Several BPM technologies, systems, and tools have emerged in the market in recent years. This course examines these various BPM technologies, information technologies, systems, tools, and architectures in supporting business processes.
*Intended Audience*:
This course is recommended for the BP analyst, BP consultant, and IT architects.
*Learning Objectives*:

- Have a basic understanding the types of BPM systems.
- Understand integration and interoperability issues among intra- and inter-organizational business processes.
- Develop an understanding of Workflow Management Systems
- Understand the current BPM technology architectures and standards
- Understand the role of Enterprise Services Architecture and Service-Oriented Architecture for BPM enablement

*Suggested Topics*:

- Evaluate BPM software and BPM suites
- Overviews of the types of BPM systems
- BPMS and Workflow Management Systems
- Integration and interoperability of intra- and inter-organizational processes
- Introduction to the BPM technology architectures and standards
- The role of Enterprise Services Architecture and Service-Oriented Architecture for BPM enablement
- BPM tools and trends

## BP12 – Process Transformation and Innovation

*Description:*
The primary focus of the course is on the integration of BP-based knowledge and skills for creating a holistic understanding and application of process innovation strategy and methods for organizational process transformation. This course aims to equip students with the state-of-the-art theory and techniques in business process strategy and innovation in order to increase successful participation in transforming traditional business processes into innovative business processes and managing it.
*Intended Audience*:
This course is highly recommended for the BP director, BP architect, and BP consultant. It is also recommended for the BP analysts in order to further their knowledge in these areas.
*Learning Objectives*:

- Be able to apply continuous improvement techniques such a Lean and Six Sigma to process initiatives.
- Understand and apply simulation techniques to process transformation
- Understand the role of BPM innovation in achieving organizational strategy
- Be able to analyze current organizational BPM maturity, identify maturity state goals of organization, and develop a transition plan for achievement.

*Suggested Topics*:

- Continuous improvement techniques for process transformation
  - Lean, SixSigma
- Process Simulation
- BPM innovation methods
  - Organizational strategy achievement through process innovation
- Develop a process transition plan for improvement

## BP13 – Sustaining the Process-Driven Organization

*Description*:
Once the organization has been able to achieve process transformation, the organization faces the challenge of sustaining the process-driven state. The key to long-term benefits from BPM is the ability to build a process-awareness culture coupled with long-term transformation practices in order to sustain the competitive

advantage of a process-driven organization. This course introduces the methods, strategies, and techniques currently used in successful BPM practices for sustainment.

*Intended Audience*:
This course is highly recommended for the BP director, BP architect, and BP consultant. It is also recommended for the BP analysts in order to further their knowledge in these areas.
*Learning Objectives*:

- Understand the critical aspects an organization needs to sustain the benefits of BPM over time
- Understand the role of process agility in sustainment
- Be able to analyze and deploy appropriate change management methods – people in the process
- Understand techniques and strategies for building a process-awareness culture
- Understand how to achieve business process communities of practice throughout the organization
- Understand methods for technology change implementations
- Identify the potential for business process outsourcing
- Understand methods and techniques to develop and cultivate appropriate process skills and positions

*Suggested Topics*:

- Reviewing success and risk factors in BPM practices, implications for sustainment
- Building organizational communities of practice
- Deploying change management practices
- Methods for building a process-awareness culture
- Preparing and implementing process change methods for enabling technologies and systems
- How do you know when you have achieved process agility?
- Understanding and identifying the potential for BP outsourcing to improve process performance
- Developing and cultivating appropriate process skills and positions
- Development of a process sustainment plan

Project or Internship:
A BP project or internship is recommended after a student has completed the BPM coursework in order to apply and practice his/her newly acquired BPM practice knowledge.

### 3.1.2 Additional Advanced Courses and Proposed Tracks

The proposed curriculum strives to integrate the business and technology aspects of BPM practices. Depending on the focus and emphasis of the desired program, advanced courses and additional courses may be included in the curriculum. One area for advanced course work would be in the area of technologies and methods as described in the following paragraphs. The addition of an advanced process analysis, design, and modeling course would be a consideration of a program designed to enforce these practices. Additional business focused courses related to BPM practices could include change management or project management as they apply to BPM.

**BP21 – Process Technologies and Methods (advanced course)**
*Description*:
This is an advanced course that investigates process technologies, systems, and methods in more depth. This course focuses on the technical and implementation aspects of BPM in order to develop process-awareness information systems. It includes an examination of process intelligence enabling technologies and support of business rules by technology. Attention is paid to process interoperability integration within and between organizations.
*Intended Audience*:
This course is recommended for the BP consultant and IT architects. The BP analysts can further their knowledge in this area.
*Learning Objectives*:

- Investigation of advanced technologies that enable BP deployment
- Understand service-enabled process management and interoperability
- In-depth analysis and use of Enterprise Resource Planning (ERP) systems as an enabler of process implementation
- Analysis and use of process automation technologies
- Understand technologies required to develop process intelligence
- Understand technologies available to support business rules.
- Understand the technologies and issues of process integration and interoperability in intra- and inter-organizational environments.

## 4 Limitations and Discussion

The proposed curriculum was based on the combination of BP analyst role definition research and several existing BPM courses, curriculum, and training programs from various universities, executive education institutions, and professional organizations. As BPM is a relatively new and evolving discipline, there is a lack of consensus on the content in the available BPM curriculum. In addition, process skills and associated positions vary in organizations, typically favoring either the business view or IT view of an organization with a lack of available research that identifies and verifies the role and activities required for holistic end-to-end BPM practices (Antonucci and Goeke 2009). These issues of existing limited BPM curriculum and lack of content consensus contribute to the main limitations of this curriculum proposal.

The primary goal of this curriculum is to integrate business and IT practices needed to develop and cultivate BP analysts. The typical MBA or business school curriculum currently lacks this integration (Fingar 2006). It can be debated on whether to have more emphasis on business or on technology depending on the outcomes desired by the organization. As such, there could be variations of this curriculum. For example, a more technical college or university may opt to include advanced courses in technology and implementation. Similarly, executive training can tailor this curriculum to a desired level of emphasis. Deployment of this curriculum is recommended to be either on-site or a scheduled on-line meeting time. The on-line training deployment of BPM curriculum needs further investigation for feasibility and effectiveness. Several of the proposed courses require a high level of interaction between participants to enforce concepts and learning, making a self-paced on-demand e-learning method difficult.

Organizations will ultimately benefit from a holistic end-to-end BPM curriculum with educated and knowledgeable BP analysts. Executive training, universities, and colleges can use this curriculum as a foundation for planning and deploying comprehensive BPM programs designed to cultivate skills for the emerging BP analyst.

## References


ABPMP Education (ed) (2008) Guide to the business process management common body of knowledge (1.0 ed.)

Antonucci YL (2006) How do we determine the skill set of a business process management expert? SAP BPX Blog column. https://www.sdn.sap.com/irj/sdn/ weblogs?blog=/pub/wlg/4944

Antonucci YL, Goeke RJ (2009) Construct validity and reliability of tasks and positions in business process management practice. Research Report, Widener University

Bandara W, Rosemann M, Davies I, Tan C (2007). A structured approach to determining appropriate content for emerging information systems subjects: an example from bpm curricula design. Paper presented at the Australasian conference on information systems, Toowoomba, Australia, 5–7 December

Burlton R (2010) Delivering business strategy through process management. In: vom Brocke J, Rosemann M (eds) Handbook on business process management, vol 2. Springer, Heidelberg

DeFee JM, Harmon P (2004) Business activity monitoring and simulation. BPTrends

Dreiling A, Rosemann M, Aalst, W v d, Sadiq W, Khan S (2005) Model-driven process configuration of enterprise systems. In: Proceedings of the 7th conference on Wirtschaftsinformatik. Bamberg, Germany, pp 691–710

Fingar P (2006) The MBA is dead, long live the MBI [Electronic Version]. BP Trends, Retrieved December

Fisher DM (2004) The business process maturity model: a practical approach for identifying opportunities for optimization. BPTrends, p 7

Hadfield W (2007) Financial services firms in grip of BPM skills shortage, says Gartner. Computer Weekly

Hammer M (2007) The process audit. Harv Bus Rev: 111–123

Hammer M (2010) What is business process management? In: vom Brocke J, Rosemann M (eds) Handbook on business process management, vol 1. Springer, Heidelberg

Hill JB, Sinur J, Flint D, Melenovsky MJ (2006). Gartner's Position on Business Process Management: Gartner Research. ID Number: G00136533

Khalil O (1997) Implications for the role of information systems in a business process reengineering environment. Inform Resour Manage J 10(1):36–43

Kokkonen A, Bandara W (2010) Expertise in business process management. In: vom Brocke J, Rosemann M (eds) Handbook on business process management, vol 2. Springer, Heidelberg

Markus ML, Jacobson DD (2010) Business process governance. In: vom Brocke J, Rosemann M (eds) Handbook on business process management, vol 2. Springer, Heidelberg

Melenovsky MJ, Hill JB (2006) Role definition and organizational structure: business process improvement (No. Report number G00141487). Stamford, CT, Gartner Research

Paim R, Caulliraux HM, Cardoso R (2008) Process management tasks: a conceptual and practical view. Bus Process Manage J 14(5):694–723

Rummler GA, Brache AP (2004) Business process management in U.S. firms today, Rummler-Brache Group

Spanyi A (2010) Business process management goverance. In: vom Brocke J, Rosemann M (eds) Handbook on business process management, vol 2. Springer, Heidelberg

# Dealing with Human-Driven Processes

**Keith Harrison-Broninski**

**Abstract** There is little evidence that current BPM deployments deliver significant return on investment (ROI), as most deployments are small-scale and tactical rather than enterprise-scale and strategic. Further, BPM/Service-oriented Architecture (SOA) deployments pose a business risk, as the necessary new management techniques are not yet well understood. The routine processes amenable to application of current BPM techniques must be integrated with high-level management work, knowledge work, and sectors in which human activity is critical. We present a means of describing collaborative, adaptive human-driven processes, and optionally supporting them with software, so as to increase individual productivity, improve organizational memory, and align human work more closely with organizational goals. A framework is provided by the theory of Human Interaction Management (HIM). HIM facilitates the management of teams, communication, knowledge, time, and plans. HIM also shows how to automate processes involving human collaboration, even those of cross-organizational boundaries. Introduction of HIM into the enterprise, as well as its integration with both organizational strategy and mainstream BPM, is via an associated methodology, Goal-Oriented Organization Design (GOOD).

## 1 Introduction

A report from BEA Systems published in March 2008 draws together their own market research with that from several analyst firms (Gartner, Forrester, and IDC) to conclude that "the BPM market is quickly growing and evolving, with a range of vendors and products spanning the market".

K. Harrison-Broninski
Role Modellers Limited, Bath, United Kingdom
e-mail: khb@rolemodellers.com

J. vom Brocke and M. Rosemann (eds.), *Handbook on Business Process Management 2*, International Handbooks on Information Systems,
DOI 10.1007/978-3-642-01982-1_21, 

However, the report is notable for what it omits – namely, a quantitative estimate of the return on investment (ROI) that can be expected from a BPM deployment. The closest the report gets is a table listing the "drivers" from which CIOs expect to get the greatest ROI. The last major research reports to provide ROI estimates were from Butler Group and Gartner, both in 2004 (Butler Group 2004; Gartner 2004). Butler Group was dismissive of the financial return on a BPM project:

> "Whatever the size and scale of the BPM implementation, companies are advised not to believe vendor hype and be prepared for little or no ROI".

By contrast, Gartner was more optimistic, stating that BPM does deliver ROI:

> "78% of the BPM projects [in the survey] yielded an internal rate of return (IRR) of over 15%".

However, while 15% makes a BPM project worth doing, it does not provide the rate of return one might expect from technology originally heralded as "disruptive". The underlying reason for this is that the management techniques underpinning current mainstream BPM, such as Lean and Six Sigma, derive from principles that have been standard practice for over 50 years: Scientific Management from the 1910s (Taylor), Statistical Quality Control from the 1930s (Shewhart), and TQM/Hoshin Kanri from the 1950s (Juran and Deming).

These techniques were designed for the improvement of production processes – routine and repetitive work such as manufacturing. Fifty years after the emergence of these techniques, most organizations now do production processes in a reasonably efficient, and often standardized, fashion. As Butler Group pointed out:

> "The main area of benefit is BPM's ability to increase the efficiency of a core business process. However, in reality, most processes have already been made efficient over time".

Further, production processes are only a part of any organization's activity. The remainder, human-driven processes, is based on humans collaborating and innovating:

(1) High-level work, such as organizational control and change
(2) Knowledge work,[1] such as R&D, sales support, team management, and customer service
(3) Sectors in which human activity is critical, such as health care, law, policing, and disaster relief

Note that the business processes known as "human-centric" (as opposed to "system-centric") are a subset of production processes, not of human-driven processes. Human-centric processes require people to get work done by relying on and interacting extensively with business applications, databases, documents, and in

[1]Davenport (2010) deals with the supporting processes of knowledge workers, which are characterized by a high degree of autonomy of the people involved in knowledge-intense processes. Karagiannis and Woitsch (2010) demonstrate how knowledge engineering methods can be generally integrated within the Business Process Management domain to also support human-centric processes.

limited ways with other people (such as to obtain approval for a document). Human-centric processes require human intuition or judgment for decision-making only as part of individual steps in a routine business process. Examples of human-centric processes include claims processing, loan approvals, accounts payable, mortgage origination, and customer service.

By some estimates, human-driven processes constitute the larger portion of organizational activity, for example, customer service. The exceptional cases typically consume the most resources – by Pareto's rule, 20% of exceptions result in 80% of the cost – and for many organizations, the number of exceptional cases is much higher than 20%.[2]

It is possible to quantify to some extent the total amount of human work. By focusing only on the above-mentioned second category (knowledge work), and ignoring developing countries (for which statistics are not readily available), we can calculate the total number of knowledge workers in the US and Europe as follows:

Estimates of the proportion of knowledge workers in the US economy vary from 59% (Woolf 2005) to 80% (Haag et al. 2006) – here we assume 59%. The size of the US workforce in 2004 was 138.5 million, giving 81 million[3] knowledge workers in the US.

A report prepared for the Knowledge Economy Programme in November 2007 concluded that "in 2005 just over 40% of the European workforce was employed in knowledge-based industries as defined by Eurostat" (Rüdiger and McVerry 2007) – here we assume 40%. We take the size of the European workforce from Eurostat figures for 2007 as 235 million (the "Active population," out of a "Total population" of 487 million),[4] giving the 94 million knowledge workers in Europe.

This gives a total number of knowledge workers in the US and Europe alone as 175 million, a significant number by any standards.

The importance of human-driven processes is not just about staff numbers, however. Management of production processes focuses on *efficiency* – reducing time and cost. It is human work that delivers *effectiveness*, resulting in high customer satisfaction and (for private sector companies) market leadership. The true rewards of BPM deployment come from extending its reach beyond small-scale, tactical improvements of production processes to enterprise-scale, strategic activity.

Human activity is also critical in the management of process improvement itself. Following a recent large SOA/BPM project at Deutsche Bank, the board member responsible for the project said:

"We underestimated how large a transformation this could be; that is, going from vertically-aligned IT operations environment to something that's trying to make much greater use of shared assets. It's not just about teaching developers how to use web services. It's changing how the funding is done for shared services. It's putting governance structures in place. It's defining engineering and process

[2]http://www.global360.com/blog/index.php/2007/11/28/democracy-aka-collaborative-bpm.

[3]heritage.org/Research/Labor/wm406.cfm.

[4]epp.eurostat.ec.europa.eu.

standards. It's creating new roles where you have actual process analysts; roles that just don't exist today".[5]

The complexity of process implementation is such that it needs to be controlled using the same principles that are used to manage organizations at a high level, for example, via balanced scorecard.[6]

Other potential problems are more subtle. For instance, the Dutch Government has created a business process in Business Process Modeling Notation (BPMN) that includes over 250,000 independent steps.[7] This represents a vastly complex piece of business software, and the chance of it being perfectly correct is infinitesimally small. However, the tools used to build it include no testing features – only simulation features, which for such a large process are of little use. It is left to the users to detect (where possible) the bugs of all impact sizes that undoubtedly exist.

To remedy the situation, we present a means of describing collaborative, adaptive human-driven processes, and optionally supporting them with software, so as to increase individual productivity, improve organizational memory, and align human work more closely with organizational goals. A framework is provided by the theory of Human Interaction Management (HIM). HIM facilitates the management of teams, communication, knowledge, time, and plans. HIM also shows how to automate processes involving human collaboration, even those of cross-organizational boundaries. We show how to introduce HIM into the enterprise, and integrate it with both organizational strategy and mainstream BPM, via an associated methodology, Goal-Oriented Organization Design (GOOD).

## 2 Human Interaction Management

Research shows that knowledge workers typically waste 28% of their time due to poor control over interactions and information. Hence, supporting human work processes requires more than the extension of current BPM systems to support current working practices – creating ad-hoc collaborations, using email and adopting Web 2.0 tools. Human workers need a *formalized approach* that has the following functions:

(1) Helps them achieve goals
(2) Structures the creation, maintenance, and re-use of knowledge
(3) Ensures the ongoing alignment of human activity with changing organizational strategy

Support for work based on human interaction requires a framework for modeling and facilitating collaborative, adaptive human-driven processes. Such a framework

[5]http://www.computerworlduk.com/technology/development/soa/in-depth/index.cfm?articleid=1792&pn=5.

[6]http://humanedjucation.com/soa/Balanced%20Scorecard%20for%20SOA%20Governance.pdf.

[7]http://findarticles.com/p/articles/mi_m0EIN/is_2006_Nov_16/ai_n27057164.

is provided by the theory of HIM,[8] which shows how to describe processes so as to facilitate management of *teams, communication, knowledge, time, and plans.*

A further concern of HIM is to provide software support for processes involving human collaboration, even those that *cross organizational boundaries*, via the definition of a new kind of software system, a Human Interaction Management System (HIMS). An HIMS is not a centralized state machine such as the current mainstream BPM software, but a means to manage distributed objects. An HIM process is a set of objects, each owned by a different player in the process. The players use an HIMS to do their work, and in the background, their HIMS synchronizes specific aspects of their own objects (such as interaction messages) with those of their peers.

Note that it is possible to take part in an HIM process without using a HIMS – as long as one player is using an HIMS, the others can use email, for example, and the sole HIMS instance will ensure that the work is structured for all players according to the process definition.

A summary of HIMS features, as well as comparison with other approaches to organizational work management, is given in Fig. 1.

The starting point of HIM is five observations that characterize collaborative human work. As an organization is effectively a manifestation of long-term human collaboration, these "principles" apply to organizations just as to any other form of

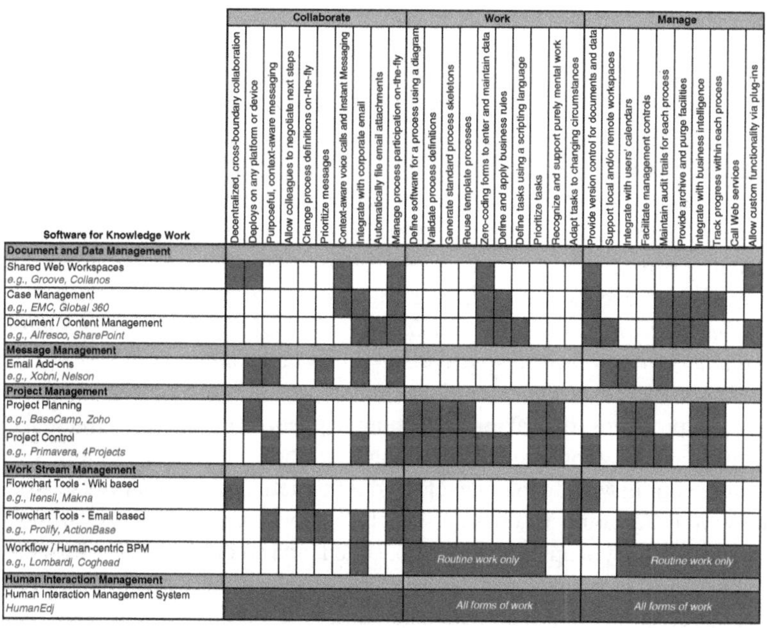


**Fig. 1** Summary of HIMS features and comparison with other approaches to work management

[8]http://www.human-interaction-management.info.

project or venture. Here are the five principles, along with their implications for any modeling framework that aims to capture human collaboration.

(1) *Team building*: To create effective teams, it must be clear who is involved in a particular process, and what each person brings to the table. As a starting point, the identity, skills, experience, and personal characteristics of each person must be captured. It is then necessary to define each individual's responsibilities, and negotiate his/her commitment to accepting these responsibilities.

    *The modeling framework must contain Role and User objects, both instances and types.*

(2) *Communication*: If people are to manage their interactions with others better, their communications must be structured and goal-directed. Within a process, there must be specific channels of communication for different purposes, each of which unifies messages transmitted via a variety of means (email, text message, FAX, voice-over-IP, etc.).

    *The modeling framework must contain interaction objects representing multiple asynchronous channels.*

(3) *Knowledge*: Organizations must learn to manage the time and mental effort their staff members invest in researching, comparing, considering, deciding, and generally turning information into knowledge and ideas. The people responsible for creating and managing this knowledge must be able to control its usage and distribution.

    *The modeling framework must contain Entity objects that can be created, versioned, and shared in a structured way.*

(4) *Empowered time management*: Humans may not sequence their activities in the manner of a software program, but there is always structure to human work, which must be understood and institutionalized so that it can be managed and improved. This means empowering people to choose and/or create their own work activities from an appropriate range, guided by understanding of organizational context (so that they can aim to deliver maximum value) and restricted by business rules that prevent contravention of applicable policies and standards.

    *The modeling framework must contain State objects that can both enable and validate Activity objects, along with the Roles that contain them.*

(5) *Collaborative, real-time planning*: Human activities are concerned often with solving problems, or making something happen. Such activities routinely start in the same fashion – by establishing a way of proceeding. Before you can design your new widget, or develop your marketing plan, you need to work out how you are going to do so – which methodology to use, which tools are required, which people should be consulted, and so on. In other words, process definition is an intrinsic part of the process itself. It takes place via negotiation between all involved parties, and is not a one-time thing but happens continually throughout the life of the process.

    *The modeling framework must support manipulation not only of objects but also of user interfaces and integration mechanisms via the process that contains them.*

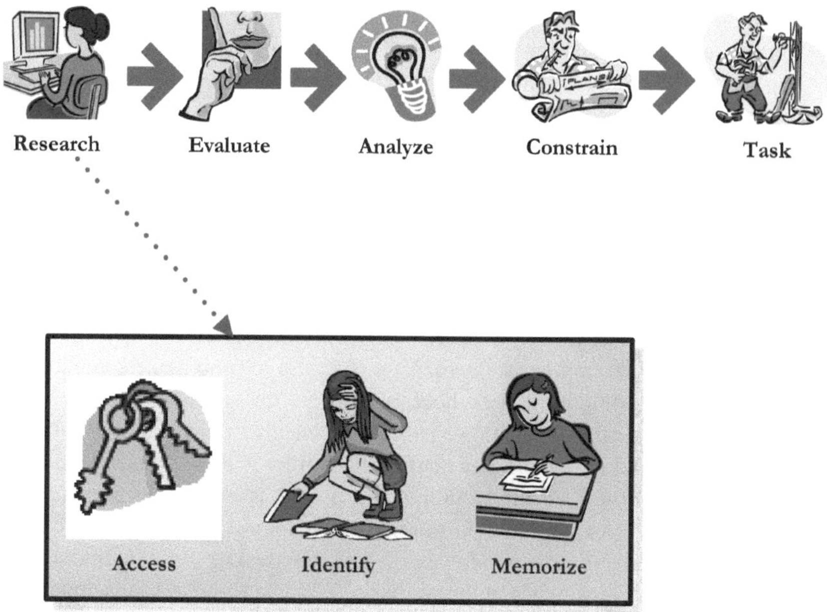


**Fig. 2** REACT and AIM

HIM includes a notation providing the necessary elements. HIM also provides guidelines on use of this notation, by identifying a number of patterns resulting from the above-mentioned principles, such as the REACT and AIM patterns that underlie any form of human activity (Fig. 2) (collaborative or not).

Here we discuss the following stages of REACT in turn:

(1) *Research*: Map out the terrain, investigate the principles, talk to those in the know, locate potential threats, and so on, in order to gain information from external sources, and turn it into personal knowledge. The external sources may be close at hand – members of a "community of practice," for example, as discussed in the following paragraphs. Alternatively, information may be acquired from an impartial expert in the field, a textbook, or a search on the Web. The details are different every time, but the principle is the same. Before you can start to work on something, it is only common sense to find out what you are getting yourself into.

(2) *Evaluate*: Step back and consider the knowledge thus acquired. Internalize it, in a sense, by making connections between different opinions or facts. Once you have discovered the general lay of the land, you need to familiarize yourself with it. You may need to carefully read a pile of papers on your desk, or to mull over some advice that you do not yet understand. This stage may take minutes or years, but it is crucial – there is no point doing an investigation unless you make an effort to take on board the information you gathered.

(3) *Analyze*: On the basis of your new-found understanding, decide on an approach to the problem. In general, the approach you settle on may result partly from applying logic to reduce the problem to more manageable subproblems – and partly from an intuitive judgment on what feels "right". The balance varies both with the type of problem and with the type of person trying to solve it. However, you arrive at a conclusion, though the decisions made at this stage are not necessarily a final say on the matter – they are simply a way forward for now; enough to let you proceed further with the work in hand. Sometimes it is hard to be sure whether you are doing the right thing, so you might choose a way forward that hedges our bets – following multiple paths at the same time, in the hope that at least one will work – or decide only on the first few steps, and leave decisions about other steps for later. But you have to make some kind of decision at this point, at least on how to start.
(4) *Constrain*: Divide the work into separate chunks, and organize them. This may be simply a matter of deciding an approximate order to do them in, or it may be a huge task involving all the techniques of project planning: dependency and impact analysis, critical path definition, resource allocation, budgeting, contingency planning, and so on. However, you are dealing with human-driven processes here – in which people rarely do things in the order laid down, and rightly see it as part of their work to determine how things should proceed. So, this stage is not about defining "workflows," in the sense of ordering activities into strict sequence – it is about laying down the constraints that govern the chunks of work, insofar as they can be understood at this point. Typically, constraints are of rather vague form: "before you can promise a delivery date for a product, make sure the component suppliers can meet it," or "it is okay in principle to take on contract staff, as long as you've made a reasonable effort to resource the project internally first".
(5) *Task*: You have determined how to break the work into chunks, and handed out these chunks to appropriate people (including yourself, perhaps), so now all those concerned can get on with the tasks at hand. For a small job, there might only be one chunk, and you might do it yourself. For a large one, this stage may involve many different people and organizations working together to deliver a product or service.

The first stage of REACT, *Research*, can be further broken down into a subpattern AIM, which describes any research activity:

(1) Access discovery services

Decide where you will go to obtain information, and obtain any necessary authorization. This might be permission to contact someone, login details for a database, or funds to use some kind of finder agency.

(2) Identify resources required

From the above-mentioned service(s), choose resources likely to be of interest. At this stage, you will have only cursory understanding of their content – what matters is that they seem likely to be useful.

(3) Memorize information obtained from particular resources

It is important to focus on committing information to memory, even if the information is only the outline of an idea you will use later on. Unless you have memorized information gathered at this first stage of REACT, it is no use in the following stage, *Evaluate* – you cannot synthesize ideas you have forgotten, or need to look up in order to understand. This stage is all about internalizing the ideas in question.

Similarly to the way REACT describes human work in general, AIM describes the particular activities of information discovery.

Taken together, the REACT and AIM patterns describe all human working behavior. The patterns capture the way that people respond to an assignment, fulfill responsibility, achieve a goal – the way they react to the work they take on. REACT and AIM help simplify complex situations, as the patterns can be repeated, overlapped, and nested in order to reduce any work assignment to the same fundamental stages.

HIM includes further patterns additional to REACT and AIM. Some examples are given in the following paragraphs.

### 2.1 Collaborative Transaction

Collaborative Transaction is an archetypal structure for describing a stage of collaborative work – a project phase, for example. The structure includes initiating and concluding interactions, separated by work activities divided among several roles. Collaborative transactions can be nested.

### 2.2 Levels of Control

Collaborative Transaction refers to a natural division of responsibility and authority between strategic, executive, and managerial roles. In brief, strategic control is about identifying goals and measures; executive control is about identifying key roles and interactions; management control is about constructing, implementing, supporting, and reporting on an executable process.

## 3 Goal-Oriented Organization Design

Introduction of HIM into the enterprise, and its integration with both organizational strategy and mainstream BPM, is facilitated by an associated methodology, GOOD. GOOD differs from mainstream BPM methodologies in being *derived from an underpinning set of consistent principles*, which are those of HIM itself.

GOOD supplies a step-by-step method for applying these and other patterns to human work, by starting from a basic observation – that the primary value delivered by humans to an organization lies in their ability to collaborate, adapt, and innovate as required to deal with changing and unexpected circumstances. As described earlier, human-driven processes are not precisely repetitive – rather, they typically evolve during usage, as the participants repeatedly collaborate to agree on next steps.

Hence, GOOD emphasizes *effectiveness* over *efficiency*. Human work should not be managed using the narrow measures of waste and cycle time typically applied for improvement of mechanistic processes. Rather, people at all levels of an organizational hierarchy must have some leeway to judge for themselves the most effective actions according to circumstances. Hence, GOOD focuses on enabling structured partial decentralization of management authority while ensuring continued alignment with strategic organizational goals.

In particular, GOOD supports process and service development, maintenance, and improvement via governance processes – human-driven processes defined using HIM notation, and inter-related via HIM levels of control. GOOD governance processes apply quality techniques drawn from HIM principles – metrics and indicators that measure the effectiveness of a process by tracking how well it makes use of the humans involved.[9]

There are three key stages of GOOD, which taken in turn provide three complementary views of organizational life:

(1) Top–down
(2) "Process Architecture" defines business strategy via a network of interacting high-level processes:
   - First draw up a process architecture, to unite business goals with business processes. This is a sine qua non – unless you start here, you will be building a house on sand. Goals are the true and only foundation of business activities – profit is simply an enabler.
   - Assess the processes in your architecture to see which are strategic, which are tactical, and which are operational.
   - On this basis, refine the architecture to reflect your organization's long-, medium- and short-term goals.
(3) Middle-out
(4) "Levels of Control" separate process governance into *Strategic*, *Executive*, and *Management*:
   - Use HIM "levels of control" to assign strategic, executive, and management responsibility for processes, and gain commitment from the right people.
   - Assess the interactions between processes in the new architecture to decide which processes can and should be outsourced.
   - For those processes you have decided to manage internally, apply HIM techniques to make best use of the humans in your organization, at all levels

[9] humanedjucation.com/white_papers/A_New_Approach_To_Quality.pdf.

of the organization chart – not in order to downsize your people away, but rather in order to leverage the skills you have on board.

(5) Bottom – up

(6) "Stories" represent collaborative work processes that the participants evolve on-the-fly as part of the work itself:
- Roles representing goals and responsibilities;
- Users representing commitment to playing roles;
- Interactions representing long-lived, purposeful communications between roles.

## 4 Respond to Request for Proposal

We will introduce the part of GOOD that shows how to describe human-driven processes and support them via software – in other words, we focus on HIM process modeling notation. We illustrate the essential characteristics of HIM notation via comparison of how simple process examples might be depicted (if possible) using the standard mainstream notation BPMN.[10]

As a first step toward exploring the depiction of human-driven processes in BPMN, we will use a very common process – responding to a request for proposal (RFP). Here is a simplified version of this work in BPMN (Fig. 3):

From a manager's perspective, there are several important questions about this process. The process as shown could be carried out exactly as depicted, yet it completely fails to deliver what the business needs. Whatever is an organization's

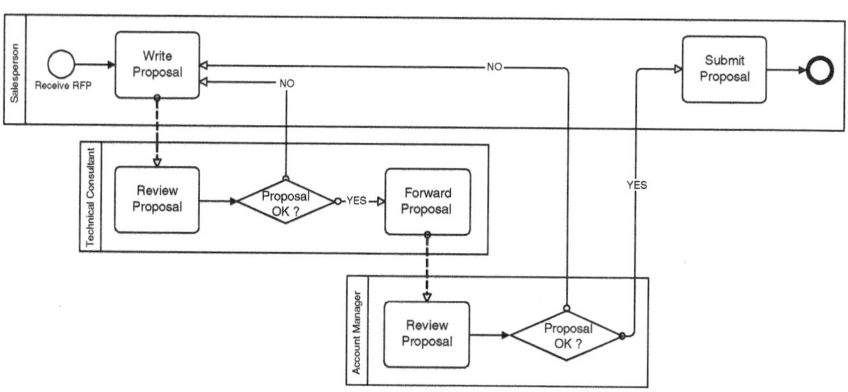


**Fig. 3** Respond to request for proposal (an attempt to capture the process using BPMN)

[10]http://www.bpmn.org.

"process maturity level," and however sophisticated is its BPM software, implementation of the process without answering these questions is more likely to harm the business than to improve it. However, the diagram itself offers no hooks on which to hang the answers.

We take these questions in turn:

*What are the goals and responsibilities of each player?* A BPMN lane or pool is simply a grouping of activities – it is not an organizational role, with associated goals and responsibilities.

*How can the Salesperson know what the others are looking for?* Starting from a diagram such as this, the proposal author is effectively working blind –he/she has no idea on what basis his/her work will be reviewed, or even by whom.

*To what policies and regulations must the players adhere?* The diagram shows no indication of organizational context – to what conditions the proposal must conform.

*What skills, experience, and personality type should each player possess?* Encoding processes in standard format can be dangerous – without providing any information about the players, it gives the false impression that the work is somehow independent of the people carrying out the activities.

*What if the Salesperson needs help from another Salesperson to write the proposal?* If the proposal turns out to be too much work for one person in the time available, he/she may need to share it with someone else – but the diagram offers no means to achieve this.

*What if the Salesperson needs to discuss matters with the others?* The most efficient way to prepare a document draft is to allow communication with reviewers prior to submission – but BPMN does not allow the depiction of interactive, multi-party communication channels, but only one-off messages sent from one pool to another as part of a workflow.

*What if other work, apart from document writing, is necessary to prepare the proposal?* Writing the proposal document is actually the tip of the iceberg compared to the research, evaluation, and analysis that underpin the document – such activities tend to be hard to predict in advance, yet BPMN makes no allowance for on-the-fly adjustment to the process.

*What supporting information is needed?* It is critical to supply each player with the reference material he/she needs – yet BPMN allows artifacts to be associated with a process only as activity inputs/outputs.

*How is material containing that supporting information made available to the participants?* It is not enough just to show a reference material – the players need to know what form it is in, where to find it, and how to access the locations (e.g., account details for a technical journal subscription).

In summary, anyone who has ever prepared a proposal in response to an RFP will see immediately that this diagram is totally unrealistic – the real world is neither so simple nor so rigid as the workflow depicted. BPMN is a fine process notation – when used for its natural purpose, which is to capture routine work in which the only human activities are data entry and low-level decision-making. Work suited to depiction using BPMN is either automated, semi-automated, or so

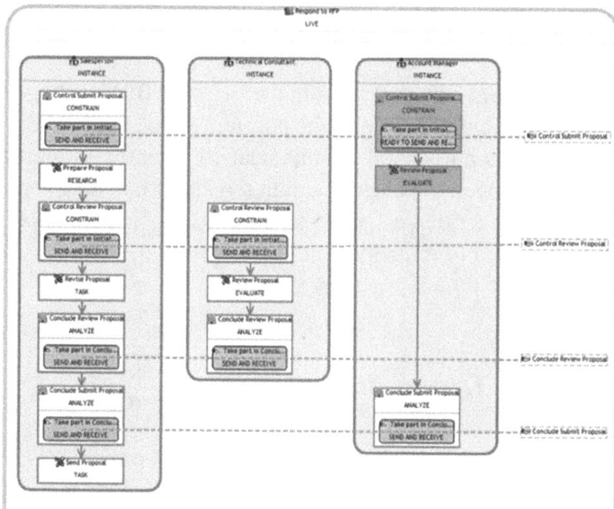

**Fig. 4** Respond to RFP (executable process diagram in HIM notation)

repetitive that one day it will be automated. Effectively, BPMN is a high-level software design notation.

When it comes to human knowledge work, a BPMN diagram simply does not contain the right information. Even if business people can be persuaded to try and understand a notation stuffed full of engineering symbols, a software design notation is the wrong tool to capture collaborative, adaptive, innovative human activity.

By contrast, given in the following paragraphs is a representation of the same process in HIM notation (Fig. 4):

The diagram looks quite different from the BPMN version, and those similarities that exist are superficial – the notational constructs are not equivalent. Here are some key aspects of the diagram.

## 4.1 Roles

Instead of lanes/pools as in a BPMN diagram, with documents/data floating about in thin air, each player in a HIM process has a role – the vertical rectangles with yellow background. A role is more than a collection of actions – it is a mini-workspace that provides you with a lot more than “things to do in a specific order”. For a start, each role has its own goals and responsibilities – which by agreeing to play a role, you commit to meeting. To help you meet the goals and responsibilities, each role has its own private documents/data that you can update and share with colleagues when appropriate. A role also contains business rules that help you decide when to do what, and that help ensure that your work stays in line with higher-level policies and regulations.

## 4.2 Interactions

Instead of messages from one party to another as in a BPMN diagram, an HIM process has interactions between roles – the purple, dashed, mainly horizontal lines. An HIM interaction is a purposeful communication channel – a means by which messages can be exchanged, repeatedly and in any direction, between any number of parties. Think of interactions as "email plus process context," although any form of messaging can be used to implement an interaction.

## 4.3 Collaborative Transactions

Instead of sub-processes as in a BPMN diagram, an HIM process has collaborative transactions – stages or phases of a process, as highlighted in the marked-up version of the diagram that follows. Collaborative transactions start with an interaction between all parties (to establish the purpose of the ensuing work), contain various actions for each party, and conclude with another interaction (to agree that the work is completed and decide on next steps). Collaborative transactions can be nested, as shown here, without introducing a hierarchical structure foreign to human interactions – in reality, people can talk to one another at any time, whatever part of a process they are supposed to be carrying out (Fig. 5).

In the above-mentioned HIM diagrams, each role (*yellow rectangle*) has the word *INSTANCE* underneath its name. This means that the role is active in the process – it represents a real, working participant. Some roles, however, are used differently. Here is another version of the HIM solution above to "Respond to RFP" (Fig. 6):

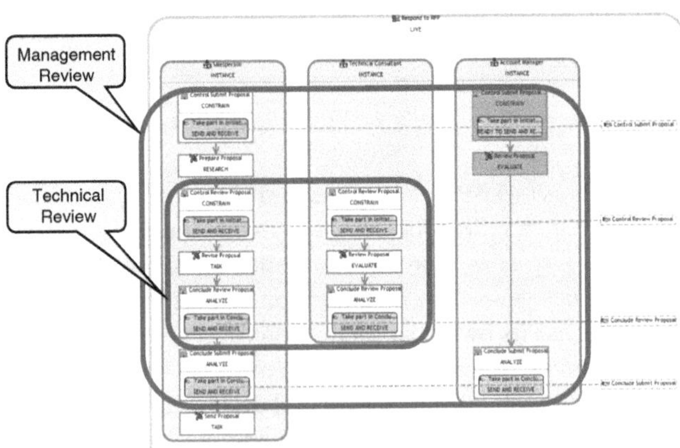


**Fig. 5** Respond to RFP (executable process diagram in HIM notation) – collaborative transactions

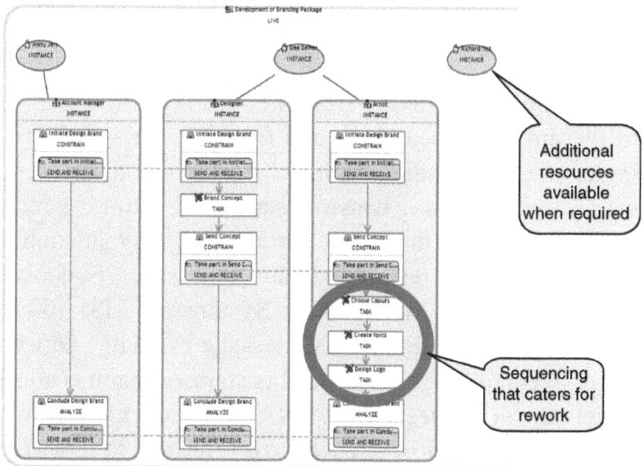


**Fig. 6** Respond to RFP (executable process diagram in HIM notation) – extended

Notice that this time the Technical Consultant Role is shown as a *TYPE* rather than an instance. Also, the Account Manager has a new Activity, to assign a Technical Consultant.

The new diagram reflects the fact that, in some cases, the salesperson will not need technical consultancy – he/she will be familiar enough with the solution to be offered to the client that he/she can prepare the proposal unaided. In the new version, the Salesperson and Account Manager can discuss this via the *Initiate Submit Proposal* Interaction – and depending on the outcome of that discussion, the Account Manager may or may not create an "instance" of the Technical Consultant Role "type".

To depict this in BPMN, one would have to create a swimlane for the technical consultancy work, and make all its activities optional in the process. In other words, work has been assigned but may never happen. Further, there is no explicit depiction of how the work will be assigned – under what circumstances, when, by whom, to whom, the sort of skills and experience required, and so on. Critical aspects of human resource planning are not part of the process definition – of necessity, as there is nowhere to put them.

## 5 Development of Branding Package

We consider another example process – development of a branding package (colors, fonts, logo, artwork, etc.), in which the following features are seen:

(1) The account manager, designer, and artist throw ideas back and forward for review and debate (concepts, images, documents, etc.), usually but not always by email
(2) The same person acts as designer and artist at the start, but has the option of handing over the artwork creation to others if his/her workload becomes too heavy

(3) It is possible to add more artists as needed during the life of the process, all of whom participate in the same communications

This process cannot be depicted in BPMN at all.

With regard to "throwing ideas back and forward," message flow in BPMN is limited to a single, one-way sending from one pool to another. The sending can be repeated if the appropriate looping constructs are used, but it is very hard to depict message flow between more than two parties, and any attempt to reproduce the flexible manner in which people exchange messages is doomed to failure. Mainstream Business Process Management System (BPMS) software currently deals with this limitation by claiming that message exchange between colleagues is not really part of a work process – rather, it is claimed that it is an ad-hoc activity on which no structure can (or needs to) be placed. In other words, what is perhaps the most fundamental tool of knowledge work is relegated to floating around under the organizational radar, in an unmanageable backwater.

With regard to "handing over work," BPMN has no concept of who does the work. It simply shows what needs to be done, by someone or something. Hence, it is impossible to include in a process diagram any indication of the people, or sorts of people, involved. Again, fundamental aspects of knowledge work (acceptance and delegation of responsibility, capabilities, personal characteristics, and so on) are quite literally out of the picture.

With regard to "adding more" of a certain role, there is no means to achieve this in a BPMN process. It is hard even to imagine how the notation could be extended to support the notion, as the flowchart principles on which BPMNs are based do not support such a concept. Yet, human resource planning is fundamental to process management, as it is to all management. How is process software supposed to support human resource planning using a notation in which it is not possible to depict, let alone adjust, the resource levels assigned to a work package?

By contrast, here is a simple diagram using HIM notation that shows all the above-mentioned constraints (Fig. 7):

As mentioned above, the *interactions* show message exchange among the three parties to the process. Messages can flow in any direction, as repeatedly as necessary.

As mentioned above, the yellow rectangles are *roles* in the process. This time another construct is shown – the ovals at the top are *users* of those roles (the user section was collapsed on the previous HIM diagram). At the start, Dee Zeiner is playing both the designer and the artist roles. However, the diagram includes an extra user, Richard Tist, to whom the artist role can be reassigned during the process if Dee takes on other work and has to delegate.

Finally, should it become necessary to add another artist as extra resource, this can be done in an HIMS simply by right-clicking on the artist's role and asking for another one. The HIMS will prompt for the details of the person to be assigned the work and then duplicate the role, automatically assigning the new role to the new person and including the new role in the same interactions as the current role.

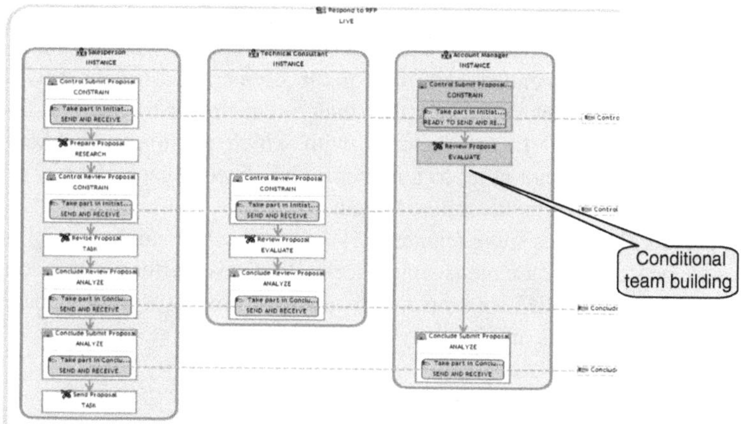


**Fig. 7** Development of branding package (executable process diagram in HIM notation)

There are many other aspects of HIM notation that make it more suitable for collaborative, adaptive human work than BPMN. For example, consider the following aspects of the above-mentioned process. The artist must create a draft set of colors before starting to create fonts. However, once one has created a draft set of colors, [the semantics of a HIM diagram mean that] one can repeat and interleave the color and font creation activities as one wishes. Similarly, he/she must create a draft set of fonts before starting to create a logo. However, once one has created a draft set of fonts, one can repeat and interleave the color, font, and logo creation activities as one wishes.

These aspects of the process are simple common sense. However, it is extremely hard to depict in BPMN, requiring highly artificial constructs in order to show, for example, how the artist can go directly from color creation to logo creation only once he/she has created fonts.

Unlike people, a flowchart has no memory. An HIMS does, however – and organizations need a memory too.

## 6 Conclusion

BPMN is a symptom of a deep problem with BPM, which is that its management practices completely ignore leading management thinking since 1960. The great figures of the last half century – Drucker, Handy, Senge, and others – all pointed out that organizations are *systems*, in which feedback loops cross boundaries. For the organization to operate effectively, people must collaborate in order to make real-time changes to running processes. This requires both visibility of what is happening at many levels and empowerment to implement such changes.

Yet, mainstream BPM practice, as it currently stands, is based on describing an organization as a hierarchical tree of processes, starting with separate value streams/chains, and descending with inexorable rigor to routine, repetitive flow-charts more suited to enactment by CPUs than to enactment by humans. Such an approach is well suited to the factories with which Deming and Juran were concerned in 1950, but not at all to a modern, globalized organization in which a huge part of the work is collaborative human activity.

This chapter illustrates some features of HIM that go beyond the capabilities of mainstream process and case management technology, even offerings that appear to be at the leading edge. HIM notation directly addresses five aspects of management with which organizations are currently struggling:

(1) Teams
(2) Communication
(3) Knowledge
(4) Time
(5) Planning

Further, the current inexorable trends toward outsourcing, partnering, and sub-contracting as the fundamental means of doing business in a globalized economy mean that in each of the five aspects of the above-mentioned management, it is critical to support decentralized, cross-boundary processes where there is not necessarily a single process "owner".

To meet these requirements, a new paradigm for process description is required – one that is based not on state machines in which the process is a clockwork mechanism that moves from stage to stage, controlled centrally by a single engine, but on object models where a process is a set of objects in different domains, whose interaction and synchronization are controlled collaboratively by agents acting on behalf of each player. This new paradigm is what HIM notation and the underpinning HIM semantics provide.

As regards why this is necessary, the global economy is undergoing a sea change, for which the deep reason is simply the advent of the Web, with the consequent rise of "Asia, Automation and Abundance". The only way to survive such change is to adapt, which means taking dramatic steps early on. For once, only the early adopters will survive – those that wait until new ideas have been fully tested will be out of business before they get a chance to put them into practice for themselves.

To meet the challenge of globalization, a conceptual breakthrough is required in business. Pareto's law tells us that the 20% of "exceptional cases" account for 80% of the costs – but it does not tell us why. To discover why, and deal with it, one must appreciate that "*exceptional* cases" are not exceptional at all – they are the norm, as they occur all the time. Further, the "exceptional" cases are what truly test your business practices.

To deal with the "long tail" – that is, to operate efficiently and effectively in a globalized economy based on an explosive proliferation of niches – one must abandon the hopeful notion that business processes can be defined once then run thousands of times with only minor change. One must create an operational environment in which change is not only possible, but structured, encouraged, and aligned with strategic objectives.

This means taking a much richer view of "process" – a view in which people, communication channels, knowledge, time, and plans are all managed along with the activities that are more easily visible – across multiple domains that include not only you and all your trading partners but also your customers. Bottom–up empowerment is not enough. Top–down control is not enough. Organizations need an enterprise management framework that supports both, at the same time, using the same approach.

Change is never easy, especially under market pressure. However, at the start of the twenty-first century, there really is little choice. Improving routine processes, using current mainstream BPM techniques, only brings you up to the level of your competitors. To stay ahead, and stay in the game, you need to improve the human-driven processes that cannot be fully planned in advance – and do it on enterprise scale.

## References


Butler Group (2004) Business Process Management – A Guide to Navigating the Process Minefield. Butler Group, England

Davenport TH (2010) Process management for knowledge work. In: vom Brocke J, Rosemann M (eds) Handbook on business process management, vol 1. Springer, Heidelberg

Edward Woolf (2005) "The growth of information workers in the US economy". New York University, Communications of the ACM

Gartner (2004) "Justifying BPM projects"

Haag et al. (2006) Management information systems for the information age. McGraw-Hill, New York

Karagiannis D, Woitsch R (2010) Knowledge engineering in business process management. In: vom Brocke J, Rosemann M (eds) Handbook on business process management, vol 2. Springer, Heidelberg

Katerina Rüdiger, Alana McVerry (2007) "Knowledge work and knowledge workers in Europe"

The state of the BPM market (2008). BEA Systems, Inc., California, USA p 28

# Knowledge Engineering in Business Process Management

**Dimitris Karagiannis and Robert Woitsch**

**Abstract** Business Process Management (BPM) is a commodity today after an evolution from the initial business process re-engineering in the 1980s to a well-established management approach. This chapter proposes three aspects of knowledge engineering (KE) in BPM. First, BPM can be seen as a domain itself focusing on the BP-framework that identifies the basic concepts of business model, domain, regulation, and model processing. Second, BPM needs to be applied by a management method. Third, BPM needs to be executed within an environment; hence, it is deployed. BPM can be the basic concept for corporate knowledge leading to knowledge-sensitive BPM. Studying the knowledge-sensitiveness according to the four dimensions (1) form, (2) content, (3) use, and (4) interpretation, KE and knowledge management support can be distinguished. In the following, the focus is on KE. KE in BP-frameworks can be established by models using the meta-model approach for integration. Knowledge-intensive actions within the BP-management method can be supported by KE techniques that are proposed on the basis of the results of demonstrations in research projects. The deployment of BPM within an execution environment that uses KE requires consideration of the KE concepts also in BPM. This chapter, therefore, argues to support BPM in the three areas, BP-framework, BP-management method, and BP-deployment. KE techniques are proposed, the experiences in the demonstration of research projects are described, and an outlook on the conceptual and technical integration, is given.

## 1 Introduction

Business Process Management (BPM) is an established management approach, although there is a controversial interpretation among the different disciplines

D. Karagiannis (✉)
Institute for Business and Knowledge Engineering, University of Vienna, Vienna, Austria
e-mail: dk@dke.univie.ac.at

J. vom Brocke and M. Rosemann (eds.), *Handbook on Business Process Management 2*, International Handbooks on Information Systems,
DOI 10.1007/978-3-642-01982-1_22, 

between information management, business informatics, or software engineering in computer science (http://www.bptrends.com).

The common understanding is to interpret working procedures as directed graphs, to map these working procedures of the real world into formal models, and to finally make them operational. There are approaches for social deployment, via organizational regulations, space management, and incentives, and approaches for technical deployment via workflows, Customer Relationship Management (CRMs), portals, or enterprise application integration.

One of the current roles of BPM can be shown in the prominent sample of business and IT alignment.

The importance of BPM can be demonstrated, as this business and IT alignment is no longer seen as a "nice to have," but as a "must-have" to ensure that IT infrastructure is aligned with business. This can be underlined by the provocative Gartner survey (Gartner 2006) that eight out of ten American dollars invested in IT are "Dead Money" as they are "...not contributing directly to business growth." European investments in IT are estimated to be 315 billions Euros per year.

The complexity of BPM can be assessed by the observation that currently there is a shift from data-rich to information-rich to service-rich (http://complexsystems.lri.fr/Portal/tiki-index.php?page=SOS+Homepage&bl) structures in economies, business, and social communities. Through the rapid development of IT, new services that share resources and configure inter-organizational workflows, have been developed. Now, this technology is "moving up" to influence not only technical computation but also tasks that require human interaction. Developments such as service-oriented architecture (SOA), service-oriented knowledge utilities (SOKUs), software as a service (SaaS), virtualization, and systems of systems[1] are influencing the way in which IT infrastructure and services are rendered for business processes (Karagiannis et al. 2008; vom Brocke 2007b).

BPM is a commodity today and is acting as a mediator between business models, regulations, application domains, and model processing, establishing the required performance as well as ensuring the required compliance. This means BPM needs to balance between assuring compliance and raising performance.

Knowledge engineering (KE) is an interesting instrument to support BPM in order to achieve this balance. This chapter proposes three different viewpoints for KE in BPM:

First, BPM is interpreted as a domain on its own.[2] As BPM includes several aspects, such as realization approaches, tools, or modeling approaches, it is necessary to focus on the basic concepts that are BPM specific. Therefore, the focus is the BP-framework

[1]A system of systems (syn. hybrid computing system) is a system composed of (super-) computing resources of different architectures. They are tightly coupled, interconnected by high-speed network and are treated as a single system.

[2]Hammer (2010) provides insights as to what the Business Process Management domain is about.

that identifies the four dimensions business model, domain, regulations, and model processing. Hence, the second Section discusses KE in BP-frameworks resulting in KE-enabled BP-frameworks.

Each BPM approach requires a concrete instantiation of the BP-framework in order to be bound to the organizational context and to enable the actual management of BPs. This is performed by applying a management method; therefore, Section 3 describes KE in BP-management methods.

Once the BP has been bound into the organizational context and is managed according the BP-management method, it needs to be deployed into an execution environment. Therefore, BPM needs to be aware of the applied KE technologies of the execution platform. Section 4, therefore, discusses KE in BP-deployment.

Figure 1 introduces KE in BP-frameworks, BP-management method, and BP-deployment. The actual knowledge space needs to be specified, according to the four dimensions, form, content, use, and interpretation. This knowledge space can

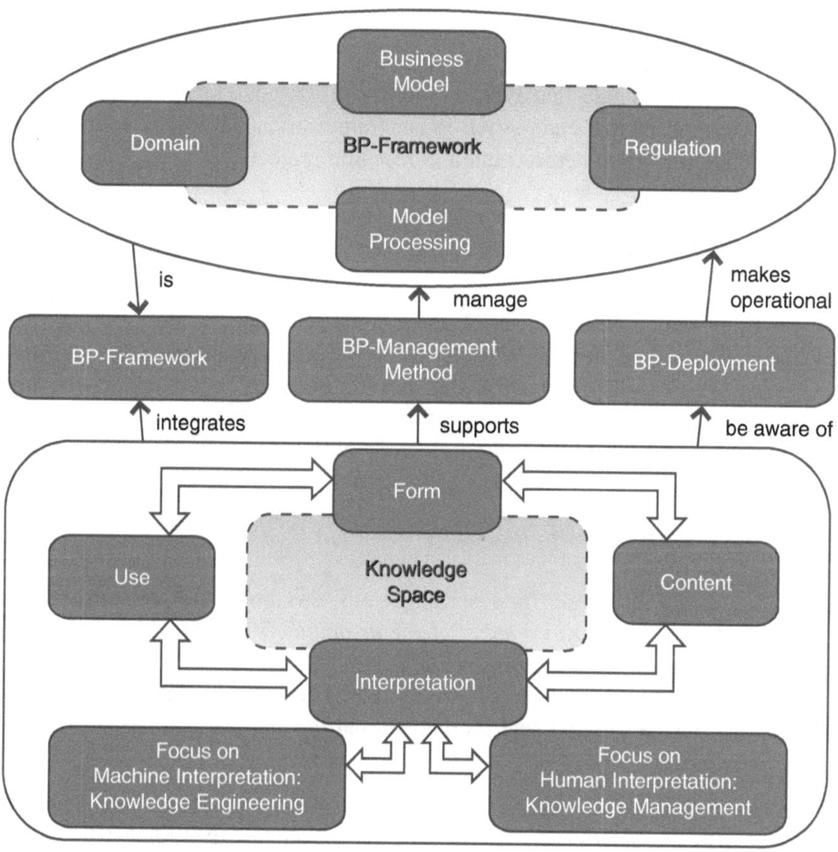


**Fig. 1** The BPM and KE alignment

be represented focusing on human interpretation – in case of knowledge management – or focusing on machine interpretation – in case of KE.[3]

In the following, the BPM knowledge space is discussed that is used for KE in BP-frameworks, KE in BP-management methods, and KE in BP-deployment.

# 2 Knowledge Engineering in BP-Framework

"The initial objective of Business Process Management is to capture the guidelines and business rules for an enterprise which govern the way it functions: how a task is processed, which jobs have to be performed, responsibilities and qualifications of actors, and so forth" (Karagiannis 1995).

These guidelines and business rules are usually very general and may be applied to different situations. BPM starts with this observation in order to capture the BP applying various acquisition techniques. Once the BPs are captured, the aim is to design the working procedures in formal representations (Junginger et al. 2000) to be used for model processing.

Hence, the question in the following chapter is how KE techniques can be used to enrich the BP-framework. First, the BP-Framework is discussed and second, KE is introduced to conclude that both can be model-based. Third, the meta model approach is proposed that enables KE in BP-frameworks, and fourth, solutions are presented that have been demonstrated in research projects.

## 2.1 *The BP-Framework*

The BP-framework is seen as a set of assumptions, concepts, values, and practices that constitute a way of viewing BPM. Hence, BPM is seen as an instance of the basic BP-framework. The BP-framework that is proposed can be divided in the four concepts: (1) business models, (2) regulations, (3) domain, and (4) model processing with a model-based approach. In the following, each concept is briefly discussed.

### 2.1.1 The Business Model

There are several frameworks for describing a business model that are seen as "*... a conceptual tool that contains a set of elements and their relationships and allows expressing the business logic of a specific firm* (Osterwalder et al. 2006)".

Independent from the selected business model framework, there are common artifacts of a business model such as the external factors, that is, market situation,

---

[3]Davenport (2010) explores a particular aspect of knowledge in BPM, i.e. how BPM can facilitate knowledge work. As opposed to the general knowledge engineering approach presented in this chapter, Davenport presents process-oriented approaches tailored to the specific requirements of autonomous knowledge workers.

competition, regulations, and social and technical environment, as well as the internal factors, that is, business strategy, business organization, and technology. These artifacts need to be defined for the concrete application scenario. The business model, therefore, defines the basics for the BPM approach.

### 2.1.2 The Domain

The generic BP-framework needs to be realized within a concrete application scenario such as the following: (1) process documentation, (2) process optimization, (3) process calculation, (4) process performance management, (5) capacity planning, (6) risk management, (7) quality management, (8) Six Sigma, (9) Sarbanes-Oxley Act (SOX), (10) software requirement engineering, (11) service-oriented architecture, and (12) IT security management.

Each of the aforementioned application scenarios puts BPM in a specific context, and therefore, requires domain-specific standards, methods, and technologies.

The domain-specific BPM instantiation is seen as a reference for a given domain, still missing the consideration of local dependencies such as regulations and organizational context.

### 2.1.3 The Regulation

The regulations define local dependencies to the application domain that can be divided into legal regulations, business regulation, or technological regulations (Karagiannis et al. 2007).

The business regulations are commonly agreed approaches and standards, such as European Foundation for Quality Management (EFQM), Common Assessment Framework (CAF), or International Organization for Standardization (ISO), as well as commonly agreed practices for safety and health, noise, or pollution control. Technological regulations use frameworks, such as Business Process Execution Language (BPMN), Event-driven Process Chain (EPC), or Unified Modeling Language (UML) for the specification and Business Process Execution Language (BPEL), Ontology Web Language for Semantic Web Service (OWL-S), or Web Service Modeling Ontology (WSMO) for the orchestration of services. Legal regulation frameworks, such as BASEL II, Sarbanes-Oxley Act (SOX), or Euro-SOX, are mandatory in a given context to be applied by organizations.

The aforementioned three viewpoints depend very much on the local context, and hence, can vary between application domains. The instantiation of the BP-framework results in a concrete BPM approach. This approach needs to be bound and managed within the organizational context via a BP-management method, which is introduced in Section 3.

### 2.1.4 The Model Processing

The model processing in this context is a series of automated operations on models that retrieve, transform, or classify information for further use.

As the processing is independent of the applied business models, the domain, and the regulations, it is reasonable to use model processing for KE in order to have a domain, business, and regulation agnostic view on KE in BP-frameworks.

1. First, KE can be used in the definition and application of the modeling language. This includes checks on the correct definition of the modeling language.
2. Another processing part is the mediation and mapping between different modeling languages. This includes the extraction of parts of the models in different formats and different contexts.
3. KE can be used in order to manage the modeling language such as managing the evolution of the language and the models as well as applying security or representation views on models and modeling languages.
4. Finally, the use of the modeling language can be supported by KE. This includes the documentation, transformation, analysis, simulations, or similarity checks within the models.

KE for model processing establishes a direct use of KE within model processing and an indirect use of KE for the whole BP-framework, as when instantiating the framework for a concrete case, all dimensions are represented in models.

## 2.2 *Knowledge Engineering for BP-Framework*

Before discussing the different knowledge approaches, it is important to distinguish between KE that is prioritizing machine interpretable knowledge and knowledge management (KM) that is prioritizing human interpretable knowledge.

The history of KE started in the 1940s with the first attempts of artificial intelligence. After the hype, disillusionment, and first commercial success, KE can be found today in semantic technology (Karagiannis and Telesko 2001). A prominent vision is the Semantic Web that is seen as the "upgrade" of the current Content Web.

KM, in contrast, evolved out of the KE community and has its origin in 1995. KM is a holistic view on the knowledge space that considers human interpretation as well as machine interpretation (Woitsch 2004; Mak 2005; vom Brocke 2007a).

In both cases, model-based approaches provide concepts for the formalization although the level of formalisms is different. Humans have the ability to interpret incomplete and partly corrupted models, whereas machines require knowledge representations in a complete and correct manner.

Hence in both cases, it is reasonable to apply a model-based approach. The knowledge space specifies the domain, encapsulates its content, and provides a semantic for its interpretation. Hence, the knowledge space identifies KE for BP-framework.

First, KE in BP-framework is discussed and second, KE mechanisms are introduced for model processing.

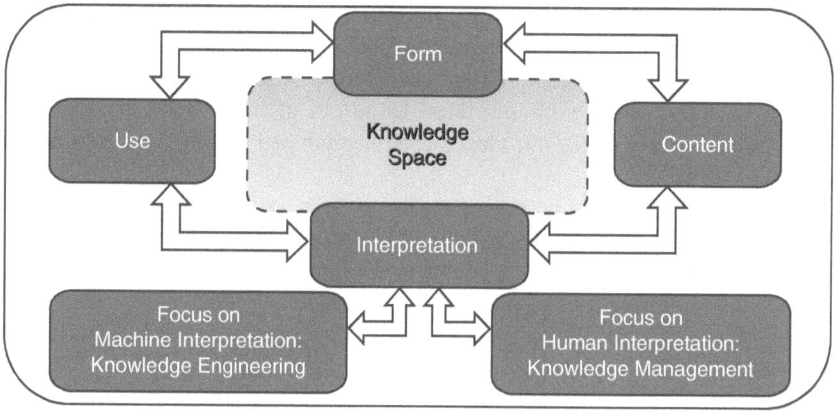


**Fig. 2** The four dimensions of the knowledge space

### 2.2.1 Analyzing Knowledge for KE in BP-Frameworks

The knowledge space defines four dimensions: (1) form, (2) content, (3) interpretation, and (4) use, which is introduced in Fig. 2.

The form represents the syntax and semantic, such as a group of human experts, text documents, models, program code, mathematical forms, or statistics.

When applying KE for model processing, the forms are BP-models. Models need to be distinguished between nonlinguistic or iconic models that use signs and symbols having an apparent similarity to the concepts of the real world and linguistic models that use basic primitives such as signs, characters, or numbers. Nearly all models in BPM are of the latter – linguistic-type. Linguistic models can be further distinguished in being realized with textual and graphical/diagrammatic languages (Kalfoglou and Schorlemmer 2003).

The content is seen as the domain, in which KE is applied. When applying KE for model processing, we interpret the concrete BPM approach that realizes the BP-framework as content.

The use defines how KE is applied for model processing such as the definition and application of the modeling language, the mediation and mapping between modeling languages, the managing and evolution of the language and the models, as well as the use of the models and modeling language considering the documentation, transformation, analysis, simulation, or similarity checks.

The representation of knowledge is either focused on machine interpretation – in terms of KE or on human interpretation – in terms of KM. KE in BP-frameworks focuses on machine interpretation, applying formalisms that represent knowledge for model processing. In the following, mechanisms and tools are discussed for KE in BP-frameworks.

### 2.2.2 Model-Based Approach for KE in BP-Framework

Models enable the externalization of knowledge in a machine interpretable form. As KE has its root in artificial intelligence, the same classification in symbolic, sub-symbolic, and fuzzy logic can be used. It can be expressed in symbols represented in form of rules, frames, logic, predicate logic, or concept maps to express static and dynamic knowledge. Often, such formal and strict representations are difficult to define when extracting knowledge out of the domain experts mind. Hence, fuzzy logic has been introduced enabling a transformation from natural text into fuzzy logic.

Knowledge that cannot be expressed in symbols require sub-symbolic techniques such as neuronal networks, which are an imitation of the human brain. KE in model processing can be used to identify similarities of model patterns. For the externalization of heuristics of domain experts about the correct use of models, the fuzzy logic can be used. For the analysis of models, symbolic mechanism such as rules can be used.

These formalisms can be expressed in models. A prominent sample is the Semantic Web evolved out of the KE community, which has the vision of programs that can support tasks by intelligent mechanisms that were formerly only thought to be solved by humans (http://www.w3.org/Submission/OWL-S/; http://www.wsmo.org/; http://lsdis.cs.uga.edu/projects/meteor-s/index.php?page=1). Hence, KE in BP-frameworks can be applied using a model-based approach. Therefore, the challenge is how to conceptually link KE in BP-frameworks with models.

## 2.3 Conceptual Integration of KE and BP-Framework

Models are considered as an instrument to formally specify the BP-framework as well as KE. Hence, a conceptual integration of BP-framework models with KE models is required for KE in BP-framework.

A solution is the use of the meta model approach for the BP-framework as well as for KE to enable the integration of the two frameworks. The meta model approach is introduced in Fig. 3 depicting the layered model stack by Strahringer, adapted by Karagiannis (Strahringer 1996; Karagiannis and Höfferer 2006).

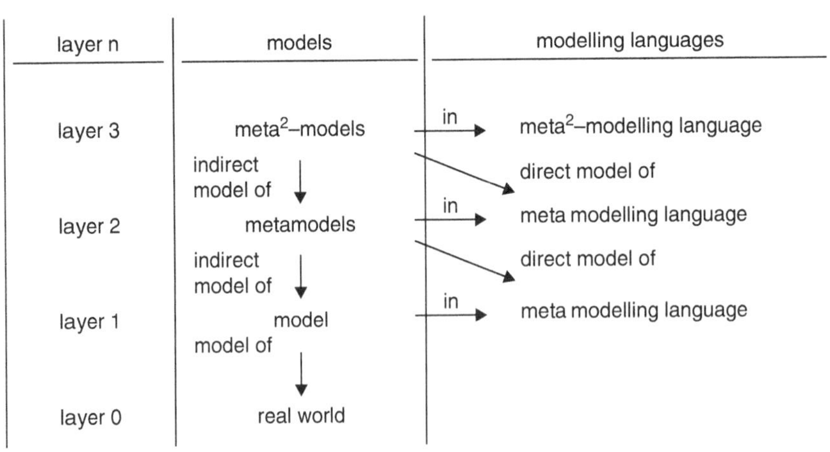


**Fig. 3** Meta Model Layers, based on Strahringer 1996 adapted by Karagiannis

Models are seen as "representation of either reality or vision" (Peters and Ozsu 1993), representing the real world in an agreed syntax and semantics. The modeling language is defined by syntax, semantics, and notation that provide the necessary modeling primitives in order to build the model. The concepts that describe the modeling language are defined in the meta meta model language, which leads to the well-known model layers depicted earlier.

The meta models are therefore seen as a modeling language that can be used to generate models. This enables to distinguish between meta models for BP-frameworks – such as BPs – and meta models for KE – such as business rules.

### 2.3.1 Meta Model Frameworks

A prominent framework for BP-Framework-meta models is the ADOxx® meta meta model, which has been researched at the University of Vienna, and implemented in the commercial tool ADONIS® (Bayer 2001; Junginger et al. 2000; Karagiannis et al. 1996; Karagiannis and Höfferer 2006).

This meta meta model provides not only the basic meta modeling classes that are necessary to define a modeling language such as class, attribute, and relation, but it also introduces several concepts for the specific BP-support, such as model types, views, attribute profiles, and predefined classes for directed graphs for business processes and nondirected graphs for organizational structure.

The commercial products ADOscore®, ADONIS®, ADOlog®, and ADOit® demonstrate the applicability of this approach.

Another prominent framework is MOF – meta object facilities (http://www.omg.org/mof/) – from which the ontology language OWL and the rule language SWRL can be deduced (http://www.w3.org/2007/OWL/wiki/OWL_Working_Group). Hence, MOF is a candidate for object-oriented enterprise modeling, and therefore, used for the object-oriented approach via ontologies.

KE techniques are currently often performed with semantic standards derived from MOF.

Hence the challenge is to integrate meta models derived from MOF – which are used for KE representations – with meta models derived from ADOxx® – which are used for BP-framework representations.

### 2.3.2 KE in BP-Framework Using the Meta Model Approach

The usage of meta models for the BP-framework as well as for KE enables the transformation, exchange, reference, and integration of meta models and other models (Kühn 2004; Kühn et al. 2003). Applying the meta modeling approach for both the BP-framework and KE, it is possible to apply meta modeling merging patterns to realize KE in BP-framework.

The patterns for modeling techniques that are suitable for KE in BP-frameworks are the *reference pattern*, the *extension pattern*, the *transformation pattern*, and the *merge pattern*.

*Reference pattern*: The reference pattern defines links that relate exactly one element in the BP-framework meta model to exactly one element in the KE meta model. A BP-framework, for example, can be further specified by providing links to an ontology to enable the semantic description of a BP object within an ontology.

*Extension pattern*: The extension pattern specifies how the BP-framework can be extended by concepts of KE. New concepts can be integrated, for example, in the form of rules. A rule model that would typically be expressed in rules can be integrated in BP-models.

*Transformation pattern*: In the transformation pattern, rules are responsible for creating parts of one or more BP-framework meta models in a KE meta model. When applying KE in BP-framework this mechanism enables for example the generation of an ontology from a business process.

*Merge pattern*: The merge pattern can be regarded as a specialization of the transformation pattern, where a merge rule generates a part of the KE model from two or more BP-framework models.

## 2.4 Solutions for KE in BP-Framework

The goal with meta models is to establish a m:n relation from different KE models to different BP-models. Hence, the aforementioned meta model reference patterns are proposed for KE in BP-frameworks. In the following, some solutions are introduced that have been realized with ADOxx® and different KE scenarios.

1. *Transformation of BP-framework models into KE* has been applied in BREIN in order to use a semi-formal description of business process models in ADONIS (http://www.boc-group.com) and related Business Process Management languages [e.g. (http://www.oasis-open.org/; ftp://www6.software.ibm.com/software/developer/library/ws-bpel.pdf; http://www-1.ibm.com/services/us/index.wss/offering/bcs/a1006593; http://www.idef.com; Keller et al. 2008)] to define application domain-specific concepts. Mapping rules have been established to allow transformation of the BP-framework models into domain ontologies.

   Parallel to this top-down approach, a continuous evaluation and improvement task has been performed by knowledge engineers, capturing and refining the derived ontologies. The combination of these approaches led to the definition of the ontologies in an iterative way (see Fig. 4), leading to a complete domain conceptualization. The result is a domain ontology that has been transformed from the original BP-framework models in order to apply KE techniques for service discovery and agent-based SLA negotiation within a grid middleware.

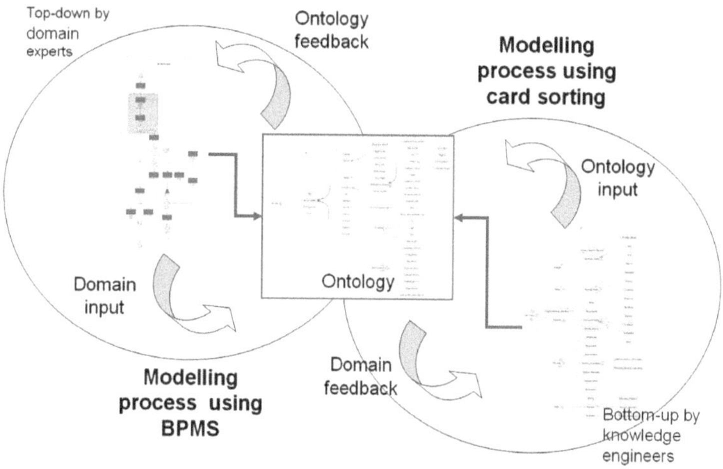


**Fig. 4** Transformation from BP-framework models to KE models (Karagiannis et al. 2008)

2. *Extension of BP-framework with KE* has been applied in FIT, where the BP-framework ADOeGov® based on ADOxx® for egovernment has been extended by business rule models and ontology models. As business rules consist of quite simple model types, the effort in extending the BP-framework was reasonable. These business rules follow the SWRL specification, and hence, require ontology for the term definition. As the use of the ontology was limited for the term definition for SWRL rules, parts of the OWL specification have been implemented in ADOeGov®. The extension of the BP-framework with KE enabled the use of rules within the BP-framework.
3. *Extension and reference of BP-framework with KE* has been applied in AsIs-Known, where the BP-framework has been extended with the OWL specification. This extended ontology in the BP-framework was used as a so-called "transit model" that enables the use of the ontology management system as an autonomous system by referencing to the corresponding concepts via the transit model. Functions such as the inference mechanisms have been performed by the ontology management system, and the ontology concepts have been referenced within the BP-framework via the transit model. The reference pattern has been applied to reference a lexicon out of the BP-models with the aim to delegate KE to the so-called term-resolver of the lexicon, which is a separate system.
4. *The reference of BP-framework with KE* has been applied in LD-Cast in order to combine the BP-framework with KE. In this setup, the BP-framework has not been extended with ontology but a so-called "RDF-Tunnel" has been introduced that is responsible for the annotation management between the BP-framework of ADOxx® and the KE-framework with ATHOS. Hence, the BP-Framework and the KE-framework have been encapsulated by the so-called modeling services and a third system called "RDF-Tunnel" manages the references between these two services. This architecture is a complex integration of BP-frameworks

and KE but provides full functionality for both the model processing within the BP-framework and the knowledge processing within the KE.

The aforementioned solutions introduced different approaches of KE in BP-frameworks, based on the meta modeling approach and the corresponding meta model transformation patterns. The result is a KE-enabled BP-framework, which can be bound into the organizational context by using management methods.

# 3 Knowledge Engineering in the BP-Management Method

This section discusses the management method to bind the previously introduced BP-framework – that may apply KE – into the organizational context. Such a BP-management method can also be supported by KE.

## *3.1 The Organizational Context of BP-Framework*

Organizations have their history, their terminology, their organizational culture, and their system environment that influence the BP-framework. Besides these organizational influences, it is necessary to bind the BP-framework to concrete actions, to concrete persons, and to concrete systems.

### 3.1.1 The BP-Management Method

The binding of the BP-framework to the concrete organization as well as the consideration of narrative organizational influence factors require a BP-management method. A method that can be interpreted as a high-level life cycle consisting of five processes that consider the balance between compliance and performance is the Business Process Management Systems (BPMS) (Karagiannis et al. 1996):

1. *Strategic decision process* is triggered by strategic decision to select the appropriate approach, identify the process in question, and specify the required resources.
2. *Re-Engineering process* is concerned with a detailed insight of the selected processes and demonstrates all activities, their links and relationships, involved persons, and connections to the external environment. This information should be carefully modeled, either from scratch when applying process engineering, or adapting already existing processes when applying re-engineering. The traditional re-engineering is widely interpreted as radical improvement (Hammer 2010). The design part is concerned with the mapping of the real world in a

modeling environment, whereas the modeling part is concerned with the change and adaptation of the models in order to achieve more efficiency.
Depending on the selected approach there are different possibilities to support knowledge engineering in the form of planning tools, animation tools, or simulation tools.
3. *Resource allocation process*: The main objective of the resource allocation is to align the business with concrete IT-infrastructure. This process became more important during the last few years, as the paradigm of a fixed IT-infrastructure changed dramatically. Model driven-architecture, service-oriented architecture, and software as a service pushed the traditional workflow paradigm into orchestration of so-called virtual organizations. Therefore, this process needs also to deal with semantic service management for smart workflows.
4. *Workflow management process*: This process deals with the concrete execution of a workflow. As mentioned, BPM enables the social as well as the technical deployment (Karagiannis 1994). One of the challenges is to interact with technical services in the same manner as with humans (http://download.boulder.ibm.com/ibmdl/pub/software/dw/specs/ws-bpel4people/BPEL4People_v1.pdf). The "virtualization" concept that has originally been used in the Grid community (http://www-fp.mcs.anl.gov/~foster/Articles/WhatIsTheGrid.pdf) now finds its way to workflows managing resources independent of their nature.
5. *Performance evaluation process*: This process collects concrete data about the execution of business processes and integrates them into different evaluation frameworks. Hard fact data collection is performed by logging of execution data to enable data mining. Current log and web mining tools extend this semantic information to make the monitoring domain-specific. Additionally, soft facts can be acquired by questionnaires allowing an integrative cockpit to monitor, evaluate, and optimize.

The knowledge that is required to execute the aforementioned processes, such as strategy knowledge, process knowledge, resource allocation knowledge, workflow knowledge, as well as performance management knowledge, can partly be formalized for engineering.

In the following, the chapter focuses on the re-engineering process that uses the aforementioned model processing from the BP-framework; hence, direct and indirect KE support is provided.

### 3.1.2 Knowledge Intensive Actions in the BP-Method

In the following, the focus is on the re-engineering phase, as it is the interface for the transformation from real world into formalisms. This phase has five knowledge-intensive actions.

Figure 5 depicts the five knowledge-intensive actions within the re-engineering process of the BPMS. The acquisition observes the current situation of the real world and transforms parts of it into a representation.

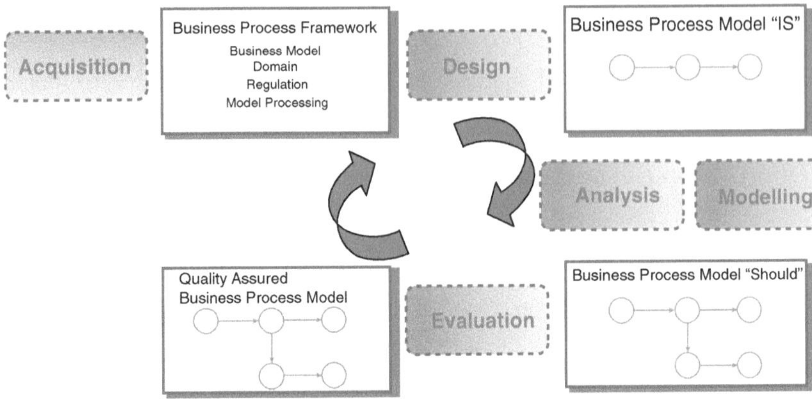


**Fig. 5** Knowledge intensive domains in the re-engineering process

The acquisition uses either quantitative acquisition methods, such as ethnographic studies, questionnaires, or mining techniques, or qualitative methods, such as interviews or workshops, to acquire information for the actual design.

Based on the collection of representation parts, the design produces a model of the real world, by taking the individual parts of the acquisition to form a complete and coherent representation as the "is-model." The analysis and modeling are two counterparts; while the analysis aims to identify weaknesses in the existing model, the modeling performs continuously changes in the model that need to be analyzed till the quality is sufficient in the form of a "should-model." Finally, the model passes the evaluation to check whether the model has been correctly generated. The result is a quality assured model.

The design, analysis, modeling, and evaluation of models use modeling languages and tools. Hence, the knowledge provided is either implemented in the modeling language, the tool, or in additional resources. The modeling language can be classified according to the level of expressiveness and the domain it is used. As the built-in knowledge support depends on the level of expressiveness, there is a different knowledge support available.

It has to be mentioned that the BP-method is a human-intensive task, and hence, KM approaches and KE are likely to be applied in combination (Telesko et al. 2001). In the following, the focus is on KE.

## 3.2 KE Solutions for BP-Management Method

In the following section, solutions for KE for BP-management method are discussed:

1. *Adaptive questionnaires* (http://www.boc-eu.com; http://www.fit-project.org) to support the acquisition have the advantage that the sequence of questions can

change according to the previously given answers. The idea is that answers are seen as objects that refer to questions. Therefore, there is a so-called "loose coupling" between the sequence of questions and the sequence of possible answers. The question sequence is primarily executed by a workflow engine, whereas the referenced possible answers are treated similar to Web – services that are bound to the questions during execution. Applying mechanisms for adaptive workflows, it is then possible to hand over the control of the question sequence to a rule engine in case an adaptive question sequence has been reached. The previously given answers are then interpreted as facts and the engine tries to find new questions that match with already provided answers. A more detailed description on the cooperation between workflow engine and rule engine is provided in the smart process execution section.

2. *Knowledge-based designer* (http://www.asisknown.org) supports homogeneous modeling from different domain experts with different implicit knowledge, cultures, and different natural languages. The domain ontology has to be generated for a common language by domain experts. To align the terminology, each term is translated into the agreed language. This glossary is used to check the correct usage of terms in models and provides reports on the compliance of the used terms. In case the term is not found, it proposes terms available within the glossary. The domain expert is involved in the evolution of the glossary, as when unsatisfying suggestions are provided, there is the possibility of insisting on new terms. The glossary evolves on the basis of the negotiation between the ontology expert and the domain expert.
3. *Formalization and transformation of models* enable the conceptual integration of models that are represented in different formats and formal expressiveness, and hence, enable conceptual integration. The transformation from, for example, a business process model into an ontology, is based on transformation rules, where each modeling concept gets a mapping to the corresponding ontology construct. It is important to consider the semantic loss, when translating from a less expressive language to a more expressive language. This challenge is tackled by using rules to transform models into ontology concepts. The technical solution is conducted either by fix-coded mappings or by transformation rules.
4. *Knowledge-based analysis of models* provides enhanced search functionality within the model repository (http://www.asisknown.org). Traditionally, a search interface is offered to enable the search for modeling constructs. In case the modeling language cannot provide a satisfactory answer, the request is translated term by term into OWL and passed to the domain ontology. An inference engine searches term by term, for example, parent-, children-, and sibling-concepts to enlarge the analysis features of the BP-models.
5. *Knowledge-based evaluation* for quality assurance deals with the challenge that an expert and a novice modeler have different competences in modeling guidelines and the correct application of the modeling language. The aim is to make implicit knowledge of the experienced modeler explicit in order to enable checks of the model generated by novices that go beyond current model analysis. Examples for model checks that can be implemented are for instance tests that

verify whether processes have exactly one start-object and heuristics that assess the quality of a model on the number of inter-model references in comparison with the number of objects in the model.

Applying the BP-management method enables the binding of the BP-framework into a concrete organizational context. In order to make the organization-specific BP-framework operational, it is necessary to deploy it into the existing platform. Hence, the next chapter discusses the BP-deployment into an organizational infrastructure to make the BP-framework operational.

# 4 KE in BP-Deployment

BPM can be either technically deployed via workflow engines that interpret machine interpretable processes, or can be socially deployed via business processes or organizational order that provides human interpretable processes.

BP-deployment requires awareness of KE technologies used in the executive platform as they become a common approach (http://www.bptrends.com/search.cfm?keyword=Kunzi&gogo=1; http://www.ip-super.org/) in order to provide the corresponding concepts. In the following, BP sample deployments that use KE techniques are introduced.

## 4.1 *Knowledge Techniques and Solutions for BP-Deployment*

In the following, solutions for KE in BP-deployment are discussed that basically use the concepts of the BP-framework and deploy them into system platforms.

1. *Smart process publishing* tackles the challenge that business process models are designed by skilled modelers, while the documentation, however, is designed for the nonexperts. So the same model information is provided for two differently skilled roles. Currently available mechanisms implement a "one to many" publishing component that distributes the content differently to separate target groups. This is seen as server-side content adaptation that requires large resources publishing the content for each of the user groups separately. On-demand, content generation enforces a paradigm change to a client-side content adaptation, where the user interface at the client interprets the content differently depending on the context of the user. The idea has its origin from the Adaptive Web (Brusilovsky 2003) that creates a user model based on the navigation behavior of the user. Once the user model has been identified, there are active content elements that change their appearance on the basis of the user model.
2. *Smart process execution* considers the combination of adaptive workflows (Leutgeb et al. 2007) and semantic service discovery (Catapano et al. 2008). The integration of the workflow engine and the business rule engine enables an

adaptive and smart workflow engine that requires semantic concept. The technical integration is performed as the business rule engine is integrated as a service and called by the workflow engine [Active BPEL Engine (http://www.activeos.com)] when a decision has to be taken. The business rule engine receives the relevant data as well as the rule-set to be executed. The results of rule execution are provided in an engine-specific format to the workflow engine. In order to make the workflow engine adaptive, a so-called "Rule Enactor" has been implemented, which transforms the application data of the workflow engine into a format for rule execution. This architecture reduces the complexity of the workflow- and the rule definition, as the Rule Enactor limits the interaction scenarios between rule engine and workflow to a predefined set of invocation types.

In order to enable a semantic service discovery, service ontology is used that maps BPs to workflows. These workflows are defined as abstract, as up to the defined point in time they have no concrete services bound to their activities/tasks. In the second step, registered concrete services, which could be used to carry out one of the activities, are annotated with the same concept from the ontology.

Figure 6 shows the required concepts for the integration of BPs, abstract workflows, and concrete services, where respective items have been annotated with corresponding concepts from the ontology (C1–C4). Once all required items have been annotated, registered, and published, the abstract workflows can be provided

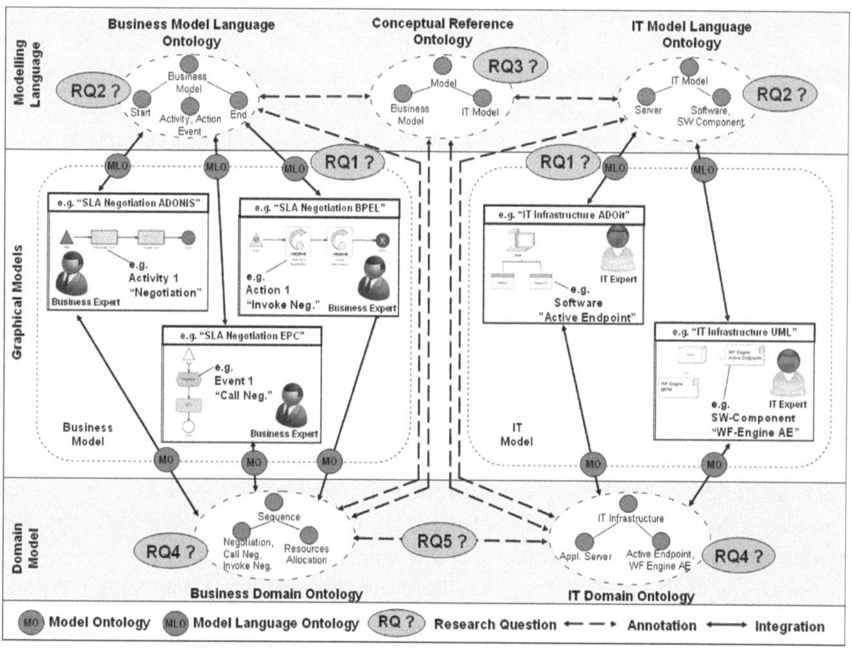


**Fig. 6** Service delivery using semantic workflows

to the end users. If an abstract workflow is accessed, it has to be bound to a concrete workflow, where semantic service discovery offers different mechanisms for lazy or ambiguous bindings.

The aforementioned sections discussed KE in BP-frameworks to enable KE sensitive BP-frameworks. In order to bind the BP-framework into the organizational context, it is necessary to apply a BP-management method, which can be supported by KE.

The previous sections concluded with concrete solutions that have been developed and demonstrated in a wide range of application scenarios. The following section gives an outlook on upcoming challenges when considering KE in BPM.

# 5 Outlooks on KE in BPM

This section gives an outlook on the conceptual and technical alignment between KE and BPM introducing the next generation modeling framework. First, the conceptual alignment between KE and BPM is introduced, and second, the technical alignment is discussed by providing a reference architecture for model-based alignment.

## *5.1 Conceptual KE and BPM Alignment*

There are different approaches, where either semantic techniques using an ontology stack (Schacher and Grässle 2006) or meta modeling patterns (http://www.athena-ip.org/) are used to establish model-based BPM alignment. This section argues for a hybrid approach, by applying the meta model patterns and realizing the transformation and integration following a semantic approach. The Semantic Integration World Animation (SIWA) (Nissen and Jarke 1999) approach as an extension to MOF is seen as an interesting multilevel modeling framework that enhances the linguistic meta modeling processing with additional semantic primitives. An appealing aspect of this approach is the automatic suggestions of meta model and the allowance of incomplete models. A concept that makes the semantics explicit is called lifting (Kappel et al. 2006) that is based on the approach of ontology anchoring.

But for the given complexity, the SIWA approach needs to be enriched, by a knowledge base for modeling languages, for models as well as translation rules. Such an enriched conceptual architecture is introduced in Fig. 7 by introducing knowledge bases for different BP-framework models, as well as for different KE models and introduces additional rules that enable the alignment.

Following such a hybrid conceptual architecture enables a technological platform to interpret meta models as well as semantics for the alignment. Such a platform enables the coherent modeling of BPM models as well as KE models with different modeling languages but using the same model base.

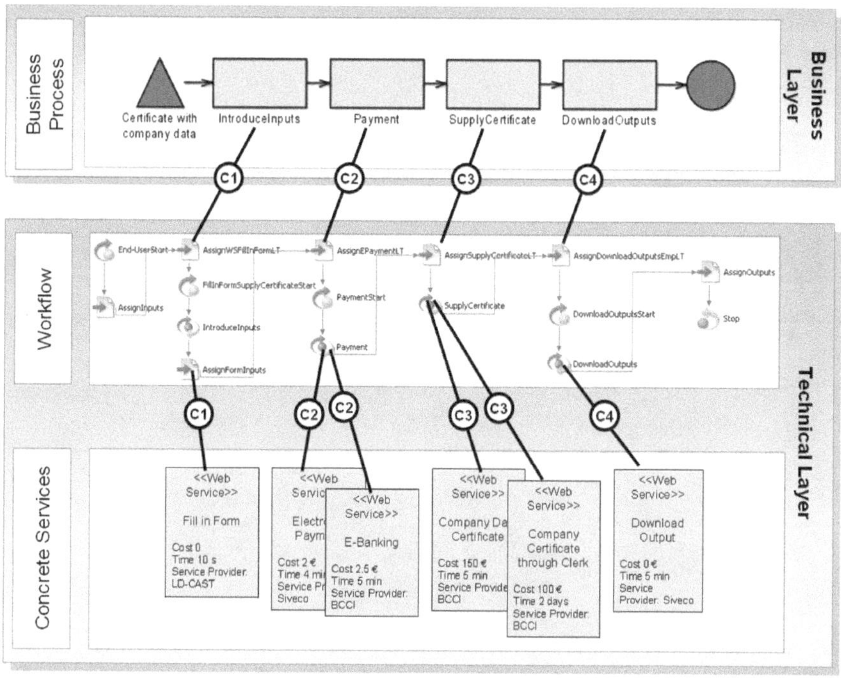


**Fig. 7** Conceptual architecture for knowledge alignment

## 5.2 *Technical KE and BPM Alignment*

The aim of the next generation modeling framework is to provide appropriate editors to represent knowledge demand and knowledge provision independent of the BPM business model, the BPM domain, the BPM regulations, or the BPM processing on one side as well as the knowledge form, the knowledge use, the knowledge content, and the knowledge interpretation on the other side.

The following reference architecture enables to apply the model-based approach for KE in BPM using a flexible and open IT-infrastructure.

There is a large variety of modeling tools, ranging from informal, unstructured, and text-based to semi-structured and formal ones. Different tools are used for different purposes and it is quite common to encounter both unstructured and structured modeling methods. As most of the tools are already in use, the challenge is therefore not to exchange the existing modeling tools, but instead use a reference architecture that integrates existing modeling tools and makes them interoperable to enable the alignment of BPM and KE.

Technically spoken, the traditional three layer architecture of meta modeling tools (Junginger et al. 2000) needs to be enriched by a fourth layer, the so-called "Semantic Modeling Kernel". In order to enable such an enrichment of existing tools, the service-oriented approach is applied. The corresponding reference

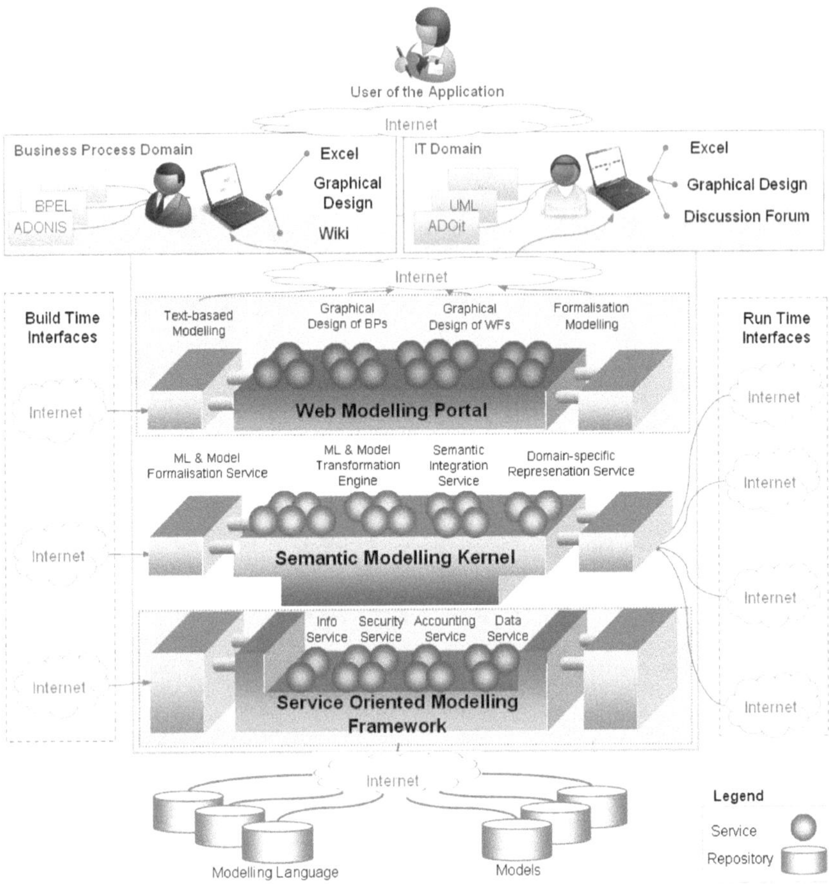


Fig. 8 Next generation Business Process Management modeling framework

architecture is depicted in Fig. 8 as the next generation modeling framework. Basically, the reference architecture identifies four different layers. The bottom layer is concerned with the transparent storage of models and modeling languages with the vision of an open model repository. The layer called service-oriented modeling framework provides middleware services such as service registration, service discovery, service orchestration as well as basic model functionality such as model access, accounting, security, or information services.

The top layer is the Web modeling portal, which provides user interfaces for modeling services and deals with the communication between the Web-applications in the Web-browser and modeling services running on the server.

The proposed next generation modeling framework introduces a new layer to this architecture, the so-called semantic modeling kernel, which is responsible for the transformation between the different modeling tools, modeling languages, and models. This layer is responsible for the transformation of syntax, semantic, and context that enables the aforementioned integration of meta models and semantics.

This modeling framework is developed within the Open Model Initiative that publishes open model approaches. The aforementioned approach is seen as one project within the Open Model Initiative (http://www.openmodels.at) that provides a solution for KE in BPM.

## 6 Summary

This chapter identified three aspects of KE in BPM. First, BPM can be seen as a domain on its own, and hence, the basic BP-framework can be enriched with KE. As the BP-framework and KE can be represented by models; the integration of KE in BP-frameworks can be realized with the meta model approach.

As the instantiation of a concrete BPM approach requires a management method that binds the BPM approach into the organizational context in order to enable the actual management, the BP-management method has been introduced. KE in BP-management method has been discussed focusing on the knowledge intensive actions during the re-engineering phase.

After the realization of BPM within a concrete organization, it is necessary to enable the execution within an environment. In case this platform uses KE techniques, the BPM approach requires awareness of these concepts. Hence, KE in BP-deployment is introduced.

This chapter considers the wide field of KE in BPM, and therefore, focuses on relevant aspects in the three viewpoints that are justified by demonstration within research projects.

The outlook discusses a conceptual and technical integration of KE and BPM that enables a discussion beyond the aforementioned solutions.

This chapter discussed approaches for KE in BPM. Considering also the human interpretation that is focused in KM, there are similarities for KM in BPM. The introduced approaches as well as the outlook considered a model-based approach for KE in BPM. As KM can also be realized using a model-based approach and the introduced mechanisms can be used for the more formal models in KE, it is possible to use the aforementioned mechanisms for the partly informal model used in KM.

## References

Active BPEL Engine. http://www.activeos.com. Accessed 10 Nov 2008
ADONIS®. http://www.boc-group.com. Accessed 15 Nov 2008
ATHENA EC-Project. http://www.athena-ip.org/. Accessed 5 May 2008
AsIsKnown EC-Project. http://www.asisknown.org. Accessed 10 Nov 2008
AWA Project, Austrian National Project. http://www.boc-eu.com. Accessed 10 Nov 2008

Bayer Franz (2001) Proceedings der Informatik'2001 – Wirtschaft und Wissenschaft in der Network Economy – Visionen und Wirklichkeit. In: Bauknecht K, Brauer W, Mück Th (Hrsg) Tagungsband II der GI/OCG-Jahrestagung, Universität Wien, 25–28 September 2001, pp S922–S927

BMI Report, Bptrend. http://www.bptrends.com/. Accessed 10 Nov 2008

BPEL for People. http://download.boulder.ibm.com/ibmdl/pub/software/dw/specs/ws-bpel4people/BPEL4People_v1.pdf. Accessed 11 Nov 2008

Brusilovsky P (2003) University of Pittsburgh, USA, From adaptive hypermedia to the adaptive web. In: Szwillus G, Ziegler J (Hrsg) Mensch & computer: Interaktion in Bewegung, Stuttgart, Teubner BG, pp S21–S24

Catapano A, D'Atri A, Hrgovcic V, Ionita AD, Tarabanis K (2008) LD-CAST: local development cooperation actions enabled by semantic technology, eastern Europe e|Gov days. Prague, Czech Republic

Davenport TH (2010) Process management for knowledge work. In: vom Brocke J, Rosemann M (eds) Handbook on business process management, vol 1. Springer, Heidelberg

FIT EC-Project. http://www.fit-project.org. Accessed 10 Nov 2008

Foster I What is grid? In: A three point checklist. http://www-fp.mcs.anl.gov/~foster/Articles/WhatIsTheGrid.pdf. Accessed 10 Nov 2008

Gartner (2006) http://www.gartner.com/it/page.jsp?id=497088. Accessed 10 Nov 2008

Hammer M (2010) What is business process management? In: vom Brocke J, Rosemann M (eds) Handbook on business process management, vol 2. Springer, Heidelberg

IBM, Business Process Execution Language For Web Services (BPEL4WS). ftp://www6.software.ibm.com/software/developer/library/ws-bpel.pdf. Accessed 20 Jun 2006

IBM, Line of Visibility Enterprise Modeling (LOVEM). http://www-1.ibm.com/services/us/index.wss/offering/bcs/a1006593. Accessed 10 Nov 2008

IDEF, Integrated Definition Methods. http://www.idef.com. Accessed 10 Nov 2008

Johnson J, Dum R SOS-Homepage. http://complexsystems.lri.fr/Portal/tiki-index.php?page=SOS+Homepage&bl. Accessed 10 Nov 2008

Junginger S, Kühn H, Strobl R, Karagiannis D (2000) Ein Geschäftsprozessmanagement-Werkzeug der nächsten Generation-ADONIS: Konzeption und Anwendungen, Wirtschaftsinformatik, Vieweg, pp 392–401

Kalfoglou Y, Schorlemmer M (2003) Ontology mapping: the state of the art. Knowl Eng Rev 18(1):1–31

Kappel G, Kapsammer E, Kargl H, Kramler G, Reiter T, Retschitzegger W, Schwinger W, Wimmer M (2006) On models and ontologies – a layered approach for model-based tool integration. In: Mayr HC, Breu R (eds) Modellierung 2006, pp 11–27

Karagiannis D (1994) Die Rolle von Workflow-Management beim Re-Engineering von Geschäftsprozessen. Dv Management 3/94, pp 109–114

Karagiannis D (1995) BPMS: business process management systems. SIGOIS Bulletin 16(1): 10–13

Karagiannis D, Höfferer P (2006) Metamodels in action: an overview. In: Filipe J, Shishkov B, Helfert M (eds) ICSOFT 2006 – First international conference on software and data technologies: IS27-36. Insticc Press, Setúbal

Karagiannis D, Junginger S, Strobl R (1996) Introduction to business process management systems concepts, business process modelling. In: Scholz-Reiter B, Stickel E (eds), Springer, ISBN 3-540-61707-8, pp 81–106

Karagiannis D, Mylopoulos J, Schwab M (2007) Business process-based regulation compliance: the case of the Sarbanes-Oxley Act. In: 15th IEEE international requirements engineering conference, 2007

Karagiannis D, Telesko R (2001) Wissensmanagement: Konzepte der künstlichen Intelligenz und des Softcomputing. Oldenbourg Wissenschaftsverlag, Germany. ISBN 3486255665

Karagiannis D, Utz W, Woitsch R, Eichner H (2008) Business process modelling for semantic service oriented infrastructure. In: Cunningham P, Cunningham M (eds) Collaboration and the knowledge economy. IOS Press, Amsterdam

Keller G, Nüttgens M, Scheer A-W Semantische Prozessmodellierung auf der Grundlage, Ereignisgesteuerter Prozessketten (EPK). In: Scheer A-W Veröffetlichungen des Instituts für Wirtschaftsinformatik (Iwi), Universität des Saarlandes, Heft 89, Jannuar 92, http://www.iwi.uni-sb.de/Download/iwihefte/heft89.pdf. Accessed 10 Nov 2008

Kühn H (2004) Methodenintegration in business engineering. PhD thesis, University of Vienna

Kühn H, Bayer F, Junginger S, Karagiannis D (2003) Enterprise model integration. In: Bauknecht K, Min Tjoa A Quirchmayer G (eds) Proceedings of the 4th international conference ec-web 2003, Dexa 2003, Prague, Czech Republic, September 2–5, 2003, lncs 2738, Springer-Verlag, Berlin, Heidelberg, pp 379–392

Leutgeb A, Utz W, Woitsch R, Fill H-G (2007) Adaptive processes in e-government – a field report about semantic-based approaches from the EU-project "FIT". In: Proceedings of the international conference on enterprise information systems (ICEIS 07), Funchal, Madeira – Portugal

Lienhard H, Künzi U-M Workflow and business rules: a common approach. In: BPTrends 2005. http://www.bptrends.com/search.cfm?keyword=Kunzi&gogo=1. Accessed 10 Nov 2008

Mak K (2005) Der Einsatz des prozessorientierten Wissensmanagementwerkzeuges PROMOTE® in der Zentraldokumentation der Landesverteidigungsakademie, Landesverteidigungsaka demie Wien

METEOR-S. Semantic web services and processes. http://lsdis.cs.uga.edu/projects/meteor-s/index.php?page=1. Accessed 10 Nov 2008

Nissen HW, Jarke M (1999) Repository support for multi-perspective requirements engineering. Information Systems 24(2):131–158

OASIS: OASIS SOA reference model. http://www.oasis-open.org/. Accessed 10 Nov 2008

Object Management Group (OMG), Meta Object Facility (MOF). http://www.omg.org/mof/. Accessed 15 Nov 2008

Open Model Initiative. http://www.openmodels.at. Accessed 10 Nov 2008

Osterwalder A, Pigneur Y, Tucci CL (2006) Clarifying business models: origins, present, and future of the concept. Communications of AIS:17

OWL Working Group. http://www.w3.org/2007/OWL/wiki/OWL_Working_Group. Accessed 15 Nov 2008

Peters RJ, Ozsu MT (1993) Reflection in a uniform behavioral object model. In: Proceedings of the 12th international conference on entity-relationship approach, pp 34–45

Schacher M, Grässle P (2006) Agile unternehmen durch business rules. Springer, Berlin

Strahringer S (1996) Metamodellierung als Instrument des Methodenvergleichs: eine Evaluierung am Beispiel objektorientierter Analysemethoden. Shaker, Aachen

SUPER, EC-Project SUPER. http://www.ip-super.org/. Accessed 01 Oct 2008

Telesko R, Karagiannis D, Woitsch R (2001) Knowledge management concepts and tools: the PROMOTE project. In: Gronau N, Wissensmanagement – Systeme – Anwendungen – Technologien, Proceedings of the 2nd Oldenburger Forum Wissensmanagement, Shaker Verlag, Aachen

vom Brocke J (2007a) Informationssysteme für Wissensnetzwerke, HMD, Praxis der Wirtschaftsinformatik

vom Brocke J (2007b) Wirtschaftlichkeit serviceorientierter Architekturen. Management und Controlling von Prozessen als Service Portfolios. HMD, Praxis der Wirtschaftsinformatik

W3C. OWL-S: semantic markup for web services. http://www.w3.org/Submission/OWL-S/. Accessed 10 Nov 2008

Woitsch R (2004) Process oriented knowledge management: a service-based approach. PhD thesis, University of Vienna

WSMO, Web Service Modeling Ontology. http://www.wsmo.org/. Accessed 10 Nov 2008

# Cultural Change in Process Management

**Ulrike Baumöl**

**Abstract** Organizational change management is an important task in the context of Business Process Management (BPM). Organizational change covers a broad range of topics, from strategy to corporate culture and performance management. BPM is at the center of change initiatives as the main lever for implementing change through process engineering. Yet, especially the cultural aspects of organizational change have not been systematically integrated into the principles of BPM. Since organizational change is mainly driven by projects, an integrated change method would be helpful to support the business process manager to achieve the goals of change. Existing methods, however, are often rather inflexible and do not cater to the situational needs of a change project. Moreover, they tend to focus on specific topics of change, for example, either strategy or processes or culture. This leads to a disregard of the interrelation of the relevant topics, and with this, the complexity of organizational change. As a consequence, an approach is required, which first of all supports the holistic analysis of an organizational change project, and secondly provides a method construction process which allows for a situational design of the change method integrating the relevant dimensions of organizational change as well as the involved "hard" and "soft" factors. This chapter introduces a corresponding approach.

## 1 Introduction

Successfully changing an organization is still one of the major challenges of today's management. A recent study by Jorgensen et al. (2007, pp. 1–19) points out that despite many approaches in theory and practice, still only 38% of the analyzed projects are considered successful. An interesting fact presented is the fairly low

U. Baumöl
Department of Information Management, University of Hagen, Hagen, Germany
e-mail: ulrike.baumoel@fernuni-hagen.de

J. vom Brocke and M. Rosemann (eds.), *Handbook on Business Process Management 2*, International Handbooks on Information Systems,
DOI 10.1007/978-3-642-01982-1_23, 

diffusion of formal change methods. In only 22% of the companies, a formal change method exists and is employed during the change process. The authors compare the maturity of change management with that of project management 20 years ago: the degree of improvisation during the process is high and the success of the change process depends on a fair amount of serendipity. However, considering the value that can be destroyed by a failed change process, the dependency on serendipity is not acceptable. The volume of only the merger and acquisition market of 200 bn. Euro in 2006 already justifies a closer look at how organizational change processes can be managed more efficiently.

Organizational change is mostly driven by Business Process Management (BPM) (cf. Oesterle 1995). Almost any effort of an organization to adapt to new requirements involves at some point of time analyzing the processes (cf. Baumöl 2008). This step results in either initializing a process reengineering or a process engineering phase, depending on the degree of change that is to be introduced. The reason for the high significance of BPM for organizational change is first of all the function of processes as direct levers for implementing the strategy. Secondly, they serve as junction between the strategy and the supporting information technology (IT) solutions by defining the business requirements for the IT solution. As a consequence, each change – be it on the strategy level or on the task level – is directly dependent on BPM.

One of the critical success factors of transforming the company by changing processes is the responsiveness of the people and their true commitment toward the new ways of doing things. As a consequence, a "process culture" with values, beliefs, and process-oriented behavior needs to be established before the change process starts [also cf. Bucher and Winter (2010)]. Moreover, the challenge today is to foster the ability to manage evolutionary, continuous change rather than driving revolutionary change. As a consequence, the "unfreeze–freeze" paradigm cannot be applied here.

The change method, in which the approach of business process engineering is ideally embedded, plays an important role for the success of the change initiative. Current BPM methods often lack a dedicated change management approach (cf. e.g., Spanyi 2006). This is probably the case because these methods are designed to focus on the content related rather than the behavior-related change. Thus, mainly the so-called "hard factors," which are much more tangible and communicable, are addressed and the "soft factors" are at most treated indirectly. This becomes very clear, when during a project meeting, the question about the way a change is addressed is answered by the process consultants by explaining the way new requirements or changes in the process design during the implementation phase are managed. This misunderstanding happens very often and shows that there is still room for improvement with respect to the awareness of the cultural issues of organizational change.

It does not help, though, to refer to change methods for solving this shortcoming. The majority of change methods proposed in theory and practice (cf. e.g., Tichy and Devanna 1990; Friedman and Gyr 1998; Vollmann 1996; Doppler and Lauterburg 2000; Burke 2002; Kotter 2008) concentrate on specific change topics, such as change of culture or change of processes.[1] This is efficient with respect to the chosen focus, but it often neglects the complexity of the entire change process with its many influencing factors. The methods promoted by consulting companies tend to be strictly standardized and fairly inflexible. As a consequence, companies facing a change process often find themselves changing the change method before even starting, and as a consequence, lose the efficiency gains a standardized approach promises (cf. Classen et al. 2003, pp. 3–12). The change process is operationalized by a portfolio of change projects. The goals and milestones of these projects are defined by the goals of the organizational change. The projects are managed by the respective project management methods of the company, for example, PRINCE2 or standards of the Project Management Institute (PMI). Since these merely have a supportive character for change methods, they are not discussed in detail in this chapter.

The hypothesis on which this chapter is based states that only a comprehensive and flexible approach toward organizational change can foster the receptiveness of the intended changes. To solve this challenge, the following objectives are pursued in this chapter:

- Explain the prerequisites for dealing with organizational change.
- Present a framework for describing change projects and the relevant influencing factors.
- Suggest an approach for constructing situational change methods called "Change Method Engineering (CME)," which caters to the requirements of the people responsible for the change process, for example, the business process manager.

Such an approach combines hard and soft factors and integrates with this the relevant dimensions of organizational change. Moreover, it has to be flexible to its construction process as opposed to trying to treat all organizations more or less the same way.

An approach like this supports the business process manager facing the challenge of dealing with organizational change in the following way:

- The business process manager needs to understand the overall consequences of the proposed changes on both the "hard" and "soft" factors: CME takes into consideration the most relevant dimensions of organizational change and integrates them. With this, it does not focus either on "contents" or on "behavior," but builds the necessary bridge to provide the full picture.
- The business process manager needs to have a framework for modeling the change process and the resulting change projects with all relevant factors: CME suggests a framework for modeling both the change process and the change project in connection with its "hard" and "soft" context to gain a detailed understanding of the prerequisites and requirements of organizational change.

---

[1]vom Brocke et al. (2010) present the case of the Hilti corporation, providing insights into how change processes are facilitated by a so called "culture journey".

- The business process manager needs to have a toolbox for constructing change methods, which answer to the respective requirements of the situation the company is in: CME provides a method construction methodology, which has been deduced from successful change projects.
- And last, but not least, the business process manager needs to identify possible barriers to accept and to adapt to the new process architecture: CME provides a concept based on keywords for the analysis of the state of acceptance in the dimension "culture & emotions."

The argumentation is first of all built on the notion that change processes are driven by a chain of individual decision processes which cannot be deterministically foreseen. Thus, following a constructivist approach toward change, a flexible construction of the change method is mandatory. Secondly, the hard factors normally drive the emotional change process, both directly and indirectly. Only by integrating the hard and the soft factors, a successful management of the change process becomes possible. Figure 1 presents the building blocks of the chapter and their relationship. It shows that there are three basic factors which have to be considered when managing organizational change. First of all, BPM has to be established as a management approach within the company, since it serves as a basis for driving the change process. It does so in two ways: On the one hand, the intended change is implemented in the business processes and BPM is the approach to manage it. On the other hand, the principles of BPM are also applied for managing the change process. Secondly, the prerequisites for organizational change must be clear and understood. The questions, what went well and what went wrong in other change projects, or are there best practices, must be considered. Thirdly, the

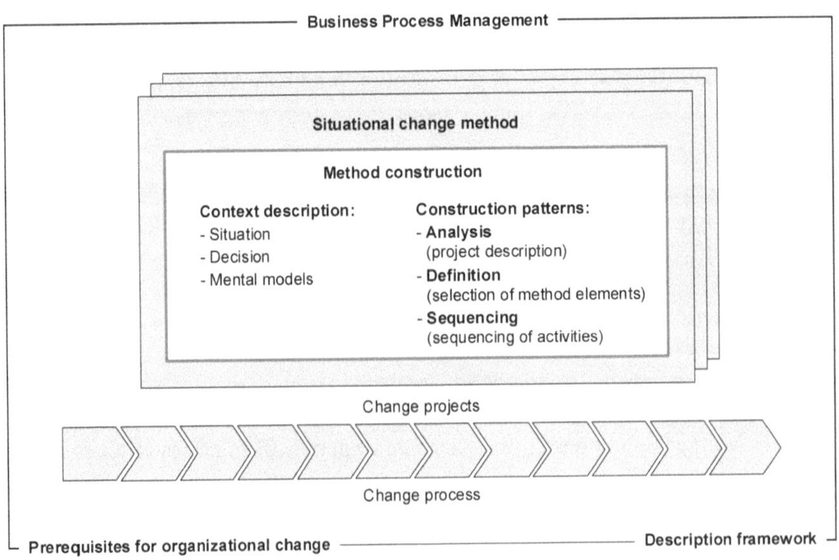


**Fig. 1** BPM and change effects in the organization

change project must be clearly defined and documented. Thus, a framework for describing change projects must exist, which could serve as an input for the method construction process.

The change process starts with the first idea or need to change the organization and it goes on until the change is established within the organization. The goals of the change process are implemented by one or more change projects, which are based on a specific method [also cf. Bucher and Winter (2010)]. This chapter suggests a change method, which consists of two major parts: a framework for describing the project context and a procedure to construct a situational change method.[2]

The chapter develops in the following way: First, evidence is presented that the success of organizational change is in most cases dependent on the "human factor." Then, results of a 2004 study by the author highlight the most important factors for successful change from the perspective of the people "being changed." Following that, factors are presented which directly address and influence the "human factor" of organizational change. These factors are taken from an in-depth analysis of several change projects in the US (i.e., California), Germany, Switzerland, and Austria. With this, the prerequisites of organizational change are discussed. In the next section, a framework for describing change projects is presented, which was also developed based on the interviews of the 2004 study. As a basis for the method construction approach, the responsiveness to change is analyzed based on the concept of mental models. In the last section, based on the business engineering approach of method engineering, a method construction process is presented, which takes into consideration the requirements of situational flexibility as well as the integration of relevant dimensions of a change project. With this integrated approach, a systematic change process becomes possible, considering both hard and soft factors. It combines techniques from the engineering and business disciplines with approaches from organizational psychology. Moreover, in addition to the theoretical concepts, a case study is presented which shows the application of the presented ideas in a real-life company context.

## 2 Prerequisites for Modeling Business Process Driven Organizational Change

To understand and in the end manage the change process successfully, it is first of all important to analyze the influencing factors on success and failure of organizational change. The second step is to model, that is, describe the change project as comprehensively as possible to make it communicable. Lastly, it is crucial to understand the mechanisms and levers for successful change. These steps are the

[2]Bucher and Winter (2010) propose a general introduction into situational method engineering in the context of Business Process Management.

groundwork for a systematic approach toward constructing a change method and thus, managing the change project. In the following sections, the basics of the three steps are presented. These are, at the same time, the foundation for the CME approach which is presented later on in the chapter.

## 2.1 Influencing Factors on Organizational Change

Recent studies have shown that the rate of success of change projects is still considerably low (cf. Jorgensen et al. 2007): only 38% of the projects analyzed are rated as successful in every aspect, 46% of the projects are considered "troubled," and 16% are rated as failure. Figure 2 sums up these results graphically.

Among the 220 projects analyzed, the reasons for troubled or failing projects are diverse, but eventually they can be traced back to mainly soft factors (cf. Jorgensen et al. 2007). To complete the picture, it is interesting to look at a different study which analyzed successful projects and the main factors for success (cf. Houben et al. 2007). Here it is interesting to note that also "hard" factors (e.g., existence of training programs, compensation, organizational structure, and performance management system) played a role in the success. These factors were not mentioned in the analysis of failure. This represents a contrast to the failure factors, which are mainly soft factors. Table 1 summarizes the failure and success factors ordered according to their relative importance.

These findings support an in-depth study of 52 companies on methods applied in change projects in the San Francisco Bay Area and the Silicon Valley, Germany, Switzerland, and Austria conducted by the author in 2004 as well as the literature analysis of 37 case studies and methodologies (cf. Baumöl 2008). The recent findings of Jorgensen et al. and Houben et al. show that the issues of organizational change management seem to be quite stable, so it seems to be safe to assume that the findings from 2004 are still valid.

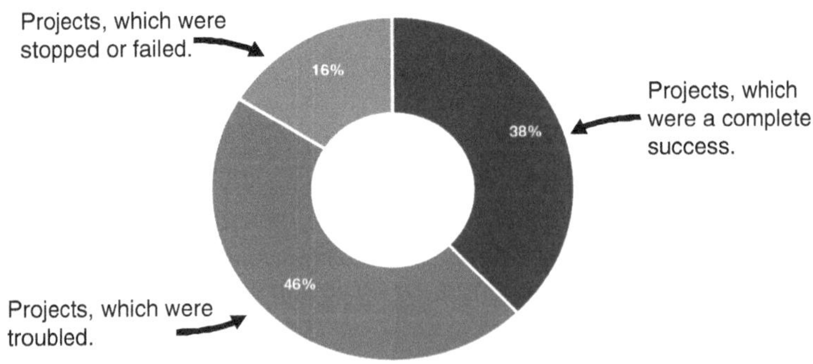


**Fig. 2** Success and failure of change projects (cf. Jorgensen et al. 2007)

**Table 1** Failure and success factors of change projects

| Failure factors | Success factors |
|---|---|
| Insufficient commitment of management (61%) | Sponsoring by top management (83%) |
| Nontransparent goals and visions of the change process (56%) | Honest and up-to-date communication (73%) |
| Lack of leadership experience of management with respect to insecurity and fear of change (56%) | Involvement of employees (69%) |
| Conflicts within management (56%) | Motivating and change-friendly corporate culture (53%) |
| Lack of management support (52%) | Existence of "change pioneers" (39%) |
| Insufficient information, e.g., too late or incomplete (50%) | Efficient organizational structure (26%) |
| Insufficient room for coping with fears and resistance (46%) | Support of change process by alignment of corporate culture (21%) |
| Neglect of psychological factors within the project planning (43%) | Efficient training programs for the new processes and/or IT solutions (19%) |
| Insufficient human resources for the project (37%) | Compensation and incentives (16%) |
| Lack of confidence in the communication process between management and employees (36%) | Support of new structures by adequate performance measurement (12%) |

One question of the interview questionnaire asked for the experiences with successful change and the relevant influencing factors according to the interviewee's opinion. Five main topics could be identified based on statements which reflect the major influencing factors on success. Similar topics have been identified, for example, by de Bruin et al. (2000). These topics are (also cf. Fig. 3):

- Strategy
- Leadership
- Sustainability
- Performance Measurement
- IT

To gain a certain degree of significance, only those factors were selected for defining the topics that were mentioned by more than 50% of the interviewees.

The main challenge stated by the interviewees was the balance of two different kinds of contexts: on the one hand, the commonly accepted and known context in which people are used to act, and on the other hand, the new and uncharted context which they are expected to adapt to within a short period of time. In other words, the balance of stable and dynamic structures within an accelerated change of context.

When people referred to strategic aspects of successful change, they mainly mentioned two things: first of all, the need for clarity about today's situation in connection with the clarity about tomorrow, that is, the target situation; and secondly, the structured transition process, which ought to be accompanied by a straightforward management of expectations, a reward system, continuous education for coping with the new structures and processes, an involvement of the people, and a clear and timely communication.

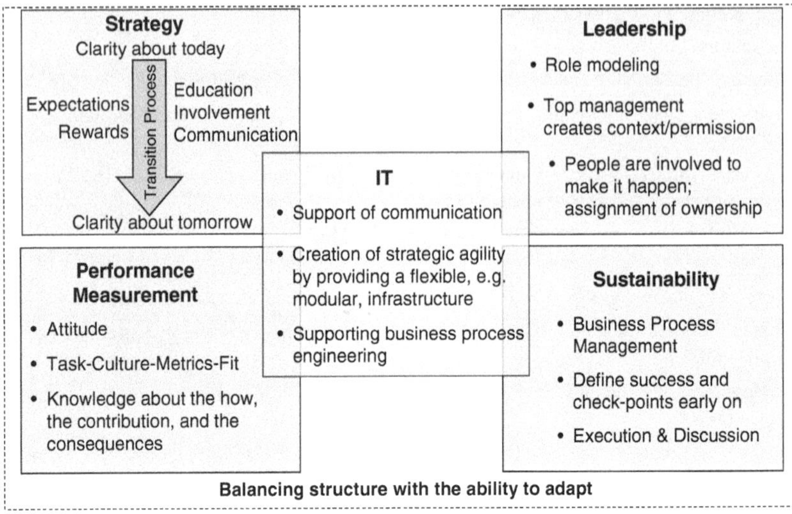


**Fig. 3** Major influencing factors on successful change

Leadership aspects mentioned were the relevance of role modeling by top management and the change team, the importance of creating the right context for change, and an explicit approval of changed behavior. The last point is important, since accepted behavior in the "old world" often does not correspond with the required behavior in the "new world." Thus, top management has to make clear what the new rules of behavior are and that it is acceptable to change to them. Moreover, the interviewees stated that the assignment of ownership in connection with the already mentioned involvement were important.

When referring to "sustainability," the interviewees indicated that one of the most important success factors was the existence of BPM to provide a systematic approach toward the change of processes as a core activity within the change projects. In addition to this, they underlined the importance of a project-specific definition of its long-term, that is, sustainable, success after having finished the project, as well as the respective metrics and checkpoints. To do this already very early on in the project is important for target-setting and expectation management. At the same time, the interviewees claimed that the focus needs to be on the execution and the discussion of the results to proactively control the success of the project.

The next topic is performance measurement. In this context, performance measurement was referred to as the philosophy as well as the system that is used for setting objectives, defining metrics, measuring success, and defining as well as deploying measures for dealing with deviations. An important success factor mentioned here was the attitude toward the company in general and change in particular. The attitude is a prerequisite for accepting the performance management system and its metrics as well as measures. It can also be said that the more positive the attitude toward the company, the more receptive the employees are toward change. Furthermore, the interviewees stressed the so-called "task-culture-metrics-fit." This means that new tasks have to be aligned with (maybe to be changed) corporate culture as well as the metrics, which are used to measure performance. If, for instance, the company decides to establish a less hierarchic decision process and empower the employees, the hierarchical culture of the old days needs to be changed and the metrics have to honor a behavior which embraces the new competencies. If these three factors are not aligned, a cognitive dissonance (cf. Festinger 1957) occurs, which keeps the employees in continuous insecurity about their performance and contribution. This statement is furthermore supported by the interviewees. They claimed that during and after change projects, it was important for them to understand the employed measurement mechanisms, their specific contribution, and the consequences of their actions with respect to overall performance. They mentioned that often it was not quite clear how their performance was actually assessed and how their individual contribution impacted the performance of the company.

The topics "sustainability" and "performance measurement" have been separated to stress a typical shortcoming of change projects: even though a performance measurement system exists, the change project is controlled by typical project management-driven parameters, such as "on time," "on budget," and "on scope," rather than addressing the long-term effects and success of the project.

The last topic IT was mainly mentioned in connection with its support and enabling function. IT contributes to the success by facilitating communication and the exchange on the progress of the change project, its results and intentions. This platform function is considered crucial for the acceptance of change initiatives. Moreover, IT's task is said to support BPM and with this the implementation of the new or changed processes. Finally, it was mentioned that IT plays an important role in enabling strategic agility by providing a flexible, for example, modular, infrastructure.

These results clearly indicate that both hard (e.g., organizational structure or performance management systems) and soft factors (e.g., role modeling, incentives) must be integrated for a holistic approach toward change. The presented topics build the basis for gaining a systematic approach for modeling change projects, and thus, facilitate the communication process.

## 2.2 *Approach for Describing Change Projects*

Communication and exchange on the change project and the intentions, which are pursued by it, are mentioned to be important success factors. The basis for facilitating communication is a description of the project, which should be as comprehensive as possible. The present approach is based on keyword clusters to fulfill this requirement. These keywords are used to trigger the description of the underlying concepts, such as, for example, business model.

In the 2004 study mentioned above, keywords for describing change projects were elicited during the interviews and an analysis of change literature. These keywords can directly be connected to the topics, which have to be addressed for successfully managing change. These topics, however, are not independent from each other. Thus, the resulting 86 significant keywords have been subsumed under four clusters, which support their clear separation (for a full list of all keywords and the explanation of their allocation to the clusters cf. Baumöl 2008):

1. *Business architecture*: The business architecture is constituted by the business strategy and the derived business model, the process architecture, the structure of the supplier network, the company's position in the value chain, the skill set of employees, products and the characteristics of the customer base. Thus, keywords, such *as business logic, implemented management system, characteristics of decision processes, roles and functions, skill profiles*, or *technical infrastructure* are subsumed into this cluster. This cluster is, compared to the other three, fairly large. This is justified by the complexity of this cluster, since it covers all the contents-related issues of the change project.[3]
2. *Culture and emotions*: The corporate culture(s) and emotional configuration represent an important basis for responsiveness to change. As a consequence, the description of the relevant factors and artifacts, which constitute this basis is crucial for the project. Keywords, such as *expectations of involved people, structure of power centers, key influencing persons and attitudes, stabilizing factors, history of the company's success, reasons for resistance,* or argumentation of *sense-making* belong to this cluster.
3. *Performance measurement*: The adaptation of the performance measurement system has been established as an important success factor during the interviews. Thus, it is not surprising that keywords for describing the performance measurement mechanisms came up in the course of the analysis. The following significant keywords are assigned to the cluster: *metrics to be used for measuring performance, activities for dealing with resistance and deviations from target values, speed of change, quality measures,* or *scenarios* for dealing with different prognoses.[4]
4. *Context*: The context into which the change project is embedded plays an important role. The context influences the options for the change project, that is, the freedom of action that is granted. Significant keywords for this cluster are: *the triggers for the change, possible discontinuities during the change phase, influence that stakeholders* are exerting, *milieu of the industry,* or the *economic situation.*[5]

[3]Burlton (2010) discusses the various aspects of planning and implementing business architectures from a process management perspective and presents a methodological framework for executing typical Business Process Management activities.

[4]Heckl and Moormann (2010) provide a comprehensive discussion of process performance measurement.

[5]Bucher and Winter (2010) discuss the significance of situational particularities which have to be accounted for by Business Process Management methods.

Since each change project has its specific characteristics and is thus almost unique, not all the keywords fit in any one case. This means that for the description of the change project, the most suitable keywords have to be selected. This immediately leads to the question which keywords are the right ones. One hypothesis of the 2004 study was that frequently occurring keywords define the so-called reference scenarios. These scenarios are used to define the general topics of change projects. By running a statistical cluster analysis of the keywords and the change projects they were connected with, it was indeed possible to confirm the hypothesis, and five reference scenarios could be identified.

These reference scenarios are:

- Strategy adaptation
- Improvement of strategic agility
- Business process engineering and business process redesign
- Communication and interaction with the customers' and business partners' networks
- Growth strategy and cultural aspects in a technological context

For each of the reference scenarios, a distinct set of keywords could be identified. As a consequence, a change project can be described based on this reference set and moreover additional relevant and situation-specific keywords can be added.

### 2.2.1 Case Study: Implementation of the Customer Service Idea Within an IT Organization; Part One: Description of the Change Project

In 2004, a mid-sized company in the financial services industry decided to reposition its IT organization toward an improved customer orientation. The goal of the change project was to establish an internal IT service provider within the IT department, but to have, at the same time, a direct interface to the business areas. Being a typical IT department, this required not only a change of the strategy together with a change in most of the processes but also a major change of its culture. To achieve this, CME in combination with the project management standards of the PMI were deployed.

The first step to describe the project and its context was to select the reference scenario: In this case, "strategy adaptation" was selected as the closest fit. Based on this, the standard set of keywords could be selected and during an initial discussion with the department head, three more keywords have been identified: *working conditions, required (target) behavior of the employees, incentives for good performance* (cf. Fig. 4).

These keywords were used to describe the status as it is, as well as the target situation for the project, for communicating the goals and for exchanging ideas and standpoints with the people involved. It was a good basis for starting the discussion among the different groups throughout the department and to give the factual as well as the emotional discussion a direction or an anchoring, respectively.

**Business Architecture**

Way of communicating
Decision processes
Method how the organization is developed
Success factors of the change project
Skills profile
Degrees of freedom to take decisions
Business logic
Challenges
Information management
Intention and implementation
Core competencies
Communication channels
Consequences of decisions
Customer satisfaction
Management system
Organizational learning
Planning of training and development of employees
Effects on products (output view)
Project scope
Project goals
Process architecture
Degree of process orientation
Roles in the organization
Way (style) of initialization
Strategy process
Subject of change project
Degree of transparency
Drivers of corporate success and change
Existing change processes
Degree of interdependencies
Vision and mission
Value added
Range in which the project takes effect
Knowledge management process

**Culture & Emotions**

Addressees of the change processes
*Working conditions*
Dominant corporate cultures and sub cultures
Leadership: employees' activities and commitment
Leadership: Assessment of own skills and abilities
Leadership: cognitive diversity
Leadership: Management commitment and role modeling
History of past successes (company)
Communication behaviour
Power centres
Mentality/attitudes
Key influencing people
Fun factor
Stabilizing factors
Structure of group processes
Structure of communication networks
Sense making
Reasons for and manifestations of resistance
Mental models
*Target behaviour*

**Performance Measurement**

Metrics for managing of department
*Incentives*
Levers of control
Measures in case of deviations from target figures
Measures in case of resistance
Milestones
Qualitative metrics for controlling
Quality measures
Securing of sustainability
Scenarios
Speed of change

**Context**

Triggers
Influence by stakeholders
Milieu
Economic situation

**Fig. 4** Example for the selection of descriptive keywords for a change project

The description framework provides an important technique, in the sense of method construction [cf. Fig. 6 and Bucher and Winter (2010)], to the business process manager. With this framework, he or she gains a holistic understanding of the project going beyond the sole focus on processes. Only with this understanding, the business process manager is able to design solutions for BPM tasks.

This section present the first step to initializing a change project – its thorough description as a basis for discussion. An interpretation of reactions and contributions to the discussion of the people involved in the change project as well as a conclusion as to their responsiveness to change, however, can only be successfully made if the underlying assumptions and beliefs are understood. Thus, the possibilities of analyzing and eliciting values, assumptions, and beliefs as constituent parts of the organizational culture needs to be discussed before constructing the situational change method.

## 2.3 *Responsiveness to Change: An Explanatory Model*

There are quite a few explanatory models with respect to employees' responsiveness to change (cf. e.g., Kotter 2008; Kanter 2003; Burke 2002; Strebel 2000; Watzlawick et al. 1974). The influencing factors which can be found in these contributions are diverse, for example, the definition and redefinition of the employment relationship, the group or rather peer structure, power centers within the company, the design of a vision of the new way to work and its communication, the importance of the "burning platform," the clear definition of the problem and its resolution, and motivational structures.

All these factors can be traced back to the way the employee perceives the current situation of the company, his or her position within the organization as well as the interpretation of the intended changes. From these pieces of information, the employee designs a model of the world and its operating mode; in other words, a mental model.

Already for some decades now, research on mental models has attempted to understand and explain human behavior (cf. e.g. Mathieu et al. 2000; Wilson and Rutherford 1989; Rouse and Morris 1986). Mental models are, in brief, a representation of the understanding of human knowledge about the world. Mental models are used to describe and explain observations as well as predict events (cf. Mathieu et al. 2000, p. 274). In this chapter, mental models are defined according to Rouse and Morris (1986, p. 360): they are "mechanism whereby humans generate descriptions of system purpose and form, explanations of system functioning and observed system states, and predictions of future system states."

The concept of mental models can also be used to support the explanation of the responsiveness to change.

Norman (1983, p. 12) explains three properties of mental models:

- *Belief system*: A mental model reflects the belief system of the individual, which is acquired through observation, instruction, or inference. The belief system is a personal instance of the perceived world and corresponds to the situation in which the individual finds himself or herself, respectively.
- *Observability*: The properties of a mental model should correspond to the properties of the observed world and support the sense making process. Otherwise, the model cannot serve as an explanatory model for the individual. An example of this property is the belief of the early Greeks in the existence of Zeus: they explained natural phenomena with the existence of higher beings and with that could explain the observable phenomenon of lightning.

- *Predictive power*: The mental model serves the understanding and anticipation of the developing target situation. Thus, it ought to build on inference rules adapted to the information processing power of the individual to support the "running" of the mental model.

As a consequence, since the three properties can have different instantiations, it is safe to assume that there are different mental models with respect to daily business and change (cf. Klimoski and Mohammed 1994, p. 432; Cannon-Bowers et al. 1993). The mental models for daily business have evolved over time and build the basis for the development of a mental model of the change project.

The reception of change has not yet been fully understood. The use of mental models could be a means to gain a better understanding on why some individuals accept and endorse change and others reject it. The evolution of a mental model centers on individuals' assessment of their own capabilities and knowledge (cf. Mathieu et al. 2000, p. 274–275).

The 2004 study and the hints during the interviews have also proved the assumptions of the above-mentioned authors that the reception of change is influenced by the existing mental model and uncertainties about capabilities and knowledge with respect to four influencing factors. These factors are briefly described in the following:

- *Future*: Not surprisingly, change projects seem to be disruptive for the expectations of the future development. Almost anyone being in a change situation starts to make predictions about the future: What role/position, which responsibilities or new peers can be expected? Thus, it is mandatory to develop the conceptual model of the target situation, as has already been described in the previous section.
- *Skills*: The individual skills must be adequate for the already known or expected tasks or for new technology that is going to be implemented during the change project. Uncertainty evolves if the employee is unsure about the suitability of his or her skill level.
- *Workplace*: Working conditions belong to the group of very important but implicit, and thus, often neglected influencing factors of responsiveness to change. The expectations (e.g., improvement of working conditions, potential relocation, or new peers) connected with the change project play a vital role on how the mental model is developed.
- *Rules*: Change normally brings new rules to an organization. These rules can either have a normative character or belong to the newly developing culture and manifest themselves either as organizational artifacts or implicit standards of behavior. Uncertainty can arise if the normative rules are not clearly documented in an early stage of the project or the new cultural rules do not become transparent and interpretable or adoptable, respectively.

The degree of uncertainty with respect to each factor influences the mental model each involved employee has of the change project. Thus, it could be a step toward a positive reception of the oncoming change to eliminate the uncertainty to a certain degree wherever possible. Since many instances of mental models can exist, which might differ only marginally, it is necessary to cluster these instances of the existing individual mental models to create profiles for efficient and targeted interventions.

The instances of these factors are moreover dependent on three other personal factors, which cannot easily be influenced, since they stem from the past:

- Technical and functional background: The employees have to be in the position to understand the intentions and objectives of the change project. A main requirement for this is their education and with this their ability to understand the technical and functional requirements of their tasks. This factor represents the required qualifications which an employee already possesses to fulfill a certain task. The factor "skills" refers to the skills which are required by the intended change and the employee might have to acquire first.
- Previous experiences, attitudes and "superstitions": Each employee has past experiences with almost any aspect of a change project, be it the technical objectives or the emotional or cultural effects. As a consequence, an attitude toward the project is developed, which can either be positive, neutral, or negative. It is important to understand the effects of the developed attitude to be able to interpret the ensuing behavior. The so-called "superstitions" or beliefs are another element of behavior. Superstitions have normally been developed over time and represent rules that seem to work even if they make no sense or cannot be validated. Nonetheless, these superstitions are deployed to the perceived intentions and objectives of the change project; especially, if the situation is new and unusual for the individual. Norman (1983, pp. 8–11) describes superstitions in connection with the use of a calculator: the observed persons pressed the clear-button several times because they were unsure of the functionality of the calculator and developed the belief that hitting the button several times for sure produces the expected result.
- Individual ability to process information: Each individual has a different capacity for processing information. This is also crucial for the responsiveness to change and needs to be addressed by selecting an adequate way of communication and providing information.

These factors need to be taken into consideration, but cannot be actively used to influence the reception of change.

To understand and influence the mental models which impact the outcome of a change project, it is necessary to form a conceptual model (i.e., an "objectified" model) of the target situation and compare this to the observed mental models of the target situation. The conceptual model tries to present the "objective" image of, for example, an IT system, which is the basis for explaining the IT system to a user and with this forming the user's mental model as to how the IT system works. Young (1983) and Greeno (1983) provided the first approach for dealing with conceptual and mental models. The conceptual model is a very important part of the effort to gain positive response to the change initiative, since it is the framework within which the employee is "trained" to understand and accept the new environment. The conceptual model has to fulfill three criteria to be of use (cf. Norman 1983, pp. 13–14):

- Learnability: The model must be easy to understand and interpret for the employees in the given context.
- Functionality: The model must provide enough input to understand the way the target situation works and the new "system" reacts.
- Usability: The model must correspond to the individual's ability to process information in the given context.

One conclusion which can be drawn from the above findings is that the design of the environment to enable employees responding to change in a positive way is the key. The employee uses the mental model as a guideline on how to act and behave in the familiar environment. To introduce new work processes or new ways of behavior, respectively, it is crucial to build on the present mental model and change it gradually. This means that new elements are added to the familiar environment rather than eliminating all familiar elements to start virtually from scratch.

One of the major requirements for an organization is, as already explained above, to be able to adapt continuously to the changing environment. Thus, the challenge for the business process manager is to balance the stable, familiar structures with new, flexible elements to foster the required ability to adapt. Information or rather the ability to process and make use of the information which is provided on the change project, its goals and the activities plays an important role. This information is processed within the mental model, which serves as the reference framework against which the new situation is assessed.

Method construction plays an important role in supporting the employees to accept change and contribute to the success of the change project. The construction process which is driven by the responsible person and addresses all employees who are involved in the change project makes the change effort visible, and with this, supports the adaptation of the mental model. At the same time, it serves as a means for communication. On the one hand, it enables the employees to deal with the change by exchanging opinions as well as fears. On the other hand, it enables management to understand the various responses to the change initiative, be it acceptance, skepticism, or rejection. This leads to the concept of shared mental models, which support the change effort by allowing the employees to build on their own mental models, compare them to those of peers, and discuss implications as well as next steps (cf. Stout et al. 1996).

Mental models are an important part of the context factors, which influence the change project, and as a consequence, are input factors for the CME. They are combined with two other input factors, "situation" and "decision," and presented in the next section.

During the case study introduced above, some observations with respect to the influence of mental models could be made. These observations, although they were not in the main focus of the change project, are discussed in the following section.

### 2.3.1 Case Study: Implementation of the Customer Service Idea Within an IT Organization; Part Two: Observations on the Impact of Mental Models

Very early in the project, it became clear that three (more or less typical) attitudes toward the intended change were manifested: the "business-as-usual- prevails-any-way" attitude, the "it-is-about-time-let's-change" attitude, and the "I-don't-know-but" attitude. The observable attitudes are a manifestation of the mental models based upon which the employees receive and react to the intended change. Although it is difficult to objectively elicit mental models, it is possible to observe specific patterns of behavior and remarks which hint at the mental model. If the observation is introduced as a systematic instrument during the change project, it might help to influence the attitude, and with this, the underlying mental models. Although it was not done systematically in this project, some activities were directed to this subject.

The discussion of the above-mentioned attitudes during meetings and personal talks seem to prove the four factors as to how these models influence the receptiveness of change. The first attitude was mainly taken by IT specialists who had already seen some change initiatives and over time had come to the conclusion that nothing ever happens if they just do as they always did. Since the service orientation required the understanding of the user's needs and requirements, which had not been in the focus in the mainly technology-driven department, it was especially important to influence this attitude. The introduction of the systematic description of the change project and method construction process helped to involve everybody in the department and catalyze discussion and engagement. This seemed to support the change of the first attitude. The second attitude is supportive of the intended change and most of the employees showing it, worked at the interface to the business areas; they could directly assess how important it was to understand the requirements. They were asked to be promoters of the change project, which worked quite well. The third attitude presents indecisiveness. The employees were skeptical about the change and mostly mentioned former, failed projects, which had already tried to introduce service orientation. It clearly helped to discuss the project and its goals in a systematic way and construct the change method with the involvement of the employees. However, not everybody could be convinced that the intended change would be beneficial in the end. As a conclusion, it can be said that the systematic and conscious handling of the existing mental models by first observing attitudes and using them for creating a conceptual model of the intended change could be advantageous for the success of the project.

## 3 Change Method Engineering: Method Construction for Organizational Change

Organizational change is driven by BPM – this is the foundation on which this chapter is based. As a consequence, BPM has to integrate not only strategic, governance or methodological, but also cultural aspects (cf. e.g., Spanyi 2006).

Change is implemented through dedicated projects, which offer the chance to integrate BPM principles with those of organizational change. Thus, each change project should be based on a method which is constructed according to the specific situation. This method serves as a guideline for the course of the project. As the above discussion proves, a holistic approach, addressing both hard and soft factors, toward change needs to be pursued. The concept of CME has been developed to cater to the specific situational needs of change projects. It provides a toolbox for firstly systematically describing the change which is intended and the context in which it is embedded. Secondly, it is based on the above-mentioned set of reference scenarios and the pool of activities which support the implementation of the intended change (cf. Sect. 2.1) to select the "right" course of action for the situational method. And finally, construction patterns are suggested to support a systematic method development.

A change initiative has three phases: the pre- or rather planning phase, where the change method is constructed, the actual project phase (implementation I), where the change is implemented, and last, but not least, the phase "implementation II" where the move to daily business is made and the intended change is anchored within the organization.

The overall responsibility for the pre- and the project phase is with the project manager. Operational responsibility is delegated to the business engineer or the business process manager, respectively. One of the two has to manage the method construction process and its deployment throughout the phases implementation I and II (Fig. 5).

## 3.1 *Basics of Method Construction*

For a situational approach toward method construction, first the elements which constitute a method have to be defined. In a second step, the construction process has to be developed. According to Gutzwiller (1994), Oesterle (1995), Winter (2003),

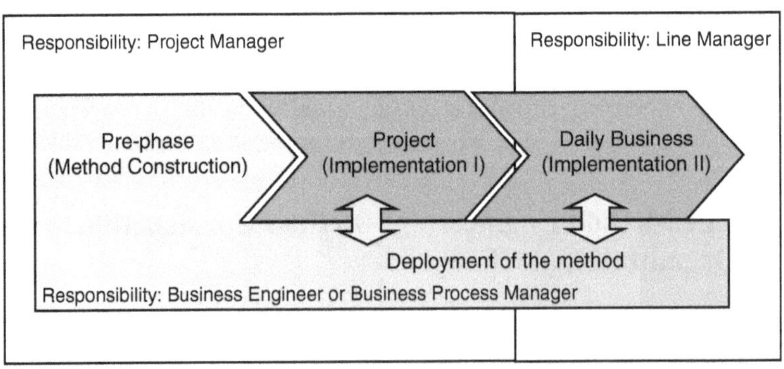


**Fig. 5** Position of method construction during the change process

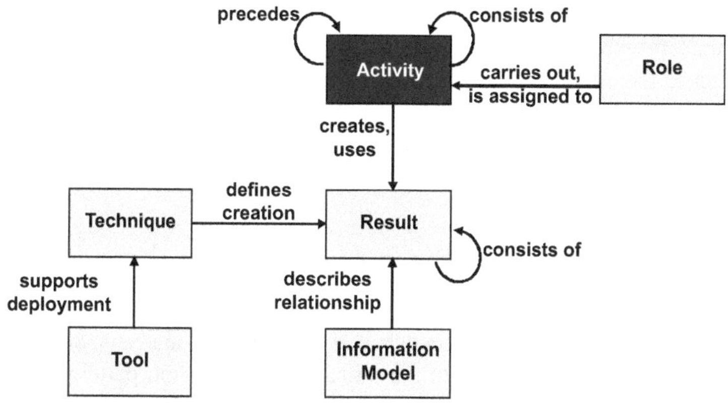


**Fig. 6** Elements of a method

and Baumöl (2005), a method consists of activities, results of these activities, roles which are assigned to the activities, techniques supporting the activities, IT tools for documenting the results and an information model that ties the results logically together. The construction of the situational method develops around activities; they define the characteristics of the method. In Fig. 6, the above described elements are presented (cf. Winter 2003; Bucher and Winter 2010).

One of the questions to be solved is how the activities are gained. For the approach suggested in this chapter, the activities are derived from the descriptive keywords presented above. Each keyword can be translated into an activity, for example, the keyword "stabilizing factors" is translated into the activity "identification and analysis of stabilizing factors for the organization." As a consequence, the set of descriptive keywords for a specific scenario defines the activities for the change method.

The sequence of the activities is dependent on two things: there are activities which set the ground for the project, that is, they serve the determination, analysis, that is and documentation of the basic framework and the status quo of the environment into which the project is embedded (e.g., history of successes, business logic, power centers, and milieu). The second group of activities addresses measures, results, or consequences of the change project (e.g., measures in case of resistance, key influencing people, scenarios). This group of activities builds upon the first group and can only be defined after the first one. The sequence of activities within these two groups has to be defined by the project team and is highly dependent on the situation.

Project management activities, as they are defined in many companies, can be found in both the groups.

Depending on the activities, the other elements of the method are defined. These are, for example, the roles which perform the activities (process owner, project manager, change manager, etc.) and the results which are to be achieved (defined and documented processes, project plan, communication plan, etc.).

The method construction process is crucial, since it reflects the situation in which the change project is embedded. Even though it must be flexible and adapted according to the situation, it cannot be a more or less random process, but has to follow a structured plan, which supports the efficiency of the change project. As a consequence, the construction process belongs to the standard procedures of CME.

## *3.2 Structured Process of Method Construction*

The method construction process consists of three phases: analysis, definition, and sequencing. These phases base on the so-called construction patterns, which are presented in detail in Baumöl (2008). In the following, the basic mechanisms of these three construction patterns are presented.

### 3.2.1 Analysis

The process of method construction is not only influenced by the context, but also by the mental model and the attitudes of the employees. As a consequence, an effective construction process has to integrate these influencing factors and start with defining them. The first step of the analysis phase is to understand and define the situation. This step requires first of all a precise description of the situation by focusing on the parameters, "complexity" and "risk," for both the current situation and the target situation. It is based on the topic of the change project and the ensuing reference scenario. Secondly, the decisions during the set-up of the project have to be analyzed. They are operationalized by the parameters "intention," "objectives," and "solution."

As a first step, the "situation" is described based on its defining parameters. The parameters, complexity and risk, are subsumed under the "problem domain." This domain represents the general definition framework for the project and the target domain (cf. Fig. 7). Complexity is operationalized by five perspectives in which complexity can manifest itself:

- *Organization perspective*, for example, a high degree of interdependencies within the organization drives complexity, and so does a very diverse background of the workforce.
- *Process perspective*, for example, a high maturity of the process architecture reduces complexity; a high number of involved process domains drive it.
- *Technology perspective*, for example, a high reusability of the IT infrastructure reduces complexity; the need for a considerable redesign drives it.
- *Control perspective*, for example, a positive attitude toward the measurement system, maybe because of an attractive incentive system, reduces complexity; and so does a high maturity of the measurement system; a high degree of interdependency between various departments drives complexity.

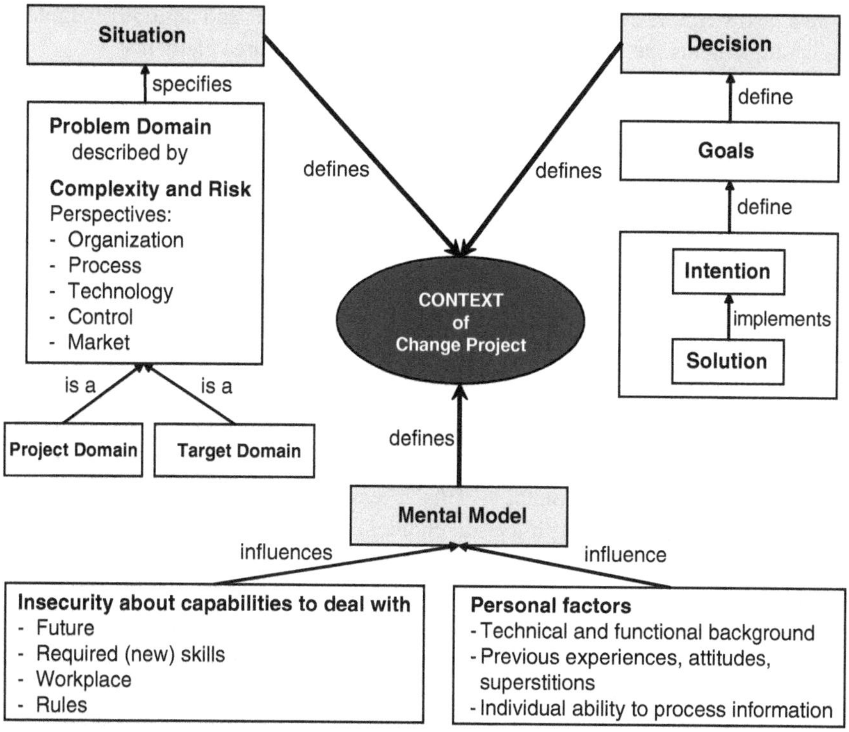


**Fig. 7** Description of the situational context by three elements "situation," "decision," and "mental model"

- *Market perspective*, for example, a high dependency on suppliers drives complexity and so does a high sensitivity of the business model for innovations.

The documented analysis of these five perspectives leads to an overall estimate of complexity measured by the attributes "high," "medium," and "low."

Risk is assessed based on the same perspectives and analyzes the probability of the occurrence of a "risky" event, for example, from the organization perspective, the failure of the project due to resistance by the employees. The documented risk analysis of the five perspectives is also measured by the three attributes "high," "medium," and "low."

The second step describes the element "decision" by three parameters. The intention is analyzed as the first parameter. This is a text-based analysis of the prior and original goals of the change project. The approach to achieve these goals, that is, the chosen solution, is also described in this context and from these two parameters, the objectives which are directly related to the change project are deduced. Thus, a hierarchy of goals is defined: first of all, the overall goals of the intended change are set and then the objectives, in the sense of sub-goals for the change project or change projects, respectively, are deduced.

In a next step, the third influencing factor "mental models and attitude of employees" complements the tuple, which is thus constituted of three elements.

This factor is operationalized by the above-mentioned dimensions of uncertainty with respect to the individual's capabilities to deal with the intended change and the personal factors.

With this, the context of the change project, which requires a situational method is adequately analyzed and documented.

Figure 7 presents the tuple and the parameters used for operationalizing the context.

### 3.2.2 Definition

The second phase of the construction process is supported by the definition pattern. The goal of this process is to select the keywords for the description of the project and the activities for the method. This is carried out based on the reference scenarios and a discussion with the stakeholders of the project. Here, the combined approach of using standards or best practices and complementing them with the situational elements takes full effect: The reference scenarios provide the keywords which were used for the respective scenario in most of the analyzed, successful change projects and with this systematically support the selection of the keywords for the required comprehensive description of the change projects (cf. Sect. 2). Further keywords which refer to the specific situation can be added during the discussion process.

Since this step is crucial, this part of the definition process is constructed as an iterative activity. Only if the relevant stakeholders have committed themselves to the way of describing the project and the planned activities, the next phase, that is, the construction of the method, can be executed. Of course, the discussion process has to be restricted to a defined time frame to avoid endless loops of new or old arguments. As a result of this first step, a set of keywords is obtained, which can be used for the comprehensive description of the change project.

The next step in the phase "definition" is the deduction of the activities from the keywords as described above. The activities are the first elements of the method, which have to be selected to be able to define the rest of the other elements of the method (e.g., roles, techniques; cf. Fig. 6). The result of the second step is a concrete instance of these elements for the situational change method.

### 3.2.3 Sequencing

After the definition has been completed successfully, the third and last phase is the sequencing of the activities. The main goal of this step is to define the right sequence of the activities, that is, the phasing of the change project. This is carried out by developing various alternatives for the sequencing and discussing their pros and cons within the team and with the stakeholders.

After this last phase of the construction process, the method with all its elements has been completed and with this the pre-phase of the change project is concluded. Then, the project phase "Implementation I" can be started.

### 3.2.4 Case Study: Implementation of the Customer Service Idea Within an IT Organization; Part Three: Extract of the Results of the Method Construction Process

In the following, an extract of the results of the method construction process for the case study is presented. Figure 8 shows the activities and their sequencing. Another result of the construction process was a comprehensive list of the other elements of the method: all expected results of the activities, the involved roles, the techniques and the tools (e.g., ARIS), which were connected to the activities. As a support for the sequencing, two dimensions have been defined: four phases with respect to time and four blocks related to contents. These served as a basis for allocating the activities. The four phases were:

- Phase 1 "Initialisation and positioning"
- Phase 2 "Implementation"
- Phase 3 "Anchoring of the results"
- Phase 4 "Monitoring of the project success"

The four contents-related blocks were:

- Block 1 "Analysis of the prerequisites for the change project"
- Block 2 "Definition of the project"
- Block 3 "Definition of target parameters"
- Block 4 "Definition of control metrics"

The overall result of the construction process is the method "Internal IT Service Provider" consisting of a comprehensive description of the situational context of the change project according to the abstract example in Fig. 7, a comprehensive description of the project itself (cf. Fig. 4), a list of activities and related elements

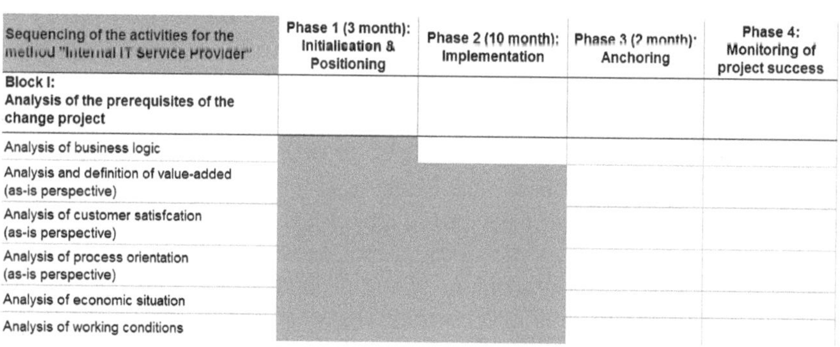


**Fig. 8** Extract of the results of the method construction process

and finally a chart with the sequencing of the activities, ordered according to time and contents.

The definition of the activities and the dependent building proved to be fairly easy, since the keywords were used as a basis and they represented already a common understanding of the change project. The sequencing, however, was much more subject to discussions and the responsible project member had to strictly guide the process. The method was then deployed and brought the expected success. Minor alterations during the process had nonetheless to be made, reacting to changes in the project context.

The application of the CME approach proved beneficial for structuring and communicating the change project and its goals. For the organization, it was the first time to explicitly model structures and openly discuss chances and risks of the intended change. The procedure to clearly describe the project and its context as well as the way to proceed during the project was well received and evaluated as a considerable improvement. Moreover, the support by the pool of method elements and the integrated approach to include all relevant dimensions of change were highly appraised. However, applying the method created a higher planning effort and increased the communication needs, thus taking up more time than other projects, especially for the responsible people. Sometimes, it was received as bureaucratic because of the need to explicitly document results in a fairly detailed way. Since it was the first time the method was applied, the learning curve was arduous although it was also steep. As a conclusion, it can be stated that to harvest the benefits of the method, it seems first of all to be necessary to follow a pragmatic approach when using the method, that is, "keep it simple and flexible." Secondly, to make use of the learning curve effect, it should be introduced as a standard and be used for each change project. A dedicated training for the people driving the method in the organization seems to be a good addition since project management or process management training does not provide the entire picture.

To continuously improve the method construction process and enhance the pool of activities, a systematic management process is necessary. This process is described in the next section.

### 3.3 Management Process for Change Method Engineering

The management process for CME focuses on two steps: on the one hand, the structured procedure for constructing the method; and on the other hand, the continuous updating of the pool of activities as well as reference scenarios and enhancing of the knowledge base. This is necessary for a systematic use of CME to take advantage of the learning curve and to establish continuous improvement. The left-hand side of Fig. 9 (cf. Baumöl 2008, p. 156; Gericke and Winter 2006, p. 234) represents the above-described phases of the method construction process. The right-hand side presents the improvement process and its elements. The existing method elements constitute the initial knowledge base for method construction. Experiences from projects, new method elements, and other lessons learnt are used

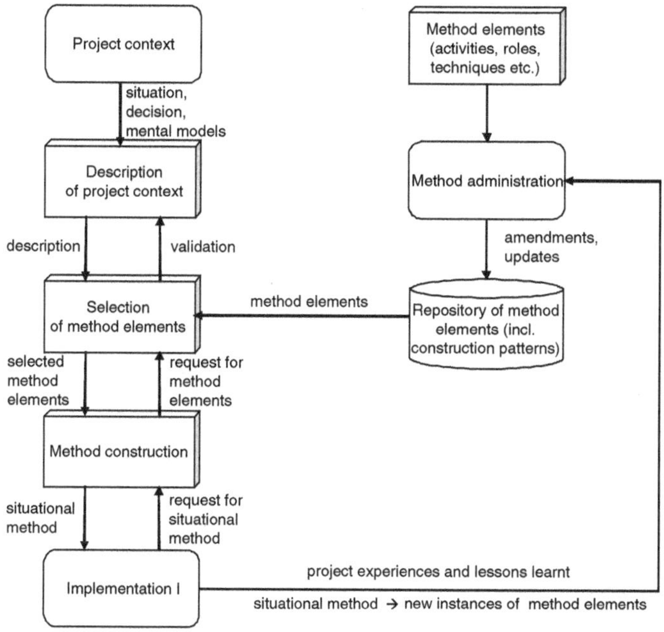


**Fig. 9** Management process for CME with respect to the construction process and a continuous improvement

to enhance the initial knowledge base. Method administration is responsible for this step and the result of method administration is a so-called "repository of method elements," which also includes the construction patterns.

# 4 Conclusion

Change is for sure necessary for the survival of each individual and each company. Nonetheless, change projects create a high amount of tension within a company and often conflicting sentiments. Even worse, change projects tend to paralyze companies for a considerable time span. The responsiveness to change, be it accepting or rejecting, is a critical success factor for each change project. As a consequence, it is important to understand which factors seem to be important for the people with respect to change, how the mental model of change is created and finally, what are the possibilities to influence the responsiveness for the good of the people as well as the company.

All three questions have been addressed in this chapter. The first objective was to explain the prerequisites for dealing with organizational change. The analysis provided a systematic basis for initiating a change project: they answer the questions "what must be considered" and "which mistakes could be prevented from the start".

The second objective was to present a framework for modeling change projects and the influencing factors. The resulting framework is the first one to support the comprehensive description of a change project considering hard (e.g., the process architecture) and soft factors (e.g., the influencing factors on mental models). Further research here is to investigate the options for eliciting and describing mental models by maybe defining certain profiles. Once mental models can be explicitly modeled and communicated, their influence on the change process can be further analyzed and activities for influencing existing change models can be added to the pool of CME activities.

The third objective was to suggest an approach for constructing change methods, which can be flexibly adapted to the specific situation. To achieve this, the concept of CME has been introduced as a means to drive change projects in a structured way by also taking into consideration the emotional prerequisites within the company. Further research in this area is necessary with respect to analyzing and complementing the reference scenarios and to complete the pool of activities without overloading the basis. Moreover, the systematic training of business engineers and business process managers with respect to the integral approach for organizational change must be driven onward by specific programs. What has already been achieved for project management must now be carried out for change management: establish standards and the communication of best practices rather than treating change management like a process whose results are serendipitous at best.

With these results, CME contributes to the domain of BPM by providing a comprehensive approach for supporting the business process manager to drive organizational change. It does not only consider the contents-related aspects of business process-driven change, but also the success-critical aspects of culture.

However, even though CME provides a framework for effective and efficient change, the business process manager has another crucial part in the change project. He (or she) is responsible for the construction of a situational change method which reflects the specific situation of the project. A thorough understanding of the system "organization," and with this also the success factors of business process-driven change, is mandatory. The business process manager is the bridge between the hard and the soft factors of change.

There is still considerable research required in this field to understand the "people factor" of change. It is important to note that this research process can only add value if companies and universities work together closely and construct solutions for successful change initiatives.

## References

Baumöl U (2005) Strategic agility through situational method construction. In: Reichwald R, Huff AS (eds) Proceedings of EURAM 2005 (European Academy of Management) "Responsible Management in an Uncertain World", Munich, 2005

Baumöl U (2008) Organisational change. Wiesbadena, Gabler Verlag

Bucher T, Winter R (2010) A taxonomy of business process management approaches. In: vom Brocke J, Rosemann M (eds) Handbook on business process management, vol 2. Springer, Heidelberg
Burlton R (2010) Delivering business strategy through process management. In: vom Brocke J, Rosemann M (eds) Handbook on business process management, vol 2. Springer, Heidelberg
Burke WW (2002) Organisation change – theory and practice. Sage Publications, Thousand Oaks, CA
Cannon-Bowers JA, Salas E, Converse SA (1993) Shared mental models in expert team decision making. In: Castellan NJ Jr (ed) Current issues in individual and group decision making. Lawrence Erlbaum Associates, Hillsdale, NJ, pp 221–246
Classen M, Alex B, Arnold S (2003) Veränderungen erfolgreich gestalten: Change Management 2003/2008, Bedeutungen, Strategien, Trends, Studie des Handelsblatts (Deutschland), des Standards (Österreich), der Handelszeitung (Schweiz) mit Cap Gemini und Ernst & Young: http://www.ch.cgey.com/servlet/PB/menu/1004221_l1/index.html Accessed 08 June 2008
de Bruin B, Verschut A, Wierstra E (2000) Systematic analysis of business processes. Knowl Proc Manage 7(2):87–96
Doppler K, Lauterburg C (2000) Managing corporate change management. Springer, Berlin
Festinger L (1957) A theory of cognitive dissonance. Stanford University Press, Stanford, CA
Friedman L, Gyr H (1998) The dynamic enterprise. Jossey-Bass, San Francisco
Gericke A, Winter R (2006) Situational change engineering in healthcare. European Conference on eHealth 2006, Fribourg, Switzerland 2006, pp 227–238
Greeno JG (1983) Conceptual entities. In: Gentner D, Stevens AL (eds) Mental models. Lawrence Erlbaum Associates, Hillsdale, NJ, pp 227–252
Gutzwiller T (1994) Das CC RIM-Referenzmodell für den Entwurf von betrieblichen, transaktionsorientierten Informationssystemen. Physica, Heidelberg
Heckl D, Moormann J (2010) Process performance management. In: vom Brocke J, Rosemann M (eds) Handbook on business process management, vol 2. Springer, Heidelberg
Houben A, Frigge C, Trinczek R, Pongratz HJ (2007) Representative study on success and failure during change management. Technical University of Munich, Munich
Jorgensen HH, Albrecht J, Neus A, Rietz C, Krahn B (2007) Making change work. Erfolgsfaktoren für die Einführung von Innovationen. Study of IBM Global Business and University of Bonn, Stuttgart
Kanter RM (2003) Leadership and the Psychology of Turnarounds. Harv Bus Rev 81(6):58–67
Klimoski R, Mohammed S (1994) Team mental model: construct or metaphor? J Manag 20:403–437
Kotter JP (2008) Leading change: why transformation efforts fail. Harv Bus Rev OnPoint Collection, October 2008
Mathieu JE, Hefner TS, Goodwin GF, Salas E, Cannon-Bowers JA (2000) The influence of shared mental models on team process and performance. J Appl Psychol 85(2):273–283
Norman DA (1983) Some observations on mental models. In: Gentner D, Stevens AL (eds) Mental models. Lawrence Erlbaum Associates, Hillsdale, NJ, pp 7–14
Oesterle H (1995) Business in the information age: heading for new processes. Springer, Berlin
Rouse WB, Morris NM (1986) On looking into the black box: prospects and limits in the search for mental models. Psychol Bull 100:349–363
Spanyi A (2006) More for less: the power of process management. Meghan-Kiffer Press, Tampa, FL
Stout RJ, Cannon-Bowers JA, Salas E (1996) The role of shared mental models in developing team situational awareness: Implications for training. Train Res J 2:85–116
Strebel P (2000) Why do employees resist change? Har Bus Rev OnPoint
Tichy NM, Devanna MA (1990) The transformational leader. Wiley, New York
Vollmann T (1996) The transformation imperative. Harvard Business School, Boston, MA
vom Brocke J, Petry M, Sinnl T, Østerberg Kristensen B, Sonnenberg C (2010) Global Processes and Data: The Cultural Journey at the Hilti Corporation. In: vom Brocke J, Rosemann M (eds) Handbook on business process management, vol 2. Springer, Heidelberg

Watzlawick P, Weakland JH, Fish R (1974) Change – principles of problem formation and problem resolution. W. W. Norton, New York

Wilson JR, Rutherford A (1989) Mental Models: Theory and Application in Human Factors. In: Human Factors: The Journal of the Human Factors and Ergonomics Society, 31(6):617–634

Winter R (2003) Modelle, Techniken und Werkzeuge im Business Engineering. In: Oesterle H, Winter R (eds) Business Engineering – Auf dem Weg zum Unternehmen des Informationszeitalters

Young RM (1983) Surrogates and mappings: two kinds of conceptual models for interactive devices. In: Gentner D, Stevens AL (eds) Mental models. Lawrence Erlbaum Associates, Hillsdale, NJ, pp 35–52

# Managing Creativity-intensive Processes: Learning from Film and Visual Effects Production

Stefan Seidel, Katherine Shortland, David Court, and Didier Elzinga

**Abstract** Creativity is of considerable importance to many organizations and can be seen as a core competitive factor in a variety of contemporary industries. Consequently, process managers are increasingly forced to ask questions such as: How can I successfully manage an organization without crushing creativity? In response to this challenge, we introduce the concept of creativity-aware process management. We propose a model of creativity-intensive processes which can be described as highly dependent on creativity, interdependent, complex, and intensively involving the client. We explain how creative organizations manage these processes in order to pursue both operational and creative process performance while simultaneously mitigating operational and creative risk. In doing so, we propose a set of guidelines that can support process managers in successfully managing creativity without systematically crushing it. We use the case of a leading Australian visual effects (VFX) company in order to illustrate our explanations.

## 1 Introduction

There has been an increasing awareness that the management of business processes that involve creativity is critical. This is true not only within the growing creative industries (Hartley 2005; Hesmondhalgh 2002), such as game development and film production, but also within industries such as software development and pharmaceuticals that increasingly rely on creativity. Creativity is commonly associated with the generation of products, services, processes, or ideas that are both novel and appropriate (Woodman et al. 1993; Amabile 1996). Amabile (1998) states that, despite its importance, "creativity is undermined unintentionally every day in work environments that were established – for entirely good reasons – to

S. Seidel (✉)
Institute of Information Systems, University of Liechtenstein, Vaduz, Principality of Liechtenstein
e-mail: stefan.seidel@uni.li

J. vom Brocke and M. Rosemann (eds.), *Handbook on Business Process Management 2*, International Handbooks on Information Systems,
DOI 10.1007/978-3-642-01982-1_24, 

maximize business imperatives such as coordination, productivity, and control" (p. 77). Managers are thus forced to ask questions such as *How can I successfully manage an organization without crushing creativity?*

In recent years, Business Process Management (BPM) has shifted the focus toward the so-called human-centric or knowledge work processes (Davenport 2005; Eppler et al. 1999; Harmon 2007).[1] BPM researchers and practitioners have increasingly been recognizing the role of knowledge, judgment, collaboration, and individual capabilities in many critical processes, ranging from financial operations to health care, art, design, and entertainment. Although the literature reveals important factors, such as high levels of required autonomy, motivation, and expertise (e.g., Davenport 2005), the role of creativity and its consequences to the management of these processes have not been investigated in depth.

Research on organizational creativity has traditionally focused on individuals, groups, and organizations as the level of analysis and treated creativity as an outcome rather than a process (exemptions can be found in Drazin et al. 1999; Ford 1996; Borghini 2005). While different studies explain how creativity can be nourished in organizations, they do not sufficiently relate the proposed practices to the underlying business processes (Styhre and Sundgren 2005; Amabile 1988; Tan 1998).

In brief, no ample answers are provided to the question of how creativity influences business processes and how processes that rely on creativity can be successfully managed. Figure 1 suggests that the recognition of the importance and impact of creativity on BPM may be framed as *creativity-aware process management*. On the contrary, the recognition of BPM as a management approach with the potential of effectively managing creativity may be framed as *process-aware creativity management*. Our research seeks to explore what has been framed as creativity-aware process management, and which is built around the concept of the creativity-intensive process.

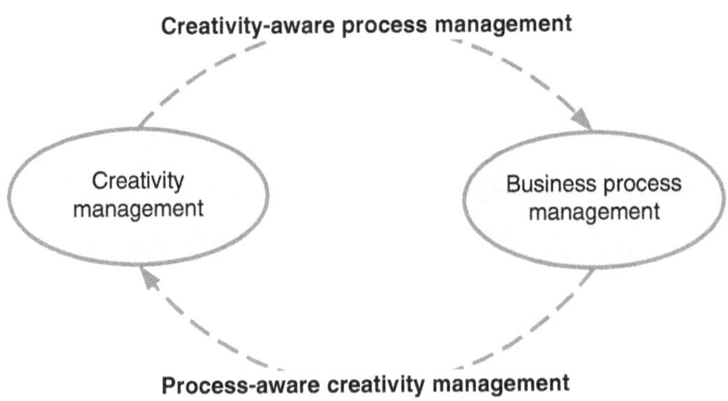


**Fig. 1** Creativity-aware process management versus process-aware creativity management

[1]Human-centric processes are discussed in detail by Harrison-Broninski (2010). Approaches to support knowledge work by means of process management are presented by Davenport (2010).

Over the last few years, we have studied organizations from the creative industries in order to explain how creativity influences business processes and their management (Seidel et al. 2008b; Seidel 2009). The creative industries are generally regarded as those which focus on creating and exploiting intellectual property (Hartley 2005). Prominent examples are the film industry, visual effects (VFX) production, and the development of computer and video games. The processes we studied can be framed as highly dependent on creativity, interdependent, complex, and intensively involving the client. We have learned that such processes are characterized both by divergent and convergent thinking as well as an often vague understanding of the requirements of the creative product. In conjunction with different subjective perceptions brought in by a variety of involved stakeholders, this leads to high uncertainty with regard to process flow, required resources, and particularly the outcome (Seidel et al. 2008b). In fact, in many cases the specifics of the outcome are not fully understood until the process is completed. As a consequence, the process manager is faced with particular challenges, such as high risk exposure and high demands for flexibility.

In this chapter, we introduce a model of creativity-intensive processes. We explain how creative organizations manage these processes in order to pursue both operational and creative process performance. In doing so, we explain how organizations can manage creativity at a process level, and propose guidelines to support process managers in successfully managing creativity without systematically crushing it. We will use the case of a leading Australian VFX company in order to illustrate our explanations.

## 2 The Case of Visual Effects (VFX) Production

Rising Sun Pictures (RSP) is an Australian VFX company exclusively dedicated to the production of effects for feature films. The company is based in Adelaide and Sydney. Clients of RSP include major Hollywood film studios, international producers, directors, and VFX supervisors. The company has contributed to films such as *The Lord of the Rings, Harry Potter,* and *Superman.*

The increased value share of VFX in film and television (TV) has contributed to more and more globalized competition which is accelerated by emerging technologies such as high definition television (HDTV) and digital intermediate (DI) postproduction paths. VFX companies that have traditionally relied on the creativity and flexibility of their resources are now increasingly forced to apply contemporary business approaches, such as BPM, to stay competitive.

The film production value chain can be roughly divided into the stages of development, preproduction, production, and postproduction (Clevé 2006). Within the development stage, tasks such as budgeting, financing, and scheduling are carried out to initiate a project. Preproduction deals with all the aspects related to the practical production needs, such as casting, location scouting, etc. Subject to the production phase is the actual shooting (Clevé 2006), that is, the production of the feature film, TV commercial, etc. The postproduction phase comprises all the steps that have to be done between production and final delivery (Clark and Sphor 1998), such as editing and sound editing. Creation of VFX is also within this phase (Wales 2005). Although the creation of VFX is often seen as a separate production process called the digital production process (e.g., Kerlow 2004), it typically begins parallel to the production phase. Figure 2 provides an overview.

The main process of RSP is the so-called VFX production pipeline, which generates digital sequences for films. The pipeline comprising complex sets of processes is characterized by innumerable interdependencies and high levels of creativity which result from the complexity of the generated products. For example, generating a VFX shot requires the creation of the so-called bones, textures, and animation. The primary outputs are computer-generated images (digital assets) that can contain characters, animations, and realistic simulations. One such example is an animated spider. Figure 3 shows the results of an intermediate process step of generating the spider (the so-called mesh). Eventually, this character will be part of a shot that includes footage from production. Thus, there are also interdependencies with production processes. For example, the spider may be dangling from a web in a barn that was shot on a "real world" set; hence the intimate connection to the production stage.

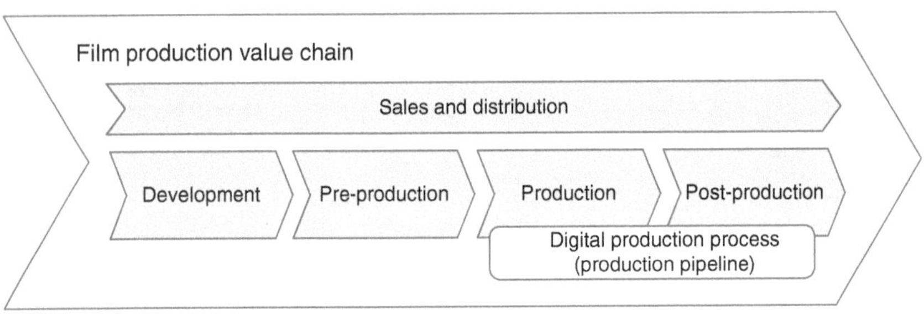


**Fig. 2** Film production value chain

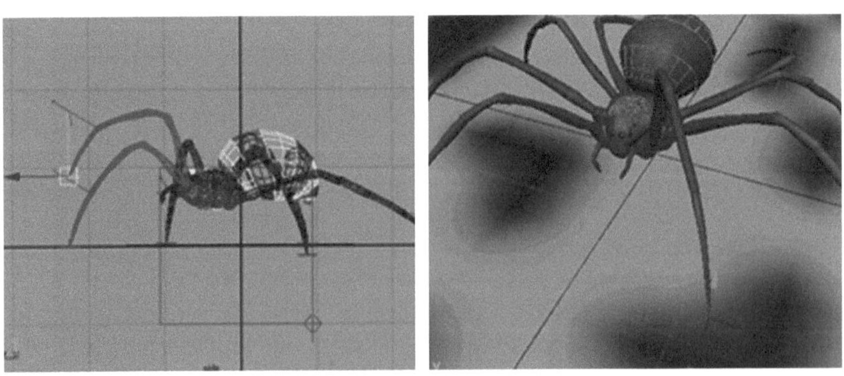

**Fig. 3** An exemplary outcome of a VFX process: an animated spider

The generation of VFX is a resource-and labor-intensive process. Even short sequences may take the work of several weeks or even months. Thus, ineffective management bears huge financial risks.

# 3 Creativity-intensive Processes

## *3.1 The Dynamics of Creativity-intensive Processes*

Mastering creativity in organizations requires us to understand the *creative process,* the *creative product,* the *creative person,* and the *creative situation,* as well as the interaction between these components (Woodman et al. 1993). We propose a process-centric view that establishes a connection between these components: Creative persons are actors in business processes who generate creative products. Thus, the creative product is a process-oriented object that is characterized by novelty and purposefulness (Firestien 1993). The business process is carried out in a creative situation, involving organizational resources and available information technology (IT).

Before we proceed to the model, let us consider a real-world example, the production of a particular shot involving the example of the spider. During the initial brief with the VFX company, the client discusses what that particular shot should look like. It is an iterative and communication-intensive process, where the VFX organization not only tries to understand the client's vision, but also stimulates the client with ideas she might not have had before. Simultaneously, the VFX company must also be conscious of matching the client's requirements to their capabilities. As a result of this process of understanding and negotiating the requirements, both the client and the representatives of the VFX house have an understanding of what the product should look like. Thus, they develop a shared understanding of the process goals. For example, although the spider's location in the scene (e.g., dangling from a web) may be known, the exact action and emotion may not. Exactly how the spider reacts is uncertain and cannot really be described until it is seen. Generally, it can be distinguished between *attributes* and *meta attributes.* While attributes refer to aspects that can be specified in advance (e.g., technical format, etc.), meta attributes refer to those specifics of a creative product that are related to esthetics and creative judgment and cannot be fully specified in advance (e.g., the spider should look "scary"). The VFX house starts to develop a first version based on their understanding of the requirements. The resulting (intermediate) product not only depends on the creative person's understanding of the requirements, but also on his/her creative and technical skills. Consequently, the product needs then to be reviewed by the client who, through seeing the actual product, may even get a better understanding of her own expectations. The result of this review may be further iterations of understanding and further negotiating the requirements, doing work, and reviewing.

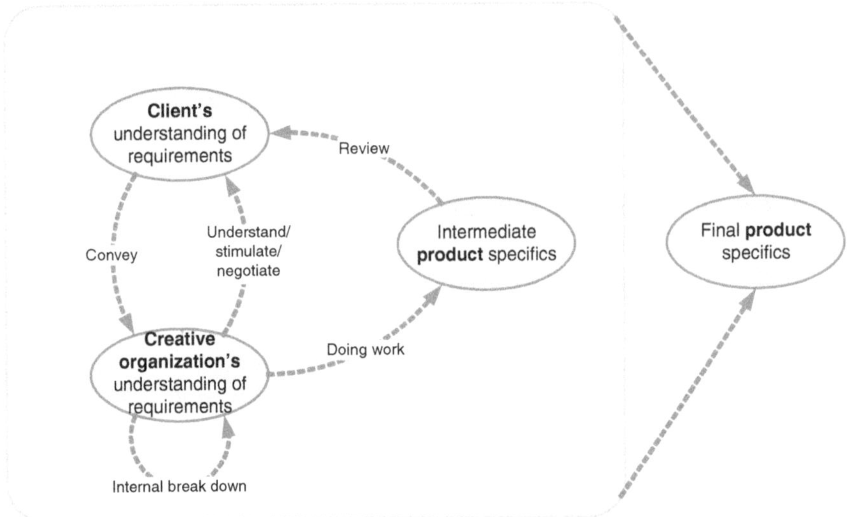


**Fig. 4** The dynamics of creativity-intensive processes (Seidel 2009)

Figure 4 suggests that creativity-intensive processes comprise a number of highly interwoven and iterative stages or phases: understanding the requirements, internally breaking the requirements down, doing work, and evaluating work. It must be noted that evaluation or review as well as doing work are part of understanding the requirements of the creative product. That is, the requirements are not entirely known before the process is completed. The completion, in turn, results in a final product and measurable process performance. Also note that the understanding of the requirements of a creative person or client is highly dependent on their expertise. Often, a senior creative person is more likely to understand the client's vision than a less experienced person. Similarly, a more experienced client will be more likely to be capable of describing what she actually expects the creative organization to do because she has a better understanding of that organization's capabilities.

## 3.2 *Structure versus Pockets of Creativity*

In reality, the rather high level view of creativity-intensive processes as introduced above translates into business processes that consist of a number of discrete elements or tasks (Fig. 5).

For example, at a high level, the production pipeline can be seen as a constant iteration between understanding the requirements of a shot, generating the shot, and evaluating the shot. However, in order to actually accomplish this, certain discrete tasks (or subprocesses) must be carried out. Some of the discrete elements can be viewed as well-structured subprocesses with defined outcomes, whereas others are

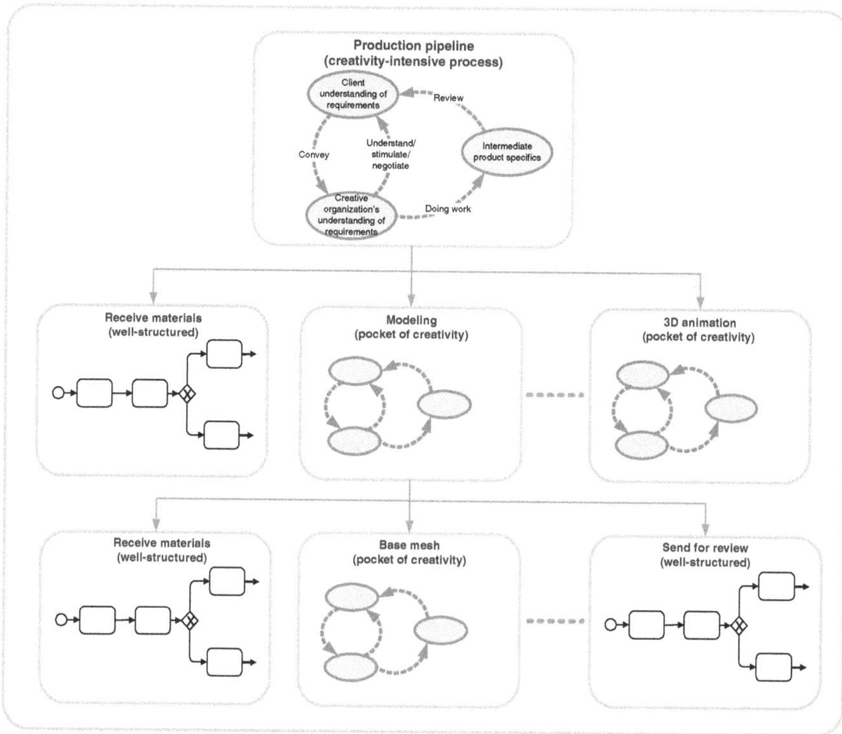


**Fig. 5** Relationships between well-structured parts and pockets of creativity (compare Seidel 2009)

highly creative. The latter one we refer to as *pockets of creativity*. An example for a well-structured element with a defined outcome may be the task of *receive materials*, where materials such as references and scans are received from different sources. *Modeling* and *3D animation* are examples for pockets of creativity, where artists generate creative products such as the spider. The dotted lines indicate that a complete production pipeline comprises many more elements than that are depicted in Fig. 5.

Figure 5 further illustrates that pockets of creativity may be further broken down. At the highest level, a pocket of creativity is a creativity-intensive process by itself. At the other end of the chain there is the individual creative process, such as generating a particular idea for a visual effect. For example, the pocket of creativity *modeling* is a quite complex process which iterates between understanding and refining the requirements, doing work, and evaluation. At the same time, this pocket of creativity will take place in another, higher level pocket of creativity in creating a particular asset or character (in this case the creativity-intensive process of the production pipeline), which also iterates between elaborating and refining requirements, doing work, and evaluation. Both the outcome of the modeling and the outcome of the whole character animation are not known until the process is concluded.

As a consequence of the above discussion, the following question emerges: How can one identify pockets of creativity within creativity-intensive processes? First of all, creative tasks are characterized by both divergent and convergent thinking as creative persons strive to generate something that is both novel and original. Moreover, pockets of creativity very much rely on the tacit knowledge and the expertise of the involved people. Yet, in order to identify pockets of creativity, more tangible factors are needed. Three main features can be identified:

- The first characteristic has already been introduced: as creativity means to produce something novel or original, the outcome is never entirely known in advance. We refer to this feature of pockets of creativity as uncertainty with regard to outcome. As indicated, those characteristics that are not fully known in advance (e.g., the emotion of the spider) may be referred to as *meta attributes*.
- Due to this uncertainty with regard to outcome and differing (subjective) perceptions of the creative product, the actual structure of the overall process or the number of iterations etc., is not known in advance. For example, in VFX production, there are certain process steps that every artifact (character, animation) goes through. However, the required elements, order, iterations, and exceptions are highly dependent on the nature of the shot. Also, different creative persons will carry out the same task in different ways. Yet, it is not the case that nothing is known about the process structure. For example, particular well-structured subprocesses, such as review processes, or aspects of data management are known in advance.
- As required process steps and iterations are not entirely predictable, so are resources and involved people not known in advance. For example, different creative people may use different resources (e.g., different systems) to carry out the same task. One example from VFX production is the so-called *matchmoving*, a process of creating a 3D camera for a particular set of images. While this process is time-consuming and expensive, often the VFX supervisor will not know whether it is required until the shot is attempted without it. Again, it is not the case that nothing is known about required resources. Certain resources that are required (e.g., particular IT systems) may be known as well as resource restrictions (e.g., available time).

Due to the above-described uncertainty, creativity-intensive processes are associated with high levels of risk. First, uncertainty in outcome can lead to customer dissatisfaction due to the subjectivity that is linked to the judgment of the quality of the creative product. We refer to this risk as *creative risk*. Second, uncertainty with regard to process structure and required resources can lead to what we refer to as *operational risk*. For example, the process may require more iterations than expected, which then results in higher costs and time consumption. Moreover, uncertainty with regard to process structure and required resources may lead to a mismatch between what is required to fulfill the customer expectations and the actual capabilities of the creative organization.

Yet, it must be noted that uncertainty in creativity-intensive processes also affords great opportunities. Creativity-intensive processes are inherently linked to

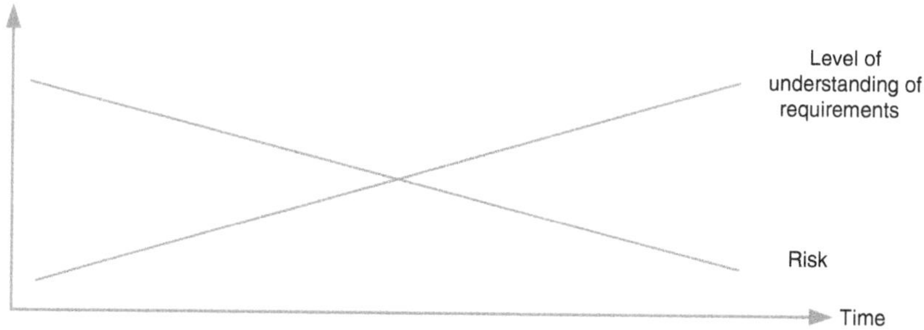


**Fig. 6** Development of level of understanding of the requirements and risk in creativity-intensive processes (Seidel 2009)

a certain creative potential which denotes the processes' capability of generating truly creative products. The creative potential is influenced by different factors, such as the level of detail of requirements specifications and available resources, including time and budget. Low levels of requirements specifications are associated with higher levels of creative potential, but also higher creative and operational risk. Generally, more time and budget allow for the exploration of more options, and thus are associated with higher levels of creative potential too.

As has been indicated, the understanding of the requirements of the creative product evolves throughout the process. Consequently, the degrees of freedom, as well as the associated risk, are highest at the outset when almost any thought is permissible. Throughout the process, various constraints are imposed upon the process, such as limited resources and a constantly evolving understanding of the requirements both on the client's and the organization's side. Figure 6 provides an overview of how requirements and risk develop throughout the process.

Note that this model is a simplification in that it describes how the understanding of the requirements and the associated risk ideally develop throughout the process, if the creative organization successfully (a) develops a good understanding of the client's vision, (b) matches the requirements with their capabilities, and (c) reviews the product throughout the process. How creative organizations accomplish this is explained later in this chapter, when various managerial practices are discussed.

Table 1 provides an overview of the main characteristics of creativity-intensive processes.

## 4 Roles in Creativity-intensive Processes

Creativity-intensive processes involve various stakeholders. Focusing on the creative aspects of such processes, at least three groups of people deserve closer attention: artists, creative supervisors, and clients. As we will see in the subsequent section, these stakeholders shape creativity-intensive processes and need to be considered when it comes to managing these processes.

**Table 1** Properties of creativity-intensive processes

| Property | Description |
|---|---|
| Uncertainty with regard to outcome | Certain characteristics of the process-oriented object (i.e., the creative product) are not known in advance. Uncertainty with regard to outcome depends on various factors, such as the level of requirements specifications. Also, creative people usually perform processes that are very much characterized by divergent thinking (Runco 2007). |
| Uncertainty with regard to process structure | The process structure (required process steps, number of iterations, process flow) of creativity-intensive processes is often not known in advance. This is mainly due to different perceptions of involved people. |
| Uncertainty with regard to required resources | Similarly, required resources (e.g., IT, time, and budget) in creativity-intensive processes are often not fully known in advance. |
| Varying levels of structure | Some parts of a creativity-intensive process have a predetermined structure, other parts do not. Thus, creativity-intensive processes comprise both flexible, hard-to-predict sections and well-structured sections. |
| Iterative nature | Creativity-intensive processes are highly iterative. They constantly iterate between understanding the requirements, doing work, and reviewing work. |
| Operational risk[2] | Creativity-intensive processes are characterized by operational risk. This property denotes the probability of the occurrence of process-related errors, such as a mismatch between the requirements of the creative product and the creative organization's capabilities. |
| Creative risk | Creativity-intensive processes are characterized by creative risk. This property denotes the probability of the occurrence of unwanted consequences that are mainly due to uncertainty with regard to process outcome and different subjective perceptions of this outcome. |
| Knowledge-intensity | Creativity-intensive processes require knowledge and expertise of the involved creative persons. Often, pockets of creativity are characterized by the application of tacit knowledge. |
| Creative potential | Creativity-intensive processes have a certain creative potential. This creative potential denotes the processes' capacity of generating products that are truly creative and thus characterized by high degrees of novelty or originality. |

## *4.1 Artists*

In the VFX industry, the creative individuals who perform the actual creative work are commonly referred to as artists. These artists, such as a compositor or an animator, will produce a particular element that contributes to a shot or series of shots. There are

[2]Risk can be defined as the probability of the occurrence of an unwanted consequence (Peltier 2004).

often multiple artists in the same role managed by a creative supervisor. They contribute their creativity in order to generate creative products. But what are the characteristics of creative individuals that in particular contribute to their ability to be creative, and that the process manager must recognize when allocating tasks? Expertise, motivation, and creative thinking skills have been proposed as key characteristics (Amabile 1998). This very much concurs with what we have learned from VFX production. Expertise, for example, is not only important with regard to a person's ability to act creatively by producing her elements, but also with regard to her ability in assessing what it takes to carry out a particular creative task (how long it will take, etc.). Given the uncertainty linked to creative processes, this capability is of high relevance in order to plan for the process. Generally speaking, higher levels of expertise of creative people are associated with lower levels of uncertainty and thus lower levels of risk. Moreover, motivating creative people is a particular challenge which goes beyond the use of financial incentives. In the next section, we discuss the so-called *creative buy-in* to motivate people and still successfully meet a project's goals. Finally, the artist's work is very much characterized by divergent thinking (Runco 2007). As indicated earlier, divergent thinking contributes to the uncertainty that is part of any creative process.

## 4.2 Creative Supervisors

Due to the complexity of creativity-intensive processes, creative organizations need to employ what can be referred to as creative supervisors. Creative supervisors are process managers who, due to the creative nature of the processes, need the ability and authorization to quickly respond to changing requirements with regard to the creative product and the process, including process design and resource allocation. Creative supervisors act as process intermediaries who are responsible for aligning the organization's processes with the client's processes and for communicating with the client. Often, creative supervisors are creative people with high expertise; that is, more senior people. More so than just experience, creative supervisors must possess the specific skill set of being able to plan, manage, and oversee a group of artists. Generally, creative supervisors must pursue two main goals: operational process performance and creative process performance. While the first goal pertains to classical measures such as time and budget, the latter refers to the quality of the creative product. Given the creative product's subjective nature, measuring the quality of a creative output is difficult. We will discuss the measurement later in this chapter. In order to pursue these goals, creative supervisors have to

- Manage the process internally (allocating resources, build teams etc.),
- Coordinate communication and manage the expectations of the creative organization and the client.

In VFX production, creative supervisors are process managers who are usually responsible for processes at different levels of granularity. For example, a so-called lead may be responsible for the production of a particular character (character lead) or sequence (sequence lead), whereas a VFX supervisor is accountable for a whole range of elements that compose a shot or scene.

## *4.3 Clients*

As has been maintained earlier, processes in VFX production are not only client-focused, but also actively involve the client. In fact, the client contributes to, and shapes, the processes in many ways. Clients of a VFX house can be producers, directors, and VFX supervisors from other organizations. Initially, the client will deliver an overview to the VFX house on the potential scope of what is required. Depending on how specific the client is at this early stage, the brief may be open to a great deal of interpretation or quite deterministic. In a highly iterative and interwoven process, the requirements of the creative product are determined and the supervisor seeks to match these with the organization's capabilities accordingly. It is also essential that the supervisor establishes a working style that suits the needs of the client. This working style depends on the client's background, expectations, as well as the particular project. Relevant issues to be dealt with by creative supervisors are:

- Where in the process shall the client be involved? Who will communicate with the client?
- How well does the client understand the VFX process and hence how early in the process can they be shown results?
- What artifacts are delivered to the client and when are they delivered?

# 5 Managing Creativity-intensive Processes: Creativity-aware Business Process Management

Having introduced the main characteristics of creativity-intensive processes, as well as the different roles, we now shed light on how to effectively manage creativity at a process level. Generally, creative supervisors need sufficient authorization to quickly respond to changing requirements with regard to the product and the underlying process, including process-design and resource allocation. We suggest the process manager to consider the following general guidelines:

1. Recognize the high uncertainty in both process and outcome and view it as a chance to generate highly creative and valuable outputs.
2. Structure the process around its pockets of creativity as these are the sections where the organization creates business value and distinguishes itself from its competitors.
3. Encourage risk mitigating strategies such as clarity in communication between all levels of the process to ensure that client expectations are met.

4. Constantly re-evaluate and re-align processes. Every process blueprint becomes irrelevant if the organization does not deliver to the client.

In the following, we introduce primary managerial practices, as well as IT systems, that are used in the creative industries in order to manage creativity-intensive processes. We proceed in analogy to the generic elements of understanding and refining the requirements, doing work, and evaluation. We use the notion of *elements* rather than *stages* so as to highlight that creativity-intensive processes are highly iterative and are not to be seen as a rigid sequence. We then introduce different IT systems that can be used in order to support these different managerial practices. Keep in mind that the three stages are highly iterative and are not more than a high level blueprint of creativity-intensive processes.

## 5.1 Understanding and Refining the Requirements

Understanding the requirements of a creative product (e.g., a VFX shot) as clearly as possible reduces uncertainty with regard to outcome, required resources, and process structure, as the creative organization can develop a better perception of what is needed to carry out the process. The challenge of understanding requirements is twofold: Firstly, the creative organization needs to understand what the client expects them to do. Secondly, it must be ensured that the organization has the technical and creative capabilities to meet the client requirements.

In our VFX example, the organization has to first understand the general requirements of each and every shot: where is the spider located, what does the spider do, and what other elements should be in the shot (e.g., trees, etc.). In order to reach high levels of client satisfaction, creative organizations must not only understand the requirements in general, but also what product features are of particular importance to the client. In some cases, it is possible to identify those pockets of creativity that are of exacting importance for a certain project and, thus, need to be treated with particular caution. At the same time, the organization must match the requirements with their technical capabilities. For example, if the shot would involve fluid dynamics, this would rely on a very sophisticated simulation pipeline. Very few companies have this capability and so taking on work that requires it depends on an understanding of the cost implied in achieving the result. This is a common and important problem for most VFX companies – understanding a priori that it will take to build creative capability. Once the requirements are understood at the highest level and the shot is broken down into discrete process steps, requirements need to be understood at the more detailed levels. One example is the 3D animation of the shot, where the animator has to understand how precisely the spider moves in that particular shot. Again, the requirements at this more detailed level must match the organizations capabilities as well as available resources, including time and budget.

Table 2 summarizes important managerial practices that creative organizations use in order to understand and refine requirements.

**Table 2** Managerial practices in understanding and refining the requirements

| Managerial practice | Description |
|---|---|
| Creative brief | The initial creative brief is done upfront and is a process of creating a common understanding between creative persons and clients with regard to what is required. This stage is not only about briefing the creative people; creative people can stimulate the client by presenting reference to encourage creativity. The creative brief is hence a practice for supporting requirements engineering in a creative way. |
| Providing stimuli | The creative organization provides stimuli to the client in order to iteratively generate a shared understanding of the project goals. As mentioned above, the practice of providing stimuli is often combined with the creative brief. |
| Showing references | Showing references supports the creative brief; it helps to generate a common understanding between creative people and client on where the project is heading. Besides, it can provide stimuli for coming up with truly creative ideas. |
| Matching requirements with capabilities | Determining the requirements also requires the creative organization to match what they are expected to do with their technical and creative capabilities. This task can be quite challenging given that required resources and process steps are hard to predict. Getting caught up in operational problems can compromise creativity. In VFX production, for example, it is relatively common to discover that an approach taken is not able to deliver the creative results required. This particularity of "temporary process failure" must thus also be considered when allocating resources. |

Summarizing, we propose the following guidelines for the process of understanding and refining the requirements of a creative product:

- Understand the requirements early in the process so as to mitigate creative risk. Use a variety of tools and techniques in order to create a mutual understanding of the requirements (in VFX production, these may include style frames and previews, for example).
- View understanding the requirements as a highly iterative process of negotiation between client and creative organization.
- Match the requirements to your capabilities. Know what can be done and validate early that you are capable of meeting the client's expectations. Being caught up in operational problems is one of the greatest risks to creativity.
- Understand what features of the product are most important to the client.

## 5.2 *Doing Work*

Our research has revealed two main types of managerial practices that are used throughout the process of doing work: *managing the scope of creativity* and *allocating resources.*

### 5.2.1 Managing the Scope of Creativity

Allowing freedom for a particular task increases variance – and thus uncertainty – and decreases predictability. This leads not only to greater creative potential, but also to greater risk. The process manager (creative supervisor) must carefully decide what freedom she allows for each and every task to achieve high creativity and innovation while still ensuring that everybody works toward one aim. As Amabile (1998) puts it, autonomy "around process fosters creativity because giving people freedom in how they approach their work heightens their intrinsic motivation and sense of ownership. Freedom about process also allows people to approach problems in ways that make the most of their expertise and their creative thinking skills" (p. 82). By defining pockets of creativity and setting up goals and constraints, creative persons are actually granted freedom where it is needed while they do not have to diverge at their own risk. Possible constraints are deadlines, clearly defined outputs (such as a certain number of alternative artifacts etc.), review processes, and regular communication among creative persons and stakeholders.

As indicated, motivation is one of the most relevant factors that impact on a person's capacity of acting creatively. Monetary incentives are in most cases not the sole source of motivation to enhance people's creative power. In fact, creative people's motivation may be fostered by means such as allowing them freedom or even putting them under time pressure. The creative supervisor must find a balance between what can be referred to as the creative people's personal creative agenda and the actual project goals in order to motivate people while simultaneously pursuing process goals and delivering to the client. This balance is called the *creative buy-in*.

Summarizing, we propose the following guidelines for managing the scope of creativity:

- Find a balance between project goals and the personal creative agenda of creative people.
- Try to not restrict creativity but channel it down the right path.

### 5.2.2 Allocating Resources

Pockets of creativity are crucial to an organization's success as this is where the organization can distinguish itself from its competitors. Yet, as has been maintained, the creative parts of processes are difficult to predict with regard to required resources. Thus, we first advocate to identify pockets of creativity and then to carefully consider what is actually needed to successfully accomplish the task. The existent literature as well as our own research clearly point out that a lack of resources for creative tasks can completely compromise creativity (e.g., Amabile 1998).

Let us consider a shot where the spider will be dangling from a web. There may be a number of animators who have the technical capabilities of completing the

**Table 3** Managerial practices in resource allocation

| Managerial practice | Description |
|---|---|
| Task allocation and team building | Creative persons who are allocated to a task must have a certain expertise to be capable of accomplishing that task. Task allocation can also be used in order to facilitate knowledge transfer between experienced and less experienced individuals. Creative parts of a process are largely characterized by the application of tacit knowledge; by putting junior and senior persons on the same task, an organization enables the transfer of tacit knowledge. Moreover, through finding a balance between creatively challenging and rather simple tasks, creative people can be given the opportunity to follow their creative agenda, which, in turn, fosters motivation. |
| Time allocation | A lack of time is often associated with a lower quality of a creative product. Thus, creative supervisors must identify the particularly complex and creative parts of a process, so as to allocate sufficient time. Generally, more time enables creative people to explore and come up with various options, which can then be used in order to create a shared understanding between client and creative organization. Although insufficient time can reduce the quality of the creative product, sometimes enforcing constraints can generate creativity under pressure. |
| Allocation of other resources | Other resources include artist systems, such as particular animation suites, for example. Again, the identification and characterization of pockets of creativity throughout the process landscape sets the baseline for resource allocation. If creative tasks with high impact on the overall process success lack resources, this may fundamentally hamper an organization's creativity and success. |

shot. However, the VFX supervisor may further ask who has particular experiences with similar animations. She might then choose the person and further ask what software that particular person would use for that shot (different people may approach the problem differently) and make sure that the software is available.

Table 3 provides an overview of managerial practices with regard to resource allocation in creativity-intensive processes.

Summarizing, we propose the following guidelines with regard to resource allocation in creativity-intensive processes:

- Do not overload key talent with trying to achieve all tasks.
- Leverage people with less experience by allocating them to challenging tasks and letting them work with more senior people.
- Avoid resource shortage particularly where you expect people to be creative. Thus, channel your resources toward the more creative parts of your processes.

## 5.3 Evaluation of the (Intermediate) Creative Product

Two main types of managerial practices for product evaluation can be distinguished: *approval processes* and *ongoing communication.*

### 5.3.1 Approval Processes/Reviews

The most important means to evaluate creative products are approval processes which ensure that the creative product meets the requirements. It can be distinguished between quality assurance (technical reviews) and creative reviews, and further between internal and external approvals. External approvals include clients while internal approvals usually involve artists and creative supervisors. Approval processes are quite a complex practice, as the process manager has to make decisions, such as: when should the approval happen? Who should be involved? Do people have to meet physically? This practice requires the identification of pockets of creativity, as these are the process sections that are characterized by high levels of uncertainty and, therefore, particularly require review.

Wrong decisions with regard to review and approval can have serious consequences for the overall process. Due to differing subjective perceptions of creative products, for example, the exclusion of key stakeholders may consequently lead to expensive product revisions.

Summarizing, we propose the following guidelines with regard to approval processes:

- Understand who you work with and what their ability is in assessing a creative product.
- Reviewing at the right stage is critical in order to mitigate creative risk.
- When reviewing, keep communication open, so as not to compromise creativity.

### 5.3.2 Ongoing Communication/Showing Work in Progress

Ongoing communication ensures that the project team works toward one aim. This practice thus aims to mitigate variance that may be caused by weak requirement specifications as well as creative freedom. As a rule of thumb, vague requirement specifications require more communication between the different stakeholders and increase risk. The identification of pockets of creativity enables the process manager to identify where within the process there is a particular need to communicate with the client.

Let us consider the spider example. After client and creative organization have developed a first (mutual) understanding of the requirements, the VFX house starts to model and animate the spider. The spider is developed step by step. The VFX house could wait until the spider is completed and then review with the client. However, if the client is dissatisfied this would mean an enormous amount of work that would have to be redone. Alternatively, the VFX house can involve the client into the process by showing them work in progress throughout the process, so as to ensure that the VFX house's understanding of the requirements and the client's understanding of the requirements indeed match. At the same time, the VFX house must understand who their client is; that is, the client's background and expertise. If the client is, due to low expertise, not capable of understanding where the process is heading when they are shown something that is far from finished, their involvement may actually hamper the process, consume time, and as a consequence, compromise creativity.

Summarizing, we propose the following guidelines for communication within creativity-intensive processes:

- Ongoing and appropriate communication is of high importance to ensure that the creative process is not heading down the wrong path.
- Communication is essential to creativity. Nominate key communicators early on to ensure clarity in briefing and feedback.
- As a rule of thumb, vague initial requirements specifications require more intensive communication.

## *5.4 The Use of Information Technology (IT)*

Davenport (2005) argues that technology may be the most important intervention in the performance of knowledge workers over the last couple of years. This observation is also likely to hold for processes in the creative industries. Yet, it must be noted that the use of IT should not be mandatory; creative people need freedom in order to act creatively. The orchestration of IT tools that are used depends on the situation at hand. Moreover, as with other resources in creativity-intensive processes, it is hard to predict what tools will actually be required throughout the process.

In the following, we provide a brief overview of the most important classes of IT that are used in VFX production processes. We also explain how these software tools can be used in order to successfully manage creativity-intensive processes.

### 5.4.1 Artist Systems

Artist systems are tools that are used by creative people in order to generate creative artifacts. Examples for artist's systems used at RSP are 2D and 3D packages, which enable artists to generate images and carry out the different tasks that are done within the production pipeline. Usually, within the production pipeline various tools need to be used in order to generate VFX for a feature film.

### 5.4.2 Groupware

Groupware systems play a prominent role in all major stages of creativity-intensive processes in order to create a mutual understanding of requirements, showing work in progress, and evaluating creative products. Groupware is a collective name for those systems that enable groups to work cooperatively. One major benefit in the usage of groupware systems can be seen in a potentially higher number of iterations of the creative product, which can ultimately reduce creative risk due to differing perceptions of the creative product. Groupware systems range from tools such as email or instant messengers to tools that are particularly tailored to the industry.

For example, RSP uses a software called *cineSync* which is a remote review and approval tool based on *Apple QuickTime* technology. By synchronizing the timeline and playback of movies, people around the world are able to view the work simultaneously. The tool supports audio-visual communication and also allows for interaction, as people can draw on the images they are seeing. Thus, the software enables rich communication between geographically distributed stakeholders. As has been indicated, the process of determining requirements of a product as well as the process of evaluation highly depends on the involved people. *cineSync* enables different people to express their thoughts in different ways and, thus, furthers the process of negotiating requirements and evaluating creative products. Consequently, it enables involved stakeholders to create a mutual understanding of process goals.

### 5.4.3 Knowledge Management Systems

As (previous) knowledge is an important factor that influences creativity (Weisberg, 1999), knowledge management systems (Alavi and Leidner 2001) are a set of technologies that are used in the creative industries for making knowledge available to accomplish creative tasks. For every pocket of creativity, it has to be considered what type of knowledge can be made available (e.g., technical guidelines on how to use a tool, previous experiences for a certain type of task, or artifacts that have been created earlier and that can now be used as reference material). Thus, the identification of pockets of creativity can help to understand where knowledge is created, where it is stored and located, and how it is transferred and applied (Seidel et al. 2008a).

Consequently, by identifying and comprehensively describing pockets of creativity, the organization is enabled to integrate knowledge into their processes. In a similar manner, Davenport (2005) suggests to embed knowledge in the technology that is used by knowledge workers.

In the VFX industry, knowledge management is of particular importance, as much of the industry's knowledge is tacit knowledge that is located in the heads of, often freelancing, creative people. Consequently, the industry seeks to explicate and store this knowledge in knowledge bases, in order to make it available for the organization.

### 5.4.4 Asset Management Systems

Asset management systems for digital assets, for example, can be used to facilitate the process of understanding the requirements of the creative product, as well as the actual work (cf. vom Brocke et al. 2010). In the process of understanding the requirements, existent digital assets can be used to support communication by showing what has been done previously and what could be done. This includes cognitively stimulating both creative people and clients by providing new options and potential associations. As a matter of fact, in many cases, being creative means to put together what has been done previously (Couger and Higgins 1993). Thus, supporting pockets of creativity with asset management systems can increase productivity and the quality of the creative output.

For example, when a particular shot with our spider is to be generated, an asset management system can be used in various ways: First, previous shots can be reviewed so as to get a better understanding of what would be possible. Second, assets (such as a tree the spider is dangling from) that have previously been designed for other shots may be re-used in this shot.

### 5.4.5 Workflow Technology

With regard to workflow technology (Ouyang et al. (2010) on workflow management) it must be noted that such systems have to be used very carefully when introduced into creative environments. As has been argued by various authors, there is a danger of straight-jacketing; the so-called production-workflow systems in particular tend to be too rigid (e.g., van der Aalst et al. 2005). Creativity-intensive processes, however, require high levels of flexibility. When a creative organization introduces workflow-related technology, they must ensure that no unnecessary constraints are imposed on pockets of creativity. Automating the well-structured parts of the processes, however, can give people more time to be creative, which can ultimately result in higher product quality. As indicated earlier, one key issue in managing creative organizations is not overloading key creative resources.

Yet, our research has shown that even simple solutions such as task lists that show the next process steps can support creativity-intensive processes in many ways. Even though creative people need freedom in order to act creatively, they also need security on what they have to deliver and when. It is up to the creative supervisor to find the appropriate balance of creative freedom and structure. Consequently, organizations in the creative industries make extensive use of such systems.

Summarizing, we propose the following guidelines with regard to the use of IT in creativity-intensive processes:

- Technology should be scalable. A lack of scalability may compromise creativity.
- Do not try to automate creative parts of the process as this may lead to too rigid processes.
- Technology should be accessible according to the pull principle; that is, creative people can access a tool in order to solve the problem at hand. Do not force the use of software tools unless it is actually required.

## 5.5 Summary of Managerial Practices and IT Used in Creativity-intensive Processes

In Fig. 7, we pick up the conceptualization of creativity-intensive processes introduced in section 3 and relate it to the above described managerial practices and IT systems. The managerial practices that are used in order to communicate with the client can be distinguished from those that are used so as to internally manage the process.

Creative organizations use these practices along with IT in order to pursue both creative and operational process performance while simultaneously mitigating operational and creative risk. The arrows in Fig. 8. illustrate how successful reviews and ongoing communication with the client can impact on the development of risk and the level of understanding of the requirements of the creative product.

## 5.6 Measuring Creativity-intensive Processes

Harmon (2007) states that it "is widely held that performance information is a key differentiator and that organizations that can obtain and use information about their markets and their processes in a timely manner can perform better" (p. 139). But does this also hold for creative organizations? Is not creative output difficult to measure? In a 2008 Harvard Business Review article, Ed Catmull, co-founder of Pixar, wrote that it is a misbelief that much of what is done in a creative

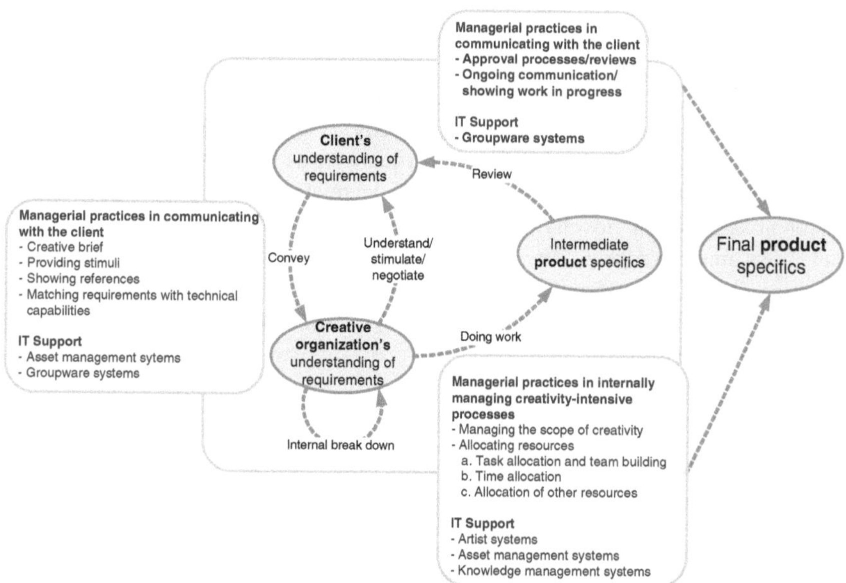


**Fig. 7** Managing creativity-intensive processes (compare Seidel 2009)

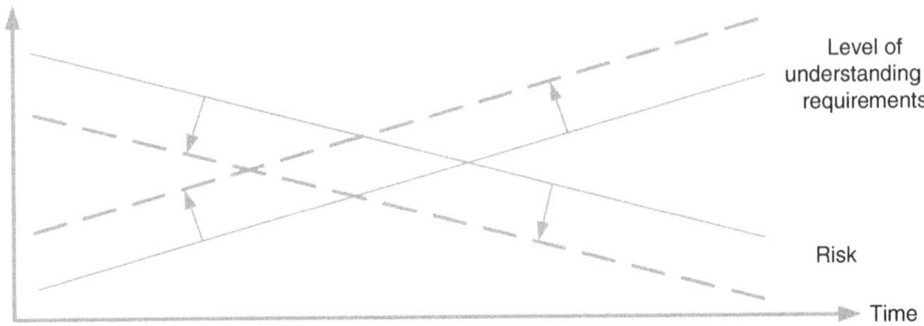


**Fig. 8** Risk mitigation in creativity-intensive processes through the application of managerial practices and IT (Seidel 2009)

organization cannot be measured (Catmull, 2008). He argues that most processes involve activities and deliverables that can be quantified. As indicated, creative organizations pursue both what may be referred to as *operational process performance* and *creative process performance*. While the first one is relatively easy to measure, the latter one is not. In fact, creative organizations must find a balance between the two. On the one hand, every organization must follow business imperatives such as time and budget in order to stay in business. On the other hand, they must pursue creative excellence, which means to meet, and even exceed, customer expectations in order to gain competitive advantage. Ultimately, both operational and creative process performance determine customer satisfaction.

*Operational process performance* refers to classical measures such as time, budget, and process efficiency [see also on process performance measurement by Heckl and Moormann (2010)]. To achieve these, organizations apply managerial practices that are known from process management, such as process automation and process optimization. Other possible measures may include the number of iterations that are necessary to generate a certain type of creative product (for example a particular type of VFX animation), for example.

*Creative process performance* refers directly to the creative product. It can be measured by its novelty/appropriateness (quality), as well as by the number of outputs generated. While purposefulness may be relatively easily identified through customer satisfaction, novelty can only be rated by experts in the particular area. In fact, measures have been developed in order to evaluate creative performance. Firestien (1993), for example, states "the evaluation [of a creative product] must occur on a number of levels; not with a single factor, or a single total effective criterion score" (p. 265).

## 6 Conclusions

Creativity influences business processes and the way we do BPM. We believe it is both relevant and timely to take a closer look at the role that creativity plays within business processes, and how it can be managed. Existent modeling techniques, software tools, and management practices may support some of the important issues in this context. However, until now there is no comprehensive approach on how to manage creativity from a business process perspective.

The processes that we discussed in this chapter can be framed as highly dependent on creativity, interdependent, complex and intensively involving the client. Other creativity-intensive processes, however, may be different. For example, they may not involve clients and may be characterized by lower levels of interdependency. However, we expect that the main characteristics, such as uncertainty with regard to outcome, process, and required resources, or operational and creative risk, can be found in many industries. Also, other industries may learn from the creative industries, as high levels of uncertainty are not only related to high operational and creative risk, but also to high creative potential. Finding a balance between risk mitigation and creative freedom can open tremendous opportunities to any organization.

## References

Alavi M, Leidner DE (2001) Review: Knowledge management and knowledge management systems: Conceptual foundations and research issues. MIS Q 25(1):107–136

Amabile TM (1988) A model of creativity and innovation in organizations. In: Staw BM, Cummings LL (eds) Research in organizational behavior. JAI Press, Greenwich, CT, pp 123–167

Amabile TM (1996) Creativity in context: Update to the social psychology of creativity: Update to the "Social psychology of creativity". Westview Press, Boulder, CO

Amabile TM (1998) How to kill creativity. Harv Bus Rev 76(5):76–87

Borghini S (2005) Organizational creativity: Breaking equilibrium and order to innovate. J Knowl Manage 9(4):19–33

Catmull E (2008) How pixar fosters collective creativity. Harv Bus Rev 86(9):65–72

Clark B, Sphor SJ (1998) Guide to postproduction for tv and film. Managing the process. Focal Press, Burlington, MA

Clevé B (2006) Film production management. Burlington, Oxford

Couger JD, Higgins LF (1993) (Un) structured creativity in information systems organizations. MIS Q 17(4):375

Davenport TH (2005) Thinking for a living: How to get better performance and results from knowledge workers. Harv Bus Sch Press, Boston, MA

Davenport TH (2010) Process management for knowledge work. In: vom Brocke J, Rosemann M (eds) Handbook on business process management, vol 1. Springer, Heidelberg

Drazin R, Glynn MA, Kazanjian R (1999) Multilevel theorizing about creativity in organizations: A sensemaking perspective. Acad Manage Rev 24(2):286–307

Eppler MJ, Seifried PM, Röpnack A (1999) Improving knowledge intensive processes through an enterprise knowledge medium. In: ACM SIGCPR Conference on Computer Personnel Research. New Orleans, LA

Firestien RL (1993) The power of product. In: Isaksen SG, Murdock MC, Firestien RL, Treffinger DJ (eds) Nurturing and developing creativity. The emergence of a discipline. Norwood, New Jersey, pp 261–277

Ford CM (1996) A theory of individual creativity in multiple social domains. Acad Manage Rev 21(4):1112–1132

Harmon P (2007) Business process change. A guide for business managers and bpm and six sigma professionals, Elsevier, Amsterdam
Harrison-Broninski K (2010) Dealing with human-driven process. In: vom Brocke J, Rosemann M (eds) Handbook on business process management, vol 2. Springer, Heidelberg
Hartley J (2005) Creative industries – introduction. In: Hartley J (ed) Creative industries. Malden, USA, pp 1–40
Heckl D, Moormann J (2010) Process performance management. In: vom Brocke J, Rosemann M (eds) Handbook on business process management, vol 2. Springer, Heidelberg
Hesmondhalgh D (2002) The cultural industries. Sage, London, Thousand Oaks
Kerlow IV (2004) The art of 3d computer animation and effects. Wiley, Hoboken, New Jersey
Ouyang C, Adams M, Wynn MT, ter Hofstede AHM (2010) Workflow management. In: vom Brocke J, Rosemann M (eds) Handbook on business process management, vol 1. Springer, Heidelberg
Peltier TR (2004) Risk analysis and risk management. EDP Audit Control Secur Newsl, 32(3):1–17
Runco MA (2007) Creativity. Research, development, and practice. Elsevier Academic Press, Burlington, MA, Theories and themes
Seidel S (2009) A theory of managing creativity-intensive processes. Münster Faculty of Business and Economics. University of Münster, Münster
Seidel S, Müller-Wienbergen F, Rosemann M, Becker J (2008a) A conceptual framework for information retrieval to support creativity in business processes. In: 16th European Conference on Information Systems, Galway, Ireland
Seidel S, Rosemann M, Becker J (2008b) How does creativity impact business processes? In: 16th European Conference on Information Systems, Galway, Ireland
Styhre A, Sundgren M (2005) Managing creativity in organizations critique and practices. Palgrave Macmillan, Houndmills, Basingstoke
Tan G (1998) Managing creativity in organizations: A total system approach. Creativ Innovat Manage 7(1):23–31
van der Aalst W, Weske M, Grünbauer D (2005) Case handling: A new paradigm for business process support. Data Knowl Eng 53(2):129–162
vom Brocke J, Seidel S, Simons A (2010) *Bridging the Gap between Enterprise Content Management and Creativity: A Research Framework*. Paper presented at the 43rd Hawaii International Conference on System Sciences (HICSS 2010), Koloa, Kauai, HI, USA
Wales LM (2005) The people and process of film and video production from low budget to high budget.. Allyn & Bacon, Boston
Weisberg RW (1999) Creativity and knowledge: A challenge to theories. In: Sternberg RJ (ed) Handbook of creativity. Cambridge University Press, Cambridge, pp 226–250
Woodman RW, Sawyer JE, Griffin RW (1993) Toward a theory of organizational creativity. Acad Manage Rev 18(2):293–321

# Global Processes and Data: The Culture Journey at Hilti Corporation

**Jan vom Brocke, Martin Petry, Theresa Sinnl, Bo Østerberg Kristensen, and Christian Sonnenberg**

**Abstract** The role of culture in business processes is often underestimated. Especially the success of Business Process Change depends to a large extent on the employees' willingness to adapt to a new work environment and eventually accept short-term losses for long-term benefits. We, therefore, engage with the Hilti Corporation analyzing the role of culture in a specific change project. After introducing the Hilti business model, we take a closer look at the measures taken at Hilti to actively manage a global culture by means of the Culture Journey. Against this background, we examine the impact culture may have on Business Process Change. The IT-driven change project Global Processes and Data (GPD) at Hilti serves as an example for exploring the way in which culture affects process change. We conclude deriving some lessons learnt from the Hilti Case on the role of culture in BPM.

## 1 Introduction

Every company has its own culture with its own values which become apparent, for example, in the actions of the employees. The culture develops along with the history of the company, and therefore represents the people's behavior. However, culture is not passive, it is not just a pattern *of* behavior. The culture of a company can actively be shaped as a pattern *for* behavior (Neuberger and Kompa 1987) – as Hilti does. Hence, it is an important step for a company to identify its core values as the origin of the corporate culture. Most of the times, these values, have led back to the vision and attitude of the founders of a company and have developed over time (Buß 2008). To understand the roots of the corporate culture, it is vital to become aware of the different levels of culture (Schein 2004).

J. vom Brocke (✉)
Martin Hilti Chair of Business Process Management, Institute of Information Systems, University of Liechtenstein, Vaduz, Principality of Liechtenstein
e-mail: jan.vom.brocke@uni.li

J. vom Brocke and M. Rosemann (eds.), *Handbook on Business Process Management 2*, International Handbooks on Information Systems,
DOI 10.1007/978-3-642-01982-1_25, 

On the surface, culture manifests itself in so-called artifacts that are visible to everyone, such as symbols of a company, its products, typical behavior and rituals, the way of dressing, or architecture. The values of a company can lie both on the surface and underneath it. It is therefore important to distinguish between espoused values, that are visible, for example, in the mission statement or in publicly expressed strategies, on the one hand and invisible, lived values on the other. The latter, the subconscious part of culture underneath the surface, accounts for the biggest part of culture. A company's implicit values, the way of verbal and nonverbal communication, time orientation, social hierarchies, finally, the implicit common assumptions that underlie every action within a company amount to the main part of culture.

> If the espoused beliefs and values are reasonably congruent with the underlying assumptions, then the articulation of those values into a philosophy of operating can be helpful in bringing the group together, serving as a source of identity and core mission. (Schein 2004, p. 30)

However, there are often inconsistencies between the "lists of values" in the mission statement and the "observed behavior" (Schein 2004). The failure to manage the cultural aspects of US companies, for example, is said to have contributed to a great extent to the US economy's decline in the 1980s (Du Gay 1997, p. 246). Since then, organizational culture has become a popular topic in the management literature. From the "Search of Excellence," Peters and Waterman (1982), originated the conclusion that an excellent organization stands out through "common ways by which its members have learned to think, feel and act" (Hofstede 1991, p. 18).

In the face of today's fast moving world, it is therefore even more important to become aware of the common values of an organization, the shared "software of the mind" (Hofstede 1991). Bringing these values to mind, helps keeping the company's spirit alive, which is an essential driver of stability.

Consciously living these values then shapes a culture of trust and honesty which is crucial for coping with external and internal challenges, and achieving set goals. A holistic appearance of a company toward all of its stakeholders will pay off in loyal employees, loyal customers, satisfied industry partners, and a good reputation in society. Especially in times of economic turbulences, or throughout internal change processes, this accounts for a vital competitive advantage.

In this chapter, we engage with the Hilti Corporation in order to further analyze the role of culture in BPM. As a global corporation, Hilti provides technology for the construction industry in more than 120 countries around the world. Hilti evolved from a family company founded in 1941 to the Hilti Group with almost 21,000 employees today. The corporation upholds a clear value orientation and has developed the concept of the Culture Journey to facilitate that its employees become aware of the corporate culture and actually live the corporate core values. Apart from various activities belonging to this concept, Hilti summarized its approach to cultural awareness within the organization in a book provided to every employee. Below, an excerpt of this book is presented, alluding to what the Culture Journey at Hilti is aiming at:

> The way we do things at Hilti is based on living strong values. We act with integrity in all we do. We demonstrate courage to go beyond the circle of habits. We outperform through teamwork and we have commitment to personal and company growth. We share a common purpose of passionately creating enthusiastic customers and building a better future. We take responsibility for the development of the business, our team, and ourselves. We encourage, coach, and support each other to achieve outstanding results.

With such a statement, Hilti may not differ much from other corporations or organizations. However, as the people and corporate core values are vital to the business model of Hilti, much effort is put into making sure that the employees at Hilti really live up to these values. The leverage of this investment can be seen in various occurrences.

In the following, we present the Hilti business model in which culture plays an essential role. We then take a closer look at the measures taken at Hilti to actively manage a global culture by means of the Culture Journey. Against this background, we analyze the impact culture may have on Business Process Change. We take the IT-driven project of Global Processes and Data (GPD) as an example and set out exploring the role of culture. As to our prior source of knowledge, we report on the results of interviews conducted with managers of Hilti. Finally, we conclude deriving some lessons learnt from the Hilti Case on the role of culture in BPM.

# 2 Culture as an Integral Part of the Hilti Business Model

## 2.1 *Introducing the Hilti Business Model*

In order to understand the relevance of corporate culture within Hilti's business processes, it is necessary to have a look at the business model of the Hilti Corporation. It can be seen that the organization's culture plays an essential role being perceived as the backbone of corporate success. In this section, we first give an overview of the business model and its various elements, before studying the mechanisms of realizing and maintaining a strong culture in more detail.

The Hilti business model is essentially framed by two elements: (1) *customer value* and *sustainable profitable growth* as the primary *objectives* (output), and (2) *passionate people sharing a motivating culture* as the essential *drivers* for business (input). Both elements span the Hilti business model displayed in Fig. 1. The various elements of the model show how Hilti aims to realize its objectives.

The model illustrates that business is initially driven by "Purposes and Values" that are shared by the "People" working at Hilti. These purposes and values are continuously communicated and further developed within the process of "Our Culture Journey." For guiding business activities the "Champion 3C strategy" is another essential pillar in the business model. Processes responsible for creating customer value and sustainable profitable growth are the engines of the business model.

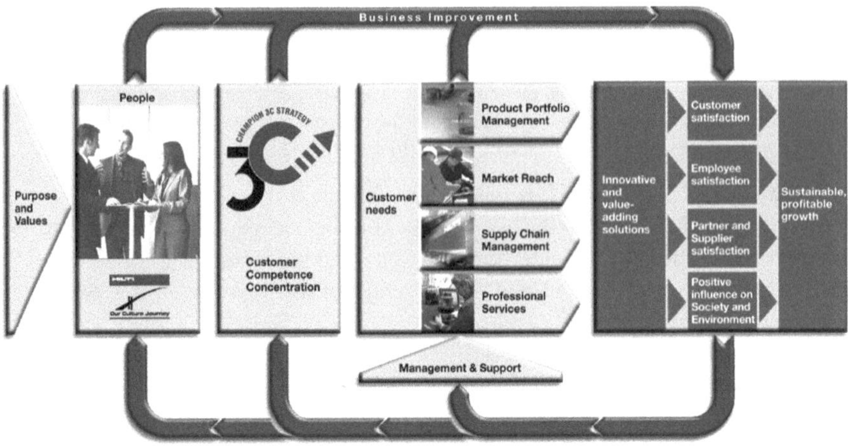


Fig. 1 The Hilti business model

All pillars of the business model are connected with a feedback loop, driving the continuous improvement of individual pillars. In the following section, these pillars are described in some more detail providing a framework for our further examination.

### 2.1.1 Purpose and Values

At Hilti, the purpose of business is summed up by the Hilti Core Purpose Statement: *We passionately create enthusiastic customers and build a better future.* This statement nicely illustrates both, objectives and drivers of business.

Regarding the objectives, Hilti goes beyond the common goal of customer satisfaction and – according to the objective of creating customer value – draws the picture of the "enthusiastic customer." This underlines the intention to create success for the customers by identifying their needs and providing innovative and value-adding solutions. In one interview, a manager puts it as follows: *It is not about selling customers a drill, it is more about providing them a complete fastening solution in a certain situation. That means: where to put that hole, how to measure it, how to make that hole, what to fill it up with, and to ensure that a building is going to stay there for 10, or 20, or 50 years – and doing all this in an efficient way and in line with highest health and safety standards.*

Enthusiastic customers already account for one aspect of Hilti's sustainability objective. Building a "better future" also relates to this objective and is further defined through the following elements: (1) to foster a company climate in which every team member is valued and able to grow, (2) to develop win-win relationships with partners and suppliers, (3) to embrace responsibility toward society and environment. In discussions with representatives of the company, it became apparent that Hilti's responsibility-driven attitude may particularly ground on the special business Hilti is active in. A manager explained it like this: *Hilti is not about putting pictures on the wall. It builds tools to hold buildings together, to make sure that bridges do not fall down, to make sure that tunnels are safe, to make sure that concrete sticks to steel or steel sticks to concrete even in the most difficult conditions and environments.* This shows that sustainable solutions are a key objective for Hilti to serve its business purpose.

With regard to the drivers in the business model, Hilti's employees share the following corporate values:

- *Integrity*: Integrity means being upright toward all people you interact with, acting according to principles, incorporating a holistic perception, and feeling responsible.
- *Courage*: Courage stands for having a backbone, being brave enough to go beyond the obvious and proven and exploit new ideas.
- *Teamwork*: Teamwork signifies pulling at one string, sharing a common goal, using synergies and therefore enlarging competence.
- *Commitment*: Commitment implies identifying with the company, feeling an inner engagement for accomplishing high performance.

Hilti's corporate values account for a motivating culture and passionate people as important drivers of the business. These values serve different goals at the operational level. They provide a basis for both selecting new personnel, and developing employees within the Culture Journey. As a manager stated: *When we recruit people we ask: Do they fit our corporate core values? And if we see this guy is not so much of a team player [...] we do not even start looking at the skills.* Furthermore, Hilti's values provide a framework on how to work together in the business processes.

The priority given to purposes and values at Hilti is visible in the Culture Journey. Its impact will be analyzed later on in this chapter.

### 2.1.2 Our Culture Journey

The Culture Journey at Hilti is a corporate initiative that intends to make sure that the corporate purposes and values described before are meaningful to all employees working at Hilti. These approximately 20,000 people work in more than 80 market organizations around the world. In this global setting, a specific process is needed in order to foster a shared understanding within the company, and to help people identifying with the company. The Culture Journey binds people to act together and is an important source of motivation and integration. A manager underlines the importance of the initiative: *We need to ensure that everybody sings the same song. And we do that through the Culture Journey, continuously working on our corporate values.*

The implications of the Culture Journey for the business model in general, and also more specifically for BPM, will be further explored in the remainder of this chapter. Before going into more detail, the other elements of the Hilti business model will be briefly introduced in order to complete the picture. This will help better understand the various effects of Hilti's corporate culture.

### 2.1.3 Customer, Competence, and Concentration

In order to be the *customers' best partner*, a manager explains, *sales people and product managers continuously listen to the specific needs of the customers*. Many innovations are driven out of customer needs reported to, or experienced by, the product managers in the field. Therefore, the overall objectives of the corporation are transformed into tangible action plans and strategic initiatives are derived. Within the Hilti business model, the *champion 3C strategy* serves that purpose. It draws on *customer*, *competency*, and *concentration* as the main strategic *drivers*. Before, we described Hilti's enthusiastic people and motivating culture as the main drivers for business and customer value as a main objective. At the same time, customers are seen as business drivers. This shows the corporation's business understanding as being process-oriented in the sense that customers represent both beginning and end of the business process. Hilti's strategic drivers are specified as follows:

- *Customer*: *We want to be our customers' best partner. Their requirements drive our actions.*
- *Competency*: *We are committed to excellence in innovation, total quality, direct customer relationships, and effective marketing.*
- *Concentration*: *We focus on products and markets where we can achieve and sustain leadership positions.*

Specific initiatives are derived from these drivers. For example, Hilti employs a direct sales model and does not sell through a distributor network, or through wholesalers. That means a customer always buys a Hilti tool from a Hilti employee and thus communicates his needs directly to Hilti. Focusing on direct customer relationships is the key for Hilti being excellent in innovation.

In order to put these strategic drivers into practice, Hilti applies a strong process oriented structure building the next pillar of the business model.

### 2.1.4 Processes

In the Hilti business model, four process areas are defined on the corporate level, each of which is further distinguished on more specific levels.

- *Product Portfolio Management*: This aspect essentially deals with the design of new products. On the top level, it comprises the management of the entire portfolio of products and services across a life-cycle. It also comprises research and design of specific products on the more detailed levels.

- *Market Reach*: Considering the Market Reach process, five different sales channels are differentiated, namely (1) Hilti centers, (2) Territorial sales people, (3) Pro Shops, (4) B2B (incl. Hilti online), and (5) Customer Services.
- *Supply Chain Management*: On a daily basis, Hilti purchases significant amounts of material and delivers a high volume of its products to its customers. Supply chain management deals with the logistics and the warehouse management by means of logistic centers. Moreover, the management of relations to its supply-chain-partners is an essential element for Hilti in order to achieve win-win situations.
- *Professional Services*: These processes include delivering after sales services. An essential part is dealing with repair services which should be provided with a favorable quality and speed. Another important part of Professional Services is fleet management: Customers pay a low monthly fee for the use of a Hilti tool and also experience a package of value added services that deliver direct business benefit.

In addition to the processes characterizing the core business, a process area for *management and support* is distinguished. In particular, IT services are located therein, supporting the four process areas.

All processes are measured in terms of outcomes in order to actively manage their contribution to the corporate purposes and values. These outcomes form the next pillar to be described as part of the business model.

### 2.1.5 Outcome

According to the primary objectives, Hilti is aiming at customer value and sustainable profitable growth. These goals can be translated into business goals at a more operative level. Sustainability translates, for example, in high quality as an undisputed element in the Hilti business model. At the same time, profitability is focused on. That means Hilti safeguards efficiency, in order to deliver high quality at reasonable costs, and in appropriate time.

For further operationalization of the objectives, visions are created covering the development of a 5–10 years life-span. In 2000, for instance, "Vision 2008" was announced named "Accelerated Profitable Growth." As part of this vision, the goal was set to have a yearly turnover of 4 billion CHF and 450 million CHF of profit by 2008. As these goals were already reached before 2008, a new vision was announced in 2006, namely "Vision 2015: Be a Great Company." One goal is to double sales to 8 billion CHF per year, and to more than double profit by 2015.

In addition to the financial operationalization of the objectives, Hilti follows a stakeholder approach (vom Brocke et al. 2009), looking at the value contribution of the processes from the perspective of all stakeholders. Considering the employees' perspective, for instance, Hilti aims at ensuring that everybody at Hilti grows into their job positions according to individual capabilities and preferences. In the same way, win-win relationships with the suppliers as service providers are an essential part of the value concept. Apart from the stakeholders directly involved in the processes, Hilti is also concerned about a positive impact on society and ecology. As a consequence, Hilti is actively involved in social welfare projects around the world, for example, in Sri Lanka and in Brazil.

Against the background of the Hilti business model, the role of corporate culture in BPM can be analyzed in more detail. In the following chapter, we examine the specific mechanisms of realizing and maintaining a corporate culture.

## 2.2 A Closer Look at Culture: The Hilti Culture Journey

It is comprehensible that "any successful process management effort requires a strong emphasis on culture, leadership and change management" (Davenport 2008, p. xvi). While there is evidence on the importance of cultural aspects in BPM (Hammer 2010; Armistead et al. 1999), little is known about specific measures to actively consider corporate culture in BPM (Baumöl 2010; Gore 1999 for some discussions on probable measures and actions to design organizational culture; Lee and Dale 1998; Zairi 1997). As to the example of the Culture Journey at Hilti, we can now study such measures in more detail and analyze the leverage of these initiatives within a global BPM project.

There are different phases toward a consciously lived corporate culture. These include the development, the realization, and the maintenance of the corporate culture and its values. Regarding the development, a company's culture is based on the values and visions of the founders for the most part, and develops over time according to various internal and external influences. Very often, neither managers, nor other employees, are aware of the corporate culture. Awareness, however, is the first step to actively shaping it, accomplishing major changes, or harmonizing it worldwide. It is the first step to realize an aspired corporate culture.

### 2.2.1 Realizing a Corporate Culture: Taking Efforts for Values

Moving toward a specific corporate culture is a very intense undertaking. The more people are involved in an organization, the bigger the challenge to integrate people of different socio-cultural backgrounds. Sustainable initiatives are required that go beyond single workshops.

Hilti's tool to realize its aspired corporate culture is the Culture Journey. That means every employee goes through several so-called "team camps." These camps are organized off-site, and intend to foster teaching and learning of corporate values. The effort taken to organize and conduct these trainings is significant. *I have never seen a corporate initiative that costs millions a year to make sure that everybody is on the same page*, a, manager states. *And we are not talking about half an hour: The first team camp takes 2 or 3 days and we continue in that fashion resulting in 2–4 days of commitment every year*, the manager keeps on reporting.

38,000 working days were spent on the Culture Journey in 2007. In 2008, the working days even increased up to 53,000 days per year.

Every new employee of Hilti attends a training called "Welcome to Hilti." This is a five day event, of which 2–3 days are solely spent focusing on a "fast track" Culture Journey. Further camps follow, according to a standardized process, making sure that everybody is going through the same training and getting new employees up to speed.

Summing up, we can conclude that quite a significant effort is made at Hilti realizing the corporate culture worldwide. Apart from building up a common understanding, initiatives for maintaining the corporate culture are also considered.

### 2.2.2 Maintaining the Corporate Culture: Making Values Relevant

Hilti's corporate culture is also embedded into the management process. Annual ratings are conducted in order to examine to what extent the corporate culture is actually lived by the employees. The degree of the aspired culture's realization is measured and consolidated – measured at the individual team member's level and consolidated at the department and group level.

For each employee "Performance Metrics for Personal Development" are evaluated by means of a scorecard, including sections for each corporate value dimension: integrity, courage, teamwork, and commitment. Based on this scorecard, regular feedback talks are conducted. As one manager reports, the corporate values are under close surveillance. If an employee, for example, lies and therefore violates integrity, the dismissal of him or her is taken into consideration. At the same time, *Commitment is strongly acknowledged* and employees receive appreciation for their contribution to the corporation's success.

Apart from the individual management of team members, the core corporate value rating also is an essential part of the performance measurement on the group and department level (see Fig. 2).

As part of the overall Performance Measurement a global employee opinion survey (GEOS) is carried out particularly capturing cultural issues. GEOS is a large scale survey that is conducted anonymously and that serves to comprise people's perspectives on the company. The survey, which nearly all employees participate in (well over 90%), includes more than 80 questions focusing on areas such as direction, execution, trust teamwork, encouragement, and recognition regarding the department, team, and individual performance level. For instance, employees are asked to evaluate the work-relations in the team. Further questions elude to what extent employees' feel they understand the link between their work and the overall business, or to what extent they have the feeling of being supported in their personal development and career.

Following up on the ratings, Hilti takes actions to make sure the corporate culture can be maintained. Within this process, the employees' feedback is a valuable source of knowledge regarding the measures to take. Continuously examining to what extend the corporate culture meets the vision of it is an essential part of

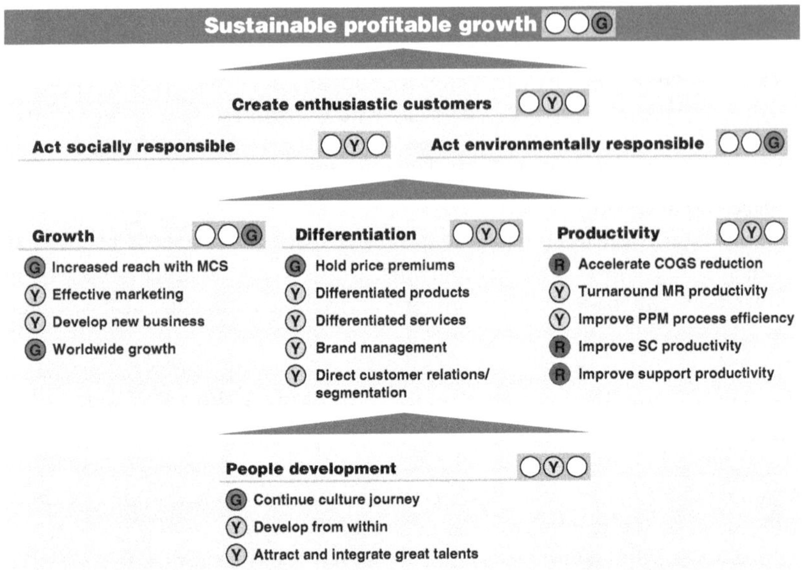


**Fig. 2** Sample of a corporate value cockpit chart (G: *green*, Y: *yellow*, R: *red*)

the Hilti business model *primarily fuelling the sustainable profitable growth at Hilti*, as one manager points out.

As a result we can observe that Hilti follows a systematic process in realizing and maintaining its aspired corporate culture worldwide. We now focus on the IT department analyzing the impact the Culture Journey has on this particular department. Subsequently, we will take a closer look at the GPD project that was mainly driven by the IT department.

## 2.3 Implications for Hilti IT: A Business-Driven IT-Strategy

Even though IT plays an important role throughout the entire business processes and, therefore, cannot be separated from "business," the alignment of business and IT is an issue. This can be seen from both theoretical discussions on the two disciplines and from the governance structure in practice where most often there are IT departments separate from other departments. Hence, the clash, or rather the alignment of business and IT, is widely discussed (Coombs et al. 1992; Guzman et al. 2008; Leidner and Kayworth 2006; Robey and Boudreau 1999).

At Hilti IT, a strong alignment with the overall corporate values can be observed ensuring that the corporation's business and IT go in the same direction. In particular, the Culture Journey had a significant impact on the Core Purpose Statement, terminology, and organization of Hilti IT.

### 2.3.1 Impact on the IT Core Purpose Statement

According to one of the IT Managers, it was within one of the team camps that people from Hilti IT created their own Core Purpose Statement. Just like the overall Hilti Corporation has a statement that describes the purpose of the corporation (*We passionately create enthusiastic customers and build a better future*) Hilti IT also started to work on the creation of such a statement. It reads as follows: *We passionately enable business excellence through global IT solutions.* The Hilti IT Core Purpose Statement was carefully derived from the Hilti Core Purpose Statement by questioning how Hilti IT can contribute to reach the overall objectives. IT is, thus, not at all seen as a means in itself, but as a means to support excellence in business.

### 2.3.2 Impact on the IT-Terminology

The Culture Journey led to a change in thinking that had an impact on the terminology used at Hilti IT. Right out of the discussions driven by the Culture Journey, there was the intention of expressing the idea of global cooperation in the wording commonly used. *We need to have the courage to completely disband having or even using the term "local IT." You are not local IT anymore, you are now "global IT."* This action was indeed a small change, but it turns out to make a specific difference. For example, the Spanish IT team is no longer a "local IT" team, but rather an "onsite IT" team, and part of the global picture.

### 2.3.3 Impact on the IT-Organization

In terms of work practices, the Culture Journey also contributed to "breaking down departmental walls" and fostering cooperation between the departments. The implementation of joint *task forces,* for example, developed directly from the attitude to take responsibility valuing teamwork. In these task forces, business and IT people, for instance, work together on innovative solutions. According to our interview partners, the task force members do not perceive themselves as representatives of individual departments. They are not *us and them*, as a business representative said. *That is not IT and this is not us. We are a team. Yes, we do not belong into the same department but we sit in the same room*, he explained further.

Summing up, we can learn that the Culture Journey has a significant effect on the way IT is carrying out business at Hilti. In particular, there is no divergent sub-culture but rather a strongly business-oriented IT. As the examples show, the shared corporate purposes and values had been a major source for the development of a new IT-Strategy. What we have not analyzed so far is the leverage of the corporate culture. In order to do so, we will look at a global BPM project at Hilti.

# 3 Global Processes and Data: An IT-Project Driven by Culture

## 3.1 Scope of the Project

Realizing the IT-Strategy of 2000, Hilti started quite a remarkable project on GPD. The objective was to overcome local data and process silos by introducing global standard business processes and standardized data structures supported by a global SAP solution, managed centrally from the headquarters in Liechtenstein. By the end of 2008, in excess of 95% of revenue, in excess of 40 sales organizations, and all eight production plants were operated on one global system. This means more than 15,000 users work with SAP ERP and 6,000 users also work with SAP Mobile.

Global standards for processes bear great potentials in terms of economies of scale. However, at the same time, these initiatives may face tremendous resistance from the local actors (Brenner and Coners 2010; Tregear 2010). While methods for modeling standardized processes and process variants may well be at hand, particularly from the field of reference modeling (vom Brocke 2007; Hallerbach et al. 2010), there are strong obstacles with regard to people giving up well established local processes for the sake of globally "dictated" ones.

Against this background, the GPD project is considered an ambitious initiative. It was conducted following multiple waves and has until now been perceived as successful. For our study, such a huge transformation project was interesting to pick as an example to reflect the role of corporate culture in this process. We mainly base our study on the assessment of the managers who were actively involved in the project.

At first, we analyze the scope of the GPD project in more detail. Driven by the IT strategy, GPD particularly required: (1) a global scope, and (2) an orientation toward the support of globally decentralized sales processes.

### 3.1.1 IT Becomes Global

One objective of the IT strategy was to globalize IT. Before the implementation of GPD, the organization of Hilti IT was fragmented, that is, having two chief information officers (CIOs), one CIO of Hilti, and another one for Hilti North America, in addition to multiple independent IT heads locally, who reported to local management teams.

A Hilti IT Manager described the need as follows: *A centrally managed IT with one global CIO was needed to properly handle a globally used, integrated business application environment for 15,000 users.*

After redesigning the organization of Hilti IT, the "onsite IT" teams would report to the regional infrastructure managers (RIM) who, then, would report to the central IT team at the headquarters which is called "global IT." The RIM are split up into five regions: the Far East region, three regions in Europe and the Americas.

To make sure that Second Level Support for all Business Applications is available at all times, three strategic locations for the Second Level support teams were selected. *We apply a follow-the-sun Second Level support concept. We went with Kuala Lumpur in the Far East, Headquarters in Schaan, and Tulsa in the US almost perfectly within an 8-8-8 h schema,* an IT manager explains.

Consequently, moving toward a global IT has not only led to economies of scale, but also accounts for Hilti's employees further growing together, practicing teamwork on a world-spanning scale. Therefore, the process change impacts Hilti's culture, providing a flow of activities that intensifies global collaboration among employees.

### 3.1.2 IT Supports Sales

The IT Strategy also had to account for the fact that Hilti is not only a production company. Actually in terms of headcount, Hilti is a service company involving most people in direct sales. One manager put it like this: *The majority of people are not making drill hammers. Actually, the majority of people are involved in direct sales. Globally we have 200,000 customer contacts every day.*

Hence, it is crucial to support the customers in the best way possible *by driving integrated marketing and sales processes through its Market Reach community, creating outstanding customer relationships and MR productivity. That's what CRM @ Hilti is all about.*

For this purpose, Hilti built a global process for CRM, which entails a comprehensive 360° customer information offering, the seamless integration of all sales channels, as well as a structured Sales Management Process (SMP). This defines the relationship between marketing and sales, the proper planning of the weekly customer visits, as well as the execution on the road. It is a natural extension of Hilti's Champion 3C strategy (Customer, Concentration, and Competence) which translates to being the customer's best partner, having the customer requirements drive actions, delivering excellence through innovation and total quality, and ensuring a direct customer relationship. To accomplish this, Hilti selected to base all customer relevant information on an integrated CRM system. This tool enables the 360° picture of the customer base, which all Hilti sales channels are utilizing, fitted to their specific needs.

The vehicle chosen to deliver and capture a significant portion of this information is an SAP based, in-house optimized solution, named TS-Mobile. With a PDA, the territorial salesperson gets the information concerning upcoming customer visits and logs customer information and sales activities, eventually synchronized into the SAP CRM and ERP solutions.

Hilti was well aware of the fact that introducing GPD was not only a matter of deciding on an information system, and therefore an IT project. On the contrary, the biggest difficulty of the process change was to have employees around the world change their daily way of work and adopted work patterns. Challenges had to be foreseen which are now discussed in more detail. The role Hilti's corporate culture played in overcoming the difficulties of the change project will be considered afterward.

## 3.2 Challenges Within the Project

Introducing GPD, brought in massive changes not only for Hilti IT, but also for all Hilti employees. Following the corporate culture, it was considered essential to integrate people in the change process from an early stage, in order to facilitate acceptance of the new system and to get support in the new processes.

In this section, we illustrate specific challenges within GPD in order to better understand the project and the changes for the employees going along with it. We differentiate between (1) organizational issues and (2) financial issues.

### 3.2.1 Organizational Issues: Restructuring Hilti IT

The organization of Hilti IT underwent significant changes initiated by the GPD project. These changes are related to business process orientation and include three perspectives: subject areas, infrastructure, and governance.

The subject areas within the IT were closely aligned to the business processes, namely the following three (in alphabetical order):

- *D-area*: comprising development, production, supply chain, and logistics. This area is aligned with *supply chain management* and *product portfolio management.*
- *F-area*: basically comprising support and management functions, finance, human resources, and back office support mechanisms. The corresponding business area is *management and support.*
- *R-area*: comprising sales channels such as Hilti online, the TS mobile, and CRM. This area corresponds with *market reach* and *professional services.*

For the support of the three areas, Hilti IT established so-called Process Competence Centers (PPCs) according to the D, F, and R-area (Rosemann 2010).

Furthermore, an effective and powerful infrastructure was considered vital. The infrastructure layer in Hilti IT is supported by a team covering technical components such as servers, storage facilities, laptops, operating systems, or application provisioning. Another layer in Hilti IT is the governance, which is concerned with enforcing business excellence, ensuring IT security, coordinating operations, and conducting performance measurement.

Accordingly, the IT leadership team, consisting of nine managers, is equally partitioned into three managers on the governance side, three managers on the infrastructure side, and three managers on the PCC (subject areas) side. That way a maximum alignment with business can be provided, consolidating the infrastructure, governance, and PCC perspective in one IT leadership team.

Restructuring the organization of Hilti IT was a difficult undertaking since it necessitated both changes in work practices, and changes in responsibilities.

#### 3.2.2 Financial Issues: Adjusting the Budgeting Structure

The new organizational structure also had implications for the budgeting. Before implementing the global IT strategy, responsibility for the IT budget was in the hands of the (now called) "onsite IT" of each market organization. This was changed to a centralized model, according to which global IT autonomously governs the entire IT budget.

This change had a significant impact on the work practices and also affected the employee's perception. For example, the salaries of the IT people working in the onsite IT department used to be paid from the local market organization, which are now paid out of the centrally managed budget. A manager gives further examples: *If the IT in France wanted to buy a server they bought a server. If they needed maintenance on a router they bought that in Paris. As a consequence of this global IT strategy that has changed.* The global IT infrastructure team, as explained above, is now centrally managing the purchases of hardware and network capacity, thus disburdening the "onsite IT" teams and achieving economies of scale.

We can conclude that the GPD project at the Hilti Corporation brought along significant changes. These changes are driven by the economic potential of GPD and they are essentially facilitated by the IT infrastructure. However, we see that the effects of the initiative are not at all limited to IT. On the contrary, the managers reported on – to some extent – dramatic changes to the way people do (and perceive) their work. Therefore, GPD seems to affect both processes, and culture and the introduced challenges can account for enough reason to have a project like GPD fail. Since most parts of the change project have already been completed by now, we are interested in the results of the project, particularly in the role Hilti's corporate culture played regarding the challenges of the project.

### *3.3 The Role of Culture: Assessing the Cultural Leverage*

Given the strong initiative at Hilti in realizing and maintaining its specific corporate culture, we are particularly interested in the role the Culture Journey played in the GPD project. Our interest is based on the fact that IT projects most commonly fail due to a lack of user acceptance (vom Brocke and Thurnher 2009; Baumöl 2010). This is the case particularly in projects which require changes in people's work practices to a large extent. Therefore, the support of these people is a crucial success factor (Anderson and Ackerman Anderson 2001; Hlupic 2003). As former IBM CEO Gerstner puts it, *culture isn't just one aspect of the game – it is the game. In the end, an organization is nothing more than the collective capacity of its people to create value* (Gerstner 2002).

With respect to previous studies, we therefore assume that (1) the Culture Journey and, especially, the shared corporate purpose fostered the support of the initiative since employees understand the benefits of the global initiative. In addition, we assume that (2) the corporate values – integrity, courage, teamwork, and commitment – have a positive influence on the people's behavior during the change project, and thus contribute to the effectiveness and efficiency of the project.

1. Overall influence of the Culture Journey on the support of the project
   Regarding the shared corporate purpose, representatives of Hilti perceived the Culture Journey as a facilitator for the change project. *We couldn't implement global solutions without Global Processes and Data and indeed without this commonly shared understanding driven by the Culture Journey, I think the project would not have turned out to be a success* a manager stated in our interviews. Of course, resistance was also part of the people's reactions in the GPD project: *No doubt that also challenges come along making people change their habits and giving up their well established practices for adapting to blueprints. But still, the corporate culture provided a means to manage these issues.* A shared corporate culture cannot prevent resistance in all cases, but it accounts for a common understanding that helps overcome those resistances.

   In addition, the corporate purpose gives a clear frame of reference explaining the need for change. Since Hilti integrated every employee right from the beginning, people felt being part of the global picture. The common corporate purpose gave meaning to the action of the single employee which in turn, for example, raised the willingness to work with the new ERP solution. People thus were able to accept single short-term discomfort for overall long-term benefits.

   As Hilti emphasizes the maintenance of its corporate culture, e.g., through its recruitment process and the Culture Journey, it ensures the sustainable success of projects like GPD. One manager put it in a nutshell: *Let's face it: you either get on or off the bus – and those people working with Hilti are happy to be on it. This has once again proven true regarding the great changes within the GPD project.*
2. Specific influence of the corporate values on the implementation process
   In addition to the overall support of the changed initiative, we further analyze the role of the corporate values as a potential facilitator for implementing change in the GPD project. In fact, the managers reported positive effects of the corporate values regarding the change process.

   **Integrity**
   The interviews revealed several effects of integrity. The organizational change of aligning the structure of Hilti IT with the structure of the corporation's business, for instance, is a stringent logic consequence of living integrity. It means that the entire corporate change serves consequently building a better future starting inside the corporation. People are likely to follow a project that is part of a bigger picture, when they already defined integrity as a value for themselves.

   As all employees incorporate a holistic perception, it was thus easier to demonstrate the usefulness of the project as one essential driver for acceptance.

Even though some changes were perceived as unfavorable for the market organization, at the same time they made sense from a holistic perception.

Integrity also facilitated the management of the project since each team concerned with the implementation of tasks was responsible for its actions. *If you say you are going to roll out a new solution, then roll out the solution. If you say you are going to do that by June 1st, then do it by June 1st.* Considering the scale of the project, a high level of accountability was crucial for project management.

Furthermore, the position toward Hilti's stakeholders was a key factor for the change management since it led to a broad understanding for the challenging situation during the project.

**Courage**

The corporate value of courage proved to be an important facilitator for the GPD project. Starting the initiative, already took courage considering the dimensions of the business process changes. While this was courage on the management side, our interviewees reported that courage was also a major source for people in the market organizations to leave the circle of their habits. *It took courage to kick of this thing at first, but also courage from all the people adapting to new ways of doing their job, without really knowing where this would lead them.*

In addition, the corporate value of courage imposed further positive effects on the management of the project. The characteristics of giving honest feedback contributed much to the efficiency and effectiveness of the initiative, as it was reported. *We have the principle, 'brutal facts, no blame' which is a matter of courage. This attitude for example, helped a lot: Obstacles appearing throughout GPD were communicated in a timely manner, and solutions were found.*

Courage set a positive climate for taking the risk of realizing the GPD project. In addition it also helped managing the required changes, particularly by means of an open and honest way of cooperating with each other. This relates to teamwork, as another important corporate value at Hilti.

**Teamwork**

The managers reported that another prerequisite for succeeding in the GPD project surely was 'sharing common goals' and 'pulling at one string' as it is referred to by the corporate value of teamwork at Hilti.

Apart from the general situation of people working together, a special quality of team work within the global change project was reported to us. This is the element of interlinking teams and building new teams involving members of different disciplinary settings worldwide: *Hilti employs high performing and specialized teams, being very good in one task but not necessarily in another. However, in order to implement a global solution by means of GPD, building multi-disciplinary teams became a vital necessity. For example, this takes accepting that I am in IT but I am going to be working in this very business related project or the other way round.*

Furthermore, the attitude of learning from each other turned out to be of major importance for the project. For that purpose, the environment of open communication and honest feedback created an atmosphere of respect and openness that helped to also learn from failures in the project. *If something is not working out as planned it has to be communicated. Learning from communicated failures of past projects and acknowledging these failures was vital for the GPD project. And even more so, it enabled Hilti IT to report a good success rate of IT projects nowadays.*

**Commitment**

The commitment of the employees involved in the GPD project was perceived as a major success factor by our interviewees. Not only the commitment of team members, but also the commitment of the senior and executive management was pointed out in the interviews. *There was definitely a need for commitment from the executive management and executive board to accept effort, impact and cost of the project. And this commitment to support IT and push GPD has always been there. It was clear for everybody right from the beginning that GPD really is of strategic importance to Hilti.*

Regarding the GPD project, the perception of the decentralized market organizations played a major role as they were directly affected by the change. Their commitment was of utmost importance in order to make people change their habits. Thinking in terms of the overall corporation and transcending, for example, departmental structures already accounted for significant commitment in the project. Interestingly, the people's commitment also affects the economic results of the units: *Right after we go live in any market organization their KPI's may deteriorate. Training is not enough, data is never fine, and change management is never prepared enough. Very seldom do you see them improve immediately, but rather it happens over time. That was strong commitment of the people believing in us and going along with the change.*

We see examples of the facilitating role of the corporate culture functioning as a driver of stability in Hilti's change project. Both corporate purpose, and values, played a significant role in supporting the GPD project. Hilti's employees living the corporate values account for a large part of the success in coping with the challenges of this change project. Against this background, we would now like to draw some conclusions and also indicate directions for future research.

## 4 Conclusion

In this chapter, we examined the role of corporate culture in BPM. Regarding our source of knowledge, we studied a real life example, reporting from interviews conducted with representatives of the Hilti Corporation. At Hilti, culture plays an essential role for business. As such, it is also incorporated as the major element in the Hilti business model. The systematic process, called ´Our Culture Journey´ helps disseminating and living the corporate culture on a global and corporation-wide scale. For the IT department, this initiative particularly led to a business-driven IT strategy.

As to the role of culture in BPM, we can conclude that the Culture Journey was both a driver and an enabler for change. It can be considered a driver regarding the GPD project as the IT Core Purpose Statement called for global solutions that could be met by managing processes and data within a global IT setting. In addition, the Culture Journey also turned out to be an important enabler for the GPD project. According to our interviews, the changes were hardly possible without the clear corporate business model. More specifically, it is this facilitating role of the corporate culture that is of foremost interest for BPM in general. Hence, we further set out analyzing the potential leverage of the Culture Journey within the GPD project.

Within our study we found several good examples showing that positive effects on the change project could be realized by the Culture Journey. We particularly analyzed to what extent the corporate purpose in general, and the corporate values more specifically, were perceived useful by the interviewed managers for conducting the GPD project. It indeed remains an open issue to quantify these effects in terms of an economic leverage.

Apart from the impact Hilti's corporate culture had on the change project, we also found that the change of processes influenced culture. Process improvement allowed for an intensified way of living the teamwork value on a global scale.

Drawing from the statements of our interviewees' one might conclude that GPD would not have been as successful in absence of the specific corporate culture. Hence, the earnings of the initiative might be kept in mind when evaluating the leverage of the Culture Journey. Just as well, the implementation efforts could be taken into account. However, such issues can hardly be calculated and were thus better left to their qualitative nature.

What we can learn in terms of value considerations, however, is that efforts in culture are investment-related in nature. Shared corporate purpose and values once realized (and continuously maintained) may well serve for multiple purposes within the corporation. In our study, we picked the GPD project as one example, while at the same time numerous other fields exist to which the corporate culture delivers value, such as avoiding high employee fluctuation and a related loss of knowledge, or arranging win-win situations with business partners.

Our findings reported in this chapter are – indeed – limited to the Hilti Case. We analyzed corporate documents and conducted interviews with managers involved in both the Culture Journey, and the GPD project. However, considering the early stage of research on culture in BPM, we aimed at utilizing this case study for setting a basis for future work, and eventually stimulating further research in this important new field in BPM.

## References

Anderson D, Ackerman Anderson LS (2001) Beyond change management: advanced strategies for today's transformational leaders. Jossey-Bass/Pfeiffer, San Francisco

Armistead C, Pritchard JP, Simon M (1999) Strategic business process management for organisational effectiveness. Long Range Plann 32(1):96–106

Baumöl U (2010) Change engineering and process management: integrating people and culture in the change process. In: vom Brocke J, Rosemann M (eds) Handbook on business process management, vol 2. Springer, Berlin

Brenner M, Coners A (2010) Process capital as strategic success factor: the Lufthansa example. In: vom Brocke J, Rosemann M (eds) Handbook on business process management, vol 2. Springer, Berlin

Buß E (2008) Managementsoziologie. Grundlagen, Praxiskonzepte, Fallstudien, München

Coombs R, Knights D, Willmott HC (1992) Culture, control and competition: towards a conceptual framework for the study of information technology in organizations. Organ Stud 13(1):51–72

Davenport TH (2008) Foreword. In: Jeston J, Nelis J (eds) Business process management. Practical guidelines to succesful implementations, 2nd edn. Elsevier, Oxford, pp xiv–xvii

Du Gay P (1997) Production of culture/cultures of production, Sage, Glasgow

Gerstner LV Jr (2002) Who says elephants can't dance? Inside IBM's historic turnaround. HarperBusiness, New York

Gore EW Jr (1999) Organizational culture, TQM, and business process reengineering an empirical comparison. Team Perform Manage 5(5):164–170

Guzman IR, Stam KR, Stanton JM (2008) The occupational culture of IS/IT personnel within organizations. Data base Adv Inf Syst 39(1):33–50

Hallerbach A et al. (2010) Configuration and management of process variants. In: vom Brocke J, Rosemann M (eds) Handbook on business process management, vol 1. Springer, Berlin

Hammer M (2010) What is business process management? In: vom Brocke J, Rosemann M (eds) Handbook on business process management, vol 1. Springer, Berlin

Hlupic V (2003) Knowledge and business process management. Idea Group Publishing, Hershey, London

Hofstede G (1991) Cultures and organizations. Software of the mind. McGraw-Hill, London

Lee RG, Dale BG (1998) Business process management: a review and evaluation. Bus Process Manage J 4(3):214–225

Leidner DE, Kayworth T (2006) A review of culture in information systems research: towards a theory of IT-culture conflict. MIS Q 30(2):357–399

Neuberger O, Kompa A (1987) Wir, die Firma. Der Kult um die Unternehmenskultur, Weinheim/Basel

Peters TJ, Waterman RH (1982) In search of excellence. Lessons from America's best-run companies. Harper & Row, New York

Robey D, Boudreau M-C (1999) Accounting for the contradictory organizational consequences of information technology: theoretical directions and methodological implications. Inf Syst Res 10(2):167–185

Rosemann M (2010) The service portfolio of a BPM center of excellence. In: vom Brocke J, Rosemann M (eds) Handbook on business process management, vol 2. Springer, Berlin

Schein EH (2004) Organizational culture and leadership, 3rd edn. Jossey Bass, San Francisco

Tregear R (2010) Business process standardization. In: vom Brocke J, Rosemann M (eds) Handbook on business process management, vol 2. Springer, Berlin

vom Brocke (2007) Design principles for reference modeling: reusing information models by aggregation, specialisation, instantiation, and analogy. In Loos P, Fettke P (eds) Reference modelling for business systems analysis. Idea Group, Hershey/PA/USA

vom Brocke J, Thurnher B (2009) On the leverage of user participation in business process transformation – learning from case studies in the IT-service sector. In: Proceedings of the Americas Conference on Information System (AMCIS 2009), San Francisco, CA

vom Brocke J, Recker J, Mendling J (2010) Value-oriented Process Modeling: Integrating Financial Perspectives into Business Process Re-design. Bus Process Manage J (BPMJ), 16(2): 333–356

Zairi M (1997) Business process management: a boundaryless approach to modern competitiveness. Bus Process Manage J 3(1):64–80

# An Organizational Approach to BPM: The Experience of an Australian Transport Provider

Tonia de Bruin and Gaby Doebeli

**Abstract** When discussing Business Process Management (BPM), there is an obvious lack of clarity in the use of the term. A consequence of these varying interpretations is confusion among practitioners and an inability to compare and contrast experiences in a meaningful way. To date, there has been no clear articulation of the distinction between these interpretations and how this distinction is reflected in practice. The chapter provides a clear explanation of three interpretations and details how a large Australian transport provider has applied a BPM Capability Framework to guide its BPM Initiative that aims at being an approach to managing the organization.

## 1 Introduction

When discussing Business Process Management (BPM), there is an obvious lack of clarity in the use of the term. Common interpretations include: (1) BPM as a solution for a business using software systems or technology to automate and manage processes, (2) BPM as a broader approach to managing and improving processes that focus on the process lifecycle and (3) BPM as an approach to managing an organization by taking a process-view or orientation.

A consequence of these varying interpretations is confusion among practitioners and an inability to compare and contrast experiences in a meaningful way. Furthermore, this lack of clarity leads to an inability to build a cumulative body of knowledge as results and experiences can appear to be conflicting and inconsistent. To date, there has been no clear articulation of the distinction between these interpretations and how this distinction reflects in practice.

T. de Bruin (✉)
BPM Group, Queensland University of Technology, Brisbane, QLD, Australia
e-mail: t.debruin@qut.edu.au

J. vom Brocke and M. Rosemann (eds.), *Handbook on Business Process Management 2*, International Handbooks on Information Systems,
DOI 10.1007/978-3-642-01982-1_26, © Springer-Verlag Berlin Heidelberg 2010

This chapter makes a unique contribution in this area. First, providing clear explanation of the three interpretations, together with examples of how the interpretations result in different decisions within BPM initiatives. Following this, the chapter details how a large Australian transport provider has applied a BPM Capability Framework to guide its BPM Initiative that aims at being an approach to managing the organization.

## 1.1 BPM as a Technology Solution

In some cases, the term BPM denotes a technology solution for an organization (McDaniel 2001). For example, before describing the "four tenets of BPM" being modeling, integrating, monitoring, and optimizing, McDaniel (2001) says:

> ...BPM entails integrating the value of each asset, providing a seamless interface, and coordinating the efforts of all assets to achieve a goal, in a given sequence, within a set time... and ...BPM provides end-to-end life cycle management of information requests or transactions made up on many steps...

In this context, McDaniel (2001) talks about the human element of BPM only in relation to the use of technology to automate manual tasks saying:

> ...executing a BPM solution is a pathway to internal employee efficiency. Enterprises can eliminate costly and slow manual steps that can be more effectively executed when automated...automating saves time for current employees and saves training costs for new employees...

The ten pillars identified by McDaniel (2001) provide further evidence of the technology focus of his use of the term BPM. The pillars include: (1) unified process automation and workflow model, (2) direct model execution and manipulation, (3) state management, (4) time-based exception management, (5) robust process monitoring and analysis, (6) nested model support, (7) concurrent model support, (8) standards based, (9) high scalability, and (10) high reliability.

Using BPM in this sense usually applies to a software solution to a given process or within a given project. While some software vendors still use the term BPM in this narrow technology sense, it is becoming increasingly common to use the terms Business Process Management Systems (BPMS) or Process-Aware Information Systems (PAIS) (Dumas et al. 2005).

## 1.2 BPM as a Lifecycle Approach

A number of researchers provide examples of the term BPM used to describe a lifecycle approach to managing and improving processes. For example:

> ...BPM is concerned with how to manage processes on an ongoing basis and not just with the one-off radical changes associated with BPR... (Armistead and Machin 1997)

> ...A BPM approach involves four key areas including process documentation, establishing accountability and ownership, managing and measuring performance and improving processes by enhancing quality or performance... (Gulledge and Sommer 2002)
>
> ...A generic BPM method of preparation, process selection, process description, process quantification, process improvement selection and implementation... (Elzinga et al. 1995)
>
> ...A systematic approach to designing, prioritizing, managing, controlling and monitoring business processes... (Zairi 1997)

A common thread in these approaches is that the view of BPM is from the perspective of managing and/or improving the operations of a process or a set of processes. Garvin (1998) indicates that this approach often neglects the ongoing management and operation of many redesigned processes, highlighting a key limitation of this view. Furthermore, Garvin (1998) found that a tendency to focus on work processes led to administrative and supporting processes being overlooked which ultimately ended in inconsistencies in information and planning.

An underlying assumption in the use of BPM as a lifecycle approach to managing and improving processes is that a generic, systematic approach to BPM is possible and preferable. However, from a theoretical perspective, Sabherwal et al. (2001) suggest that taking such a narrow view will not capture the dynamics of organizations including the internal variances and external contextual situations.

### *1.3 BPM as an Organizational Approach*

In addition to Pritchard and Armistead (1999), a number of researchers consider BPM to be an approach to organizational management that takes a process-view. For example, DeToro and McCabe (1997) indicate that BPM is a new way of managing an organization, which is different to a functional, hierarchical management approach. Similarly, at this level Harmon (2003) states:

> ...In the Nineties, a number of management gurus, for different reasons, began to argue that it was more efficient to conceptualize a company in terms of a set of value chains or business processes. This approach has been given many names, but the most popular, today, seems to be the Process-Centric Company...

Harmon (2003) claims a process-centric organization is one whose:

> ...managers conceptualize it as a set of business processes. Most process-centric companies, like most traditional organizations, still have departments and divisions. Unlike traditional organizations, however, process-centric companies place their primary emphasis on maximizing the efficiency of processes, and not on maximizing the efficiency of departmental or functional units. In effect, departments or functions contribute employees, knowledge and management skills to processes...Ultimately, however, the core business processes are managed and evaluated as wholes, and departments are rewarded for their effective contributions to successful processes...

At this level, the emphasis is on the management of the organization as opposed to using a standardized approach to managing the processes within the organization.

## 1.4 Distinguishing a Lifecycle from an Organizational Approach

Thus, the use of BPM at a process level and at an organizational level is fundamentally different. The following example highlights how this distinction could manifest within an organization.

Consider the notion of *documenting or designing*, a step in all of the above *BPM as a Lifecycle Approaches*. At this level, these steps lead to the visual representation of a process. Potential issues that individuals within an organization would address during this step could include:

- What level of detail does the representation of the process require?
- Who are the relevant stakeholders?
- How are their requirements captured?
- What technology is available for representing the model?

With the interpretation of *BPM as an Organizational Approach*, this step would result in different considerations. For example, from an organizational perspective the key issues in *documenting and designing processes* would include:

- What technology is the organization going to make available for modeling processes?
- Which people need to have access to this technology?
- Do these people need training in the technology?
- Who is going to be responsible for the maintenance of the model library?
- Where are the funds for purchasing the technology going to come from?

These examples show that there is a clear difference in the intent and consequence of BPM using these two different interpretations. Furthermore, applying a systematic lifecycle approach to the processes within an organization does not necessarily mean that individuals within the organization view the organization as a set of processes. Hence, being successful at adopting a BPM lifecycle approach does not automatically translate to being successful at an organizational BPM approach.

Arguably, the distinction between a *lifecycle* approach and an *organizational* approach may contribute to explaining why earlier process endeavors such as BPR and BPI were often unable to provide sustainable change within organizations. The authors contend that a major reason may be that, while endeavors such as BPR and BPI focus on changing *processes* and *process capability* within organizations, they do not focus on changing the *organizational capability* required to support process thinking at an organizational level. In other words, they do not challenge or change the fundamental way in which people think about how the organization operates. For example, approaches such as BPR and BPI do not focus on assisting to depict the organization as a series of interrelated processes. Nor do they assist in determining how to prioritize process projects for the organization as a whole or how to develop and implement appropriate governance mechanisms to guide process decisions throughout the organization.

This distinction marks the uniqueness of this chapter. While there is significant literature on a BPM as lifecycle approach, little deals with BPM as an organizational approach. This chapter addresses this shortfall by showing how one organization applies a BPM Capability Framework to guide the development of capability and to progress its (organizational) BPM Initiative.

## 2 Background to Company Q

Company Q is one of Australia's largest and most modern transport providers. Company Q has annual revenue in excess of $AUD 3 billion and managed assets of $AUD 10 billion. Operating for 143 years, Company Q is among the nation's longest running service enterprises with approximately 15,000 employees throughout the country. Company Q is a Government-Owned Corporation (GOC) directed by a Board that is accountable to two shareholding ministers.

Changes in the Queensland State Government in the late 1990s led to major organizational changes within Company Q. In 1999, a move to increase the commercialization of some State Government operations resulted in Company Q effectively moving from a monopoly government provider to becoming a national commercial operation in a competitive business environment. Since that time, Company Q has expanded operations by acquiring further subsidiary companies, and it is now a major player in the transport and logistics industry within Australia.

By 2002, following the move to commercialization, Company Q knew it had serious problems with its operations. Disparate projects were having a counteractive effect. Changing legislation and regulations were increasing reporting requirements and competition. Increased usage of its transport networks were resulting in scheduling difficulties, delays, and customer dissatisfaction.

Like many organizations, Company Q had actively tried to improve operations by applying methods like Quality Assurance (QA), Total Quality Management (TQM), Business Process Reengineering (BPR), and Business Process Improvement (BPI). Such endeavors had met with limited success reflecting in high levels of frustration and a lack of progress. Paradoxically, the failure of these earlier endeavors compounded in an inability to gain the necessary levels of executive support required to develop a long-term and sustainable approach to process thinking because of an inability to show early returns on investment.

### *2.1 BPM Within Company Q*

In 2002, Company Q's Board and Senior Executives assigned the Chief Strategy Officer (CSO) to lead a major change program to establish a sound platform to achieve service excellence and allow further growth of the business. The overall objectives were to (1) gain transparency of processes and cost, (2) achieve accountability throughout the different levels of management, and (3) operate as a successful organization that makes profit.

At the time, this undertaking was ambitious because of the culture of Company Q being typical of a public sector, monopoly organization where the need for continuous performance improvement and change was not at the forefront of people's minds. This was evident within Company Q in a lack of recognition and understanding of process; the existence of functional silos; rules-based governance; and heavy unionization. Company Q considered the change program to be a *cultural* change program, with the aim of changing the mindset of staff members and moving toward a commercial framework.

Consequently, the CSO established three program streams. The three streams were *Performance through Governance, Performance through Business*, and *Performance through People*. The program stream of *Performance through Business* included a project that was to investigate *Business Process and Systems*. Company Q established a BPM team which was led by the Business Process Design Adviser (BPDA)[1] to progress this project. The BPDA reported directly to the CSO.

The first phase of the *Business Process and Systems* project led to the identification of an enterprise-wide BPM approach as a means of addressing a number of the operational and strategic issues facing the organization. This included a need for Company Q to become more competitive and more focused on its customers. Due to the failings of past endeavors arising from the implementation and use of methods including TQM, BPR, and BPI, the BPDA believed that an organizational BPM approach that focused on building sustainable capability within the organization was appropriate to addressing Company Q's needs.

In coming to this conclusion, Company Q conducted literature reviews, interviews, and study tours with other organizations facing similar issues in order to identify different management and operational concepts. Internally, the BPDA conducted workshops throughout the organization to engage key stakeholders in the development of a framework for the implementation of BPM within Company Q. However, getting support for adopting a BPM approach and developing the initial frameworks was difficult because of (1) conflicting literature and practice regarding what constituted an enterprise-wide BPM approach and (2) a lack of guidance as to how to go about adopting such an enterprise-wide approach.

The second phase of the project included making the frameworks operational in order to embed BPM principles and practices within the organization. In the first instance, the BPDA was responsible for the establishment of the methods and techniques within the framework, and the introduction of these to the organization. In this phase, the first deliverable from the BPDA was the development of the Enterprise Process Model that formed the base of the Process Architecture and provided Company Q with a tool to develop their new Business Model. The development of the Enterprise Process Model was not to the extent of an Enterprise Process Architecture but rather was a list of known processes in Company Q

[1]The BPDA is co-author of this chapter.

clustered by either function or end-to-end process. The second deliverable was the first version of Company Q's BPI and BPR Framework including initial principles, tools and methods (also referred to as Company Q's BPM Concept) and a proposed implementation plan. The implementation plan included the need to perform an organizational wide assessment to baseline the current state and identify potential organizational change arising from the adoption of a BPM approach.

The BPDA received approval to investigate BPM capability assessment methods to gain a deeper understanding of an organizations maturity in BPM. This investigation resulted in an early appreciation of the differences between a BPM approach that was focused on the management of processes (i.e., what this chapter calls a lifecycle approach) and an approach that was focused on the management of the organization (i.e., what this chapter calls an organizational approach). However, subsequent investigation revealed a lack of a suitable means by which to (1) understand existing practices and to gain guidance on progressing and embedding BPM practices within the organization and (2) an inability to measure the progression of BPM practices adopted within the organization.

In addressing these issues, the BPDA approached Queensland University of Technology (QUT) for assistance. This initial contact from Company Q's BPDA led to a study at QUT investigating the progression and measurement of BPM Initiatives within organizations.

## 3 Developing a BPM Capability Framework

Since 2004, researchers at QUT have worked to develop a model for assessing the maturity of BPM within organizations. One of the key outcomes from this research was a so-called BPM Capability Framework. The journey to develop this framework is documented in a number of existing publications including Rosemann et al. (2004), Rosemann and de Bruin (2004, 2005), Rosemann et al. (2006), de Bruin and Rosemann (2007), and de Bruin (2007).[2]

Since its development, the Principal Researcher[3] has used the BPM Capability Framework to explore the BPM Initiatives of a number of organizations. Furthermore, within industry, a number of organizations have independently applied the BPM Capability Framework to guide the development of their BPM Initiatives. In this chapter, the discussion centers on the application of the BPM Capability Framework by Company Q.

[2]The core elements of this BPM capability framework are also presented by Rosemann and vom Brocke (2010).

[3]The Principal Researcher is co-author of this chapter.

# 4 Applying the BPM Capability Framework in Company Q

Representatives from Company Q developed a deeper understanding of the BPM Capability Framework because of the ongoing relationship with the researchers and participation in BPM forums including the BPM Roundtable and the Queensland BP Trends Chapter. On this basis, Company Q's BPDA started using the BPM Capability Framework to develop a roadmap to guide Company Q's BPM journey.

In particular, the BPDA used the BPM Capability Framework to guide Company Q's (1) BPM communication, (2) BPM strategy development and implementation, and (3) internal BPM consultancy engagements. The following sections provide details on this application while Fig. 1 summarizes the key projects in Company Q's BPM journey and the timeframe in which they occurred.

## 4.1 BPM Communication

In late 2006, application of the BPM Capability Framework within Company Q resulted in an overhaul of the BPM portal site. The subsequent redesign of this communication media reflects the BPM Capability Framework. An underlying directory structure, mapped to the Framework, stores all BPM documentation available through the portal. Staff members within Company Q access this documentation

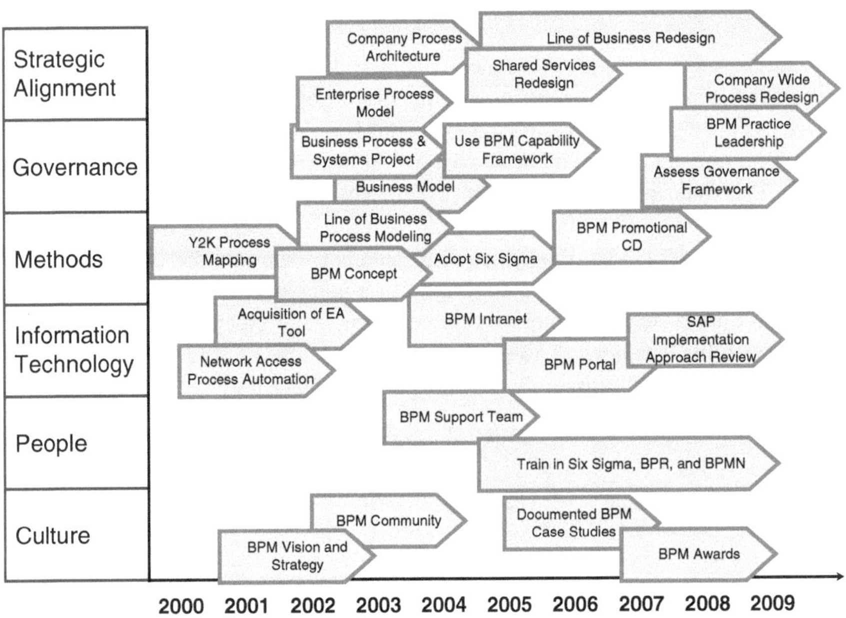


**Fig. 1** Key projects in company Q's implementation of a BPM approach

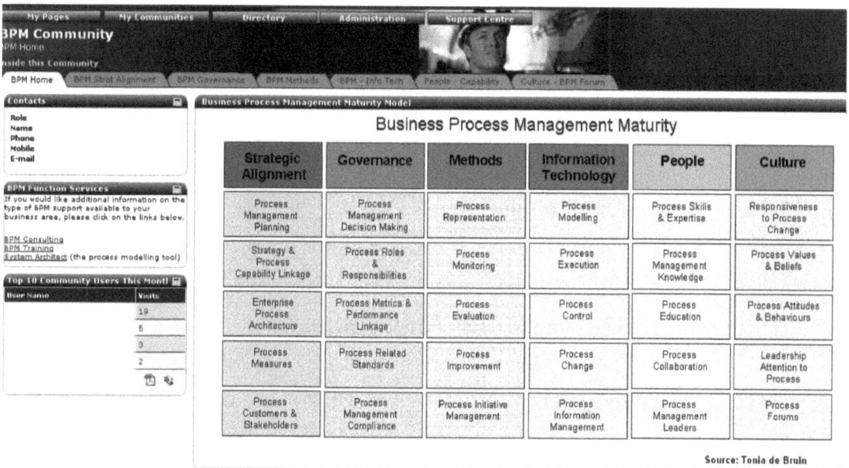


**Fig. 2** Company Q's BPM community portal using the BPM capability framework

within the portal by clicking on the relevant Capability Area button to drill down to the available information. In doing so, the Framework provides Company Q with the ability to develop a common language among its staff members. In addition, the site acts as a corporate repository and single point of truth for "all things process."

The BPM team also uses the portal to provide management and staff with access to a range of education materials. For example, the portal provides access to:

- Company Q internal Case Studies of BPM projects
- BPM Book List
- BPM Conference Resources and Papers
- BPM Research areas structured according the BPM Capability Framework
- Links to major BPM Internet sites

Figure 2 shows the BPM Community Portal that utilizes the BPM Capability Framework at the core of its design and functionality.

## 4.2 *BPM Strategy Selection and Implementation*

Since 2006, Company Q's BPM team has used the BPM Capability Framework to progressively implement, refine, and build upon strategies to develop capability in various areas. For example, the BPDA uses the BPM Capability Framework to provide direction on which capability areas to give attention. In doing this, the BPDA uses the capability area definitions to understand the intent of the capability areas, and knowledge of the organization to determine an informal level of maturity in the capability areas within business units and/or projects. From there, the BPDA determines which capability areas will deliver the greatest immediate benefit to achieving the goals and objectives of Company Q. In doing so, the BPDA is able to allocate resources and develop capability that will optimize the benefit to the organization from adopting a BPM approach. The Principal Researcher is not directly involved in the determination or implementation of these strategies, however, the Principal Researcher and the BPDA meet regularly to discuss or clarify issues regarding the intent and interpretation of the capability areas and possible strategies and their implications.

## 4.3 Internal BPM Consulting Engagements

Following a restructure in 2005, Company Q's BPM team moved into the Shared Services Group with the responsibility to deliver BPM services to the different business areas using an internal consultancy arrangement. The team uses the BPM Capability Framework to guide the conduct of its consulting engagements, including the subsequent recording and documentation of the engagements and their outcomes.

Every consulting assignment is carefully scoped, and the initiation phase includes an internal BPM capability assessment. This assessment enables the consulting team to plan additional activities to further improve BPM capability as part of the project delivery. Once the consulting project is finalized, a session of reflection is facilitated by the BPDA to identify the project results as well as the progression of BPM capability in the particular business area. Every project is treated as a case study, with a summary capturing the findings and adding to the progression of Company Q's BPM journey. Each project contributes to the improvement of different capability areas within the BPM Capability Framework. The project summaries are an effective tool to further consolidate and communicate the BPM progress to the rest of the organization and for the BPDA to further set strategies to enhance capability areas within the model.

An example of one of the key projects delivered by the BPM team using the BPM Capability Framework in this way is the review and redesign of the strategic planning process for Company Q's Corporate Strategy area. This project was twofold, delivering the design of the *to-be* process while at the same time enabling the BPM team to incorporate the necessary links to BPM into the strategic planning process. The project's focus was on building the capability in Strategic Alignment and Governance. The project delivered a streamlined, integrated process for strategic planning including associated tools to make the process operational (e.g., a Process Priority Matrix). The project also provided the Corporate Strategy area with a clear customer value proposition, and established the process performance requirements to build the capability required. For example, the BPM team provided Corporate Strategy with an approach to identify and define their current value chains including how to redesign and redefined their business to meet the expected future needs of the market and to deliver value to their customers by being better able to meet requirements.

## 5 Benefits of Adopting BPM as an Organizational Approach

Since commencing its BPM journey in 2002, Company Q has gained many benefits from adopting an organizational approach to BPM. These benefits include an increase in customer focus, greater alignment in strategy and between areas of the business, changes in the way people within the organization work, improved governance structures, and increased recognition in the BPM community, as discussed in the following sections.

### *5.1 Increased Customer Focus*

Within the last few years, customer surveys have shown that Company Q has become more customer-focused. The organization has dedicated resources to review and improve the service delivery processes within each Line of Business. Company Q refers to these dedicated resources (i.e., process professionals) as the BPM community. Members of the BPM community work together with the marketing and sales professionals and strategic planners to ensure that the proposed improvements to service delivery processes will meet customer needs.

### *5.2 Improved Strategic Planning and Strategy Deployment*

The BPM team was engaged by the CSO to redesign the strategic planning process, together with the organization's strategic planning professionals. The overall objective was to design an integrated strategic planning process that would enable successful deployment.

To further improve the strategic deployment process, the BPM community assisted in building the necessary mechanisms in the Lines of Business to successfully deploy strategic initiatives. The BPM community is working to improve their program and project management across their BPI and BPR efforts to ensure maximized results. The efforts of the BPM team have resulted in a strong community of process professionals across the organization that are aligned in their thinking and who utilize common methods for BPI and BPR. The majority of Company Q's Lines of Business have recognized the importance of selecting and managing the critical programs and projects to improve service delivery from an end-to-end perspective and adopt these common methods within their own programs and projects.

The Chief Information Officer assigned the BPM team and the Enterprise Architect to develop the frameworks, methods, and tools to link business strategies and ICT. The efforts of the BPM team and the Enterprise Architect have resulted in a standard approach toward ICT Planning and Enterprise Architecture for Company Q. This approach minimizes the divide between business strategy and design and IT strategy and design. Consequently, Company Q is experiencing improvements in technology selection and solution development. The two teams provide an integrated service to the business, delivering future roadmaps, and designs in the areas of: business/process, information, application, and technology. All artifacts are consistent, reusable, centrally managed and recognized as key components of the organization's DNA.

## *5.3 Changing Human Resource Capability*

The efforts of the BP community and the BPM team have contributed to breaking down the functional silos in the organization. Process projects have triggered ongoing discussions around further improving the service delivery processes from an end-to-end perspective and challenged accountability structures, organizational structures, cost structures, roles and responsibilities, and capability development. Cross-functional teams have been able to prove the concept of (cross-functional) process collaboration by demonstrating positive results in overall performance and customer focus.

Company Q has adopted a (People) Capability Framework including a Performance Management process for its staff (at all levels) that is based on the BPM principles. Under this framework, individuals are now accountable for the outcomes of a process and Company Q recognizes and rewards teamwork that aims to optimize the end-to-end process. The BPDA reviewed the (People) Capability Framework and provided guidance on the incorporation of capabilities required to move the current culture toward a *process-thinking* culture.

Consequently, the BPM team is now in a position to review their BPM training package in line with business needs as there is better linkage between current capability and the required future capability. This piece of work has also highlighted that additional methods and tools are required for the adoption of BPM at different levels of the organization, that is, Strategic, Tactical, and Operational levels.

## *5.4 Increased Recognition in BPM Community*

In recent years, Company Q has nominated a number of the BPM projects for the Australasia BPM Awards. The categories of the award are aligned with the organization's current efforts in its BPM journey, calling for nominations in the areas of (1) Strategic Alignment and Governance, (2) Methods and Information Technology, and (3) People and Culture. In 2006, Company Q nominated one of their Business Process Architecture projects in the category *Strategic Alignment and Governance* and won the award. In 2007, Company Q nominated one of their

Business Process Redesign and Systems Implementation projects in the category of *Methods and Information Technology* and won an award for a second year.

Within Company Q, winning these awards has given the BPM community and the BPM team an increased profile. This has resulted in more proactive engagement of BPM professionals by senior management leading to greater involvement of the BPM team in emerging business issues. This external recognition of their success has also led the BPM community process professionals to be more motivated in working with the BPM team to progress the adoption of an organizational approach to BPM throughout Company Q. The BPM team in Shared Services is now the Practice Leader for BPM in Company Q, setting the overall BPM governance and providing support to upper level management in how to embed the BPM approach throughout the organization. Winning the awards has also given Company Q an increased profile in the Australian BPM Community.

## 6 Issues in Adopting BPM as an Organizational Approach

Despite the advances that Company Q has made, the progression of an organizational approach to BPM is not without issues. Recent changes within Company Q that have influenced the progression of the BPM approach include (1) changes in Company Q's business model and (2) changes to the organizational structure. These examples show that the progression of an organizational BPM approach requires an ongoing focus and needs to evolve to keep pace with changes that occur within the organization and its environment.

### *6.1 Changes in Business Model*

In 2008, a change in the Board and senior management of Company Q led to a significant change in its business model, taking it from a model of an integrated transport provider to being a multiple company model. The new business model was designed to increase the flexibility and agility of Company Q, with stronger accountability to making it more competitive in the market place. Changes to the Corporate Governance Framework were necessary to enable the organization to implement the new business model.

Company Q revised their Corporate Governance Framework from a strongly rule-based to a principle-based focus to achieve the following benefits:

- Applying Principles as appropriate in the individual Businesses as one size does not fit all
- Making management more empowered in the decision-making process and having greater accountability in business outcomes

As a part of the new Corporate Governance Framework, the Practice Leaders (i.e., the functional and process owners) within Company Q developed Governance Principles for all practices (i.e., function and processes). Subsequently, the

Governance Principles underwent a peer review prior to implementation throughout the Businesses. However, since the new Corporate Governance Framework has been put in place, questions have arisen about its effectiveness.

Consequently, the Company Secretary asked the BPDA to assist in a review of the organization's new Corporate Governance Framework. The purpose of the review was to ensure that the design of the accountability structure and decision-making process was effective. The BPDA assessed the new Corporate Governance Framework against the BPM Principles to identify any gaps. The review found that, despite the involvement of the Practice Leaders, the basis for the accountability structure was more on functional demarcations. Furthermore, the review revealed that not all Practice Leaders were included in the initial development and peer review. The review by the BPDA also found that there was no alignment of the overall decision-making process within some end-to-end processes and that links between business areas and/or levels of business were missing.

An independent external reviewer analyzed the BPDA's findings and proposed an appropriate Corporate Governance Framework for Company Q. Company Q envisages that a subsequent redevelopment of the Corporate Governance Framework to address the issues found will create further challenges due to potential changes in accountability and organizational structure, and a lack of capability for executing the new framework. The success of this redevelopment will depend in part on the re-education of senior management and the development of Practice Leaders in the deployment of the practices based on the BPM Principles.

The low level of understanding of Information Management that exists within Company Q will also influence the change in the Corporate Governance Framework from rule-based to principle-based. A past compliance-driven culture has resulted in mechanisms for record keeping being in place; however, to assist the organization in becoming more competitive and to enable improved performance, a stronger information management focus needs to be established.

## 6.2 Changes in Organizational Structure

Since commencing its BPM journey in 2002, a number of organizational restructures have led to significant changes in the roles and responsibilities of the BPM team. At times, these changes have affected the manner in which the team operates or is resourced, while at other times, these changes have affected the location of the BPM team within the organization.

In mid-2007, the BPM team commenced their most recently defined role as the Practice Leader for BPM in the organization. Process professionals from the BPM community are now part of the individual support teams within the different Businesses. The process professionals work closely with people from within the strategic planning, human resource, finance, and IT functions as well as the areas of risk and project management. This change includes the BPM team working closely with other leadership teams of the organization to build BPM capability to support and enable a more enterprise wide and top-down approach to BPM. An example of this is the BPM team working closely with Practice Leaders and Line of Business management. This work is building BPM capabilities within the factors of Strategic Alignment and Governance. The expected consequence of the work is that it will set boundaries for the future development and implementation of Methods and IT and that it will activate the cultural change needed to achieve higher levels of capability in the People and Culture factors.

A further consequence of the multiple company restructures is that the IT systems that support the activities of end-to-end processes lack integration. The CIO is currently tasked with rationalizing the IT systems (where appropriate). However, moves to rationalize IT systems will present a challenge to business units as interim solutions are applied in order to manage the high business risks associated with the changes.

## 6.3 *Lessons Learnt During Company Q's BPM Journey*

Company Q has learnt numerous lessons that relate to the development and execution of strategies for implementing BPM as an organizational approach. The following points provide an overview of the key lessons learnt by Company Q during its journey. In keeping with the approach adopted within Company Q, these points are mapped to the *factors* from the BPM Capability Framework.

### 6.3.1 Strategic Alignment

Company Q found that a strong connection between strategy formulation and the selection of BPI initiatives needs to occur to optimize resource allocation. It recognized that a lot of effort was wasted throughout the organization by undertaking numerous improvement projects that were not business critical or strongly linked to the overall strategic objectives. These projects often came to a standstill or did not deliver value to the organization. The company has now determined that the strategic planners and BPM professionals work together, undertaking a business risk assessment and clearly defining the business critical improvement projects. This drives subsequent resourcing of projects and ensures projects undertaken are more effective and enable strategic objectives to be delivered.

Within Company Q, processes need to be clearly defined in order to be successfully measured. It was recognized that if the organizational processes were not defined from an end-to-end perspective, ownership and accountability for process performance could not be clearly assigned. When processes were not clearly defined, the process measures used related to only discrete components of the process and the performance outcome of the entire process was not managed successfully. The end result for Company Q was often unhappy customers. The experiences of the BPM community found that it was good practice to use the customer requirements to define the process and measures to ensure success.

It was acknowledged that Company Q had to become more customer focused to be able to compete in the market place and in doing so had to clearly understand customer requirements. Ultimately, Company Q had to decide which market segments were to be targeted as they found it was no longer feasible to cater to everyone as the cost of delivery was often higher than the return to the organization. Company Q investigated its service delivery processes and its cost to gain a better understanding of the market segments they should focus on considering the business environment they are working within.

### 6.3.2 Governance

Company Q found that BPM Governance needs to be put in place early to ensure clear direction and leadership and common terminology as people within Company Q only follow leadership when clear directions, boundaries, and rewards are set and properly interpreted and communicated. Furthermore, Company Q found that BPM Governance needs to be integrated into an overarching corporate governance framework as BPM is a management philosophy and not a standalone practice.

In Company Q's experience, transparency is a key element to gaining accountability as they found that few people would take accountability if they were not fully aware of "what the accountability is for." This meant that processes had to be well defined and furthermore, that the individuals accountable for the processes had a solid understanding of what was involved in achieving this outcome. Company Q also found that process leaders within the businesses needed support from their functional counterparts within an integrated BPM governance framework to ensure that optimal (process) decision making occurs.

In the experience of Company Q, linking individual performance measures with the overall end-to-end process performance acted to focus attention on continuous process improvement.

### 6.3.3 Methods

With respect to modeling processes, Company Q found that there needs to be a common process-modeling notation in use across the business to ensure consistent, reusable models. At the time of commencing their BPM journey, the notation selected was not as important as the consistent application of the notation and the ability for the notation to be supported by an associated modeling tool.

Company Q found that the use of multiple process improvement methods (in their case Six Sigma and Lean Manufacturing) was beneficial. This enabled the matching of the most appropriate method dependent on the different purpose and types of the improvement project. Company Q has developed guidelines on the selection of the most appropriate methods for use in different situations, and these form a part of their process review.

In Company Q's experience, strong program and project management capability needs to be in place to track the benefits for the business. Company Q found that this applied to process improvement and/or review projects as well as the overall BPM program of works that aims to deliver supporting BPM capability.

### 6.3.4 Information Technology

Company Q found that a common process repository/modeling tool is essential when progressing with BPM. The system itself (i.e., whether it was System Architect, ARIS or other similar software) was not important in the initial start up of BPM in Company Q. However, being able to match the suitability of the tool to the different purposes of the modeling has increased in importance when implementing different process improvement and review projects.

### 6.3.5 People

Company Q found that the most effective way for many of their staff members to learn was by them being involved in doing the work. Hence, the BPM team built BPM capabilities through discrete projects. Selection of projects was on their strategic importance and the level of energy senior management placed on the project. Every project provided the company with the required process improvement; however, as an additional value add, the projects also provided an increase in particular BPM capabilities as they served to develop the process related skills and abilities of the people selected to work on the project.

Prior to adopting BPM as an organizational approach, sharing of information within the organization was limited, despite endeavors to improve processes in numerous projects. Company Q found that an increase in the sharing of information and a new openness in the way in which people communicated with each other following involvement in process improvement projects that used the new BPM Principles and allowed different project teams to reuse information across the organization. This reduced cycle time and the cost of certain tasks.

Company Q's staff did not positively connect with the notion of process or BPM, nor did they like the use of BPM terms. Hence, members of the BPM community had to convey their messages in a language filled with analogies and stories to build acceptance in the wider organization.

### 6.3.6 Culture

Company Q found that top-down leadership is essential to achieve a holistic implementation that includes a BPM approach throughout the entire organization (as opposed to within discrete components of it). Within Company Q, acceptance of the BPM Principles required many staff and management to change their mindset – creating a need for a program of cultural change. Without strong leadership from the top and clear guidance, the required change in people will not happen.

In adopting BPM, the strategies used need to be communicated in a manner that is meaningful for all management and staff. This requires different approaches at the different levels of the organization and not just a uniform approach. In part, this is because the implementations of strategies that happen in the operation of the organization are not the same as those on the executive management level. However, it is also because the appropriateness of the communication medium and/ or channel varies between the levels.

## 7 Conclusion

This chapter presents the experiences of an Australian Transport Provider in adopting BPM as an organizational approach. In doing so, the chapter clearly distinguishes such an approach to one that focuses on technology solutions or to one that focuses on the management of processes throughout the process lifecycle.

The experiences of Company Q showed the value in adopting a BPM Capability Framework to develop a roadmap to guide the progression of BPM. This roadmap included direction for BPM communication, BPM strategy development and implementation, and internal BPM consultancy engagements.

Company Q found numerous benefits flowing from the adoption of an organizational approach. These included an increase in customer focus, an increased ability to change human resource capability, and increased recognition of BPM both within the organization and within the broader business community.

Finally, the lessons learnt during Company Q's BPM journey show that often it is necessary to match the strategies for developing these capabilities to the individuals within, and experiences of, the organization itself for them to be successful. This suggests that a single, generic methodology for adopting BPM as an organizational approach is unlikely to lead to widespread success, and that organizations will find value in developing a capability "roadmap" that suits their unique needs and circumstances.

**Acknowledgments** The authors wish to acknowledge the vital role of all contributors to the ongoing program of research that supports this chapter. This includes the associated researchers from QUT and the individuals from Company Q.

## References

Armistead C, Machin S (1997) Implications of business process management for operations management. Int J Oper Prod Manage, 17(9), 886–898

de Bruin T (2007) Insights into the Evolution of BPM in Organisations. In: 18th Australasian Conference on Information Systems. Toowoomba, Australia, 4–6 Dec 2007

de Bruin T, Rosemann M (2007) Identifying BPM capability areas using the delphi technique. In: 18th Australasian conference on information systems toowoomba, Australia, 4–6 Dec 2007

DeToro I, McCabe T (1997) How to stay flexible and elude fads. Qual Prog 30(3):55–60
Dumas M, van der Aalst WMP, ter Hofstede AHM (eds) (2005) Process aware information systems: bridging people and software through process technology. Wiley, Hoboken, NJ
Elzinga DJ, Horak T, Lee C-Y, Bruner C (1995) Business process management: survey and methodology. IEEE Trans Eng Manage 42(2):119–128
Garvin DA (1998) The process of organisation and management. Sloan Manage Rev 39(4):33–50
Gulledge TR Jr, Sommer RA (2002) Business process management: public sector implications. Bus Proc Manage J 8(4):364–376
Harmon P (2003) Business Process Architecture and the Process-Centric Company. http://www.buisnessprocesstrends.com
McDaniel T (2001) Ten pillars of business process management. eAI J, November, 30–34
Pritchard J-P, Armistead C (1999) Business process management – lessons from European business. Bus Proc Manage J 5(1):10–32
Rosemann M, de Bruin T (2004) Application of a holistic model for determining BPM. In: AIM Pre-ICIS workshop on process management and information systems, Washington DC, Dec 2004, pp 46–60
Rosemann M, de Bruin T (2005) Towards a business process management maturity model. In: 13th European conference on information systems. Regensburg, Germany, May 26–28
Rosemann M, vom Brocke J (2010) The six core elements of business process management. In: vom Brocke J, Rosemann M (eds) Handbook on business process management, vol 1. Springer, Heidelberg
Rosemann M, de Bruin T, Hueffner T (2004) A model for business process management maturity. In: 15th Australasian conference on information systems, Hobart, Dec 1–3
Rosemann M, de Bruin T, Power B (2006) A model to measure BPM maturity and improve performance. In: Business Process Management, Jeston J, Nelis J (eds) Butterworth-Heinemann 2006, Chapter 27
Sabherwal R, Hirschheim R, Goles T (2001) The dynamics of alignment: insights from a punctuated equilibrium model. Organ Sci 12(2):179–197
Zairi M (1997) Business process management: a boundaryless approach to modern competitiveness. Bus Proc Manage J 3(1):64–80

# Who Is Who

## Dr. Chris Aitken

Enterprise Architect
QIC
Brisbane, Australia
c.aitken@qic.com

Chris Aitken holds a PhD in Psychophysiology and has worked with a variety of government agencies over the last 15 years in both clinical and IM and IT roles. During the last 11 years, he has held a number of quality improvement and IM- and IT-related positions within the public sector, health, and financial industries and is currently Enterprise Architect with QIC in Brisbane, Australia. Chris' clinical applied research background means that he brings a combination of a strong human service delivery perspective and a keen logical rigor to his approach to enterprise architecture and IM and IT planning and implementation. Chris' current interests include topics as varied as: the development of an abstract enterprise meta-model, Business Process Management and the psychology of human behavior, enterprise interoperability, and the integration of IM and IT strategic planning, and BPM with enterprise architecture.

## Dr. Wasana Bandara

Senior Lecturer
Business Process Management Group
Faculty of Science and Information Technology
Queensland University of Technology
Brisbane, Australia
w.bandara@qut.edu.au

Dr. Bandara is a Senior Lecturer in Information Systems, specializing in BPM, in the Faculty of Science and Technology at the Queensland University of Technology, Brisbane, Australia. Dr. Bandara received her PhD from Queensland University of

Technology in 2007 for the thesis titled "Process Modelling Critical Success Factors and Measures". She was the winner of the Australian Council of Professors and Heads of Information Systems (ACPHIS) Information Systems Doctoral Thesis Award Competition in 2007. Her research interests include Business Process Management, Process Modeling, BPM Expertise, and BPM Education. She is author/co-author of over 30 refereed publications. Dr. Bandara is a regularly invited speaker at BPM practitioner conferences and forums. Dr. Bandara has been a BPM educator for 9 years. In this time, she has received six university awards for teaching and learning, and a national award from the Australian Learning and Teaching Council for teaching excellence.

## Prof. Dr. Ulrike Baumöl

Professor of Information Management
University of Hagen
Hagen, Germany
ulrike.baumoel@fernuni-hagen.de

Ulrike Baumöl is a Professor of Information Management at the University of Hagen. Her research areas are Business Engineering, Business Process Management, Organizational Change Management, and Intelligent Decision Systems. Before joining the University of Hagen, she worked as vice director for an insurance company and was responsible for Business/IT-Alignment projects. She is co-publisher of a journal on performance management and accounting. Dr Baumöl´s PhD students work on subjects such as process management for organizational flexibility, collective intelligence in value networks, quality management and architecture design patterns for service networks, and the simulation of large networks with various graphs. She regularly conducts executive trainings in business engineering, process management, and information management, as well as business intelligence and provides advice to organizations from the financial services industry, retail, and logistics.

## Jyoti M. Bhat

BPM Research Group, SETLabs
Infosys Technologies Limited
Bangalore, India
JYOTIMB@infosys.com

Jyoti Bhat leads the BPM Research Group within the Software Engineering and Technology Labs (SETLabs) of Infosys. Jyoti heads a team that is currently researching business transaction monitoring, simulation, process innovation, BPM governance and BPM-SOA methodologies. She has 16 years of industry experience in software delivery, research and process consulting. She has expertise in several areas of Process Management, change management, software engineering, including Object Oriented Analysis and Design, Requirements Analysis and Business Process Management. Jyoti has been the Program Manager for Infosys Strategic Initiatives, Metrics Program, and several Process Improvement initiatives. She program-managed the creation of the business process repository and project management platform for Infosys. She is a certified CMMI Assessor and ISO Auditor. She has several publications on Process Management, Requirements Engineering, and software engineering. Jyoti has a Bachelor's degree in Engineering (Electronics and communication) from Bangalore University, India.

## Eric Brabänder

Head of Product Management Enterprise BPM
IDS Scheer AG
Saarbrücken, Germany
eric.brabaender@ids-scheer.com

Eric Brabänder studied Industrial Engineering and Business Administration at the University of Kaiserslautern. After working in the marketing department of Porsche, he started at IDS Scheer in 1999 in the area of ARIS product management. He was involved in the development of several ARIS products (i.e. ARIS for SAP, ARIS Risk and Compliance Manager etc.). In 2004, he worked together with SAP in a development cooperation on ARIS and SAP Solutions. Since 2005, he was working in ARIS product marketing. Today as Head of Product Management Enterprise BPM, he is responsible for the product roadmap and the rollout of the ARIS EBPM products of IDS Scheer. Eric Brabänder has written numerous articles for books and magazines about Balanced Scorecard, risk management, and process-based SAP implementation. Furthermore, he is an active member of the ARIS community (www.ariscommunity.com) and invented ARIS TV as a BPM YouTube Channel (www.youtube.com/aristv). Together with Rob Davis, he is the author of the book "ARIS Design Platform – Getting started with BPM".

## Markus Brenner

Principal
Horváth and Partners Management Consultants
Stuttgart, Germany
mbrenner@horvath-partners.com

Markus Brenner is Principal at Horváth and Partners Management Consultants and is responsible for the business segment Business Process Management. He has more than 10 years' experience as a Management Consultant regarding Strategic Management, Business Process Management, and Controlling.

In addition, he has a strong teaching background as a lecturer at several universities. He published several articles covering activity-based costing and Business Process Management. Furthermore, he is researching the field of process controlling and working on a PhD thesis.

## Ryan Brinkworth

Enterprise Architect
Emirates Group
Dubai, United Arab Emirates
ryan.brinkworth@emirates.com

Ryan Brinkworth is an Enterprise Solution Architect working for Emirates Group. Ryan has experience in the public sector, working as a developer, system administrator, business analyst, information manager, and combining these roles as enterprise architect.

## Tobias Bucher

Institute of Information Management
University of St. Gallen
St. Gallen, Switzerland
tobias.bucher@unisg.ch

Tobias Bucher is research assistant and doctoral student at the Institute of Information Management, Chair of Prof. Dr. Robert Winter, University of St. Gallen. He holds a Master's degree in economics (concentration in information systems and econometrics) from the University of Freiburg, Germany. His research interests include business engineering methods and models, data warehousing, business intelligence, and Business Process Management.

## Roger Burlton

BPTrends Associates
Process Renewal Group
Vancouver, BC, Canada
rburlton@uniserve.com

Roger is the founder of the pioneering Process Renewal Group (1993). He is also a co-founder of BPTrends Associates the services firm partnered with the BPTrends knowledge portal. Roger's insights can be found in his book "Business Process Management: Profiting from Process" and other publications including his column in BPTrends.com. To date, he has conducted over seven hundred working sessions and has presented to over 35,000 professionals globally. His seminars are the longest continuous BPM series in the world running since 1991. Not only does he present these advanced BPM concepts to managers and professionals around the world but he has also worked with over a hundred leading organizations to refine and implement BPM.

## Prof. DSc. Heitor Caulliraux

Professor of Industrial Engineering
Federal University of Rio de Janeiro
Rio de Janeiro, Brazil
heitor.caulliraux@gpi.ufrj.br

Heitor Caulliraux is a Professor of Industrial Engineering at Federal University of Rio de Janeiro (UFRJ), Brazil. He holds a Doctoral Degree in Electric Engineering at Pontifical Catholic University, Rio de Janeiro, Brazil (1990), and specializations at the Instituto Per La Ricostruzioni Italiana, Italy (1983) and Politecnico Di Milano, Italy (1988). Prof. Caulliraux coordinates a Research Group within UFRJ and has several publications in the fields of Operations Management and Business Process Management. He is an Editorial Board Member for international workshops and conferences.

## Jim Champy

Chairman
Perot Systems Corporation's
Boston, MA, USA
Jim.Champy@ps.net

Jim Champy, Chairman of Perot Systems' consulting practice, is recognized throughout the world for his work on leadership and management issues and on organizational change and business reengineering. He is the co-author with Michael Hammer of REENGINEERING THE CORPORATION: A Manifesto for Business Revolution, the book that introduced the world to the concept of reengineering. That book sold more than 3 million copies and spent more than a year on The New York Times best seller list. Champy was also a founder and CEO of Index Systems, later CSC/Index. Much of the original research and practice of reengineering was developed at Index, in collaboration with Hammer. Champy's latest writing is a series of books for the Financial Times Press. The first volume – OUTSMART! – was published in April of 2008, and shows how to achieve breakthrough growth by consistently outsmarting your competition. The second volume in the series, INSPRE!, Why Customers Come Back, was published in April 2009. Champy earned his BS in 1963 and his MS in Civil Engineering in 1965 from M.I.T., and a JD degree from Boston College Law School in 1968. Champy is a life member of the MIT Corporation, Massachusetts Institute of

Technology's Board of Trustees, and serves on the Board of Overseers of the Boston College Law School. He is also a member of the Board of Directors of Analog Devices, Inc.

## Prof. Dr. André Coners

Professorship for Controlling and Process Management
South Westphalia University of Applied Sciences
Hagen, Germany
Coners@fh-swf.de

Dr. Coners is a Professor at South Westphalia University of Applied Sciences, Germany. Before joining the South Westphalia University of Applied Sciences he was Principal at Horváth and Partners Management Consultants and responsible for the business segment Business Process Management. André Coners has more than 10 years experience as a Management Consultant regarding Strategic Management, Business Process Management, and Controlling. In addition, he holds a lectureship at the University of Münster. He published books and articles about strategic management, process mining, activity-based costing, cost management and process management.

## Paul Coogans

Business Process Analyst
QIC
Brisbane, Australia
p.coogans@qic.com

Paul Coogans is a Business Process Analyst for QIC (Queensland Investment Corporation), an institutional fund manager with over $60 billion funds under management. He is a qualified Six Sigma Black Belt and prior to joining QIC, honed his skills in this field with 5 years in the financial services industry in the UK, first in stockbroking and subsequently offshore wealth management.

## David Court

Director
Centre for Screen Business
Australian Film, Television and Radio School (AFTRS)
Sydney, Australia
david.court@aftrs.edu.au

David Court is the founding director of the AFTRS Centre for Screen Business. David is an experienced film industry practitioner who has been involved in the financing of more than a dozen film and television productions (including Strictly Ballroom, The Bank and the IMAX film Antarctica). He was the founder and publisher of the authoritative industry newsletter Entertainment Business Review. He was also a director of the licensed film investment company Content Capital Ltd. With accounting firm KPMG, David conducted the feasibility study that led to the development of Fox Studios at the Sydney Showgrounds. As the author of Film Assistance: Future Options (Allen and Unwin, Sydney, 1986), he was the policy architect of the Film Finance Corporation, established by the Australian Government in 1988.

## Dr. Tonia de Bruin

BPM Group
Faculty of Science and Technology
Queensland University of Technology
Brisbane, Australia
t.debruin@qut.edu.au

BPM – Manager
Shared Service Agency
Department of Public Works
Brisbane, Australia
tonia.debruin@ssa.qld.gov.au

Tonia de Bruin completed her PhD entitled Business Process Management: Theory on Progression and Maturity with Queensland University of Technology, Brisbane, Australia in 2009. Tonia is currently the BPM — Manager at the Shared Service Agency within the Department of Public Works in Queensland State Government, and a CPA-qualified accountant. Her research interest lies in the progression and measurement of BPM Initiatives including the development of organizational capability to enable such progression. Tonia has more than 20 conference papers and book chapters and has presented her research in America, Europe, and Australia. Tonia conducts executive training in BPM (www.bpm-training.com) and provides advice to organizations regarding the adoption and implementation of BPM Initiatives. She is an active member of the Australian BPM Roundtable and the Queensland BPTrends Chapter.

## Gaby Doebeli

Business Architect Process Design Advisor
Brisbane, Australia
gaby.doebeli@onthenet.com.au

Gaby is a member of Australia's Business Process Management and Business Architecture Communities. She is actively contributing to Australia's BPM Roundtable, Queensland's Enterprise Architecture Council (QEAC) and has been chairing the BPLink Brisbane Community since 2005. She has presented at several conferences and published articles in the last few years, sharing her knowledge and experience with others. Gaby's current focus is on BPM Governance and Strategy, where she is further investigating the capability areas of Process Management Decision Making and Roles and Responsibilities.

## Didier Elzinga

CEO/Founder
Culture Amp
Melbourne, Australia
didier@cultureamp.com

Didier Elzinga is an entrepreneur with a wide range of experience in building media and technology companies. Trained as a software engineer (BA Maths and Computer Science, Adelaide University), he is the CEO and founder of software startup Culture Amp, focusing on improving the performance of people related processes in fast growing companies. He is the ex CEO of Hollywood visual effects company Rising Sun Pictures (Australian National Export Awards winner for 2006) and co-founder and chairman of visual software company Rising Sun Research (Anthill's "Coolest company in Australia 2007"). Didier is a Director of the Atlassian Foundation, Slingsby Theatre Company Ltd and Brink Productions and also acts in an advisory capacity for several startups.

## Jude Fernandez

BPM Research Group, SETLabs
Infosys Technologies Limited
Bangalore, India
judef@infosys.com

Jude leads research projects within the BPM Research Group at the Software Engineering and Technology Labs (SETLabs) in Infosys. His current research focuses on areas of Distributed Work patterns,

Process-based Compliance, among others. Jude has about 15 years of varied experience in the process arena both as an internal and as an external consultant. He was a key member of the Corporate Quality team at Infosys and anchored key initiatives such as the Malcolm Baldrige assessments for Infosys and Six Sigma-based BPR projects for key Infosys business processes. He also helped set up the Infosys Customer Satisfaction Survey process. Jude's consulting experience covers different areas including Balanced Scorecard, Process Analysis and Improvement, BPR, etc. He was the chairperson of the first International Workshop on BPM Governance (co-located with BPM 2007 in Brisbane).

## Dr. Peter Fettke

German Research Center for Artificial Intelligence (DFKI)
Institute for Information Systems (IWi)
Saarbrücken, Germany
peter.fettke@iwi.dfki.de

Peter Fettke obtained a Master's Degree in Information Systems from the University of Münster, Germany, and a PhD Degree in Information Systems from the Johannes Gutenberg-University Mainz, Germany. Since April 2006, he is a Senior Researcher in Information Systems, Institute for Information Systems (IWi) at the German Research Center for Artificial Intelligence (DFKI), Saarbrücken. Peter has taught and researched previously at the Technical University of Chemnitz and the University Mainz, Germany. His research interests include information systems analysis and design, especially the use of conceptual modeling and component-based system paradigm. Peter has published numerous articles on reference modeling, conceptual modeling, and component-based engineering in both national and international journals and conference proceedings. Furthermore, he is a member of the editorial board of the Journal of Cases on Information Technology (JCIT) as well as the Journal of System and the Management Sciences (JSMS). Recently, he has finished his Habilitation thesis on empirical Business Engineering.

## Sukriti Goel

BPM Research Group, SETLabs
Infosys Technologies Limited
Bangalore, India
sukriti_goel@infosys.com

Sukriti Goel is a member of BPM Research Group, at the Software Engineering and Technology Labs (SETLabs) at Infosys Technologies Limited, Bangalore, India. Her research areas are Business Process Management Systems (BPMS), Process Monitoring, and Process Extraction. She is also the Architect for the BPM technology team working on different tools, including BPM execution engine and process monitoring among others. She has considerable experience in BPM and BPMS implementations in different scenarios.

## Dr. Guido Governatori

Associate Education Director
NICTA, Queensland Research Laboratory
Brisbane, Australia
guido.governatori@nicta.com.au

Guido Governatori received his PhD in Computer Science and Law from the University of Bologna in 1997. Since then he has held academic and research positions at Imperial College, Griffith University, Queensland University of Technology, the University of Queensland, and NICTA. He has published more than 160 scientific papers in logic, artificial intelligence, and database and information systems. His current research interests include modal and nonclassical logics, defeasible reasoning and its application to normative reasoning and e-commerce, agent systems, and business process modeling for regulatory compliance. He is a member of the editorial board of Artificial Intelligence and Law.

## Alain Guillemain

Principal Consultant
inexure
Brisbane, Australia
a.guillemain@inexure.com

Alain Guillemain is Principal Consultant at inexure, a strategy management consulting firm. In his role, Alain works with managers and decision-makers to assist with the development and implementation of strategy. Prior to this, Alain was Operations Strategy Manager at QIC. Alain has been involved in a number of process improvement projects, ranging from project prioritization to reporting automation and information delivery. Alain has an MBA from the University of Newcastle and a Master of Commerce from Deakin University. He is the President of Alumni Brisbane Chapter for the University of Newcastle.

## Keith Harrison-Broninski

CTO
Role Modellers Limited
Bath, United Kingdom
khb@rolemodellers.com

Keith Harrison-Broninski's 2005 book "Human Interactions" introduced the theory of Human Interaction Management (HIM). HIM is now taught on MBA and Computer Science courses and is the subject of research worldwide. Keith regularly gives keynote lectures to business, IT, and academic audiences, most recently in Poland, India, the Netherlands, the UK, Finland, and Portugal. Keith is CTO of Role Modellers, whose software supports innovative, collaborative human work. Keith also stays active as a consultant, via which he continues to refine and extend the HIM theory.

## Dr. Diana Heckl

Frankfurt School of Finance & Management
Research Fellow, ProcessLab
Frankfurt/a.M., Germany
d.heckl@frankfurt-school.de

Diana Heckl is a research associate and postgraduate at the research center ProcessLab at Frankfurt School of Finance & Management. Her studies support the idea of increasing productivity in banks and bank-related companies through Business Process Management. Diana analyzes concepts that are already used successfully in the manufacturing industry and retail trade. These concepts (Capacity Management, Business Reengineering, Six Sigma etc.) are tested for the specific conditions of the Financial Services Industry.

## Alexandra Kokkonen

BPM Group
Faculty of Science and Technology
Queensland University of Technology
Brisbane, Australia
akokkone@yahoo.com.au

Alex Kokkonen is currently with Johnson and Johnson, working in the Information Technology Global Finance Business Relationship and Strategy team as Business Relationship Director. She is also the Consumer Sector Finance Global Process Owner (GPO). Alex has significant international and multiindustry experience in the BPM field. Prior to joining Johnson and Johnson, she held a variety of commercial, financial, and project management positions with other multinational companies in Europe, North America, and the Asia/Pacific regions. Alex is finalizing her PhD in Information Systems: Business Process Management with Queensland University of Technology and her MBA with Deakin University. She is a Fellow of the Chartered Institute of Management Accountants (CIMA), and member of the Association of Corporate Treasurers

(ACT). She holds a Master in Educational Leadership and Management from RMIT, Melbourne, and a Master in Applied Social Science (Counseling) and Graduate Diploma in Counseling (Performance Psychology) from the Australian College of Applied Psychology.

## Dax D. Jacobson

PhD Candidate
Information and Process Management Department
Bentley University
Waltham, MA, USA
djacobson@bentley.edu

Dax D. Jacobson is a PhD Candidate in the Information and Process Management Department at Bentley University and a Research Associate on a National Science Foundation-funded team studying public safety networks. Dax's research interests include IT governance, interorganizational systems, organization design, and the diffusion of administrative innovations and he has taught, written, and presented in all these areas. He is a member of the Academy of Management and the Association for Information Systems. Dax spent several years working in acquisitions for the United States Air Force and holds an MBA from Bentley University.

## Leandro Jesus

Lecturer and Researcher
Federal University of Rio de Janeiro
Co-Leader at ELO Group
Rio de Janeiro, Brazil
leandro.jesus@elogroup.com.br

Leandro Jesus is a Researcher and Lecturer at Federal University of Rio de Janeiro, Brazil, and holds a Master's degree in Industrial Engineering. His research is currently focused on Business Process Management and Service Engineering and Management. He regularly conducts BPM classes and executive training in Brazil. He is a co-leader and consultant at ELO Group, a Brazilian consulting firm focused on BPM and Risk Management solutions. He is a Vice-President for the Brazil Chapter at the Association of Business Process Management Professionals (ABPMP).

## Prof. Dr. Dimitris Karagiannis

Professor
Head of the Institute for Business and Knowledge Engineering
University of Vienna
Vienna, Austria
dk@dke.univie.ac.at

Dimitris Karagiannis studied Computer Science at the Technical University of Berlin and was visiting scientist at research institutions in the USA and Japan. From 1987 to 1992, he was scientific director for Business Information Systems at the Research Institute for Applied Knowledge Management in Ulm. Since 1993, he has been full professor at the Faculty of Computer Science at the University of Vienna. As head of the Institute for Business and Knowledge Engineering, his main research areas are Knowledge Management, Business Intelligence, and Meta-Modeling. Besides his engagement in national and EU-funded research projects, Dimitris Karagiannis is the author of research papers and books on Knowledge Databases, Expert Systems, Business Process Management, Workflow-Systems, and Knowledge Management. He is the founder of the European software- and consulting company BOC (http://www.boc-group.com), which implements software tools based on the meta-modeling approach. Recently, he established the Open Model Initiative (www.openmodels.at) in Austria.

## Daniel Karrer

Lecturer and Researcher
Federal University of Rio de Janeiro
Co-Leader at ELO Group
Rio de Janeiro, Brazil
daniel.karrer@elogroup.com.br

Daniel Karrer is a Researcher and Lecturer at the Federal University of Rio de Janeiro, Brazil, and holds a Master's degree in Industrial Engineering. He currently teaches classes on BPM, Strategic Management, and Risk Management. He is a co-leader and consultant at ELO Group, a Brazilian business consulting firm focused on BPM and Risk Management solutions. He regularly provides BPM consulting services to Brazilian organizations from various industries, including banking, insurance, utility, telecommunications, retail, and public sector.

## Dr. Mathias Kirchmer

Executive Partner
Accenture
Philadelphia, PA, USA
mathias.kirchmer@accenture.com

Dr. Mathias Kirchmer is Executive Partner for Process Excellence at Accenture. He leads the global Business Process Lifecycle Management Practice, as well as the program for the development of Accenture's Business Process Reference Models across industries and functional areas. Before joining Accenture, Dr. Kirchmer had been for almost 18 years with IDS Scheer, a leading provider of business process excellence solutions, known for its BPM Software, the ARIS Platform. His last position was Chief Innovation and Marketing Officer. Before that he managed the Americas and the Japan operations of the company. During his professional career, Dr. Kirchmer has developed deep knowledge in approaches, methods, and software for process management. He has applied this know-how in companies of various sizes around the world. Dr. Kirchmer is an affiliated faculty member of the University of Pennsylvania as well as a faculty member of the Business School of Widener University, Philadelphia. In 2004, he won a research fellowship from the Japan Society for the Promotion of Science. He is the author of numerous publications, including five books. Dr. Kirchmer holds a PhD in Information Systems from Saarbrücken University (Germany), a Master in Business Administration and Computer Science from Karlsruhe Technical University (Germany), and a Master in Economics from Paris-IX-Dauphine University (France).

## Bo Østerberg Kristensen

Head of Global IT Performance and Risk Management
Hilti Corporation
Schaan, Principality of Liechtenstein
bo.kristensen@hilti.com

Mr. Bo Østerberg Kristensen has been Head of Global IT Performance and Risk Management since 2007. This department includes the Global IT Security team, the Access Security and Control team, the Global IT Operations team, and the Global IT Controlling team. Since joining the Hilti Corporation in 2004, Mr. Kristensen had been responsible for putting into effect a Change Management process to support the GPD/H2 solution (Global Process and Data – Hilti's implementation of SAP). Before 2004, he worked in London as a Technical Development Manager with BBC's project to implement SAP R/3. He holds a Master of International Management from Thunderbird – School of Global Management, with a focus in International Marketing. Immediately following graduation, he joined Royal Greenland as a Product Manager and was based in Greenland and Denmark.

## Dr. Manish Kumar

BPM Research Group, SETLabs
Infosys Technologies Limited
Bangalore, India
manish_kumar28@infosys.com

Manish Kumar leads Business Process Simulation research in the Software Engineering and Technology Labs (SETLabs) of Infosys. He is currently involved in developing business process simulation tools for process design and process monitoring. He is also involved in consulting around Information Technology Strategy and Change Management. Manish was earlier a faculty member at the Management Development Institute Gurgaon, India, where he taught management graduates, consulted organizations on IT Strategy and also conducted management development programs for senior executives on Knowledge Management (KM). He has published in the areas of BPM and Knowledge Management. Manish has considerable experience of over 13 years with the Indian Railways and was involved in institutionalization of processes for managing large numbers of employees across several locations with minimal monitoring. Manish Kumar is a Fellow of the Indian Institute of Management, Calcutta, and holds a Master's degree in Technology from the Indian Institute of Technology, Delhi.

## Dr. Yvonne Lederer Antonucci

Assoc. Professor of MIS and Decision Sciences
Director, SAP/IDS Scheer Business Process
Innovation Center of Excellence
School of Business
Widener University
Chester, PA, USA
yantonucci@widener.edu

Yvonne Lederer Antonucci, Ph.D., is an Associate Professor at Widener University in Chester, Pennsylvania, USA, where she is also the director of the SAP/IDS Scheer Business Process Innovation Center of Excellence. Yvonne has developed and taught courses on process analysis, modeling, and automation for over 15 years, and has received several teaching awards and industry grants related to Business Process Management, process analysis, and business-to-business collaboration. She has published in numerous international journals, books, and conferences in the area of BPM, IT outsourcing, interorganizational trust and collaboration, workflow management, and enterprise systems, and has been a frequently invited speaker to various international BPM industry events. Yvonne works with the BPM community where she has been involved in several BPM consulting and training activities. She is one of the founders and current board member of the Philadelphia Association of Business Process Management Professionals (ABPMP) chapter, and a contributor to the USA National ABPMP BPM CBOK$^{TM}$.

## Prof. Dr. Peter Loos

German Research Center for Artificial Intelligence (DFKI)
Director, Institute for Information Systems (IWi)
Saarland University
Saarbrücken, Germany
peter.loos@iwi.dfki.de

Peter Loos is director of the Institute for Information Systems (IWi) at the German Research Institute for Artificial Intelligence (DFKI) and head of the chair for Business Administration and Information Systems at Saarland University. His research activities include Business Process Management, information modeling, enterprise systems, and software development as well as implementation of information systems. During his earlier career, Prof. Loos had been chair of information systems and management at University of Mainz, chair of information systems and management at Chemnitz University of Technology, deputy chair at University of Münster as well as lecturer (Privatdozent) at Saarland University. Furthermore, he had worked for 6 years as manager of the software development department at the software and consulting company IDS Scheer. Prof. Loos has written several books, contributed to 30 books and published more than 100 papers in journals and proceedings.

## André Macieira

Lecturer and Researcher
Federal University of Rio de Janeiro
Co-Leader at ELO Group
Rio de Janeiro, Brazil
andre.macieira@elogroup.com.br

André Macieira is a Researcher and Lecturer at the Federal University of Rio de Janeiro, Brazil, and holds a Master's degree in Industrial Engineering. Member of international risk management discussion groups at ABNT/ISO and OCEG. His main areas of interest are Risk Management and Business Process Management. Co-leader and consultant at ELO Group, a Brazilian business consulting firm focused on BPM and Risk Management solutions.

## Prof. Dr. M. Lynne Markus

The John W. Poduska Sr. Professor of
Information and Process Management
Bentley University
Waltham, MA, USA
mlmarkus@bentley.edu

M. Lynne Markus is the John W. Poduska, Sr. Professor of Information and Process Management at Bentley University and a Research Affiliate at MIT Sloan's Center for Information Systems Research. Professor Markus's teaching, research, and consulting interests include enterprise and interenterprise systems and IT-enabled organization change. She is the author/editor of five books and over one hundred articles; her research has been supported by numerous government and industry grants. She was named Fellow of the Association for Information Systems in 2004 and received the AIS LEO award for Exceptional Lifetime Achievement in Information Systems in 2008.

## Prof. Dr. Jürgen Moormann

Professor of Banking
Head of ProcessLab
Frankfurt School of Finance & Management
Frankfurt/a.M., Germany
j.moormann@frankfurt-school.de

Jürgen Moormann is Professor of Banking at Frankfurt School of Finance & Management. He has a strong research and practice background in Bank Management. After completing an apprenticeship at Commerzbank AG, he studied business administration at the universities of Kiel and Zurich. Jürgen worked for 5 years as a consultant in the Financial Services Industry before joining Frankfurt School of Finance & Management. Areas of teaching and research are Bank Strategy, Business Process Management, and IT Management in banks. He is the founder and head of ProcessLab – a research center focusing on bank-related Business Process Management (www.processlab.info). Jürgen has been a Visiting Professor at the University of Colorado at Colorado Springs, USA, the University of New South Wales, Sydney, Australia, the Hong Kong University, China and the Queensland University of Technology, Brisbane, Australia. He is author and editor of seven books and numerous articles in academic and practice-oriented journals. He presented papers at international conferences like BPM, HICSS, and ICEIS.

## Dr.-Ing Stefan Novotny

Divison Manager Quality and Processes
ThyssenKrupp Presta AG
Eschen, Principality of Liechtenstein
stefan.novotny@thyssenkrupp.com

Stefan Novotny is Divison Manager for Quality and Processes at ThyssenKrupp Presta AG, a manufacturer of steering systems for cars supplying big OEMs. He is responsible for Quality and Process Management throughout the Presta Group with 15 locations worldwide. This comprises the buildup and corporate governance of the global Business Process Management System, internal consulting for process improvement across the companies' disciplines, post merger integration projects for acquired companies, and the respective internal and external auditing. With his group, Stefan drives Presta's process maturity along ISO TS 16949, ASPICE (ISO 15504), ISO 14001, and other international standards. BPM at Presta is done using a model-based and document-oriented approach to share knowledge about processes, compliances, and the related organizational structure corporate wide. His process knowledge is based on his technical background, including a PhD in manufacturing engineering and work experience in product management and engineering as well as ERP-systems implementation. He also works as BPM-Expert for the University of Liechtenstein and contributes his knowledge to process management trainings.

## Dr. Martin Petry

Chief Information Officer
Hilti Corporation
Schaan, Principality of Liechtenstein
martin.petry@hilti.com

Dr. Martin Petry holds a Ph. D. in Applied Mathematics from Georg-August University in Göttingen, Germany, and has worked for the Hilti Corporation since 1993. Initially, his job assignments were Project Manager Customer Software Development (1993–1995) and ERP Implementation Manager Oracle Applications (1995–1999) in Japan and Great Britain. Dr. Petry then took the lead for the Business Driven Hilti IT Strategy development. As Head of Hilti's global process, data and system initiative, he implemented a global SAP environment with ERP, BI, CRM, and SCM now being used by >15,000 users in more than 50 countries. Since the beginning of 2005, he has worked as CIO for the Hilti group (400 IT people and in three strategic locations: Schaan (Liechtenstein), Tulsa (Oklahoma, US), and Kuala Lumpur (Malaysia)). In addition, Dr. Petry took responsibility of Business Excellence at Hilti starting from 2009.

## Nicholas Rohmann

Consultant
4C Group AG
Elsenheimerstrasse 55a
Munich, Germany
nrohmann@4cgroup.com

Nicholas Rohmann is a consultant at one of the leading and independent Top-Management consulting firms specialized in cost and performance management and innovative corporate management systems. With a unique broad approach – starting from the business concept and covering all organizational and

IT-technological implementation aspects as well as tailormade management coaching – 4C Group ensures a lasting effect on overall corporate performance for companies in different industries. During his time at the ThyssenKrupp Presta, a leading automotive supplier for steering systems, Nicholas Rohmann was involved in setting up a department for corporate governance on Business Process Management. Within that department, he had with his team the responsibility for the corporate process management system. He developed a combined model-based and document-oriented approach to sharing knowledge about processes, compliances, and the related organizational structure corporate wide. Besides, he implemented an integrated lean product-portfolio management and management reporting system as well as a resource and order management system in the prototype shops. Today he focuses on project governance for large process and IT-system renewal programs.

## Prof. Dr. Michael Rosemann

Professor of Information Systems
Co-Leader of the BPM Group
Faculty of Science and Technology
Queensland University of Technology
Brisbane, Australia
m.rosemann@qut.edu.au

Michael Rosemann is a Professor and Co-Leader of the Business Process Management Group at Queensland University of Technology, Brisbane, Australia. His research areas are Business Process Management, Enterprise Systems, and conceptual modeling. He is the author/editor of seven books and more than 140 refereed papers (incl. MISQ, IEEE TKDE, JAIS, DSS, Information Systems) and Editorial Board member of seven international journals. His publications have been translated into German, Russian, Portuguese, and Mandarin. Dr Rosemann's PhD students have won the Australian award for the best PhD thesis in Information Systems in 2007 and in 2008. He is the founder and chair of the Australian BPM Community of Practice (http://bpm-collaboration.com) and he has been the Chair of the 5th International Business Process Management Conference in 2007. He regularly conducts executive training in BPM (www.bpm-training.com) and provided BPM-related advice to organizations from various industries, including telecommunications, banking, insurance, utility, retail, public sector, logistics, and film industry.

## Dr. Shazia Sadiq

Associate Professor
School of Information Technology and Electrical Engineering
The University of Queensland
Brisbane, Australia
shazia@itee.uq.edu.au

Shazia Sadiq is currently working in the School of Information Technology and Electrical Engineering at The University of Queensland, Brisbane, Australia. She is part of the Data and Knowledge Engineering (DKE) research group and is involved in teaching and research in databases and information systems. Shazia holds a PhD from The University of Queensland in Information Systems and a Master's degree in Computer Science from the Asian Institute of Technology, Bangkok, Thailand. Her main research interests are innovative solutions for Business Information Systems that span several areas, including Business Process Management, governance, risk and compliance, data quality management, workflow systems, and service-oriented computing.

## Prof. Dr. August-Wilhelm Scheer

Institute for Information Systems (IWi)
German Research Center for Artificial Intelligence
Saarbrücken, Germany
scheer@iwi.uni-sb.de

Dr. August-Wilhelm Scheer founded the firm known today as IDS Scheer AG in 1984. From the IPO in 1999 until September 2009, he has been the chairman of the Supervisory Board as well as principal shareholder of the company. He was director of the Institute for Information Systems (IWi) at Saarland University from 1975 until 2005. His research activities focus on information and Business Process Management in industry, the services sector, and in public administration. His publications, translated into eight languages, have gained worldwide attention. In 1997, Prof. Scheer founded the imc, information multimedia communication AG. Today he is the chairman of the Supervisory Board. In 2003, he received the Philip Morris Research award and was named Entrepreneur of the Year. From 2006 to 2008, he was member of the council for innovation and growth of the Federal Government. Professor Scheer is member of the senate of the Fraunhofer-Gesellschaft, president of the German Federal Association for Information Economy, Telecommunications, and New Media (BITKOM), and vice president of the Bundesverband der Deutschen Industrie e.v. (BDI).

## Dr. Stefan Seidel

Assistant Professor
Martin Hilti Chair of Business Process Management
Institute of Information Systems
University of Liechtenstein
Vaduz, Principality of Liechtenstein
stefan.seidel@uni.li

Stefan Seidel is Assistant Professor at the Institute of Information Systems at the University of Liechtenstein. His current areas of research include innovative and creative business processes as well as the role of Business Process Management in the context of sustainable development. His work has been published in a number of academic journals and presented at international conferences. Since 2007 he is an Associated Researcher to the BPM Group at Queensland University of Technology (QUT) and to the ARC Center of Excellence for Creative Industries and Innovation (CCI) and, since 2009, he has been teaching in the international Master Program in Business Process Management at the University of Liechtenstein (www.bpm-master.com). Stefan has a research background in qualitative methods and design science research.

## Robert Shapiro

Process Analytica
Wellfleet, MA, USA
rshapiro@processanalytica.com

Robert Shapiro is founder and manager of Process Analytica. He is also Senior Vice President: Research, for Global 360. He founded Cape Visions, which was acquired by Global in 2005. At Cape Visions, he directed the development of Analytics and Simulation software used by FileNet/IBM, Fujitsu, PegaSystems, and Global 360 Business Process Management products. Prior to founding Cape Visions, as founder and CEO of Meta Software Corporation, he directed the implementation of a unique suite of graphical modeling and optimization tools for enterprise-wide business process improvement. Products based on these tools are used by Bank America, Wells Fargo, JPMChase, and other major banks to optimize their check processing and Lock Box operations. As a participant in the Workflow Management Coalition and chair of the working groups on conformance and process definition interchange, he plays a critical role in the development of international standards for workflow and Business Process Management. In 2005, he was awarded the Marvin L. Manheim Award for outstanding contributions in the field of workflow.

## Katherine Shortland

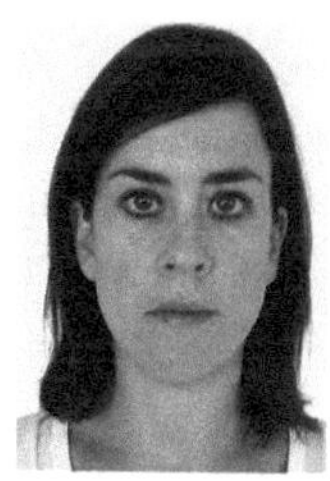

Business Affairs Manager/Producer
Centre for Screen Business
Sydney, Australia
katherine.shortland@gmail.com

Katherine Shortland has worked across all aspects of the arts, including arts funding, digital broadcasting, publicity and marketing, public broadcasting, and film production. Katherine completed her BA (Hons) at the University of NSW, after receiving a research scholarship to the

University of Exeter, UK. In 2005, she completed her MA in Film Producing at AFTRS. She was the inaugural Research Fellow with Centre for Screen Business, AFTRS, where she successfully implemented the film production software developed in association with the BPM Group QUT, on the feature film "Prime Mover." Katherine also worked with Caltech, California, into Predictive Market theory. Katherine has been published in a number of academic journals and presented at international conferences on new approaches to the screen industry. Katherine continues to work as a freelance producer with advertising agencies and film/TV production companies. She is currently the Business Affairs Manager at both The Wiggles and Cordell Jigsaw Productions in Sydney. In 2009, Katherine, along with her partner, launched a wine label, Seven Sundays.

## Theresa Sinnl

Research Assistant
Martin Hilti Chair of Business Process Management
Institute of Information Systems
University of Liechtenstein
Vaduz, Principality of Liechtenstein
theresa.sinnl@uni.li

Theresa Sinnl is a research assistant at the Institute of Information Systems of the University of Liechtenstein. She holds a Diploma in economics from the University of Hohenheim, Stuttgart, Germany, and conducted her studies focused on sociology, controlling, and monetary economics at the University of Hohenheim and York University, Toronto, Canada. Since 2009 she has been teaching in the international Master Program in Business Process Management at the University of Liechtenstein (www.bpm-master.com). She has worked as a student and graduate assistant at the Department for Sociology and Empirical Social Research, University of Hohenheim, and as a research and teaching assistant at the Centre for Cultural and General Studies, Universität Karlsruhe (TH), Karlsruhe, Germany. Her research interests focus on the interconnection of culture and Business Process Management.

## Christian Sonnenberg

Research Assistant
Martin Hilti Chair of Business Process Management
Institute of Information Systems
University of Liechtenstein
Vaduz, Principality of Liechtenstein
christian.sonnenberg@uni.li

Christian Sonnenberg is a PhD student at the Martin Hilti Chair of Business Process Management at the University of Liechtenstein. He holds a

Master's degree in Information Systems with specialization in Business Administration from the Westfälische Wilhelms-Universität Münster. Christian's main research interests are in the area of business process analysis and the analysis of IT value. He is IT systems architect of the "EU Network of Excellence on Global Governance, Regionalization and Regulation (GARNET)" and assists the teaching in the Bachelor and Master study programs in Information Systems at the University of Liechtenstein. Since 2008 he has been teaching in the international Master Program in Business Process Management at the University of Liechtenstein (www.bpm-master.com). Before Christian joined the research group at the University of Liechtenstein, he worked as a research assistant at the European Research Center for Information Systems (ERCIS).

## Andrew Spanyi

Founder and Director
Spanyi International Inc.
Oakville, Ontario, Canada
andrew@spanyi.com

Andrew Spanyi's work in the area of Business Process Management is recognized internationally. His focus is on assisting companies in transformation and advising on the behavioral aspects of process ownership. He is the author of two books on Process Management: *More for Less: The Power of Process Management and Business Process Management is a Team Sport: Play It to Win!* He has delivered keynote speeches at conferences in Canada, the USA, and in Europe (England, Ireland, Belgium, and Slovenia). He has published articles on process issues in a broad cross-section of magazines. He has managed and/or consulted on over 100 major improvement projects and has participated in the development and delivery of dozens of sales and management training programs. He is an editorial board member with the BPM Institute, and a Research Associate at the Process Management Research Center, Babson College. He was formerly a Director at the Association of Business Process Management Professional and chaired the Education committee. He regularly conducts executive training in BPM (www.spanyi.com) and provides advice to organizations in industries such as telecommunications, banking, insurance, electric utilities, pharmaceuticals, and chemicals.

## Christine Stephenson

Manager Enterprise Architecture
Emirates Group
Dubai, United Arab Emirates
christine.stephenson@emirates.com

Christine Stephenson is the Manager of Enterprise Architecture for the Emirates Group of Companies in Dubai, which includes Emirates Airlines. She has a vast knowledge of Enterprise Architecture, having worked in the public and private sector as a practitioner in Australia and now overseas. Christine has a background in Business Analysis and is passionate about integrating Business Process Management and Enterprise Architecture frameworks to get better alignment between the business and IT.

## Roger Tregear

Consulting Director
Leonardo Consulting
Canberra, Australia
r.tregear@leonardo.com.au

Roger Tregear is a Consulting Director with Australian BPM services company, Leonardo Consulting. Often working as a "thinking partner" and mentor, he provides BPM consulting and education services in Australia and overseas. Roger's consulting work over the years has covered a wide variety of situations and organization types. The common thread in all of this diversity has been the identification and resolution of complex business problems. Whether in strategic planning, project rescue, performance analysis, or innovation, the key task has been to first determine what the real questions are and then to answer them in meaningful and pragmatic ways. An active educator in BPM, Roger has delivered training courses and presentations in Saudi Arabia, Bahrain, UK, Africa, Australia, and New Zealand. A frequent writer on BPM topics, Roger is a regular columnist at www.bptrends.com.

## Prof. Dr. Jan vom Brocke

Martin Hilti Chair of Business Process Management
Director, Institute of Information Systems
University of Liechtenstein
Vaduz, Principality of Liechtenstein
jan.vom.brocke@uni.li

Jan vom Brocke holds the Martin Hilti Chair in Business Process Management (BPM) at the University of Liechtenstein. He is Director of the Institute of Information Systems and President of the Liechtenstein Chapter of the Association of Information Systems (AIS). Jan has more than ten years of experience in BPM projects and serves as an advisor to a wide range of institutions. He has published his work in more than 150 refereed papers at internationally perceived conferences and journals, and is an invited speaker on BPM at a number of universities, such as the University of St. Gallen in Switzerland, the LUISS University in Italy, or the University of California at Berkeley. In Liechtenstein, Jan is initiator and academic director of Europe's first international university Master Program in Business Process Management (www.bpm-master.com). His PhD students regularly take part in doctoral consortiae, two of which have just recently been awarded junior research fellows of the Third Lindau Nobel Prize Laureates Meeting in Economic Sciences.

## Prof. Dr. Robert Winter

Full Professor of Business and Information Systems Engineering
Director, Institute of Information Management
University of St. Gallen
St. Gallen, Switzerland
robert.winter@unisg.ch

Prof. Dr. Robert Winter is full professor of Business and Information Systems Engineering at the University of St. Gallen (HSG), director of HSG's research institute of information management (IWI-HSG), and founding academic director of HSG's Executive Master of Business Engineering program (EMBE HSG). After master studies in business administration and business education at Goethe University, Frankfurt (Germany), he joined Frankfurt's institute of information systems for 10 years before being tenured in St. Gallen in 1996. His primary research responsibilities are consortial projects ("competence centres") in the areas of information logistics, enterprise architecture, integration management, healthcare, and corporate controlling systems. He is co-editor of "BIT – Banking and Information Technology" as well as member of the editorial boards of four journals.

## Dr. Robert Woitsch

University of Vienna, Faculty of Computer Science
Department of Knowledge and Business Engineering
Vienna, Austria
robert.woitsch@dke.univie.ac.at

Robert Woitsch holds a PhD in business informatics and is currently responsible for European and National research projects within the consulting company BOC (www.boc-group.com) in Vienna, in the domain of knowledge management and technology-enhanced learning. He has been dealing with KM-projects since 2000, starting with the EU-funded projects ADVISOR, PROMOTE, and EKMF and has recently been working on KM-aspects within a number of EU-projects. Mr. Woitsch is involved in commercial projects in the design of documentation processes, skill management, and knowledge balances and is a member of the Austrian Standardization Institute contributing to the ON-Workshop 1144 "Knowledge Management". Besides his engagement at BOC, he teaches at the Department of Knowledge and Business Engineering at the Faculty of Computer Science at the University of Vienna. The tight coupling between BOC and the University of Vienna is expressed in about 40 joined papers, including the best-paper award at the eChallenges 08 and the involvement as reviewer and member of program committees in KM-conferences.

## Prof. Dr. Michael zur Mühlen

Associate Professor of Information Systems
Director, Center of Excellence in Business Process Innovation
Stevens Institute of Technology
Hoboken, NJ, USA
mzurmuehlen@stevens.edu

Michael zur Mühlen is Associate Professor of Information Systems at Stevens Institute of Technology, where he directs the Research Center on Business Process Innovation and is responsible for the graduate curriculum in Business Process Management and Service Innovation. Michael has over 15 years of experience in process automation and workflow management and has conducted numerous reengineering projects in the public and private sector, both in the United States and Europe. He serves as an advisor to the Chief Architect and Chief Technology Officer of the U.S. Department of Defense's Business Mission Area. Michael actively participates in BPM standardization efforts and in 2004 was named a fellow of the Workflow Management Coalition, where he chairs the working group "Management and Audit". His research focuses on the practical use of process modeling standards, techniques to manage operational risks in business processes, and the integration of business processes and business rules. He is the author of a book on workflow-based process controlling and numerous articles on process management and workflow automation.

## Jörg Zwicker

German Research Center for Artificial Intelligence (DFKI)
Institute for Information Systems (IWi)
Saarbrücken, Germany
joerg.zwicker@iwi.dfki.de

Jörg Zwicker received a Master's Degree in Information Systems from the Chemnitz University of Technology, Germany in 2004. He worked as a research assistant at the Chair of Information Systems and Business

Administration, Johannes Gutenberg-University Mainz, Germany. Since 2005, he has been researcher and PhD student at the Institute for Information Systems (IWi) at the German Research Center for Artificial Intelligence (DFKI). There, he manages and works on research and consulting projects in the field of Information System sciences and public administration. Jörg's research interests include Business Process Management, especially BPM assessment and optimization, using maturity models, Electronic Government, and conceptual modeling. Jörg has published several papers at national and international conferences, and in journals. Furthermore, he organized the First European eGovernment Symposium SaarLorLux in 2008.

# Index

**Note: Page numbers in Roman represent Volume 1. Those in italics are in Volume 2.**

## Q

FSC
www.fsc.org
MIX
Papier | Fördert
gute Waldnutzung
FSC® C083411

Kolibri 360 GmbH
Ferdinand-Jühlke-Straße 7
99095 Erfurt, Deutschland
produktsicherheit@kolibri360.de